Artificial Intelligence in Social Work

Ruopeng An • Michael A. Lindsey
Editors

Artificial Intelligence in Social Work

Bridging Technology and Humanity

Springer

Constance and Martin Silver Center
on Data Science and Social Equity
NYU | SILVER SCHOOL OF SOCIAL WORK

Editors
Ruopeng An
Silver School of Social Work
New York University
New York, NY, USA

Michael A. Lindsey
Silver School of Social Work
New York University
New York, NY, USA

ISBN 978-3-032-18442-9 ISBN 978-3-032-18443-6 (eBook)
https://doi.org/10.1007/978-3-032-18443-6

This work was supported by the Constance and Martin Silver Center on Data Science and Social Equity at the Silver School of Social Work, New York University.

This Springer imprint is published by the registered company Springer Nature Switzerland AG
The registered company address is: Gewerbestrasse 11, 6330 Cham, Switzerland

Preface

Artificial intelligence (AI) is no longer a distant frontier for social work. Across agencies, clinics, schools, community organizations, and policy arenas, algorithmic systems are already shaping how need is identified, how resources are allocated, and how care is delivered. Social workers encounter predictive risk models in child welfare, chatbots in mental health and sexual violence services, digital companions for older adults, and immersive simulations in social work education. At the same time, these tools raise profound questions about equity, surveillance, professional judgment, and the human relationships at the heart of our profession.

We conceived this edited volume as a response to this pivotal moment. Our aim is not to celebrate technology uncritically, nor to reject it outright. Instead, we hope to offer a rigorous, accessible, and ethically grounded roadmap for how social work can engage with AI in ways that advance dignity, justice, and social equity. Throughout the book, the contributors ask a shared question: how can AI be developed, governed, and used so that it strengthens, rather than undermines, social work's core commitments?

Why This Book, and Why Now

The chapters in this volume collectively argue that AI is best understood not as a single tool, but as an evolving ecosystem of socio-technical systems: machine learning and deep learning models, natural language processing, computer vision, recommender systems, conversational agents, robotics, and virtual and augmented reality. These systems are increasingly embedded in the infrastructures of service delivery, education, research, and governance. They can enable earlier and more precise identification of need, support personalized interventions, and expand access to information and care. They can also reproduce and amplify structural inequalities encoded in data and model design, narrow professional discretion, normalize surveillance, and displace relational practice.

Our opening and concluding chapters underscore that AI's impact on social work will depend less on what the technology can do and more on how we, as a profession, choose to understand, govern, and co-create these systems. That choice requires AI literacy and competency, critical reflection, participatory governance, and an unwavering commitment to social work's mission of promoting human rights, social justice, and the well-being of individuals, families, groups, organizations, and communities.

How the Book Is Organized

To help readers navigate this landscape, the book is organized into five parts that move from foundational concepts to applications across practice domains, to broader social contexts, and finally to education, research, ethics, governance, and the road ahead.

Part I: Foundations of AI in Social Work (Chaps. 1–2)

Part I provides the conceptual and ethical grounding for the volume. Chapter 1, "Introduction—The Role of AI in Transforming Social Work Practice, Education, and Research," situates AI within the historical trajectory of technology use in human services and clarifies foundational concepts such as machine learning, deep learning, natural language processing, predictive analytics, and computer vision. It surveys emerging applications in direct practice, education, and research, while emphasizing ethical dimensions such as bias, equity, privacy, transparency, and human oversight. The chapter closes with a call for cautious optimism, arguing that social workers must cultivate AI literacy, interdisciplinary collaboration, and robust governance so that AI augments professional judgment and strengthens human relationships.

Chapter 2, "Ethical Foundations of AI in Social Work," anchors AI firmly within longstanding ethical traditions, including the NASW Code of Ethics and core professional values. Drawing on trustworthy AI and value-sensitive design frameworks, the chapter articulates cross-cutting principles such as beneficence, non-maleficence, justice, autonomy, privacy, transparency, and accountability. It examines domains of ethical concern ranging from data protection and fairness to explainability, informed consent, and mechanisms for redress, and it highlights global and cultural dimensions of AI governance. Together, these chapters frame AI as both an opportunity and a test of social work's ethical resolve.

Part II: AI Applications Responding to Social Needs (Chaps. 3–15)

Part II presents a comprehensive view of how AI is being applied across core domains of social work practice. Chapters 3 through 5 explore AI's role in combating poverty and economic inequality, child welfare and family services, and health care and health disparities. These chapters show how predictive analytics and decision-support tools can help identify at-risk populations, guide case planning, improve resource allocation, and map AI to workflows such as screening, care planning, service delivery, and quality improvement. They also underscore persistent concerns: algorithmic bias, misalignment with professional judgment, gaps in regulation and theory, and the need for participatory design that keeps communities at the center.

Chapters 6 through 8 examine AI for physical, cognitive, and developmental challenges; in supporting LGBTQ+ populations; and in sexual and intimate partner violence. They illustrate how AI-powered robotics, adaptive interfaces, computer vision, multimodal analytics, and chatbots can enhance mobility, communication, early detection, and survivor support. At the same time, they highlight specific vulnerabilities, including risks to data privacy and safety for LGBTQ+ communities, the dangers of deepfakes and re-identification in sexual and intimate partner violence, and the need for trauma- and violence-informed, safety-by-design approaches that foreground survivor empowerment and co-design.

Chapters 9 through 11 focus on mental health services, school social work, and substance use disorder treatment and prevention. These chapters synthesize evidence on digital phenotyping, deep learning, large language models, socially assistive robotics, and other modalities used for earlier detection, more precise diagnosis, adaptive treatment, continuous monitoring, and rapid crisis response. They address school-based applications in customized learning, social-emotional supports, and early risk identification, as well as digital therapeutics and clinical decision support in substance use treatment. Across these areas, the authors stress the importance of methodological rigor, interpretability, clinician and educator acceptance, privacy protections, and client autonomy, along with harm-reduction–oriented, stakeholder-engaged implementation.

Chapters 12 through 15 turn to older adults, communities at risk and housing stability, criminal justice and rehabilitation, and human trafficking prevention and safety. Here, AI supports real-time health monitoring, cognitive training, and social robots in elder care; early identification of housing instability and neighborhood risk; risk assessment and rehabilitation in criminal justice; and the detection and disruption of human trafficking through spatial prediction, image and text analysis, and supply-chain monitoring. These chapters consistently highlight that AI can help address loneliness, prevent adverse events, and enhance safety and accountability, but can also deepen surveillance, discriminatory profiling, and data misuse if deployed without strong ethical design, cultural adaptability, and community engagement.

Taken together, Part II demonstrates both the breadth of AI applications and the consistency of the questions they raise about fairness, power, and human dignity.

Part III: AI and Social Justice in Changing Contexts (Chaps. 16–19)

Part III broadens the lens to consider social, environmental, workplace, and global contexts in which AI and social work intersect. Chapter 16, "AI in Advocacy and Social Justice," reviews how AI methods—including web and social media mining, natural language processing, computer vision, remote sensing, virtual reality, and chatbots—are being used in advocacy and human rights efforts. It shows how these tools can help organizations understand complex social problems, mobilize support, and document abuses, while also confronting challenges related to cultural sensitivity, reach in low-resource settings, misinformation, bias, and risks to marginalized communities.

Chapter 17, "AI in Environmental Social Work and Climate Change," introduces Eco-Social Work and explores how AI can expose and address unequal environmental harms. Through examples such as wildfire detection, water management, deforestation monitoring, and flood prediction, the chapter shows how AI can support both immediate crisis response and structural interventions in communities disproportionately affected by climate change. It also addresses ethical questions related to data quality, algorithmic bias, and the digital divide, and it stresses the need to center vulnerable populations and challenge systems that produce environmental injustice.

Chapter 18, "AI in the Evolving Workplace," traces how successive technological revolutions have reshaped labor markets and examines AI as the hallmark of a new era. The chapter details how AI systems not only automate tasks but also introduce algorithmic management, workplace surveillance, and new forms of job polarization, raising critical questions about employment stability, workers' rights, and social equity. It also identifies ways social workers can respond—by advocating for technological fairness, supporting displaced workers, and engaging in policy and ethical debates—to help shape a more just and inclusive AI-driven workplace.

Chapter 19, "AI in International Social Work and Global Issues," turns to cross-border crises and global inequality. It reviews AI applications in migration management, humanitarian aid, and global health emergencies, including forecasting displacement, mapping disaster impacts, and supporting outbreak detection, diagnostics, and telehealth. The chapter analyzes key risks such as algorithmic bias, data privacy and security threats, and digital and global divides, especially when tools built in the Global North are exported elsewhere. It places cultural competence, ethical collaboration, and capacity building at the center, emphasizing participatory design, AI literacy, community self-determination, and decolonizing approaches that foreground cultural humility, Indigenous knowledge, data sovereignty, and community ownership of technological infrastructures. In doing so, it shows how AI can either reinforce or disrupt global inequities, depending on how it is governed and by whom.

Part IV: AI in Social Work Education and Research (Chaps. 20–21)

Part IV turns inward to the profession's own systems of learning and knowledge production. Chapter 20, "AI in Social Work Education," examines how simulation-based learning, immersive virtual reality, and tools such as large language models, conversational tutors, and documentation assistants are reshaping social work education. Grounded in experiential and constructivist pedagogies, the chapter reviews evidence that AI-enhanced simulations can strengthen clinical interviewing, crisis response, interprofessional collaboration, and competency-based education, including virtual field placements and scaffolded learning. It also analyzes ethical, legal, and equity concerns related to bias, privacy, professional judgment, accessibility, and shifting regulatory standards, and it outlines a forward-looking research agenda on emotional intelligence in AI, interoperability, longitudinal evaluation, critical AI literacy, and participatory co-design with students and service users.

Chapter 21, "AI in Social Work Research," synthesizes how AI is being used across descriptive, predictive, experimental, and conceptual research designs. It describes how data mining and natural language processing help analyze population data and narrative records, how predictive models identify complex risk patterns and support decisions in human service systems, and how socially assistive robots, conversational agents, and computer vision are used to test technology-mediated interventions. Conceptually, it discusses large language models, retrieval-augmented generation, and agentic AI as tools for new forms of synthesis, theory development, and epistemological reflection. The chapter stresses that AI's value in research depends on methodological rigor, ethical safeguards, and alignment with professional values, and it highlights ongoing challenges related to participatory research, reproducibility, interpretability, privacy, consent, and algorithmic bias.

Part V: Ethical Considerations and Future Directions (Chaps. 22–24)

The final part of the volume brings ethics, governance, literacy, and future directions into sharp focus. Chapter 22, "Ethical Challenges and AI Governance in Social Work," reviews global and regional AI governance frameworks, including the OECD AI Principles, UNESCO recommendations, GDPR, the EU AI Act, the U.S. AI Action Plan, and the NIST AI Risk Management Framework. It then proposes an institutional, risk-tiered governance model tailored to social work, detailing requirements for data governance, privacy protection, transparency, accountability, fairness, and participatory decision-making. The chapter underscores social workers' roles as ethical leaders, co-designers, and evaluators of AI systems, and it identifies gaps and capacity needs that must be addressed to align AI with dignity, justice, and social equity.

Chapter 23, "Building AI Literacy and Competency in Social Work," argues that AI literacy and AI competency are now essential for ethical practice. It defines these constructs, adapts general frameworks to social work's relational, data, organizational, and equity commitments, and offers working definitions that distinguish broad, values-attuned understanding from role-specific, performance-based abilities. Aligning AI literacy and competency with the NASW Code of Ethics and CSWE EPAS—including a proposed tenth competency on engaging AI and algorithmic systems—the chapter introduces a three-tier professional development model spanning foundational literacy for all social workers, intermediate applied competencies, and advanced leadership capacities. It concludes with a professional agenda that integrates literacy and competency to confront algorithmic injustice and guide human-centered AI.

Chapter 24, "Conclusion—Challenges and Opportunities for AI in Social Work," synthesizes themes across the volume. It emphasizes that AI is now embedded in the infrastructures of service delivery, research, education, and governance; that it creates opportunities for earlier identification of need, improved coordination, and expanded access; and that it simultaneously poses risks related to surveillance, data injustice, and the narrowing of human judgment. The chapter identifies three cross-cutting challenges: safeguarding relational practice in increasingly automated environments, addressing structural inequalities encoded in data and model design, and building participatory governance that enables practitioners and communities to shape AI systems that affect them. It concludes that the future of AI in social work will be determined less by technological capability than by the profession's capacity for critical literacy, ethical accountability, and collective agency.

Intended Audiences and Uses

We envision this book serving multiple audiences at different stages of engagement with AI. Practitioners and agency leaders can use it to better understand how AI already intersects with their work, evaluate tools they are being asked to adopt, and advocate for clients and communities in AI-related decisions. Educators and students can draw on the chapters for conceptual frameworks, case examples, and practice-relevant applications that integrate AI literacy and competency into curricula and field education. Researchers and methodologists can use it to explore how AI supports descriptive, predictive, experimental, and conceptual work that is firmly aligned with social work values. Policymakers, technologists, and interdisciplinary partners can turn to it for a grounded account of social work perspectives on AI governance, ethics, and implementation.

The chapters can be read sequentially or selectively, depending on readers' interests and roles. They can support coursework and professional development, inform organizational planning and policy design, and serve as a springboard for community dialogue and cross-sector collaboration.

A Note of Thanks—and an Invitation

As co-editors, we are deeply grateful to the chapter authors who contributed to this volume. They bring together expertise from social work, public health, economics, data science, environmental studies, and beyond. Their scholarship, practice experience, and commitment to justice have made this book possible. We also thank our students, colleagues, and community partners whose questions, critiques, and hopes for technology in human services have continually pushed us to think more clearly and act more responsibly.

We offer this book with cautious optimism and with confidence in the profession's capacity to lead. AI will not, on its own, solve the entrenched inequities that social workers confront every day. Yet, if approached with critical literacy, ethical accountability, and collective agency, AI can be one of many tools that social work harnesses to advance equity, dignity, and social justice—rather than a force that deepens harm.

We invite you to read these chapters as a call to learn, to question, to collaborate, and to help shape the future of social work together.

New York, NY, USA — Ruopeng An
New York, NY, USA — Michael A. Lindsey

Acknowledgments

This work was supported by the Constance and Martin Silver Center on Data Science and Social Equity at the Silver School of Social Work, New York University.

Contents

About the Editors and Contributors

Editors

Ruopeng An, PhD, MPP, is a leading expert in obesity epidemiology and policy evaluation, a noted interdisciplinary data scientist, and an internationally recognized scholar in applying artificial intelligence to address public health disparities and social inequities. He currently holds the Constance and Martin Silver Endowed Professorship in Data Science and Prevention and serves as the Director of the Constance and Martin Silver Center on Data Science and Social Equity at NYU Silver School of Social Work. He is the founding Editor-in-Chief of the SAGE journal *Translational Data Science for Social Impact* and is also an elected Fellow of the American Academy of Health Behavior and the American College of Epidemiology. Recognized as one of Elsevier's top 2% most-cited scientists, his work has been featured by major media outlets such as *TIME, New York Times, Los Angeles Times, Washington Post, Reuters, USA Today, Bloomberg, Forbes, The Atlantic, The Guardian*, FOX, NPR, and CNN. He is the author of the forthcoming book *Building an AI-Ready University: A Holistic Strategy for Higher Education Leaders*, to be published by Routledge. He serves on research grant review and expert panels for the NIH, CDC, NSF, HHS, USDA, and the French National Research Agency. Before joining NYU, he was the Faculty Lead in Public Health Sciences and Faculty Fellow for AI Innovations in Education at Washington University in St. Louis, where he founded two certificate programs in artificial intelligence and data science. He holds a PhD in Policy Analysis from the RAND School of Public Policy, a Master of Public Policy from the National Graduate Institute for Policy Studies, and a BA in Political Science and Public Administration from Peking University.

Michael A. Lindsey, PhD, MSW, MPH, is a noted scholar in child and adolescent mental health and a leader in the search for knowledge and solutions to generational poverty and inequality. He is the Dean and Paulette Goddard Professor of Social Work at NYU Silver School of Social Work, and an Aspen Health Innovators Fellow. Additionally, he led the working group of experts supporting the Congressional Black Caucus Emergency Taskforce on Black Youth Suicide and Mental Health, which created the report Ring the Alarm: The Crisis of Black Youth Suicide in America. He is the President of the American Academy of Social Work and Social Welfare and a Distinguished Fellow of the National Academies of Practice in Social Work. He was also appointed by the Centers for Disease Control and Prevention to the Community Preventive Services Task Force. In 2023, he was appointed to the New York City Board of Health. Before being named NYU Silver's Dean, he was the Constance and Martin Silver Professor of Poverty Studies and Executive Director of the NYU McSilver Institute for Poverty Policy and Research. His current research is funded by the National Institutes of Health, and he has been ranked among the top 2% of most-cited scientists by Elsevier. The political news outlet *City & State New York* has recognized him as a 2025 Trailblazer in Higher Education and on their 2024 Health Care Power 100 list, the 2022 and 2023 Higher Education Power 100 lists, and the 2021 Mental Health Power 50 list. Additionally, *PoliticsNY/amNY* named him both a 2025 Power Player in Health Care and a 2025 Power Player in Education. He is a Life Member of Alpha Phi Alpha Fraternity, Inc. He holds a PhD in social work and an MPH from the University of Pittsburgh, an MSW from Howard University, and a BA in sociology from Morehouse College. He also completed a two-year postdoctoral fellowship in public health at the Johns Hopkins Bloomberg School of Public Health.

Contributors

Eunhye Ahn School of Human Ecology, University of Wisconsin-Madison, Madison, WI, USA

Charles Alba Division of Computational and Data Sciences, Washington University in St. Louis, St. Louis, MO, USA

Ruopeng An Silver School of Social Work, New York University, New York, NY, USA

Beth Angell School of Social Work, University of Michigan–Ann Arbor, Ann Arbor, MI, USA

Sara S. Bachman School of Social Policy & Practice, University of Pennsylvania, Philadelphia, PA, USA

Melissa D. Begg School of Social Work, Columbia University, New York, NY, USA

Ramona Denby-Brinson School of Social Work, University of North Carolina at Chapel Hill, Chapel Hill, NC, USA

Dget L. Downey Sliver School of Social Work, New York University, New York, NY, USA

Cao Fang School of Social Work, The University of Texas at Austin, Austin, TX, USA

Yue Fang Silver School of Social Work, New York University, New York, NY, USA

Noelle E. Fearn School of Social Work, St. Louis University, St. Louis, MO, USA

Kirk A. Foster School of Social Work, The University of Texas at Arlington, Arlington, TX, USA

Peiqi Guo School of Public Health, The University of Texas Health Science Center at Houston, Houston, TX, USA

Philip Young P. Hong School of Social Work, University of Georgia, Athens, GA, USA

Jingyi Huang Sliver School of Social Work, New York University, New York, NY, USA

David A. Jenkins College of Social Work, The Ohio State University, Columbus, OH, USA

Sheara Jennings School of Social Work, Howard University, Washington, DC, USA

Mengmeng Ji Division of Public Health Sciences, Washington University School of Medicine in St. Louis, St. Louis, MO, USA

Joyce Lee College of Social Work, The Ohio State University, Columbus, OH, USA

George Leibowitz School of Social Work, Rutgers University, New Brunswick, NJ, USA

Janet M. Liechty School of Social Work, University of Illinois Urbana-Champaign, Urbana, IL, USA

Michael A. Lindsey Silver School of Social Work, New York University, New York, NY, USA

Benjamin Lough School of Social Work, University of Illinois Urbana-Champaign, Urbana, IL, USA

Siva Mathiyazhagan School of Social Policy and Practice, University of Pennsylvania, Philadelphia, PA, USA

Henrika McCoy Graduate School of Social Work, University of Denver, Denver, CO, USA

Judy L. Postmus School of Social Work, University of Maryland–Baltimore, Baltimore, MD, USA

Vaiju Raja Mailman School of Public Health, Columbia University, New York, NY, USA

Shaddy Saba Silver School of Social Work, New York University, New York, NY, USA

Jing Shen Department of Physical Education, China University of Geosciences Beijing, Beijing, China

Jong Cheol Shin Department of Population Health, Lehigh University, Bethlehem, PA, USA

Jon E. Singletary Diana R. Garland School of Social Work, Baylor University, Waco, TX, USA

Susan Stone School of Social Welfare, University of California–Berkeley, Berkeley, CA, USA

Dorian Traube Brown School, Washington University in St. Louis, St. Louis, MO, USA

Junjie Wang School of Kinesiology and Health Promotion, Dalian University of Technology, Dalian, China

Xi Wang School of Social Work, Boston College, Chestnut Hill, MA, USA

Shuo Xu School of Social Research, Ren Ming University of China, Beijing, China

Gautam N. Yadama School of Social Work, Boston College, Chestnut Hill, MA, USA

Fan Yang School of Social Work, University of Illinois Urbana-Champaign, Urbana, IL, USA

Yuyi Yang Division of Computational and Data Sciences, Washington University in St. Louis, St. Louis, MO, USA

Yingying Zeng School of Social Work, University of Georgia, Athens, GA, USA

Liwei Zhang School of Social Work, University of Georgia, Athens, GA, USA

List of Figures

List of Tables

Part I
Foundations of AI in Social Work

Chapter 1
Introduction: The Role of AI in Transforming Social Work Practice, Education, and Research

Ruopeng An and Michael A. Lindsey

1 Contextualizing AI Within the Evolving Landscape of Social Work Practice

Artificial intelligence (AI) has rapidly emerged as a defining force shaping service delivery, organizational management, and policy development in the human services sector (Mikhaylov et al., 2018). Broadly understood as a set of computational techniques designed to perform tasks that typically require human intelligence—such as perceiving patterns, learning from experience, and making informed decisions—AI now intersects with many facets of social work. The profession's enduring commitment to social justice, client empowerment, and ethical practice faces both opportunities and challenges in an era marked by technological disruption (Dziegielewski & Holliman, 2019). As a historically adaptive field incorporating a wide range of tools—from telehealth platforms to sophisticated case management software—social work now confronts the complex task of integrating AI-driven tools into practice and policy environments while preserving its core human-centered values (Dali & Caidi, 2023).

The rapidly evolving digital world has prompted social workers to engage critically with new technologies that shape how services are planned, delivered, and evaluated. At the systemic level, organizations and agencies increasingly rely on AI for tasks such as predictive analytics in child welfare decision-making, automated triage in mental health hotlines, and the optimization of resource allocation in community-based programs (Kawakami et al., 2022; Zidaru et al., 2021). Beyond direct practice, AI influences policy formation by offering data-driven insights into

R. An (✉) · M. A. Lindsey
Silver School of Social Work, New York University, New York, NY, USA
e-mail: ra4605@nyu.edu; michael.lindsey@nyu.edu

R. An, M. A. Lindsey (eds.), *Artificial Intelligence in Social Work*,
https://doi.org/10.1007/978-3-032-18443-6_1

patterns of social problems, informing legislative priorities, and guiding strategic investments in social infrastructure (Van Ooijen et al., 2019). These technological shifts are not neutral: they reflect institutional priorities, embedded values, and patterns of economic investment that can either reduce or exacerbate inequalities (Chan & Holosko, 2016). For instance, while AI-driven analytics may help identify high-risk cases more quickly, they may also inadvertently reinforce systemic biases if models are trained on datasets that are skewed or historically discriminatory (Eubanks, 2018).

The current landscape invites social workers to consider the central place of AI in shaping client outcomes, professional roles, and organizational cultures. AI tools can enhance efficiency by streamlining administrative burdens, allowing practitioners to invest more time in building therapeutic rapport and crafting person-centered interventions (McCoyd et al., 2016). At the same time, introducing algorithmic decision-support systems requires social workers to develop a critical awareness of how data are generated, interpreted, and transformed into recommendations. The ethical application of AI is not merely technical but deeply relational: it depends on whether the professionals who use these tools understand their limitations, challenge their assumptions, and ensure alignment with ethical codes and regulatory standards (National Association of Social Workers, 2021).

A key consideration is that social work historically has operated within sociopolitical contexts characterized by structural inequities, cultural diversity, and chronic resource constraints. Integrating AI into these contexts requires a nuanced understanding of how technology intersects with various dimensions of identity, including race, gender, socioeconomic status, and others (Joyce et al., 2021). For example, predictive models used to determine child welfare interventions might inadvertently produce disparate outcomes for families from marginalized communities if the training data, datasets used to train AI models, reflect historical patterns of surveillance in these populations (Hall et al., 2023). Thus, the task is not simply to adopt AI but to do so with a vigilant eye toward the potential for unintended harm.

As social workers engage with AI, they must navigate a complex landscape of technological innovation, ethical imperatives, and professional identity. The National Association of Social Workers (NASW) Code of Ethics emphasizes a responsibility to advance clients' well-being, foster social justice, and ensure the dignity and worth of all individuals (National Association of Social Workers, 2021). These principles are as relevant as ever, guiding the integration of AI to enhance human capacities rather than diminish them. This involves ongoing interdisciplinary dialogue, professional development in digital competencies, and advocacy for policies and best practices that protect client rights and agency. By contextualizing AI within the evolving tapestry of social work practice, the profession can advance into this new technological landscape with cautious optimism, ensuring that the integration of AI remains anchored in the ethical and humanistic values that have long defined social work.

2 Foundational Concepts: Defining AI, Machine Learning, and Related Technologies

AI encompasses a broad class of computational methods and systems designed to perform tasks that typically require human intelligence—such as perceiving the environment, reasoning, learning, and making informed decisions (Dwivedi et al., 2021). Rather than referring to a single technology, AI can be understood as an umbrella term for various tools, techniques, and approaches. For social work professionals, gaining a foundational understanding of AI's key concepts is critical to engaging thoughtfully with emerging technologies and evaluating their potential impact on practice, policy, education, and research (Asakura et al., 2020; Villamil et al., 2019).

A fundamental building block of AI is machine learning (ML). This approach enables computer systems to learn from data patterns rather than relying on explicit, rule-based instructions (Mohri et al., 2018). For example, in traditional software development, humans write detailed instructions specifying how a program should operate. In contrast, ML algorithms detect trends, correlations, and relationships within large datasets, adjusting their internal parameters to improve the accuracy of predictions or classifications over time. For social workers, ML-driven tools might analyze historical service outcomes to identify which clients are most likely to benefit from a particular intervention, thus informing resource allocation and personalized support.

Within ML, a prominent subset of techniques known as deep learning leverages layered artificial neural networks inspired by the structure and function of the human brain (Goodfellow et al., 2016). Deep learning models excel at processing unstructured data—such as text, images, or audio—and have achieved state-of-the-art performance in tasks like image recognition, language understanding, and speech synthesis. In social work, this could mean automated analysis of case notes, rapid screening of digital images for signs of abuse or neglect, or natural language processing (NLP) to assist practitioners in quickly reviewing large volumes of textual information. It is crucial, however, to emphasize that these technologies are intended to enhance, not replace, the role of social workers. While AI tools can provide valuable insights and improve efficiency, the empathy, human judgment, and contextual understanding that social workers bring remain irreplaceable. Thus, the true potential of these innovations lies in their ability to augment human practice, rather than supplant the crucial human touch in service delivery.

NLP, a specialized area of AI, focuses on enabling computers to understand, interpret, and generate human language. NLP technologies can sort through case records, policy documents, and online community forums to identify relevant themes, sentiments, or emerging trends. For example, social workers may rely on NLP-driven tools to quickly distill insights from client narratives, enabling them to understand community concerns, detect patterns of trauma, or identify areas where policy advocacy is needed (Zhang et al., 2023).

Beyond these core concepts, AI includes various additional techniques that can be applied to social work. Reinforcement learning, for instance, involves training models by rewarding correct actions and penalizing mistakes, making it well-suited for environments where decisions unfold over time. Predictive analytics, a more application-driven concept, uses historical data to forecast future outcomes, informing preventive strategies in child welfare, homelessness prevention, or mental health screening (Hall et al., 2023). Computer vision, another AI subfield, empowers systems to interpret visual information, which can be harnessed to identify signs of environmental hazards in housing or to monitor community health conditions in areas affected by natural disasters.

Social workers need to distinguish between the capabilities and limitations of these technologies. AI is not a monolithic solution but a toolkit that can augment professional judgment, improve efficiency, and broaden service reach—if employed responsibly. Social workers must remember that AI models are only as good as the data on which they are trained. Biased or incomplete data can lead to skewed analyses and inequitable decision-making. Moreover, despite their sophistication, AI systems often operate as "black boxes," making it challenging to understand the rationale behind specific predictions or classifications (Dwivedi et al., 2021). This underscores the need for transparency, explainability, and human oversight, which resonate with social work's ethical principles.

By establishing a clear understanding of AI's foundational concepts—its broad scope, the roles of ML and deep learning, and the significance of language processing and other specialized techniques—social work professionals are better positioned to assess how these technologies fit into their professional landscapes. Subsequent sections of this chapter and book will explore how this literacy enables practitioners, educators, and researchers to engage in meaningful dialogue with technologists, policymakers, and communities, ultimately guiding the ethical and effective integration of AI into the social work field.

3 Historical Trajectories of Technology Use in Social Work

The integration of technology into social work has evolved gradually, reflecting shifts in professional needs, the availability of tools, and broader societal changes. Early applications of technology in the field primarily focused on administrative and record-keeping functions, as rudimentary computer systems were introduced in the late twentieth century to streamline case documentation and agency management (Malekoff, 2023). These basic, often text-based interfaces helped social workers catalog client information, track service utilization, and maintain consistent records—functions that, while modest by today's standards, represented a significant modernization of practice administration at the time.

As the Internet gained prominence in the 1990s and early 2000s, social work practitioners and organizations began exploring online resources and databases to access research, identify best practices, and coordinate inter-agency collaboration

(Warmington et al., 2004). This digital shift facilitated an expanding repertoire of tools, including email consultations, online support groups, and emerging telehealth platforms that connected clients to resources with unprecedented efficiency and reach. Over time, advanced information and communication technologies further enabled remote service delivery, allowing social workers to broaden their client bases, overcome geographic barriers, and improve the availability of culturally tailored interventions (Chan & Holosko, 2016).

Parallel to these developments, the advent of "big data" and advanced analytics in the early twenty-first century opened new horizons for data-driven decision-making. Social workers and agencies have begun to identify patterns and trends with greater clarity by collecting and analyzing large volumes of information, including demographic data, program outcomes, and community-level indicators (Beheshti et al., 2022). These efforts aimed to inform evidence-based practice, guide resource allocation, and influence organizational strategies and policy formulation.

As the scale and sophistication of data processing grew, predictive analytics and ML models started to shape prevention and early intervention strategies. These techniques have helped agencies identify at-risk families in fields such as child welfare, enabling more targeted and timely services (Kawakami et al., 2022). In mental health contexts, online screening tools and teletherapy platforms provide more flexible and user-friendly ways to deliver care and support (Malekoff, 2023). Even research in social work began to leverage emerging analytical methods, examining vast datasets to uncover social patterns, test interventions, and refine theoretical frameworks (Van Ooijen et al., 2019).

This trajectory sets the stage for integrating AI tools into the field of social work. AI-driven applications build on earlier technological innovations, drawing from the historical lessons of data collection, digital communication, and analytics, and extend their capabilities in novel directions. Where early systems were limited to essential data management, AI-enabled technologies can detect subtle patterns, learn from complex datasets, and offer real-time decision support. Such tools hold promises for enhancing the precision of assessments, improving resource distribution, and potentially reducing administrative burdens, allowing social workers more time for therapeutic engagement and advocacy.

However, this transition is neither seamless nor purely technical. As technology in social work has advanced, concerns about ethical practice, data privacy, equity, and human oversight have also evolved (Malekoff, 2023). The history of technology use in social work reveals that while digital tools can amplify impact and efficiency, they also necessitate ongoing vigilance, critical reflection, and adaptive professional standards. Understanding this historical backdrop is crucial for appreciating the complexities of AI adoption today. It underscores that each new technological wave brings both opportunities and challenges, requiring practitioners, educators, and policymakers to remain grounded in the profession's core values and to ensure that human well-being, dignity, and justice guide every step forward.

4 Transformative Potential of AI in Direct Practice

AI offers substantial potential to transform direct social work practice, promising tools and applications to enhance efficiency, improve personalization, and strengthen client engagement. At the assessment stage, for example, AI-driven platforms can help practitioners process large amounts of client data, identify critical risk factors, and streamline the intake process. Rather than relying solely on manual chart review and subjective interpretation, social workers can leverage predictive analytics that draw on demographic, clinical, and contextual information to produce more accurate and timely insights (Zetino & Mendoza, 2019). By providing early warnings or highlighting patterns that may otherwise go unnoticed, AI can empower practitioners to make more informed judgments and prioritize cases that require immediate attention.

In intervention planning, AI-driven recommender systems and decision-support tools can bridge the gap between research evidence and on-the-ground practice. ML models can suggest evidence-based interventions or highlight best practices suited to a client's unique circumstances, including cultural background, language preferences, and identified support networks (McCoyd et al., 2016; Villamil et al., 2019). For instance, a mental health clinic might utilize AI to analyze historical treatment outcomes and propose personalized care plans that incorporate effective therapeutic modalities, service referrals, and supportive resources. This data-informed approach does not replace practitioner judgment; instead, it provides a supplementary layer of guidance that can enhance the relevance and effectiveness of services.

Client engagement also benefits from AI's capabilities. For example, chatbots, virtual assistants, and interactive apps can provide real-time support and information, allowing clients to access help outside conventional working hours or formal office settings (Zumstein & Hundertmark, 2017). Such tools can reduce barriers to care for individuals who face mobility constraints, linguistic challenges, or geographical isolation. Additionally, AI-driven NLP systems can interpret and respond empathetically to user input, prompting clients to share experiences or concerns they may have difficulty articulating in traditional settings. Social workers can then review transcripts, sentiment analyses, or highlight reports to understand client needs better and calibrate their face-to-face interventions more effectively.

Another promising area is the personalization of services. AI can help tailor interventions based on learning style, communication preferences, or life context. For example, a family receiving parenting support might benefit from short, AI-curated informational videos that use culturally congruent examples. In contrast, another family might respond better to text-based coaching messages delivered via a mobile application. As services become more individualized, clients may experience a stronger sense of agency and alignment with the support they receive, potentially leading to improved outcomes and satisfaction (Dwivedi et al., 2021).

Despite these benefits, the use of AI in direct practice must be approached with a keen awareness of ethical considerations. Issues around privacy, data security, and potential algorithmic biases demand rigorous oversight and continuous evaluation

(National Association of Social Workers, 2021; UNESCO, 2021). Practitioners must remain transparent about these technologies, informing clients how their data is processed and offering opt-out provisions. This human-in-the-loop model ensures that while AI drives efficiency and insight generation, practitioners must be responsible for interpreting results, challenging assumptions, and upholding the client's best interests.

5 Implications of AI for Social Work Education and Training

As AI continues to reshape various dimensions of social work practice, it likewise holds significant implications for professional education and training. By integrating AI-driven tools and methodologies into learning environments, social work programs can better prepare students for an increasingly data-informed and technology-mediated practice landscape. Virtual simulations, for instance, offer realistic, scenario-based learning experiences that can refine students' clinical judgment, interpersonal skills, and ethical decision-making before they engage with clients in real-world settings (Dali & Caidi, 2023). These simulations, enriched by AI's capacity to respond to student inputs adaptively, can provide tailored feedback that accelerates skill acquisition and fosters deeper learning.

Beyond simulations, adaptive learning platforms enabled by AI-driven analytics can personalize educational content, pacing, and complexity to meet each student's unique needs. Instead of adopting a one-size-fits-all curriculum, these platforms can assess learners' strengths, identify areas for improvement, and deliver targeted instructional materials. Such systems not only support more efficient skill development but also empower students to take greater ownership of their learning. As social work students confront complex practice challenges—ranging from crisis intervention to culturally responsive community engagement—accessing finely tuned learning resources can enhance their preparedness and confidence upon entering the workforce (Holmes et al., 2019).

The growing presence of AI in social work practice underscores the need to incorporate digital competencies and AI literacy into social work curricula. For example, some child welfare agencies employ predictive analytics to identify families at heightened risk of abuse, and mental health providers are experimenting with AI-powered chatbots to streamline client intake. In both cases, social workers require the skills to interpret algorithmic outputs, question model accuracy, and uphold ethical standards regarding data privacy, bias, and client consent (Asakura et al., 2020; Reamer, 2019). Students should graduate not only with a theoretical understanding of human behavior and social justice principles, but also with the ability to critically evaluate technology-driven assessments and advocate for safeguards. Without foundational literacy in these domains, future practitioners risk being unprepared to leverage AI responsibly or to challenge inequitable systems when AI tools are deployed in human services settings.

Social work educators must continually update teaching practices, materials, and evaluation methods in response to these evolving demands. Incorporating hands-on exercises with AI tools—such as analyzing open-source datasets or critiquing AI-based mental health applications—can help demystify these technologies and foster ethical vigilance. Examining case studies of both successful and problematic AI implementations highlights how issues of bias, client welfare, and confidentiality manifest in real-world practice. Facilitating open dialogues about professional responsibilities in a digital age further reinforces the obligation to prioritize human dignity and cultural competence. Moreover, training faculty to integrate and evaluate AI-based educational resources is crucial for maintaining consistent standards and ensuring high-quality instruction across programs (McInroy, 2021).

By aligning educational approaches with the unlimited opportunities offered through AI-enhanced practice, the profession reinforces its longstanding commitments to evidence-informed practice, ethical rigor, and social justice. Investing in comprehensive AI literacy and skill development within social work education not only supports the next generation of practitioners but also ultimately benefits clients and communities, ensuring that the field remains responsive, competent, and resilient in the face of ongoing technological change.

6 AI as a Catalyst for Innovations in Social Work Research

AI has begun significantly shaping social work research, offering methods and tools that enhance data analysis, predictive modeling, and evidence-based practice. Social work researchers have traditionally relied on surveys, interviews, and manual data coding to identify patterns and evaluate program outcomes. While these methods remain essential, the introduction of AI-driven approaches expands the scope and depth of inquiry. ML algorithms, for example, can process large volumes of complex, multi-sourced data more efficiently than human analysts, illuminating trends that may have been overlooked using conventional research techniques (Dwivedi et al., 2021; Villamil et al., 2019).

One prominent innovation involves using predictive modeling to anticipate trends and inform intervention strategies. In child welfare, predictive analytics can help identify families at elevated risk of adverse outcomes, guiding the allocation of preventive services before a crisis occurs (Kawakami et al., 2022). Similarly, in homelessness prevention research, AI-driven models can pinpoint the factors contributing to housing instability, informing the design of targeted, evidence-based policies. By refining our ability to forecast, these tools encourage a more proactive, preventive orientation to social problems rather than reactive measures.

Beyond predictive capabilities, AI also facilitates more nuanced analyses of qualitative data. NLP techniques can be applied to large sets of text—from case notes to policy documents—extracting themes, sentiment, and linguistic patterns. This capacity enriches research methodologies by combining the depth of qualitative inquiry with the scale afforded by computational approaches. It enables a more comprehensive understanding of client experiences, community feedback, and policy discourse (Munford & Sanders, 2011).

The integration of AI in social work research also supports knowledge production by enabling the rapid synthesis of multifaceted data sources. For instance, AI-driven literature mining tools can streamline systematic reviews, searching scholarly databases to identify relevant studies faster and more consistently. These technologies expedite the translation of knowledge into practice by reducing the time and labor required to gather and analyze research findings. As a result, social workers and policymakers can access timely evidence to inform their decision-making, ultimately enhancing service delivery and improving client outcomes (Van Ooijen et al., 2019).

In evaluating outcomes, AI can help build more rigorous and dynamic feedback loops. Real-time data analysis enables researchers to monitor program effectiveness continuously, rather than waiting for the completion of lengthy evaluation cycles. This iterative process fosters ongoing improvements to interventions, ensuring that social work practice remains responsive to client needs and contextual shifts. Additionally, automated data validation—an AI-driven process that checks for inconsistencies or errors in data—and anomaly detection, which flags unusual patterns or outliers signaling potential issues, can enhance the reliability of research findings, reducing the risk of bias, human error, or incomplete information (Beheshti et al., 2022).

7 Ethical Dimensions and Value Alignment in AI Adoption

As AI technologies become increasingly integrated into social work practice, adhering to the profession's ethical foundations is paramount. Social work's core values—service, social justice, dignity and worth of the person, importance of human relationships, integrity, and competence—offer a vital framework for guiding responsible AI use (National Association of Social Workers, 2021). These principles help ensure that AI-driven decisions and interventions advance human well-being rather than undermining it.

At the forefront is the obligation to promote fairness and equity: AI models must be carefully examined for biases in their training data that could lead to discrimination or disparate outcomes for historically marginalized communities (Eubanks, 2018; Hall et al., 2023). Examples of such biases include risk assessment tools in child welfare systems that inadvertently target lower-income families through overly simplistic metrics (e.g., using ZIP codes as proxies for socioeconomic status) or mental health applications that fail to account for linguistic and cultural nuances, systematically misinterpreting user inputs. Indicators of algorithmic bias often appear when certain demographic groups repeatedly receive unfavorable decisions or when neutral-sounding variables correlate with outcomes that reflect historical inequities.

To identify bias, practitioners and researchers can conduct regular audits of AI outputs, analyze subgroup performance metrics to detect unusual patterns, and solicit feedback from community stakeholders who can reveal context-specific harms. Mitigation efforts may involve refining training data sets, adjusting model parameters to reduce disparate impacts, or introducing "human-in-the-loop" review processes for critical decisions. Continuous monitoring—through routine evaluation and periodic "stress testing" of the models—ensures that biases do not resurface over time. Ultimately, training practitioners, researchers, and developers to recognize these warning signs and conduct targeted analyses is key to preventing the reproduction of social inequalities in AI-driven social work interventions.

Confidentiality and data protection represent another crucial dimension of ethical AI adoption. Social workers must ensure that sensitive client data is not compromised or misused in a field built on trust and relational depth. This includes implementing strong data governance practices, secure storage solutions, and strict access controls, as well as establishing policies to limit data sharing and handle breaches responsibly (Boppana, 2021). The complexities of digital data mean that maintaining client confidentiality now requires technical literacy and vigilance to uphold professional standards in a new era of information exchange.

Even when collecting data for anomaly detection—an AI-driven practice that flags suspicious or unusual patterns that may indicate fraud or data breaches—robust safeguards must remain at the forefront. In particular, data minimization (collecting only what is necessary), de-identification of sensitive fields, and explicit consent procedures help reduce the risk of inadvertently revealing personal information. Encryption and secure user authentication can further protect these sensitive data streams. Equally important is regularly auditing who has access to the data and for what purposes, alongside ongoing risk assessments to evaluate potential re-identification scenarios or misuse. By establishing these layered protections, social workers can utilize advanced digital tools to detect anomalies while maintaining the confidentiality and trust that underpin social work practice.

Safeguarding human rights is integral to the value-aligned use of AI. If left unchecked, automated decision-making tools can influence eligibility for vital services or accelerate outcomes in areas such as housing, healthcare, and child welfare. When not subjected to ethical oversight, such systems risk stripping individuals and communities of their agency and eroding the humanistic element of care (Eubanks, 2018). Ensuring that human rights remain central involves maintaining human-in-the-loop approaches, whereby trained professionals oversee, interpret, and, if necessary, override AI-generated recommendations. The profession is committed to empowering clients and respecting their autonomy by keeping humans at the core of decisions.

Transparency and explainability are also vital to cultivating trust in AI systems. Clients, practitioners, and stakeholders must understand how algorithms make decisions, what data they rely upon, and what safeguards are in place to prevent harmful outcomes. Openness about the capabilities and limitations of AI tools allows for meaningful engagement with clients, fosters accountability, and helps ensure that technology aligns with social work's ethical standards (Chan & Holosko, 2016).

Another essential component is ongoing professional development and interdisciplinary collaboration. As AI tools evolve, social workers must remain informed about emerging ethical challenges and best practices to ensure that AI supports, rather than undermines, the profession's mission. This may involve seeking technical training, collaborating with technologists, and contributing to policy dialogues that shape regulatory standards for AI in human services (Dwivedi et al., 2021). By taking an active role in shaping the ethical frameworks that govern AI, social workers can influence the trajectory of technological development and deployment to prioritize human welfare and social justice.

8 Global Perspectives and Cultural Variations in AI Integration

As AI technologies spread globally, their understanding, implementation, and governance vary widely. Different regions face unique socioeconomic conditions, policy frameworks, and cultural values that influence how AI is applied in social work contexts (Dwivedi et al., 2021; Villamil et al., 2019). While some high-resource nations have well-established regulatory structures, abundant data infrastructures, and ample funding to drive cutting-edge AI applications, other countries may face constraints stemming from limited digital infrastructure, heightened concerns about data sovereignty, or cultural norms that influence perceptions of technology and authority (Jobin et al., 2019).

A key challenge for social workers and organizations operating in international or cross-cultural settings is ensuring that AI tools respect local norms, client perspectives, and community priorities. For instance, interventions designed for one cultural context may not translate seamlessly into another, as the meanings attached to concepts such as well-being, family structures, or community problem-solving vary from place to place. This necessitates involving local stakeholders—such as clients, community leaders, and practitioners—in AI development and adaptation. Such participatory approaches help to ensure that language models, predictive analytics, or decision-support tools are grounded in relevant cultural references, ethical principles, and indigenous knowledge systems (UNESCO, 2021).

Policy landscapes, too, diverge significantly across regions. While the European Union's Ethics Guidelines for Trustworthy AI emphasize human rights, transparency, and accountability, other jurisdictions may prioritize economic growth, innovation, or national security concerns in shaping their AI regulatory frameworks (EU High-Level Expert Group on AI, 2019; Morley et al., 2020). For social workers, understanding these differing priorities is essential for navigating ethical practice. In some contexts, stringent data protection laws might limit the use of specific predictive models or data-sharing initiatives, whereas, in others, looser regulations could enable rapid experimentation—but also raise the risk of inadequate oversight. Tailoring AI solutions to local policy contexts requires technical adjustments and an understanding of how legal and political environments influence client rights and service delivery.

Global differences in language, social hierarchies, and historical power imbalances underscore the importance of culturally sensitive AI integration even more. Tools that rely on NLP or sentiment analysis must be attuned to linguistic subtleties, idioms, and dialects. Similarly, systems that rank or score clients for service eligibility must account for entrenched social inequities, including social determinants of health, to ensure that biased algorithms do not exacerbate existing disadvantages. Achieving this requires interdisciplinary collaboration among social workers, technologists, linguists, cultural anthropologists, and community representatives, all of whom bring critical insights into how AI can be responsibly introduced and maintained in varied contexts (Dwivedi et al., 2021; Jobin et al., 2019).

The global trajectory of AI integration in social work is not a one-size-fits-all story. Instead, it requires ongoing dialogue, mutual learning, and ethical vigilance. By recognizing cultural nuances, engaging local expertise, and aligning with region-specific legal and value systems, social workers can help ensure that AI-driven interventions promote equity, respect community autonomy, and enhance well-being wherever deployed. Such context-sensitive approaches to technology will support a future in which AI does not merely replicate existing social patterns but instead serves as a tool for empowerment and social justice worldwide.

9 Risks, Limitations, and Unintended Consequences of AI in Social Work

While AI holds immense promise for enhancing social work practice, it is crucial to acknowledge that its deployment can yield outcomes that diverge from professional intentions and goals. One prominent concern lies in algorithmic bias—a situation in which patterns learned from historical data disadvantage certain groups or reinforce existing inequities. Although data are often presented as neutral, they invariably reflect societal imbalances, resulting in predictive models that may disproportionately label, classify, or allocate resources in ways that undermine equity (Hall et al., 2023). Rather than simply acknowledging this risk, social work professionals must approach algorithmic outputs with a healthy skepticism and a willingness to interrogate underlying assumptions.

Data privacy and security constitute another significant limitation. Despite efforts to safeguard client information, large datasets aggregated from multiple sources are more susceptible to breaches, unauthorized access, and malicious use. The rich, sensitive details required for robust AI models—ranging from socioeconomic indicators to mental health histories—make privacy a moving target that demands constant vigilance. Technical encryption solutions, strict data governance protocols, and limited-access data enclaves help mitigate these risks; however, they cannot eliminate the possibility of harm, especially in rapidly evolving digital landscapes (Beheshti et al., 2022; Dwivedi et al., 2021).

The human element in social services is also vulnerable to erosion. If practitioners over-rely on automated processes and time-saving AI tools, they can unintentionally reduce interpersonal contact. Without careful calibration, clients may feel distanced by an invisible layer of technology or perceive that their unique narratives are being reduced to data points. This loss of relational depth could diminish trust, client engagement, and the therapeutic alliance that underpins effective social work practice (Dalziel et al., 2024).

Another unintended consequence arises from model drift and data quality issues. As social conditions, policies, and client populations evolve, algorithms trained on outdated or incomplete data may produce misleading predictions. What worked under one set of circumstances may fail under another, leading to flawed decision-making if models are not regularly updated and validated. Regular audits, external peer reviews, and ongoing refinement of training datasets can help maintain model accuracy and relevance (Patchipala, 2023).

To mitigate these challenges, several strategies emerge. First, transparent model documentation—sometimes referred to as "model cards" or "nutrition labels"—can demystify how an AI tool functions, elucidate its limitations, and highlight contexts in which it should not be applied. Second, interdisciplinary oversight committees can bring together practitioners, data scientists, ethicists, and community representatives to continuously review and refine the use of AI. Such committees can set thresholds for acceptable accuracy, scrutinize performance disparities across subgroups, and recommend remedies when harms are detected (Dwivedi et al., 2021). Third, agencies can invest in capacity-building initiatives that equip social workers with the knowledge and skills necessary to critically interpret algorithmic results, adapt practice guidelines as new technologies emerge, and maintain a balanced integration of AI into their professional toolkit.

10 Balancing Optimism with Responsible Use: Charting a Path Forward

As AI continues to influence the core realms of social work—from direct practice and research to education and policy—it is essential to strike a balance between embracing technological potential and upholding the profession's enduring commitments to social justice, equity, and human well-being. This chapter shows that AI can streamline administrative processes, enhance personalized interventions, guide evidence-based decisions, and reveal patterns previously hidden in complex datasets (Dwivedi et al., 2021). However, we have also acknowledged the associated risks: algorithmic bias, data privacy concerns, cultural mismatches, and unintended consequences that can compromise trust and subvert core social work values (Eubanks, 2018; Hall et al., 2023).

This complexity calls for cautious optimism. Rather than dismissing AI out of fear or adopting it uncritically, social workers can approach new technologies with curiosity, humility, and a commitment to responsible innovation. Such responsibility entails ongoing evaluation of AI tools within specific service contexts, carefully considering the populations they affect, and continuous dialogue with stakeholders—clients, community members, ethicists, policy experts, and technologists. Professional development in AI literacy, interdisciplinary collaboration, and robust governance frameworks can help practitioners interpret algorithmic outputs, challenge biases, and respond when systems produce misleading or harmful results (Chan & Holosko, 2016).

Moreover, as AI continues to evolve, the field must remain vigilant in championing human rights and social justice. These guiding principles ensure that technological progress aligns with social work's moral compass. By advocating for transparent AI design, participatory model development, and rigorous oversight, social workers can influence the direction of innovation, ensuring that it addresses human needs rather than corporate interests or state surveillance. Whenever AI-driven processes risk marginalizing vulnerable populations or reinforcing existing power imbalances, social workers can step in—armed with data literacy and ethical resolve—to demand accountability and push for transformative solutions that uplift rather than oppress (Dwivedi et al., 2021; Eubanks, 2018).

In the face of complexity and change, embracing AI in social work is less about achieving a final state of technological perfection and more about cultivating a dynamic, reflective approach to practice. Just as clinical approaches evolve with new evidence and social policies adapt to shifting landscapes, so should AI integration remain fluid, iterative, and open to revision. Researchers can design studies that examine the real-world impacts of AI interventions, educators can continuously update curricula to include digital competencies, and policy leaders can shape legislation that protects clients' rights and data integrity.

The path forward is one of deliberate, value-driven engagement with technology. By upholding the principles that have guided social work through past innovations—service, social justice, dignity, and integrity—practitioners can help ensure that the AI revolution does not lead to a diminished vision of care but to one that is expanded, more equitable, and more profoundly human.

Competing Interests The authors have no conflicts of interest to declare that are relevant to the content of this chapter.

References

Asakura, K., Occhiuto, K., Todd, S., Leithead, C., & Clapperton, R. (2020). A call to action on artificial intelligence and social work education: Lessons learned from a simulation project using natural language processing. *Journal of Teaching in Social Work, 40*(5), 501–518. https://doi.org/10.1080/08841233.2020.1813234

Beheshti, A., Ghodratnama, S., Elahi, M., & Farhood, H. (2022). *Social data analytics*. CRC Press.

Boppana, V. R. (2021). Ethical considerations in managing PHI data governance during cloud migration. *Educational Research (IJMCER), 3*(1), 191–203.

Chan, C., & Holosko, M. J. (2016). A review of information and communication technology enhanced social work interventions. *Research on Social Work Practice, 26*(1), 88–100. https://doi.org/10.1177/1049731515578884

Dali, K., & Caidi, N. (2023). Social work education for the digital age: Insight from information science. *Social Work Education, 42*(5), 663–693. https://doi.org/10.1080/02615479.2022.2057942

Dalziel, M. V., Schaffer, K., & Martin, N. (2024). *Navigating AI in social work and beyond: A multidisciplinary review*. arXiv preprint https://arxiv.org/abs/2411.07245

Dwivedi, Y. K., Hughes, L., Ismagilova, E., Aarts, G., Coombs, C., Crick, T., et al. (2021). Artificial intelligence (AI): Multidisciplinary perspectives on emerging challenges, opportunities, and agenda for research, practice and policy. *International Journal of Information Management, 57*, 101994. https://doi.org/10.1016/j.ijinfomgt.2019.08.002

Dziegielewski, S. F., & Holliman, D. C. (2019). *The changing face of health care social work: Opportunities and challenges for professional practice*. Springer Publishing Company.

EU High-Level Expert Group on AI. (2019). *Ethics guidelines for trustworthy AI*. European Commission. https://digital-strategy.ec.europa.eu/en/library/ethics-guidelines-trustworthy-ai

Eubanks, V. (2018). *Automating inequality: How high-tech tools profile, police, and punish the poor*. St. Martin's Press.

Goodfellow, I., Bengio, Y., & Courville, A. (2016). *Deep learning*. MIT Press.

Hall, S. F., Sage, M., Scott, C. F., & Joseph, K. (2023). A systematic review of sophisticated predictive and prescriptive analytics in child welfare: Accuracy, equity, and bias. *Child and Adolescent Social Work Journal, 41*, 831–847. https://doi.org/10.1007/s10560-023-00931-2

Holmes, W., Bialik, M., & Fadel, C. (2019). *Artificial intelligence in education: Promises and implications for teaching and learning*. Center for Curriculum Redesign. https://curriculumredesign.org/our-work/artificial-intelligence-in-education/

Jobin, A., Ienca, M., & Vayena, E. (2019). The global landscape of AI ethics guidelines. *Nature Machine Intelligence, 1*(9), 389–399. https://doi.org/10.1038/s42256-019-0088-2

Joyce, K., Smith-Doerr, L., Alegria, S., Bell, S., Cruz, T., Hoffman, S. G., et al. (2021). Toward a sociology of artificial intelligence: A call for research on inequalities and structural change. *Socius, 7*, 2378023121999581. https://doi.org/10.1177/2378023121999581

Kawakami, A., Sivaraman, V., Cheng, H.-F., Stapleton, L., Cheng, Y., Qing, D., … & Holstein, K. (2022). Improving human-AI partnerships in child welfare: Understanding worker practices, challenges, and desires for algorithmic decision support [Paper presentation]. *Paper Presented at the Proceedings of the 2022 CHI Conference on Human Factors in Computing Systems*. https://doi.org/10.1145/3491102.3517439

Malekoff, A. (2023). A look back and ahead. *Social Work With Groups, 46*(2), 101–102. https://doi.org/10.1080/01609513.2023.2179220

McCoyd, J. L., Lee, J. E., & Kerson, T. S. (2016). *Social work in health settings: Practice in context*. Routledge.

McInroy, L. B. (2021). Teaching technology competencies: A social work practice with technology course. *Journal of Social Work Education, 57*(3), 545–556. https://doi.org/10.1080/10437797.2019.1671272

Mikhaylov, S. J., Esteve, M., & Campion, A. (2018). Artificial intelligence for the public sector: Opportunities and challenges of cross-sector collaboration. *Philosophical Transactions of the Royal Society A: Mathematical, Physical and Engineering Sciences, 376*(2128), 20170357. https://doi.org/10.1098/rsta.2017.0357

Mohri, M., Rostamizadeh, A., & Talwalkar, A. (2018). *Foundations of machine learning* (2nd ed.). MIT Press.

Morley, J., Floridi, L., Kinsey, L., & Elhalal, A. (2020). From what to how: An initial review of publicly available AI ethics tools, methods and research to translate principles into practices. *Science and Engineering Ethics, 26*(4), 2141–2168. https://doi.org/10.1007/s11948-019-00165-5

Munford, R., & Sanders, J. (2011). Embracing the diversity of practice: Indigenous knowledge and mainstream social work practice. *Journal of Social Work Practice, 25*(1), 63–77. https://doi.org/10.1080/02650533.2010.532867

National Association of Social Workers. (2021). *Code of ethics*. NASW Press.
Patchipala, S. (2023). Tackling data and model drift in AI: Strategies for maintaining accuracy during ML model inference. *International Journal of Science and Research Archive, 10*(2), 1198–1209. https://doi.org/10.30574/ijsra.2023.10.2.0855
Reamer, F. G. (2019). Social work education in a digital world: Technology standards for education and practice. *Journal of Social Work Education, 55*(3), 420–432. https://doi.org/10.1080/10437797.2019.1567412
UNESCO. (2021). *Recommendation on the ethics of artificial intelligence*. UNESCO Publishing. https://unesdoc.unesco.org/ark:/48223/pf0000380455.locale=en
Van Ooijen, C., Ubaldi, B., & Welby, B. (2019). *A data-driven public sector: Enabling the strategic use of data for productive, inclusive, and trustworthy governance*. In OECD Working Papers on Public Governance, Vol. 33. OECD.
Villamil, V., Deloria, R., & Wolbring, G. (2019). Artificial intelligence and machine learning: What is the role of social workers, occupational therapists, audiologists, nurses and speech language pathologists according to academic literature and Canadian newspaper coverage?. *In Proceedings of the 5th Workshop on ICTs for improving Patients Rehabilitation Research Techniques* (pp. 83–87). https://doi.org/10.1145/3364138.3364158
Warmington, P., Daniels, H., Edwards, A., Brown, S., Leadbetter, J., Martin, D., & Middleton, D. (2004). *Interagency collaboration: A review of the literature*. Learning in and for Interagency Working Project.
Zetino, J., & Mendoza, N. (2019). Big data and its utility in social work: Learning from the big data revolution in business and healthcare. *Social Work in Public Health, 34*(5), 409–417. https://doi.org/10.1080/19371918.2019.1614508
Zhang, W., Shi, J., Wang, X., & Wynn, H. (2023). AI-powered decision-making in facilitating insurance claim dispute resolution. *Annals of Operations Research, 334*, 1–30. https://doi.org/10.1007/s10479-023-05631-9
Zidaru, T., Morrow, E. M., & Stockley, R. (2021). Ensuring patient and public involvement in the transition to AI-assisted mental health care: A systematic scoping review and agenda for design justice. *Health Expectations, 24*(4), 1072–1124. https://doi.org/10.1111/hex.13299
Zumstein, D., & Hundertmark, S. (2017). Chatbots—An interactive technology for personalized communication transactions and services. *IADIS International Journal on WWW/Internet, 15*(2017), 96–109.

Chapter 2
Ethical Foundations of AI in Social Work

Ruopeng An and Michael A. Lindsey

1 Introduction to Ethical Principles in AI and Social Work

Ethics has long been at the heart of social work practice, research, and education. The National Association of Social Workers (NASW) Code of Ethics articulates the profession's core values—service, social justice, dignity and worth of the person, the importance of human relationships, integrity, and competence—and frames ethical decision-making as an ongoing process of balancing obligations to individuals, communities, and society at large (National Association of Social Workers [NASW], 2021). Building on this foundation, social work ethicists have developed rich traditions of care-based, justice-oriented, and human rights-based approaches that guide practitioners as they confront dilemmas involving scarce resources, structural oppression, and competing duties (Barsky, 2019; Reamer, 2025). In this view, ethics is not merely compliance with rules but a reflective, dialogical, and context-sensitive practice grounded in social work's distinctive mission.

The rapid diffusion of artificial intelligence (AI) introduces a qualitatively new set of ethical questions within this long-standing tradition. AI systems—ranging from predictive analytics in child welfare to large language models used in education, counseling, and policy analysis—shape how information is generated, interpreted, and acted upon in ways that may be opaque even to experienced practitioners. Recent social work scholarship highlights that AI is not merely a neutral "tool," but a socio-technical infrastructure that can reconfigure power dynamics, exacerbate structural inequities, and alter fundamental aspects of professional judgment (Garkisch & Goldkind, 2025; Reamer, 2023; Victor et al., 2023). At the same time, AI may offer new capabilities for early risk identification, personalized services, enhanced information accessibility, and administrative efficiency. Ethical analysis,

R. An (✉) · M. A. Lindsey
Silver School of Social Work, New York University, New York, NY, USA
e-mail: ra4605@nyu.edu; michael.lindsey@nyu.edu

R. An, M. A. Lindsey (eds.), *Artificial Intelligence in Social Work*,
https://doi.org/10.1007/978-3-032-18443-6_2

therefore, must grapple with both the possibilities AI creates and the ways it may deepen or re-inscribe harms that social work has historically sought to remedy.

Emerging work in social work explicitly calls for the development of AI-related knowledge, skills, and ethical sensibilities as part of core professional competence. Ahn et al. (2025), for example, argue that AI literacy should be integrated into social work education, conceptualizing this literacy as encompassing a critical understanding of algorithmic bias, transparency, accountability, and the implications of data practices for marginalized communities. Victor and Herrenkohl (2025) describe how AI is becoming a central focus of social work scholarship and outline the need for discipline-specific frameworks that are grounded in social work values and responsive to evolving technologies. Complementing these calls, social work researchers have begun to evaluate generative AI in concrete professional contexts—for example, using ChatGPT to interrogate the validity and equity of licensing exams (Victor et al., 2023)—thereby illustrating both the promise and the risks of delegating aspects of professional reasoning to AI systems.

Alongside these AI-specific contributions, social work scholars have proposed multidimensional ethical frameworks for technology that foreground equity, transparency, human-centeredness, inclusion, accountability, and sustainability as interrelated guiding principles for the design and use of AI in social work research and practice (Lee et al., 2025). Taken together, this emerging literature suggests that ethical reflection about AI cannot be "bolted on" after technical systems are built. Instead, it must be woven into how problems are framed, which data are collected, how models are developed and deployed, and how impacted communities participate in shaping and governing AI applications. These insights closely align with social work's long-standing commitments to participatory practice, cultural humility, and the structural analysis of power and privilege.

At the same time, social work can draw on established cross-disciplinary ethical frameworks that have been influential in biomedical ethics and AI governance. One widely used framework is the principlist model advanced by Beauchamp and Childress (2019), which identifies four mid-level principles—respect for autonomy, beneficence, non-maleficence, and justice—as a shared vocabulary for analyzing ethical issues across domains. When interpreted through social work values, respect for autonomy highlights clients' rights to informed, meaningful participation in decisions about how AI affects them, including understandable explanations of automated recommendations and accessible paths to contest or refuse automated decisions. Beneficence and non-maleficence emphasize that AI applications should demonstrably promote client and community well-being while minimizing foreseeable harms, such as misclassification, stigmatization, or intensified surveillance. Justice directs attention to how AI systems may reproduce or challenge structural inequities—for instance, by embedding biased historical data into risk prediction models or by intentionally designing systems to identify and remediate disparities.

More recently, policy-oriented frameworks have articulated criteria for "trustworthy" or "responsible" AI that resonate with social work's ethical commitments. The European Commission's Ethics Guidelines for Trustworthy AI outline requirements such as human agency and oversight, technical robustness and safety, privacy and data governance, transparency, diversity and non-discrimination, societal and environmental well-being, and accountability (High-Level Expert Group on Artificial Intelligence, 2019). From a social work perspective, these requirements underscore the importance of maintaining human judgment and relational practice at the core of AI-enabled decision-making, examining how technical choices may differentially impact marginalized groups, and ensuring that mechanisms for redress and public accountability are in place when harms occur. Trustworthiness, in this sense, is not only a technical property of AI systems but also a relational and institutional achievement that depends on transparency, participation, and responsiveness to community concerns.

The Value-Sensitive Design (VSD) framework offers a complementary orientation by treating human values as integral to the entire technology design and implementation process rather than as after-the-fact constraints (Friedman & Hendry, 2019). VSD calls for iterative conceptual, empirical, and technical investigations that identify stakeholders (including those indirectly affected), surface the values at stake, and translate those values into specific design features and organizational practices. This approach aligns closely with social work's emphasis on the co-production of knowledge with service users, attention to power differentials, and responsiveness to context. Applying VSD in social work AI projects might involve, for example, engaging clients, community organizations, and front-line practitioners in defining what "fairness," "safety," or "usefulness" mean in a given setting and incorporating their perspectives into model objectives, evaluation metrics, and governance structures.

Synthesizing these perspectives, several overarching ethical principles emerge as particularly salient for AI in social work: respect for autonomy and self-determination; commitments to justice, equity, and non-discrimination; non-maleficence and beneficence; robust protections for privacy and confidentiality; and strong expectations of transparency and accountability in the design, implementation, and oversight of AI systems. Principlist, "trustworthy AI," and value-sensitive design frameworks each offer complementary tools for articulating and operationalizing these principles. Still, they must be interpreted through the lens of social work's mission, codes of ethics, and lived realities of practice. The remainder of this chapter builds on this integrated foundation by examining how core social work values can guide AI adoption and by exploring specific ethical issues—related to fairness, privacy, consent, and accountability—that arise as AI becomes more deeply embedded in social work practice and policy.

2 Core Social Work Values and the AI Context

Building on this integrated ethical foundation, social work's core professional values—social justice, the dignity and worth of the person, the importance of human relationships, self-determination, and professional integrity—offer a concrete, practice-oriented lens for evaluating how AI should be developed, implemented, and governed in social work contexts.

Social work is guided by core values that underpin its practice, including social justice, the inherent dignity of individuals, self-determination, and professional integrity. These values not only define the profession's ethical obligations but also offer critical insights into how AI should be integrated into social work. As AI technologies become increasingly prominent in social service delivery, evaluating their alignment with these principles is essential. This requires a nuanced understanding of how adopting AI can shape core values.

2.1 *Social Justice*

The principle of social justice is a cornerstone of social work, emphasizing the need to challenge systemic inequalities and promote equity for all individuals, particularly those who are marginalized and vulnerable. When applied thoughtfully, AI can advance social justice by identifying inequities, improving access to resources, and streamlining services for underserved communities. For example, predictive analytics can help allocate resources to neighborhoods with higher rates of homelessness or identify clients at risk of adverse outcomes due to social determinants of health (Eubanks, 2018). These tools, however, have their risks.

Algorithmic bias remains a significant challenge to ensuring social justice in AI systems. Many algorithms rely on historical data, which can reflect and reinforce societal inequities. For instance, data used in child welfare systems have been criticized for disproportionately flagging families of color for intervention, perpetuating racial disparities (Barocas et al., 2023). Addressing these issues requires deliberate efforts to ensure fairness, such as diversifying training datasets, auditing algorithms for bias, and involving marginalized groups in the design process (Mehrabi et al., 2021). Without these measures, the integration of AI could inadvertently exacerbate the inequities that social work seeks to eliminate.

2.2 *Dignity and Worth of the Person*

Social work's commitment to the dignity and worth of every individual underscores the importance of respecting clients' humanity and unique circumstances. By their nature, AI systems operate on patterns and generalizations, which can sometimes conflict with this principle. For instance, an AI model designed to predict client needs may prioritize efficiency over personal context, reducing individuals to data points (Dignum, 2019). Such reductionism risks dehumanizing clients and undermines social work's relational and person-centered ethos.

To align AI with the value of dignity, practitioners must emphasize transparency and interpretability in AI systems. Clients should be able to understand how decisions are made and have opportunities to contest or override AI-driven recommendations. Moreover, the design of AI tools should consider clients' diverse cultural, social, and personal contexts, ensuring that systems are adaptable to individual needs rather than imposing one-size-fits-all solutions (Floridi et al., 2018). By embedding dignity into AI design and application, social workers can ensure that technological advancements enhance, rather than diminish, respect for clients.

2.3 *Self-Determination*

The principle of self-determination recognizes individuals' right to make decisions about their lives, which is central to ethical social work practice. AI systems, particularly those involving predictive analytics or automated decision-making, can challenge this principle. For example, an AI tool might predict that a client is unlikely to benefit from a particular intervention, potentially influencing practitioners to deprioritize that client's preferences (Banks et al., 2020).

Preserving self-determination in the context of AI requires transparency, informed consent, and the availability of alternatives. Clients must be fully informed about how AI systems operate and their implications for service delivery. They should also be able to opt out of AI-driven processes or request a human review of decisions that affect their lives. For instance, AI chatbots are increasingly used to provide initial support in mental health services. However, these systems must operate alongside, not as substitutes for, human professionals to preserve clients' agency (Boucher et al., 2021). When self-determination is upheld, AI can be a powerful tool for empowering individuals rather than constraining their choices.

2.4 *Professional Integrity*

Professional integrity is critical in guiding social workers to act ethically and uphold the profession's values. Integrating AI into social work introduces new ethical dilemmas that test this commitment. For example, using client data in AI systems raises questions about confidentiality and the appropriate boundaries of data usage. Professionals must navigate these dilemmas while maintaining transparency, accountability, and adherence to ethical standards (Beauchamp & Childress, 2019).

Integrity also demands that social workers critically evaluate the tools they adopt. Practitioners must understand the limitations and potential biases of AI systems and ensure that their use does not compromise the quality of care. For example, if an AI system recommends cost-cutting measures that conflict with clients' best interests, social workers have an ethical obligation to challenge those recommendations. Professional integrity requires that practitioners advocate for systems that align with social work values rather than passively accepting technological solutions (Mittelstadt et al., 2016).

2.5 *Balancing Core Values and Technological Potential*

Integrating AI into social work creates opportunities to advance the profession's core values, but it also introduces tensions that require careful navigation. Social justice, dignity, self-determination, and integrity are not static ideals but dynamic principles that must evolve to address the complexities of modern technology. For instance, while AI can enhance equity by identifying underserved populations, it can also reinforce systemic biases if not carefully designed. Similarly, while AI can improve efficiency, it must not do so at the expense of client dignity or agency.

Social workers must reconcile these tensions by engaging in ongoing dialogue with technologists, policymakers, and clients. Interdisciplinary collaboration is crucial to ensuring that AI systems are designed and implemented in ways that reflect social work values. This includes advocating for ethical standards in AI development, participating in the design of human-centered technologies, and holding institutions accountable for the consequences of AI use (Friedman et al., 2013).

3 Privacy, Confidentiality, and Data Protection

Privacy and confidentiality are fundamental ethical obligations in social work, forming the bedrock of trust between practitioners and clients. Integrating AI into social work introduces unprecedented challenges to these principles, as AI systems often rely on collecting, storing, and analyzing vast amounts of personal data. Safeguarding client information in the context of AI requires a thorough understanding of data governance principles and adherence to relevant regulatory standards.

The challenge of maintaining confidentiality in AI-driven social work begins with the sheer scale and scope of data collection. AI systems designed for predictive analytics, case management, or resource allocation often require access to sensitive client information, such as health records, financial data, or behavioral patterns (Floridi et al., 2018). This reliance on data introduces risks, including unauthorized access, data breaches, and misuse of information. For instance, a violation in an AI-powered case management system could expose intimate details of a client's life, causing significant harm to their well-being and trust in the system (Wachter & Mittelstadt, 2019).

One of the primary concerns in this context is the potential for re-identification of anonymized data. Even when datasets are stripped of personally identifiable information, sophisticated AI algorithms can sometimes infer individual identities by cross-referencing or identifying unique patterns (Narayanan & Shmatikov, 2010). This raises questions about whether anonymization alone safeguards confidentiality and highlights the need for more robust data protection strategies, such as differential privacy techniques, which add statistical noise to datasets to obscure individual data points while preserving aggregate patterns (Dwork & Roth, 2014).

Data governance principles are critical in addressing these challenges, providing a framework for responsible data management. These principles emphasize accountability, transparency, and stewardship, ensuring data is collected, stored, and used ethically and securely. Effective data governance requires clearly defined roles and responsibilities, robust cybersecurity measures, and regular audits to detect vulnerabilities (van den Hoven et al., 2015). For social work organizations, this means implementing data access controls, encrypting sensitive information, and establishing protocols for responding to data breaches.

Regulatory standards are crucial in shaping data governance practices by establishing legal frameworks that safeguard client information. In the European Union, the General Data Protection Regulation (GDPR) sets a high standard for data protection, requiring organizations to obtain explicit consent for data collection, ensure data portability, and uphold the "right to be forgotten." These provisions align with social work's ethical obligation to respect client autonomy and dignity (GDPR, 2016). Similarly, in the United States, the Health Insurance Portability and Accountability Act (HIPAA) establishes safeguards for the confidentiality of health information and mandates the secure handling of electronic health records (Office for Civil Rights, 2013).

However, regulatory compliance alone is insufficient to address AI's ethical complexities in social work. For example, while GDPR emphasizes transparency, the opacity of AI algorithms—often referred to as the "black box" problem—can obscure how client data is used and decisions are made (Wachter et al., 2017). This lack of explainability poses a significant ethical challenge, as clients may be unable to understand or challenge the outcomes generated by AI-driven systems. Ensuring transparency in AI systems requires developing interpretable models and providing clear, accessible explanations for AI-driven decisions.

Cultural and contextual factors further complicate the ethics of data protection in AI. For example, in low-resource settings, the infrastructure and expertise required to implement robust data protection measures may be lacking, increasing the risk of data breaches and misuse (Mittelstadt et al., 2016). Additionally, cultural norms around privacy and data sharing vary widely, influencing how confidentiality is perceived and practiced. Social workers must navigate these differences sensitively, adapting data governance practices to align with local values while upholding universal ethical standards.

AI also introduces unique challenges to the principle of minimization, which requires collecting only the data necessary for a specific purpose. The predictive nature of AI often incentivizes the collection of extensive datasets to improve model accuracy, potentially conflicting with the goal of minimizing data. This tension underscores the need for clear guidelines on data collection and usage, ensuring that the benefits of AI are achieved without compromising client privacy.

To address these challenges, interdisciplinary collaboration is essential. Social workers must collaborate with data scientists, ethicists, and policymakers to design AI systems that prioritize privacy and confidentiality. This includes advocating for technologies that incorporate privacy-preserving mechanisms, such as federated learning, which enables AI models to be trained on decentralized data without transferring sensitive information to a central server (McMahan et al., 2017). By embedding ethical considerations into the development and deployment of AI systems, social workers can help mitigate risks while harnessing the potential of technology to enhance practice.

4 Fairness, Equity, and Non-Discrimination in AI Systems

Fairness, equity, and non-discrimination are foundational principles in social work, deeply intertwined with its mission to advance social justice and protect vulnerable populations. Integrating AI into social work presents opportunities to promote these principles while also risking the exacerbation of systemic inequities.

4.1 Algorithmic Bias and Its Implications

AI systems, particularly those using ML algorithms, are only as unbiased as the data and assumptions that underlie them. Algorithmic bias refers to systematic and repeatable errors in AI systems that lead to unfair outcomes, often disproportionately affecting marginalized groups. Such biases usually originate in the data used to train algorithms. Historical data, which reflects existing societal inequalities, can reinforce and amplify those inequities when used without critical scrutiny (Barocas et al., 2023). For example, predictive policing systems trained on crime data have been shown to disproportionately target Black and low-income communities due to historical over-policing, perpetuating cycles of discrimination (Eubanks, 2018).

In social work, algorithmic bias poses significant risks, as AI systems are increasingly used for tasks such as eligibility screening, resource allocation, and risk assessment. If left unchecked, biased algorithms can lead to discriminatory practices, such as denying unfair service or implementing disproportionate interventions in specific populations. For example, research on AI decision aids in rental housing markets has shown that biases in these systems can lead to unfair human decisions across racial groups, exacerbating inequities in housing access (Wang et al., 2023).

4.2 Methods to Detect and Mitigate Inequities

Detecting and addressing algorithmic bias is critical in ensuring fairness and equity in AI systems. Bias detection involves examining the outcomes of AI models to identify unfair treatment patterns across different demographic groups. Statistical fairness metrics, such as demographic parity and equalized odds, can help evaluate whether an AI system treats individuals equitably (Mehrabi et al., 2021). For example, demographic parity ensures that an algorithm's decisions are distributed proportionally across demographic groups, while equalized odds require that outcomes are equally accurate across all groups.

Mitigating bias begins with the data used to train AI models. Ensuring diverse, representative datasets can help reduce biases, but achieving true representativeness can be challenging. Marginalized groups are often underrepresented in data, leading models to need to account for their unique needs and circumstances. Techniques such as data augmentation, which generate synthetic data to balance representation, can help address this issue (Binns, 2018).

Algorithmic fairness can be improved beyond data through model adjustments. Techniques like reweighting data to balance outcomes across groups, adversarial debiasing to penalize discriminatory patterns during training, and post-processing adjustments to correct biased outputs are effective methods for reducing bias (Zemel et al., 2013). Fairness-aware ML frameworks explicitly incorporate fairness constraints into the optimization process, ensuring the model adheres to ethical principles during development (Corbett-Davies et al., 2023).

4.3 Ensuring Equitable Outcomes

Equity in AI systems goes beyond the absence of bias; it involves actively working to reduce disparities and promote justice. In the context of social work, this means designing AI systems that prioritize the needs of historically underserved and marginalized populations. Strategies for ensuring equitable outcomes include participatory design, transparency, and accountability.

Participatory design involves engaging diverse stakeholders, including marginalized communities, in the development of AI systems. By incorporating the perspectives and lived experiences of those affected by AI, designers can create systems that better address the unique challenges faced by these groups (Friedman et al., 2013). For example, involving clients in the design of an AI-powered resource allocation tool can help ensure that the system reflects their priorities and avoids unintended harm.

Transparency is another essential component of equitable AI. Clients and practitioners must understand how AI systems make decisions, particularly when those decisions have significant consequences for individuals' lives. Transparent AI systems build trust and enable scrutiny, allowing stakeholders to identify and challenge inequities. Enhancing transparency includes using interpretable models, providing clear documentation of algorithms, and offering accessible explanations of AI-driven outcomes (Wachter et al., 2017).

Accountability mechanisms are crucial for addressing the impacts of AI systems. Clear lines of responsibility must be established to ensure that practitioners, organizations, and developers are held accountable for inequitable outcomes. This includes implementing policies for regular audits, creating avenues for redress when harm occurs, and mandating impact assessments to evaluate the social consequences of AI systems (Floridi et al., 2018).

5 Transparency, Explainability, and Informed Consent

Transparency, explainability, and informed consent are critical components of ethical AI deployment in social work. These principles ensure that AI-driven decisions are understandable, accessible, and aligned with clients' rights and autonomy. As AI systems increasingly influence decisions in social work, practitioners must address the challenges of opaque algorithms, client comprehension, and ethical consent processes.

5.1 The Need for Interpretable AI Models

Transparency in AI involves revealing how algorithms process data and arrive at specific outcomes. This principle is especially crucial in social work, where decisions frequently have profound consequences for individuals and communities. Opaque or "black box" algorithms, which process data in ways that are difficult to understand even for their developers, create significant ethical challenges. These models risk undermining trust and accountability, as neither clients nor practitioners can scrutinize or challenge their decisions (Wachter et al., 2017).

Interpretable AI models provide a solution by offering insights into the decision-making process. These models allow practitioners to understand which factors influenced a particular outcome, enabling them to explain these decisions to clients. For example, interpretable models in child welfare systems can clarify why certain families were flagged as high-risk, ensuring practitioners can contextualize and validate the algorithm's recommendations (Chouldechova et al., 2018). Social workers can maintain accountability and effectively address client concerns by making AI decisions transparent.

Tools such as SHAP (Shapley Additive Explanations) and LIME (Local Interpretable Model-Agnostic Explanations) are commonly used to enhance the interpretability of complex models. These methods identify the contribution of individual variables to a model's output, offering actionable explanations for AI-driven decisions (Ribeiro et al., 2016). Adopting these tools in social work can help ensure that AI systems are technically robust and ethically sound.

5.2 Ensuring Client Understanding of AI-Driven Decisions

In social work, understanding the client is paramount to ethical practice. Clients have the right to know how decisions affecting their lives are made, yet the complexity of AI systems often poses barriers to comprehension. This lack of understanding can lead to disempowerment, particularly for individuals in vulnerable or marginalized groups, who may already face challenges in navigating bureaucratic systems (Floridi et al., 2018).

To address these issues, social workers must advocate for clear and accessible communication of AI-driven decisions. Simplified explanations, visual aids, and analogies can help bridge the gap between technical complexity and client understanding. For example, practitioners might explain AI outcomes in concrete scenarios rather than presenting clients with abstract probabilities and emphasize the rationale behind specific recommendations (Dignum, 2019). This approach not only empowers clients but also fosters trust in AI systems.

5.3 *Upholding Informed Consent in Data Use*

Informed consent is a cornerstone of ethical social work. It ensures that clients are aware of and agree to how their information is collected, used, and shared. Integrating AI introduces new complexities to this process, as clients must consent to data collection and understand how AI systems analyze and act on their information. Achieving informed consent in the context of AI requires a careful balance of transparency, accessibility, and respect for client autonomy (van den Hoven et al., 2015).

One challenge is explaining the implications of data use in AI systems. For example, clients may consent to sharing their data for a specific purpose, such as assessing eligibility for a housing program. However, they may not fully understand that the same data could be used to train algorithms for other purposes. This raises questions about whether consent can genuinely be informed if clients lack a clear picture of how their data might be repurposed (Wachter & Mittelstadt, 2019).

Social workers must prioritize clarity and specificity in communication to uphold informed consent. Consent forms should clearly outline the immediate use of data, potential secondary uses, associated risks, and relevant safeguards. Practitioners should also allow clients to ask questions, withdraw consent, or opt out of AI-driven processes without fear of discrimination or reduced access to services. This ensures consent is a dynamic and ongoing process rather than a one-time transaction.

Furthermore, innovative technologies such as blockchain can enhance consent processes by creating immutable records of client agreements. These records ensure that clients' preferences are respected and provide accountability for the use of their data. For instance, if a client withdraws consent, blockchain can provide a transparent mechanism for verifying that their data is no longer in use (Zhang et al., 2018). Such tools exemplify how technology can support ethical practice in AI-driven social work.

6 Accountability and Responsibility for AI Outcomes

Accountability and responsibility are critical ethical considerations in integrating AI into social work. These principles determine who is answerable for AI-driven outcomes and ensure that mechanisms are in place to address errors, biases, or harms resulting from AI systems. Social work's ethical framework, which emphasizes transparency, justice, and the protection of vulnerable populations, offers a valuable lens for examining accountability in the context of AI.

6.1 Shared Accountability Across Stakeholders

Ethical accountability for AI outcomes is inherently distributed among stakeholders, each with distinct roles and responsibilities. Integrating AI into social work requires a shared approach to accountability, as no single entity operates in isolation in the design, deployment, or use of AI systems.

- **Individual Practitioners:** Social workers who use AI tools are responsible for understanding their limitations, ensuring they align with ethical standards, and making informed decisions based on AI recommendations. Practitioners cannot delegate their moral obligations to AI systems; instead, they must critically evaluate the outputs of these tools and exercise professional judgment. For instance, a predictive analytics tool may suggest a course of action for a client. However, the social worker is ultimately responsible for determining whether it is appropriate, considering the client's unique context and needs (Banks et al., 2020).
- **Organizations:** Institutions employing AI in their operations bear significant responsibility for the outcomes of these systems. Organizations are accountable for selecting, deploying, and maintaining AI tools that adhere to ethical principles. This includes conducting impact assessments, providing adequate staff training, and establishing policies for the ethical use of AI. Organizations also play a key role in addressing systemic biases in AI, ensuring that these tools do not perpetuate or exacerbate inequities (Eubanks, 2018).
- **Developers and Designers:** AI developers and designers are responsible for creating systems prioritizing fairness, transparency, and inclusivity. They must identify and mitigate biases in training data, ensure algorithms are interpretable, and incorporate safeguards against misuse. Developers also have an ethical obligation to engage with stakeholders, including social workers and clients, during the design process to ensure the system reflects the values and needs of its intended users (Friedman et al., 2013).
- **Policymakers and Regulators:** Policymakers and regulators are responsible for establishing frameworks and guidelines that govern the ethical use of AI. This includes setting standards for transparency, accountability, and fairness and enforcing compliance through audits and penalties. Regulatory frameworks, such as the European Union's GDPR, provide mechanisms to hold organizations

and developers accountable for breaches of ethical standards (GDPR, 2016). In social work, policymakers must also consider the unique vulnerabilities of the populations served and adapt regulations accordingly.

6.2 *Mechanisms for Redress*

Mechanisms for redress are essential to ensure that harms resulting from AI systems are identified, addressed, and remedied. These mechanisms must be accessible, transparent, and responsive to the needs of affected individuals and communities. Several key approaches can help establish accountability and provide avenues for redress:

- **Impact Assessments:** Conducting social impact assessments before deploying AI systems helps identify potential risks and unintended consequences. These assessments evaluate how an AI tool might affect diverse populations, allowing organizations to address concerns proactively (Floridi et al., 2018).
- **Audit Trails:** Comprehensive audit trails are essential for tracing AI systems' decisions. This involves documenting the data inputs, algorithms, and decision-making processes that led to specific outcomes. Audit trails enable stakeholders to investigate and understand errors or biases, providing a basis for corrective actions (Wachter & Mittelstadt, 2019).
- **Appeal Mechanisms:** Establish transparent processes that allow clients to appeal AI-driven decisions, ensuring they have a voice in correcting errors or addressing grievances. For example, if an AI system incorrectly denies a client access to a service, the client should be able to challenge this decision through a transparent and fair process (Raji et al., 2020).
- **Liability Frameworks:** Clear liability frameworks delineate who is responsible when AI systems cause harm. These frameworks can allocate responsibility across practitioners, organizations, and developers based on their roles and the specific circumstances of the case. For instance, if harm arises from a developer's failure to address known biases, they may bear greater liability than the practitioner who relied on the tool (Mittelstadt et al., 2016).
- **Ethics Oversight Committees:** Organizations can establish ethics oversight committees to monitor AI use and address related ethical concerns. These committees bring diverse perspectives, including those of practitioners, clients, and technologists, to evaluate the moral implications of AI systems and recommend improvement actions (Dignum, 2019).

6.3 Challenges in Establishing Accountability

Despite these mechanisms, several challenges complicate accountability for AI outcomes. One major issue is the opacity of AI systems, particularly those involving deep learning algorithms, which operate in complex ways that are difficult to interpret or explain. This lack of transparency can make it challenging to determine who is responsible when things go wrong, leading to a "responsibility gap" (Floridi et al., 2018).

Another challenge is the diffusion of responsibility across stakeholders. With multiple parties involved in an AI system's lifecycle, accountability can become fragmented, making it challenging to determine who should be held responsible for specific outcomes. Addressing this requires clearly defining roles and responsibilities at every stage of AI development and use.

Additionally, power imbalances between stakeholders can hinder accountability. Vulnerable populations, such as clients of social work services, may require additional resources or knowledge to challenge AI-driven decisions. At the same time, developers and organizations may disproportionately influence how these systems are designed and deployed (Eubanks, 2018).

7 Balancing Innovation with Ethical Vigilance

Integrating AI into social work offers immense innovation potential, from improving service delivery to addressing systemic inequities. However, these advancements bring significant ethical challenges that necessitate vigilance to ensure that innovation does not compromise ethical principles. The tension between technological progress and ethical caution necessitates a deliberate and thoughtful approach to navigating the risks associated with rapid AI development, including the "ethics washing" phenomenon and the challenge of ensuring genuine accountability.

7.1 The Tensions Between Technological Advancement and Ethical Caution

Technological advancements in AI often prioritize efficiency, scalability, and predictive accuracy—goals that can conflict with the nuanced and human-centered nature of social work practice. For instance, predictive analytics in child welfare systems can more efficiently identify at-risk families than traditional methods. However, these models may overlook the context-specific factors critical to ethical decision-making (Eubanks, 2018). This tension highlights the need to carefully assess whether the benefits of AI innovation align with social work's ethical responsibilities.

A key concern is that the speed of AI development often outpaces the establishment of ethical guidelines and regulatory frameworks. As AI technologies become more sophisticated, the risk of unintended consequences grows, mainly when systems are deployed without rigorous evaluation. For example, facial recognition technologies have been criticized for their high error rates in identifying individuals from racial minority groups, raising questions about their fairness and appropriateness in public services (Buolamwini & Gebru, 2018). In social work, such issues can lead to discriminatory practices, undermining the profession's commitment to equity and justice.

Another challenge is the ethical gray areas that emerge in AI development. Many AI applications involve trade-offs, such as balancing the need for accurate predictions with the risks of privacy intrusion. These trade-offs require careful consideration of social work values to ensure that technological innovation does not overshadow ethical priorities (Floridi et al., 2018).

7.2 *The Risks of "Ethics Washing"*

"Ethics washing" refers to superficially addressing ethical concerns to gain public trust while failing to make substantive changes in the design or use of AI systems. This phenomenon often manifests as vague or unenforced ethical statements, the creation of ethics boards with limited authority, or the adoption of frameworks that lack accountability mechanisms (Binns, 2018). Ethics washing poses a significant threat to the responsible integration of AI, as it can obscure harmful practices and undermine efforts to hold developers and organizations accountable.

In social work, ethics washing can occur when organizations adopt AI systems with stated commitments to fairness or transparency but fail to address underlying biases or operationalize these principles effectively. For instance, a case management system may claim to use "ethical AI" but rely on biased data that disproportionately flags specific demographics as high-risk. Such practices can erode trust and perpetuate harm, particularly for marginalized communities.

Social work organizations and practitioners must demand measurable and enforceable ethical standards to counter ethics washing. This includes requiring developers to demonstrate how AI systems uphold principles such as fairness and accountability, conducting independent audits of AI tools, and refusing to adopt technologies that fail to meet ethical criteria (Raji et al., 2020).

7.3 Ensuring Genuine Responsibility in AI Innovation

Genuine responsibility in AI innovation involves embedding ethical considerations into every stage of the technology lifecycle, from design to deployment and evaluation. Several strategies can help achieve this goal:

- **Interdisciplinary Collaboration:** Ethical AI requires collaboration between technologists, social workers, ethicists, and policymakers. By bringing diverse perspectives, these stakeholders can identify potential risks and ensure that AI systems align with social work values (Friedman et al., 2013). For example, involving social workers in the design of predictive analytics tools can help ensure that these systems consider the complexities of client needs.
- **Ethics-by-Design Approaches:** Ethics-by-design involves integrating ethical principles into the technical architecture of AI systems. This approach goes beyond compliance, directly embedding fairness, transparency, and inclusivity into algorithms and workflows (van den Hoven et al., 2015). For instance, incorporating bias detection mechanisms into ML models can help prevent discriminatory outcomes before they occur.
- **Continuous Monitoring and Evaluation:** AI systems must be subject to ongoing scrutiny to identify and address unintended consequences. This includes regular audits, impact assessments, and feedback loops that involve practitioners and clients. Continuous monitoring ensures that AI systems remain aligned with ethical standards even as contexts and use cases evolve (Floridi et al., 2018).
- **Transparent Reporting:** Transparency ensures accountability in AI innovation. Organizations must document how AI systems are designed, trained, and deployed, and disclose their limitations and potential risks. This transparency enables stakeholders to make informed decisions and hold developers accountable for their practices (Wachter et al., 2017).
- **Education and Advocacy:** Social workers have a unique role in advocating for ethical AI practices within their organizations and broader policy discussions. Education on AI ethics and advocacy for robust regulatory frameworks can help ensure that the profession remains a strong voice for justice and accountability amid technological change (Banks et al., 2020).

7.4 The Role of Regulatory Frameworks

Regulatory frameworks are crucial in ensuring that ethical principles guide innovation. Standards such as the GDPR and emerging guidelines for trustworthy AI emphasize accountability, transparency, and fairness as prerequisites for responsible innovation (GDPR, 2016). In social work, these frameworks can provide a foundation for evaluating AI tools and holding organizations accountable for their ethical obligations.

However, existing regulations often lag behind technological advancements, underscoring the need for proactive policymaking. Policymakers must engage with social work practitioners to understand the unique challenges posed by AI in this field and develop regulations that address these concerns. By shaping the regulatory landscape, social workers can help ensure that innovation aligns with the profession's commitment to social justice and ethical practice.

8 Global and Cultural Dimensions of AI Ethics

Integrating AI into social work occurs within a diverse and interconnected global context. Cultural norms, legal frameworks, and resource disparities are critical in shaping ethical considerations for AI and influencing how these technologies are designed, deployed, and perceived worldwide. Ethically integrating AI requires a culturally responsive, globally inclusive approach that addresses disparities and adapts to diverse socio-legal environments.

8.1 The Role of Cultural Norms in AI Ethics

Cultural values and norms significantly influence perceptions of ethical behavior and acceptable practices, including those related to AI. In some societies, collective values emphasize community well-being, whereas in others, individual autonomy and privacy are prioritized. These differences affect how AI systems are implemented and the ethical principles that guide their use.

For example, in collectivist cultures, integrating AI into social services may prioritize community-level outcomes, such as resource allocation for the shared benefit of all, over individual-level considerations. In contrast, societies that emphasize individualism may prioritize privacy, informed consent, and personal autonomy in AI applications (Triandis, 1995). Social workers in these contexts must navigate these cultural nuances, ensuring that AI systems align with local values while upholding universal ethical principles such as fairness and justice (Floridi et al., 2018).

Culturally responsive approaches to AI also involve recognizing and addressing implicit biases embedded in technology. AI systems trained on datasets rooted in specific cultural or geographic contexts often struggle to generalize effectively across diverse populations. For instance, language processing models primarily developed using Western languages frequently fail to perform adequately with non-Western languages or dialects, resulting in inequitable outcomes for underrepresented groups (Bender et al., 2021). Social workers must advocate for AI systems that are inclusive and representative of the populations they serve, ensuring cultural sensitivity in design and application.

8.2 *Legal Frameworks and Ethical Standards Across Jurisdictions*

Legal and regulatory frameworks governing AI vary significantly across countries, reflecting different societal priorities and levels of technological development. The GDPR establishes stringent data protection standards in the European Union, emphasizing transparency, accountability, and individual rights (GDPR, 2016). In contrast, countries with less robust regulatory safeguard frameworks may require more comprehensive frameworks to protect privacy and ensure the ethical use of AI, creating challenges for social workers in these contexts.

In some regions, the absence of clear legal standards can lead to the unchecked deployment of AI systems, resulting in ethical lapses and potential harm. For instance, AI-driven surveillance technologies have been criticized for infringing on civil liberties and disproportionately targeting marginalized groups, particularly in countries with weak protections against misuse (Feldstein, 2021). Social workers must be vigilant in these environments, advocating for stronger regulatory oversight and adherence to international ethical standards.

International organizations, such as UNESCO and the IEEE, have developed guidelines and frameworks to promote the ethical use of AI globally. UNESCO's Recommendation on the Ethics of Artificial Intelligence emphasizes the importance of inclusivity, accountability, and sustainability in AI systems, providing a valuable reference for practitioners navigating diverse legal contexts (UNESCO, 2021). These global frameworks can serve as benchmarks for social workers seeking to uphold ethical standards across jurisdictions.

8.3 *Resource Disparities and Ethical Implications*

Resource disparities across countries and communities create significant challenges to the equitable integration of AI into social work. High-income countries often have greater access to advanced AI technologies, robust infrastructure, and technical expertise, enabling them to implement sophisticated systems that improve service delivery. In contrast, low- and middle-income countries may face resource constraints that limit their ability to develop or adopt ethical AI systems, exacerbating global inequities (Mittelstadt et al., 2016).

For example, rural or under-resourced communities may need more digital infrastructure to support AI-driven social work tools, such as case management systems or predictive analytics. This digital divide not only limits the benefits of AI for these populations but also raises ethical concerns about the fairness and inclusivity of technological advancements. Social workers in resource-limited settings must prioritize accessible, context-appropriate solutions and advocate for investments in infrastructure and capacity building to bridge these gaps.

Open-source AI tools and collaborative initiatives offer promising avenues for addressing resource disparities. Social work organizations can develop cost-effective solutions that align with local needs and ethical standards by leveraging open-access platforms and fostering international partnerships. For instance, community-driven datasets and models can help ensure that AI systems are culturally and contextually relevant while minimizing reliance on proprietary technologies (Hsu et al., 2022).

8.4 Culturally Responsive Approaches to AI Ethics

Culturally responsive approaches emphasize tailoring AI systems to the specific values, needs, and circumstances of diverse populations. This requires ongoing engagement with stakeholders, including clients, community leaders, and cultural experts, to ensure that AI systems respect and reflect local contexts.

Participatory design methods are particularly effective in fostering cultural responsiveness. By involving stakeholders in the development process and ensuring that AI systems align with the communities' priorities, social workers can identify potential cultural and ethical concerns early (Friedman et al., 2013). For example, in Indigenous communities, where collective decision-making and respect for traditional knowledge are paramount, participatory design can help integrate these principles into AI applications.

Cultural responsiveness also involves challenging assumptions embedded in AI systems. Developers and practitioners must critically examine the cultural biases inherent in datasets, algorithms, and evaluation metrics and address them through strategies such as dataset diversification and culturally sensitive training (Binns, 2018). Additionally, social workers must advocate for the inclusion of diverse voices in AI governance, ensuring that a broad range of cultural perspectives informs the development of ethical standards.

8.5 Global Collaboration and Ethical Leadership

The global and cultural dimensions of AI ethics require collaborative efforts to address shared challenges and promote equitable outcomes. International partnerships among governments, organizations, and civil society can facilitate knowledge exchange, capacity building, and the development of ethical standards that transcend cultural and geographic boundaries (Floridi et al., 2018).

Social workers play a vital role in these collaborative efforts. By leveraging their expertise in cultural competence and ethical practice, they can help develop inclusive, equitable, and culturally sensitive AI systems. Moreover, social workers can serve as ethical leaders in advocating for global policies and frameworks that prioritize social justice and human rights in AI development.

9 Developing Ethical Competencies and Guidelines

Integrating AI into social work demands the development of robust ethical competencies and guidelines to navigate its complexities. As AI systems become increasingly central to social work practice, practitioners, organizations, and policymakers must ensure that these technologies are deployed responsibly, ethically, and equitably. This requires ongoing training, interdisciplinary collaboration, adherence to professional codes of ethics, and alignment with emerging standards for the responsible use of AI.

9.1 The Role of Ongoing Training in Ethical AI Competency

Ongoing training is crucial for equipping social workers with the knowledge and skills necessary to utilize AI technologies ethically. Many practitioners lack familiarity with AI's technical underpinnings, including its capabilities, limitations, and ethical risks. Without this understanding, social workers may struggle to assess AI systems or advocate for their clients.

Ethical training should address several core areas, including data privacy, algorithmic bias, and the ethical implications of automated decision-making. For instance, training programs can explore real-world scenarios, such as predictive analytics in child welfare, to help practitioners recognize and address potential harms (Chouldechova et al., 2018). These programs should also emphasize transparency and informed consent, ensuring that social workers can communicate effectively with clients about AI-driven decisions.

Interdisciplinary collaboration is essential for practical training. Involving data scientists, ethicists, and legal experts in the development and delivery of training programs can provide social workers with diverse perspectives on AI ethics. For example, a workshop led by a team of technologists and social work practitioners can illuminate the technical and ethical dimensions of bias in AI systems, thereby fostering a deeper understanding of how to mitigate such issues (Friedman et al., 2013).

9.2 Interdisciplinary Collaboration for Ethical AI Development

Collaboration across disciplines is crucial for developing AI systems that align with social work's values and ethical principles. As experts in human behavior and ethical practice, social workers bring a unique perspective to AI development that can help ensure these technologies address the needs of diverse populations. Social workers can advocate for integrating ethical considerations into the design, deployment, and evaluation of AI systems by collaborating with data scientists, engineers, and policymakers.

Participatory design is a key interdisciplinary collaboration approach involving stakeholders at every stage of the AI lifecycle. For example, social workers can collaborate with developers to create transparent, fair, and responsive case management tools. This collaborative process enhances the ethical quality of AI systems, fostering trust and accountability among stakeholders (Binns, 2018).

Professional organizations and academic institutions can play a pivotal role in facilitating interdisciplinary collaboration. Conferences, joint research initiatives, and cross-disciplinary committees provide platforms for dialogue and knowledge exchange, enabling practitioners and technologists to address ethical challenges collectively. For instance, the IEEE Global Initiative on Ethics of Autonomous and Intelligent Systems brings together experts from diverse fields to develop frameworks and guidelines for ethical AI (IEEE, 2019).

9.3 Professional Codes of Ethics and AI Integration

Professional codes of ethics provide a foundational framework for ethical decision-making in social work, offering guidance on navigating the challenges posed by AI. The National Association of Social Workers (NASW) Code of Ethics emphasizes principles such as respect for client dignity, commitment to social justice, and the importance of informed consent—all of which are directly relevant to the ethical use of AI (NASW, 2021). Social workers can draw on these principles to critically evaluate AI systems, ensuring they align with the profession's core values.

However, existing codes of ethics may not fully address the complexities of AI. As AI evolves, professional organizations must update their codes to reflect emerging ethical challenges. This includes incorporating guidelines on data ethics, accountability for AI-driven decisions, and the moral implications of automated processes. By aligning their ethical frameworks with the realities of AI, social work organizations can equip practitioners with the necessary tools to navigate this rapidly evolving landscape.

9.4 Building a Culture of Ethical AI Practice

Developing ethical competencies and guidelines is not only a technical or procedural task but also a cultural one. Social work organizations must foster ethical AI practices, prioritizing reflection, accountability, and continuous improvement. This involves creating spaces for dialogue about moral dilemmas, encouraging critical engagement with AI systems, and recognizing the value of diverse perspectives in shaping ethical standards.

Leadership plays a critical role in cultivating this culture. Organizational leaders can set the tone by prioritizing ethical considerations in decision-making, investing in training and capacity building, and promoting a vision of AI that aligns with the mission and values of the social work profession. By embedding ethics into the organizational ethos, leaders can ensure that ethical AI becomes a collective responsibility rather than an individual obligation.

10 Anchoring AI in Social Work's Ethical Foundations

Integrating AI into social work presents an unprecedented opportunity to enhance service delivery, decision-making, and social justice outcomes. However, this potential can only be realized if AI systems are developed, implemented, and monitored within a robust ethical framework that aligns with social work's core values. This chapter has provided a comprehensive exploration of the ethical dimensions of AI, emphasizing the importance of embedding ethics at every stage of the AI lifecycle. By grounding AI in the ethical foundations of social work, practitioners and organizations can navigate the complexities of this emerging field responsibly and effectively.

Key insights from this chapter highlight the multifaceted nature of ethical considerations in AI. Ethical principles such as privacy, fairness, accountability, and cultural responsiveness provide essential guardrails for navigating the challenges posed by AI technologies. Privacy and data protection remain critical, given the sensitive nature of client information. Fairness and equity must guide efforts to address algorithmic bias and ensure inclusive outcomes. Accountability mechanisms distribute responsibility across practitioners, developers, organizations, and policymakers, ensuring that AI systems align with the values of social work. Furthermore, the global and cultural dimensions of AI ethics emphasize the importance of context-sensitive approaches that respect local cultural norms and address disparities in access to resources.

The chapter also examined the crucial role of ethical competencies and guidelines in promoting responsible AI use. Ongoing training equips practitioners with the knowledge necessary to critically evaluate AI systems, while interdisciplinary collaboration fosters ethically grounded and technically robust innovation. Professional codes of ethics and emerging global standards offer a foundation for assessing and guiding the use of AI in social work, ensuring that technological advancements remain aligned with the profession's mission.

As AI continues to evolve, it is imperative to anchor its development and application in the ethical foundations of social work. This involves adhering to established ethical principles and actively shaping the future of AI to reflect the profession's commitment to dignity, justice, and human rights. Subsequent chapters will build on these insights, examining specific applications of AI in social work and exploring how ethical frameworks can be operationalized to address the unique challenges and opportunities in diverse practice settings. Through this ongoing dialogue, social workers can ensure that AI is a tool for empowerment and equity, advancing the profession's mission in an increasingly digital world.

Competing Interests The authors have no conflicts of interest to declare that are relevant to the content of this chapter.

References

Ahn, E., Choi, M., Fowler, P. J., & Song, I. H. (2025). Artificial intelligence (AI) literacy for social work: Implications for core competencies. *Journal of the Society for Social Work and Research, 16*(1), 9–26. https://doi.org/10.1086/735187

Banks, S., Cai, T., de Jonge, E., Shears, J., Shum, M., Sobočan, A. M., Strom, K., Truell, R., Úriz, M. J., & Weinberg, M. (2020). *Ethical challenges for social workers during COVID-19: A global perspective.*

Barocas, S., Hardt, M., & Narayanan, A. (2023). *Fairness and machine learning: Limitations and opportunities.* MIT Press.

Barsky, A. E. (2019). *Ethics and values in social work: An integrated approach for a comprehensive curriculum* (2nd ed.). Oxford University Press.

Beauchamp, T. L., & Childress, J. F. (2019). *Principles of biomedical ethics* (8th ed.). Oxford University Press.

Bender, E. M., Gebru, T., McMillan-Major, A., & Shmitchell, S. (2021). On the dangers of stochastic parrots: Can language models be too big? *Proceedings of the 2021 ACM Conference on Fairness, Accountability, and Transparency* (pp. 610–623). https://doi.org/10.1145/3442188.3445922

Binns, R. (2018). Fairness in machine learning: Lessons from political philosophy. In *Conference on fairness, accountability and transparency* (pp. 149–159). PMLR.

Boucher, E. M., Harake, N. R., Ward, H. E., Stoeckl, S. E., Vargas, J., Minkel, J., et al. (2021). Artificially intelligent chatbots in digital mental health interventions: A review. *Expert Review of Medical Devices, 18*(sup1), 37–49. https://doi.org/10.1080/17434440.2021.2013200

Buolamwini, J., & Gebru, T. (2018). Gender shades: Intersectional accuracy disparities in commercial gender classification. In *Conference on fairness, accountability and transparency* (pp. 77–91). PMLR.

Chouldechova, A., Benavides-Prado, D., Fialko, O., & Vaithianathan, R. (2018, January). A case study of algorithm-assisted decision making in child maltreatment hotline screening decisions. In *Conference on fairness, accountability and transparency* (pp. 134–148). PMLR.

Corbett-Davies, S., Gaebler, J. D., Nilforoshan, H., Shroff, R., & Goel, S. (2023). The measure and mismeasure of fairness. *The Journal of Machine Learning Research, 24*(1), 14730–14846.

Dignum, V. (2019). *Responsible artificial intelligence: How to develop and use AI in a responsible way* (Vol. 2156). Springer. https://doi.org/10.1007/978-3-030-30371-6

Dwork, C., & Roth, A. (2014). The algorithmic foundations of differential privacy. *Foundations and Trends in Theoretical Computer Science, 9*(3–4), 211–407. https://doi.org/10.1561/0400000042

Eubanks, V. (2018). *Automating inequality: How high-tech tools profile, police, and punish the poor.* St. Martin's Press.

European Commission, High-Level Expert Group on Artificial Intelligence. (2019). *Ethics guidelines for trustworthy AI.* European Commission.

Feldstein, S. (2021). *The rise of digital repression: How technology is reshaping power, politics, and resistance.* Oxford University Press.

Floridi, L., Cowls, J., Beltrametti, M., Chatila, R., Chazerand, P., Dignum, V., et al. (2018). AI4People—An ethical framework for a good AI society: Opportunities, risks, principles, and recommendations. *Minds and Machines, 28*, 689–707. https://doi.org/10.1007/s11023-018-9482-5

Friedman, B., & Hendry, D. G. (2019). *Value sensitive design: Shaping technology with moral imagination*. MIT Press.
Friedman, B., Kahn, P. H., Borning, A., & Huldtgren, A. (2013). Value sensitive design and information systems. In *Early engagement and new technologies: Opening up the laboratory* (pp. 55–95).
Garkisch, M., & Goldkind, L. (2025). Considering a unified model of artificial intelligence enhanced social work: A systematic review. *Journal of Human Rights and Social Work, 10*, 23–42. https://doi.org/10.1007/s41134-024-00326-y
General Data Protection Regulation (GDPR). (2016). Regulation (EU) 2016/679 of the European parliament and of the council of 27 April 2016. *Official Journal of the European Union*. https://eur-lex.europa.eu/eli/reg/2016/679/oj
Hsu, Y. C., Verma, H., Mauri, A., Nourbakhsh, I., & Bozzon, A. (2022). Empowering local communities using artificial intelligence. *Patterns, 3*(3), 100449. https://doi.org/10.1016/j.patter.2022.100449
IEEE Global Initiative on Ethics of Autonomous and Intelligent Systems. (2019). *Ethically aligned design: A vision for prioritizing human well-being with autonomous and intelligent systems*. https://ethicsinaction.ieee.org
Lee, J. Y., Pace, G. T., Cha, H., Rao, S., Hahm, H. C., An, R., & Denby-Brinson, R. (2025). ETHICS: An ethical framework for artificial intelligence (AI) use in social work research. *Journal of the Society for Social Work and Research, 16*, 1. https://doi.org/10.1086/739116
McMahan, B., Moore, E., Ramage, D., Hampson, S., & y Arcas, B. A. (2017). Communication-efficient learning of deep networks from decentralized data. In *Artificial intelligence and statistics* (pp. 1273–1282). PMLR.
Mehrabi, N., Morstatter, F., Saxena, N., Lerman, K., & Galstyan, A. (2021). A survey on bias and fairness in machine learning. *ACM Computing Surveys (CSUR), 54*(6), 1–35. https://doi.org/10.1145/3457607
Mittelstadt, B. D., Allo, P., Taddeo, M., Wachter, S., & Floridi, L. (2016). The ethics of algorithms: Mapping the debate. *Big Data & Society, 3*(2), 1. https://doi.org/10.1177/2053951716679679
Narayanan, A., & Shmatikov, V. (2010). Myths and fallacies of "personally identifiable information". *Communications of the ACM, 53*(6), 24–26. https://doi.org/10.1145/1743546.1743558
National Association of Social Workers (NASW). (2021). *Code of ethics of the national association of social workers*. https://www.socialworkers.org/About/Ethics/Code-of-Ethics/Code-of-Ethics-English
Office for Civil Rights. (2013). *Summary of the HIPAA privacy rule*. U.S. Department of Health and Human Services. https://www.hhs.gov
Raji, I. D., Smart, A., White, R. N., Mitchell, M., Gebru, T., Hutchinson, B., … & Barnes, P. (2020). Closing the AI accountability gap: Defining an end-to-end framework for internal algorithmic auditing. *Proceedings of the 2020 Conference on Fairness, Accountability, and Transparency*, (pp. 33–44). https://doi.org/10.1145/3351095.3372873
Reamer, F. G. (2023). Artificial intelligence in social work: Emerging ethical issues. *International Journal of Social Work Values and Ethics, 20*(2), 52–71. https://doi.org/10.55521/10-020-205
Reamer, F. G. (2025). *Ethical standards in social work: A review of the NASW code of ethics* (3rd ed.). NASW Press.
Ribeiro, M. T., Singh, S., & Guestrin, C. (2016). "Why should I trust you?": Explaining the predictions of any classifier. *In Proceedings of the 22nd ACM SIGKDD international conference on knowledgediscoveryanddatamining*(pp.1135–1144).https://doi.org/10.1145/2939672.2939778
Triandis, H. C. (1995). *Individualism and collectivism*. Westview Press.
UNESCO. (2021). *Recommendation on the ethics of artificial intelligence*. United Nations Educational, Scientific and Cultural Organization.
van den Hoven, J., Vermaas, P. E., & van de Poel, I. (2015). Design for values: An introduction. In J. van den Hoven, P. Vermaas, & I. van de Poel (Eds.), *Handbook of ethics, values, and technological design*. Springer. https://doi.org/10.1007/978-94-007-6970-0_40

Victor, B. G., & Herrenkohl, T. I. (2025). Introducing a new JSSWR specialty series on artificial intelligence and social work. *Journal of the Society for Social Work and Research, 16*(1), 5–8. https://doi.org/10.1086/735286

Victor, B. G., Kubiak, S., Angell, B., & Perron, B. E. (2023). Time to move beyond the ASWB licensing exams: Can generative artificial intelligence offer a way forward for social work? *Research on Social Work Practice, 33*(5), 511–517. https://doi.org/10.1177/10497315231166125

Wachter, S., & Mittelstadt, B. (2019). A right to reasonable inferences: Re-thinking data protection law in the age of big data and AI. *Columbia Business Law Review,* 494. https://ssrn.com/abstract=3248829

Wachter, S., Mittelstadt, B., & Floridi, L. (2017). Transparent, explainable, and accountable AI for robotics. *Science Robotics, 2*(6), eaan6080. https://doi.org/10.1126/scirobotics.aan6080

Wang, X., Liang, C., & Yin, M. (2023). The effects of AI biases and explanations on human decision fairness: A case study of bidding in rental housing markets. *In IJCAI* (pp. 3076–3084). https://doi.org/10.24963/ijcai.2023/343

Zemel, R., Wu, Y., Swersky, K., Pitassi, T., & Dwork, C. (2013). Learning fair representations. In *International conference on machine learning* (pp. 325–333). PMLR.

Zhang, P., White, J., Schmidt, D. C., Lenz, G., & Rosenbloom, S. T. (2018). FHIRChain: Applying blockchain to securely and scalably share clinical data. *Computational and Structural Biotechnology Journal, 16*, 267–278. https://doi.org/10.1016/j.csbj.2018.07.004

Part II
AI Applications Responding to Social Needs

Chapter 3
AI in Combating Poverty and Economic Inequality

Yingying Zeng and Jon E. Singletary

1 Introduction

Artificial intelligence (AI) has emerged as a transformative tool across various domains, including healthcare, finance, and increasingly, social welfare. Its potential to address complex societal challenges, such as poverty and economic inequality, is gaining recognition. AI-driven solutions offer promising pathways to enhance social welfare by optimizing resource distribution, identifying at-risk populations, and improving financial inclusion. As global economic disparities continue to widen, leveraging AI to address poverty is an urgent necessity rather than a technological luxury. Governments, non-profit organizations, and the private sector are turning to AI-powered predictive analytics and targeted interventions to develop data-driven policies and programs to mitigate economic hardship.

1.1 Poverty and Economic Inequality Worldwide and in the United States: Current Statistics

Understanding the current landscape of poverty and economic inequality worldwide and in the United States is crucial for contextualizing the role of AI in addressing these issues. Globally, poverty and economic inequality remain pressing challenges. As of 2023, over 1 billion people worldwide live in acute poverty, with more than

Y. Zeng (✉)
School of Social Work, University of Georgia, Athens, GA, USA
e-mail: yzeng@uga.edu

J. E. Singletary
Diana R. Garland School of Social Work, Baylor University, Waco, TX, USA
e-mail: Jon_Singletary@baylor.edu

R. An, M. A. Lindsey (eds.), *Artificial Intelligence in Social Work*,
https://doi.org/10.1007/978-3-032-18443-6_3

half being children and nearly 40% residing in conflict-affected areas (United Nations, 2024). According to the U.S. Census Bureau's 2023 report, the official poverty rate decreased by 0.4 percentage points to 11.1% in 2023, meaning 36.8 million people were living in poverty. However, the Supplemental Poverty Measure (SPM), which accounts for additional factors such as tax payments and in-kind benefits, increased by 0.5 percentage points to 12.9% during the same period (U.S. Census Bureau, 2024a). This indicates that while traditional metrics show a decline in poverty, broader measures suggest an increase, highlighting the complexity of assessing economic well-being. Income inequality remains a significant concern, with the Gini index showing no statistically significant change between 2022 and 2023, indicating persistent disparities in income distribution. Median household income rose to $80,610 in 2023, marking a 4% increase from the previous year and the first significant annual rise since 2019 (Guzman & Kollar, 2024). However, this increase was not uniform across all demographics. While white households experienced notable income gains, median incomes for Black, Asian, and Hispanic households remained statistically unchanged, underscoring enduring racial disparities in economic outcomes (Guzman & Kollar, 2024). In 2023, Native Americans had the highest poverty rate at 22%; for Black individuals, the rate was 17.9%; for Hispanics, it was 17.1%; for Asian Americans, it was 9.4%, while for non-Hispanic Whites, the rate was 7.7% (U.S. Census Bureau, 2024b).

1.2 The Exacerbation of Economic Inequality Post-COVID-19

The COVID-19 pandemic has exacerbated global economic disparities, disproportionately affecting low-income populations and marginalized communities. It not only intensified pre-existing inequalities in healthcare access, education, and financial stability but also underscored the urgent need for innovative solutions to mitigate its long-term impacts. In the current economic and political climate, these challenges are further compounded by inflationary pressures, policy debates over social safety nets, and uncertainties in global markets. The expiration of pandemic--era support programs has placed additional financial strain on many households, making AI-driven interventions more critical than ever.

AI has become an increasingly vital tool in combating poverty and mitigating the socioeconomic impacts of COVID-19. The crisis has demonstrated the need for data-driven, adaptive solutions that can efficiently allocate resources and identify those most in need. According to Goralski and Tan (2023), AI-driven interventions have played a significant role in post-pandemic recovery by enhancing financial inclusion, optimizing social assistance programs, and supporting economic resilience. AI applications such as predictive analytics for targeted aid distribution, automated job-matching systems, and real-time economic risk assessments have been instrumental in addressing systemic inequalities exacerbated by COVID-19.

Furthermore, AI has facilitated data-driven decision-making in social policy, ensuring that relief efforts effectively reach those most in need while enhancing the efficiency of governmental and non-profit interventions (Goralski & Tan, 2023). For example, AI models using remote sensing and spatial data were deployed to detect areas of concentrated poverty and economic distress—allowing governments and aid organizations to direct support where it was most needed. These innovations are particularly impactful in rural or under-resourced areas, where conventional data infrastructure is often weak. By enabling high-resolution poverty mapping and predictive modeling, AI contributes to more responsive and equitable post-pandemic recovery planning (Agyemang et al., 2023). As the economic landscape continues to evolve, AI's role in poverty alleviation and economic stability will likely expand, shaping the future of social welfare programs and economic inclusion efforts.

1.3 The Role of AI in Addressing Poverty and Economic Inequality

Given this backdrop, AI presents both opportunities and challenges in the fight against poverty and economic inequality. Its applications range from predictive analytics that identify at-risk populations to systems that optimize the allocation of social services. However, deploying AI must be approached with caution to avoid perpetuating existing biases and ensure that technological advancements translate into equitable social benefits.

This chapter explores AI applications in combating poverty and economic inequality, focusing on predictive analytics, resource optimization, and financial inclusion. The discussion employs an intersectional lens to examine how AI-driven interventions affect diverse demographic groups, particularly along racial, gender, and immigration-status lines. Additionally, the chapter addresses the ethical implications of AI in social welfare, including algorithmic bias, data privacy concerns, and the need for accountability in AI-driven decision-making. Finally, the chapter concludes with recommendations for policymakers, AI practitioners, and social work professionals on implementing AI responsibly in poverty alleviation efforts. By critically analyzing the opportunities and risks associated with AI in this context, this chapter aims to provide a nuanced understanding of how technology can be leveraged to foster economic justice while ensuring that AI systems remain equitable, inclusive, and socially responsible.

2 AI and Economic Disparities: An Intersectional Framework

Economic inequality is shaped by income disparities, wealth concentration, and structural barriers that limit access to education, employment, and essential services. These disparities disproportionately affect marginalized groups, reinforcing cycles of poverty and limiting economic mobility. While AI has been proposed as a tool to address these challenges, it can also deepen existing inequalities if it inherits biases from historical data and flawed decision-making processes. This section examines the scope of economic inequality, the intersectional nature of poverty, and the ways in which AI can both exacerbate and mitigate disparities.

2.1 The Scope of Economic Inequality: Income Gaps, Wealth Disparities, and Structural Barriers

Economic inequality is a defining challenge of the twenty-first century, shaped by long-standing disparities in income, wealth, and opportunity. In the United States, the top 1% of earners control more wealth than the bottom 90% combined (Saez & Zucman, 2019), reflecting a concentration of assets that limits upward mobility for most households. A critical distinction exists between income poverty—defined by inadequate earnings to meet basic needs—and asset poverty, in which families lack the financial buffers to withstand economic shocks. As of 2021, approximately 19% of U.S. households are asset poor, placing them at heightened risk of housing instability, debt accumulation, and long-term insecurity (Prosperity Now, 2022). The COVID-19 pandemic further exposed and widened these divides. While wealthy individuals benefited from asset growth driven by stock and real estate markets, millions of low- and middle-income workers faced layoffs, income loss, and financial distress, with 16 million unemployment claims filed in a single 3-week period in early 2020 (Congressional Research Service, 2021). Although the post-pandemic recovery has favored asset holders, others continue to struggle with inflation, rising housing costs, and stagnant wages (Wong, 2024), contributing to what many now describe as a shrinking, increasingly precarious middle class.

Structural barriers perpetuate these economic divides. Racial and ethnic minorities, immigrants, and people with disabilities continue to face systemic disadvantages in education, employment, and healthcare access, limiting their ability to accumulate wealth or access stable jobs (Chetty & Hendren, 2018). The burden of student loan debt also represents a significant hurdle, particularly for younger adults and first-generation college students. Despite educational attainment, many face delayed wealth accumulation due to unsustainable debt obligations (Elliott & Rauscher, 2016).

Amid these conditions, AI is increasingly being positioned as a solution to improve resource allocation, enhance public service delivery, and flag populations at risk of economic hardship. However, AI is also deeply intertwined with the same systems of inequality it seeks to reform. For instance, studies show that machine learning models used in hiring decisions often encode biases that disadvantage women, racial minorities, and applicants with non-traditional work histories (Raghavan et al., 2020). Similarly, AI-driven credit-scoring models have been found to systematically assign lower creditworthiness to Black and Hispanic applicants, even when controlling for financial behavior (Bartlett et al., 2022). These outcomes arise from training data that reflect long-standing discrimination and structural exclusion.

Emerging research underscores the importance of transparency and interpretability in AI design, especially when these tools are used in high-stakes environments such as finance, employment, or housing. Interpretable machine learning models, for instance, have shown promise in diagnosing the structural features of urban inequality—such as uneven access to public transportation, green spaces, and zoning practices (Fan et al., 2023). However, without safeguards, even the most sophisticated models can unintentionally replicate social hierarchies.

Ultimately, addressing economic inequality requires not only closing income and wealth gaps through policy reform, but also subjecting new technologies to critical scrutiny. As AI becomes more embedded in public and private decision-making, it is essential to ensure that these tools do not reinforce systemic disadvantage under the guise of objectivity.

2.2 An Intersectional Perspective on AI and Economic Inequality: Bridging Gaps or Reinforcing Barriers?

Economic inequality does not affect all populations equally; it is deeply intertwined with race, gender, immigration status, and disability. Structural barriers—such as discriminatory hiring practices, restricted access to education and healthcare, and financial exclusion—prevent marginalized groups from achieving economic mobility (Chetty & Hendren, 2018). Black and Hispanic families in the U.S. have significantly lower median wealth than white families due to historic and systemic discrimination in employment, homeownership, and banking (Pew Research Center, 2021). Women, particularly women of color, continue to experience wage gaps and barriers to career advancement, while immigrants face additional hurdles such as legal restrictions and language barriers. These disparities are often reflected in the development of AI systems themselves, where the underrepresentation of marginalized groups in the tech workforce contributes to algorithms that reinforce existing patterns of exclusion (West et al., 2019).

AI is often positioned as a tool for analyzing and addressing these disparities. Predictive analytics can help policymakers identify at-risk populations, allocate resources efficiently, and design targeted interventions. For example, machine learning models can yield higher accuracy and fairness in identifying low-income households, therefore increasing the efficiency of social welfare (Wobcke & Mariyah, 2023). AI-driven employment platforms claim to improve job-matching efficiency, and alternative credit-scoring models offer financial access to individuals traditionally excluded from banking systems (Bartlett et al., 2022). However, these applications often fail to address the root causes of inequality, and worse, they may reproduce and amplify existing biases.

A key issue lies in AI's reliance on historical data, which often reflects systemic discrimination. Machine learning models trained on biased hiring, lending, and criminal justice datasets risk reinforcing past inequalities. AI-powered resume screening tools, for instance, have been shown to favor male candidates over equally qualified women due to patterns in past hiring decisions (Raghavan et al., 2020). Similarly, facial recognition technology has been found to misidentify Black and Hispanic individuals at disproportionately higher rates, leading to wrongful arrests and other forms of systemic bias (Buolamwini & Gebru, 2018). Even financial AI models can reflect discriminatory lending practices, as seen in algorithms that assign lower creditworthiness scores to minority borrowers despite similar financial behaviors to those of white applicants (Richardson et al., 2019). In public services, AI-based systems used to determine eligibility for social welfare programs have exhibited biases that disproportionately exclude minority and low-income applicants. In Los Angeles, an AI-driven housing assistance system initially trained on biased historical data underestimated the vulnerability of Black and Latino individuals, leading to unfair housing allocations (Eubanks, 2018).

These examples illustrate the dual nature of AI—while it offers tools for analyzing inequality, it can also exacerbate economic disparities if not designed with fairness and accountability in mind. Without intervention, algorithmic decision-making risks automating discrimination at an unprecedented scale, widening the economic gap between privileged and marginalized communities. This raises urgent questions about algorithmic harms, the topic of the next section, where we explore how AI, when unchecked, perpetuates systemic bias in hiring, lending, housing, and public services.

2.3 *Mitigating Algorithmic Bias and Promoting Inclusive AI*

To ensure that AI contributes to reducing economic disparities rather than reinforcing them, proactive steps must be taken to address algorithmic bias. One crucial approach is increasing diversity in AI development systems, ensuring that training data used as the foundation of AI tools is representative of diverse populations. Research has emphasized that the lack of diversity in AI development teams contributes to biased systems and that increasing representation is critical to addressing algorithmic harms (West et al., 2019).

Bias audits and fairness evaluations are essential in AI deployment to detect and mitigate discriminatory patterns before systems are widely implemented. Independent audits can uncover biases that may not be apparent to developers, ensuring that AI systems operate fairly across diverse populations. For instance, Raji et al. (2020) emphasize the importance of such audits in identifying and addressing biases in AI models. Transparency and accountability mechanisms, including explainable AI models and third-party oversight, are crucial for making AI-driven decisions understandable and contestable, allowing for corrections when necessary.

Policymakers play a pivotal role in regulating AI to prevent discriminatory outcomes. The European Union's Artificial Intelligence Act (European Commission, 2024), which entered into force in August 2024, serves as a comprehensive framework to ensure fairness in high-risk AI applications. This legislation categorizes AI systems by risk level and imposes stricter regulations on those deemed high-risk, including applications affecting health, education, and critical infrastructure. In the United States, advocacy groups are pushing for similar regulations to address AI-driven discrimination across sectors such as hiring, lending, and public services (Akselrod, 2021). Without such safeguards, AI risks perpetuating economic inequality rather than alleviating it.

3 AI Applications in Poverty Alleviation

AI has shown promise in poverty alleviation; however, its effectiveness depends on equitable design and implementation. This section explores four key AI applications for poverty reduction: predictive analytics to identify at-risk populations, AI-driven resource optimization, employment and workforce development, and financial inclusion.

3.1 Predictive Analytics for Identifying At-Risk Populations

AI's capacity to analyze vast and complex datasets enables governments and organizations to identify individuals and communities most vulnerable to economic hardship. Machine learning models can synthesize data from diverse sources—including employment histories, income trends, housing stability, and geographic indicators—to detect early signs of financial distress. These tools have been used to flag individuals at risk of eviction, food insecurity, or homelessness, enabling earlier, more targeted interventions (Huang et al., 2021).

In regions where traditional economic data are limited or outdated, AI has expanded the possibilities for poverty monitoring through satellite imagery, remote sensing, and geospatial analysis. By detecting patterns in infrastructure, nighttime lighting, and land use, AI systems can generate timely, subnational poverty estimates that support resource allocation at scale. When combined with ensemble learning methods and mobile data, these approaches allow organizations to direct aid more precisely and efficiently—especially in rural or underserved areas (Agyemang et al., 2023; Arnold, 2025; Shah & Tallam, 2023).

These developments are particularly valuable in fragile or data-scarce environments where surveys are infrequent or costly. For example, recent models have integrated geospatial and temperature data to estimate household poverty with high accuracy. Other models have demonstrated that combining mobile phone metadata with environmental indicators can enhance the granularity of poverty targeting.

While these innovations offer promise, their effectiveness depends on the contextual relevance and quality of input data, as well as ethical safeguards to prevent misclassification or surveillance.

Together, these predictive tools signal a shift toward more proactive and data-informed poverty alleviation strategies. When integrated into policy systems that prioritize transparency and equity, they can improve outreach, reduce exclusion errors, and support more resilient social protection frameworks.

3.2 *AI-Driven Resource Optimization and Targeted Interventions*

Beyond identifying need, AI is increasingly used to optimize the delivery of resources in social assistance programs. Traditional welfare systems often rely on rigid eligibility rules and bureaucratic processes, leading to delays, inefficiencies, and the misallocation of aid. AI offers a more dynamic alternative by enabling data-driven identification of geographic poverty patterns, particularly in areas with limited administrative data. For example, convolutional neural networks trained on satellite imagery have been used to estimate poverty rates at the municipal level in Mexico, offering a scalable tool to inform targeted interventions (Babenko et al., 2017).

One area of advancement involves improving how poverty is measured and defined for program eligibility purposes. Machine learning-enhanced proxy means tests have demonstrated superior accuracy in estimating household welfare, especially in contexts where complete income data are unavailable. By identifying underreporting or inconsistencies in applications and constructing multidimensional poverty profiles, AI systems can help match individuals to appropriate benefits more effectively and reduce exclusion and inclusion errors (Wobcke & Mariyah, 2023). In China, big data mining and machine learning are also applied to improve the precision of China's poverty alleviation efforts (Wang, 2021).

AI has also been deployed to enhance the targeting of humanitarian aid in regions where social registries or population data are sparse. In such cases, remote sensing and mobile data serve as proxies for income, housing conditions, and consumption behavior, enabling the identification of households in extreme poverty. These approaches have been used to inform cash transfer programs and disaster relief operations, offering a flexible way to reach people who traditional systems might otherwise overlook (Yeh et al., 2020). In child welfare contexts, predictive models have been used to uncover distinct subgroups experiencing financial hardship, helping service providers design more nuanced support strategies. Such applications suggest that AI can play a valuable role not only in scaling program delivery but also in personalizing interventions for populations with varying needs and vulnerabilities (Johnson et al., 2024).

While these innovations show promise, they also raise questions about transparency and accountability. Ensuring that AI systems used in public assistance operate fairly requires ongoing evaluation, especially when algorithms are used to make eligibility determinations or prioritize beneficiaries. Without such oversight, there is a risk that resource optimization may inadvertently reinforce existing inequities rather than alleviate them.

3.3 *Employment and Workforce Development*

AI is playing an increasing role in workforce development by facilitating job matching, skills training, and reskilling programs for low-income workers. Many job seekers, particularly those from disadvantaged backgrounds, face barriers to accessing employment due to mismatches in skills or a lack of professional networks. AI-powered platforms analyze labor-market trends, identify in-demand skills, and match individuals with suitable job opportunities (World Bank, 2023).

AI has also played a role in improving the delivery of educational content and productivity in low-resource environments. For example, lesson-planning tools powered by machine learning have helped educators tailor instruction to students' needs, particularly in underserved rural areas. Similarly, generative AI chatbots have been deployed to deliver agricultural and vocational guidance in local languages, expanding access to practical knowledge and technical skills in communities with limited infrastructure (Chow, 2024).

While AI offers tools to expand employment access, its use in hiring processes also raises concerns. Automated screening systems may penalize applicants with interrupted work histories or non-linear career paths—disproportionately affecting women, caregivers, people with disabilities, and immigrants. Without transparency into how job-matching or resume-filtering algorithms operate, there is a risk that exclusionary labor-market dynamics will be encoded into ostensibly neutral systems (Raghavan et al., 2020; West et al., 2019).

3.4 *Financial Inclusion and Access to Credit*

Access to financial services is critical for economic stability, yet millions of low-income individuals remain excluded from traditional banking systems due to insufficient credit histories. AI is transforming financial inclusion by enabling alternative credit-scoring models that assess creditworthiness using non-traditional data sources, such as utility payments, mobile phone usage, and social network behavior (Neal et al., 2023).

In Latin America, fintech companies are using machine learning to evaluate borrowers without formal credit histories. These AI models analyze spending patterns, transaction histories, and behavioral data to assess loan eligibility, allowing financial institutions to extend credit to previously unbanked populations (Briggs, 2023). AI-driven lending models have also been deployed in the United States to improve financial access for minority borrowers, reducing biases inherent in traditional credit-scoring systems (Neal et al., 2023).

The cases discussed in this section represent only a fraction of AI's applications in poverty alleviation. In reality, AI is being deployed across numerous other domains, including healthcare access for low-income populations, disaster response for communities vulnerable to climate change, and education initiatives for children in underserved areas (Arnold, 2025). While AI holds promise in these areas, it is essential to recognize its limitations and the need for continuous monitoring to prevent unintended consequences, such as reinforcing systemic biases or deepening inequalities. The following section will delve into ethical challenges and algorithmic harms, highlighting how AI, if not properly managed, can reinforce existing disparities in economic opportunity, lending, hiring, and public services.

4 Ethical Challenges and Algorithmic Harms

While AI holds promise in addressing economic inequality, its implementation also raises serious ethical concerns. If not properly designed and monitored, AI systems can reinforce existing disparities rather than alleviate them. Issues such as algorithmic bias, data privacy risks, and the lack of accountability in AI decision-making pose significant challenges, particularly for marginalized communities. This section explores how AI-driven models can perpetuate discrimination, the ethical concerns surrounding data collection and surveillance, and the urgent need for greater transparency in AI decision-making.

4.1 Bias and Discrimination in AI Models

AI systems employed in social services are susceptible to biases that can reinforce systemic discrimination. When AI models are trained on historical data imbued with societal prejudices, they may replicate these biases, leading to unjust outcomes.

4.1.1 Example 1: Welfare Fraud Detection Systems

In France, the government utilized algorithms to identify errors in welfare payments. However, these systems have been challenged legally for allegedly discriminating against vulnerable groups, such as disabled individuals and single mothers. The algorithms assigned risk scores based on personal data, potentially leading to biased, intrusive investigations that disproportionately affect marginalized populations (Meaker, 2024).

4.1.2 Example 2: Housing Allocation in Los Angeles

Los Angeles explored using machine learning to prioritize housing for its homeless population. The previous system often misjudged vulnerability, with Black and Latino clients underrepresented. The new AI-driven approach aimed to correct these biases by refining assessments using historical data. However, concerns remain about the ethical implications of relying heavily on algorithms for such critical decisions (Stern, 2024).

4.2 Data Privacy and Surveillance Risks

The deployment of AI in social services necessitates extensive data collection, raising significant privacy and surveillance concerns. Low-income and marginalized communities are particularly vulnerable to intrusive data practices.

4.2.1 Example 3: AI in Social Work Documentation

In England, social workers have begun using an AI system called Magic Notes to record conversations and draft documents. While intended to reduce administrative burdens, this technology raises concerns about the accuracy of AI-generated summaries and the potential misuse of sensitive information. Ensuring that AI tools do not compromise the confidentiality and integrity of social work is crucial (Booth, 2024).

4.2.2 Example 4: Algorithmic Surveillance in Welfare Systems

The use of AI to monitor welfare recipients has led to allegations of excessive surveillance and discrimination. In the United Kingdom, concerns have been raised about AI tools used by the government potentially being "racist and biased," prompting the publication of a public register to increase transparency. Such practices can disproportionately target marginalized groups, subjecting them to heightened scrutiny and reinforcing existing inequities (Ungoed-Thomas & Abdulahi, 2024).

4.3 Algorithmic Accountability and Explainability

The opacity of AI decision-making processes poses challenges to accountability and transparency in social services. When algorithms operate as "black boxes," it becomes difficult to understand, challenge, or rectify their decisions.

4.3.1 Example 5: AI in Health Insurance Claims

In the United States, health insurers have faced scrutiny for using AI to determine claim coverage, leading to allegations of unfair denials. AI systems developed by companies like UnitedHealth's NaviHealth have been criticized for reducing human oversight in coverage decisions, potentially leading to unjust outcomes for patients. This underscores the need for transparency and accountability in AI-driven decision-making processes (Jack, 2025).

The integration of AI into social services necessitates a careful examination of ethical challenges to prevent the perpetuation of existing social inequities. Addressing bias and discrimination in AI models, safeguarding data privacy, and ensuring algorithmic accountability are critical steps toward ethical AI deployment. Implementing robust oversight mechanisms and involving diverse stakeholders in AI development can help mitigate these risks, ensuring that AI serves as a tool for social good rather than harm.

5 Future Directions and Recommendations

Artificial Intelligence (AI) is rapidly evolving and holds immense potential for advancing poverty reduction strategies. Recent trends indicate that AI is not only being used to enhance existing social services but is also creating new avenues for addressing deep-rooted socioeconomic disparities. Emerging applications include AI-driven financial inclusion, personalized education, healthcare accessibility, agricultural optimization, and more efficient social welfare distribution. These developments are transforming the landscape of social policy and practice—particularly in healthcare, agriculture, and poverty monitoring—by enabling more precise targeting of interventions and more effective resource allocation (Huang et al., 2021; Kshetri, 2022).

One significant trend is the use of AI to drive financial inclusion. Machine learning models are increasingly employed to analyze non-traditional data sources—such as mobile phone usage, utility payments, and transactional histories—to assess creditworthiness. This innovative approach enables financial institutions to extend credit and other financial services to individuals who have been historically excluded from the formal banking sector (Neal et al., 2023).

In education, AI is increasingly used to provide personalized learning experiences, particularly in developing countries, thereby bridging educational gaps and enhancing employability. For example, initiatives such as Kabakoo Academies in West Africa employ AI-enabled virtual mentors to deliver customized learning experiences and mentorship, preparing youth for self-employment in informal economies (World Economic Forum, 2024). Similarly, AI's role in healthcare is expanding rapidly. Diagnostic tools that utilize AI algorithms can analyze medical images and patient data to detect diseases early, while telemedicine platforms enable remote consultations, thereby extending healthcare services to underserved communities (Ghiasi et al., 2021).

Agricultural optimization represents another promising area. AI models that forecast weather patterns, detect crop diseases, and monitor soil conditions are helping farmers maximize yields and manage resources more efficiently. Such applications not only increase food security but also contribute to poverty alleviation by improving the livelihoods of smallholder farmers (Kshetri, 2022). Moreover, governments are increasingly incorporating AI into the administration of social welfare programs. By employing AI systems to identify eligible beneficiaries and detect fraudulent activities, social programs can become more efficient and responsive. These technologies have the potential to reduce administrative burdens and ensure that limited resources reach those most in need.

An emerging frontier in AI is the development and deployment of large language models (LLMs), such as GPT-3 and GPT-4. LLMs have demonstrated unprecedented capabilities in natural language processing and understanding, which can be leveraged to support social services. For example, LLMs can assist social workers by analyzing unstructured case files to extract relevant insights, generating personalized support recommendations, and providing real-time language translation for multilingual client interactions. Additionally, these models can monitor social media and public forums for early signals of economic distress, helping identify emerging needs in near real time. As LLMs continue to advance, their integration into social programs could further enhance decision-making and service delivery. However, it remains critical to address the risks of bias and misinterpretation inherent in these models (Bommasani et al., 2021).

Given these emerging trends, various stakeholders need to adapt and collaborate in harnessing the full potential of AI for poverty reduction. Policymakers must develop inclusive AI policies that ensure the benefits of these technologies extend to marginalized communities. This involves investing in digital infrastructure in underserved areas and establishing robust regulatory frameworks to ensure transparency, fairness, and accountability in AI applications. Regulatory efforts, such as the European Union's Artificial Intelligence Act, offer promising models for how governments can safeguard the rights of vulnerable populations while fostering innovation (European Commission, 2024).

For AI developers, integrating ethical considerations into the design and deployment process is imperative. Developers should engage closely with target communities to understand their unique challenges and co-create culturally relevant solutions. This collaborative approach, coupled with multidisciplinary input from ethicists, social scientists, and legal experts, can help ensure that AI systems are designed with fairness and inclusivity at their core. Moreover, developers must prioritize robust data protection measures to secure sensitive personal information, especially in domains such as healthcare and finance.

Social work practitioners, who operate on the front lines of service delivery, have a crucial role in leveraging AI tools to enhance outcomes for vulnerable populations. By integrating AI-driven insights into case management and resource allocation, social workers can better identify at-risk individuals and tailor interventions accordingly. Practitioners must remain vigilant about the ethical risks associated with AI—such as data privacy concerns and algorithmic bias—and advocate for transparent, accountable AI applications in their practice (Eubanks, 2018). Participation in interdisciplinary collaborations can further empower social workers to influence the development of AI systems, ensuring that these tools align with the principles of social justice.

An overarching recommendation for all stakeholders is the need for continued ethical oversight and interdisciplinary collaboration. As AI becomes more deeply embedded in poverty alleviation efforts, establishing ethics committees and review boards can provide ongoing assessment and accountability for AI projects. Regular bias audits and impact evaluations are necessary to identify and mitigate unintended consequences. Furthermore, interdisciplinary teams that combine expertise from computer science, social work, ethics, and law can proactively address challenges and develop more robust, socially responsible AI solutions (Raji et al., 2020). Community involvement in the design and implementation process is also vital; participatory approaches not only ensure that AI interventions are culturally appropriate but also build trust and increase the likelihood of successful adoption.

Global cooperation is critical as well. International collaborations can facilitate the sharing of best practices, resources, and knowledge, accelerating the development of AI solutions for poverty reduction. By standardizing ethical guidelines and regulatory frameworks globally, countries can work together to harness AI's potential in an innovative and just manner (European Commission, 2024).

In summary, while the potential of AI to reduce poverty is vast, its successful application requires deliberate, coordinated action from policymakers, developers, and social work practitioners alike. Continuous ethical oversight, interdisciplinary collaboration, and active community involvement are indispensable for ensuring that AI catalyzes social equity rather than reinforcing existing disparities. As we move forward, integrating emerging technologies—including large language models—into social programs offers new opportunities to transform poverty alleviation efforts and create a more equitable future.

6 Conclusion

This chapter has explored the role of AI in poverty reduction, highlighting its applications in predictive analytics, financial inclusion, education, healthcare, agriculture, and social welfare. AI has the potential to enhance economic justice by optimizing resource allocation, improving service delivery, and expanding access to essential services. However, while AI offers significant opportunities, it also presents risks, particularly in areas of bias, privacy, and accountability.

The transformative power of AI lies in its ability to process vast amounts of data, uncover patterns of need, and support more targeted interventions. From AI-driven credit assessments that expand financial access to predictive models that improve social service delivery, AI has the potential to increase efficiency and equity in economic and social policies. Recent advances, such as large language models (LLMs), further extend AI's capabilities by assisting social workers, analyzing case files, and improving communication in multilingual contexts.

However, realizing AI's potential requires strong ethical oversight. Without proper regulation and transparency, AI systems may perpetuate discrimination and exclusion rather than alleviate inequality. Addressing these risks requires collaboration among policymakers, AI developers, and social work practitioners. Policies that ensure fairness, regular bias audits, and participatory design approaches can help mitigate harmful effects while maximizing AI's benefits.

As AI continues to shape poverty alleviation efforts, balancing innovation with ethical responsibility is crucial. By fostering interdisciplinary collaboration, engaging communities in AI design, and enforcing accountability measures, AI can serve as a powerful tool for social equity. Moving forward, a collective commitment to responsible AI development will be essential in ensuring that technology advances economic justice rather than reinforcing disparities.

Competing Interests The authors have no conflicts of interest to declare that are relevant to the content of this chapter.

References

Agyemang, F. S., Memon, R., Wolf, L. J., & Fox, S. (2023). High-resolution rural poverty mapping in Pakistan with ensemble deep learning. *PLoS One, 18*(4), e0283938. https://journals.plos.org/plosone/article?id=10.1371/journal.pone.0283938

Akselrod, O. (2021). *How artificial intelligence can deepen racial and economic inequities.* American Civil Liberties Union (ACLU). https://www.aclu.org/news/privacy-technology/how-artificial-intelligence-can-deepen-racial-and-economic-inequities

Arnold, C. (2025). Can AI help beat poverty? Researchers test ways to aid the poorest people. *Nature, 638*(8052), 878–880. https://www.nature.com/articles/d41586-025-00565-7

Babenko, B., Hersh, J., Newhouse, D., Ramakrishnan, A., & Swartz, T. (2017). *Poverty mapping using convolutional neural networks trained on high and medium resolution satellite images, with an application in Mexico.* arXiv preprint arXiv:1711.06323. https://doi.org/10.48550/arXiv.1711.06323

Bartlett, R., Morse, A., Stanton, R., & Wallace, N. (2022). Consumer-lending discrimination in the FinTech era. *Journal of Financial Economics, 143*(1), 30–56. https://doi.org/10.1016/j.jfineco.2021.05.047

Bommasani, R., Hudson, D. A., Adeli, E., Altman, R., Arora, S., von Arx, S., … & Liang, P. (2021). *On the opportunities and risks of foundation models.* arXiv preprint arXiv:2108.07258. https://doi.org/10.48550/arXiv.2108.07258

Booth, R. (2024). *Social workers in England begin using AI system to assist their work.* The Guardian. https://www.theguardian.com/society/2024/sep/28/social-workers-england-ai-system-magic-notes

Briggs, B. (2023). *"We have to solve the problem": How three fintechs are boosting financial inclusion in Latin America.* Microsoft (Source). https://news.microsoft.com/source/features/ai/fintech-ai-financial-inclusion-latin-america/

Buolamwini, J., & Gebru, T. (2018). Gender shades: Intersectional accuracy disparities in commercial gender classification. In *Conference on fairness, accountability, and transparency* (pp. 77–99). PMLR.

Chetty, R., & Hendren, N. (2018). The impacts of neighborhoods on intergenerational mobility I: Childhood exposure effects. *The Quarterly Journal of Economics, 133*(3), 1107–1162. https://doi.org/10.1093/qje/qjy007

Chow, A. (2024). *Inside the new nonprofit ai initiatives seeking to aid teachers and farmers in rural Africa*. Times. https://time.com/7160849/opportunity-international-ai-farmers-teachers/

Congressional Research Service. (2021). *Unemployment rates during the COVID-19 pandemic*. https://www.congress.gov/crs-product/R46554#:~:text=The%20unemployment%20rate%20peaked%20at,to%20February%202020%20(3.5%25)

Elliott, W., & Rauscher, E. (2016). *When does my future begin? Student debt and intragenerational mobility*. https://aedi.ssw.umich.edu/sites/default/files/publications/publication-working-papers-brief-2.pdf

Eubanks, V. (2018). *Automating inequality: How high-tech tools profile, police, and punish the poor*. St. Martin's Press.

European Commission. (2024). *AI act enters into force*. https://commission.europa.eu/news/ai-act-enters-force-2024-08-01_en

Fan, C., Xu, J., Natarajan, B. Y., & Mostafavi, A. (2023). Interpretable machine learning learns complex interactions of urban features to understand socio-economic inequality. *Computer-Aided Civil and Infrastructure Engineering, 38*(14), 2013–2029. https://doi.org/10.1111/mice.12972

Ghiasi, A., Gu, Y., & Zhou, J. (2021). AI in healthcare: A review of current applications and future directions. *Global Health Journal, 5*(2), 85–99.

Goralski, M. A., & Tan, T. K. (2023). Artificial intelligence: Poverty alleviation, healthcare, education, and reduced inequalities in a post-COVID world. In *The ethics of artificial intelligence for the sustainable development goals* (pp. 97–113). Springer International Publishing.

Guzman, G., & Kollar, M. (2024). *Income in the United States: 2023* (Report No. P60-282). U.S. Census Bureau. https://www.census.gov/library/publications/2024/demo/p60-282.html

Huang, L. Y., Hsiang, S. M., & Gonzalez-Navarro, M. (2021). Using satellite imagery and deep learning to evaluate the impact of anti-poverty programs (No. w29105). *National Bureau of Economic Research*. https://www.nber.org/system/files/working_papers/w29105/w29105.pdf

Jack, A. (2025). *US health insurers face pressure over AI role in claim decisions*. Financial Times. https://www.ft.com/content/600e53b6-963b-4c62-9548-b2b98788a950

Johnson, I. C., Achulo, S. H., Brevard, K. C., & Ansong, D. (2024). Examining financial hardship and caregiver subgroups in kinship foster placements: A machine learning approach. *Societies, 14*(3), 38. https://doi.org/10.3390/soc14030038

Kshetri, N. (2022). Data and artificial intelligence as tools to fight poverty: Some notable applications in agriculture and health care. *Computer, 55*(12), 134–139. https://doi.org/10.1109/MC.2022.3207602

Meaker, M. (2024). *Algorithms policed welfare systems for years. Now they're under fire for bias*. https://www.wired.com/story/algorithms-policed-welfare-systems-for-years-now-theyre-under-fire-for-bias/

Neal, M., Zhu, L., Young, C., Perry, V., & Pruitt, M. (2023). *Harnessing artificial intelligence for equity in mortgage finance*. Urban Institute. FHL Bank San Francisco. https://www.urban.org/research/publication/harnessing-artificial-intelligence-equity-mortgage-finance

Pew Research Center. (2021). *Wealth gaps within racial and ethnic groups*. https://www.pewresearch.org/2023/12/04/wealth-gaps-within-racial-and-ethnic-groups/

Prosperity Now. (2022). *Prosperity Now scorecard: Data by issue–Financial assets and income*. https://scorecard.prosperitynow.org/data-by-issue#finance/outcome/asset-poverty-rate

Raghavan, M., Barocas, S., Kleinberg, J., & Levy, K. (2020). Mitigating bias in algorithmic hiring: Evaluating fairness in machine learning. In *Conference on fairness, accountability, and transparency* (pp. 469–481).

Raji, I. D., Smart, A., White, R. N., Mitchell, M., Gebru, T., Hutchinson, B., … & Barnes, P. (2020). Closing the AI accountability gap: Defining an end-to-end framework for internal algorithmic auditing. In *Proceedings of the 2020 conference on fairness, accountability, and transparency* (pp. 33–44).

Richardson, R., Schultz, J. M., & Crawford, K. (2019). Dirty data, bad predictions: How civil rights violations impact police data, predictive policing systems, and justice. *NYUL Rev. Online, 94*, 15.

Saez, E., & Zucman, G. (2019). *The triumph of injustice: How the rich dodge taxes and how to make them pay*. WW Norton & Company.

Shah, O., & Tallam, K. (2023). *Novel machine learning approach for predicting poverty using temperature and remote sensing data in ethiopia*. arXiv preprint arXiv:2302.14835. https://doi.org/10.48550/arXiv.2302.14835

Stern, C. (2024). *LA thinks AI could help decide which homeless people get scarce housing—And which don't*. Vox. https://www.vox.com/the-highlight/388372/housing-policy-los-angeles-homeless-ai

The U.S. Census Bureau. (2024a). *Income, poverty and health insurance coverage in the United States: 2023*. https://www.census.gov/newsroom/press-releases/2024/income-poverty-health--insurance-coverage.html?daily=

The U.S. Census Bureau. (2024b). *Income in the United States: 2023*. https://www.census.gov/library/publications/2024/demo/p60-282.html

Ungoed-Thomas, J. & Abdulahi, Y. (2024). *Warning AI tools used by government on UK public are "racist and biased."* The Guardian. https://www.theguardian.com/technology/article/2024/aug/25/register-aims-to-quash-fears-over-racist-and-biased-ai-tools-used-on-uk-public

United Nations. (2024). *Nearly half the world's 1.1 billion poor live in conflict settings*. https://news.un.org/en/story/2024/10/1155821

Wang, L. (2021). Improving the performance of precision poverty alleviation based on big data mining and machine learning. *Journal of Intelligent & Fuzzy Systems, 40*(4), 6617–6628.

West, S. M., Whittaker, M., & Crawford, K. (2019). *Discriminating systems: Gender, race, and power in AI*. AI Now Institute. https://ainowinstitute.org/publication/discriminating-systems-gender-race-and-power-in-ai-2

Wobcke, W., & Mariyah, S. (2023). Machine learning and data augmentation in the proxy means test for poverty targeting. *Statistical Journal of the IAOS, 39*(4), 961–977. https://doi.org/10.3233/SJI-230033

Wong, V. (2024). *As the wealthy keep spending, here's why the middle class is in for a tough year*. Market Watch. https://www.marketwatch.com/story/as-the-wealthy-keep-spending-heres-why-the-middle-class-is-in-for-a-tough-2025-5e5b3a0b

World Bank. (2023). *The use of advanced technology in job matching platforms: Recent examples from public agencies*. https://thedocs.worldbank.org/en/doc/ceb5c5792ad0d874e9b1c3cc71362f46-0460012023/original/Digital-Job-Matching-Platforms-S4YE-Draft-Note-for-Discussion.pdf

World Economic Forum. (2024). *Revolutionizing classrooms: How AI is reshaping global education*. https://www.weforum.org/press/2024/04/revolutionizing-classrooms-how-ai-is-reshaping-global-education/

Yeh, C., Perez, A., Driscoll, A., Azzari, G., Tang, Z., Lobell, D., et al. (2020). Using publicly available satellite imagery and deep learning to understand economic well-being in Africa. *Nature Communications, 11*(1), 2583.

Chapter 4
AI in Child Welfare and Family Services

Liwei Zhang and Ramona Denby-Brinson

1 Introduction

Child abuse and neglect, or child maltreatment, is a pressing and costly public health issue with negative lifelong consequences. According to the nationwide administrative data (U.S. Department of Health & Human Services, 2025), during the federal fiscal year 2023, about 7.8 million children received child protective services investigations for child abuse and neglect in the United States. Of these, about 546,159 cases were confirmed, and 2000 children died from child abuse and neglect. While all child maltreatment is detrimental and should be prevented and addressed, child neglect is the most pervasive form of maltreatment. Of the 546,159 confirmed cases of maltreatment, approximately 75% were due to neglect. This means that out of the 546,159 confirmed cases, around 409,000 were instances of child neglect. It is important to parse out the difference between categories of maltreatment, given the elusive nature of child neglect and the challenges associated with the use of risk assessments to predict the same. The field has historically come under scrutiny for its inability to differentiate child neglect from family poverty (Gibbs et al., 2024; Milner & Kelly, 2020) and the resulting harm that such failures cause families. As will be discussed later in this chapter, AI and assessment technology are often used not only to identify those children most at risk for maltreatment but also to make critical judgments about resource and service allocations. Unlike other forms of child maltreatment, child neglect is often intertwined with a range of socioeconomic conditions, many of which child welfare and family services (CWFS) have limited capacity to change in any substantive way. Given the

L. Zhang (✉)
School of Social Work, University of Georgia, Athens, GA, USA
e-mail: liwei.zhang@uga.edu

R. Denby-Brinson
School of Social Work, University of North Carolina at Chapel Hill, Chapel Hill, NC, USA
e-mail: rdenby-brinson@unc.edu

R. An, M. A. Lindsey (eds.), *Artificial Intelligence in Social Work*,
https://doi.org/10.1007/978-3-032-18443-6_4

complexities inherent in child neglect—many of them socio-structural in nature—yet the predominantly individual-level focus of most interventions, we must consider how to use AI in ways that fully capture the challenging dynamics of prediction in this context.

Child welfare and family services (hereafter, CWFS) provide a continuum of services to ensure that children are safe and that families have the support they need to care for them successfully. These services typically include receiving and investigating possible child maltreatment reports, providing services to families that need assistance and support in the safety and care of their children, arranging for children to live with foster families or relatives when they are considered to be not safe at home, and arranging for reunification, adoption, or other permanent family placements for children and youth leaving foster care. During each step of the process, CWFS workers are expected to document their observations and decisions. At some points, they also need to retrieve historical information to help determine which service options to choose.

While helpful in most respects, the CWFS system has historically been criticized for administrative burdens, reporting inconsistencies, and disparities in service and resource distribution. Racial disparities in families' involvement in the system, such as the overrepresentation of Black/African American and Native American children in the system, have been at the center of the debate (Dettlaff & Boyd, 2020; Edwards, 2025; Drake et al., 2023). While these critiques and discussions are not new, researchers and policymakers have been calling for efforts and reforms that can identify risk earlier, ensure supports are provided with precision to those in need, and ultimately prevent system involvement and child maltreatment for families at risk. Recognizing the potential to make unbiased, evidence-based decisions, CWFS is increasingly integrating artificial intelligence (AI) tools into its decision-making and service-delivery systems to improve risk assessments and reduce human bias. AI-assisted tools, such as machine learning technologies, help CWFS workers identify potential child maltreatment cases and support them in making informed decisions. While many current AI applications have shown some success, they also face significant challenges and criticisms.

To critically examine the current applications, benefits, challenges, and ethical considerations of AI in CWFS, we conducted a comprehensive literature review on AI tools used in CWFS. We recognize that there are existing literature reviews on AI and CWFS (Gibbs et al., 2024b; Hall et al., 2024). However, these studies generally focus on a specific area overlapping with AI use, such as predictive and prescriptive analytics in child welfare or the birth match policy. Also, we would like to acknowledge the use of AI tools in the copyediting process of this chapter. However, this chapter is fundamentally human-centered, developed through the efforts of the authors and research assistant students who conducted the literature search, review, and writing. Below, we review the use of AI in CWFS by answering the following questions: How is AI currently utilized in child welfare and family services? What are the benefits associated with its implementation? What challenges and concerns arise from AI's use in this field? What are the future directions and implications of AI use in child welfare and family services?

2 AI in Child Welfare and Family Services: Current Applications

Over the past decades, CWFS has increasingly used AI across various operations, including risk assessment, child abuse and neglect detection, and service recommendations such as placement decisions and matching children with foster parents. Below, we detail the current uses of AI in CWFS, highlighting applications, AI models, data sources, and operational settings.

2.1 Risk Assessment and Decision Support

In the context of CWFS, risk assessment typically refers to predictive risk modeling that evaluates the likelihood that a child may experience maltreatment in the future (Hall et al., 2024). This process considers factors related to the children, their family, and their broader environment. When a relatively higher risk is identified, CWFS agencies can respond by prioritizing support and resources for families most in need, ideally intervening before harm occurs. Modern predictive risk modeling is a growing approach that uses machine learning methods to analyze large, diverse datasets, such as social service records, health care information, and demographic data, to estimate the probability of adverse outcomes related to child maltreatment (Schwartz et al., 2017). Unlike traditional statistical models, which are often built around pre-defined variables and assumptions, AI techniques such as machine learning models are more flexible. They can learn and adapt over time, helping identify new patterns and relationships as more data becomes available. These AI-driven models can incorporate numerous variables and are often used for so-called prescriptive analytics (Hall et al., 2024), which goes beyond predicting outcomes to guide decision-making by suggesting potential actions. For this section, we focus specifically on studies that implemented sophisticated, data-driven machine learning algorithms in CWFS. While we acknowledge that the field also uses more traditional tools, such as actuarial checklists and structured decision-making instruments, we did not include those in this review. These conventional tools are typically based on a fixed set of historical and current risk factors and do not evolve with new data inputs (Gleeson, 1987).

Currently, AI-assisted risk assessment tools are being increasingly used in the CWFS sector across the United States and internationally. A 2021 survey by the American Civil Liberties Union found that 26 U.S. states have considered using predictive analytics in child welfare, while jurisdictions in at least 11 states are actively doing so (Samant et al., 2021). A well-known example that has received extensive attention in research and practice is Allegheny County, Pennsylvania, which implemented a predictive risk model to assess hotline reports (Allegheny County Department of Human Services, 2019). The Allegheny Family Screening Tool is an AI-assisted tool introduced to Allegheny County, PA's Office of Children,

Youth, and Families Intake/Call Screening Department. It has since been adapted in many other states. The tool was designed to assist child protection hotline call screeners in assessing child maltreatment risk by providing a risk score indicating the likelihood that a child may be placed out of the home in 2 years. The AI model processes historical administrative data and generates risk scores based on predictive analytics. The model analyzes data from various sources, including previous child maltreatment reports, family demographics (e.g., socioeconomic status, family history), criminal records of parents or guardians, substance abuse and mental health history, and emergency hotline call records. Another example is California's predictive analytics model in Los Angeles County, which was modeled closely on the Allegheny Family Screening Tool but used only historical administrative data that the child welfare agency already held to improve screening decisions for child protective service investigations (Putnam-Hornstein et al., 2022). Other examples in the U.S. CWFS agencies include Florida (Schwartz et al., 2017).

Common features of the above tools include adaptive algorithms trained to predict future maltreatment risks using an extensive database, including prior case histories and social service reports. These assessment tools demonstrate how AI-based risk assessment tools can improve risk prediction and support CWFS caseworkers. However, they also generated concerns about how to avoid biases, ensure fairness, and maintain human oversight. For example, in 2017, Illinois's Department of Children and Family Services discontinued the use of a predictive analytics tool due to its ineffectiveness in accurately identifying children at high risk of harm (Drake et al., 2020). In the sections below, we will detail concerns about false positives arising from AI-assisted tools.

2.2 AI-Assisted Service Recommendations

AI also supports CWFS providers in service planning and decision-making, such as out-of-home placement decisions and matching children with foster parents, by analyzing data patterns and predicting outcomes. Out-of-home placement decisions are particularly important for a child's well-being, as placement instability and frequent moves can lead to adverse outcomes, including delayed permanency, poorer educational outcomes, and increased behavioral and mental health issues. During the federal fiscal year 2022, a total of 569,879 children were served by the foster care system (U.S. Department of Health and Human Services, 2023). With this large number, CWFS has been exploring ways to improve placement outcomes. There are many factors to consider in CWFS decision-making (Chor, 2013), including child safety, family dynamics, and service availability, making AI techniques an ideal approach to addressing this challenge by leveraging multiple data sources. Currently, the most used tools by states to inform placement recommendations include the Child and Adolescent Functional Assessment Scales (Hodges & Kim, 2000), Child and Adolescent Level-of-Care Utilization System (Sowers et al., 2003), Child and Adolescent Needs and Strengths (Lyons, 2008), and Treatment Outcome Package

(TOP; Kraus et al., 2005). The first three tools are mostly traditional, rule-based, human-scored assessment tools that use scoring rubrics to inform placement recommendations. The TOP, however, received some modern implementations, including machine learning for early detection of poor emotional and behavioral outcomes. TOP provides a multidimensional assessment of children's behavioral health and well-being across multiple domains from various informers. A recent study used TOP's detailed assessments as critical input features to develop machine learning models that can predict the probability of treatment success in psychiatric residential care versus other placements (Trudeau et al., 2023). By integrating TOP into their methodology, the study demonstrates the promise of machine learning for predicting positive placement outcomes and informing future placement decisions for youth in care. Overall, while promising, studies are still rare in using AI-assisted tools for out-of-home placement recommendations.

Child-foster parent matching focuses on the compatibility between a child's specific needs and a caregiver's capabilities. Existing research consistently indicates that matching children with foster parents who are emotionally involved and well-prepared to meet children's behavioral and emotional needs can lead to increased stability and well-being for children (Carnochan et al., 2013). By analyzing past placement data, caregiver profiles, and child characteristics, AI can recommend stable matches. Recent research shows that a web-based matching algorithm implemented in Kansas helps pull together child and placement information to inform placement decisions. The study shows the promise of the matching system in improving permanency and reducing disruptions by using temperament and caregiving styles (Moore et al., 2016). However, the specific computational methods employed by the algorithm are not detailed in the available literature. Although there are potential benefits, AI-assisted child-foster parent matching remains under-researched.

2.3 *Detection of Child Abuse and Neglect*

Although AI implementation in child abuse and neglect detection remains limited compared to other fields, its applications are expanding. Image recognition models, particularly deep learning techniques, have been used to distinguish abuse from non-abuse in children based on the radiology reports of head computed tomography, brain MRIs, skeletal surveys, and child self-figure drawing (Tsai & Kleinman, 2022). Other tools, such as natural language processing, have also been used to distinguish child abuse from non-abuse based on electronic medical records (Annapragada et al., 2021). For example, a recent study (Shahi et al., 2021) explored the application of deep learning and natural language processing to identify cases of child physical abuse. The researchers used clinical notes and radiology reports from pediatric hospital data to train deep learning models. The models showed that AI could assist clinicians in identifying potential cases of abuse more efficiently and accurately. There are also studies focused on text mining and machine learning to detect child maltreatment or domestic violence from unstructured data, such as narrative case reports (Amrit et al., 2017; Victor et al., 2021). Collectively, these studies underscore the growing role of AI in detecting child maltreatment. However, despite the positive results, the implementation of such tools is still rare.

2.4 AI-Assisted Training for CWFS Practice

AI has also been used to train CWFS professionals, especially in investigative interviewing training. Trainees in CWFS often require opportunities to practice in realistic settings with immediate feedback (Lamb, 2016). Importantly, AI-driven avatars enable the simulation of child interviewees, offering dynamic conversational practice and AI-generated feedback. Several recent studies have explored the creation of AI-powered avatars as realistic, conversational CWFS training tools designed to simulate interactions with children who may have experienced maltreatment (Baugerud et al., 2021; Salehi et al., 2022; Hassan et al., 2022a, 2022b). These technologies provide professionals a safe, controlled, and consistent environment to build interviewing skills, receive feedback, and improve child-centered communication. For example, Salehi et al. (2022) explored how synthesized avatars can be used to develop questioning skills in trainees. The study demonstrated that these avatars could simulate realistic dialogue and provide feedback in line with best interview practices. Hassan et al. (2022a) further integrated a virtual reality environment with a talking avatar. Together, these tools have contributed to a growing body of research on AI-powered training tools that can address the shortage of practical training opportunities in investigative interviewing.

3 Benefits of AI in Child Welfare and Family Services

When properly trained, AI technologies have shown promise in assisting decision-making, reducing operational costs, and delivering better outcomes for children and families. Studies have applied AI-assisted predictive analytics to examine child maltreatment-related outcomes, such as foster care placement, maltreatment re-reports, aging out of out-of-home care, birth outcomes, service use of child-welfare-involved caregivers, and cases requiring judicial or preventive intervention (Ahn et al., 2021; Chor et al., 2025; Chouldechova et al., 2018; Janczewski & Nitkowski, 2023; Schwartz et al., 2017; Vaithianathan et al., 2020). These studies all showed promising results in the predictive power of AI-assisted tools. Below, we summarize several key benefits of AI in CWFS from the existing literature.

3.1 Data-Driven Decision-Making with Reduced Human Bias

A key advantage of AI in CWFS is its predictive power that can provide early identification of families and children in need of services and supports before harms escalate. Traditional human decision-making in CWFS has been criticized for the influence of implicit biases on outcomes (Miller et al., 2013). Although racial disproportionality in child welfare system involvement is widely documented, the factors contributing to these issues have been the subject of debate over the past decades (Dettlaff & Boyd, 2020; Drake et al., 2023; Edwards, 2025). Clearly, however, the debate regarding these factors has led to efforts to address human biases that may particularly affect families of color and those from lower socioeconomic backgrounds. When trained on diverse, representative datasets, AI models can reduce subjectivity by offering data-driven, evidence-based recommendations. Data-driven AI techniques also uncover complex, multidimensional patterns in data that traditional statistical methods may miss. Research assessing AI tools in risk prediction has shown that machine learning techniques could significantly improve the accuracy and utility of the risk assessment instrument (Hall et al., 2024). For example, a recent study in Broward County found that AI tools significantly improved accuracy in identifying cases likely to re-enter the system. The study found that 57% of recurrences occurred within 1 year of case closure, and AI models were effective at flagging these high-risk cases (Schwartz et al., 2017). These tools also assisted in classifying cases requiring judicial action, preventive services, or intensive intervention. By improving risk differentiation, AI enabled systems helped match services more effectively to family needs, potentially improving child safety and long-term well-being.

3.2 Improved Case Management and Administrative Efficiency

CWFS workers often need to make decisions and provide service within a tight timeline with potentially life-changing consequences for children and families. Also, the administrative burden on CWFS workers is overwhelming, as they must manage large volumes of case files and sometimes perform repetitive tasks. Without immediate access to critical information and with the emotional strain, errors can arise that carry serious consequences. As a result, families may be wrongly targeted, children at risk may be overlooked, and workers may face heightened burnout, all of which can strain public trust and resources. At worst, failures in decision-making can jeopardize child safety.

AI tools have the potential to address these challenges by reducing administrative workloads, automating data entry and analysis, reducing manual errors, and expediting case assessments. Predictive risk models, as mentioned above, analyze historical case data, case worker assessments, and demographic information to estimate the likelihood of child abuse or neglect (Vaithianathan, 2019). These tools can instantly analyze large volumes of data, from the point of hotline intake to service recommendations, using system-stored information available before a call is made. Unlike humans, AI tools can scan all relevant records without fatigue or oversight, which ensures no data point is overlooked. These tools enable CWFS workers to access critical data promptly and allocate resources proactively, thereby reducing false negatives and false positives. AI tools also bring efficiency benefits. By automating repetitive tasks, AI reduces administrative burden and allows social workers to focus more on family engagement than paperwork (Gillingham, 2020). These tools streamline workflows, enhance data access, and support real-time decision-making, thereby improving both worker efficiency and service delivery in emotionally charged, information-rich environments.

3.3 Strategic Service Recommendation and Resource Allocation

In addition to minimizing biases and human errors in decision-making, AI models can effectively allocate CWFS resources when making service recommendations, such as out-of-home placement decisions and child-foster parent matching. Machine learning algorithms offer decision support to CWFS workers by providing data-driven recommendations. These tools analyze an extensive database of case histories and provide insights into the best service or intervention based on past successful cases. By offering case recommendations based on previously successful interventions, these AI-based tools also improve consistency and reduce variability in assessments and, eventually, achieve equitable outcomes (Trudeau et al., 2023). AI also helps direct CWFS workers, financial support, and prevention programs to where they are most needed by predicting which geographic regions or populations are at higher risk. For example, deep learning models can forecast surges in neglect or maltreatment cases. These systems, integrated with Geographic Information Systems, can locate high-risk communities using crime statistics, economic indicators, and historical child welfare data. Still, as stated in other sections of this chapter, the use of the technology in this manner should be done judiciously, given the biased assumptions often made about children and families whose neighborhoods or communities of origin, demographics, or other macro conditions depict a picture that may not accurately convey their unique experiences and needs. Theoretically, by predicting which communities may have a high risk of child maltreatment, resources such as shelters, foster care placements, and counseling services can be allocated more effectively. While this is an aim of the technology, we know that help-seeking and the receipt of needed services can be frustrating and elusive for many families.

3.4 *Facilitating Communication and Training Tools*

AI-powered chatbots and virtual assistants can also provide immediate support to both families and CWFS professionals. These systems provide access to parenting resources, legal information, and crisis support, helping families navigate services in real time. Regarding CWFS professionals, AI tools, such as chatbot-based training tools, help them practice critical skills in child interviews in an interactive environment. These interactive tools support emotional, cognitive, and behavioral engagement among professionals and enable continuous learning and skill retention (Røed et al., 2023). In addition, although primarily studied outside CWFS, developing engaging AI-supported platforms can help educators prepare students for careers in high-pressure, real-world settings.

4 Concerns and Challenges

While studies generally embrace the strengths of AI in CWFS, its implementation also raises a host of concerns across technical and ethical domains (Gillingham, 2020; Saxena & Guha, 2024). Many of these concerns are not only hypothetical but have been demonstrated in real-world cases, as evidenced by critiques from researchers, practitioners, and communities that have experienced unintended harms and challenges arising from the use of algorithmic systems in CWFS services. Complicating the full embrace of AI in child welfare is a level of practice tension that predates technology and is not necessarily caused by AI. Failure to recognize this tension can stagnate progress or increase skepticism about AI in child welfare. The three current points of tension are crucial for understanding how AI is perceived and approached.

Practice Dilemma 1: The existence of a remove-and-place system and the absence of a support system. AI advancement in child welfare must be examined within the contested goals of Child Welfare and Family Assistance (CWFA) systems. The child welfare system aims to protect, promote well-being, and ensure permanency (U.S. Department of Health and Human Services, Administration for Children and Families, 2023). However, critics argue that the system overemphasizes family surveillance and child removal, focusing less on providing services to families in need. This belief suggests the system punishes parents by removing children, even when challenges stem from socio-structural phenomena beyond individual control. Some scholars differentiate abuse and neglect and, in doing so, advocate for a different response system for child neglect (Feely et al., 2020). Other advocates call for policy-level interventions to provide economic security and reduce maltreatment rates (Berger & Slack, 2021). Additionally, care coordination and cross-system collaboration have long been advanced as mechanisms to improve child and family outcomes (Mariscal et al., 2024). AI advancements that coordinate services across the continuum of care are needed. AI can be valuable when data and learning models account for broader environmental conditions and identify appropriate response patterns. Predicting adverse conditions without providing practitioners with tools to respond and support families limits progress.

Practice Dilemma 2: Inadequacy of child removal. AI as an assessment aid raises concerns about its impact on human decision-making. Predictive analytics may lead child welfare professionals to substantiate maltreatment and remove children, but this may not improve decision-making. Proponents argue that AI tools offer objectivity, aiding difficult decisions, while skeptics question whether this is, in fact, the very problem. About 50% of children removed by child protective services are reunited within a short period (USDHHS-ACF, 2023). This issue is problematic due to the family disruption, trauma, and inherent bias and institutionalized racism it produces (Merritt et al., 2025; Roberts, 2014, 2019, 2022). High-touch case management and authentic engagement with children and parents should be service-delivery objectives. Reconciling AI use in critical service decisions requires demonstrating its myriad purposes, downplaying its current use as a marker for child removal.

Practice Dilemma 3: The need to predict and respond to adverse community conditions. Families in the child welfare system are often deemed inadequate rather than suffering from strained community conditions. Decision-makers should prioritize child and family well-being. Decision-making tools frequently fail to account for the community adversity associated with foster care risks (White-Wolfe & Denby, in press). Increased reliance on AI tools in child welfare settings will occur when they decipher pathways to reverse economic hardships and structural issues associated with child welfare involvement. AI could help explain racial disparities in child welfare and formulate policies to reduce harm to impoverished or minoritized families.

Below, we summarize several additional key concerns and challenges raised in the literature.

4.1 Data-Driven Bias and Unintended Consequences

One of the most significant challenges in applying AI to CWFS is the potential for algorithmic bias. AI systems are objective only when the data on which they are trained is objective. If the data already embed existing biases, the AI system will accurately predict them and ultimately reproduce systematic inequalities. For example, many risk-prediction tools are highly dependent on administrative data (Putnam-Hornstein et al., 2022). When the historical child welfare data reflects deep-rooted systemic racial/ethnic and socioeconomic inequities, predictive risk models may inadvertently reinforce these disparities rather than correct them. Although scholars have proposed a range of fairness metrics, such as calibration, predictive parity, and error rate balance, these definitions are often incompatible with one another in practice (Chouldechova et al., 2018; Corbett-Davies & Goel, 2018; Dwork et al., 2012). A tool might be equally accurate across two racial groups but still have a higher false-positive rate for one group. In the CWFS context, this can translate into disproportionate scrutiny or intervention for certain populations, such as Black and African American families.

Despite growing awareness, relatively few child welfare studies explicitly assess bias and fairness during model development (Chouldechova et al., 2018; Lanier et al., 2019; Ahn et al., 2021; Purdy & Glass, 2023; Chor et al., 2025). A recent review study found that less than half of the reviewed published work in the child welfare field considered ethics, equity, or participatory design principles (Hall et al., 2024). Also, administrative data often contain errors, inconsistencies, or duplicate records (Vogl, 2020; Allard et al., 2018). Without robust mechanisms for uniquely identifying individuals across systems, data can be fragmented or misleading, further undermining the reliability of AI predictions. While AI may help deduplicate records, current systems struggle when individuals withhold information or when only partial data is available. These challenges are especially problematic at the frontline level, where decisions made with flawed data can have life-altering consequences for children and families.

In fact, while many child welfare agencies continue to explore the AI tools in CWFS, several state or local agencies, including Illinois, Los Angeles County, and, most recently, Oregon, have shut down predictive analytics programs due to concerns over poor outcomes and racial bias. In Allegheny County, as we mentioned above, while the AI-assisted family screening tool supported objective decision-making, it was also found to produce biased risk scores, which caseworkers frequently had to override (Kawakami et al., 2022b). Ironically, the tool meant to reduce bias may end up adding layers of complexity and mistrust.

4.2 *AI Misalignment with Human Judgement*

Although AI tools are designed to assist practitioners' decision-making, studies indicate a persistent misalignment between the long-term predictive goals of AI systems and the immediate, context-driven needs of CWFS professionals. For example, in a 2-year ethnographic study with child welfare agencies, researchers found that algorithms predicting long-term risks may not provide actionable insights for addressing immediate family needs, leading to skepticism and reduced trust in these tools (Saxena & Guha, 2024). Many studies found that caseworkers often report that AI tools do not reflect their professional judgment (Kawakami et al., 2022a, 2022b; Saxena et al., 2020). In some cases, algorithmic design choices, such as aggregating household-level risk or including static variables like criminal justice involvement, have amplified systemic discrimination rather than mitigated it. CWFS practitioners expressed frustration when predictions are based on proxy indicators, such as prior child welfare system involvement, that feel misaligned with their day-to-day decision-making (Saxena & Guha, 2024). Also, tools such as the Child and Adolescent Needs and Strengths assessment require workers to collect and enter detailed data, often without providing them with increased decision-making power in return. As a result, AI was initially intended to reduce workload and improve efficiency, but in many cases, it has added new layers of data entry and administrative burden for caseworkers (Saxena & Guha, 2024).

4.3 Regulatory and Theoretical Gaps

Despite the growing adoption of AI tools, the CWFS field lacks clear regulatory frameworks to guide the ethical development and use of these tools (Saxena & Guha, 2024). There are few federal or state-level guidelines on how such tools should be used, evaluated, or overseen. This lack of guidelines creates significant ethical risks, particularly in a field already marked by racial and socioeconomic disparities. Without a clear regulatory framework, CWFS and AI tool developers also must navigate the process in a gray zone, which can raise concerns about data privacy and bias that reinforce systemic inequalities. Equally important is the absence of a firm theoretical grounding. A review study found that, among 50 studies on computational systems used in CWFS, only one used a theoretical model grounded in the child welfare literature (Saxena et al., 2020). The review study found that several studies have acknowledged this gap and proposed frameworks, such as cumulative risk models, causal models, or revised SDM models grounded in risk and resilience theory, to conduct research in AI and child welfare. Yet, such models have not been implemented within existing literature. Without theoretical frameworks that meaningfully guide the practice of AI tools, AI tools may risk oversimplifying the multidimensional factors influencing family well-being into binary classifications based on risk scores. For example, the authors argued that many AI tools used predictors based on readily available, quantifiable child and family characteristics. Yet, many such factors, such as the severity of abuse, have little indication that they are related to the recurrence of abuse (Saxena et al., 2020). Also, such factors are often based on individual- or family-level characteristics rather than on broader social contexts, such as structural or historical factors. The absence of interdisciplinary, child welfare-specific theoretical models only reduces the validity and fairness of AI tools and limits their potential to support preventive approaches in CWFS. In short, without models that reflect the realities of family life and systemic challenges, AI tools risk oversimplifying complex social issues.

4.4 Human Trust and Transparency

Beyond technical issues, AI introduces ethical concerns around consent, surveillance, and stigmatization (Drake et al., 2020). Many families are unaware that their data is being used in algorithmic systems, raising important questions about privacy and confidentiality. When data is collected for one purpose and used for another without informed consent, it not only undermines public trust but also risks harming those it was intended to help. This inevitably led to a trust issue, which remains a significant barrier to successful AI integration in CWFS. For technology to support, not replace, human decision-making, both users and the public must fully understand how the system works, how to interpret its outputs, and when to question or override its recommendations. While the public provides a mixed response to the use of AI in CWFS, the trust within CWFS itself has been mixed. Research has found that practitioners are generally skeptical and distrustful of AI's judgment (Kawakami et al., 2022a). When workers do not trust these tools, organizational pressures may push them to rely on AI recommendations to avoid liability or to comply with policy requirements. The significant impact of the algorithm-generated score on their decision-making has been shown not only among CWFS professionals but also in the legal context (Trail, 2024). Therefore, while external transparency (e.g., public documentation of a tool's design) is essential, internal transparency and training are equally important. Also, the lack of transparency in how these tools operate has confused CWFS practitioners (Kawakami et al., 2022a). Many practitioners reported not receiving adequate training or information on how the models function and how the system responds to different inputs (Gibbs et al., 2024a). Taken together, workers need ongoing support to engage meaningfully with AI tools, and agencies need to foster environments that respect professional judgment alongside technological guidance.

5 Recommendations and Future Directions

Overall, despite the concerns around the use of AI tools in CWFS, most studies suggested these concerns can catalyze thoughtful, interdisciplinary dialogue and innovation, not as a reason to abandon the potential of these technologies altogether (Drake et al., 2020; Hall et al., 2024; Lanier et al., 2019). If designed and implemented with care, transparency, and collaboration, AI can help strengthen decision-making, reduce disparities, and ultimately improve outcomes for children and families. Below, we provide a summary of key recommendations to guide future work based on the current literature review.

5.1 Improve Accuracy and Account for Human Misalignment

While predictive tools should be accurate, it is equally important to recognize that accuracy alone is not enough. In the predictive risk model context, for instance, studies have suggested that differences in prediction targets led to misalignment between AI recommendations and workers' actual decision-making objectives (Drake et al., 2020; Kawakami et al., 2022a). Comparing human decisions to algorithmic outputs without understanding the underlying purpose of each can be misleading. If an algorithm misidentifies families due to structural biases (e.g., poverty, racial disparities), it risks reinforcing the very inequities the child welfare system seeks to address (Drake et al., 2020). Some studies have highlighted the importance of human oversight in algorithmic decision-making, such as in reducing racial disparities (Cheng et al., 2022). While algorithms, such as those in the predictive risk model, can provide valuable data-driven insights, incorporating human judgment is also crucial for interpreting these recommendations within appropriate social and historical contexts. Furthermore, any AI system used in CWFS needs to undergo comprehensive and ongoing evaluation (Chor et al., 2025; Lanier et al., 2019). It is essential to ask whether predictive tools are reducing rates of serious harm, such as fatal maltreatment, in the jurisdictions where they have been implemented. These evaluations should be based on high-quality longitudinal data and incorporate causal inference methods to determine whether the tools are meeting their intended goals or unintentionally causing harm.

5.2 Build Internal and External Transparency

Transparency is also needed to be both intentional and continuous. This means engaging families, communities, and CWFS practitioners throughout the design and use of AI tools and clearly documenting the rationale, development, and implementation processes. Allegheny County serves as a promising example of external transparency, with publicly available documentation detailing how its predictive model was built, validated, and monitored (Allegheny County Department of Human Services, 2019). However, internal transparency remains an issue. Workers need to understand the tools they are expected to use, such as what data drives them, how scores are generated, and when to trust (or question) their outputs. True transparency also means creating space for public oversight and community dialogue. Jurisdictions should solicit feedback from affected families, frontline workers, and advocacy groups before and after implementation. Those families' lived experiences must also inform technologies that impact families. It is critical to involve parents, caregivers, and children, especially those from historically marginalized communities, in conversations around AI-assisted tools such as predictive screening and service recommendations.

Notably, there is an apparent disconnect between the number of AI systems built and how frontline professionals work. Many studies suggest that most AI-assisted tools lack a grounding in child welfare theory and are rarely co-designed with the people who use them daily (Kawakami et al., 2022a). They have recommended bridging AI and human-computer interaction through participatory design (Ahn et al., 2024b; Gibbs et al., 2024; Hall et al., 2024). This approach actively involves CWFS workers in both the design and evaluation of tools, thereby ensuring that systems are aligned with their needs and professional judgment. Professionals expected to use these tools, including social workers and healthcare providers, should also be part of shaping how systems are designed, monitored, and refined. Engaging these groups ensures a deeper understanding of intended benefits and unintended consequences and supports more ethical, inclusive policymaking. Many child welfare agencies lack in-house data science capacity. One way to close this gap is to invest in interdisciplinary partnerships among CWFS organizations, computer science departments, and policy schools (Hall et al., 2024; Kum et al., 2015). These collaborations could support training, research, and even the creation of internship pipelines for students in CS, informatics, and social work. Extending Title IV-E funding to support workforce development in AI and data-informed practice could also equip CWFS professionals with the skills needed to engage critically with these tools. For example, understanding model performance and its implications, such as how 75% accuracy might sound impressive in a research paper but fall short in high-stakes decisions, requires both technical and contextual expertise.

5.3 *Promote Equal and Ethical Frameworks*

Finally, research suggested that we need to ensure that systems work equitably and ethically across all groups (Ahn et al., 2024a; Drake et al., 2020). Any tool that produces significantly higher false-positive rates for a specific racial/ethnic group or socioeconomic group is ethically problematic. Concerns about equity are not new in child welfare. They arise at every decision point, from screening and investigation to service delivery and out-of-home care placement. While AI may help reduce child maltreatment or improve risk assessment, it also introduces new risks, such as over-surveillance or biased intervention (Saxena & Guha, 2024). These trade-offs should be made explicit and debated publicly. Predictive tools should be audited and evaluated regularly to assess performance across subpopulations, and adjustments should be made to address disparities when they appear. Additionally, algorithmic design needs to consider legal and ethical boundaries, such as limits on the use of sensitive information (e.g., juvenile justice records and histories of abuse) in prediction models. Regarding data privacy and consent, some scholars argued that AI tools, such as predictive risk models, should be treated similarly to other methods. Therefore, in cases where the child welfare agency has granted data sources use, the use of those data sources would not pose new ethical concerns (Drake et al., 2020). While debates continue over this issue, policies related to risk assessment should also address accountability, transparency, and fairness.

6 Conclusion

Taken together, AI can play an influential role in CWFS, but only if implemented with care, transparency, and a commitment to equity. It is not enough for these tools to be accurate. They should also be fair, ethical, and aligned with the needs of both families, children, and the professionals who serve them. Achieving this balance requires not only technical expertise but also meaningful collaboration across disciplines and communities. That said, it is essential to ensure that these AI systems do not replicate the systemic biases already embedded in historical data. To address this, researchers are exploring fairness-aware machine learning and ethical AI governance frameworks that can improve transparency and accountability in CWFS (e.g., Ahn et al., 2021; Purdy & Glass, 2023). The use of AI in CWFS should never be about replacing human judgment. It should be about supporting it. By thoughtfully integrating ethical design, rigorous evaluation, inclusive collaboration, and transparent governance, we can move toward AI systems that serve children and families, especially those who have historically been underserved or harmed by the system.

Competing Interests The authors have no conflicts of interest to declare that are relevant to the content of this chapter.

References

Ahn, E., An, R., Jonson-Reid, M., & Palmer, L. (2024a). Leveraging machine learning for effective child maltreatment prevention: A case study of home visiting service assessments. *Child Abuse & Neglect, 151*, 106706. https://doi.org/10.1016/j.chiabu.2024.106706

Ahn, E., Gil, Y., & Putnam-Hornstein, E. (2021). Predicting youth at high risk of aging out of foster care using machine learning methods. *Child Abuse & Neglect, 117*, 105059. https://doi.org/10.1016/j.chiabu.2021.105059

Ahn, E., Morstatter, F., Waters-Roman, D., Palmer, L., & McCroskey, J. (2024b). Qualitative exploration of child welfare workers' decision-making experiences and perspectives on fairness. *Journal of Public Child Welfare, 19*(1), 229–252. https://doi.org/10.1080/15548732.2024.2312846

Allard, S. W., Wiegand, E. R., Schlecht, C., Datta, A. R., Goerge, R. M., & Weigensberg, E. (2018). State agencies' use of administrative data for improved practice: Needs, challenges, and opportunities. *Public Administration Review, 78*(2), 240–250. https://doi.org/10.1111/puar.12883

Allegheny County Department of Human Services. (2019). *Developing predictive risk models to support child maltreatment hotline screening decisions* https://www.alleghenycountyanalytics.us/2019/05/01/developing-predictive-risk-models-support-child-maltreatment-hotline-screening-decisions/

Amrit, C., Paauw, T., Aly, R., & Lavric, M. (2017). Identifying child abuse through text mining and machine learning. *Expert Systems with Applications, 88*, 402–418. https://doi.org/10.1016/j.eswa.2017.06.035

Annapragada, A. V., Donaruma-Kwoh, M. M., Annapragada, A. V., & Starosolski, Z. A. (2021). A natural language processing and deep learning approach to identify child abuse from pediatric electronic medical records. *PLoS One, 16*(2), e0247404. https://doi.org/10.1371/journal.pone.0247404

Baugerud, G. A., Johnson, M. S., Røed, R. K., Lamb, M. E., Powell, M. B., Thambawita, V., et al. (2021). Multimodal virtual avatars for investigative interviews with children. In M. Dao, D. Dang-Nguyen, & M. Riegler (Eds.), *Proceedings of the 2021 workshop on intelligent cross-data analysis and retrieval* (pp. 2–8). ACM.

Berger, L. M., & Slack, K. S. (2021). The contemporary U.S. child welfare system(s): Overview and key challenges. *The Annals of the American Academy of Political and Social Science, 692*(1), 7–25. https://doi.org/10.1177/00027162209693

Carnochan, S., Moore, M., & Austin, M. J. (2013). Achieving placement stability. *Journal of Evidence-Based Social Work, 10*(3), 235–253. https://doi.org/10.1080/15433714.2013.788953

Cheng, H. F., Stapleton, L., Kawakami, A., Sivaraman, V., Cheng, Y., Qing, D., … & Zhu, H. (2022). How child welfare workers reduce racial disparities in algorithmic decisions. In *Proceedings of the 2022 CHI Conference on Human Factors in Computing Systems* (pp. 1–22). https://doi.org/10.1145/3491102.3501831

Chor, K. H. B. (2013). Overview of out-of-home placements and placement decision-making in child welfare. *Journal of Public Child Welfare, 7*(3), 298–328. https://doi.org/10.1080/15548732.2013.779357

Chor, K. H. B., Luo, Z., Rodolfa, K. T., & Ghani, R. (2025). Exploring machine learning to support decision-making for placement stabilization and preservation in child welfare. *Journal of Child and Family Studies, 34*(1), 282–297. https://doi.org/10.1007/s10826-024-02993-x

Chouldechova, A., Benavides-Prado, D., Fialko, O., & Vaithianathan, R. (2018). A case study of algorithm-assisted decision making in child maltreatment hotline screening decisions. In *Proceedings of the Conference on Fairness, Accountability and Transparency* (pp. 134–148). PMLR.

Corbett-Davies, S., & Goel, S. (2018). The measure and mismeasure of fairness: A critical review of fair machine learning. *arXiv Preprint*. https://arxiv.org/abs/1808.00023

Dettlaff, A. J., & Boyd, R. (2020). Racial disproportionality and disparities in the child welfare system: Why do they exist, and what can be done to address them? *The Annals of the American Academy of Political and Social Science, 692*(1), 253–274. https://doi.org/10.1177/0002716220980329

Drake, B., Jones, D., Kim, H., Gyourko, J., Garcia, A., Barth, R. P., Font, S. A., Putnam-Hornstein, E., Duerr Berrick, J., Greeson, J. K. P., Cook, V., Kohl, P. L., & Jonson-Reid, M. (2023). Racial/ethnic differences in child protective services reporting, substantiation and placement, with comparison to non-CPS risks and outcomes: 2005–2019. *Child Maltreatment, 28*(4), 683–699. https://doi.org/10.1177/10775595231167320

Drake, B., Jonson-Reid, M., Ocampo, M. G., Morrison, M., & Dvalishvili, D. (2020). A practical framework for considering the use of predictive risk modeling in child welfare. *The Annals of the American Academy of Political and Social Science, 692*(1), 162–181. https://doi.org/10.1177/0002716220978200

Dwork, C., Hardt, M., Pitassi, T., Reingold, O., & Zemel, R. (2012). Fairness through awareness. In *Proceedings of the 3rd Innovations in Theoretical Computer Science Conference* (pp. 214–226). Association for Computing Machinery. https://doi.org/10.1145/2090236.2090255

Edwards, F. (2025). Bias, risk, racism: Reconciling critical and quantitative approaches to understanding racial inequality in child welfare system outcomes. *Journal of Policy Analysis and Management, 44*(2), 693–706. https://doi.org/10.1002/pam.70001

Feely, M., Raissian, K. M., Schneider, W., & Bullinger, L. R. (2020). The social welfare policy landscape and child protective services: Opportunities for and barriers to creating systems synergy. *The Annals of the American Academy of Political and Social Science, 692*(1), 140–161. https://doi.org/10.1177/0002716220973566

Gibbs, D. J., Lanier, P., McNellan, C., & Bryant, K. (2024b). Identifying children at risk for maltreatment fatalities: Assessing the current landscape of birth match policies in the United States. *Journal of Public Child Welfare, 19*, 1–29. https://doi.org/10.1080/15548732.2024.2319732

Gibbs, D. J., Loper, A., Farley, A., Afkinich, J. L., Johnson, I. C., & Metz, A. J. (2024a). Implementing algorithmic decision-making tools in child welfare systems: Practitioner perspectives on use and usefulness. *Journal of Technology in Human Services, 42*(4), 277–311. https://doi.org/10.1080/15228835.2024.2402982

Gibbs, J., Coughlan, B., Morgan, T., Mikushnica, A., Phippard, S., Crozier-Roche, F., Drayak, T., Graham, D., Smith, J., & Duschinsky, R. (2024). Social workers' perceptions of the nature of child neglect: A systematic literature review. *The British Journal of Social Work, 54*(8), 3619–3637. https://doi.org/10.1093/bjsw/bcae102

Gillingham, P. (2020). Algorithmically based decision support tools: Skeptical thinking about the inclusion of previous involvement in child protection matters. *Journal of Social Work Practice, 34*(4), 409–419. https://doi.org/10.1080/09503153.2020.1749584

Gleeson, J. P. (1987). Implementing structured decision-making procedures at child welfare intake. *Child Welfare, 66*(2), 101–112.

Hall, S. F., Sage, M., Scott, C. F., & Joseph, K. (2024). A systematic review of sophisticated predictive and prescriptive analytics in child welfare: Accuracy, equity, and bias. *Child and Adolescent Social Work Journal, 41*(6), 831–847. https://doi.org/10.1007/s10560-023-00931-2

Hassan, S. Z., Salehi, P., Riegler, M. A., Johnson, M. S., Baugerud, G. A., Halvorsen, P., et al. (2022a). A virtual reality talking avatar for investigative interviews of maltreated children. In *Proceedings of the 19th International Conference on Content-Based Multimedia Indexing* (pp. 201–204). ACM.

Hassan, S. Z., Salehi, P., Røed, R. K., Halvorsen, P., Baugerud, G. A., Johnson, M. S., et al. (2022b). Towards an AI-driven talking avatar in virtual reality for investigative interviews of children. In *Proceedings of the 2nd Edition of the Game Systems Workshop (GameSys '22)* (pp. 9–15). ACM.

Hodges, K., & Kim, C. S. (2000). Psychometric study of the Child and Adolescent Functional Assessment Scale: Prediction of contact with the law and poor school attendance. *Journal of Abnormal Child Psychology, 28*(3), 287–297.

Janczewski, C. E., & Nitkowski, J. (2023). Predicting mental and behavioral health service utilization among child welfare-involved caregivers: A machine learning approach. *Children and Youth Services Review, 155*, 107150. https://doi.org/10.1016/j.childyouth.2023.107150

Kawakami, A., Sivaraman, V., Cheng, H. F., Stapleton, L., Cheng, Y., Qing, D., & Holstein, K. (2022a). Improving human-AI partnerships in child welfare: Understanding worker practices, challenges, and desires for algorithmic decision support. In *Proceedings of the 2022 CHI Conference on Human Factors in Computing Systems* (pp. 1–18). ACM. https://doi.org/10.1145/3491102.3517439

Kawakami, A., Sivaraman, V., Stapleton, L., Cheng, H. F., Perer, A., Wu, Z. S., Zhu, H., & Holstein, K. (2022b). "Why do I care what's similar?" Probing challenges in AI-assisted child welfare decision-making through worker-AI interface design concepts. In *Proceedings of the 2022 ACM Designing Interactive Systems Conference* (pp. 454–470). https://doi.org/10.1145/3532106.3533556

Kraus, D. R., Seligman, D. A., & Jordan, J. R. (2005). Validation of a behavioral health treatment outcome and assessment tool designed for naturalistic settings: The treatment outcome package. *Journal of Clinical Psychology, 61*(3), 285–314. https://doi.org/10.1002/jclp.20084

Kum, H. C., Stewart, C. J., Rose, R. A., & Duncan, D. F. (2015). Using big data for evidence based governance in child welfare. *Children and Youth Services Review, 58*, 127–136. https://doi.org/10.1016/j.childyouth.2015.09.014

Lamb, M. E. (2016). Difficulties translating research on forensic interview practices to practitioners: Finding water, leading horses, but can we get them to drink? *American Psychologist, 71*(7), 710–718. https://doi.org/10.1037/amp0000039

Lanier, P., Maguire-Jack, K., Welch, H., & Lombardi, B. (2019). Preventing infant maltreatment with predictive analytics: Applying ethical principles to evidence-based child welfare policy. *Journal of Family Violence, 34*(6), 475–485. https://doi.org/10.1007/s10896-019-00074-y

Lyons, J. S. (2008). *Manual for the Child and Adolescent Needs and Strengths (CANS)*. University of Illinois at Chicago. https://www.hca.wa.gov/assets/billers-and-providers/child-adolescent-needs-strengths-cans-screening-tool.pdf

Mariscal, E. S., Victor, B. G., Elliot, J. M., Smith, J., Commodore-Mensah, M., & Sabina, C. (2024). Preventing foster care entry at the community, systems, and societal levels: Recommendations from the child-serving workforce. *Children and Youth Services Review, 163*, 107811. https://doi.org/10.1016/j.childyouth.2024.107811

Merritt, D. H., Ludeke, R. D., Halverson, J., Chewe, J., & Kaul, U. (2025). Mandated reporting and child welfare surveillance: Protection or subordination. *Families in Society, 106*(2), 480–499. https://doi.org/10.1177/10443894251322200

Miller, K. M., Cahn, K., Anderson-Nathe, B., Cause, A. G., & Bender, R. (2013). Individual and systemic/structural bias in child welfare decision making: Implications for children and families of color. *Children and Youth Services Review, 35*(9), 1634–1642. https://doi.org/10.1016/j.childyouth.2013.07.002

Milner, J., & Kelly, D. (2020, January 17). *It's time to stop confusing poverty with neglect.* The Imprint. https://imprintnews.org/child-welfare-2/time-for-child-welfare-system-to-stop-confusing-poverty-with-neglect/40222

Moore, T. D., McDonald, T. P., & Cronbaugh-Auld, K. (2016). Assessing risk of placement instability to aid foster care placement decision making. *Journal of Public Child Welfare, 10*(2), 117–131. https://doi.org/10.1080/15548732.2016.1140697

Purdy, J., & Glass, B. (2023). The pursuit of algorithmic fairness: On "correcting" algorithmic unfairness in a child welfare reunification success classifier. *Children and Youth Services Review, 145*, 106777. https://doi.org/10.1016/j.childyouth.2022.106777

Putnam-Hornstein, E., Vaithianathan, R., McCroskey, J., & Webster, D. (2022). *Los Angeles County risk stratification model: Methodology & implementation report.* University of California. https://dcfs.lacounty.gov/wp-content/uploads/2022/08/Risk-Stratification-Methodology-Report_8.29.22.pdf

Roberts, D. E. (2014). Child protection as surveillance of African American families. *Journal of Social Welfare and Family Law, 36*(4), 426–437. https://doi.org/10.1080/09649069.2014.967991

Roberts, D. E. (2019). How the child welfare system polices Black mothers. *S&F Online, 15*(3). https://sfonline.barnard.edu/how-the-child-welfare-system-polices-black-mothers/

Roberts, D. E. (2022). *Torn apart: How the child welfare system destroys Black families—and how abolition can build a safer world.* Basic Books.

Røed, R. K., Baugerud, G. A., Hassan, S. Z., Sabet, S. S., Salehi, P., Powell, M. B., et al. (2023). Enhancing questioning skills through child avatar chatbot training with feedback. *Frontiers in Psychology, 14*, 1198235. https://doi.org/10.3389/fpsyg.2023.1198235

Salehi, P., Hassan, S. Z., Lammerse, M., Sabet, S. S., Riiser, I., Røed, R. K., et al. (2022). Synthesizing a talking child avatar to train interviewers working with maltreated children. *Big Data and Cognitive Computing, 6*(2), 62. https://doi.org/10.3390/bdcc6020062

Samant, A., Horowitz, A., Xu, K., & Beiers, S. (2021). *Family surveillance by algorithm: The rapidly spreading tools few have heard of.* American Civil Liberties Union. https://www.aclu.org/news/womens-rights/family-surveillance-by-algorithm-the-rapidly-spreading-tools-few-have-heard-of

Saxena, D., Badillo-Urquiola, K., Wisniewski, P. J., & Guha, S. (2020). A human-centered review of the algorithms used within the U.S. child welfare system. In *Proceedings of the 2020 CHI Conference on Human Factors in Computing Systems* (pp. 1–13). https://doi.org/10.1145/3313831.3376229

Saxena, D., & Guha, S. (2024). Algorithmic harms in child welfare: Uncertainties in practice, organization, and street-level decision-making. *ACM Journal on Responsible Computing, 1*(1), 1–32. https://doi.org/10.1145/3616473

Schwartz, I. M., York, P., Nowakowski-Sims, E., & Ramos-Hernandez, A. (2017). Predictive and prescriptive analytics, machine learning and child welfare risk assessment: The Broward County experience. *Children and Youth Services Review, 81*, 309–320. https://doi.org/10.1016/j.childyouth.2017.08.020

Shahi, N., Shahi, A. K., Phillips, R., Shirek, G., Lindberg, D. M., & Moulton, S. L. (2021). Using deep learning and natural language processing models to detect child physical abuse. *Journal of Pediatric Surgery, 56*(12), 2326–2332. https://doi.org/10.1016/j.jpedsurg.2021.03.007

Sowers, W., George, C., & Thompson, K. (2003). *Level of care utilization system for psychiatric and addiction services (LOCUS) and Child and Adolescent Level of Care Utilization System*

(CALOCUS). American Association of Community Psychiatrists. https://www.communitypsychiatry.org/locus#:~:text=Both%20LOCUS%20and%20CALOCUS%20have,facilitate%20clinical%20management%20and%20documentation

Trail, M. (2024). Child welfare predictive risk models and legal decision making. *Child Abuse & Neglect, 154*, 106943. https://doi.org/10.1016/j.chiabu.2024.106943

Trudeau, K. J., Yang, J., Di, J., Lu, Y., & Kraus, D. R. (2023). Predicting successful placements for youth in child welfare with machine learning. *Children and Youth Services Review, 183*, 107117. https://doi.org/10.1016/j.childyouth.2023.107117

Tsai, A., & Kleinman, P. K. (2022). Machine learning to identify distal tibial classic metaphyseal lesions of infant abuse: A pilot study. *Pediatric Radiology, 52*, 1095–1103. https://doi.org/10.1007/s00247-022-05287-w

U.S. Department of Health and Human Services, Administration for Children and Families. (2023). *Child welfare outcomes 2020: Report to Congress*. https://www.govinfo.gov/app/details/CMR-HE25-00182856

U.S. Department of Health and Human Services, Administration for Children and Families, Administration on Children, Youth and Families, Children's Bureau. (2023). *The AFCARS report: Preliminary FY 2022 estimates as of May 9, 2023—No. 30*. https://acf.gov/sites/default/files/documents/cb/afcars-report-30.pdf

U.S. Department of Health and Human Services, Administration for Children and Families, Administration on Children, Youth and Families, Children's Bureau. (2025). *Child maltreatment 2023*. https://www.acf.hhs.gov/cb/data-research/child-maltreatment

Vaithianathan, R. (2019). *Implementing a child welfare decision aide in Douglas County: Methodology report*. Centre for Social Data Analytics. https://csda.aut.ac.nz/__data/assets/pdf_file/0009/347715/Douglas-County-Methodology_Final_3_02_2020.pdf

Vaithianathan, R., Putnam-Hornstein, E., Chouldechova, A., Benavides-Prado, D., & Berger, R. (2020). Hospital injury encounters of children identified by a predictive risk model for screening child maltreatment referrals: Evidence from the Allegheny family screening tool. *JAMA Pediatrics, 174*(11), e202770. https://doi.org/10.1001/jamapediatrics.2020.2770

Victor, B. G., Perron, B. E., Sokol, R. L., Fedina, L., & Ryan, J. P. (2021). Automated identification of domestic violence in written child welfare records: Leveraging text mining and machine learning to enhance social work research and evaluation. *Journal of the Society for Social Work and Research, 12*(4), 631–655. https://doi.org/10.1086/712734

Vogl, T. M. (2020). Artificial intelligence and organizational memory in government: The experience of record duplication in the child welfare sector in Canada. In *Proceedings of the 21st Annual International Conference on Digital Government Research* (pp. 223–231). https://doi.org/10.1145/3396956.339697

White-Wolfe, H., & Denby, R. (In press). Expanding policy frames to acknowledge links between community adversity and foster care entry for county, White, Black, and Hispanic/Latino populations. *Journal of Public Child Welfare*.

Chapter 5
AI in Health Care and Health Disparities

Mengmeng Ji, Shuo Xu, Fan Yang, and Sara S. Bachman

1 AI in Health Care and Social Work

1.1 Health and Social Determinants of Health

Health is widely recognized as a fundamental human right, a principle enshrined in foundational global documents like the Universal Declaration of Human Rights and the Constitution of the World Health Organization (United Nations, 1948). Traditionally, the realization of this right has been equated with health care, the system of diagnosis, treatment, and prevention delivered across settings ranging from acute care hospitals to community clinics. However, despite the universal ideal of health as a right, profound inequities persist, revealing a critical disconnect between the promise of medical care and the reality of population health outcomes (Institute of Medicine, 2008).

This disconnect is most evident in the persistence of health disparities, defined as preventable differences in health outcomes experienced by socially disadvantaged populations. These inequities are not random occurrences; instead, they are

M. Ji (✉)
Division of Public Health Sciences, Washington University School of Medicine in St. Louis, St. Louis, MO, USA
e-mail: j.mengmeng@wustl.edu

S. Xu
School of Social Research, Ren Ming University of China, Beijing, China
e-mail: shuoxu27@outlook.com

F. Yang
School of Social Work, University of Illinois Urbana-Champaign, Urbana, IL, USA
e-mail: fany16@illinois.edu

S. S. Bachman
School of Social Policy & Practice, University of Pennsylvania, Philadelphia, PA, USA
e-mail: deansoffice@sp2.upenn.edu

R. An, M. A. Lindsey (eds.), *Artificial Intelligence in Social Work*,
https://doi.org/10.1007/978-3-032-18443-6_5

systematically driven by social, economic, and environmental determinants, such as poverty, structural racism, and unequal access to resources (National Academies of Sciences, Engineering, and Medicine (NASEM), 2017). The consequences are stark: globally, billions lack access to essential health services, and even within wealthy nations like the United States, life expectancy varies dramatically between high- and low-income groups. For instance, a 40-year-old American man in the poorest 1% of the income distribution dies an average of 14.6 years sooner than a man in the wealthiest 1% (Chetty et al., 2016).

To address these disparities, we must look beyond clinical healthcare. While the United States spends far more per capita on medical services than other nations, it spends significantly less on social services, a disproportionate investment that correlates with lagging health indicators compared to peer countries. This suggests that "health" must be defined more broadly than the absence of disease or the presence of medical intervention. It requires a shift in focus toward the social determinants of health (SDOH).

SDOH are the broad socio-economic and environmental factors in which people "are born, grow, work, live, and age" that affect a wide range of health outcomes (CDC, 2024). These include conditions such as income level, housing stability, neighborhood safety, education, employment opportunities, access to nutritious food, transportation, social support, and discrimination. Research indicates that medical care accounts for only a minority of modifiable health outcomes, whereas SDOH influence 80% or more of these outcomes (Magnan, 2017). In other words, SDOH are responsible for most health disparities.

1.2 Social Work and SDOH

Social workers have long been integral to the healthcare system, addressing not only the psychosocial dimensions of health but also the broader social, economic, and structural factors that shape health outcomes, alongside medical care. They work across the continuum of care, including prevention and public health, primary care, acute and specialty care, rehabilitation, home health, long-term care, and hospice. Building on this traditional focus on psychosocial dimensions, contemporary social work practice emphasizes the broader biopsychosocial and spiritual needs of patients. In each setting, social workers attend to biopsychosocial-spiritual needs using a person-in-environment framework, complementing medical professionals' work by focusing on patients' social contexts and supports.

A defining feature of healthcare social work is its commitment to health equity (NASW, 2016). Social workers recognize that reducing these health disparities requires addressing both individual biopsychosocial needs and the systemic issues that drive poor outcomes. In other words, healthcare social work operates at both the micro level (e.g., supporting patients and families through illness, treatment, and recovery) and the macro level (e.g., advocating for policies and programs to eliminate inequities in health care). Social workers bring a holistic, justice-oriented perspective that complements the medical model. This makes them crucial leaders in integrating social care into health care delivery.

Addressing SDOH is imperative for improving population health and reducing disparities. Healthcare organizations are increasingly screening patients for social needs and partnering with community services. Social workers often lead these efforts. For instance, a social worker may implement a brief SDOH screening tool in a primary care clinic to identify patients who are struggling with food insecurity or housing instability. Upon finding a need, the social worker can intervene by connecting the patient to a food pantry, a medical-legal partnership to prevent eviction, or a transportation assistance program. In hospital settings, social workers ensure safe discharge plans by arranging home health services or rehabilitation, recognizing that without stable home supports, a patient's recovery may be compromised. In macro roles, social work administrators advocate for policies, such as expanded Medicaid or paid sick leave laws, that address social determinants at a systemic level. The 2019 National Academies of Sciences, Engineering, and Medicine (NASEM) report, *Integrating Social Care into the Delivery of Health Care*, affirmed that factors like stable housing, economic security, food security, and transportation play a key role in health outcomes (NASEM, 2019). The NASEM consensus study recognized social workers as specialists in identifying and addressing social needs in healthcare settings.

1.3 Current Applications of AI in Health-Focused Social Work Practice

We conducted a scoping review of recent articles from mainstream social work journals to identify studies linking artificial intelligence (AI) with health-related practice. Most of the identified work aligns with three major thematic areas. In the following section, we summarize the papers within each theme and synthesize the insights emerging from this literature.

1.3.1 Mental Health Assessment and Risk Detection

A substantial number of AI-and-social-work studies focus on using AI for mental health screening, diagnosis, or risk prediction. Local LLM architectures can analyze confidential mental health narratives with high fidelity while preserving privacy safeguards (Perron et al., 2025). Studies on youth populations further show that digital traces, such as Reddit or Twitter posts, contain identifiable linguistic patterns of depression, anxiety, and discrimination (Choi et al., 2025; Sinha et al., 2025). Behavioral health research confirms that machine-learning models can detect suicidal ideation and early deterioration signals more rapidly than routine screening methods (Ballı et al., 2025; Ji et al., 2021). Some studies also indicate mixed readiness to integrate these systems, often expressing concerns about explainability and the clinical consequences of potential AI errors (Creswell Báez et al., 2025). These findings underscore AI's growing capacity to enhance mental health risk identification while also highlighting the ethical imperatives, especially around fairness and contextual interpretation, that must accompany such applications.

1.3.2 Child Welfare, Parenting Support, and Family Health

Child and family services are among the most active areas of AI experimentation in the social work field. Large language models have demonstrated the ability to classify complex child-protective case reports with accuracy comparable to trained humans, enabling scalable synthesis of abuse narratives (Stoll et al., 2025). Efforts to evaluate the reliability of AI judgment in interpreting children's statements further illustrate both the promise and sensitivity of these tools (Karataş, 2025). Machine-learning studies examining resilience and caregiving environments offer new insights into family-system factors in childcare and occupational health (Duan et al., 2025). AI-enabled parenting support platforms have the potential to enhance parental skills and support early intervention through tailored guidance (Escoredo et al., 2025). These developments resonate with broader child-welfare scholarship documenting how predictive models can help with the early detection of maltreatment risks while simultaneously raising concerns about bias, surveillance, and equity. Overall, these studies demonstrate both the promise and tensions of AI in child and family systems, positioning technology as a potential enhancer of safety and support, so long as its implementation remains grounded in social work values and ethical safeguards.

1.3.3 Communication, Social Media, and Online Behavior Monitoring

AI-driven analysis of communication and digital behavior has become an important methodological direction for understanding youth well-being, risk behavior, and social environments. NLP models can identify emotional expressions, discrimination experiences, and mental health signals in youth digital communication (Choi et al., 2025; Zhang et al., 2025). AI-supported interpretations of sexting, sextortion, and broader online sexual-risk patterns provide additional avenues for digital-safety intervention (Pater et al., 2025). Parental engagement and youth-safety applications also leverage online communication streams to detect risk and provide structured support (Escoredo et al., 2025). These developments mirror broader research showing that AI can detect cyberbullying, self-harm indicators, and social isolation patterns in adolescents' digital footprints (Milosevic et al., 2022). At the same time, the literature emphasizes the ethical challenges of monitoring minors' online behavior, including privacy expectations, consent boundaries, and potential disparate impacts on marginalized youth.

1.4 *Current Applications of AI in Healthcare*

AI is transforming nearly all sectors of health and medicine, including but not limited to higher-quality disease diagnosis, personalized treatment, drug discovery, public health forecasts, mental health support, remote patient monitoring, patient self-care, and healthcare administrative processes (Alowais et al., 2023; Bajwa et al., 2021). In this section, we briefly highlight several major areas where AI has had the most significant impact.

1.4.1 Diagnosis

One of the most mature applications of AI in healthcare is disease diagnosis. AI has the potential to accelerate and improve disease diagnosis by assisting clinicians in interpreting diverse patient data, including imaging, lab results, and clinical notes (Niazi et al., 2019). A well-known example is a deep neural network trained on over 129,000 skin lesion images, which achieved a classification accuracy equivalent to that of board-certified dermatologists in discriminating malignant melanomas from benign lesions (Esteva et al., 2017). AI systems are also being implemented to assist in detecting abnormalities such as lung nodules on chest X-rays, tumors on CT/MRI, and breast cancer on mammograms (Khalifa & Albadawy, 2024; McKinney et al., 2020). There is also growing use of AI in laboratory testing and clinical microbiology. ML models trained on genomic and metagenomic data can detect pathogens, predict antibiotic susceptibility, and improve workflow efficiency, thereby increasing the speed and accuracy of infectious disease diagnosis (Peiffer-Smadja et al., 2020; Vandenberg et al., 2020).

1.4.2 Treatment Planning

Clinicians often need to consider a range of relevant variables when developing a treatment plan, including the patient's medical history, disease stage, comorbidities, and preferences. AI tools could serve as decision-support tools by employing algorithms to process and evaluate relevant variables and recommend evidence-based strategies (Alowais et al., 2023). In the example of sepsis management, it was reported that the treatment selected by the AI model is, on average, reliably higher than that of human clinicians, and patients had the lowest mortality when both the human physician and the AI clinician recommended the strategy (Komorowski et al., 2018). AI has significantly improved treatment planning for cancer radiotherapy, a traditionally complex, time-intensive process that aims to deliver sufficient radiation to the tumor while preserving healthy tissue (Wang et al., 2019).

1.4.3 Drug Discovery

AI is widely regarded as a powerful accelerator and enhancer of drug discovery and development. One well-known example is the deep learning–based identification of a new antibiotic compound, later named Halicin (Trafton, 2020). Another landmark advance is AlphaFold, an AI system developed by DeepMind that accurately predicts protein folding; in 2021, it released predicted structures for almost all human proteins (Jumper et al., 2021). AlphaFold now serves as an increasingly valuable structural biology resource, helping drive drug development. AI can also contribute through drug repurposing—the process of identifying new indications for existing drugs (Pushpakom et al., 2019). Instead of focusing solely on novel compounds, AI can uncover new therapeutic uses by recognizing patterns in large, complex datasets (Cortial et al., 2024; Yan et al., 2024).

1.4.4 Precision Medicine

Precision medicine, sometimes known as "personalized medicine", is an innovative approach to tailoring disease prevention and treatment that considers differences in people's genes, environments, and lifestyles (Ashley, 2016). The intersection of AI and precision medicine presents "remarkable opportunities" to identify disease at early stages or give patients the right therapy they would most likely benefit from (Matheny et al., 2019). AI approaches are applied to genomic, clinical, electronic health records, medical imaging, and other "omics" (e.g., proteomics, metabolomics) datasets to identify phenotypes or predictors that guide more individualized therapeutic pathways (Johnson et al., 2021). For example, AI systems can analyze tumor genomic sequences to identify genetic mutations or expression patterns to guide targeted therapies (El-Deiry et al., 2019; Huang et al., 2018).

1.4.5 Predictive Analytics and Population Health

In healthcare, predictive analytics are used to forecast infectious disease outbreaks, identify patients at high risk for certain conditions, and inform preventive care and policy interventions. Predictive models driven by AI could evaluate patient demographics, clinical history, comorbidities, and social determinants of health to identify higher-risk individuals for chronic disease management and/or specific complications and hospitalizations (Dixon et al., 2024). For instance, AI systems have demonstrated remarkable efficacy in predicting the occurrence of specific cancers and cardiovascular diseases (Singh et al., 2024), as well as hospitalization and hospital readmission risk (Riis et al., 2023; Silva et al., 2024). AI is also employed to estimate population health trends and outbreaks by integrating different data sources such as weather, travel patterns, health surveillance data, and social media to quickly identify emerging infectious disease threats and alert public health officials (Ding et al., 2025).

1.5 *Harnessing AI to Address SDOH*

AI has emerged as a powerful tool for identifying and addressing SDOH, with the potential to reduce global health disparities. AI could help identify and monitor SDOH. Machine learning and predictive analytics integrate data from electronic health records, public health surveillance, and socioeconomic and environmental datasets to uncover hidden patterns linked to SDOH (Basu et al., 2020). For example, AI models have linked food insecurity and substandard housing to higher chronic disease rates, and flagged pollution-heavy areas with elevated asthma risk. AI is also being used in public health surveillance to forecast disease outbreaks and map social vulnerabilities. Natural language processing and advanced language models can mine unstructured text for SDOH, vastly extending the reach of social needs identification beyond structured records (Guevara et al., 2024).

AI could also help with intervention design and policymaking. AI-generated insights enable health systems and governments to implement targeted interventions on upstream factors. Predictive risk scores incorporating SDOH help clinicians proactively identify vulnerable patients and connect them with resources like housing or food assistance. At the community level, AI can pinpoint which neighborhoods would benefit most from new services, guiding more equitable allocation of resources. Nonetheless, using AI for SDOH demands careful ethical oversight. Ensuring diverse, representative data and mitigating algorithmic bias are essential so that these tools help mitigate, rather than exacerbate, disparities.

2 AI for Social Work Across Healthcare Settings

The Social Work Health Impact Model illustrates how social workers can act across multiple domains of intervention: clinical practice, prevention and health promotion, systems alignment, and broader policy advocacy (Cederbaum et al., 2018). Against this backdrop, AI technologies could play a transformative role across these domains. Whether through predictive analytics in healthcare settings, natural language processing for case documentation, or AI-enabled tools that support advocacy with big data evidence, AI is becoming intertwined with the mission of healthcare social work. This section discusses social work practice in various healthcare settings, highlighting the unique contributions of social workers and the implications of AI in each setting.

2.1 Prevention and Public Health

In prevention and public health, social workers focus on community-level and population-level interventions to improve health outcomes and reduce risks before illness occurs. This can include roles in public health departments, community health centers, schools, and nonprofit agencies that address issues such as vaccination, obesity, HIV prevention, substance abuse, and more. Social workers bring to these efforts an understanding of community dynamics, engagement strategies, and policy advocacy, making them natural leaders for prevention initiatives that require both social and medical strategies.

AI is revolutionizing this work by enabling "Precision Public Health", i.e., the use of data to target interventions more effectively to those most in need (Cordeiro, 2024). Rather than treating health solely as a medical issue, AI tools allow social workers to analyze complex interactions between social environments and health outcomes. AI can help identify communities or subpopulations with elevated health risks. Machine learning models combining data on SDOH indicators can predict which neighborhoods might experience spikes in issues like asthma exacerbations or opioid overdoses. A public health social worker could use this information to allocate resources proactively, such as organizing an asthma awareness and home-cleanup drive in an area with high asthma-related emergency department visits. Social workers leveraging AI-driven platforms can enhance outreach and education. AI systems can scan data, including unconventional sources such as Google search trends and social media mentions, for early signs of public health issues. A well-known example is using Google search query patterns to detect flu outbreaks faster than traditional reporting (Yang et al., 2015).

Prevention is an area where global collaboration often occurs. Tools like AI-driven GIS mapping help identify communities globally that lack access to clean water or basic healthcare, guiding interventions. Social workers' intersectional lens ensures that prevention programs consider factors like gender, race, and socioeconomic status, which AI data can incorporate if well-designed. For example, in a vaccination campaign, AI might optimize the locations of vaccine sites (Musa et al., 2025). Still, a social worker will ensure those sites are accessible and welcoming to minority communities that historically faced discrimination in healthcare.

Crucially, social workers bring an intersectional lens to these technologies. While AI might optimize logistical resource distribution, such as mapping the most efficient locations for vaccine sites, social workers ensure these locations are culturally accessible and trusted by marginalized communities. By integrating AI's analytical power with social work's community engagement strategies, the profession can advance a holistic vision of health that addresses the root causes of disparity.

2.2 *Primary Care, Acute Care, and Specialty Care*

Primary, acute, and specialty care social work is dynamic and directly patient-facing. Across all settings, social workers address both clinical and SDOH to improve patient outcomes and care continuity. The social worker's challenge and opportunity are to use these tools to enhance patient care, such as faster identification of needs and more personalized interventions, while also humanizing the care, making sure technology does not eclipse empathy and individualized support.

Many hospitals have adopted AI predictive models, such as risk scores for readmission, falls, and complications (González-Castro et al., 2024). These models often trigger automatic consults or alerts to social work. For instance, a readmission risk model might flag a patient with heart failure who lives alone and has multiple comorbidities as high risk. This means social workers can focus on patients who most need attention rather than purely on those who happen to ask or be referred late.

Primary and specialty care have embraced telehealth, especially post-2020. AI often underpins telehealth platforms, such as routing patients to providers, summarizing patient input for providers, and translating language (Chaturvedi et al., 2025). Social workers providing tele-behavioral health might use AI tools for scheduling, even for elements of therapy, such as tracking progress. These augmentations can improve continuity but also risk turning social workers into data monitors, so balance is needed.

2.3 *Rehabilitation*

Social workers in rehab facilities perform many familiar functions, but in the context of patients dealing with significant life changes. They provide psychosocial support to patients adjusting to new physical limitations or chronic disability, addressing grief, identity issues, family strain, and motivation for the hard work of rehab. They educate patients and families about coping strategies and available long-term resources (e.g., vocational rehab, disability benefits, and home modifications). Discharge planning is a major task, as patients often cannot return to their previous living situation without modifications or help. Social workers coordinate with insurance and community agencies to arrange durable medical equipment, home care, and follow-up services. They might run peer support groups, for example, connecting new spinal cord injury patients with others who have lived with such injuries. They are also key in family education, preparing family caregivers for the patient's needs and linking them to support like respite care or caregiver training programs.

In rehabilitation, perhaps more than anywhere else, the interplay between mindset and physical progress is strong. AI can support physical training and planning, but *mindset* is the domain of human support. As one might say, "rehab is 10% physical, 90% mental." Social workers ensure that while PTs and OTs work on the body, someone's caring for the soul. AI won't provide a patient with empathetic listening or the therapeutic alliance that helps them find meaning after a life-altering injury, which remains the sacred work of the social worker. Suppose AI offloads paperwork or finds the best accessible housing option faster. In that case, the social worker has more time to sit with a patient who is mourning the loss of their former abilities and help them envisage a fulfilling life ahead. That is the real "value-add" that technology should enable in rehab social work.

2.4 *Long-Term Care*

In long-term care (LTC) settings, social workers perform psychosocial assessments upon admission and periodically thereafter, develop care plans addressing mood, behavior, and social adjustment, provide or coordinate counseling to cope with aging, loss, and transition, and lead group programs. They are problem-solvers across a range of issues, from roommate conflicts to residents refusing care to family dynamics in decision-making. Social workers also address quality-of-life domains, e.g., helping residents maintain autonomy, engage in meaningful activities, and stay connected to their community or family. They often handle end-of-life planning and advocate for residents' preferences during care plan meetings. Ensuring culturally competent and person-centered care is a core function.

Falls are a big concern in LTC. AI-powered camera systems or wearable sensors that detect falls or analyze gait patterns to predict fall risk are being introduced in some facilities (Subramaniam et al., 2022). For example, there are camera systems that can alert staff if a resident gets out of bed at night. Social workers might not operate these systems directly, but they change their practice environment by potentially reducing falls and raising privacy considerations. Many LTC residents have dementia or cognitive impairments and may exhibit behavioral symptoms. AI can help track patterns of agitation, such as through movement trackers or by analyzing vocalizations via microphones to detect stress indicators, to address triggers preemptively.

Social workers are often liaisons to families. Tech is now bridging families and residents, for example, with secure messaging apps for updates and video call setups for families who can't visit. AI could assist by automatically sending families updates (e.g., "Your mom participated in bingo today and had a good appetite at lunch"), thereby relieving family anxiety. Also, AI sentiment analysis could gauge family satisfaction from messages or survey responses, flagging those needing follow-up (Taherdoost & Madanchian, 2023). A social worker could receive a nudge, such as "the daughter of Resident X expressed concern about care quality in her last message," so they can reach out promptly instead of waiting for a quarterly survey result.

3 AI for Social Work Across Healthcare Practice

Healthcare social workers fulfill a variety of roles and responsibilities that can be grouped into key functional areas: screening and assessment, care planning, service delivery and intervention, advocacy, quality evaluation, and record-keeping. These correspond to core practice standards for social work in health settings (NASW, 2016). In each of these activity domains, AI and related technologies are beginning to play a transformative role. This section explores how AI can be applied in healthcare social work practice.

3.1 *Screening and Assessment*

Screening and assessment are often the first steps in social work practice with clients. In healthcare settings, this involves gathering a psychosocial history, identifying patient needs (practical, emotional, and social), assessing risks (such as risk of abuse, suicide, readmission, etc.), and determining eligibility for various services. Social workers also conduct SDOH screenings, asking questions about factors like housing, food, transportation, and social support (Gehlert & Browne, 2011; NASEM, 2019).

AI is increasingly augmenting these processes. Machine learning algorithms can analyze EHR data and other patient information to predict who is at high risk of certain adverse outcomes. NLP algorithms can digest large volumes of unstructured text, such as clinical notes, social worker case notes, or even social media posts, to surface insights for assessment. In healthcare, AI could be used in collaborative documentation in behavioral health to evaluate the quality of person-centered care. For example, in child welfare, predictive analytic tools ingest case narratives and structured data to estimate the likelihood of child maltreatment recurrence, aiding social workers in screening high-risk cases. While these tools are still emerging, they point to a future where AI can comb through data that would be impossible for an individual to read, giving social workers a "heads up" about potential issues.

Some health systems have begun deploying chatbot-style questionnaires accessible on tablets or phones that ask patients about social needs in a friendly, conversational manner. These AI-driven screening tools can increase the rate of disclosure of sensitive needs by providing a private, stigma-free interface. For instance, a patient may feel more comfortable typing into a tablet that they have trouble affording food than telling a clinician face-to-face, especially if the chatbot normalizes these questions for all patients. The social worker then receives an alert or report on any needs identified. This doesn't replace the social worker's comprehensive assessment, but it makes the process more efficient by front-loading information gathering.

3.2 Care Planning

Care planning in social work involves crafting a tailored plan with the client to address identified needs and goals. In healthcare settings, a social work care plan might include linkages to community services, therapeutic interventions, education, and coordination with the medical team's treatment plan. It is often a collaborative process: social workers partner with clients to set goals, and with other professionals to align services.

AI can assist care planning in several ways, mainly by providing decision support and information management. A common challenge for social workers is keeping track of the ever-changing landscape of community resources. AI-enabled resource directory platforms now exist that can suggest optimal referrals based on a client's specific profile. For instance, if a client is a low-income older adult living alone with diabetes, the system might automatically suggest a nearby Meals on Wheels program, a transportation service for medical appointments, and a diabetes self-management class. Some platforms incorporate AI search algorithms that learn from past referrals and outcomes, which resources tend to be most effective. Rather than thumbing through binders or static databases, the social worker can enter key parameters to receive a curated list of resources. This is especially helpful when working with issues like housing, where multiple programs have different criteria; the AI can quickly filter them. It effectively functions as a specialized "recommender system" for social care services.

Beyond concrete services, AI can parse research and aggregate client data to recommend intervention strategies. For example, consider a hospital social worker planning discharge for a patient with congestive heart failure and limited family support. An AI tool might analyze similar past cases of patients with heart failure living alone, with certain risk factors, and suggest a set of interventions that led to better outcomes, such as enrolling the patient in a remote monitoring program, scheduling a home health nurse visit within 48 h of discharge, and ensuring a social work follow-up call within a week. It might even prioritize which factor (e.g., transportation, medication management) to address first using predictive modeling. Another scenario is in mental health care planning: an AI might identify that a client with moderate depression and social isolation could benefit most from a combination of a peer support group and a digital CBT app, in addition to therapy. This combination could reduce depressive symptoms significantly. These kinds of insights can guide social workers in crafting more effective, evidence-informed plans faster than manually sifting through the literature or relying on anecdotal memory.

It's important to stress that the human element remains central in care planning. AI can provide options or even optimal pathways based on generalized data. However, the social worker and client must decide together what truly fits the client's preferences, culture, and unique situation (NASW, 2017). When thoughtfully integrated, AI can significantly enhance care planning. It can reduce the clerical load and provide data-driven insights, allowing social workers to spend more time in conversation with clients. The social worker remains the driver steering the course in partnership with the client.

3.3 Service Delivery and Systems Integration

Social workers do not only assess and plan; they also deliver interventions and coordinate action. In healthcare, this can range from brief counseling and psychoeducation with a patient, to arranging concrete services, to leading care coordination meetings, to macro-level interventions like community health initiatives. The NASEM (2019) report provides a framework for action that classifies health and social care integration activities into five categories: Awareness, Adjustment, Assistance, Alignment, and Advocacy. Here, we discuss how AI tools could be applied across the five categories.

Awareness refers to activities to identify social risks and needs. AI tools can increase awareness by systematically identifying needs. Whether it's through patient-level SDOH screening chatbots or analysis of community-level data, AI expands the scope and speed of identifying where intervention is needed. For example, an AI might analyze demographic, socioeconomic, and claims data to produce a "heat map" of a city showing neighborhoods with the highest preventable hospitalization rates and correlated social issues. A health system's social work department could use this to guide community health workers to those areas.

Adjustment refers to making changes in clinical care to accommodate patients' social barriers. AI can help inform care design adjustments. For instance, using machine learning to analyze appointment data, a clinic might discover, via an algorithm, that a significant number of patients from a certain low-income ZIP code miss morning appointments. In response, the clinic extends hours into evenings or offers telehealth for that community. AI could also assist on the fly: a scheduling system might automatically suggest a telehealth option to a patient who lives far from the clinic. Additionally, AI-driven translation tools can help adjust communication for patients with limited English proficiency, enabling more linguistically appropriate service delivery.

Assistance refers to connecting patients directly with social resources and support, often through referrals or navigation. When providing direct aid, such as connecting a client to resources, AI can streamline referral and navigation tasks. Voice-activated assistants might walk patients through application forms for social programs. Social services agencies could use robotic process automation to quickly determine eligibility for benefits, reducing wait times. Some hospitals have experimented with AI-based texting services that "assist" patients post-discharge, for example, by checking whether they have obtained their medications or need help, and then alerting a social worker if an issue arises. These intelligent follow-ups increase the reach of assistance beyond the clinic visit. Importantly, because social needs often require quick action, AI's ability to operate 24/7 is a boon for timely aid, e.g., a chatbot that provides emergency shelter addresses after hours.

Alignment refers to aligning healthcare with community resources by partnering with organizations, investing in community capacity, or otherwise strengthening the resource landscape. Social workers in leadership may use AI analytics to align programs with community needs. For instance, if an AI analysis finds that many diabetes patients are food-insecure and there's no healthy food program in the area, a social work administrator might establish a partnership with a food nonprofit (alignment) or start a hospital-based produce prescription program. Alignment often involves forming intersectoral partnerships. Here, AI's contribution might even be in matchmaking: platforms can identify potential community partners by mining data on local organizations to recommend where a health system should invest or collaborate to strengthen the social care infrastructure. The caveat is that smaller community organizations might not have robust data for AI to analyze, so personal relationship-building remains key.

Advocacy involves promoting policies and broader system changes to address SDOH and improve community health equity. AI empowers social workers' advocacy by providing robust evidence and narratives. Big data can illustrate problems that were previously hidden. For example, analyzing millions of health records might reveal that a particular policy led thousands of vulnerable patients to skip care. Visualizing this data makes a compelling case to policymakers. Without oversight, algorithms can increase racial bias in care, but with proper use, data can also uncover bias and spur reform. The aforementioned case of the racially biased health algorithm is a prime example. Once exposed, it not only prompted the company to fix the tool but also fueled broader advocacy around algorithmic fairness in healthcare. Social workers have joined coalitions calling for algorithmic accountability in public services to protect clients from unjust outcomes. Internally, social work leaders advocate within health systems for ethical guardrails on AI, emphasizing core values like equity, transparency, and client privacy. NASW itself has called for an AI Commission to ensure social work has a voice in shaping AI's impact on our field and those we serve. On a community level, AI data can support classic social work advocacy for resources: e.g., open data on housing and neighborhood conditions, when analyzed, can "empower communities to fight disinvestment and predatory lending" by pinpointing patterns of neglect and harm.

3.4 *Quality Improvement and Learning Health Systems*

Continuous practice evaluation and quality improvement are essential in healthcare social work. Social workers strive to evaluate the outcomes of their interventions, measure program performance, and use data to improve services. In the era of big data and AI, social workers have powerful new means to conduct these evaluations and contribute to a learning health system. AI enhances the learning loop in healthcare social work. It enables more rigorous, rapid analysis of the effectiveness of interventions, supports a data-driven culture of improvement, and helps quantify the value that social work adds to healthcare outcomes. As healthcare moves toward value-based care, demonstrating and improving quality is crucial. Social workers, armed with AI insights, can both improve services and solidify their role as key players in achieving the "Triple Aim" of better care, improved population health, and lower costs (NASW, 2017). In practice, that could mean showing that adding a social needs screening and intervention program not only improves patient satisfaction but also reduces costly hospital utilization for vulnerable groups, making a strong case for sustainability.

On a larger scale, social workers contribute to practice-based research. AI is accelerating social work research by enabling the analysis of "big data" from health systems, government databases, and even social media relevant to community health. For example, researchers have merged large administrative datasets (child welfare, social services, and public health) to study how policy changes affect outcomes. Social work scholars are using AI to examine how large social datasets correlate with health measures, potentially identifying novel community-level indicators. The generation of new knowledge through such interdisciplinary research feeds back into practice improvement. The findings from AI analyses can highlight best practices and model programs that can be replicated.

4 Ethical Challenges and Role of Social Workers

While AI holds great potential to augment social work practice in health care, integrating AI introduces significant ethical hurdles, particularly regarding algorithmic bias, which can perpetuate the very health disparities that social workers strive to eliminate (Ferrara, 2024; Hanna et al., 2025). AI systems learn from historical data, and thus they risk absorbing and amplifying societal biases, potentially leading to discriminatory outcomes in which care is unequally allocated based on race or socioeconomic status. Social workers are uniquely positioned to advocate for equity by demanding that AI development include diverse, representative data and undergo rigorous bias testing.

Recognizing this, critical thinking has emerged as an essential social work competency in the age of AI. Practitioners must actively interrogate algorithmic outputs, questioning what might be missing or misrepresented rather than accepting recommendations at face value. Experts caution that overreliance on AI can erode professional judgment and empathy, making it vital for social workers to maintain human oversight and advanced critical thinking when using these tools. Indeed, social workers will require extremely high levels of critical thinking to evaluate and critique AI systems effectively and to spot biases, epistemic gaps, or cultural misinterpretations in algorithmic information. To this end, the profession must invest in structured AI-related training and digital literacy education. Social workers should be trained to recognize AI's limitations and to challenge algorithmic outputs when necessary, and recent scholarship calls for integrating AI literacy, i.e., knowledge and skills to understand, use, and critically evaluate AI, into core social work training competencies. Such preparation will enable practitioners to engage with AI tools in an equitable, person-centered manner while mitigating potential harms.

Competing Interests The authors have no conflicts of interest to declare that are relevant to the content of this chapter.

References

Alowais, S. A., Alghamdi, S. S., Alsuhebany, N., Alqahtani, T., Alshaya, A. I., Almohareb, S. N., Aldairem, A., Alrashed, M., Bin Saleh, K., Badreldin, H. A., Al Yami, M. S., Al Harbi, S., & Albekairy, A. M. (2023). Revolutionizing healthcare: The role of artificial intelligence in clinical practice. *BMC Medical Education, 23*(1), 689. https://doi.org/10.1186/s12909-023-04698-z

Ashley, E. A. (2016). Towards precision medicine. *Nature Reviews Genetics, 17*(9), 507–522. https://doi.org/10.1038/nrg.2016.86

Bajwa, J., Munir, U., Nori, A., & Williams, B. (2021). Artificial intelligence in healthcare: Transforming the practice of medicine. *Future Healthc J, 8*(2), e188–e194. https://doi.org/10.7861/fhj.2021-0095

Ballı, M., Dogan, A. E., Senol, S. H., & Eser, H. Y. (2025). Machine learning based identification of suicidal ideation using non-suicidal predictors in a university mental health clinic. *Scientific Reports, 15*(1), 13843. https://doi.org/10.1038/s41598-025-97387-4

Basu, S., Faghmous, J. H., & Doupe, P. (2020). Machine learning methods for precision medicine research designed to reduce health disparities: A structured tutorial. *Ethnicity & Disease, 30*(Suppl 1), 217–228. https://pmc.ncbi.nlm.nih.gov/articles/PMC7138444

CDC. (2024). *Social determinants of health.* https://www.cdc.gov/about/priorities/why-is-addressing-sdoh-important.html

Cederbaum, J. A., Ross, A. M., Ruth, B. J., & Keefe, R. H. (2018). Public health social work as a unifying framework for social work's grand challenges. *Social Work, 64*(1), 9–18. https://doi.org/10.1093/sw/swy045

Chaturvedi, U., Chauhan, S. B., & Singh, I. (2025). The impact of artificial intelligence on remote healthcare: Enhancing patient engagement, connectivity, and overcoming challenges. *Intelligent Pharmacy, 3*(5), 323–329. https://doi.org/10.1016/j.ipha.2024.12.003

Chetty, R., Stepner, M., Abraham, S., Lin, S., Scuderi, B., Turner, N., Bergeron, A., & Cutler, D. (2016). The association between income and life expectancy in the United States, 2001–2014. *JAMA, 315*(16), 1750–1766. https://doi.org/10.1001/jama.2016.4226

Choi, S., Park, H., Ausbrooks, A., Huntt, M. B., Mendenhall, R., Harwood, S. A., & Gough, H. (2025). A machine learning approach to Asian & Asian-American young adults' racial microaggressions and depressive symptoms. *Studies in Clinical Social Work: Transforming Practice, Education and Research, 95*(2), 122–149. https://doi.org/10.1080/28376811.2024.2424412

Cordeiro, J. V. (2024). Artificial intelligence and precision public health: A balancing act of scientific accuracy, social responsibility, and community engagement. *Portuguese Journal of Public Health, 42*(1), 1–5. https://doi.org/10.1159/000538141

Cortial, L., Montero, V., Tourlet, S., Del Bano, J., & Blin, O. (2024). Artificial intelligence in drug repurposing for rare diseases: A mini-review. *Frontiers in Medicine (Lausanne), 11*, 1404338. https://doi.org/10.3389/fmed.2024.1404338

Creswell Báez, J., Victor, B. G., Dysart, C., & Goldkind, L. (2025). "I Don't understand it, but okay": An empirical study of mental health practitioners' readiness to use large language models. *Journal of Technology in Human Services, 43*(2), 142–160. https://doi.org/10.1080/15228835.2025.2479475

da Silva, N. C., Albertini, M. K., Backes, A. R., & Pena, G. d. G. (2024). Machine learning for hospital readmission prediction in pediatric population. *Computer Methods and Programs in Biomedicine, 244*, 107980. https://doi.org/10.1016/j.cmpb.2023.107980

Ding, X., Shang, B., Xie, C., Xin, J., & Yu, F. (2025). Artificial intelligence in the COVID-19 pandemic: Balancing benefits and ethical challenges in China's response. *Humanities and Social Sciences Communications, 12*(1), 245. https://doi.org/10.1057/s41599-025-04564-x

Dixon, D., Sattar, H., Moros, N., Kesireddy, S. R., Ahsan, H., Lakkimsetti, M., Fatima, M., Doshi, D., Sadhu, K., & Junaid Hassan, M. (2024). Unveiling the influence of AI predictive analytics on patient outcomes: A comprehensive narrative review. *Cureus, 16*(5), e59954. https://doi.org/10.7759/cureus.59954

Duan, H., Tian, B., Levine, D. T., & Kaul, H. (2025). Investigating resilience in the childcare context through the agent-based paradigm. *Child Abuse & Neglect, 163*, 107402. https://doi.org/10.1016/j.chiabu.2025.107402
El-Deiry, W. S., Goldberg, R. M., Lenz, H. J., Shields, A. F., Gibney, G. T., Tan, A. R., Brown, J., Eisenberg, B., Heath, E. I., Phuphanich, S., Kim, E., Brenner, A. J., & Marshall, J. L. (2019). The current state of molecular testing in the treatment of patients with solid tumors, 2019. *CA: A Cancer Journal for Clinicians, 69*(4), 305–343. https://doi.org/10.3322/caac.21560
Escoredo, M. C., Mostovoy, K., Schickler, R., Bechtel, A., Shagan, J., & Bunge, E. L. (2025). Enhancing parental skills through artificial intelligence-based conversational agents: The PAT initiative. *Family Relations, 74*(3), 1250–1265. https://doi.org/10.1111/fare.13158
Esteva, A., Kuprel, B., Novoa, R. A., Ko, J., Swetter, S. M., Blau, H. M., & Thrun, S. (2017). Dermatologist-level classification of skin cancer with deep neural networks. *Nature, 542*(7639), 115–118. https://doi.org/10.1038/nature21056
Ferrara, E. (2024). Fairness and bias in artificial intelligence: A brief survey of sources, impacts, and mitigation strategies. *The Sciences, 6*(1), 3. https://www.mdpi.com/2413-4155/6/1/3
Gehlert, S., & Browne, T. (2011). *Handbook of health social work*. John Wiley & Sons.
González-Castro, A., Leirós-Rodríguez, R., Prada-García, C., & Benítez-Andrades, J. A. (2024). The applications of artificial intelligence for assessing fall risk: Systematic review. *Journal of Medical Internet Research, 26*, e54934. https://doi.org/10.2196/54934
Guevara, M., Chen, S., Thomas, S., Chaunzwa, T. L., Franco, I., Kann, B. H., Moningi, S., Qian, J. M., Goldstein, M., Harper, S., Aerts, H. J. W. L., Catalano, P. J., Savova, G. K., Mak, R. H., & Bitterman, D. S. (2024). Large language models to identify social determinants of health in electronic health records. *npj Digital Medicine, 7*(1), 6. https://doi.org/10.1038/s41746-023-00970-0
Hanna, M. G., Pantanowitz, L., Jackson, B., Palmer, O., Visweswaran, S., Pantanowitz, J., Deebajah, M., & Rashidi, H. H. (2025). Ethical and bias considerations in artificial intelligence/machine learning. *Modern Pathology, 38*(3), 100686. https://doi.org/10.1016/j.modpat.2024.100686
Huang, C., Clayton, E. A., Matyunina, L. V., McDonald, L. D., Benigno, B. B., Vannberg, F., & McDonald, J. F. (2018). Machine learning predicts individual cancer patient responses to therapeutic drugs with high accuracy. *Scientific Reports, 8*(1), 16444. https://doi.org/10.1038/s41598-018-34753-5
Institute of Medicine. (2008). *Evidence-based medicine and the changing nature of health care: 2007 IOM annual meeting summary*. The National Academies Press. https://doi.org/10.17226/12041
Ji, S., Pan, S., Li, X., Cambria, E., Long, G., & Huang, Z. (2021). Suicidal ideation detection: A review of machine learning methods and applications. *IEEE Transactions on Computational Social Systems, 8*(1), 214–226. https://doi.org/10.1109/TCSS.2020.3021467
Johnson, K. B., Wei, W. Q., Weeraratne, D., Frisse, M. E., Misulis, K., Rhee, K., Zhao, J., & Snowdon, J. L. (2021). Precision medicine, AI, and the future of personalized health care. *Clinical and Translational Science, 14*(1), 86–93. https://doi.org/10.1111/cts.12884
Jumper, J., Evans, R., Pritzel, A., Green, T., Figurnov, M., Ronneberger, O., Tunyasuvunakool, K., Bates, R., Žídek, A., Potapenko, A., Bridgland, A., Meyer, C., Kohl, S. A. A., Ballard, A. J., Cowie, A., Romera-Paredes, B., Nikolov, S., Jain, R., Adler, J., et al. (2021). Highly accurate protein structure prediction with AlphaFold. *Nature, 596*(7873), 583–589. https://doi.org/10.1038/s41586-021-03819-2
Karataş, Z. (2025). Can a large language model judge a child's statement?: A comparative analysis of ChatGPT and human experts in credibility assessment. *Journal of Evidence-Based Social Work (2019), 23*(1), 1–16. https://doi.org/10.1080/26408066.2025.2547211
Khalifa, M., & Albadawy, M. (2024). AI in diagnostic imaging: Revolutionising accuracy and efficiency. *Computer Methods and Programs in Biomedicine Update, 5*, 100146. https://doi.org/10.1016/j.cmpbup.2024.100146

Komorowski, M., Celi, L. A., Badawi, O., Gordon, A. C., & Faisal, A. A. (2018). The artificial intelligence clinician learns optimal treatment strategies for sepsis in intensive care. *Nature Medicine, 24*(11), 1716–1720. https://doi.org/10.1038/s41591-018-0213-5

Magnan, S. (2017). *Social determinants of health 101 for health care: Five plus five*. NAM Perspectives. https://nam.edu/social-determinants-of-health-101-for-health-care-five-plus-five

Matheny, M., Israni, S. T., Ahmed, M., & Whicher, D. (2019). *Artificial intelligence in health care: The hope, the hype, the promise, the peril* (p. 10). National Academy of Medicine.

McKinney, S. M., Sieniek, M., Godbole, V., Godwin, J., Antropova, N., Ashrafian, H., Back, T., Chesus, M., Corrado, G. S., Darzi, A., Etemadi, M., Garcia-Vicente, F., Gilbert, F. J., Halling-Brown, M., Hassabis, D., Jansen, S., Karthikesalingam, A., Kelly, C. J., King, D., et al. (2020). International evaluation of an AI system for breast cancer screening. *Nature, 577*(7788), 89–94. https://doi.org/10.1038/s41586-019-1799-6

Milosevic, T., Van Royen, K., & Davis, B. (2022). Artificial intelligence to address cyberbullying, harassment and abuse: New directions in the midst of complexity. *International Journal of Bullying Prevention, 4*(1), 1–5. https://doi.org/10.1007/s42380-022-00117-x

Musa, S. M., Haruna, U. A., Aliyu, L. J., Zubairu, M., & Lucero-Prisno, D. E., 3rd. (2025). Leveraging AI to optimize vaccines supply chain and logistics in Africa: Opportunities and challenges. *Frontiers in Pharmacology, 16*, 1531141. https://doi.org/10.3389/fphar.2025.1531141

NASW. (2016). *NASW standards for social work practice in health care settings*. https://www.socialworkers.org/Practice/NASW-Practice-Standards-Guidelines/NASW-Standards-for-Social-Work-Practice-in-Health-Care-Settings

NASW. (2017). *NASW, ASWB, CSWE, & CSWA standards for technology in social work practice*. National Association of Social Workers. https://www.socialworkers.org/Practice/NASW-Practice-Standards-Guidelines/Standards-for-Technology-in-Social-Work-Practice

National Academies of Sciences, Engineering, and Medicine. (2017). *Communities in action: Pathways to health equity*. The National Academies Press. https://doi.org/10.17226/24624

National Academies of Sciences, Engineering, and Medicine. (2019). *Integrating social care into the delivery of health care: Moving upstream to improve the nation's health*. The National Academies Press. https://doi.org/10.17226/25467

Niazi, M. K. K., Parwani, A. V., & Gurcan, M. N. (2019). Digital pathology and artificial intelligence. *The Lancet Oncology, 20*(5), e253–e261. https://doi.org/10.1016/s1470-2045(19)30154-8

Pater, J., McDaniel, B. T., Nova, F. F., Drouin, M., O'Connor, K., & Zytko, D. (2025). A commentary on sexting, sextortion, and generative AI: Risks, deception, and digital vulnerability. *Family Relations, 74*(3), 1109–1120. https://doi.org/10.1111/fare.13152

Peiffer-Smadja, N., Dellière, S., Rodriguez, C., Birgand, G., Lescure, F.-X., Fourati, S., & Ruppé, E. (2020). Machine learning in the clinical microbiology laboratory: Has the time come for routine practice? *Clinical Microbiology and Infection, 26*(10), 1300–1309. https://doi.org/10.1016/j.cmi.2020.02.00

Perron, B. E., Rivenburgh, K. A., Victor, B. G., Qi, Z., & Luan, H. (2025). A primer on word Embeddings: AI techniques for text analysis in social work. *Journal of the Society for Social Work and Research, 16*(2), 241–273. https://doi.org/10.1086/735577

Pushpakom, S., Iorio, F., Eyers, P. A., Escott, K. J., Hopper, S., Wells, A., Doig, A., Guilliams, T., Latimer, J., McNamee, C., Norris, A., Sanseau, P., Cavalla, D., & Pirmohamed, M. (2019). Drug repurposing: Progress, challenges and recommendations. *Nature Reviews Drug Discovery, 18*(1), 41–58. https://doi.org/10.1038/nrd.2018.168

Riis, A. H., Kristensen, P. K., Lauritsen, S. M., Thiesson, B., & Jørgensen, M. J. (2023). Using explainable artificial intelligence to predict potentially preventable hospitalizations. A population-based cohort study in Denmark. *Medical Care, 61*(4), 226–236. https://doi.org/10.1097/mlr.0000000000001830

Singh, M., Kumar, A., Khanna, N. N., Laird, J. R., Nicolaides, A., Faa, G., Johri, A. M., Mantella, L. E., Fernandes, J. F. E., Teji, J. S., Singh, N., Fouda, M. M., Singh, R., Sharma, A., Kitas, G., Rathore, V., Singh, I. M., Tadepalli, K., Al-Maini, M., et al. (2024). Artificial intelligence for cardiovascular disease risk assessment in personalised framework: A scoping review. *EClinicalMedicine, 73*, 102660. https://doi.org/10.1016/j.eclinm.2024.102660

Sinha, G. R., Graaf, G., Larrison, C. R., & Brooks, I. (2025). Gender disparities and mental health manifestations in twitter discourse on student loan debts. *Social Work in Mental Health, 23*(3), 272–286. https://doi.org/10.1080/15332985.2024.2425306

Stoll, D., Wehrli, S., & Lätsch, D. (2025). Case reports unlocked: Harnessing large language models to advance research on child maltreatment. *Child Abuse & Neglect, 160*, 107202. https://doi.org/10.1016/j.chiabu.2024.107202

Subramaniam, S., Faisal, A. I., & Deen, M. J. (2022). Wearable sensor Systems for Fall Risk Assessment: A review. *Frontiers in Digital Health, 4*, 921506. https://doi.org/10.3389/fdgth.2022.921506

Taherdoost, H., & Madanchian, M. (2023). Artificial intelligence and sentiment analysis: A review in competitive research. *Computer, 12*(2), 37. https://www.mdpi.com/2073-431X/12/2/37

Trafton, A. (2020). *Artificial intelligence yields new antibiotic*. https://news.mit.edu/2020/artificial-intelligence-identifies-new-antibiotic-0220

United Nations. (1948). *Universal declaration of human rights*. https://www.un.org/en/about-us/universal-declaration-of-human-rights

Vandenberg, O., Durand, G., Hallin, M., Diefenbach, A., Gant, V., Murray, P., Kozlakidis, Z., & van Belkum, A. (2020). Consolidation of clinical microbiology laboratories and introduction of transformative technologies. *Clinical Microbiology Reviews, 33*(2), e00057. https://doi.org/10.1128/cmr.00057-19

Wang, C., Zhu, X., Hong, J. C., & Zheng, D. (2019). Artificial intelligence in radiotherapy treatment planning: Present and future. *Technology in Cancer Research & Treatment, 18*, 1–11. https://doi.org/10.1177/1533033819873922

Yan, C., Grabowska, M. E., Dickson, A. L., Li, B., Wen, Z., Roden, D. M., Michael Stein, C., Embí, P. J., Peterson, J. F., Feng, Q., Malin, B. A., & Wei, W.-Q. (2024). Leveraging generative AI to prioritize drug repurposing candidates for Alzheimer's disease with real-world clinical validation. *npj Digital Medicine, 7*(1), 46. https://doi.org/10.1038/s41746 024 01038 3

Yang, S., Santillana, M., & Kou, S. C. (2015). Accurate estimation of influenza epidemics using Google search data via ARGO. *Proceedings of the National Academy of Sciences, 112*(47), 14473–14478. https://doi.org/10.1073/pnas.1515373112

Zhang, Y., Fang, J., Luo, X., Lindsay, D., Madre, N., Paredes, J., Penna, A., Melley, E., & Garcia, T. (2025). Exploring the efficacy of ChatGPT in understanding and identifying intimate partner violence. *Family Relations, 74*(3), 1233–1249. https://doi.org/10.1111/fare.13176

Chapter 6
AI for Physical, Cognitive, and Developmental Challenges

Junjie Wang and Melissa D. Begg

1 Introduction

The World Health Organization (WHO) has reported that approximately 1.3 billion individuals worldwide—equating to about 16% of the global population, or 1 in 6 persons—experience significant disabilities. Empirical evidence suggests that some individuals with disabilities face a reduction in life expectancy of up to 20 years compared to their non-disabled counterparts. Furthermore, they are at a twofold increased risk for developing chronic health conditions, including depression, asthma, diabetes, stroke, obesity, and poor oral health. Substantial systemic and logistical barriers compound these health disparities; for instance, they experience difficulties in accessing transportation—both in terms of availability and affordability—at a rate 15 times greater than those without disabilities. These pervasive inequities are largely attributable to structural factors such as stigma, discrimination, poverty, and exclusion from educational and employment opportunities, as well as inherent barriers within the healthcare system itself (WHO, 2023).

Artificial intelligence (AI) is a transformative technology with significant implications across diverse sectors, particularly healthcare and business operations (Dhopte & Bagde, 2023). AI encompasses technologies that enable computers and machines to simulate human cognitive functions, such as learning, comprehension, problem-solving, decision-making, creativity, and autonomy (Stryker & Kavlakoglu, 2024). Its rapid advancements offer transformative potential to enhance support systems for persons with disabilities. In healthcare, AI-driven innovations—such as diagnostic tools and predictive analytics—enable the early detection of chronic

J. Wang (✉)
School of Sports and Health Promotion, Dalian University of Technology, Dalian, China
e-mail: wangjunjie@dlut.edu.cn

M. D. Begg
School of Social Work, Columbia University, New York, NY, USA
e-mail: mdb3@columbia.edu

R. An, M. A. Lindsey (eds.), *Artificial Intelligence in Social Work*,
https://doi.org/10.1007/978-3-032-18443-6_6

conditions like depression, diabetes, and cardiovascular disease. These innovations facilitate timely, personalized interventions that help reduce premature mortality (Davenport & Kalakota, 2019) and promote systemic changes in diagnostic and clinical management processes (Thacharodi et al., 2024). In transportation, AI applications can optimize route planning and service scheduling, thereby improving the accessibility and affordability of mobility solutions for individuals facing logistical challenges (Olawade et al., 2025). Furthermore, AI-based assistive technologies—including speech recognition software, smart home devices, and adaptive interfaces—can improve independent living and daily navigation, fostering greater participation in education and employment and ultimately contributing to enhanced social inclusion (Boscardin et al., 2024).

Addressing the multifaceted challenges posed by AI in the physical, cognitive, and developmental domains for individuals with disabilities, this chapter focuses on key considerations. Specifically, it examines adaptive devices, communication tools, and rehabilitation technologies. Furthermore, it explores the crucial aspects of accessibility and user-centered design. Most importantly, it interrogates the ethical considerations of reliance on AI and the importance of incorporating the perspectives of those with lived experience. Central to all of this is the notion that AI can be deployed in ethical and valuable ways, so long as we are mindful of who is at the table and how biases can be mitigated—making the role of social workers critical in its development and impact. In the words of Tim Wu (2025), "Instead of asking which future is coming, we should be asking which future we want" (para. 4). Now is the time to think about how to craft that future.

2 AI in Addressing Physical Challenges

Physical challenges among individuals with disabilities encompass difficulties in performing everyday tasks due to impairments in movement, strength, coordination, and overall physical function. Recent advances in AI have led to significant improvements in the detection, diagnosis, and management of these challenges. AI-based techniques are increasingly being developed and implemented to address issues such as muscle degeneration, impaired mobility, and the need for enhanced rehabilitation strategies across diverse patient populations. These innovations facilitate earlier diagnosis and support personalized treatment planning, ultimately having the potential to improve patient outcomes and quality of life.

2.1 Advancements in AI-Driven Adaptive Devices

AI-powered assistive technologies integrate advanced AI—encompassing machine learning (ML), computer vision, and natural language processing—with conventional support devices to enhance functionality, personalization, and adaptability for individuals with disabilities. By processing real-time data from sensors, cameras, and other sources, these systems detect user needs, predict behaviors, and provide tailored assistance across domains such as mobility, communication, and daily living tasks.

Recent AI advancements have significantly expanded the range of assistive technology applications. These breakthroughs span various categories, from wearable devices that augment sensory perception to sophisticated communication tools and the integration of AI into everyday smart environments (Table 6.1). Significant scientific interest has emerged in the development of AI-driven robotic exoskeletons for upper-limb applications. For example, an AI-driven universal exoskeleton system has been designed to dynamically switch assistance types across walking modes, modulate support based on ground slope, and provide timely intervention during specific gait phases. Such innovations have the potential to markedly improve the quality of life for individuals with physical disabilities by promoting independence and social inclusion (Lee et al., 2024). Similarly, AI-driven knee exoskeletons that utilize integrated sensors to gather pressure, movement, and force data have

Table 6.1 AI-powered assistive technologies

Technology name	Disability addressed	Key AI features
Ray-Ban Meta glasses (Bikkani, 2025)	Visual impairment	Real-time audio descriptions of environments
Orion (Bikkani, 2025)	Visual impairment	Multitasking assistance, holographic displays
NeuroVision Pro (Carr, 2024)	Blindness/visual impairment	"Digital sight" via neural signals from cameras, sensors, and AI
BionicM's Bio Leg (Bikkani, 2025)	Mobility impairment	Adapts to user movements, learns gait patterns
ExoWalk (Carr, 2024)	Mobility disabilities	Lighter, more sensitive exoskeleton with AI-based motion prediction
Auracast (Bikkani, 2025)	Hearing impairment	Broadcasts audio to multiple devices simultaneously without individual pairing
Otter.ai (Bikkani, 2025)	Hearing/language barriers	Real time multilingual translation
Samsung's Bulging TV (Bikkani, 2025)	Sensory disabilities	Tactile 3D screens with haptic feedback
SoundSphere (Carr, 2024)	Hearing impairment	Personalized 360-degree soundscape with AI filtering
Accessible Google Maps (Bikkani, 2025)	Mobility/visual impairment	Wheelchair-friendly routes, better live view, disabled-owned business labels
GPT-4 + Be my Eyes (Bikkani, 2025)	Visual impairment	AI-powered virtual volunteer assistance
NanoGlove (Carr, 2024)	Limited hand mobility	AI-based adaptability tailors
Alinker (Carr, 2024)	Mobility impairment	Non-motorized walking bike for social inclusion and physical activity
HoverChair (Carr, 2024)	Mobility impairment	Omnidirectional movement and standing with AI control

been developed to deliver adaptive gait assistance (Puyuelo-Quintana et al., 2020). Another system leverages electromyography signals to enable human-robot cooperative movement, providing assistance tailored to user needs (Lyu et al., 2019).

Furthermore, AI-powered assistive technologies extend beyond mobility support. For instance, an eye-tracking control system for assistive robotics has demonstrated a 100% task-completion rate among individuals with motor impairments, thereby enhancing the efficacy of wheelchair and robotic manipulator control while promoting user engagement and motivation (Sunny et al., 2021). In the realm of in--home care, AI systems that analyze real-time sensor data have shown promise in predicting falls and other adverse health events among seniors, thereby facilitating timely interventions and improving overall care (Momin et al., 2022). Integrating AI with various agents—including electronics, robotics, and software—continues to revolutionize assistive technologies, enabling people with disabilities to achieve greater independence in daily activities, access community and healthcare services more effectively, and enhance productivity in educational and employment settings (Pancholi et al., 2024).

AI-driven adaptive devices can significantly enhance the quality of life for individuals with disabilities by offering personalized assistance, real-time environmental adaptation, and improved accessibility. These technologies, such as AI-powered prosthetics, speech-to-text systems, and smart navigation tools, foster greater independence and social inclusion.

2.2 AI Application in Physical Therapy

The transformative potential of AI, and specifically ML, for clinical practice is increasingly evident. In neurorehabilitation, AI is revolutionizing treatment paradigms by offering personalized, data-driven interventions that enhance recovery outcomes in patients with neurological disorders such as stroke, spinal cord injury, and Parkinson's disease (PD) (Morelli, 2024). By analyzing intricate patterns within diverse datasets, AI algorithms can identify subtle indicators that inform both diagnosis and treatment planning (Calderone et al., 2024). A notable development in this area is the synergistic integration of wearable technologies with AI. These devices provide continuous data streams by monitoring patient movements and physiological responses outside traditional clinical environments. These data, when incorporated into ML models, enable real-time assessment of intervention efficacy and facilitate timely adjustments to treatment protocols (Swarnakar & Yadav, 2023). This iterative process of monitoring and refinement is particularly valuable in therapies aimed at regaining muscle strength and improving balance, where incremental gains can significantly enhance a patient's quality of life (Sardari et al., 2023).

Furthermore, AI-powered decision support systems are being developed to assist clinicians in formulating optimal intervention strategies. By analyzing historical data from large patient cohorts—including imaging studies, wearable sensor outputs, and patient demographics—these systems forecast which individuals are most likely to benefit from specific therapeutic approaches. This holistic assessment not only augments clinical decision-making but also promotes more efficient allocation of healthcare resources, potentially reducing the overall disease burden (Johnson et al., 2021; Morelli, 2024). Despite these advancements, it remains imperative that AI and ML tools complement rather than replace human expertise in clinical settings. The integration of these technologies into routine practice should support healthcare providers in delivering more effective, personalized care while ensuring that the nuanced judgment and empathy inherent to human practitioners remain central to patient management (Fiorente et al., 2024). The development and deployment of AI technologies must ensure that care decisions and care delivery continue to center on the individual patient.

Future directions in AI for addressing physical challenges are likely to focus on enhancing the interoperability of wearable devices, improving data security and privacy, and refining algorithmic models for even more precise predictions. As AI continues to evolve, its integration with Internet of Things (IoT) and personalized rehabilitation strategies is expected to lead to more adaptive, responsive, and effective treatment modalities. This integration will pave the way for a new era in physical healthcare, where continuous, data-driven insights empower clinicians and patients alike to achieve better health outcomes through tailored, proactive interventions (Sumner et al., 2023).

3 AI in Addressing Cognitive Challenges

Cognitive challenges refer to impediments to efficient cognitive processing, including deficits in attention, memory, problem-solving, and decision-making. These challenges manifest in educational, professional, and everyday contexts, affecting performance and overall satisfaction. Recognizing and addressing these limitations is essential for optimizing personal development, productivity, and learning strategies. Given that individuals experience cognitive challenges to varying degrees, tailored interventions are necessary to enhance cognitive efficacy (Anderson, 2024).

Recent advancements in AI have significantly contributed to the detection, diagnosis, and management of cognitive impairments. AI-based techniques are increasingly applied to address a spectrum of challenges—from autism spectrum disorder (ASD) and PD to rehabilitation in diverse patient populations. These innovations not only improve healthcare delivery but also enable personalized learning experiences by adapting to individual needs and pacing. By analyzing performance data, AI systems can offer customized content and feedback, thereby enhancing cognitive skills and promoting better knowledge retention (Gupta et al., 2023), which is essential to patient-centered care.

3.1 AI in Detection and Diagnosis

Recent advances in AI have demonstrated significant promise in the early detection and diagnosis of various cognitive disorders, including PD, ASD, Alzheimer's disease (AD), Attention-Deficit Hyperactivity Disorder (ADHD), addiction, and sleep disorders (Bazoukis et al., 2023; Namasse et al., 2025; Perju-Dumbrava et al., 2022; Sun et al., 2023; Suva & Bhatia, 2024; Winchester et al., 2023).

For example, in PD detection, AI models have achieved an area under the curve of 0.90 on held-out test sets and 0.85 on external test sets. These models also reliably estimate disease severity and progression using established clinical benchmarks such as the Movement Disorder Society Unified Parkinson's Disease Rating Scale (Yang et al., 2022). Data mining of prodromal markers—ranging from cognitive disturbances to cerebrospinal fluid measurements—has yielded diagnostic accuracies as high as 96%, with sensitivities and specificities reaching 97% and 95%, respectively (Prashanth et al., 2016). Moreover, ML models capturing non-linear and overlapping disease trajectories have provided a comprehensive view of early PD progression (Severson et al., 2021).

In the realm of neurodevelopmental disorders, the standard diagnostic process for ASD has traditionally relied on clinician-administered behavioral observations, a method often hampered by subjectivity and time constraints. In contrast, MRI-based AI techniques have demonstrated improved objectivity, speed, and accuracy in early detection of ASD (Helmy et al., 2023). Similarly, early indicators of AD, such as speech and language alterations, have been effectively analyzed using AI-driven natural language processing. This non-invasive and cost-effective approach facilitates the timely initiation of management strategies and interventions (Jahan et al., 2024). This can lead to substantial patient benefits.

Additional ML models further underscore AI's diagnostic potential. One model, integrating support vector machines (SVMs) with principal component analysis (PCA), was developed to predict cognitive decline in PD using clinical data, biomarkers, and neuropsychological tests. This model achieved 92.3% accuracy with 32 parameters, which improved to 100% after feature selection reduced the parameter set to 13 (Chen et al., 2022a). Another model demonstrated high logistic classification performance, achieving 91.67% accuracy in classifying mild cognitive impairment subtypes using gait data (Chen et al., 2020).

Overall, integrating AI into early detection and diagnosis not only improves the precision of traditional assessments but also accelerates the diagnostic process, paving the way for earlier and more effective interventions.

3.2 AI in Cognitive Rehabilitation Therapy

In March 2020, the National Institute on Aging (NIA) launched the Artificial Intelligence and Technology Collaboratory for Aging Research to accelerate the adoption of AI and digital technologies. This initiative specifically targets improvements in health and quality of life for older adults, particularly those affected by dementia and AD (Abadir et al., 2024).

AI has emerged as a transformative tool in cognitive rehabilitation by enhancing the adaptability of therapeutic interventions. ML algorithms now adjust exercise difficulty in real time according to individual patient performance, ensuring that challenges remain optimally calibrated to patient-identified needs and preferences. In addition, AI's predictive capabilities facilitate early identification of setbacks or plateaus in recovery, enabling timely, proactive modifications to treatment plans (Bhattarai et al., 2023; Campagnini et al., 2022; Chen et al., 2023).

Cognitive Rehabilitation Therapy (CRT) is a non-pharmacological intervention that employs both restorative and compensatory strategies to enhance functional cognition in daily living activities (Khalid et al., 2024). The integration of AI into CRT has led to the development of advanced AI-powered robots designed to enhance essential cognitive functions, such as memory retention, focus, attention span, and executive skills. Notably, AI-enabled social robots like PARO have demonstrated tangible benefits by offering continuous support and personalized cognitive assistance across various settings, including healthcare and social care (Lu et al., 2021). Furthermore, AI-driven socially assistive robots—whether designed in animal, robotic, or humanoid forms—have shown promising results in improving cognitive function and can serve as a digital and social prescription program, providing 24-h engagement for older adults (Lee et al., 2022).

In addition, virtual reality (VR) systems powered by AI create immersive environments that simulate real-life scenarios, thereby stimulating neuroplasticity and enhancing cognitive recovery. The synergistic application of VR and Brain–Computer Interface (BCI) enables targeted neuromodulation of specific brain areas, potentially eliciting neurochemical shifts and influencing cognitive functions, including memory, perception, and motor skills (Drigas & Sideraki, 2024). Integrating AI and VR into chronic pain cognitive therapy shows promise for enhanced management and improved patient outcomes (Mazzolenis et al., 2024). Similarly, AI-driven VR platforms personalize cognitive rehabilitation, monitor progress, and show promising results for dementia (Velagaleti, 2025). These advancements exemplify AI's enormous potential to bridge the gap between clinical expertise and innovative technology, ultimately leading to more effective and efficient cognitive rehabilitation strategies.

Despite these advancements, challenges remain, and the greatest promise of AI in addressing cognitive challenges may lie in personalized cognitive augmentation. AI, converging with cognitive science, will evolve beyond pattern recognition to offer real-time, non-disruptive interventions for cognitive biases—which are systematic and predictable deviations from rational judgment or decision-making

(Blanco, 2017)—and limitations. Personalized platforms will tailor support for executive functions, benefiting neurodivergent and aging populations by preserving cognitive autonomy. Overall, the strategic incorporation of AI in CRT holds significant promise for revolutionizing patient care and advancing the field of neurorehabilitation (Gupta, 2024).

4 Accessibility, User-Centered Design, and the Digital Divide

4.1 Accessibility Challenges in AI

The integration of AI into various facets of life necessitates a critical examination of its accessibility for individuals with disabilities. Digital accessibility, as defined by established initiatives, ensures equitable access to digital content and services for everyone, regardless of ability. This relies on the POUR principles: perceivable, operable, understandable, and robust design (Chemnad & Othman, 2024). While AI holds immense potential to enhance accessibility and improve the quality of life for people with disabilities, its current trajectory presents several challenges that demand scholarly attention (Liyanage et al., 2019). The increasing reliance on AI in decision-making processes further underscores the importance of ensuring these systems are comprehensible and usable by all, including those with disabilities. Failure to prioritize accessibility in the development and deployment of AI risks creating new forms of exclusion and discrimination, underscoring the ethical imperative to address these challenges proactively (Fjeld & Brynn, 2024).

A significant logistical hurdle in creating accessible AI is the availability of diverse, representative datasets for training models. AI algorithms learn from patterns in data, and if disability is underrepresented or inaccurately categorized, the resulting models will not effectively serve individuals with disabilities (Lay-Flurrie, 2025). Similarly, speech recognition systems may perform poorly for individuals with speech impairments due to the lack of diverse speech samples in their training data (Goudarzi & Moya-Galé, 2021). Many readily available datasets tend to reflect the most common data, inadvertently excluding individuals with disabilities who have unique accessibility requirements. This lack of representative labeling can also lead to misclassifications in crucial accessibility features like alternative text for images, impacting nonbinary individuals and those with disabilities (Bennett & Trewin, 2023). The scarcity of comprehensive disability data, termed a "disability data desert," significantly limits AI utility and can inadvertently perpetuate harmful stereotypes and amplify existing biases.

Furthermore, high costs and market failures limit access to advanced AI-assistive technologies. The necessity for sophisticated hardware and extensive computational resources creates an economic barrier, particularly for low-income regions and underserved populations. Complex interfaces requiring high technical literacy further restrict adoption (Botelho, 2021). Infrastructural deficits, encompassing limited network connectivity and intermittent power supply, pose significant impediments (Deo & Anjankar, 2023). These limitations create substantial challenges for the deployment and effective operation of AI in various contexts.

4.2 User-Centered Design Principles in AI

User-centered design (UCD) emphasizes placing the user at the heart of the development process. This approach involves iterative cycles of prototyping, testing, and refinement to ensure that solutions are tailored to real-world needs (Luna et al., 2015). In the context of AI, UCD requires a rigorous analysis of user behaviors, contextual challenges, and environmental factors (McDermott et al., 2023). It promotes empathy, usability, and accessibility by focusing on the users' experiences and limitations. Methodologies such as contextual inquiry, heuristic evaluation, and participatory design are essential. These techniques help uncover hidden requirements and contextual nuances that may be overlooked in traditional design approaches, ensuring that the final product is both intuitive and accessible (El et al., 2024) and tailored and responsive to the needs and preferences of those affected.

Direct engagement with disabled users is paramount to creating inclusive AI systems. Involving these users from the conceptual stage through to the final evaluation helps identify specific challenges that may not be evident to designers without lived experiences of disability. This participatory design process not only enriches the product's development but also empowers users by validating their input (Jung et al., 2025). For example, incorporating user feedback on interface adjustments, navigation methods, and accessibility features enables designers to address diverse needs effectively. From the very start of the design process, regular workshops, focus groups, and usability testing sessions provide platforms for dialogue and collaborative problem-identification and problem-solving. Moreover, such involvement ensures that design decisions are informed by practical experiences rather than theoretical assumptions, thereby increasing the likelihood of adoption and long-term user satisfaction.

The effectiveness of AI-based solutions depends heavily on their ease of use, flexibility, and adaptability. Ease of use is achieved through intuitive interfaces that reduce cognitive load and learning curves. This is particularly important for users with varying levels of digital literacy or who require assistive technologies. Flexibility and adaptability, on the other hand, refer to the system's ability to accommodate a wide range of user needs and contexts. This involves creating modular systems that can be customized based on individual requirements, such as adjustable display settings, voice-controlled commands, or alternative input modalities. Additionally, adaptive algorithms that learn from user interactions can further refine system performance over time. These design considerations not only enhance usability but also ensure that AI solutions remain relevant in rapidly changing technological landscapes (Prince et al., 2024).

4.3 The Digital Divide in AI

The pervasive integration of digital technologies has fundamentally reshaped societal structures, yet this transformation has not been uniformly experienced across all demographics and regions. The term "digital divide" traditionally describes the unequal access to digital technologies, encompassing disparities in Internet connectivity, device availability, infrastructure, skills, and affordability, which consequently result in unequal opportunities for information access and digital participation (Lythreatis et al., 2022; Wong et al., 2025). As AI rapidly advances and its applications become increasingly widespread, a new dimension of this disparity has emerged: the "AI divide" (i.e., AI-related access, capability, or outcome divide among users) (Carter et al., 2020). This evolving divide signifies unequal access to, benefits from, and opportunities presented by AI across regions, communities, and socioeconomic strata (Rajpurkar et al., 2022).

The AI divide manifests across several interconnected facets, creating a complex web of disparities. One significant aspect is the unequal access to AI technologies. The development and deployment of AI are concentrated primarily in wealthy nations and major technology companies. Developed countries typically enjoy robust technological infrastructure, substantial investment in research and development, and higher digital literacy rates, which collectively facilitate the integration of AI in assistive devices. In contrast, developing countries often face outdated or inadequate digital infrastructure, high costs of modern technology, and limited access to technical training. This concentration exacerbates the global imbalance, creating a digital hierarchy that marginalizes underdeveloped areas (Ahmad et al., 2024).

Another critical facet of the AI digital divide lies in the disparities in AI education and skills (Nagi et al., 2023). A substantial gap exists between the growing demand for AI expertise and the current supply. This gap exhibits demographic imbalances, with studies indicating lower AI training and proficiency among women and older adults than among men and younger adults, respectively (Randstad, 2025). Educational barriers in underserved regions further exacerbate this issue by limiting access to foundational digital literacy and AI-related skills. Psychological factors, such as technology resistance (which may be partly rooted in mistrust stemming from persistent societal inequities), also hinder engagement, particularly among those with limited prior exposure.

The third critical dimension of the AI divide lies in the unequal availability of relevant data for AI development. Fundamentally data-driven, effective AI systems rely on large, diverse, and high-quality datasets for training and improvement (Tripathi et al., 2023). Consequently, limited access to such data creates a significant disadvantage. A key concern is the pervasive issue of bias within training data, which can lead to discriminatory outcomes for marginalized groups. This bias manifests through geographical limitations, underrepresentation of racial and ethnic minorities and medically underserved populations, and other vulnerable groups, and linguistic and cultural barriers—ultimately hindering the development of fair and inclusive AI applications, especially in critical domains like healthcare (Dankwa-Mullan, 2024).

5 Ethical Considerations in Inclusive AI Development

The development of AI prediction algorithms involves several stages, each of which may introduce bias (Nazer et al., 2023). Algorithms do not create biases themselves but may perpetuate (or even amplify) societal inequities and cultural prejudices. Bias can enter at different stages of development and deployment, including data sets, algorithms, and systems (Chen, 2023). The reasons may vary, including a lack of access to data for target populations, unconscious and conscious bias within the developing team, and organizational structure and practices. As a result, algorithms may provide inaccurate predictions and outputs for certain subsets of the population or discriminate against particular groups (Pasipamire & Muroyiwa, 2024). AI algorithm development stages and potential bias sources are outlined for ethical consideration.

5.1 Formulating the Research Problem

This initial stage focuses on defining the research question or problem. Potential biases introduced here include:

- **Racial/Ethnic Bias:** Societal prejudices rooted in race and ethnicity can introduce framing bias. This influences the conceptualization of problems and potential solutions (Skinner-Dorkenoo et al., 2023).
- **Gender Bias:** Bias arising from societal stereotypes and inequalities related to gender that can influence the research question (Kotek et al., 2023).
- **Age Bias:** Bias resulting from age-related stereotypes or the exclusion of specific age groups within the problem definition, leading to skewed outcomes (Reio, 2011).
- **Disability Bias:** Bias that occurs when the problem formulation does not adequately consider or address the needs and perspectives of individuals with disabilities (Antonopoulos et al., 2023).
- **Linguistic Bias:** Linguistic bias is a systematic preference for specific language forms that leads to inequitable treatment or evaluation of individuals or groups based on their language use, potentially through the language used to define the problem (Beukeboom & Burgers, 2017).
- **Global Misrepresentation Bias:** Bias arises from the underrepresentation or inaccurate portrayal of specific populations or regions within a research problem (Shahbazi et al., 2023).

5.2 Data Collection

This stage involves gathering the data needed to train and evaluate the machine learning model. Biases that can arise during data collection are:

- **Sampling Bias:** Bias introduced when the collected data is not representative of the overall population of interest (Chen et al., 2022b).
- **Measurement Bias:** Bias resulting from systematic errors or inconsistencies in how data is measured or recorded (Hernán & Cole, 2009).
- **Exclusion Bias:** Bias caused by the intentional or unintentional exclusion of certain groups or data points from the dataset (Favier et al., 2023).
- **Label Bias:** Bias present in the labels assigned to the data, which can reflect existing societal biases or flawed annotation processes (Favier et al., 2023).
- **Social Bias:** Bias embedded in the data that reflects and potentially amplifies societal stereotypes and prejudices (Shin et al., 2024).

5.3 Data Pre-Processing

This stage involves cleaning, transforming, and preparing the collected data for model training. Potential biases introduced during pre-processing include:

- **Aggregation Bias:** Bias that occurs when data is combined in a way that masks or distorts essential differences between subgroups (Voss, 2005).
- **Feature Selection Bias:** Bias introduced when the features chosen to train the model are more relevant or accurate for some groups than others (Singhi & Liu, 2006).
- **Outlier Bias:** Bias caused by the disproportionate influence of outliers in the dataset, which might not be representative of all groups (Ding et al., 2024).
- **Confounding Bias:** Bias arising when a hidden or unobserved variable is correlated with both the input features and the outcome, leading to misleading associations (Schuster et al., 2021).

5.4 Model Development and Validation

This stage involves selecting a model architecture, training it on the pre-processed data, and evaluating its performance. Biases at this stage can include:

- **Training Dataset Bias:** Bias present in the data used to train the model, leading it to learn and perpetuate existing inequalities (Mac Namee et al., 2002).
- **Test Dataset Bias:** Bias in the data used to evaluate the model, potentially leading to an inaccurate assessment of its performance across different groups (Hou et al., 2024).

- **Algorithmic Bias:** Bias inherent in the design or assumptions of the machine learning algorithm itself, which might favor certain outcomes or groups (Hooker, 2021).
- **Confirmation Bias:** Bias where the model development or evaluation process is influenced by pre-existing beliefs or expectations, leading to the overlooking of potential biases (Taehyun & Sangyeon, 2023).
- **Validation Bias:** Bias introduced during model validation, potentially leading to an overly optimistic estimate of the model's performance on unseen data (Nazer et al., 2023).

5.5 *Model Implementation*

This final stage involves deploying the trained model for real-world use. Biases that can emerge during implementation include (Nazer et al., 2023):

- **Concept Drift:** Bias that occurs when the statistical properties of the data processed by the model change over time, leading to degraded performance or unfair outcomes.
- **Covariate Shift:** Bias that arises when the distribution of input features in the deployment environment differs significantly from that in the training data.

6 Conclusion

AI has demonstrated its potential to significantly enhance the quality of life for people with disabilities through a variety of applications and technologies. AI-powered assistive technologies offer the promise of more personalized, adaptive, and effective support tailored to each individual's unique circumstances. The integration of AI into assistive technologies is poised to revolutionize the lives of individuals with disabilities, making accessibility more effortless and breaking down barriers that once seemed insurmountable. The focus of innovation is on creating tools that are not only technologically advanced but also simple, accessible, and versatile, catering to a wide range of needs and preferences. The concept of assistive augmentation, which envisions technology as an integrated and seamless extension of human ability, represents a key direction for future development in this field (Tan et al., 2025). However, realizing this potential hinges on careful navigation of ethical considerations, incorporating the perspectives of those with lived experience, and a steadfast commitment to ensuring accessibility for all. Continued collaboration between researchers, developers, policymakers, and, most importantly, individuals with disabilities is crucial for realizing the full transformative potential of AI-based assistive technologies. The overarching trend is toward the development of more integrated, personalized, and intelligent assistive solutions that will empower individuals with disabilities to lead more independent, fulfilling, and engaged lives.

Competing Interests The authors have no conflicts of interest to declare that are relevant to the content of this chapter.

References

Abadir, P., Oh, E., Chellappa, R., Choudhry, N., Demiris, G., Ganesan, D., Karlawish, J., Marlin, B., Li, R. M., Dehak, N., Arbaje, A., Unberath, M., Cudjoe, T., Chute, C., Moore, J. H., Phan, P., Samus, Q., Schoenborn, N. L., Battle, A., & Walston, J. D. (2024). Artificial intelligence and technology Collaboratories: Innovating aging research and Alzheimer's care. *Alzheimer's & Dementia, 20*(4), 3074–3079. https://doi.org/10.1002/alz.13710

Ahmad, A., Liew, A. X. W., Venturini, F., Kalogeras, A., Candiani, A., Di, B. G., Ajibola, S., Cartujo, P., Romero, P., Lykoudi, A., De, G. M. M., Xouris, C., Lo, B. R., Doddy, I., Elegbede, I., D'Urso, L. G. F., García, D. M. L. F., & Martos, V. (2024). AI can empower agriculture for global food security: Challenges and prospects in developing nations. *Frontiers in Artificial Intelligence, 7*, 1328530. https://doi.org/10.3389/frai.2024.1328530

Anderson, C. (2024, September 19). *What is cognitive challenges?* https://focuskeeper.co/glossary/what-is-cognitive-challenges/#:~:text=Cognitive%20challenges%20refer%20to%20obstacles,workplace%20environments%2C%20and%20everyday%20life

Antonopoulos, C. R., Sugden, N., & Saliba, A. (2023). Implicit bias toward people with disability: A systematic review and meta-analysis. *Rehabilitation Psychology, 68*(2), 121–134. https://doi.org/10.1037/rep0000493

Bazoukis, G., Bollepalli, S. C., Chung, C. T., Li, X., Tse, G., Bartley, B. L., Batool-Anwar, S., Quan, S. F., & Armoundas, A. A. (2023). Application of artificial intelligence in the diagnosis of sleep apnea. *Journal of Clinical Sleep Medicine, 19*(7), 1337–1363. https://doi.org/10.5664/jcsm.10532

Bennett, C., & Trewin, S. (2023, March 28). *AI for accessibility: Opportunities and challenges*. https://equalentry.com/ai-for-accessibility-opportunities-and-challenges

Bhattarai, K., Rajaganapathy, S., Das, T., Kim, Y., & Chen, Y. (2023). Using artificial intelligence to learn optimal regimen plan for Alzheimer's disease. *The Journal of the American Medical Informatics Association, 30*(10), 1645–1656. https://doi.org/10.1093/jamia/ocad135

Bikkani, A. (2025, February 20). *The broader impact of AI on accessibility in 2025*. AEL Data. https://aeldata.com/the-broader-impact-of-ai-on-accessibility-in-2025/#GPT-4_and_Be_my_Eyes_Merger

Blanco, F. (2017). Cognitive bias. In J. Vonk & T. Shackelford (Eds.), *Encyclopedia of animal cognition and behavior* (pp. 1–7). Springer. https://doi.org/10.1007/978-3-319-47829-6_1244-1

Boscardin, C. K., Gin, B., Golde, P. B., & Hauer, K. E. (2024). ChatGPT and generative artificial intelligence for medical education: Potential impact and opportunity. *Journal of the Association of American Medical Colleges, 99*(1), 22–27. https://doi.org/10.1097/ACM.0000000000005439

Botelho, F. H. F. (2021). Accessibility to digital technology: Virtual barriers, real opportunities. *Assistive Technology, 33*(sup1), 27–34. https://doi.org/10.1080/10400435.2021.1945705

Beukeboom, C. J., & Burgers, C. F. (2017). Linguistic bias. In H. Giles, & J. Harwood (Ed.), Oxford Encyclopedia of Communication (Living ed., pp. 1-19). Oxford University Press. https://doi.org/10.1093/acrefore/9780190228613.013.439

Calderone, A., Latella, D., Bonanno, M., Quartarone, A., Mojdehdehbaher, S., Celesti, A., & Calabrò, R. S. (2024). Towards transforming neurorehabilitation: The impact of artificial intelligence on diagnosis and treatment of neurological disorders. *Biomedicine, 12*(10), 2415. https://doi.org/10.3390/biomedicines12102415

Campagnini, S., Arienti, C., Patrini, M., Liuzzi, P., Mannini, A., & Carrozza, M. C. (2022). Machine learning methods for functional recovery prediction and prognosis in post-stroke rehabilitation: A systematic review. *Journal of Neuroengineering and Rehabilitation, 19*(1), 54. https://doi.org/10.1186/s12984-022-01032-4

Carr, D. (2024, December 31). *Revolutionizing accessibility the latest innovations in assistive technology 2025*. https://www.nabroward.com/2024/12/31/517401/revolutionizing-accessibility-the-latest-innovations-in-assistive-technology-2025

Carter, L., Liu, D. P., & Caley, C. (2020). Exploring the intersection of the digital divide and artificial intelligence: A hermeneutic literature review. *AIS Transactions on Human-computer Interaction, 12*(4), 253–275. https://doi.org/10.17705/1thci.00138

Chemnad, K., & Othman, A. (2024). Digital accessibility in the era of artificial intelligence-bibliometric analysis and systematic review. *Frontiers in Artificial Intelligence, 7*, 1349668. https://doi.org/10.3389/frai.2024.1349668

Chen, P., Lien, C. W., Wu, W. C., Lee, L. S., & Shaw, J. S. (2020). Gait-based machine learning for classifying patients with different types of mild cognitive impairment. *Journal of Medical Systems, 44*(6), 107. https://doi.org/10.1007/s10916-020-01578-7

Chen, P. H., Hou, T. Y., Cheng, F. Y., & Shaw, J. S. (2022a). Prediction of cognitive degeneration in Parkinson's disease patients using a machine learning method. *Brain Sciences, 12*(8), 1048. https://doi.org/10.3390/brainsci12081048

Chen, S. W., Keglovits, M., Devine, M., & Stark, S. (2022b). Sociodemographic differences in respondent preferences for survey formats: Sampling bias and potential threats to external validity. *Archives of Physical Medicine and Rehabilitation, 4*(1), 100175. https://doi.org/10.1016/j.arrct.2021.100175

Chen, Y. W., Lin, K. C., Li, Y. C., & Lin, C. J. (2023). Predicting patient-reported outcome of activities of daily living in stroke rehabilitation: A machine learning study. *Journal of Neuroengineering and Rehabilitation, 20*(1), 25. https://doi.org/10.1186/s12984-023-01151-6

Chen, Z. (2023). Ethics and discrimination in artificial intelligence-enabled recruitment practices. *Humanities and Social Sciences Communications, 10*(1), 567. https://doi.org/10.1057/s41599-023-02079-x

Dankwa-Mullan, I. (2024). Health equity and ethical considerations in using artificial intelligence in public health and medicine. *Preventing Chronic Disease, 21*(21), E64. https://doi.org/10.5888/pcd21.240245

Davenport, T., & Kalakota, R. (2019). The potential for artificial intelligence in healthcare. *Future Healthcare Journal, 6*(2), 94–98. https://doi.org/10.7861/futurehosp.6-2-94

Deo, N., & Anjankar, A. (2023). Artificial intelligence with robotics in healthcare: A narrative review of its viability in India. *Cureus, 15*(5), e39416. https://doi.org/10.7759/cureus.39416

Dhopte, A., & Bagde, H. (2023). Smart smile: Revolutionizing dentistry with artificial intelligence. *Cureus, 15*(6), e41227. https://doi.org/10.7759/cureus.41227

Ding, X. Y., Xi, R., & Akoglu, L. (2024). Outlier detection bias busted: Understanding sources of algorithmic biasthrough data-centric factors. In *Proceedings of the Seventh AAAI/ACM Conference on AI, Ethics, and Society*. https://doi.org/10.48550/arXiv.2408.13667

Drigas, A., & Sideraki, A. (2024). Brain neuroplasticity leveraging virtual reality and brain–computer Interface technologies. *Sensors, 24*(17), 5725.

El, M. C., Singh, D., Sawhney, V., Fernandes, S., El-Lahib, Y., & Gorman, R. (2024). Exploring the intersection of AI and inclusive Design for People with disabilities. *Studies in Health Technology and Informatics, 316*, 556–559. https://doi.org/10.3233/SHTI240475

Favier, M., Calders, T., Pinxteren, S., & Meyer, J. (2023). How to be fair? A study of label and selection bias. *Machine Learning, 112*(12), 5081–5104. https://doi.org/10.1007/s10994-023-06401-1

Fiorente, N., Mojdehdehbaher, S., & Calabrò, R. S. (2024). Artificial intelligence and neurorehabilitation: Fact vs. fiction. *Innovations in Clinical Neuroscience, 21*(1–3), 10–12.

Fjeld, E. K., & Brynn, R. (2024). AI in software development and its potential influence on accessibility compliance. *Studies in Health Technology and Informatics, 320*, 493–500. https://doi.org/10.3233/SHTI241046

Goudarzi, A., & Moya-Galé, G. (2021). Automatic speech recognition in noise for Parkinson's disease: A pilot study. *Frontiers in Artificial Intelligence, 4*, 809321. https://doi.org/10.3389/frai.2021.809321

Gupta, R. (2024). AI-based technologies, challenges, and solutions for neurorehabilitation: A systematic mapping. In D. J. Hemanth (Ed.), *Computational intelligence and deep learning methods for neuro-rehabilitation applications* (pp. 1–25). Academic Press. https://doi.org/10.1016/B978-0-443-13772-3.00014-5

Gupta, R., Kumari, S., Senapati, A., Ambasta, R. K., & Kumar, P. (2023). New era of artificial intelligence and machine learning-based detection, diagnosis, and therapeutics in Parkinson's disease. *Ageing Research Reviews, 90*, 102013. https://doi.org/10.1016/j.arr.2023.102013

Helmy, E., Elnakib, A., ElNakieb, Y., Khudri, M., Abdelrahim, M., Yousaf, J., Ghazal, M., Contractor, S., Barnes, G. N., & El-Baz, A. (2023). Role of artificial intelligence for autism diagnosis using DTI and fMRI: A survey. *Biomedicine, 11*(7). https://doi.org/10.3390/biomedicines11071858

Hernán, M. A., & Cole, S. R. (2009). Invited commentary: Causal diagrams and measurement bias. *American Journal of Epidemiology, 170*(8), 959–962. https://doi.org/10.1093/aje/kwp293

Hooker, S. (2021). Moving beyond "algorithmic bias is a data problem". *Patterns, 2*(4), 100241. https://doi.org/10.1016/j.patter.2021.100241

Hou, R., Lo, J. Y., Marks, J. R., Hwang, E. S., & Grimm, L. J. (2024). Classification performance bias between training and test sets in a limited mammography dataset. *PLoS One, 19*(2), e0282402. https://doi.org/10.1371/journal.pone.0282402

Jahan, Z., Khan, S. B., & Saraee, M. (2024). Early dementia detection with speech analysis and machine learning techniques. *Discover Sustainability, 5*(1), 65. https://doi.org/10.1007/s43621-024-00217-2

Johnson, K. B., Wei, W. Q., Weeraratne, D., Frisse, M. E., Misulis, K., Rhee, K., Zhao, J., & Snowdon, J. L. (2021). Precision medicine, AI, and the future of personalized health care. *Clinical and Translational Science, 14*(1), 86–93. https://doi.org/10.1111/cts.12884

Jung, I. C., Schuler, K., Zerlik, M., Grummt, S., Sedlmayr, M., & Sedlmayr, B. (2025). Overview of basic design recommendations for user-centered explanation interfaces for AI-based clinical decision support systems: A scoping review. *DIGITAL HEALTH, 11*, 20552076241308298. https://doi.org/10.1177/20552076241308298

Khalid, U. B., Naeem, M., Stasolla, F., Syed, M. H., Abbas, M., & Coronato, A. (2024). Impact of AI-powered solutions in rehabilitation process: Recent improvements and future trends. *International Journal of General Medicine, 17*, 943–969. https://doi.org/10.2147/IJGM.S453903

Kotek, H., Dockum, R., & Sun, D. (2023). Gender bias and stereotypes in large language models. *Proceedings of the ACM Collective Intelligence Conference*. https://doi.org/10.1145/3582269.361559

Lay-Flurrie, J. (2025, March 17). *Disability data: Improving representation to drive AI innovation*. https://blogs.microsoft.com/on-the-issues/2024/10/17/disability-data-improving-representation-to-drive-ai-innovation

Lee, D., Lee, S., & Young, A. J. (2024). AI-driven universal lower-limb exoskeleton system for community ambulation. *Science Advances, 10*(51), eadq0288. https://doi.org/10.1126/sciadv.adq0288

Lee, H., Chung, M., Kim, H., & Nam, E. W. (2022). The effect of cognitive function health care using artificial intelligence robots for older adults: Systematic review and meta-analysis. *JMIR Aging, 5*(2), e38896. https://doi.org/10.2196/42312

Liyanage, H., Liaw, S. T., Jonnagaddala, J., Schreiber, R., Kuziemsky, C., Terry, A. L., & de Lusignan, S. (2019). Artificial intelligence in primary health care: Perceptions, issues, and challenges. *Yearbook of Medical Informatics, 28*(1), 41–46. https://doi.org/10.1055/s-0039-1677901

Lu, L. C., Lan, S. H., Hsieh, Y. P., Lin, L. Y., Lan, S. J., & Chen, J. C. (2021). Effectiveness of companion robot Care for Dementia: A systematic review and meta-analysis. *Innovation in Aging, 5*(2), igab013. https://doi.org/10.1093/geroni/igab013

Luna, D., Quispe, M., Gonzalez, Z., Alemrares, A., Risk, M., Garcia, A. M., & Otero, C. (2015). User-centered design to develop clinical applications. Literature review. *Studies in Health Technology and Informatics, 216*, 967.

Lythreatis, S., Singh, S. K., & El-Kassar, A.-N. (2022). The digital divide: A review and future research agenda. *Technological Forecasting and Social Change, 175*, 121359. https://doi.org/10.1016/j.techfore.2021.121359

Lyu, M., Chen, W.-H., Ding, X., & Wang, J. (2019). Knee exoskeleton enhanced with artificial intelligence to provide assistance-as-needed. *Review of Scientific Instruments, 90*(9), 094101. https://doi.org/10.1063/1.5091660

Mac Namee, B., Cunningham, P., Byrne, S., & Corrigan, O. I. (2002). The problem of bias in training data in regression problems in medical decision support. *Artificial Intelligence in Medicine, 24*(1), 51–70. https://doi.org/10.1016/S0933-3657(01)00092-6

Mazzolenis, M. V., Mourra, G. N., Moreau, S., Mazzolenis, M. E., Cerda, I. H., Vega, J., Khan, J. S., & Thérond, A. (2024). The role of virtual reality and artificial intelligence in cognitive pain therapy: A narrative review. *Current Pain and Headache Reports, 28*(9), 881–892. https://doi.org/10.1007/s11916-024-01270-2

McDermott, M. B. A., Nestor, B., & Szolovits, P. (2023). Clinical artificial intelligence: Design principles and fallacies. *Clinics in Laboratory Medicine, 43*(1), 29–46. https://doi.org/10.1016/j.cll.2022.09.004

Momin, M. S., Sufian, A., Barman, D., Dutta, P., Dong, M., & Leo, M. (2022). In-home older adults' activity pattern monitoring using depth sensors: A review. *Sensors (Basel), 22*(23), 9067. https://doi.org/10.3390/s22239067

Morelli, N. (2024). Seeing past the event horizon: A framework for integrating artificial intelligence and machine learning into physical therapy. *Physical Therapy, 105*(2), pzae137. https://doi.org/10.1093/ptj/pzae137

Nagi, F., Salih, R., Alzubaidi, M., Shah, H., Alam, T., Shah, Z., & Househ, M. (2023). Applications of artificial intelligence (AI) in medical education: A scoping review. *Studies in Health Technology and Informatics, 305*, 648–651. https://doi.org/10.3233/SHTI230581

Namasse, Z., Tabaa, M., Hidila, Z., & Mouchawrab, S. (2025). Explainable artificial intelligence for predicting attention deficit hyperactivity disorder in children and adults. *Healthcare, 13*(2), 155. https://doi.org/10.3390/healthcare13020155

Nazer, L. H., Zatarah, R., Waldrip, S., Ke, J. X. C., Moukheiber, M., Khanna, A. K., Hicklen, R. S., Moukheiber, L., Moukheiber, D., Ma, H., & Mathur, P. (2023). Bias in artificial intelligence algorithms and recommendations for mitigation. *PLOS Digitial Health, 2*(6), e0000278. https://doi.org/10.1371/journal.pdig.0000278

Olawade, D. B., Bolarinwa, O. A., Adebisi, Y. A., & Shongwe, S. (2025). The role of artificial intelligence in enhancing healthcare for people with disabilities. *Social Science & Medicine, 364*, 117560. https://doi.org/10.1016/j.socscimed.2024.117560

Prashanth, R., Dutta Roy, S., Mandal, P. K., & Ghosh, S. (2016). High-accuracy detection of early Parkinson's disease through multimodal features and machine learning. *International Journal of Medical Informatics, 90*, 13–21. https://doi.org/10.1016/j.ijmedinf.2016.03.001

Pancholi, S., Wachs, J. P., & Duerstock, B. S. (2024). Use of artificial intelligence techniques to assist individuals with physical disabilities. *Annual Review of Biomedical Engineering, 26*(1), 1–24. https://doi.org/10.1146/annurev-bioeng-082222-012531

Pasipamire, N., & Muroyiwa, A. (2024). Navigating algorithm bias in AI: Ensuring fairness and trust in Africa. *Frontiers in Research Metrics and Analytics, 9*, 1486600. https://doi.org/10.3389/frma.2024.1486600

Perju-Dumbrava, L., Barsan, M., Leucuta, D. C., Popa, L. C., Pop, C., Tohanean, N., & Popa, S. L. (2022). Artificial intelligence applications and robotic systems in Parkinson's disease (review). *Experimental and Therapeutic Medicine, 23*(2), 153. https://doi.org/10.3892/etm.2021.11076

Prince, E. W., Mirsky, D. M., Hankinson, T. C., & Görg, C. (2024). Current state and promise of user-centered design to harness explainable AI in clinical decision-support systems for patients with CNS tumors. *Frontiers in Radiology, 4*, 1433457. https://doi.org/10.3389/fradi.2024.1433457

Puyuelo-Quintana, G., Cano-de-la-Cuerda, R., Plaza-Flores, A., Garces-Castellote, E., Sanz-Merodio, D., Goñi-Arana, A., Marín-Ojea, J., & García-Armada, E. (2020). A new lower limb portable exoskeleton for gait assistance in neurological patients: A proof of concept study. *Journal of Neuroengineering and Rehabilitation, 17*(1), 60. https://doi.org/10.1186/s12984-020-00690-6

Rajpurkar, P., Chen, E., Banerjee, O., & Topol, E. J. (2022). AI in health and medicine. *Nature Medicine, 28*(1), 31–38. https://doi.org/10.1038/s41591-021-01614-0

Randstad. (2025, March 5). *Understanding talent scarcity: AI and equity*. https://www.randstad.com/s3fs-media/rscom/public/2024-11/Randstad_understanding_talent_scarcity_AI_equity.pdf?VersionId=M6f0G9oUwNRvHjNvBUv4VRXkmmWURmyk

Reio, T. G. (2011). Age Bias. In S. Goldstein & J. A. Naglieri (Eds.), *Encyclopedia of child behavior and development* (pp. 59–60). Springer US. https://doi.org/10.1007/978-0-387-79061-9_327

Sardari, S., Sharifzadeh, S., Daneshkhah, A., Nakisa, B., Loke, S. W., Palade, V., & Duncan, M. J. (2023). Artificial intelligence for skeleton-based physical rehabilitation action evaluation: A systematic review. *Computers in Biology and Medicine, 158*, 106835. https://doi.org/10.1016/j.compbiomed.2023.106835

Schuster, N. A., Twisk, J. W. R., ter Riet, G., Heymans, M. W., & Rijnhart, J. J. M. (2021). Noncollapsibility and its role in quantifying confounding bias in logistic regression. *BMC Medical Research Methodology, 21*(1), 136. https://doi.org/10.1186/s12874-021-01316-8

Severson, K. A., Chahine, L. M., Smolensky, L. A., Dhuliawala, M., Frasier, M., Ng, K., Ghosh, S., & Hu, J. (2021). Discovery of Parkinson's disease states and disease progression modelling: A longitudinal data study using machine learning. *Lancet Digital Health, 3*(9), e555–e564. https://doi.org/10.1016/S2589-7500(21)00101-1

Shahbazi, N., Lin, Y., Asudeh, A., & Jagadish, H. V. (2023). Representation bias in data: A survey on identification and resolution techniques. *ACM Computing Surveys, 55*(13s), 293. https://doi.org/10.1145/3588433

Shin, J., Song, H., Lee, H., Jeong, S., & Park, J. (2024). *Ask LLMs directly, "What shapes your bias?": Measuring social bias in large language models*. https://doi.org/10.48550/arXiv.2406.04064

Singhi, S. K., & Liu, H. (2006). Feature subset selection bias for classification learning. In *Proceedings of the 23rd International Conference on Machine Learning*. https://doi.org/10.1145/1143844.1143951

Skinner-Dorkenoo, A. L., George, M., Wages, J. E., 3rd, Sánchez, S., & Perry, S. P. (2023). A systemic approach to the psychology of racial bias within individuals and society. *Nature Reviews Psychology, 2*, 1–15. https://doi.org/10.1038/s44159-023-00190-z

Stryker, C., & Kavlakoglu, E. (2024, August 9). *What is artificial intelligence (AI)?* https://www.ibm.com/think/topics/artificial-intelligence

Sumner, J., Lim, H. W., Chong, L. S., Bundele, A., Mukhopadhyay, A., & Kayambu, G. (2023). Artificial intelligence in physical rehabilitation: A systematic review. *Artificial Intelligence in Medicine, 146*, 102693. https://doi.org/10.1016/j.artmed.2023.102693

Sun, J., Dong, Q.-X., Wang, S.-W., Zheng, Y.-B., Liu, X.-X., Lu, T.-S., Yuan, K., Shi, J., Hu, B., Lu, L., & Han, Y. (2023). Artificial intelligence in psychiatry research, diagnosis, and therapy. *Asian Journal of Psychiatry, 87*, 103705. https://doi.org/10.1016/j.ajp.2023.103705

Sunny, M. S. H., Zarif, M. I. I., Rulik, I., Sanjuan, J., Rahman, M. H., Ahamed, S. I., Wang, I., Schultz, K., & Brahmi, B. (2021). Eye-gaze control of a wheelchair mounted 6DOF assistive robot for activities of daily living. *Journal of Neuroengineering and Rehabilitation, 18*(1), 173. https://doi.org/10.1186/s12984-021-00969-2

Suva, M., & Bhatia, G. (2024). Artificial intelligence in addiction: Challenges and opportunities. *Indian Journal of Psychological Medicine, 46*, 602. https://doi.org/10.1177/02537176241274148

Swarnakar, R., & Yadav, S. L. (2023). Artificial intelligence and machine learning in motor recovery: A rehabilitation medicine perspective. *World Journal of Clinical Cases, 11*(29), 7258–7260. https://doi.org/10.12998/wjcc.v11.i29.7258

Taehyun, H., & Sangyeon, K. (2023). Improving trust in AI with mitigating confirmation bias: Effects of explanation type and Debiasing strategy for decision-making with explainable AI. *International Journal of Human–Computer Interaction, 40*(24), 8562–8573. https://doi.org/10.1080/10447318

Tan, F. F.-Y., Gupta, C., Rajendran, D. P. D., Maes, P., & Nanayakkara, S. (2025). Assistive augmentation: Fundamentally transforming human ability. *Interactions, 32*(1), 22–27. https://doi.org/10.1145/3702656

Thacharodi, A., Singh, P., Meenatchi, R., Tawfeeq, A. Z. H., Kumar, R. R. S., Neha, V., Kavish, S., Maqbool, M., & Hassan, S. (2024). Revolutionizing healthcare and medicine: The impact of modern technologies for a healthier future-a comprehensive review. *Health Care Science, 3*(5), 329–349. https://doi.org/10.1002/hcs2.115

Tripathi, S., Gabriel, K., Dheer, S., Parajuli, A., Augustin, A. I., Elahi, A., Awan, O., & Dako, F. (2023). Understanding biases and disparities in radiology AI datasets: A review. *Journal of the American College of Radiology, 20*(9), 836–841. https://doi.org/10.1016/j.jacr.2023.06.015

Velagaleti, S. B. (2025). A study on feasibility and acceptability of an AI-powered VR/AR cognitive rehabilitation platform for patients with Alzheimer's disease and dementia. *Proceedings of the 5th International Conference on Data Science, Machine Learning and Applications*. Volume 2.

Voss, D. S. (2005). Aggregation. In K. Kempf-Leonard (Ed.), *Encyclopedia of social measurement* (pp. 33–42). Elsevier. https://doi.org/10.1016/B0-12-369398-5/00044-X

WHO. (2023, March 7). *Disability*. https://www.who.int/news-room/fact-sheets/detail/disability-and-health

Winchester, L. M., Harshfield, E. L., Shi, L., Badhwar, A., Khleifat, A. A., Clarke, N., Dehsarvi, A., Lengyel, I., Lourida, I., Madan, C. R., Marzi, S. J., Proitsi, P., Rajkumar, A. P., Rittman, T., Silajdžić, E., Tamburin, S., Ranson, J. M., & Llewellyn, D. J. (2023). Artificial intelligence for biomarker discovery in Alzheimer's disease and dementia. *Alzheimer's & Dementia, 19*(12), 5860–5871. https://doi.org/10.1002/alz.13390

Wong, E., Bermudez-Cañete, A., Campbell, M. J., & Rhew, D. C. (2025). Bridging the digital divide: A practical roadmap for deploying medical artificial intelligence Technologies in low-Resource Settings. *Population Health Management, 28*(2), 105–114. https://doi.org/10.1089/pop.2024.0222

Wu, T. (2025, June 24). A 'white collar blood bath' doesn't have to be our fate. *The New York Times*. https://www.nytimes.com/2025/06/24/opinion/ai-job-loss-white-collar.html

Yang, Y., Yuan, Y., Zhang, G., Wang, H., Chen, Y. C., Liu, Y., Tarolli, C. G., Crepeau, D., Bukartyk, J., Junna, M. R., Videnovic, A., Ellis, T. D., Lipford, M. C., Dorsey, R., & Katabi, D. (2022). Artificial intelligence-enabled detection and assessment of Parkinson's disease using nocturnal breathing signals. *Nature Medicine, 28*(10), 2207–2215. https://doi.org/10.1038/s41591-022-01932-x

Chapter 7
AI in Supporting LGBTQIA+ Populations

Dget L. Downey and David A. Jenkins

1 Introduction

Artificial intelligence (AI) has transformed many aspects of daily life. As AI technologies increasingly intersect with social work and human services, it is vital to ensure these systems are designed to address the unique needs of marginalized communities, including lesbian, gay, bisexual, transgender, queer/questioning, intersex, and asexual (LGBTQIA+) populations. Despite increased recognition of health and mental healthcare disparities for queer and transgender, gender non-conforming (TGNC) individuals, AI solutions often reflect the same biases that appear in the larger societal context.

Further, this chapter explores how AI can be designed and deployed to effectively support LGBTQIA+ communities by examining the ethical, cultural, and technical considerations that arise when integrating AI into social work practice, emphasizing the need to center queer and trans-lived experiences in both the development and implementation of AI tools. This chapter gives special attention to privacy, cultural sensitivity, and bias mitigation, particularly in the context of increasing surveillance and algorithmic discrimination.

AI can promote and advance equity and inclusion when approached critically and collaboratively (Nixon et al., 2024; Roshanaci et al., 2023). This chapter highlights the tensions and opportunities that AI introduces for LGBTQIA+ social work, drawing from interdisciplinary research in psychology, computer science, queer and gender theory, and public health. By demonstrating and exploring current uses, ethical concerns, and future directions of AI, this chapter offers a roadmap for

D. L. Downey (✉)
Sliver School of Social Work, New York University, New York, NY, USA
e-mail: dld382@nyu.edu

D. A. Jenkins
The Ohio State University, Ohio State University, Columbus, OH, USA
e-mail: jenkins.1443@osu.edu

R. An, M. A. Lindsey (eds.), *Artificial Intelligence in Social Work*,
https://doi.org/10.1007/978-3-032-18443-6_7

technologists, researchers, and practitioners seeking to build AI that affirms and protects LGBTQIA+ lives.

1.1 The Problem of Algorithmic Bias Against LGBTQIA+ Communities

Bias in AI is not an accident; it is a product of data infrastructures, technical design choices, and institutional power dynamics (Arora et al., 2023; Scatiggio, 2022). Oyeniran et al. (2022) categorized several types of bias relevant to LGBTQIA+ communities, including label bias, measurement bias, and historical bias, each of which can distort how LGBTQIA+ people are identified, evaluated, and served by algorithms. For example, predictive models in mental health or social service platforms may misinterpret sexual or gender identity markers as anomalies or risk factors (e.g., suicide or mental illness risk), leading to harmful misclassification or denial of care.

Kuhlman et al. (2020) emphasized that such harms are particularly severe when AI systems are used in public health and social welfare contexts. In these spaces, algorithmic decisions are often treated as objective, even when they encode existing disparities. Their paper advocated for "no computation without representation"—a principle that demands LGBTQIA+ inclusion not only as data subjects but as co-developers of systems that affect their lives.

This problem is compounded by the fact that AI systems frequently rely on data that erases or misrepresents LGBTQIA+ identities (Katyal & Jung, 2021). Myles et al. (2023a) mapped the "algorithmic imaginary" imposed by platform companies, where queer content is often flagged as inappropriate. In their study of platform moderation and surveillance, they show how social media platforms use opaque algorithms that sort LGBTQIA+ lives into categories that serve advertising and control—not safety or care.

1.1.1 From Queering Algorithmic Imaginaries to Ethical Re-Design

To disrupt this trend, researchers and advocates argue for a queering of algorithmic imaginaries (Chartrand & Duguay, 2025). Myles et al. (2023b) suggested that LGBTQIA+ people must not only be consulted but also empowered to reimagine what AI systems can do—and what they should be prevented from doing. This includes questioning outcomes and assumptions that shape what gets measured, modeled, and acted upon.

A key insight from this work is that ethical AI cannot be limited to technical fairness metrics. As Sloane (2019) argued, the current AI ethics discourse often functions as a "smokescreen" for real accountability. Tech companies may adopt fairness toolkits or publish diversity statements without addressing the deeper political and economic structures that shape inequality. Sloane called for an ethics agenda that centers power analysis, participatory design, and structural change.

This view aligns closely with social work ethics, as it is also grounded in the principles of dignity, equity, and self-determination. They ask: Does this system reinforce marginalization? Does it increase autonomy for those who have historically been denied it? Who decides how this technology is used, and to what end?

1.1.2 Structural Inequality, Representation, and Social Context

Bias in AI systems may seem like a technical flaw, but it reflects longstanding social hierarchies (Zajko, 2022). As Kuhlman et al. (2020) noted, machine learning models are shaped by the historical exclusion of marginalized voices from data science and public policy. Underrepresentation in datasets, lack of LGBTQIA+ experts and community members in development teams, and the prioritization of efficiency over equity all contribute to systems that fail LGBTQIA+ users.

This structural perspective is vital for computational social science, AI research, and social work practice. Rather than framing inclusion as a data-labeling task or a means to an end, scholars must interrogate how identities intersect within the architecture of AI. Myles et al. (2023a) emphasized the importance of queering algorithmic systems not just at the levels of application and intervention but at the level of epistemology.

For example, content moderation algorithms suppress LGBTQIA+ speech under the guise of "safety" (Sulmicelli, 2023). Studies show that these tools reproduce societal stigma by treating LGBTQIA+ identity as risky, offensive, or adult-only. This is not just a misclassification issue—it is a form of digital violence that echoes long histories of surveillance and silencing.

1.1.3 Toward Ethical, Community-Governed AI Systems

To build AI systems that serve LGBTQIA+ communities equitably, scholars and practitioners must shift from reactive fairness fixes to proactive justice-oriented design. That means centering the needs, expertise, and leadership of LGBTQIA+ people in every stage of system development. Participatory and community-driven approaches—like those advocated by Queer in AI and other grassroots tech justice groups—offer models for this work.

Social work provides a robust foundation for guiding these efforts. Its ethical frameworks prioritize the protection of vulnerable groups, the right to self-determination, and a holistic understanding of human experience. In an AI context, this translates to tools that are: 1) context-aware (i.e., designed with an understanding of the structural forces affecting users), 2) transparent and accountable (i.e., with visible mechanisms for redress and oversight), 3) dynamic (able to evolve as understandings of identity and oppression shift over time), and 4) governed via participatory methods to encourage and reorient control to those most impacted.

While technological fixes can address some biases, lasting change will require institutional and epistemic transformation. That includes rethinking funding priorities, revising education and hiring practices in STEM fields, and challenging dominant narratives that treat marginalized communities as "edge cases" rather than as those to be centered.

1.1.4 Ethics as Praxis, Not Performance

Promoting ethical and inclusive AI for LGBTQIA+ communities requires reimagining and redirecting the purpose, priorities, and power dynamics of technology. Current approaches to AI ethics often fall short because they frame harm as a technical issue rather than a reflection of embedded social injustice. Research shows that addressing bias requires more than audits or datasets; it demands new forms of accountability, collective care, and redistribution (Vecchione et al., 2021).

By grounding ethical AI work in the values of social work and the insights of computational social science, we can move from individual fairness metrics to collective liberation frameworks. LGBTQIA+ communities deserve agency, safety, justice, and, of course, visibility in AI.

2 Meeting and Protecting LGBTQIA+ Needs Using AI

2.1 Health and Mental Health Needs

To effectively support LGBTQIA+ communities, AI systems must be responsive to the complex needs of those they aim to serve. These include addressing mental health disparities, combating violence and hate speech, enhancing educational inclusion, and building safer online and offline spaces for community and care. AI cannot be a "one-size-fits-all" solution. As studies like Tawiah and Monestime (2024) and Bragazzi et al. (2023) emphasized, technology must be attuned to intersecting identities and shaped by community participation at every step, from data collection to design to deployment.

LGBTQIA+ individuals experience disproportionately high rates of depression, anxiety, suicidal ideation, and substance use, compounded by systemic discrimination, stigma, and social exclusion (Rojas et al., 2019; Williams et al., 2021). These disparities are particularly potent for TGNC individuals (Price-Feeney et al., 2020), youth (Wilson & Cariola, 2020), and LGBTQIA+ people of color (Garcia-Perez, 2020; Sutter & Perrin, 2016). Although social work interventions can often address these concerns, structural barriers such as cost, stigma, lack of affirming providers, and language access continue to impede care (Romanelli & Hudson, 2017).

AI technologies offer new opportunities to bridge these gaps. AI-driven chatbots, virtual therapists, and symptom-monitoring systems can expand access to support, especially for people who may not have access to or thrive in traditional mental health service models. Recent research by Ma et al. (2024) found that large language model (LLM)-based chatbots, when designed and attuned to the particular needs of the LGBTQIA+ community, can provide a safe and accessible space for LGBTQIA+ users to discuss mental health concerns. Notably, LGBTQIA+ participants in the study reported appreciating the non-judgmental nature of chatbots and the ability to access support without fear of interpersonal discrimination.

However, these tools also come with risks. Some users noted that LLMs often defaulted to cisnormative or heteronormative assumptions, especially when responding to questions about gender identity or relationships (Ma et al., 2024). This aligns with broader concerns in the literature about algorithmic bias and lack of training data that reflect LGBTQIA+ lived experiences (D'Alfonso, 2020). AI systems trained on non-diverse data can misgender users, fail to recognize culturally specific expressions of distress, or offer inappropriate advice rooted in bias.

One of the most pressing needs identified in recent literature is the development of culturally tailored and linguistically accessible AI tools (Xia et al., 2024). Language is a crucial barrier for many LGBTQIA+ individuals, especially for those who speak languages other than English and for finding services that use up-to-date and appropriate language when referring to the LGBTQIA+ community. Ma et al. (2024) and Fowler et al. (2023) highlighted growing evidence that AI chatbots are most effective when multilingual and culturally adaptive. They argued that translation alone is insufficient and that AI systems must understand and respond to the cultural contexts in which mental health and identity are expressed.

Moreover, the participatory design of these tools is critical. Joyce et al. (2023) proposed a consensus process for developing LGBTQIA+-affirming AI tools, emphasizing the importance of involving diverse stakeholders, including community members, clinicians, and technology developers, in shaping tool functionality and ethical guidelines. Similarly, Joyce et al. (2024) described a toolkit for guiding ethical data practices and community-informed standards for digital mental health interventions.

These frameworks support integrating values-based and person-centered design into AI systems. As digital mental health tools become more prevalent, it is crucial that they not only be accessible but also affirm users' identities and lived experiences.

In sum, AI technologies hold promise for increasing access to mental health care among LGBTQIA+ populations through chatbots and digital interventions. However, their effectiveness depends on attention to cultural responsiveness, linguistic inclusivity, participatory development, and bias mitigation. As social work integrates these tools, practitioners and researchers must ensure that AI-driven care remains affirming, ethical, and grounded in the realities of those it serves.

2.2 Hate Speech and Threat Detection

Machine learning models are being used to detect hate speech, flag threats, and moderate harmful content across social media and online platforms. However, LGBTQIA+ users have long experienced censorship and misclassification by these systems. Terms like “trans,” “queer,” or “nonbinary” have been flagged as inappropriate content by AI models, while overt hate speech often evades detection. This phenomenon reflects a broader issue of algorithmic bias rooted in training data and sociocultural blind spots.

Research by Chan et al. (2024) demonstrated that hate speech detection models perform best in English and significantly worse across non-English languages—particularly when detecting LGBTQIA+-targeted slurs and harassment. This gap exposes many global LGBTQIA+ communities to unmoderated harm. Similarly, Wong (2024) highlighted that sociocultural context profoundly shapes the expression and detection of hate speech and must be integrated into monitoring systems. Models built on Western conceptions of violence often fail to recognize culturally coded harm in multilingual settings (Ricaurte, 2022).

To address these shortcomings, studies like Reyero Lobo (2022) have proposed knowledge-grounded approaches that incorporate a context-specific understanding of LGBTQIA+ identities and local languages, and have argued that these models perform better at detecting nuanced, culturally embedded threats but require meaningful collaboration with affected communities. Macias et al. (2023) added that preprocessing choices in machine learning pipelines can erase identity markers or misinterpret language, leading to inaccurate or inequitable moderation outcomes.

Ethical design principles must, therefore, guide hate speech detection. Rather than outsourcing safety to black-box machine learning models, both developers and social workers should involve LGBTQIA+ individuals in shaping moderation norms, defining harm, and co-creating hate speech detection logic. Participatory design not only improves accuracy but also builds trust and accountability in the system.

2.3 Predictive Analysis for Safety Planning

Beyond content moderation, AI tools are also being explored for predictive analyses of physical violence. By aggregating public data sources, AI can identify risk hotspots, enabling social workers and community organizers to develop interventions that accurately assess and address the needs of the LGBTQIA+ community. For example, real-time data analytics can reveal spikes in hate-based incidents or geographic patterns of harassment, which can then inform mental health resources, mutual aid hubs, or public awareness campaigns.

However, predictive tools carry the risk of over-policing. AI for safety planning can be most effective when it balances visibility with privacy and is grounded in the self-determined safety strategies of LGBTQIA+ communities. Community-led data collection is one pathway toward ethical and impactful implementation.

2.4 Support Tools for Survivors

AI is also being applied in survivor support platforms, such as mobile apps and chatbots that offer crisis counseling, legal aid, and safety planning (Aldkheel, 2024; Saglam et al., 2024). These tools can enhance access to support for LGBTQIA+ individuals who may hold medical and mental health mistrust due to prior discrimination or fear of being outed. However, the effectiveness of such tools depends on their cultural responsiveness, trauma-informed design, and privacy protections. Survivors from different racial, linguistic, and gender identities may express distress in unique ways that generalized AI systems are ill-equipped to interpret. The work of Dacon et al. (2022) shows that large language models, when appropriately fine-tuned, can effectively engage with diverse expressions of emotion and support, especially when trained on representative data and robust community input.

2.5 Advocacy and Community Building

LGBTQIA+ communities have long relied on digital spaces for identity exploration, social connection, mutual aid, and political mobilization. As AI becomes more integrated into these platforms through content moderation, trend surfacing, and amplification or suppression of voices, it is crucial to ask who these tools serve and whom they silence. AI offers opportunities to strengthen digital advocacy and community building, but it also presents risks of erasure, bias, and harm when designed without LGBTQIA+ participation.

2.6 Strengthening Digital Spaces

Community safety and visibility on online platforms increasingly depend on AI-based moderation systems. Monea (2021) examined how platform algorithms censor LGBTQIA+ expression under the guise of content moderation, a practice described as "digital closet-keeping." Similarly, Simpson and Semaan (2021) found that TikTok's For You Page algorithm created contradictory experiences for LGBTQIA+ users—amplifying preferred types of queer visibility while burying those viewed as "non-normative" or "political."

These findings highlight the need for community-centered moderation frameworks that distinguish between hate speech and LGBTQIA+ self-expression. AI moderation systems can do so by being trained on inclusive data and evaluated for unintended discriminatory effects. Moreover, transparency about moderation logic and avenues for contesting removals can help reclaim digital space for LGBTQIA+ users.

2.7 *Supporting LGBTQIA+ Advocacy Through AI-Driven Analysis*

AI-powered social media analysis tools are increasingly used to identify public sentiment, track policy conversations, and map discourse around LGBTQIA+ rights. These tools can help organizers understand when and where LGBTQIA+ issues are gaining or losing visibility and support and can inform mobilization.

Bragazzi et al. (2023) emphasized that AI can also support mental health advocacy by monitoring discourse related to LGBTQIA+ well-being, including moments of collective trauma (e.g., anti-LGBTQIA+ legislation or mass violence) or celebration (e.g., Pride events). Real-time AI analytics enable staying attuned to emotional trends within queer communities and responding with tailored care. However, the beneficial impact of AI use in advocacy can be hindered by surveillance logic. Systems that monitor social media sentiment should prioritize privacy, consent, and community ownership, as opposed to policing queer and trans joy, by ensuring that data insights are used to support—not control—marginalized groups.

2.8 *Storytelling and Digital Belonging*

Beyond moderation and analytics, AI can also elevate LGBTQIA+ narratives through creative applications, such as AI-generated storytelling and digital avatars. Pillis et al. (2024) explored how virtual AI-generated characters can support LGBTQIA+ youth in exploring identity in affirming, low-risk environments. These digital companions offer emotional validation and identity mirroring that many queer individuals lack in their daily lives.

Queer in AI (2023) provides a powerful example of how community-led participatory design can ensure that AI tools reflect the values, voices, and ethics of the communities they intend to serve. Their work demonstrates how intersectional, grassroots collaboration can lead to more effective, ethical, and liberatory AI tools.

2.9 *Challenges and Considerations*

While AI can support LGBTQIA+ advocacy and community resilience, its benefits are contingent on how, by whom, and for whom it is built. Systems must be designed with attention to the intersectional realities of LGBTQIA+ users, the need for community feedback loops and responsive governance, and the potential for platform bias, data misuse, and algorithmic silencing. AI's role in LGBTQIA+ advocacy is not neutral. It can act as a conduit for collective empowerment or as a mechanism for perpetuating marginalization. To ensure the former, queer and trans people must not only be consulted as users but also empowered as co-creators and stewards of the tools shaping their digital futures.

2.10 *Education and Awareness*

From curriculum design to student safety policies, students (especially TGNC youth) are disproportionately affected by exclusion, erasure, and discrimination in learning environments. As artificial intelligence becomes increasingly embedded in classrooms, learning platforms, and administrative systems, it presents both opportunities and dangers for LGBTQIA+ students and educators.

2.11 *Promoting Inclusion Through AI-Enabled Platforms*

AI-driven learning systems are frequently used to personalize education by tailoring content to individual student needs, potentially closing achievement gaps by providing equitable educational opportunities to historically marginalized students (Roshanaei et al., 2023). However, personalization must extend beyond learning style or ability to include cultural identity and gender diversity.

AI systems that recognize and affirm students' names and pronouns and that incorporate diverse examples in their content can help foster inclusion and reduce dropout rates among LGBTQIA+ learners. Yet few platforms are designed with these considerations in mind. As Pawar and Khose (2024) argued, most AI systems are not built with an intersectional lens, which limits their capacity to serve students equitably.

Wong (2024) similarly emphasized the role of AI in STEM education, where LGBTQIA+ students (particularly TGNC youth) face ongoing exclusion. They advocate for inclusive AI tools that normalize queer participation in gatekept fields, as well as curricular tools that actively counteract cisnormative biases in educational content.

2.12 *The Risks of Bias and Reinforcement of Inequity*

While AI holds promise, it can also reinforce existing biases in education. Barnes and Hutson (2024) warned that educational AI systems trained on biased or incomplete data may perpetuate gendered, racialized, or heteronormative assumptions—from how student performance is assessed to what types of content are deemed appropriate or "neutral." Without careful auditing, these systems risk codifying discriminatory norms under a veneer of technological neutrality.

Viberg et al. (2024) explored how AI-powered educational decision-support systems can embed systemic inequities when developers fail to consider how marginalized groups are represented in their models. They called for a socio-technical approach that includes ethical frameworks, stakeholder input, and mechanisms of institutional accountability to mitigate harm.

These findings are especially urgent in the U.S. context, where LGBTQIA+ (largely TGNC) students are increasingly under attack through state-level legislation that limits access to bathrooms, pronoun usage, healthcare, and inclusive curricula. In this climate, AI systems used in schools must be proactively inclusive to avoid becoming passive tools of marginalization.

2.13 *Ethical Design for Inclusive Education Summary*

To support LGBTQIA+ inclusion meaningfully, educational AI must be designed with 1) community-led development processes, 2) transparency, 3) feedback mechanisms that allow users to report bias or harm and suggest improvements, and 4) dynamic content generation that adapts to evolving understandings of gender, identity, and equity.

As multiple studies in this review point out, diversity and ethics cannot be retroactive, additive "solutions." They must be embedded in the foundation of AI development in education. Equity-oriented innovation must challenge normative assumptions and reimagine education as a space where all students can thrive.

3 Promoting Ethical and Inclusive AI Usage for the LGBTQIA+ Community

AI systems have occasionally been characterized as less biased than human biases, but in practice, they inherit and amplify the values embedded in their design, data, and deployment (Ntoutsi et al., 2020). For LGBTQIA+ communities, AI's promise of inclusion is too often eclipsed by systems that reproduce structural inequalities and social harm. This section draws on recent work in computational social science, LGBTQIA+ studies, and social work ethics to explore how AI systems replicate bias and how social work-centered ethical frameworks can guide more just and equitable AI development and use.

3.1 *Privacy Concerns for LGBTQIA+ Individuals in AI Systems*

Artificial intelligence systems depend on vast amounts of data about identities, behaviors, geographies, and interactions. For LGBTQIA+ individuals whose visibility in datasets has often been fraught with risk, this creates both opportunities and obstacles. As AI becomes more integrated into healthcare, social work, education, and public systems, it is critical to examine how data collection, storage, and usage practices can expose LGBTQIA+ people to surveillance, erasure, or unintended harm.

This section explores the ethical implications of AI data practices through the lens of privacy, confidentiality, and client dignity, drawing on social work values and critical data ethics. This section highlights the importance of community-informed data governance, the role of anonymization and data minimization, and the need to move beyond compliance toward transformative data justice.

3.1.1 Surveillance, Misuse, and the Legacy of Data Harm

Historically, LGBTQIA+ individuals have been subject to state, medical, and social surveillance, ranging from pathologizing diagnoses and anti-LGBTQIA+ laws to police monitoring, outing, and algorithmic censorship (Daum, 2019). In the digital age, these forms of surveillance are embedded in datasets, platform analytics, and biometric tools. AI systems trained on such data may not only reflect these harms but amplify them at scale.

Schneider (2022) found that many social work professionals intentionally omit LGBTQIA+ data from records to protect clients from exposure, especially in contexts where disclosure might lead to discrimination, forced outings, or violence. While this may conflict with some data completeness standards in tech development, it aligns with the social work ethic of protecting client autonomy and dignity. This tension reveals the need for AI development guided not just by data efficiency but by relational and harm-reduction ethics.

Hermansyah et al. (2023) further warned that current AI infrastructures are often ill-equipped to ensure data protection for vulnerable communities. They emphasized that ethics cannot be retrofitted. Privacy, especially for LGBTQIA+ people, must be a foundational design principle. Their work calls for a shift from "privacy by default" toward privacy by community co-design, where affected populations shape what data is collected and how it's used.

3.1.2 Anonymization and the Limits of De-Identification

Anonymization is often presented as a solution to data risk, but research shows that de-identified data can still be re-identified, especially when multiple datasets are combined (El Emam et al., 2011). This poses unique risks for LGBTQIA+ individuals who may be the only "out" person in a given ZIP code, demographic group, or service system. Data that seems anonymous on the surface may still reveal queer identity markers.

The Delphi protocol proposed by Joyce et al. (2024) provided a promising approach to this challenge. Their study outlined a participatory tool for assessing AI readiness in LGBTQIA+ mental health contexts, emphasizing the need for community-defined thresholds for data sensitivity. Instead of applying generalized privacy standards, developers should consult with LGBTQIA+ users on what types of information they feel are invasive, harmful, or safe to share.

This is especially important when collecting sexual and gender identity data, which can be highly context-dependent. Joyce et al. noted that trust, choice, and transparency are essential to ethical data collection. LGBTQIA+ individuals must be informed not just about what is collected but why, how long it will be stored, and how it will be used. Without this, even well-intentioned AI tools may reinforce feelings of vulnerability and systemic mistrust.

3.1.3 Social Work Values and the Ethics of Data Stewardship

Some principles of social work (confidentiality, dignity, harm reduction, and empowerment) offer a compelling framework for thinking about ethical AI. As Schneider (2022) argued, these values compel practitioners to evaluate the risks and benefits of data collection critically. When applied to AI, they support the idea that not all data should be collected, nor is it all ethically usable, especially when its use could harm the communities it aims to help.

Radanliev et al. (2024) emphasized this point in their review of ethical AI deployment. They argued that technical safeguards alone are insufficient without an interdisciplinary ethical framework that includes law, social science, and lived experience. Their model called for continuous ethical auditing, scenario testing for harm, and incorporating mechanisms for redress if data is misused. These collaborative processes are essential to move beyond abstract data ethics and into the realm of collective care and accountability.

3.1.4 Building Community-Centered Privacy in AI Systems

To protect LGBTQIA+ users in AI systems, it is crucial to consider informed consent practices beyond legal compliance by supporting meaningful understanding and minimizing the sharing of sensitive data. The field of computational social science can be enhanced by transparency about data flows, storage, and sharing practices. It can do so by applying social work principles to incorporate regulatory models that enable LGBTQIA+ users to influence how data about them is used.

Ethical data practices are not just technical challenges; they are cultural and political commitments. This means working against extractive data logics that treat LGBTQIA+ people as case studies, affirming their rights to digital self-determination and refusal despite the cost to power analyses and sample size. It includes conducting data collection methods that oversample to compensate for these problematic yet essential challenges.

In the age of AI, protecting privacy is not just about safeguarding personal data. It's about honoring identity, dignity, and agency, particularly for communities that have been historically surveilled, erased, or harmed by data systems. LGBTQIA+ individuals deserve more than anonymity; they deserve to be active participants in shaping how technology sees and understands them.

4 Access and Equity in LGBTQIA+ AI Systems

AI is often imagined as a tool of efficiency, but without intentional design, it frequently reproduces the inequities of the systems from which it draws data (Costanza-Chock, 2018). For underrepresented LGBTQIA+ populations, particularly queer and trans people of color (QTPOC), low-income individuals, and those at the intersection of other multiple forms of marginalization, AI systems may be inaccessible, exclusionary, and harmful.

This section draws on critical and intersectional scholarship to examine the barriers to access to AI technologies for marginalized LGBTQIA+ communities, highlighting the technical and sociopolitical challenges to inclusion. Rather than treating access as merely a matter of digital infrastructure or device availability, this section calls for equity through structural design, representational justice, and community voice.

4.1 Exclusion by Design: The Roots of Inaccessibility

Park and Humphry (2019) introduced the concept of "exclusion by design," showing how digital systems often reinforced structural inequities through decisions that seem technical but are deeply political. In their study of smart city technologies and automation, they highlighted how design choices (e.g., language models, user accessibility, and default identity fields) systematically exclude those whose lives don't align with dominant assumptions about gender, race, ethnicity, class, or ability.

For QTPOC or those with limited digital access, AI tools designed without them are alienating. These tools may make inaccurate assumptions about names or pronouns or fail to function on low-bandwidth devices commonly used in lower-income communities. This results in a double exclusion: from the benefits of the technology itself and from the data it uses to improve and adapt.

4.2 *The Matrix of Power in AI Fairness Research*

Ovalle et al. (2023) critiqued the field of AI fairness for conflating intersectionality with demographic diversity rather than engaging with the matrix of power that shapes people's lived experiences. Their review of 30 fairness-focused papers found that most AI research treats QTPOC individuals as edge cases, if at all.

This superficial treatment of identity often leads to inadequate, irrelevant, or harmful fairness interventions. For example, an AI tool might claim racial equity without acknowledging the compounded effects of being both Black and queer. To address this, the authors proposed an intersectional fairness framework that centers relational, structural, and historical dimensions of oppression (Ovalle et al., 2023).

4.3 *Queering the Ethics of AI*

Fosch-Villaronga and Malgieri (2023) took this critique further by arguing that AI ethics must be "queered." That is, instead of attempting to plug LGBTQIA+ concerns into existing frameworks, they suggested radically rethinking how AI defines normalcy, legitimacy, and value. Their work critiqued the normative logics of AI development, which presume fixed, binary categories of gender, sexuality, and ability.

Instead, they advocated for a fluid, inclusive ethics framework that embraces multiplicity. This means giving marginalized users power over the design, purpose, and evaluation of AI systems. Such an approach would help dismantle the structures that make AI inaccessible to QTPOC and other multiply-marginalized groups.

4.4 *Intersectional AI as Essential Infrastructure*

Ciston (2019) echoed this call for radical transformation and proposed that intersectionality is not an add-on to AI development but rather an essential infrastructure. Intersectional design, Ciston argued, can guide every step of the development pipeline, from research framing to interface aesthetics, naming, and addressing power rather than abstracting it away through technical language.

Importantly, Ciston identified that access is also about linguistic accessibility, cultural resonance, safety, and autonomy. A chatbot may be technically available to a transgender Latine teenager. Still, if the chatbot doesn't speak their language, recognize their pronouns, or offer guidance grounded in their lived reality, it's not truly accessible. Intersectional AI pushes us to ask, “Accessible for whom, and at what cost?”

4.5 *Educational Gatekeeping and Ethical Literacy*

McDonald and Pan (2020) offered an important complement to these arguments in their study of graduate students learning about AI ethics. They found that students often failed to grasp the structural implications of AI bias, defaulting to individualized, decontextualized interpretations of fairness. Thus, if AI developers are not trained to understand systemic inequity, they are unlikely to design tools that serve those at the margins.

This work suggested that ethical AI development must include training on intersectionality, lived experience, and anti-oppressive design, as well as the inclusion of LGBTQIA+ individuals in the development process. This aligns with a growing push in both social work and AI fields to decenter dominant narratives and treat ethical awareness as a collective, community-engaged practice (Raman, 2024).

4.6 *Toward Equitable Access: Strategies for Change*

AI development must move beyond inclusion to redistribution and co-creation. This can include funding and supporting grassroots AI projects led by LGBTQIA+ people from marginalized backgrounds; redesigning data collection and system training pipelines to reflect lived experiences and avoid the flattening of intersectional identities; creating open-source, low-resource AI tools that are mobile-accessible, multilingual, and culturally grounded; and embedding participatory governance structures that allow LGBTQIA+ users to shape how AI tools are built, deployed, and maintained.

This also means confronting institutional barriers. As McDonald and Pan (2020) showed, the failure to educate developers in structural thinking is a systemic shortcoming. Universities, funders, and tech companies must take responsibility for ensuring that equity is critical, not optional, in AI development.

Access to AI tools is about whether the systems one encounters see, hear, and serve them. For many queer and trans people of color, current AI tools are built on assumptions that exclude, flatten, or pathologize their identities. If we are serious about equity, we must build AI that is not only technically inclusive but structurally accountable. By integrating education on intersectional design frameworks, community-led development, and anti-oppressive ethics into AI infrastructures, we can move toward tools that redistribute power, reflect lived realities, and serve as resources for justice.

5 Future Directions for AI in LGBTQIA+ Social Work

As AI technologies continue to evolve, so too must the frameworks we use to guide their development, deployment, and evaluation. For LGBTQIA+ populations, especially queer and trans people of color, the future of AI in social work is not merely a matter of technical optimization but one of ethical innovation, shared control, and structural transformation.

This section outlines promising directions for AI in LGBTQIA+ social work, emphasizing the need for community-driven evaluation metrics, participatory design, and interdisciplinary collaborations. These strategies ask how LGBTQIA+ people can shape the future of AI.

5.1 Expanding the Role of AI in Social Work Practice

AI offers significant potential to support LGBTQIA+ individuals across domains such as mental healthcare, housing navigation, crisis response, and legal support. Dey (2023) emphasized that AI can enhance service delivery by enabling real-time, need-based responses, for instance, through generative tools that produce personalized referrals or guidance. These tools, deployed with a nuanced understanding of identity, social context, and systemic inequality, can optimize and enhance culturally and individually tailored support.

Lin et al. (2024) further noted that LGBTQIA+ organizations are often excluded from the development of civic tech systems despite their critical role in frontline advocacy and community care. This exclusion reproduces dynamics of marginalization by centralizing technological expertise in academic and practice spaces. Future applications of AI in social work would benefit from a design that centers collaboration with grassroots organizations, ensuring that the technologies developed accurately reflect community needs and values.

5.2 Community-Driven Evaluation Metrics

A critical gap in current AI development is the absence of community-defined success criteria. Too often, AI tools are evaluated using generalized metrics like accuracy, speed, or efficiency—standards that may overlook whether tools actually promote safety, dignity, or empowerment for LGBTQIA+ users.

As argued in this chapter, participatory methods must bring together diverse stakeholders—including LGBTQIA+ individuals, clinicians, developers, and ethicists—to define what success in AI for mental health looks like, thereby enabling more effective and supportive tools. Rather than imposing external standards, this approach grounds evaluation in lived experience and prioritizes collective care over predictive performance.

Similarly, Wan et al. (2023) advocated for community-driven AI development to build trust, improve adoption, and develop tools that work for the people they aim to serve. This work underscored the importance of reparative data practices, in which communities hold power to shape system goals, test outcomes, and govern future iterations.

5.3 Participatory Design as Ongoing Practice

Incorporating community voices into AI development is an ongoing, embedded practice. Lin et al. (2024) showed how community organizations working with LGBTQIA+ youth, people of color, and survivors of violence have developed informal but powerful forms of technological critique and innovation. Formal research and development pipelines rarely capture these insights, but they offer essential feedback for ethical, responsive AI systems.

Future AI development should support participatory research infrastructures, including co-designed workshops for system ideation and testing, feedback loops built into platform interfaces, compensation for community labor in evaluating and improving tools, and public dashboards or zines that make system logic transparent and contestable. These strategies help demystify AI and redistribute power over the systems that increasingly shape people's lives.

5.4 Interdisciplinary Collaborations for Equity and Innovation

No single field can build ethical, effective AI for LGBTQIA+ communities. The future of this work lies in collaborative, interdisciplinary teams that bring together technologists, social workers, technology designers, and, most importantly, community members with lived experience.

As Dey (2023) pointed out, AI developers often lack training in trauma-informed care, intersectionality, and systems of oppression. Similarly, social work practitioners may not be equipped to assess or critically evaluate emerging technologies. Bridging this gap requires mutual education, cross-sector dialogue, and institutional support for truly collaborative knowledge production.

McDonald and Pan (2020) argued that ethical AI development is a pedagogical and political process. Future professionals must be trained to view AI as a social system, engage in reflexive practice, and center marginalized voices at every stage of design. Universities, nonprofits, and tech companies should invest in cross-disciplinary curricula that unite data science, critical theory, and social justice, fund collaborative projects between community organizations and research labs, and support LGBTQIA+ technologists, researchers, and community leaders.

5.5 *Reimagining Success: From Risk Reduction to Liberation*

The most transformative future for AI in LGBTQIA+ social work lies not in risk mitigation alone but in the possibility of liberation. What if AI systems were designed not only to reduce harm but also to amplify queer and trans joy, resilience, and community power?

Centering LGBTQIA+ voices in AI means shifting from reactive (e.g., flagging hate speech) to proactive systems that tell our stories, support collective memory, and help us imagine alternative futures. It means moving from minimizing disparity to maximizing flourishing. And it means defining success by how well AI systems challenge dominant norms.

6 Summary and Calls to Action

Artificial intelligence holds enormous potential to advance equity in social work practice, especially for LGBTQIA+ communities who continue to face systemic barriers to safety, health, education, and visibility. But without intention and ethical design, AI tools risk reinforcing the very harms they hope to solve.

This chapter has outlined both the risks and the possibilities of AI integration, emphasizing the need for community-centered, participatory, and justice-driven approaches. From digital mental health tools to hate speech detection systems, inclusive educational platforms to storytelling technologies, we have shown how AI can either exclude or empower LGBTQIA+ individuals depending on whose voices are included, what values are prioritized, and who holds decision-making power.

This chapter offers three final calls to action:

- *For Technologists, Policymakers, and Researchers*: Prioritizing equity and inclusion at every stage of AI design, deployment, and evaluation can elevate the technology itself and those it serves. LGBTQIA+ communities—especially queer and trans people of color—must not be treated as afterthoughts, edge cases, or data points. Their participation, knowledge, and leadership are essential to creating ethical, inclusive technologies.
- *For the Social Work Profession*: Embrace AI as a tool for advancing social justice while remaining vigilant about its risks. Social workers have a critical role to play in shaping how AI is used to serve vulnerable communities. This means advocating for ethical frameworks, participating in interdisciplinary development, and continuing to prioritize client dignity, privacy, and autonomy.
- *For Social Work Education*: Integrate AI literacy and critical technology studies into social work curricula. As AI becomes more integrated into mental health, housing, child welfare, and other domains, social workers must be prepared to engage with emerging technologies. This includes understanding algorithmic bias, data justice, and participatory design—skills essential for the twenty-first-century practice.

Ethical AI for LGBTQIA+ communities is not only possible—it is necessary. Building it requires deep collaboration across disciplines and unwavering commitment to equity. By grounding our technologies in LGBTQIA+, anti-oppressive, and community-led ethics, we can ensure AI serves innovation and liberation.

Competing Interests The authors have no conflicts of interest to declare that are relevant to the content of this chapter.

References

Aldkheel, A. (2024). *Design and evaluation of a conversational agent for supporting domestic violence survivors*. Doctoral Dissertation, The University of North Carolina at Charlotte. https://www.proquest.com/docview/3069930303/abstract/3FE4B45289C044FCPQ/1

Arora, A., Barrett, M., Lee, E., Oborn, E., & Prince, K. (2023). Risk and the future of AI: Algorithmic bias, data colonialism, and marginalization. *Information and Organization, 33*(3), 100478. https://doi.org/10.1016/j.infoandorg.2023.100478

Barnes, E., & Hutson, J. (2024). Navigating the ethical terrain of AI in higher education: Strategies for mitigating bias and promoting fairness. *Forum for Education Studies, 2*(2) https://doi.org/10.59400/fes.v2i2.1229

Bragazzi, N. L., Crapanzano, A., Converti, M., Zerbetto, R., & Khamisy-Farah, R. (2023). The impact of generative conversational artificial intelligence on the lesbian, gay, bisexual, transgender, and queer community: Scoping review. *Journal of Medical Internet Research, 25*, e52091. https://doi.org/10.2196/52091

Chan, F. L., Nguyen, D., & Joshi, A. (2024). "Is hate lost in translation?": Evaluation of multilingual LGBTQIA+ hate speech detection. *arXiv*. https://doi.org/10.48550/arXiv.2410.11230

Chartrand, A., & Duguay, S. (2025). Sexual and geocultural algorithmic imaginaries: Examining approaches of participatory resignation among LGBTQ+ Instagrammers in Berlin and Montreal. *International Journal of Cultural Studies, 28*(1), 241–259. https://doi.org/10.1177/13678779241267292

Ciston, S. (2019). Intersectional AI is essential: Polyvocal, multimodal, experimental methods to save artificial intelligence. *Journal of Science and Technology of the Arts, 11*(2), 3–8. https://doi.org/10.7559/citarj.v11i2.665

Costanza-Chock, S. (2018). Design justice, AI, and escape from the matrix of domination. *Journal of Design and Science, 3*(5), 1–14.

D'Alfonso, S. (2020). AI in mental health. *Current Opinion in Psychology, 36*, 112–117. https://doi.org/10.1016/j.copsyc.2020.04.005

Dacon, J., Shomer, H., Crum-Dacon, S., & Tang, J. (2022). Detecting harmful online conversational content towards LGBTQIA+ individuals. *arXiv*. https://doi.org/10.48550/arXiv.2207.10032

Daum, C. W. (2019). *Violence against and policing of LGBTQ communities: A historical perspective*. Oxford University Press. https://doi.org/10.1093/acrefore/9780190228637.013.1221

Dey, N. C. (2023). Unleashing the power of artificial intelligence in social work: A new frontier of innovation. *SSRN Electronic Journal*. https://doi.org/10.2139/ssrn.4549622

El Emam, K., Jonker, E., Arbuckle, L., & Malin, B. (2011). A systematic review of re-identification attacks on health data. *PLoS One, 6*(12), e28071. https://doi.org/10.1371/journal.pone.0028071

Fosch-Villaronga, E., & Malgieri, G. (2023). Queering the ethics of AI. *arXiv*. https://doi.org/10.48550/arXiv.2308.13591

Fowler, J. A., Buckley, L., Muir, M., Viskovich, S., Paradisis, C., Zanganeh, P., & Dean, J. A. (2023). Digital mental health interventions: A narrative review of what is important from the perspective of LGBTQIA+ people. *Journal of Clinical Psychology, 79*(11), 2685–2713. https://doi.org/10.1002/jclp.23571

Garcia-Perez, J. (2020). Lesbian, gay, bisexual, transgender, queer + Latinx youth mental health disparities: A systematic review. *Journal of Gay & Lesbian Social Services, 32*(4), 440–478. https://doi.org/10.1080/10538720.2020.1764896

Hermansyah, M., Najib, A., Farida, A., Sacipto, R., & Rintyarna, B. S. (2023). Artificial intelligence and ethics: Building an artificial intelligence system that ensures privacy and social justice. *International Journal of Science and Society, 5*(1), 154–168. https://doi.org/10.54783/ijsoc.v5i1.644

Joyce, D. W., Kormilitzin, A., Hamer-Hunt, J., McKee, K. R., & Tomasev, N. (2023). Protocol for a Delphi consensus process for PARticipatory Queer AI Research in Mental Health (PARQAIR-MH). *medRxiv*. https://doi.org/10.1101/2023.08.07.23293764

Joyce, D. W., Kormilitzin, A., Hamer-Hunt, J., McKee, K. R., & Tomasev, N. (2024). Defining acceptable data collection and reuse standards for queer artificial intelligence research in mental health: Protocol for the online PARQAIR-MH Delphi study. *BMJ Open, 14*(3), e079105. https://doi.org/10.1136/bmjopen-2023-079105

Katyal, S. K., & Jung, J. Y. (2021). The gender Panopticon: AI, gender, and design justice. *UCLA Law Review, 68*, 692.

Kuhlman, C., Jackson, L., & Chunara, R. (2020). No computation without representation: Avoiding data and algorithm biases through diversity. In *Proceedings of the 26th ACM SIGKDD international conference on knowledge discovery & data mining*, 3593. https://doi.org/10.1145/3394486.3411074

Lin, H., Karusala, N., Okolo, C. T., D'Ignazio, C., & Gajos, K. Z. (2024). "Come to us first": Centering community organizations in artificial intelligence for social good partnerships. *Proceedings of the ACM on Human-Computer Interaction, 8*(CSCW2), 1–28. https://doi.org/10.1145/3687009

Ma, Z., Mei, Y., Long, Y., Su, Z., & Gajos, K. Z. (2024). Evaluating the experience of LGBTQ+ people using large language model based chatbots for mental health support. In *Proceedings of the 2024 CHI conference on human factors in computing systems* (pp. 1–15). https://doi.org/10.1145/3613904.3642482

Macias, C., Soto, M., Alcántara, T., & Calvo, H. (2023). *Impact of text preprocessing and feature selection on hate speech detection in online messages towards the LGBTQ+ community in Mexico*.

McDonald, N., & Pan, S. (2020). Intersectional AI: A study of how information science students think about ethics and their impact. *Proceedings of the ACM on Human-Computer Interaction, 4*(CSCW2), 1–19. https://doi.org/10.1145/3415218

Monea, A. P. (2021). The digital closet: Platform censorship and LGBTQIA+ independence online. *AoIR Selected Papers of Internet Research*. https://doi.org/10.5210/spir.v2021i0.11987

Myles, D., Chartrand, A., & Duguay, S. (2023a). 'If we look at it from an LGBT point of view…' mobilizing LGBTQ+ stakeholders to queer algorithmic imaginaries. *AoIR Selected Papers of Internet Research*. https://doi.org/10.5210/spir.v2023i0.13467

Myles, D., Duguay, S., & Echaiz, L. F. (2023b). Mapping the social implications of platform algorithms for LGBTQ+ communities. *Journal of Digital Social Research, 5*(4), 1–30. https://doi.org/10.33621/jdsr.v5i4.162

Nixon, N., Lin, Y., & Snow, L. (2024). Catalyzing equity in STEM teams: Harnessing generative AI for inclusion and diversity. *Policy Insights From the Behavioral and Brain Sciences, 11*(1), 85–92. https://doi.org/10.1177/23727322231220356

Ntoutsi, E., Fafalios, P., Gadiraju, U., Iosifidis, V., Nejdl, W., Vidal, M.-E., Ruggieri, S., Turini, F., Papadopoulos, S., Krasanakis, E., Kompatsiaris, I., Kinder-Kurlanda, K., Wagner, C., Karimi, F., Fernandez, M., Alani, H., Berendt, B., Kruegel, T., Heinze, C., et al. (2020). Bias in data-driven artificial intelligence systems—An introductory survey. *WIREs Data Mining and Knowledge Discovery, 10*(3), e1356. https://doi.org/10.1002/widm.1356

Organizers of QueerInAI, Ovalle, A., Subramonian, A., Singh, A., Voelcker, C., Sutherland, D. J., Locatelli, D., Breznik, E., Klubicka, F., Yuan, H., Hetvi, J., Zhang, H., Shriram, J., Lehman, K., Soldaini, L., Sap, M., Deisenroth, M. P., Pacheco, M. L., Ryskina, M., et al. (2023). Queer in AI: A case study in community-led participatory AI. In *Proceedings of the 2023 ACM conference on fairness, accountability, and transparency* (pp. 1882–1895). https://doi.org/10.1145/3593013.3594134

Ovalle, A., Subramonian, A., Gautam, V., Gee, G., & Chang, K.-W. (2023). Factoring the matrix of domination: A critical review and reimagination of intersectionality in AI fairness. In *Proceedings of the 2023 AAAI/ACM conference on AI, ethics, and society* (pp. 496–511). https://doi.org/10.1145/3600211.3604705

Oyeniran, O. C., Adewusi, A. O., Adeleke, A. G., Akwawa, L. A., & Azubuko, C. F. (2022). Ethical AI: Addressing bias in machine learning models and software applications. *Computer Science & IT Research Journal, 3*(3). https://doi.org/10.51594/csitrj.v3i3.1559

Park, S., & Humphry, J. (2019). Exclusion by design: Intersections of social, digital and data exclusion. *Information, Communication & Society*. https://www.tandfonline.com/doi/full/10.1080/1369118X.2019.1606266

Pawar, G., & Khose, J. (2024). Exploring the role of artificial intelligence in enhancing equity and inclusion in education. *International Journal of Innovative Science and Research Technology (IJISRT)*, 2180–2185. https://doi.org/10.38124/ijisrt/ijisrt24apr1939

Pillis, D., Pataranutaporn, P., Maes, P., & Sra, M. (2024). AI comes out of the closet: Using AI-generated virtual characters to help individuals practice LGBTQIA+ advocacy. In *Proceedings of the 29th international conference on intelligent user interfaces* (pp. 686–698). https://doi.org/10.1145/3640543.3645213

Price-Feeney, M., Green, A. E., & Dorison, S. (2020). Understanding the mental health of transgender and nonbinary youth. *Journal of Adolescent Health, 66*(6), 684–690. https://doi.org/10.1016/j.jadohealth.2019.11.314

Radanliev, P., Santos, O., Brandon-Jones, A., & Joinson, A. (2024). Ethics and responsible AI deployment. *Frontiers in Artificial Intelligence, 7*. https://doi.org/10.3389/frai.2024.1377011

Raman, D. (2024). *Empowering community-driven determination of values for language models*. Thesis, Massachusetts Institute of Technology. https://dspace.mit.edu/handle/1721.1/157021

Reyero Lobo, P. (2022). Bias in hate speech and toxicity detection. In *Proceedings of the 2022 AAAI/ACM conference on AI, ethics, and society* (pp. 910–910). https://doi.org/10.1145/3514094.3539519

Ricaurte, P. (2022). Ethics for the majority world: AI and the question of violence at scale. *Media, Culture & Society, 44*(4), 726–745. https://doi.org/10.1177/01634437221099612

Rojas, J. I., Leckie, R., Hawks, E. M., Holster, J., del Carmen Trapp, M., & Ostermeyer, B. K. (2019). Compounded stigma in LGBTQ+ people: A framework for understanding the relationship between substance use disorders, mental illness, trauma, and sexual minority status. *Psychiatric Annals, 49*(10), 446–452. https://doi.org/10.3928/00485713-20190912-01

Romanelli, M., & Hudson, K. D. (2017). Individual and systemic barriers to health care: Perspectives of lesbian, gay, bisexual, and transgender adults. *American Journal of Orthopsychiatry, 87*(6), 714–728. https://doi.org/10.1037/ort0000306

Roshanaei, M., Olivares, H., & Lopez, R. R. (2023). Harnessing AI to foster equity in education: Opportunities, challenges, and emerging strategies. *Journal of Intelligent Learning Systems and Application, 15*, 123–143. https://www.scirp.org/journal/paperinformation?paperid=128922

Saglam, R. B., Nurse, J. R. C., & Sugiura, L. (2024). Designing chatbots to support victims and survivors of domestic abuse. *arXiv*. https://doi.org/10.48550/arXiv.2402.17393

Scatiggio, V. (2022). Tackling the issue of bias in artificial intelligence to design AI-driven fair and inclusive service systems: How human biases are breaching into AI algorithms, with severe impacts on individuals and societies, and what designers can do to face this phenomenon and change for the better. https://www.politesi.polimi.it/handle/10589/186118?mode=complete

Schneider, D. (2022). Ensuring privacy and confidentiality in social work through intentional omissions of information in client information systems: A qualitative study of available and non-available data. *Digital Society, 1*(3), 26. https://doi.org/10.1007/s44206-022-00029-9

Simpson, E., & Semaan, B. (2021). For you, or for "you"? Everyday LGBTQ+ encounters with TikTok. *Proceedings of the ACM Human Computer Interaction, 4*(CSCW3), 252:1–252:34. https://doi.org/10.1145/3432951

Sloane, M. (2019). Inequality is the name of the game: Thoughts on the emerging field of technology, ethics and social justice. *Weizenbaum Conference*. https://doi.org/10.34669/WI.CP/2.9

Sulmicelli, S. (2023). Algorithmic content moderation and the LGBTQ+ community's freedom of expression on social media. *BioLaw Journal—Rivista Di BioDiritto*, 471–472. https://iris.unitn.it/retrieve/378e5c68-356a-4f49-b007-06bf7fc41137/document.pdf

Sutter, M., & Perrin, P. B. (2016). Discrimination, mental health, and suicidal ideation among LGBTQ people of color. *Journal of Counseling Psychology, 63*(1), 98–105. https://doi.org/10.1037/cou0000126

Tawiah, N., & Monestime, J. P. (2024). Promoting equity in AI-driven mental health care for marginalized populations. *Proceedings of the AAAI Symposium Series, 4*(1), 1. https://doi.org/10.1609/aaaiss.v4i1.31810

Vecchione, B., Levy, K., & Barocas, S. (2021). Algorithmic auditing and social justice: Lessons from the history of audit studies. *Proceedings of the 1st ACM conference on equity and access in algorithms, mechanisms, and optimization* (pp. 1–9). https://doi.org/10.1145/3465416.3483294

Viberg, O., Kizilcec, R. F., Wise, A. F., Jivet, I., & Nixon, N. (2024). Advancing equity and inclusion in educational practices with AI-powered educational decision support systems (AI-EDSS). *British Journal of Educational Technology, 55*(5), 1833–2418. https://doi.org/10.1111/bjet.13507

Wan, R., Alvarado Garcia, A., Saxena, D., Vajiac, C., Kawakami, A., Stapleton, L., Zhu, H., Holstein, K., Candello, H., & Badillo-Urquiola, K. (2023). Community-driven AI: Empowering people through responsible data-driven decision-making. In *Companion publication of the 2023 conference on computer supported cooperative work and social computing* (pp. 532–536). https://doi.org/10.1145/3584931.3611282

Williams, A. J., Jones, C., Arcelus, J., Townsend, E., Lazaridou, A., & Michail, M. (2021). A systematic review and meta-analysis of victimisation and mental health prevalence among LGBTQ+ young people with experiences of self-harm and suicide. *PLoS One, 16*(1), e0245268. https://doi.org/10.1371/journal.pone.0245268

Wilson, C., & Cariola, L. A. (2020). LGBTQI+ youth and mental health: A systematic review of qualitative research. *Adolescent Research Review, 5*(2), 187–211. https://doi.org/10.1007/s40894-019-00118-w

Wong, S. G.-J. (2024). Sociocultural considerations in monitoring anti-LGBTQ+ content on social media. *arXiv*. https://doi.org/10.48550/arXiv.2407.01149

Xia, Y., Shin, S.-Y., & Kim, J.-C. (2024). Cross-cultural intelligent language learning system (CILS): Leveraging AI to facilitate language learning strategies in cross-cultural communication. *Applied Sciences, 14*(13), 5651. https://doi.org/10.3390/app14135651

Zajko, M. (2022). Artificial intelligence, algorithms, and social inequality: Sociological contributions to contemporary debates. *Sociology Compass, 16*(3), e12962. https://doi.org/10.1111/soc4.12962

Chapter 8
AI in Sexual and Domestic Partner Violence

Yue Fang and Judy L. Postmus

1 Introduction

Sexual and intimate partner violence (S/IPV) are persistent and complex global public health problems, and they are violations of human rights. The term "Sexual Violence" (SV) comprises numerous acts that are committed or attempted by another person without freely given consent of the victim or against someone unable to consent or refuse, including penetration, forced touching, non-contact sexual acts, and situations where the victim is compelled to engage with a third party, whether through force, intoxication, or nonphysical pressure (Basile et al., 2014). It can be committed by any perpetrator (e.g., stranger, friend, person in a position of power, family member, or intimate partner) and occurs in and outside of the context of intimate partner violence (Basile et al., 2022). Intimate Partner Violence (IPV) is a form of violence that occurs between a current or former intimate partner (i.e., spouse, boyfriend/girlfriend, dating partner, or ongoing sexual partner) and includes physical violence, sexual violence, stalking, and psychological aggression (including coercive tactics) (Breiding et al., 2015). IPV may also vary in severity or duration and does not require sexual intimacy (Leemis et al., 2022). Both forms of violence transcend cultural, economic, and geographic boundaries, affecting individuals across the lifespan and perpetuating cycles of trauma within communities. This chapter will primarily discuss these two forms of violence collectively, with special notes when they are discussed separately.

The personal and societal impact of S/IPV is profound and multifaceted. Beyond the short-term physical injuries and death, S/IPV contributes to long-term health

Y. Fang (✉)
Silver School of Social Work, New York University, New York, NY, USA
e-mail: yf2938@nyu.edu

J. L. Postmus
School of Social Work, University of Maryland–Baltimore, Baltimore, MD, USA
e-mail: dean@ssw.umaryland.edu

R. An, M. A. Lindsey (eds.), *Artificial Intelligence in Social Work*,
https://doi.org/10.1007/978-3-032-18443-6_8

consequences such as difficulty with daily activities, memory loss, chronic pain, gastrointestinal disorders, gynecological signs like transmitted diseases, and mental health conditions, including depression, anxiety, post-traumatic stress disorder (PTSD), and suicidal thoughts (Campbell, 2002; Ellsberg et al., 2008). Also, IPV has a negative physical and emotional impact on family members, especially children (Chan et al., 2021). Econometric methods, including direct medical costs and indirect productivity losses, have quantified these health consequences. Peterson et al. (2018) estimated the lifetime cost of IPV at $103,767 per female victim and $23,414 per male victim, with a total economic burden for the population of nearly $3.6 trillion over victims' lifetimes. Medical costs (59%, $2.1 trillion), lost productivity (37%, $1.3 trillion), criminal justice activities (2%, $73 billion), and other costs, including property loss or damage (2%, $62 billion), comprised the total lifetime economic burden, with 37% ($1.3 trillion) paid by government sources. Similarly, developing countries bear IPV costs equivalent to 1%–2% of GDP (Duvvury, 2013). These impacts highlight the importance of intervention and prevention of S/IPV.

Moreover, substantial data indicate that the number of individuals victimized by S/IPV is exceedingly large, with its impact extending across all countries worldwide. A World Health Organization-led analysis (WHO, 2021) of prevalence data from 2000 to 2018 across 161 countries and areas for the UN Interagency Working Group on Violence Against Women revealed that globally, approximately 30% of women have experienced physical and/or sexual violence by an intimate partner or non-partner sexual violence or both. According to the statistics discovered by The National Intimate Partner and Sexual Violence Survey (2016-2017) (Basile et al., 2022; Leemis et al., 2022) in the United States, almost 1 in 2 women and more than 2 in 5 men reported experiencing contact with sexual violence, physical violence, and/or stalking victimization by an intimate partner at some point in their lifetime; meanwhile, 1 in 4 women reported completed or attempted rape during her lifetime, and 1 in 9 men reported being made to penetrate someone during his lifetime, highlighting the pervasive nature of this public health crisis.

During the COVID-19 pandemic, IPV escalated due to measures like social distancing and shelter-in-place orders, particularly among marginalized groups. Collecting IPV data has been challenging, with traditional sources often underestimating the true scale of victimization. Amid these challenges, social media platforms like Reddit have emerged as crucial alternatives, offering IPV survivors a safe space to share experiences and seek support anonymously. Researchers (Buchner et al., 2023; Hodgkinson et al., 2023; Kim et al., 2023; Manzoor et al., 2022; Oyebode et al., 2021) have leveraged these platforms to collect data, thereby gaining a more comprehensive understanding of the situations of IPV victims. This has not only highlighted the potential of social media in IPV surveillance and intervention but also laid the groundwork for future AI-related IPV research.

Although there is growing recognition of the seriousness of S/IPV, researchers and practitioners still face significant barriers. Generating robust evidence, such as randomized controlled trials, is hampered by funding limitations and challenges in accessing sensitive data (Taft & Campbell, 2024). At the same time, practitioners must implement survivor-centered and trauma-informed care in settings that often lack resources, especially in marginalized communities affected by poverty, racism, and gender inequality. Prevention efforts, while well-intentioned, are frequently fragmented and not fully integrated into public health strategies (Niolon et al., 2017).

In this evolving landscape, artificial intelligence (AI) offers a transformative opportunity to address these challenges. Because of its scalability, AI can provide solutions across different populations and locations without requiring additional human resources. AI systems can rapidly process large volumes of data, identify patterns, and predict risks with impressive speed and accuracy, offering insights that strengthen current support systems and enhance the efforts of S/IPV researchers and practitioners. However, to realize this potential, careful attention must be paid to ethical design and practical implementation to avoid worsening existing structural or systemic issues. AI deployment should always be grounded in a clear understanding of its benefits and limitations, and be accompanied by ongoing efforts in policy, practice, and advocacy.

This chapter examines how AI technologies can be integrated to support survivors of S/IPV. We discuss key AI applications, including risk detection, surveillance, prediction, intervention tools, AI chatbots, and survivor empowerment, and explore their practical value for both research and practice. Alongside the potential benefits, we address major ethical issues, including privacy, bias, re-traumatization, and transparency. Throughout, we emphasize the importance of trauma-informed, survivor-centered approaches and the need for ethical frameworks to guide responsible AI adoption in this sensitive field.

2 AI Applications in S/IPV Response

The integration of AI into support systems for survivors of S/IPV represents a transformative shift in addressing this pervasive societal issue. AI now plays a critical role across multiple phases of S/IPV support, from prevention and intervention to long-term survivor assistance. Drawing on evidence from sources such as social media, clinical records, telehealth, and legal documents, we explore how these technologies can enhance services while also considering important ethical and practical implications.

2.1 *Risk Detection, Surveillance, and Prediction*

Recent advances in natural language processing (NLP) have enabled innovative approaches to identifying risks associated with S/IPV through non-traditional data sources. This section presents relevant research findings aligned with the technological objectives, progressing from risk detection to monitoring and prediction. The discussion transitions from identifying existing incidents to forecasting future risks, structured to illustrate how these technologies systematically address challenges in S/IPV risk assessment. This approach aims to provide readers with a clear understanding of the technological progression in resolving complex issues within this domain. Nevertheless, it's important to note that while these categories are distinct, some AI applications may span multiple stages. For example, a system that detects instances of violence on social media can also contribute to risk surveillance by tracking the frequency and nature of such mentions over time.

2.1.1 Risk Detection: Identifying Threats Across Data Sources

Risk detection in the context of S/IPV refers to the use of AI to identify current or recent individual-level instances of S/IPV. This involves analyzing data to pinpoint situations where violence is occurring, has recently occurred, or where individuals are currently experiencing abuse or are in immediate danger. These tools are designed not to replace human decision-making, but to complement it by helping service providers, healthcare professionals, and researchers detect violence that might otherwise remain hidden or underreported.

The detection of S/IPV relies heavily on advanced AI methodologies, particularly NLP and machine learning. NLP techniques, such as keyword extraction, topic modeling (e.g., Latent Dirichlet Allocation, LDA), and word embeddings (e.g., Doc2Vec, Word2Vec), are instrumental in analyzing unstructured text data from diverse sources, including social media, news articles, and electronic health records (EHRs). These methods enable the identification of linguistic patterns and contextual cues that may indicate violence. Supervised machine learning models, such as logistic regression and transformer-based models (e.g., BERT, BioBERT, RoBERTa), are trained on labeled datasets to classify text or encounters as related to S/IPV. These models can achieve high accuracy in detecting violence-related content, as demonstrated in several studies. Additionally, rule-based systems, which rely on predefined lists of keywords or patterns, provide a structured approach to identifying potential cases of violence, particularly in clinical or crisis response settings.

For healthcare providers, risk-detection systems embedded in EHRs or chat-based platforms can help detect risks early. For instance, Botelle et al. (2022) evaluated an NLP model (BioBERT) for extracting violence-related information from EHRs. The model demonstrated high precision (89%–98%) and recall (89%–97%), underscoring its effectiveness in healthcare environments. Similarly, Tabaie et al. (2022) developed an NLP algorithm for identifying IPV cases in emergency department (ED) settings using predefined situational terms. The algorithm achieved 99.5% precision in detecting IPV cases, demonstrating the value of unstructured EHR data in identifying socially stigmatized conditions. These tools can serve as passive alerts for clinicians—flagging at-risk patients even when violence is not explicitly disclosed—thus enabling timely inquiry or referrals.

In crisis response settings, AI-enhanced chat platforms can help reduce delays in identifying urgent cases. Swaminathan et al. (2023) developed the Crisis Message Detector-1 (CMD-1), a two-stage NLP system that uses keyword filtering and logistic regression to detect crisis messages in existing clinical telehealth chat workflows. By flagging high-risk messages in real time, the system enabled humans to triage crisis messages.

AI systems can also assist in detecting disclosures of violence on social media platforms, where survivors may share their experiences anonymously. Al-Garadi et al. (2022) designed an automated system using NLP and machine learning to detect IPV-related content on Twitter, now known as X. Their model, which is based on Robustly Optimized BERT (RoBERTa), achieved an F1 score of 0.76 in classifying personal IPV reports compared to other models, highlighting how social media can supplement traditional detection pathways. Although this tool is currently in research stages, Al-Garadi's team calls for the practical applications of this effective, low-bias, and reliable model to classify self-reported IPV on social media, which could lay the foundation for designing evidence-based interventions, supporting IPV victims, and potentially addressing IPV in near real time through social media.

Although primarily designed for individual-level detection, such tools may also contribute to broader surveillance efforts when applied at scale over time—an area discussed further in the next section. Thanks to these tools, we can see undisclosed violence, but the further question is: are these risks expanding? Are they concentrated in certain populations or time periods?

2.1.2 Risk Surveillance: Tracking Population-Level Trends and Patterns

While risk detection focuses on identifying individual instances of violence, risk surveillance refers to the systematic, ongoing use of AI tools to observe patterns, fluctuations, and disparities in S/IPV incidents at the population level. These tools and evidence help public health professionals and policymakers gain insight into how violence evolves across time and thus inform public health or policy responses.

One example of AI-enabled surveillance is the GBVMeter tool developed by Manzoor et al. (2022), which analyzed 12,693 English-language news articles on gender-based violence (GBV) across Pakistan, India, and the UK. The researchers applied Latent Dirichlet Allocation (LDA) for topic modeling and introduced a word embedding technique, GBV2Vec, built on Doc2Vec, to classify and assess the sensitivity of GBV-related content. Their analysis found that rape was the most frequently reported form of GBV, followed by domestic violence, violence against women, and sexual violence. In a case study during the COVID-19 pandemic, results indicated a global increase in GBV, with women disproportionately affected. By identifying reporting patterns, topic salience, and narrative shifts during crisis periods, the GBVMeter tool provides actionable insights for policymakers and human rights advocates, enabling timely interventions and advancing Sustainable Development Goals (SDGs) such as gender equality and inclusive societies.

Another example comes from Hodgkinson et al. (2023), who analyzed 43,488 domestic abuse crime records from a UK police force during the COVID-19 pandemic. Using NLP to extract insights from free-text fields and combining change-point analysis with anomaly detection, the study tested hypotheses about reporting behavior, cohabitation effects, and timing of abuse trends. Contrary to expectations, the data showed no increase in domestic abuse during the first national lockdown, but a significant and sustained rise after restrictions were lifted. Notably, the increase did not appear to reflect changes in reporting rates or cohabitation patterns. These findings demonstrate how AI-enhanced surveillance can reveal complex, time-sensitive patterns in administrative data, thereby informing more adaptive, evidence-based policy responses.

In another example, Chen et al. (2023) addressed the challenge of underreported IPV prevalence by applying machine learning to the Third Wave Survey on the Social Status of Women in China. Using a random forest algorithm to impute missing data, they found significantly higher rates of physical (7.10%), verbal (13.74%), and cold violence (21.35%) than in traditional survey responses (4.05%, 11.21%, and 17.95%, respectively). Here, cold violence is an emotional form of domestic violence characterized by a complete withdrawal of all verbal and physical communication by one member of an intimate relationship toward the other (McLaren, 2016). This highlights how AI can enhance surveillance accuracy by estimating the true prevalence of sensitive social issues and correcting for non-response bias.

These examples highlight how AI can help answer key public health questions: Where does violence occur? Is it increasing or decreasing? Which groups are most at risk? Importantly, surveillance systems are not intended to identify individual victims or intervene directly, but rather to inform service planning, funding allocation, and prevention programming. When applied ethically and transparently, AI-supported surveillance enables a shift from reactive responses to a proactive strategy, empowering institutions to recognize macro-level signals and respond with data-informed policies. The following section builds on this by exploring how AI can move even further upstream: predicting who might be at greatest risk and intervening before violence occurs.

2.1.3 Risk Prediction: Survivor and Perpetrator

AI-based risk prediction tools aim to estimate the likelihood of future S/IPV victimization or perpetration by identifying patterns in population-level historical data. Unlike detection and surveillance tools that focus on identifying existing incidents or tracking trends, predictive models are typically used in research contexts to explore population-level risk factors and inform prevention-oriented strategies. These tools are not intended for individual-level decision-making in clinical or legal settings, and their use raises important ethical considerations, including privacy, consent, and the agency of survivors and at-risk individuals.

From a survivor-centered perspective, researchers have explored the use of predictive models to improve early identification of individuals who may be at heightened risk of severe harm. For example, Garcia-Vergara et al. (2023) trained a machine learning classifier using legal documents to distinguish between lethal and non-lethal IPV cases, achieving an accuracy of 83.16%. The goal of this model was not to label individuals, but to support risk stratification in research that could inform resource allocation or the design of lethality screening tools. However, any application of predictive models to identify potential victims must be approached with caution. Survivors may choose not to disclose abuse for valid and personal reasons, and systems that infer risk without their consent risk undermining their agency and privacy. Therefore, current models are developed with de-identified, aggregate data, and their outputs are used for population-level insights, not individual monitoring or intervention.

Recent studies have also explored predicting violent behavior from the perpetrator's perspective, building on the intergenerational transmission of violence theory (Widom & Wilson, 2015) derived from Bandura's (1977) social learning theory. This framework posits that exposure to violence during childhood, either as a victim or witness, increases the likelihood of using violence as a conflict resolution tactic in adulthood. Childhood maltreatment or abuse is identified as the most common predictor of youth intimate partner violence (IPV) perpetration. Petering et al. (2018) examined this phenomenon among homeless youth, aiming to identify key variables that determine the likelihood of IPV perpetration and developed an AI-based triage tool to predict such behavior. The study used supervised machine learning algorithms to analyze data from 353 homeless youth, focusing on physical perpetration ranging from minor (e.g., slapping) to severe (e.g., kicking). Key findings indicate that PTSD, depression, prior violence engagement, hard drug use, and loneliness are among the most influential predictors of IPV perpetration. Support Vector Machines (SVMs) with a Radial Basis Function (RBF) kernel demonstrated superior performance compared to other algorithms (e.g., Random Forests and Neural Networks), achieving the highest F1-score (0.53) and ROC AUC (0.69). However, it is essential to clarify that such models are currently limited to research contexts, often focused on high-risk or already-identified populations (such as homeless youth), rather than being broadly applied to all youth or used in routine screening. Their main contribution is in identifying population-level risk patterns and supporting the development of early prevention strategies, rather than labeling or profiling individuals for intervention. In practice, these tools are not intended for practitioners to use directly to screen or label individual perpetrators in real-world settings. Instead, they help inform policy, shape targeted interventions, and expand our understanding of risk pathways. The use of such models raises critical ethical questions, particularly around privacy, potential bias, and the dangers of misclassification or stigmatization if predictive results are misapplied outside research environments. Responsible implementation demands clear boundaries, robust data governance, and ongoing ethical oversight to prevent unintended harm.

While perpetrator-focused AI modeling shows promise for research and program design, practical deployment for case-level decision-making remains premature. Continued evaluation, transparency, and co-design with stakeholders are necessary to ensure these tools empower, rather than endanger, those most affected by IPV.

2.2 AI Tools for Assessment and Intervention

According to World Health Organization guidelines (WHO, 2013), immediate support (first-line support) is strongly advised for women disclosing sexual or intimate partner violence (S/IPV). A systematic review (Novitzky et al., 2023) classifies S/IPV interventions into three levels: primary, secondary, and tertiary. Primary prevention targets reducing health threats before they occur, typically via school, community, and digital platforms aimed at adolescents and families to tackle the root causes of IPV. Secondary prevention focuses on early intervention post-exposure, encompassing IPV screening, shelter relocation, counseling, legal support, and perpetrator interventions such as diversion programs and anger management. Tertiary prevention addresses the long-term impacts of past IPV experiences, emphasizing psychological support, recidivism reduction, and community reintegration.

Accurate recognition of survivors' specific needs is fundamental for effective intervention. Traditional screening tools rely on fixed checklists or manual triage, which can miss or delay the nuanced, rapidly changing requests survivors make online or during clinical encounters. Recent large-language-model (LLM) studies show that AI can bridge this gap by classifying survivors' self-described information needs in real time. Hui et al. (2024) fine-tuned a large language model to successfully predict 66.6% of the informational needs of domestic violence victims from online posts on Reddit. Guan et al. (2025) recently improved this prediction model to 2216 posts using GPT-3.5–generated synthetic examples and achieved an F1-score of 0.705 across eight need categories (e.g., shelters, legal aid, childbearing, safety planning, DV knowledge, etc.). These findings have the potential to be translated into practice. Guan et al. (2025) outlined how such LLMs could be embedded in electronic health-record portals to trigger real-time, need-matched recommendations, enabling community nurses, social workers, and counselors to deliver personalized resources without delay. These findings have the potential to be translated directly into clinical practice: when embedded in electronic health-record portals or NGO chatbots, LLM-based triage can automatically surface tailored resources, field routine queries, and flag ambiguous or high-risk messages, enabling nurses, social workers, and counselors to focus their expertise where it matters most. The authors also emphasize that development and deployment must be co-designed with survivors and service agencies to ensure all interventions remain trauma-informed, culturally appropriate, and ethically sound.

AI also contributes significantly to assessing the severity of violence, ensuring fairness and consistency in evaluations. In a study by Sikstrom et al. (2023), researchers compared human and machine assessment of severity in physical and psychological IPV events. Participants who experienced violence rated its severity, while another group assessed the same events. Results showed that human evaluations were affected by bias, particularly underestimating the severity of psychological violence. In contrast, a computational model trained on word embeddings and supervised learning not only achieved higher predictive accuracy but also mitigated calibration bias between self-report and observer ratings. These findings suggest that AI tools could support legal decision-making, prioritize services, and ensure fair media representation—particularly in domains where violence is often subjectively judged.

In addition to identifying and assessing survivors' needs, technology can enhance the scalability and accessibility of interventions. Al-Alosi (2020) outlines five key areas where technology can play a positive role: delivering resources and services, combating loneliness and isolation, supporting safety planning, documenting abuse, and empowering victims. AI in this context emerges as a promising technique to enhance traditional digital service delivery tools.

One application is assisting healthcare providers through AI-enabled triage systems. For instance, Swaminathan et al. (2023) developed an NLP-based model that can reliably identify crisis-related messages (including domestic violence and self-harm), decreasing the median triage time from 9 h to 8–13 min. This integration demonstrates AI's practical utility in streamlining clinical workflows and promptly addressing survivors' urgent needs.

Another application is direct client-facing chatbots. The current S/IPV-targeted AI chatbots include Aimee Says, Keepit, and ChattyCuz. Aimee Says, a web-based chatbot, has supported over 70,000 domestic violence survivors by offering confidential guidance, legal information, and safety planning referrals. It securely documents abuse incidents, enabling survivors to navigate legal processes safely and privately. Despite its effectiveness, the platform acknowledges limitations in handling deeply emotional or sensitive issues, reinforcing the ongoing need for human intervention (Gambino, 2024). Similarly, Keepit, developed by Nigerian activist Bukky Shonibare, leverages NLP, machine learning, and cloud computing to offer a confidential, empathetic space where survivors of sexual violence can safely document their experiences. It aims to empower survivors by preserving their testimonies for potential legal actions, providing emotional support, and facilitating evidence collection, legal preparation, and referrals. Recognizing that survivors may prefer interacting without being judged, Keepit ensures survivors' comfort and autonomy during sensitive disclosures (Segal, 2025).

While there is limited research on the effectiveness and safety of models like Aimee Says and Keepit, an empirical intervention study (De Filippo et al., 2023) highlights the potential of a behaviorally informed gamified chatbot called ChattyCuz (a WhatsApp chatbot intervention) as a low-cost intervention to improve gender-equitable attitudes and reduce intimate partner violence (IPV) exposure among young women in South Africa. The research examined the efficacy of behaviorally informed digital chatbots, *Attention Treatment, Gamified Treatment, and Narrative Treatment*, in enhancing gender-equitable attitudes and reducing IPV exposure among South African young women. All chatbot interventions improved gender attitudes, with the gamified version showing the most significant effect. This gamified chatbot also modestly yet significantly reduced the experience of past-month IPV exposure, especially technological and psychological IPV, with an 8% decrease as reported by women. Moreover, it enhanced users' ability to identify unhealthy relationship behaviors. Despite no impact on depressive symptoms, the chatbots' safety was ensured with a counselor link. Although promising, the researchers emphasize the need to expand future studies beyond heteronormative frameworks and single-platform contexts to strengthen generalizability and applicability.

These AI-based tools illustrate transformative potential in IPV interventions, shifting from passive support to active, personalized, and scalable strategies. Ethical implementation, rigorous evaluation, and survivor-centered design remain critical as technology increasingly shapes IPV intervention paradigms.

2.3 Survivor Empowerment

As described in previous sections, AI tools have transformed the landscape of S/IPV response by enhancing both provider-driven interventions and direct survivor access to support. Yet, the most far-reaching potential of AI in this context lies in its capacity to empower survivors. In the context of S/IPV, a "survivor" is an individual who has lived through and overcome experiences of sexual and intimate partner violence. Survivor empowerment is a cornerstone of effective responses to IPV. Empowerment, as defined by Dutton's empowerment theory (Dutton, 1992), recognizes the survivor's inherent strength and aims to equip them with the choice, knowledge, skills, resources, and sense of control necessary to ensure their safety, promote their healing, and rebuild their lives.

First, AI significantly enhances survivors' autonomy by making critical information and resources more accessible, timely, and personalized. Research by Hui et al. (2024) and Guan et al. (2025) demonstrated the capability of fine-tuned large language models to classify survivors' expressed informational needs from online disclosures accurately. Such AI applications would provide survivors with immediate, confidential access to tailored information, empowering them to independently navigate their help-seeking journey without stigma, judgment, or logistical barriers inherent to traditional service environments.

Second, AI interventions contribute to survivors' psychological resilience, self-efficacy, and proactive safety planning. Technology-based interventions, potentially incorporating AI elements, can provide discretionary and reliable support, psychoeducation, and information that empowers survivors to make informed decisions about their safety and well-being (Emezue et al., 2022). These interventions can be tailored to specific populations, such as immigrant women, to address their unique needs and increase their sense of agency (Sabri et al., 2021). Features can include information on relationship red flags, danger assessment, and personalized safety plans with links to local and national resources (Emezue et al., 2022; Sabri et al., 2021). As Aimee Says, Keepit, and ChattyCuz, these AI chatbots are designed for direct survivor interaction, providing confidential, judgment-free spaces for users to share experiences, seek guidance, and receive support at any hour. These digital assistants enable survivors to document incidents securely, preserve testimony for potential future legal action, and engage in conversational scenarios that build confidence in recognizing and responding to unhealthy relationships. By lowering the barriers to disclosure, offering step-by-step safety planning, and connecting users to relevant resources without the need for face-to-face interaction, such chatbots expand the autonomy and reach of support for those who may be hesitant, isolated, or marginalized. Nevertheless, these interventions are most effective when complemented by human oversight and are developed with survivor feedback to ensure ethical, culturally sensitive, and trauma-informed care.

Third, AI can reduce structural barriers and foster equitable access to support for marginalized or underserved populations. For example, Tabaie et al. (2022) demonstrated that NLP techniques analyzing electronic medical record notes could identify IPV cases with much greater precision than traditional ICD code-based methods. In practice, these AI systems are most often integrated into healthcare providers' electronic record workflows, where they flag potential IPV indicators for clinicians, social workers, or case managers. This allows healthcare professionals to proactively offer survivors referrals to local resources, legal aid, or counseling that they might not otherwise access—directly aligning with the World Health Organization's recommendations for connecting survivors to community services (WHO, 2013).

Drawing on the AI intervention tools discussed in Sect. 2.2, we can envision that the pathway to improved community resource access can be both healthcare-provider- and survivor-driven. In healthcare provider-facing models, AI serves as a decision-support tool: once a possible IPV case is identified, clinicians are prompted to initiate sensitive conversations and refer patients to appropriate services, with real-time, locally tailored information supplied by the AI system. Alternatively, as patient-facing tools become more common, survivors themselves may use AI-enabled portals to learn about confidentiality or to request services covered by their healthcare plans or available in their communities. In both models, the value of AI lies in its ability to deliver up-to-date, individualized, and human-reviewed recommendations, ensuring that survivors are matched with accurate, contextually relevant resources. As large language models evolve and "human-in-the-loop" designs mature, these systems will increasingly bridge the gap between detection and actionable support, making equity and personalized access to resources a practical reality for more survivors.

3 Ethical Considerations in AI Applications

The intersection of AI with S/IPV presents complex ethical challenges that demand careful consideration. Current literature reveals significant concerns regarding privacy violations through AI-enabled deepfakes, the potential for technology to exacerbate trauma, and risks of misidentification that can perpetuate harm. Research indicates that malicious AI applications can create realistic, indistinguishable fabricated content, while AI-based re-identification attacks render traditional anonymization measures increasingly ineffective. Moreover, emerging evidence suggests that trauma-informed approaches in S/IPV-related AI design are essential to prevent technology from becoming another vector for abuse. This section discusses the ethical considerations around privacy violations, the risk of retraumatization, bias, and a lack of transparency. It underscores the importance of ethically deploying AI to empower survivors and enhance support services through trauma- and violence-informed approaches, highlighting both the evolving threats and potential protective frameworks.

3.1 Privacy Violations from General AI Technologies

AI technologies have enabled unprecedented capabilities for creating fabricated content that violates privacy and dignity. Deepfakes, which are "images or recordings that have been convincingly altered and manipulated to misrepresent someone as doing or saying something that they did not actually do or say," have become particularly problematic in the context of sexual abuse (Okolie, 2023). AI technologies are extensively misused in the pornography industry, where women's faces are digitally mapped onto other bodies to create non-consensual sexual content. This form of technology-facilitated abuse constitutes a severe privacy violation with lasting psychological impacts on victims. The hyper-realism of AI-generated materials makes them nearly indistinguishable from authentic content, amplifying their harm. Moreover, the permanence and replicability of AI-generated content allow this abuse to persist indefinitely, perpetuating trauma and intensifying long-term psychological effects such as PTSD, depression, and reduced personal security (Abdulai, 2025). Another research (Hawkes et al., 2024) highlights the vulnerability of image-based sexual abuse removal tools to generative AI attacks, which can approximately reconstruct original image material. This result emphasizes the need for stronger data protection measures, such as cryptographic protocols like private set intersection (PSI). By enabling secure hash matching without exposing sensitive data, PSI offers a privacy-focused solution for removing harmful content and safeguarding vulnerable users. This approach not only counters adversarial AI attacks but also enhances privacy protection in combating technology-facilitated abuse.

Beyond the creation of fabricated content, AI systems present substantial privacy risks through person re-identification (Platzer, 2022). Traditional data masking and anonymization approaches have proven increasingly vulnerable to sophisticated AI algorithms that can re-identify individuals based on behavioral patterns. This concept has attracted increasing attention from the research community due to its vital role in security applications such as tracking robberies and preventing terrorist attacks (Yadav & Vishwakarma, 2023). However, the implications for survivors of S/IPV are particularly concerning, as maintaining privacy and confidentiality can be essential for safety. If S/IPV abusers can leverage AI re-identification techniques to locate or gather information about survivors, this technological vulnerability becomes a physical safety threat.

In addition to the intentional use of malicious AI models, general AI technologies may increase the risk for technology-mediated trauma in two other ways. First, the training of AI algorithms often relies on underrepresented, biased, and inaccurate datasets, which can perpetuate harm. Second, general AI-powered chatbots may provide inappropriate health advice, further endangering vulnerable populations (Abdulai, 2025). Thus, general AI technologies may expand avenues for sexual exploitation and abuse, but also are not suitable for supporting survivors of S/IPV without careful ethical consideration and safeguards.

3.2 *Ethical Challenges in AI Tools Designed for S/IPV Response*

Following the discussion of general-purpose AI misuse in S/IPV contexts (Sect. 3.1), this section shifts focus to the distinct ethical challenges associated with AI tools intentionally developed for S/IPV prevention and survivor support. While AI tools designed for S/IPV response (AI-S/IPV) hold promise for preventing S/IPV and survivor empowerment, as stated in Sect. 2, the absence of clear ethical governing principles and implementation guidelines poses a significant hurdle. Professionals lack comprehensive guidance on how to deploy these emerging technologies responsibly in such a sensitive domain.

First, the risk of retraumatization is a critical concern. Generative AI in digital health interventions could inadvertently trigger, perpetuate, or exacerbate prior traumatic experiences among vulnerable populations and could widen health inequities (Abdulai, 2025). Tabaie et al. (2022) acknowledge the potential for survivor retraumatization if the identification and subsequent interventions related to IPV are not handled sensitively.

Second, bias and fairness issues arise from the datasets used to train AI/ML models. These datasets often exhibit a bias toward gender-based violence against women, potentially neglecting other forms of IPV (Novitzky et al., 2023). This bias can skew the effectiveness of interventions and marginalize victims whose experiences fall outside the narrow scope of the training data, thereby undermining the equity and inclusivity of these technologies.

Third, the lack of transparency and explainability presents a significant trust challenge. Crooks et al. (2024) highlight the challenge of building trust in AI output, particularly when the AI relies on opaque techniques. If users, including survivors and healthcare providers, do not understand how an AI arrived at a recommendation or action, they may not trust or utilize it effectively. This lack of transparency can be an ethical concern, especially in sensitive contexts like S/IPV, where understanding the rationale behind AI interventions is essential.

These interconnected ethical challenges call for a comprehensive and responsible approach to the development and deployment of AI technologies in the domain of S/IPV. Addressing these challenges is essential to ensure that AI interventions are not only effective but also ethical and empowering for survivors.

3.3 Trauma- and Violence-Informed Approaches in AI-S/IPV Development

As recommended by the WHO, a trauma-informed approach is essential for S/IPV services. Traditional trauma-informed care (TIC) emphasizes that trauma affects all aspects of a person's life—including families and communities—and that providers must recognize trauma's signs, respond sensitively at both the individual and organizational level, and actively resist retraumatization (Palmieri & Valentine, 2021).

Trauma- and violence-informed care (TVIC) expands upon these foundations by explicitly addressing the role of structural violence and systemic inequities in survivors' lives (Wathen & Mantler, 2022). TVIC is guided by four core principles: (1) understanding and awareness of trauma and violence, especially structural violence, and their impacts; (2) prioritizing the physical, emotional, and cultural safety of all involved; (3) fostering person-centered connection, collaboration, and choice; and (4) building on individuals' strengths and supporting their skill and capacity development (Wathen & Varcoe, 2023). This paradigm shift is crucial, as it places responsibility on organizations and systems, not just individuals, to adapt services, policies, and environments for survivors, rather than expecting survivors to adjust to rigid or potentially harmful systems.

When considering integrating AI into S/IPV interventions, embedding TVIC principles is both a challenge and an opportunity. Conventional support systems often require survivors to formally disclose IPV and retell their experiences multiple times to access care, a process that can perpetuate harm and retraumatization (Wathen & Mantler, 2022). AI-enabled tools, especially the chatbots introduced in the previous sections, can help address this by allowing survivors to securely share their story once with informed consent and then facilitate the transfer of necessary information across authorized providers as needed. This approach aligns closely with TVIC's emphasis on minimizing retraumatization, safeguarding privacy, and maximizing survivor choice and autonomy.

To fully realize these benefits, AI tools for S/IPV response must be designed, implemented, and evaluated through a TVIC lens. This means prioritizing survivor safety, empowerment, and cultural sensitivity throughout the AI development lifecycle and ensuring that the technology is adaptable to diverse needs and contexts. TVIC also demands that organizations proactively address systemic and institutional barriers, including policies or digital practices that might inadvertently perpetuate inequity or harm.

Recent innovations demonstrate the need for robust ethical governance. For instance, a team at the University of Queensland has initiated the co-design of an AI trauma-informed audit framework to assess the extent to which AI-driven decisions may cause new trauma or retraumatization. Notably, such frameworks should inform the design of digital interventions from inception, rather than only retrospectively assessing harm after deployment. While the details of this particular framework are yet to be published, its development signals a promising direction for future AI governance.

Another forward-thinking principle is "Safety-by-Design" (Thorn & All Tech Is Human, 2024). They indicate that proactive approaches centered on safety-by-design principles are essential for mitigating potential harm. While this particular reference focuses on child sexual abuse, the principle could extend to adult survivors of S/IPV. The safety-by-design frameworks should be "tactical, actionable, and multidisciplinary," enabling technical, policy, product, and trust and safety teams to implement protective measures with minimal friction. These approaches represent a shift from reactive responses to harm toward proactive prevention of technology-facilitated abuse. This shift is fundamental given that the "prevalence of AI-generated child sexual abuse material is small, but growing," suggesting a critical window for intervention before these problems become more widespread.

As AI becomes increasingly integrated into S/IPV support, grounding technology-mediated interventions in TVIC and related frameworks is essential for advancing equity, effectiveness, and survivor well-being. Embedding these principles, supported by strong organizational commitment and ongoing ethical reflection, will help ensure that digital innovation empowers rather than inadvertently harms those it is designed to serve.

The literature on ethical considerations around AI applications related to S/IPV reveals several insights. First, AI technologies present significant privacy threats through deepfakes, re-identification attacks, and other forms of technology-mediated trauma. These threats can perpetuate trauma and create ongoing safety risks for survivors. Second, AI systems face challenges of bias and a lack of transparency. Biased datasets can reduce intervention effectiveness and marginalize some victims. Also, AI's unclear decision-making process makes it hard to trust, especially in S/IPV cases where understanding AI's logic is key. This shows the need for ethical rules that focus on fairness and accountability in AI use. Third, implementing trauma- and violence-informed approaches to AI design and deployment is essential but currently underdeveloped. Safety-by-design principles offer a new framework for proactively preventing harm, but they must be tailored to address the vulnerabilities of individuals experiencing S/IPV.

4 Discussion and Future Directions

This chapter has explored the transformative opportunities that AI brings to the field of sexual and intimate partner violence (S/IPV) prevention and survivor support. Rather than serving as a replacement for established practices, AI offers new tools to augment and diversify approaches for detection, intervention, and survivor empowerment. However, as the preceding sections make clear, integrating AI into S/IPV services cannot be straightforward or unproblematic.

4.1 Critical Reflections on the Current Evidence Base

The literature reviewed in this chapter demonstrates promising use cases for AI, including NLP for risk detection, large language models for triaging information needs, and chatbots for preliminary support. Yet, much of the available evidence remains limited in scope. Most AI-enabled interventions have only been evaluated as research prototypes or in narrowly defined pilot settings, often with modest sample sizes and limited demographic diversity. For example, while studies have shown that machine learning models can predict risk factors for perpetration among specific high-risk groups, these findings are not easily generalizable to broader populations or to routine practice. Furthermore, there is a lack of longitudinal and real-world impact evaluations.

Another key limitation lies in the conceptual framing of risk and intervention. Some AI models, in their attempt to "predict" or classify risk, may inadvertently shift the focus onto individual behaviors or characteristics, potentially reinforcing the misperception that survivors are responsible for their victimization or that perpetrators can be reduced to a set of risk factors. Such framings risk obscuring the intersectional drivers of S/IPV. It is essential for future research to adopt frameworks that respect survivors and realities, and to avoid reinforcing stigma or blame.

4.2 Ongoing Challenges in Implementation

Despite the rapid evolution of AI technologies, integrating AI into real-world S/IPV services faces formidable hurdles. Most current applications, such as AI chatbots, have not yet achieved seamless linkage with community resources, legal advocacy, or healthcare systems. Initiatives like Aimee Says demonstrate the potential for digital support, but more work is needed to ensure that these tools are embedded within a holistic, trauma- and violence-informed care ecosystem. Projects such as Keepit, while innovative, have yet to move beyond development and into sustainable practice.

Additionally, unresolved concerns remain regarding data privacy, informed consent, bias mitigation, and the risk of retraumatization. The "last mile" problem, ensuring that AI-generated insights translate into tangible, survivor-centered action within complex social systems, remains acute. Service providers must be vigilant to ensure that the introduction of AI does not inadvertently widen disparities or introduce new barriers, particularly for marginalized populations.

4.3 Future Directions for Research, Practice, and Policy

For researchers and developers:

- Foster interdisciplinary and multi-institutional collaboration to design and validate AI tools grounded in real-world needs and trauma- and violence-informed care (TVIC) principles.
- Conduct large-scale, longitudinal, and cross-cultural studies to ensure AI interventions are inclusive, robust, and responsive to the diverse experiences of survivors.
- Embrace participatory, survivor-centered co-design at every stage of development, actively addressing bias, privacy, consent, and the risk of retraumatization.

For practitioners and service providers:

- Build capacity to leverage AI tools as complements to professional judgment, emphasizing human–AI collaboration in screening, triage, and resource navigation.
- Uphold survivor choice, informed consent, and respect throughout AI-assisted workflows, and contribute real-time feedback to improve tool safety and relevance.
- Build institutional standards for ethical review, data security, and trauma- and violence-informed practice, ensuring technology always serves the safety and empowerment of those affected by S/IPV.

For policy-makers and regulators:

- Develop and enforce ethical, privacy, and accountability standards for AI use in S/IPV settings, prioritizing transparency and "safety-by-design" principles.
- Support and scale up multi-sector pilot projects that model collaborative, survivor-centered AI implementation.
- Promote equitable access and funding for inclusive AI solutions, ensuring that innovations do not deepen existing disparities or exclude marginalized communities.
- Establish ongoing mechanisms for feedback, monitoring, and policy adaptation as technologies and service needs evolve.

In summary, AI presents a transformative opportunity for S/IPV researchers, service providers, policymakers, and survivors alike. Its responsible integration demands a commitment to rigorous evidence, ethical reflexivity, survivor-centered design, and collaborative, multidisciplinary practice. As technology continues to advance, the field must remain vigilant to ensure that innovation serves not just the promise of efficiency, but the reality of safety, dignity, and empowerment for all survivors.

Competing Interests The authors have no conflicts of interest to declare that are relevant to the content of this chapter.

References

Abdulai, A. (2025). Is generative AI increasing the risk for technology-mediated trauma among vulnerable populations? *Nursing Inquiry, 32*(1), e12686. https://doi.org/10.1111/nin.12686

Al-Alosi, H. (2020). Fighting fire with fire: Exploring the potential of technology to help victims combat intimate partner violence. *Aggression and Violent Behavior, 52*, 101376. https://doi.org/10.1016/j.avb.2020.101376

Al-Garadi, M. A., Kim, S., Guo, Y., Warren, E., Yang, Y.-C., Lakamana, S., & Sarker, A. (2022). *Natural language model for automatic identification of intimate partner violence reports from twitter* (Vol. 15, p. 100217). Array (New York, N.Y.). https://doi.org/10.1016/j.array.2022.100217

Bandura, A. (1977). *Social learning theory*. (pp. viii, 247). Prentice-Hall.

Basile, K. C., Smith, S. G., Breiding, M. J., Black, M. C., & Mahendra, R. R. (2014). *Sexual violence surveillance: Uniform definitions and recommended data elements. Version 2.0.* National Center for Injury Prevention and Control, Centers for Disease Control and Prevention.

Basile, K. C., Smith, S. G., Kresnow, M., Khatiwada, S., & Leemis, R. W. (2022). *The National Intimate Partner and sexual violence survey: 2016/2017 report on sexual violence*. National Center for Injury Prevention and Control, Centers for Disease Control and Prevention.

Botelle, R., Bhavsar, V., Kadra-Scalzo, G., Mascio, A., Williams, M. V., Roberts, A., Velupillai, S., & Stewart, R. (2022). Can natural language processing models extract and classify instances of interpersonal violence in mental healthcare electronic records: An applied evaluative study. *BMJ Open, 12*(2), e052911. https://doi.org/10.1136/bmjopen-2021-052911

Breiding, M. J., Basile, K. C., Smith, S. G., Black, M. C., & Mahendra, R. R. (2015). *Intimate partner violence surveillance: Uniform definitions and recommended data elements, version 2.0.* National Center for Injury Prevention and Control, Centers for Disease Control and Prevention.

Buchner, V. L., Hamm, S., Medenica, B., & Molendijk, M. L. (2023). Linguistic analysis of online domestic violence testimonies in the context of COVID-19. *SAGE Open, 13*(1), 21582440221146135. https://doi.org/10.1177/21582440221146135

Campbell, J. C. (2002). Health consequences of intimate partner violence. *The Lancet, 359*(9314), 1331–1336. https://doi.org/10.1016/S0140-6736(02)08336-8

Chan, K. L., Lo, R., & Ip, P. (2021). From exposure to family violence during childhood to depression in adulthood: A path analysis on the mediating effects of intimate partner violence. *Journal of Interpersonal Violence, 36*(9–10), 4431–4450. https://doi.org/10.1177/0886260518790596

Chen, Z., Ma, W., Li, Y., Guo, W., Wang, S., Zhang, W., & Chen, Y. (2023). Using machine learning to estimate the incidence rate of intimate partner violence. *Scientific Reports, 13*(1), 5533. https://doi.org/10.1038/s41598-023-31846-8

Crooks, C. L., Talwalkar, S., Sharma, T., Arora, K., & Venkatesh, K. (2024). Designing human-centered artificial intelligence to assist with domestic abuse recovery: Mitigating technology enabled coercive control. *SoutheastCon, 2024*, 934–941. https://doi.org/10.1109/SoutheastCon52093.2024.10500080

De Filippo, A., Bellatin, P., Tietz, N., Grant, E., Whitefield, A., Nkopane, P., Devereux, C., Crawford, K., Vermeulen, B., & Hatcher, A. M. (2023). Effects of digital chatbot on gender attitudes and exposure to intimate partner violence among young women in South Africa. *PLOS Digital Health, 2*(10), e0000358. https://doi.org/10.1371/journal.pdig.0000358

Dutton, M. A. (1992). *Empowering and healing the battered woman: A model for assessment and intervention*. (pp. xx, 202). Springer Publishing Co.

Duvvury, N. C. (2013). *Intimate partner violence: Economic costs and implications for growth and development (English)*. The World Bank.

Ellsberg, M., Jansen, H. A., Heise, L., Watts, C. H., & Garcia-Moreno, C. (2008). Intimate partner violence and women's physical and mental health in the WHO multi-country study on women's health and domestic violence: An observational study. *The Lancet, 371*(9619), 1165–1172. https://doi.org/10.1016/S0140-6736(08)60522-X

Emezue, C., Chase, J. D., Udmuangpia, T., & Bloom, T. L. (2022). Technology-based and digital interventions for intimate partner violence: A systematic review and meta-analysis. *Campbell Systematic Reviews, 18*(3), e1271. https://doi.org/10.1002/cl2.1271

Gambino, D. (2024, December 04). *How AI could help victims of domestic violence, other crimes*. Government Technology. https://www.govtech.com/public-safety/how-ai-could-help-victims-of-domestic-violence-other-crimes

Garcia-Vergara, E., Almeda, N., Fernández-Navarro, F., & Becerra-Alonso, D. (2023). Artificial intelligence extracts key insights from legal documents to predict intimate partner femicide. *Scientific Reports, 13*(1), 18212. https://doi.org/10.1038/s41598-023-45157-5

Guan, S., Hui, V., Stiglic, G., Constantino, R. E., Lee, Y. J., & Wong, A. K. C. (2025). Classifying the information needs of survivors of domestic violence in online health communities using large language models: Prediction model development and evaluation study. *Journal of Medical Internet Research, 27*, e65397. https://doi.org/10.2196/65397

Hawkes, S., Weinert, C., Almeida, T., & Mehrnezhad, M. (2024). Perceptual hash inversion attacks on image-based sexual abuse removal tools. *IEEE Security & Privacy, 2–12*. https://doi.org/10.1109/MSEC.2024.3485497

Hodgkinson, S., Dixon, A., Halford, E., & Farrell, G. (2023). Domestic abuse in the covid-19 pandemic: Measures designed to overcome common limitations of trend measurement. *Crime Science, 12*(1), 12. https://doi.org/10.1186/s40163-023-00190-7

Hui, V., Guan, S., Zhang, B., Lee, Y. J., & Constantino, R. E. (2024). Predicting the information need for domestic violence survivors based on the fine-tuned large language model. *Studies in Health Technology and Informatics, 315*, 691–692. https://doi.org/10.3233/SHTI240282

Kim, S., Warren, E., Jahangir, T., Al-Garadi, M., Guo, Y., Yang, Y.-C., Lakamana, S., & Sarker, A. (2023). Characteristics of intimate partner violence and survivor's needs during the COVID-19 pandemic: Insights from subreddits related to intimate partner violence. *Journal of Interpersonal Violence, 38*(17–18), 9693–9716. https://doi.org/10.1177/08862605231168816

Leemis, R. W., Friar, N., Khatiwada, S., Chen, M. S., Kresnow, M., Smith, S. G., Caslin, S., & Basile, K. C. (2022). *The National Intimate Partner and sexual violence survey: 2016/2017 report on intimate partner violence*. National Center for Injury Prevention and Control, Centers for Disease Control and Prevention.

Manzoor, M. A., Hassan, S.-U., Muazzam, A., Tuarob, S., & Nawaz, R. (2022). Social mining for sustainable cities: Thematic study of gender-based violence coverage in news articles and domestic violence in relation to COVID-19. *Journal of Ambient Intelligence and Humanized Computing*, 1–12. https://doi.org/10.1007/s12652-021-03401-8

McLaren, H. (2016). Domestic violence in Chinese families: Cold violence by men towards women. *Journal of International Women's Studies, 17*(4), 1–15. https://vc.bridgew.edu/jiws/vol17/iss4/1

Niolon, P., Kearns, M., Dills, J., Rambo, K., Irving, S., Armstead, T., & Gilbert, L. (2017). *Intimate partner violence prevention resource for action: A compilation of the best available evidence*. National Center for Injury Prevention and Control, Centers for Disease Control and Prevention.

Novitzky, P., Janssen, J., & Kokkeler, B. (2023). A systematic review of ethical challenges and opportunities of addressing domestic violence with AI-technologies and online tools. *Heliyon, 9*(6), e17140. https://doi.org/10.1016/j.heliyon.2023.e17140

Okolie, C. (2023). Artificial intelligence-altered videos (Deepfakes), image-based sexual abuse, and data privacy concerns. *Journal of International Women's Studies, 25*(2), 11. https://vc.bridgew.edu/jiws/vol25/iss2/11

Oyebode, O., Ndulue, C., Adib, A., Mulchandani, D., Suruliraj, B., Orji, F. A., Chambers, C. T., Meier, S., & Orji, R. (2021). Health, psychosocial, and social issues emanating from the COVID-19 pandemic based on social media comments: Text mining and thematic analysis approach. *JMIR Medical Informatics, 9*(4), e22734. https://doi.org/10.2196/22734

Palmieri, J., & Valentine, J. L. (2021). Using trauma-informed care to address sexual assault and intimate partner violence in primary care. *The Journal for Nurse Practitioners, 17*(1), 44–48. https://doi.org/10.1016/j.nurpra.2020.08.028

Petering, R., Um, M., Alipourfard, N., Tavabi, N., Kumari, R., & Nasihati Gilani, S. (2018). Artificial intelligence to predict intimate partner violence perpetration. In I. M. Tambe & E. Rice (Eds.), *Artificial intelligence and social work*. Cambridge University Press.

Peterson, C., Kearns, M. C., McIntosh, W. L., Estefan, L. F., Nicolaidis, C., McCollister, K. E., Gordon, A., & Florence, C. (2018). Lifetime economic burden of intimate partner violence among U.S. adults. *American Journal of Preventive Medicine, 55*(4), 433–444. https://doi.org/10.1016/j.amepre.2018.04.049

Platzer, M. (2022, April 22). *AI-based re-identification attacks—And how to protect against them*. Retrieved from Mostly AI: https://mostly.ai/blog/synthetic-data-protects-from-ai-based-re-identification-attacks

Sabri, B., Glass, N., Murray, S., Perrin, N., Case, J. R., & Campbell, J. C. (2021). A technology-based intervention to improve safety, mental health and empowerment outcomes for immigrant women with intimate partner violence experiences: It's weWomen plus sequential multiple assignment randomized trial (SMART) protocol. *BMC Public Health, 21*(1), 1956. https://doi.org/10.1186/s12889-021-11930-2

Segal, A. E. (2025, January 14). *Global activist—Now a U of T PhD student—Uses AI to combat sexual violence*. University of Toronto. https://www.utoronto.ca/news/global-activist-now-u-t-phd-student-uses-ai-combat-sexual-violence

Sikstrom, S., Dahl, M., & Claesdotter-Knutsson, E. (2023). Removing biases in communication of severity assessments of intimate partner violence: Model development and evaluation. *Journal of Medical Internet Research, 25*, e43499. https://doi.org/10.2196/43499

Swaminathan, A., López, I., Mar, R. A. G., Heist, T., McClintock, T., Caoili, K., Grace, M., Rubashkin, M., Boggs, M. N., Chen, J. H., Gevaert, O., Mou, D., & Nock, M. K. (2023). Natural language processing system for rapid detection and intervention of mental health crisis chat messages. *npj Digital Medicine, 6*(1), 213. https://doi.org/10.1038/s41746-023-00951-3

Tabaie, A., Zeidan, A. J., Evans, D. P., Smith, R. N., & Kamaleswaran, R. (2022). A novel technique to identify intimate partner violence in a hospital setting. *The Western Journal of Emergency Medicine, 23*(5), 781–788. https://doi.org/10.5811/westjem.2022.7.56726

Taft, C. T., & Campbell, J. C. (2024). Promoting the use of evidence-based practice for those who engage in intimate partner violence. *American Journal of Preventive Medicine, 66*(1), 189–192. https://doi.org/10.1016/j.amepre.2023.08.017

Thorn & All Tech Is Human. (2024). *Safety by design for generative AI: Preventing child sexual abuse*. https://info.thorn.org/hubfs/thorn-safety-by-design-for-generative-AI.pdf?hsCtaAttrib=165037384300

Wathen, C. N., & Mantler, T. (2022). Trauma- and violence-informed care: Orienting intimate partner violence interventions to equity. *Current Epidemiology Reports, 9*(4), 233–244. https://doi.org/10.1007/s40471-022-00307-7

Wathen, C. N., & Varcoe, C. (Eds.). (2023). *Implementing trauma- and violence-informed care: A handbook*. University of Toronto Press.

WHO. (2013). *Responding to intimate partner violence and sexual violence against women: WHO clinical and policy guidelines*. World Health Organization. https://iris.who.int/handle/10665/85240

WHO. (2021). *Violence against women prevalence estimates, 2018. Global, regional and national prevalence estimates for intimate partner violence against women and global and regional prevalence estimates for non-partner sexual violence against women*. WHO.

Widom, C. S., & Wilson, H. W. (2015). Intergenerational transmission of violence. In J. Lindert & I. Levav (Eds.), *Violence and mental health* (pp. 27–45). Springer. https://doi.org/10.1007/978-94-017-8999-8_2

Yadav, A., & Vishwakarma, D. K. (2023). Deep learning algorithms for person re-identification: State-of-the-art and research challenges. *Multimedia Tools and Applications, 83*(8), 22005–22054. https://doi.org/10.1007/s11042-023-16286-w

Chapter 9
AI in Mental Health Services

Yuyi Yang and Dorian Traube

1 Introduction

1.1 The Digital Revolution in Mental Health

Rapid advances in digital technology have positioned artificial intelligence (AI) as a catalyst for new approaches to predicting, detecting, and treating mental disorders. Digital mental health is now an established field that continues to expand through rigorous research and a growing portfolio of AI-enabled interventions (D'Alfonso, 2020). Yet, uptake of such technologies in routine psychiatric practice has lagged behind other medical specialties, largely because mental health care depends heavily on interpersonal relationships and qualitative assessments (Graham et al., 2019).

Recent evidence indicates that AI can enhance accessibility, efficiency, and evidence-based decision-making across the mental-health spectrum (Olawade et al., 2024). Machine-learning models improve diagnostic precision, while natural language processing (NLP) tools help clinicians monitor treatment response in real time (Dehbozorgi et al., 2025; Graham et al., 2019). By extracting meaningful patterns from large, heterogeneous data sets, AI supports population-level surveillance, explains biological mechanisms, and informs personalized care plans. Remote delivery platforms and self-assessment applications further extend the reach of evidence-based interventions.

Despite these opportunities, implementation remains constrained by technological, clinical, and ethical challenges. Limitations include sparse real-world training

Y. Yang (✉)
Division of Computational and Data Sciences, Washington University in St. Louis, St. Louis, MO, USA
e-mail: y.yuyi@wustl.edu

D. Traube
Brown School, Washington University in St. Louis, St. Louis, MO, USA
e-mail: traube@wustl.edu

R. An, M. A. Lindsey (eds.), *Artificial Intelligence in Social Work*,
https://doi.org/10.1007/978-3-032-18443-6_9

data, gaps between algorithmic outputs and clinical workflows, and the need to safeguard patient privacy while ensuring transparency and fairness (Koutsouleris et al., 2022; Tavory, 2024). Addressing these issues is critical to realizing AI's potential in mental-health services.

1.2 Aims and Objectives

This chapter critically surveys how contemporary AI—ranging from multimodal deep-learning diagnostics and digital phenotyping to large-language-model chatbots and socially assistive robots (SAR)—is reshaping mental-health care across early detection, diagnosis, treatment personalization, monitoring, crisis response, and population-specific services. It synthesizes current evidence on accuracy, clinical benefit, user engagement, and cost-effectiveness, while interrogating persistent barriers such as data bias, privacy threats, opacity, workforce readiness, and epistemic blind spots. Building on these insights, it delineates research, implementation, and governance priorities needed to integrate next-generation systems, particularly retrieval-augmented large language models (LLMs), into routine practice. Throughout, the analysis underscores that early and sustained co-production with patients, caregivers, clinicians, technologists, and policymakers is indispensable for developing AI that is clinically effective, ethically sound, and socially just.

1.3 Defining AI in Mental Health

AI encompasses computational techniques, such as machine learning, deep learning, and reinforcement learning, that enable computer systems to perform tasks that conventionally require human cognition (Carr, 2020). While widely applied to diagnostic imaging, patient monitoring, and electronic health records (EHR), mental-health contexts demand sensitivity to emotion, culture, and lived experience (Gabbard & Crisp-Han, 2017). Accordingly, AI systems should augment rather than replace therapeutic relationships, providing transparent, interpretable, and ethically grounded decision support.

2 Scope and Core Concepts

2.1 *Evolution of AI Applications in Mental Health*

The integration of AI in mental healthcare has evolved significantly over recent decades, beginning with simple cognitive models such as the early chatbot ELIZA and progressing to sophisticated AI-driven interventions currently available (Bassett, 2019). Machine-learning-driven tools now underpin screening instruments, relapse-prevention systems, and adaptive digital therapeutics, signaling a shift from trial-and-error approaches to data-informed precision psychiatry (D'Alfonso, 2020).

2.2 *Cognitive and Clinical Foundations*

By modeling complex interactions among biological, psychological, and social determinants, machine-learning algorithms support more nuanced risk stratification and earlier detection of prodromal states (Koutsouleris et al., 2022). Continued refinement may eventually yield diagnostic taxonomies that supplement—or surpass—conventional nosology such as the DSM-5 (Alhuwaydi, 2024).

2.3 *Digital Phenotyping and Ecological Momentary Assessment*

Smartphones, wearables, and other sensor-laden devices now enable two complementary approaches to real-world data capture. Digital phenotyping converts passively collected streams, such as GPS traces, accelerometry, and heart-rate variability (HRV), into objective markers of mood, cognition, and social activity (Rogan et al., 2024). Ecological momentary assessment (EMA), by contrast, relies on brief active self-reports (e.g., "How anxious do you feel right now?") delivered several times a day. When combined, these passive and active signals reveal patterns—such as irregular mobility, fragmented sleep, and fluctuating self-rated affect—that precede depressive or bipolar episodes and can trigger just-in-time (JIT) interventions (de Lacy et al., 2023; Patel et al., 2024).

2.4 *NLP in Mental Health*

NLP models analyze textual and spoken language to detect linguistic cues associated with psychopathology, including suicidal ideation and affective instability (Flanagan et al., 2021). Large-language-model-based conversational agents (e.g.,

GPT variants) can deliver psychoeducation and preliminary triage, but there are still unresolved concerns about privacy, bias, and clinical validity (Hua et al., 2024; Park & Han, 2018). Rigorous evaluation and stakeholder oversight are essential before widespread deployment.

2.5 *Stakeholder-Centered Co-Production*

Meaningful AI solutions are co-produced through sustained collaboration between technical developers and those who use or are impacted by the technology. Patients contribute lived experience and behavioral data; clinicians bridge AI insights with clinical practice; data scientists integrate domain knowledge with technical modeling; and policymakers safeguard equity through governance. As depicted in Fig. 9.1, this interdependence forms a dynamic closed-loop system. The Data Loop: Patient-generated data fuel AI model development. The Support Loop: AI-generated insights trigger clinician actions, which in turn yield new behavioral data to refine models. The Governance Loop: Policymakers iteratively regulate the system in response to researcher-identified risks and feedback. Early stakeholder involvement—via participatory design or advisory boards—surfaces critical priorities (e.g., workflow constraints, equity barriers) that shape the AI lifecycle. Empirical evidence confirms that such co-production enhances feasibility, sharpens risk identification, and mitigates algorithmic harm (Broadbent et al., 2024; Patel et al., 2024; Zidaru et al., 2021).

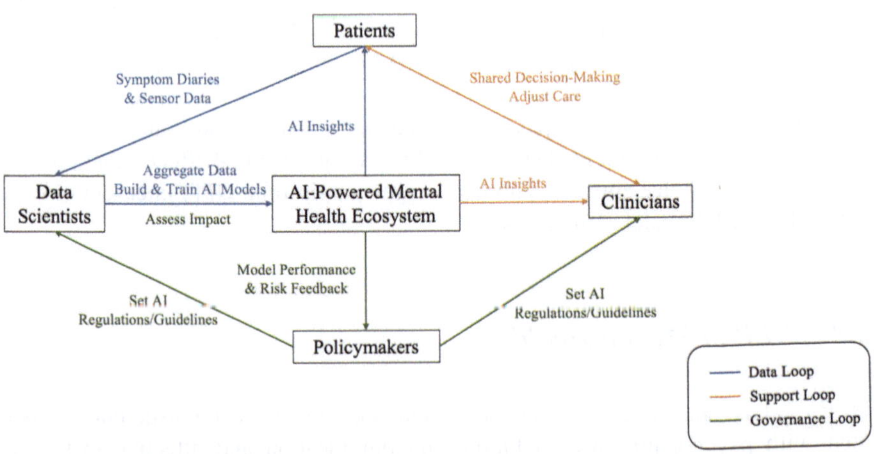

Fig. 9.1 Stakeholder loops governing AI-enabled mental-health services

3 Key Applications and Use Cases

Table 9.1 consolidates AI applications that operate not only across the core stages of the mental-health care continuum—ranging from early detection to crisis response—but also within population-specific domains such as adolescent care, geriatric care, PTSD, and addiction.

Table 9.1 AI applications and representative tools across the mental-health care spectrum

Subsection	Primary AI modalities	Illustrative use cases / tools
Early detection & prediction	Multimodal ML on speech, text, facial affect, EHR; micro-expression & paralinguistic analysis	Cogito voice analytics; Affectiva vision models; EHR suicide-risk DL models; multimodal genomic-wearable models
Clinical diagnosis & decision support	High-dimensional pattern recognition; decision-support dashboards; automated EHR summarization	FDA-cleared autism diagnostic aid; EHR mood-disorder detectors
Treatment & therapy enhancements	Pharmacogenomic classifiers; adaptive digital therapeutics; typing-dynamics wearables; LLM chatbots	Wysa CBT; Mindstrong typing-dynamics monitor; Woebot postpartum-depression chatbot
Monitoring & follow-up	Passive sensing (wearables, smartphones); EMA fusion; anomaly detection vs. personal baseline	Oura ring HRV early-warning; alcohol-use relapse EMA predictor
Chatbots & conversational agents	LLM-based context-aware dialogue platforms	Kai.AI (ACT); Woebot (CBT: Substance use and depression)
Crisis response & suicide prevention	Real-time NLP triage classifiers on crisis text/voice	Crisis text line
Adolescent mental health	Social-media sentiment; sleep & activity tracking; school digital screeners	Youth social-media mood map; school referral screener (co-designed)
Elderly mental health care	Socially assistive robots; smart-home sensors + NLP companions	ElliQ robot adherence coach; internet-of-things framework
PTSD & trauma treatment	Physio-adaptive VR exposure therapy; biosensor feedback; NLP analysis of therapy transcripts	VR exposure auto-titration; biosensor anxiety classifier; NLP trauma-cue tracker
Addiction therapy	JIT adaptive interventions; geospatial pattern recognition in recovery apps	Addict free context-aware prompts

3.1 Early Detection and Prediction

The early identification of mental health disorders increasingly depends on AI-driven analysis of speech, text, facial affect, and longitudinal EHRs. For example, micro-expression recognition algorithms now detect prodromal symptoms that frequently escape clinician observation (Zhao et al., 2023). Commercial platforms such as Cogito employ paralinguistic analysis during tele-psychiatry visits to flag subtle vocal changes, whereas Affectiva's vision models screen for depressive affective states (Affectiva, 2025; Cogito, 2025). By integrating heterogeneous data streams, machine-learning pipelines generate personalized risk scores that outperform traditional single-modality screeners.

Population-scale studies likewise demonstrate the value of multimodal modeling. Hilbert et al. (2017) distinguished generalized anxiety disorder from major depressive disorder by fusing endocrine markers with structural MRI data. Deep-learning models trained on EHR predict suicide attempts up to 1 year in advance, facilitating proactive outreach (Walsh et al., 2021; Zheng et al., 2020). Most recently, de Lacy et al. (2023) achieved area-under-the-curve (AUC—a 0-to-1 measure of overall diagnostic accuracy) values above 0.90 by jointly modeling clinical, genomic, and wearable-sensor data for three common disorders. Although external validation remains limited, these findings underscore the feasibility of moving from reactive to preventive psychiatry (Ehtemam et al., 2024; Olawade et al., 2024).

3.2 Clinical Diagnosis and Decision Support

In diagnostic practice, pattern-recognition capabilities enable AI systems to process the high-dimensional data generated by routine care. Decision-support dashboards display differential diagnoses, estimate prognoses, and recommend evidence-based treatment pathways (Dehbozorgi et al., 2025). When embedded into shared decision-making workflows, such systems have shortened assessment time, reduced waiting lists, and improved recovery rates (Rollwage et al., 2023). Importantly, clinicians report that automated summarization of patient-reported outcomes frees them to focus on the therapeutic relationship rather than data entry (De Angel et al., 2023).

Regulatory agencies are beginning to recognize clinical AI. In 2021, the U.S. Food and Drug Administration (FDA) granted breakthrough designation to an autism diagnostic aid that combines caregiver questionnaires with clinician inputs and achieves 98% sensitivity (Broadbent et al., 2024). Comparable gains have been documented for automated detection of depressive and anxiety disorders in EHRs (Higgins & Wilson, 2025). To sustain clinician trust, however, model transparency and interpretability remain essential (Warrier et al., 2023).

3.3 Treatment and Therapy Enhancements

Precision therapeutics leverage machine-learning models to match interventions with individual biological and psychosocial profiles. Pharmacogenomic classifiers, for instance, forecast antidepressant response by analyzing single-nucleotide variants (Bobo et al., 2022). Digital companions such as Wysa deliver evidence-informed cognitive-behavioral content and mood-tracking functions (Wysa, 2025), while adaptive internet-delivered cognitive behavioral therapy (CBT) adjusts session sequencing in real time (Thieme et al., 2023). Wearable-enabled platforms like Mindstrong infer cognitive fluctuations from typing dynamics, enabling just-in-time clinical review (Gruber, 2025). The FDA's breakthrough designation for the Woebot postpartum depression chatbot illustrates regulators' growing openness to digital therapeutics (Patel et al., 2024).

3.4 Monitoring and Follow-Up

Continuous passive sensing—via smartphones, wearables, and ambient sensors—provides high-frequency behavioral and physiological data. AI models detect departures from personal baselines and trigger alerts well before clinical deterioration becomes obvious (Khoo et al., 2024; Rollwage et al., 2023). For example, Oura Ring analytics link reduced HRV and fragmented sleep to impending depressive episodes (Kristiansson et al., 2023). Ecological momentary-assessment apps that fuse mood diaries with sensor streams can predict relapse in alcohol-use disorder with high precision (Alowais et al., 2023). By continuously monitoring patient data and automatically prioritizing follow-up, AI frees clinicians to devote their time to complex therapeutic work.

3.5 Chatbots and Conversational Agents

Conversational agents have evolved from rule-based scripts to LLM-based systems capable of context-aware dialogue (Thapa & Adhikari, 2024). Randomized trials report moderate reductions in depressive and anxiety symptoms after 4–8 weeks of guided interaction (Loveys et al., 2023). Special-purpose chatbots expand access to mental health support for underserved groups. For example, Kai.ai, an acceptance and commitment therapy (ACT)-based texting companion, improved well-being in more than 10,000 adolescents awaiting psychiatric intake (Vertsberger et al., 2022). Moreover, a study of a CBT-based postpartum chatbot showed modest reductions in depressive symptoms among new mothers, suggesting such tools can widen access to perinatal mental-health support (Suharwardy et al., 2023). Preliminary evidence indicates that users perceive these sophisticated interactions as beneficial for managing stress and loneliness (Yang et al., 2025). While promising, large-scale effectiveness studies and robust safeguarding protocols are still required.

3.6 Crisis Response and Suicide Prevention

Natural language classifiers embedded in crisis-text platforms can triage users within seconds, prioritizing those at imminent risk of self-harm. For example, Crisis Text Line's NLP-driven triage model correctly flags 86% of texters at severe imminent risk on their very first message (Filbin, 2018) and has cut the median wait for a counselor response from 8 min under human-only triage to just 3 min—almost a 50% reduction (Swaminathan et al., 2023). Reliance on language alone, however, poses ethical and technical dilemmas. Sarcasm, cultural idioms, and code-switching can confuse models and lead to both missed crises and false alarms; recent benchmark studies show markedly lower accuracy on African American English and other underrepresented dialects (Mire et al., 2025). False positives may trigger unwarranted police wellness checks that traumatize callers or exhaust scarce emergency resources, whereas false negatives leave texters waiting in silence.

Privacy risks further complicate deployment. In 2022, Crisis Text Line faced public backlash for sharing anonymized conversation data with its for-profit spin-off, prompting the hotline to terminate the arrangement and request deletion of all previously transferred data (Crisis Text Line, 2022). The episode underscores why crisis platforms must adopt transparent governance, opt-in data policies, human-in-the-loop overrides, and regular bias audits to complement the speed and scale of algorithms.

3.7 Adolescent Mental Health

Recent work shows that multimodal, developmentally tuned AI can flag emerging mood problems in teens days, sometimes weeks, before they meet clinical cut-offs. In a U.S. cohort of 9- to 17-year-olds, de Lacy et al. (2023) trained meta-learning ensembles on 160 psychosocial, physiological, and environmental features and achieved held-out AUCs ≥0.94 for depression, anxiety, attention-deficit/hyperactivity disorder (ADHD), disruptive behavior, and post-traumatic stress disorder (PTSD), with everyday behavioral signals outperforming neuro-imaging inputs. When these passive streams (social-media sentiment, sleep–wake regularity, and activity rhythms) are layered into real-time dashboards, clinicians can intervene earlier and more precisely.

In school settings, digital screeners have moved beyond static questionnaires: Olawade et al. (2024) report that an adaptive triage engine increased referral precision without adding false positives, ensuring counselor time goes to students who need it most. Sustained engagement, however, hinges on participatory governance.

A mixed-methods study of AI-enabled mental-health apps for young people found that adolescents will share sensitive data only when they help set privacy rules, see clear value, and can veto unwanted personalization (Nicol et al., 2022); similar themes emerged in a German co-design study that highlighted transparency and user control as non-negotiables (Götzl et al., 2022). Best practice now pairs youth-led design reviews with parent–teacher steering groups so that alert thresholds, escalation protocols, and tone remain both developmentally appropriate and culturally sensitive.

3.8 *Elderly Mental Health Care*

SARs and voice-enabled virtual agents are moving from pilot studies to real-world elder-care programs. A systematic review of eight trials by Boumans et al. (2022) found that socially assistive systems most often deliver timed medication reminders, brief cognitive games, and conversational check-ins. Home deployments achieved the highest usability scores, yet hearing-related speech-recognition errors remained a persistent barrier. Building on this evidence, Broadbent et al. (2024) describe the roll-out of the tabletop robot ElliQ across 15 U.S. and Canadian ageing-service agencies. Early field data show sustained daily engagement and self-reported reductions in loneliness, while weekly summary reports allow clinicians to integrate robot-captured insights into routine care.

Ambient sensing provides a complementary safety net. Feng et al. (2017) describe a cognitive Internet-of-Things framework that integrates heterogeneous smart-home sensors, such as motion, acoustic, light, temperature, and even furniture-pressure, into a unified data stream. An adaptive control layer then analyses these real-time traces, flags behavioral deviations, and sends plain-language alerts to caregivers. When paired with the dialogue capabilities highlighted by Boumans et al., such systems help older adults remain independent while keeping families informed. Crucially, all three studies stress that age-inclusive usability testing—covering interface legibility, error recovery, and user-tunable alert thresholds—is essential to prevent technology-driven exclusion as these AI tools scale.

3.9 *PTSD and Trauma Treatment*

Machine-learning tools now support trauma care across physiological and textual modalities. A systematic review of clinical studies by Ehtemam et al. (2024) found that suicide-risk prediction algorithms—many trained on PTSD-enriched cohorts—achieve moderate-to-high discrimination, laying the groundwork for automated safety-planning flags. Within virtual-reality exposure therapy, Mevlevioğlu et al. (2024) showed that biosensor streams captured inside the headset (e.g., electrodermal activity, HRV) classify moment-to-moment anxiety with 75% accuracy, enabling physiologically adaptive stimulus dosing. Complementing these physiological signals, NLP pipelines mine free text—from adolescent earthquake narratives (Yuan et al., 2024) to electronic medical records (Miranda et al., 2024)—to surface trauma cues and track symptom trajectories, provided that stringent confidentiality safeguards remain in place throughout the data lifecycle.

3.10 Addiction Therapy

JIT adaptive interventions that fuse smartphone sensing with reinforcement-learning policies can issue coping prompts exactly when relapse risk peaks. Gönül et al. (2021) showed that a personalized scheduling algorithm consistently outperformed fixed-rule baselines in simulated craving scenarios, demonstrating the value of continuous risk forecasting. Geospatial context adds another layer: Yang et al. (2019) use GPS and temporal patterns in the Addict Free app to detect high-risk "smoking zones" and nudge users toward alternative activities, while a deep-learning early-warning engine for suicide attempts built on EHRs (Zheng et al., 2020) illustrates how similar predictive frameworks transfer to comorbid self-harm risks.

Automated chatbots employing motivational-interviewing scripts can maintain therapeutic continuity outside clinic hours, but experience so far indicates they work best when tightly integrated with peer and clinician support. Long-term recovery, therefore, hinges on combining machine-generated prompts with human accountability, regular professional check-ins, and access to community resources that reinforce behavior change.

4 Limitations, Challenges, and Ethical Considerations

4.1 Technical and Implementation Barriers

Developing robust AI tools for mental health is constrained foremost by data quality and scope. Small, homogeneous samples promote over-fitting and undermine external validity (Schnack & Kahn, 2016), while missing or inconsistent records can distort predictions and jeopardize clinical recommendations (Tsvetanova et al., 2021). Even well-performing models often falter once deployed beyond the datasets on which they were trained (Graham et al., 2019). Under-representation of racial and ethnic minorities, older adults, and socio-economically diverse populations compounds these issues by embedding structural bias in algorithmic outputs (Franklin et al., 2024).

Despite rapid methodological advances, precision psychiatry remains in its infancy. Many machine-learning studies are conceived without the early involvement of clinicians, patients, or health-system leaders, leading to tools that are technically impressive yet clinically awkward (Wiens et al., 2019). Current prototypes rarely align with standard psychiatric assessment frameworks and cannot reproduce the empathetic exchanges fundamental to therapeutic practice (Ray et al., 2022). When model outputs are derived from questionable sensor data or self-reports, clinicians' skepticism is justified: over-reliance can delay intervention or overlook clinical deterioration (Malik et al., 2025; Rogan et al., 2024). Ensuring transparent reporting, continuous monitoring, and human oversight is therefore imperative.

4.2 *Ethical and Regulatory Considerations*

4.2.1 Algorithmic Bias and Data Protection

Training data mirror the inequities of the societies that generate them, and algorithms can magnify those inequities if safeguards are absent (Chen et al., 2019). Discriminatory outputs have been observed when diagnostic labels correlate spuriously with ethnicity or income. Regulatory regimes are beginning to respond: the EU Artificial Intelligence Act, for example, mandates bias audits and minimum performance thresholds for high-risk medical systems (Higgins & Wilson, 2025). Given the sensitivity of mental-health information, robust encryption, differential-privacy techniques, and explicit consent protocols are non-negotiable (Cruz-Gonzalez et al., 2025).

4.2.2 Explainability and Clinical Trust

Deep learning architectures often operate as opaque "black boxes (their internal reasoning is hidden from users)," limiting clinicians' willingness to rely on them in high-stakes decisions (Olawade et al., 2024). Explainable-AI (XAI) methods—such as attention maps, counterfactual explanations, and Shapley values—can expose the logic of a model's prediction, enabling users to detect bias or error (Albahri et al., 2023). Future research must prioritize solutions that balance predictive accuracy with interpretability to sustain accountability and promote adoption.

4.2.3 Global Governance Gaps

While the FDA's Software-as-a-Medical-Device framework and the EU AI Act provide a starting point, neither addresses the nuances of mental-health contexts—ranging from crisis-hotline triage to longitudinal mood monitoring (Broadbent et al., 2024; Warrier et al., 2023). The World Health Organization (WHO) has urged member states to establish sector-specific standards that encompass privacy, safety, and cultural appropriateness. Harmonized international guidelines would help ensure that vulnerable populations benefit from AI without incurring disproportionate risks.

4.3 Clinical and Human-Centered Concerns

Therapeutic effectiveness in mental health depends on empathy, rapport, and subtle non-verbal communication—capacities that current AI systems only approximate (Gabbard & Crisp-Han, 2017). When assessment or treatment planning is delegated wholesale to automated decision aids, care can become depersonalized, and the clinician–patient alliance weakened. Misalignment between algorithmic recommendations and professional judgment or lived experience may, in turn, erode trust (Koutsouleris et al., 2022; Rashid & Sharma, 2025). A growing body of user-centered design research demonstrates that engaging service users, carers, and frontline clinicians throughout development mitigates these risks. Participatory workshops, iterative prototyping, and in-situ simulations surface context-specific safety concerns, improve perceived helpfulness, and reduce attrition in digital interventions (Bernaerts et al., 2024). Such co-production has proved especially important for tailoring chatbot tone, escalation thresholds, and interface accessibility for older adults, adolescents, and linguistically minoritized populations (Peng et al., 2024).

As conversational agents adopt naturalistic voices and avatars, users increasingly attribute human-like understanding and intentions to them—a variant of the "ELIZA effect." Experimental comparisons of anthropomorphic "digital humans" with text-only chatbots show higher perceived empathy but also inflated expectations of clinical competence, which can lead to unsafe reliance during crises (Peter et al., 2025). Designers therefore face a trade-off: richer social cues may enhance engagement, yet excessive anthropomorphism can blur the boundary between tool and therapist. LLMs further complicate the picture. Recent evaluations reveal that state-of-the-art systems still generate inaccurate or unsafe advice in a minority of self-harm scenarios despite guardrails (Kolding et al., 2024). Embedding explicit usage boundaries, real-time risk-detection triggers, and human-in-the-loop escalation pathways is therefore essential. Transparent disclosure of an agent's non-human status, combined with continuous bias audits and user-centered design principles, can help preserve relational quality while minimizing the dangers of both depersonalized care and misplaced anthropomorphic trust.

4.4 Practical and Workforce Implications

Successful implementation depends on clinician literacy in data science and on thoughtfully re-engineered workflows. Targeted training should equip mental-health professionals to interpret model outputs while maintaining patient-centered values

(Higgins & Wilson, 2025). Participatory design, iterative prototyping, and simulation exercises can surface bottlenecks before deployment (Scheinker & Brandeau, 2020). Where appropriately integrated, AI may automate administrative tasks, streamline triage, and expand capacity for high-need patients (Warrier et al., 2023).

Attention to health equity is essential. People with intellectual or developmental disabilities, for example, are frequently excluded from digital-health research, thereby widening existing disparities (Zidaru et al., 2021). Inclusive data strategies and culturally attuned interface design can help ensure that AI reinforces rather than undermines equitable access to mental-health services. Emerging work on intelligent resource matching—such as directing users to linguistically appropriate crisis lines—illustrates how algorithmic tools can advance, rather than hinder, justice in mental-health care (Ehtemam et al., 2024).

4.5 Epistemological Reflexivity

Despite the growing enthusiasm for data-driven precision psychiatry, scholars in critical psychiatry and disability studies traditions caution that an exclusive focus on quantifiable markers of distress risks marginalizing lived experiences that resist easy instrumentation. Qualitative narratives of trauma, cultural idioms of distress, and personal recovery stories can be flattened when reduced to sensor streams or symptom counts. Embracing epistemological pluralism—where algorithmic outputs are complemented by participatory, phenomenological, and narrative methods—can mitigate this blind spot and foster more inclusive mental health AI (Kirmayer & Gómez-Carrillo, 2019; Shakespeare, 2013).

5 Future Directions

5.1 Research Agendas and Mechanistic Understanding

Prospective investigations should elucidate the mechanisms through which AI-enabled interventions improve mental-health outcomes. While conventional predictive models may be adequate for discrete, point-of-care tasks, the multifactorial nature of mental disorders demands interpretable approaches that facilitate accountability and clinician trust (Koutsouleris et al., 2022). Accordingly, forthcoming work ought to privilege methods that achieve both analytic precision and explanatory clarity. Leveraging large-scale multimodal datasets in this manner will allow researchers to surface clinically actionable patterns, refine treatment pathways, and identify opportunities for earlier intervention.

Despite increasing experimentation, the science of AI-supported mental healthcare remains emergent. Few studies track long-term implementation or cross-site generalizability (Auf et al., 2025). Rigorous longitudinal and multi-center designs—supplemented by rich case studies—are required to generate evidence that informs sustainable deployment for diverse populations and settings.

5.2 *Implementation Science and Stakeholder Involvement*

Patient and public involvement are increasingly recognized as prerequisites for responsible AI innovation. Treating service users and caregivers as domain experts throughout the design and evaluation cycle promotes equity, fosters trust, and aligns tools with lived experience (Zidaru et al., 2021). Empirical work demonstrates that early stakeholder engagement—via prototype testing, advisory boards, or citizen-science methods—enhances feasibility and acceptability (Broadbent et al., 2024; Patel et al., 2024).

Standardized research methodologies and reporting guidelines remain urgently needed to facilitate evidence synthesis and cross-study comparability (Dehbozorgi et al., 2025). Interdisciplinary partnerships—linking computational scientists, clinicians, implementation researchers, and ethicists—can help ensure methodological rigor and smooth translation from algorithm to workflow.

5.3 *Integration of Large Language Models*

LLMs have rapidly expanded the frontier of conversational support tools in psychiatry. By modeling nuanced linguistic cues, contemporary systems can simulate empathic dialogue, deliver psychoeducation, and triage distress (Kolding et al., 2024). Promising lines of work, such as multi-agent reinforcement learning (Liu et al., 2024), further suggest avenues for collaborative, context-aware interventions.

These advances, however, are counter-balanced by substantive concerns around privacy, factual reliability, and clinical safety. LLM outputs may be linguistically persuasive yet substantively inaccurate. Retrieval-augmented generation (RAG), which first fetches supporting documents from a knowledge base and then conditions the language model on them, can mitigate hallucinations (Li et al., 2025), while calibration techniques seek to temper unwarranted confidence (Huang et al., 2025; Leng et al., 2024). Nevertheless, robust validation in real-world mental-health contexts is still limited.

Future evaluations must articulate transparent development pipelines, benchmark performance in routine clinical environments, and incorporate iterative feedback from service users and clinicians. Special attention is warranted in high-risk scenarios—including suicide-prevention chatbots—where escalation protocols and external oversight are indispensable (Heston, 2023; Kiseleva et al., 2022).

5.4 *Beyond the Clinic—Education and Capacity Building*

Effective translation of algorithms into routine care is hindered by gaps between algorithmic performance and clinical utility, limited access to representative datasets, and insufficient integration into existing workflows (Koutsouleris et al., 2022). Addressing these issues requires blended human–machine systems co-designed by clinicians and data scientists. Curriculum reform and continuous professional development should equip mental-health professionals to interpret AI outputs, while sensitizing technologists to ethical, cultural, and relational dimensions of care. Shared infrastructure, common standards, and open benchmarking will accelerate the shift from proof-of-concept to sustainable practice.

5.5 *Governance Futures for Ethical AI*

Looking ahead, regulatory landscapes are crystallizing yet remain uneven. In the United States, the FDA already treats most mental health software as a Software-as-a-Medical-Device. Across the Atlantic, the European Artificial Intelligence Act—Regulation (EU) 2024/1689, in force since 1 August 2024, formally classifies clinical-decision support, digital phenotyping, and conversational agents used in mental-health care as high-risk. By 2026, manufacturers seeking access to the European market must complete conformity assessments, implement post-market monitoring plans, and provide documented human-oversight safeguards (European Union, 2024). Future governance will depend on translating such statutory duties into day-to-day practice. The process-oriented ISO/IEC 42001:2023 management system standard provides a ready template for continuous risk assessment and quality improvement. Pilot programs such as NHS England's AI & Digital Regulations Service—which maps ISO 42001 clauses onto national clinical-safety standards—demonstrate how health systems can operationalize global norms while retaining local accountability (NHS England, 2025).

At the multilateral level, the International Telecommunication Union (ITU) and WHO Focus Group on AI for Health have launched an open benchmarking pipeline that supplies reference datasets and performance thresholds; extending this model to mental-health use-cases would create a common evidentiary baseline for regulators, payers, and developers (ITU & WHO, 2023). Complementing these technical mechanisms, the WHO's 2021 guidance on the ethics and governance of AI for health articulates cross-cutting principles—safety, inclusiveness, explainability, and sustainability—that can anchor future national strategies (WHO, 2021).

Taken together, these layered instruments—binding regulation, voluntary international standards, sector-specific benchmarking, and ethics frameworks—sketch a path toward convergent governance, in which mental-health AI systems are accompanied by interoperable "safety cases" that follow each product across jurisdictions, are revised through post-market surveillance, and are audited against globally shared metrics. Realizing such a system will depend on continued investment in regulatory science, the expansion of shared test beds, and participatory oversight mechanisms capable of keeping pace with rapid technical change.

6 Conclusion

6.1 *Key Takeaways*

Across detection, diagnosis, treatment, personalization, and population surveillance, AI-enabled tools are reshaping mental-health services. Mobile applications, conversational agents, and immersive platforms demonstrate the capacity to analyze multimodal data streams and deliver timely, targeted interventions. Use cases spanning adolescent care, ageing populations, PTSD, and substance-use disorders illustrate both breadth and depth of application. Yet persistent challenges—algorithmic bias, limited generalizability, data inequities, and tension with relational models of care—underscore the need for cautious, evidence-driven adoption.

6.2 *Final Remarks and Call to Action*

Harnessing AI for mental-health benefit will demand sustained interdisciplinary collaboration, rigorous evaluation, and meaningful stakeholder partnership. Priorities include:

- *Interpretability and Safety*: Develop transparent models, calibrate uncertainty, and embed escalation pathways for crisis contexts.
- *Inclusive Governance*: Implement regulatory and professional frameworks that balance innovation with patient protection and data justice.
- *Capacity Building*: Provide clinicians, researchers, and technologists with training that bridges technical and human-centered competencies.
- *Longitudinal Evidence*: Conduct multi-site, real-world studies that track clinical effectiveness, implementation barriers, and equity impacts over time.

By foregrounding equity, trust, and therapeutic alliance, AI can augment—not supplant—human expertise, contributing to more responsive, accessible, and just mental-health systems.

Competing Interests The authors have no conflicts of interest to declare that are relevant to the content of this chapter.

References

Affectiva. (2025). *Humanizing technology to bridge the gap between humans and machines*. Affectiva. https://www.affectiva.com/

Albahri, A. S., Duhaim, A. M., Fadhel, M. A., Alnoor, A., Baqer, N. S., Alzubaidi, L., et al. (2023). A systematic review of trustworthy and explainable artificial intelligence in healthcare: Assessment of quality, bias risk, and data fusion. *Information Fusion, 96*, 156–191. https://doi.org/10.1016/j.inffus.2023.03.008

Alhuwaydi, A. M. (2024). Exploring the role of artificial intelligence in mental healthcare: Current trends and future directions—A narrative review for a comprehensive insight. *Risk Management and Healthcare Policy, 17*, 1339–1348. https://doi.org/10.2147/RMHP.S461562

Alowais, S. A., Alghamdi, S. S., Alsuhebany, N., Alqahtani, T., Alshaya, A. I., Almohareb, S. N., et al. (2023). Revolutionizing healthcare: The role of artificial intelligence in clinical practice. *BMC Medical Education, 23*(1), 689. https://doi.org/10.1186/s12909-023-04698-z

Auf, H., Svedberg, P., Nygren, J., Nair, M., & Lundgren, L. E. (2025). The use of AI in mental health services to support decision-making: Scoping review. *Journal of Medical Internet Research, 27*, e63548. https://doi.org/10.2196/63548

Bassett, C. (2019). The computational therapeutic: Exploring Weizenbaum's ELIZA as a history of the present. *AI & Society, 34*(4), 803–812. https://doi.org/10.1007/s00146-018-0825-9

Bernaerts, S., Van Daele, T., Carlsen, C. K., Nielsen, S. L., Schaap, J., & Roke, Y. (2024). User involvement in digital mental health: Approaches, potential and the need for guidelines. *Frontiers in Digital Health, 6*, 1440660. https://doi.org/10.3389/fdgth.2024.1440660

Bobo, W. V., Van Ommeren, B., & Athreya, A. P. (2022). Machine learning, pharmacogenomics, and clinical psychiatry: Predicting antidepressant response in patients with major depressive disorder. *Expert Review of Clinical Pharmacology, 15*(8), 927–944. https://doi.org/10.1080/17512433.2022.2112949

Boumans, R., van de Sande, Y., Thill, S., & Bosse, T. (2022). Voice-enabled intelligent virtual agents for people with amnesia: Systematic review. *JMIR Aging, 5*(2), e32473. https://doi.org/10.2196/32473

Broadbent, E., Loveys, K., Ilan, G., Chen, G., Chilukuri, M. M., Boardman, S. G., et al. (2024). Elliq, an ai-driven social robot to alleviate loneliness: Progress and lessons learned. *The Journal of Aging Research & Lifestyle, 13*, 22–28. https://doi.org/10.14283/jarlife.2024.2

Carr, S. (2020). 'AI gone mental': Engagement and ethics in data-driven technology for mental health. *Journal of Mental Health, 29*(2), 125–130. https://doi.org/10.1080/09638237.2020.1714011

Chen, I. Y., Szolovits, P., & Ghassemi, M. (2019). Can AI help reduce disparities in general medical and mental health care? *AMA Journal of Ethics, 21*(2), 167–179. https://doi.org/10.1001/amajethics.2019.167

Cogito. (2025). *Training data solutions for AI and machine learning*. Cogitotech. https://www.cogitotech.com/

Crisis Text Line. (2022, January 31). *An update on data privacy, our community and our service*. Crisis Text Line. https://www.crisistextline.org/blog/2022/01/31/an-update-on-data-privacy-our-community-and-our-service/

Cruz-Gonzalez, P., He, A. W. J., Lam, E. P., Ng, I. M. C., Li, M. W., Hou, R., et al. (2025). Artificial intelligence in mental health care: A systematic review of diagnosis, monitoring, and intervention applications. *Psychological Medicine, 55*, e18. https://doi.org/10.1017/S0033291724003295

D'Alfonso, S. (2020). AI in mental health. *Current Opinion in Psychology, 36*, 112–117. https://doi.org/10.1016/j.copsyc.2020.04.005

De Angel, V., Adeleye, F., Zhang, Y., Cummins, N., Munir, S., Lewis, S., et al. (2023). The feasibility of implementing remote measurement technologies in psychological treatment for depression: Mixed methods study on engagement. *JMIR Mental Health, 10*, e42866. https://doi.org/10.2196/42866

de Lacy, N., Ramshaw, M. J., McCauley, E., Kerr, K. F., Kaufman, J., & Nathan Kutz, J. (2023). Predicting individual cases of major adolescent psychiatric conditions with artificial intelligence. *Translational Psychiatry, 13*(1), 314. https://doi.org/10.1038/s41398-023-02599-9

Dehbozorgi, R., Zangeneh, S., Khooshab, E., Nia, D. H., Hanif, H. R., Samian, P., et al. (2025). The application of artificial intelligence in the field of mental health: A systematic review. *BMC Psychiatry, 25*, 132. https://doi.org/10.1186/s12888-025-06483-2

Ehtemam, H., Sadeghi Esfahlani, S., Sanaei, A., Ghaemi, M. M., Hajesmaeel-Gohari, S., Rahimisadegh, R., et al. (2024). Role of machine learning algorithms in suicide risk prediction: A systematic review-meta analysis of clinical studies. *BMC Medical Informatics and Decision Making, 24*(1), 138. https://doi.org/10.1186/s12911-024-02524-0

European Union. (2024). Regulation (EU) 2024/1689 of the European Parliament and of the Council of 13 June 2024 laying down harmonised rules on artificial intelligence (Artificial Intelligence Act). *Official Journal of the European Union*, L 2024/1689, 12 July 2024. http://data.europa.eu/eli/reg/2024/1689/oj

Feng, S., Setoodeh, P., & Haykin, S. (2017). Smart home: Cognitive interactive people-centric internet of things. *IEEE Communications Magazine, 55*(2), 34–39. https://doi.org/10.1109/MCOM.2017.1600682CM

Filbin, B. (2018, March 28). Detecting Crisis: An AI Solution. *Crisis Text Line Blog*. https://www.crisistextline.org/blog/2018/03/28/detecting-crisis-an-ai-solution/

Flanagan, O., Chan, A., Roop, P., & Sundram, F. (2021). Using acoustic speech patterns from smartphones to investigate mood disorders: Scoping review. *JMIR mHealth and uHealth, 9*(9), e24352. https://doi.org/10.2196/24352

Franklin, G., Stephens, R., Piracha, M., Tiosano, S., Lehouillier, F., Koppel, R., & Elkin, P. L. (2024). The sociodemographic biases in machine learning algorithms: A biomedical informatics perspective. *Life, 14*(6), 652. https://doi.org/10.3390/life14060652

Gabbard, G. O., & Crisp-Han, H. (2017). The early career psychiatrist and the psychotherapeutic identity. *Academic Psychiatry, 41*, 30–34. https://doi.org/10.1007/s40596-016-0627-7

Gönül, S., Namlı, T., Coşar, A., & Toroslu, İ. H. (2021). A reinforcement learning based algorithm for personalization of digital, just-in-time, adaptive interventions. *Artificial Intelligence in Medicine, 115*, 102062. https://doi.org/10.1016/j.artmed.2021.102062

Götzl, C., Hiller, S., Rauschenberg, C., Schick, A., Fechtelpeter, J., Fischer Abaigar, U., et al. (2022). Artificial intelligence-informed mobile mental health apps for young people: A mixed-methods approach on users' and stakeholders' perspectives. *Child and Adolescent Psychiatry and Mental Health, 16*(1), 86. https://doi.org/10.1186/s13034-022-00522-6

Graham, S., Depp, C., Lee, E. E., Nebeker, C., Tu, X., Kim, H. C., & Jeste, D. V. (2019). Artificial intelligence for mental health and mental illnesses: An overview. *Current Psychiatry Reports, 21*, 1–18. https://doi.org/10.1007/s11920-019-1094-0

Gruber, T. (2025). *Patient, know thyself: AI-powered digital brain biomarkers*. https://tomgruber.org/mindstrong-story/

Heston, T. F. (2023). Safety of large language models in addressing depression. *Cureus, 15*(12). https://doi.org/10.7759/cureus.50729

Higgins, O., & Wilson, R. L. (2025). Integrating artificial intelligence (AI) with workforce solutions for sustainable care: A follow up to artificial intelligence and machine learning (ML) based decision support Systems in Mental Health. *International Journal of Mental Health Nursing, 34*(2), e70019. https://doi.org/10.1111/inm.70019

Hilbert, K., Lueken, U., Muehlhan, M., & Beesdo-Baum, K. (2017). Separating generalized anxiety disorder from major depression using clinical, hormonal, and structural MRI data: A multimodal machine learning study. *Brain and Behavior, 7*(3), e00633. https://doi.org/10.1002/brb3.633

Hua, Y., Na, H., Li, Z., Liu, F., Fang, X., Clifton, D., & Torous, J. (2024). Applying and evaluating large language models in mental health care: A scoping review of human-assessed generative tasks. *arXiv*. https://doi.org/10.48550/arXiv.2408.11288.

Huang, C., Huang, L., Leng, J., Liu, J., & Huang, J. (2025). Efficient test-time scaling via self-calibration. *arXiv*. https://doi.org/10.48550/arXiv.2503.00031

International Telecommunication Union & World Health Organization. (2023). *Focus Group on Artificial Intelligence for Health (FG-AI4H)*. https://www.itu.int/go/fgai4h

Khoo, L. S., Lim, M. K., Chong, C. Y., & McNaney, R. (2024). Machine learning for multimodal mental health detection: A systematic review of passive sensing approaches. *Sensors, 24*(2), 348. https://doi.org/10.3390/s24020348

Kirmayer, L. J., & Gómez-Carrillo, A. (2019). Agency, embodiment and enactment in psychosomatic theory and practice. *Medical Humanities, 45*(2) https://mh.bmj.com/content/45/2/169

Kiseleva, A., Kotzinos, D., & De Hert, P. (2022). Transparency of AI in healthcare as a multilayered system of accountabilities: Between legal requirements and technical limitations. *Frontiers in Artificial Intelligence, 5*, 879603. https://doi.org/10.3389/frai.2022.879603

Kolding, S., Lundin, R. M., Hansen, L., & Østergaard, S. D. (2024). Use of generative artificial intelligence (AI) in psychiatry and mental health care: A systematic review. *Acta Neuropsychiatrica*, 1–14. https://doi.org/10.1017/neu.2024.50

Koutsouleris, N., Hauser, T. U., Skvortsova, V., & De Choudhury, M. (2022). From promise to practice: Towards the realisation of AI-informed mental health care. *The Lancet Digital Health, 4*(11), e829–e840. https://doi.org/10.1016/S2589-7500(22)00153-4

Kristiansson, E., Fridolfsson, J., Arvidsson, D., Holmäng, A., Börjesson, M., & Andersson-Hall, U. (2023). Validation of Oura ring energy expenditure and steps in laboratory and free-living. *BMC Medical Research Methodology, 23*(1), 50. https://doi.org/10.1186/s12874-023-01868-x

Leng, J., Huang, C., Zhu, B., & Huang, J. (2024). Taming overconfidence in LLMs: Reward calibration in RLHF. *arXiv*. https://doi.org/10.48550/arXiv.2410.09724

Li, H., Huang, J., Ji, M., Yang, Y., & An, R. (2025). Use of retrieval-augmented large language model for COVID-19 fact-checking: Development and usability study. *Journal of Medical Internet Research, 27*, e66098. https://doi.org/10.2196/66098

Liu, Q., Ye, J., Ma, X., Yang, J., Liang, B., & Zhang, C. (2024). Efficient multi-agent reinforcement learning by planning. In *Proceedings of the twelfth international conference on learning representations (ICLR)*. https://openreview.net/forum?id=CpnKq3UJwp

Loveys, K., Antoni, M., Donkin, L., Sagar, M., & Broadbent, E. (2023). Comparing the feasibility and acceptability of a virtual human, teletherapy, and an e-manual in delivering a stress management intervention to distressed adult women: Pilot study. *JMIR Formative Research, 7*, e42390. https://doi.org/10.2196/42390

Malik, P. K., Bhatt, H., & Sharma, M. (2025). AI integration in healthcare systems—A review of the problems and potential associated with integrating AI in healthcare for disease detection and diagnosis. *AI in Disease Detection: Advancements and Applications, 191-213*. https://doi.org/10.1002/9781394278695.ch9

Mevlevioğlu, D., Tabirca, S., & Murphy, D. (2024). Real-time classification of anxiety in virtual reality therapy using biosensors and a convolutional neural network. *Biosensors, 14*(3), 131. https://doi.org/10.3390/bios14030131

Miranda, O., Kiehl, S. M., Qi, X., Brannock, M. D., Kosten, T., Ryan, N. D., et al. (2024). Enhancing post-traumatic stress disorder patient assessment: Leveraging natural language processing for research of domain criteria identification using electronic medical records. *BMC Medical Informatics and Decision Making, 24*(1), 154. https://doi.org/10.1186/s12911-024-02554-8

Mire, J., Aysola, Z. T., Chechelnitsky, D., Deas, N., Zerva, C., & Sap, M. (2025). Rejected dialects: Biases against African American language in reward models. *arXiv*. https://arxiv.org/pdf/2502.12858

NHS England. (2025, May 2). *AI knowledge repository*. NHS Digital. https://digital.nhs.uk/services/ai-knowledge-repository

Nicol, G., Wang, R., Graham, S., Dodd, S., & Garbutt, J. (2022). Chatbot-delivered cognitive behavioral therapy in adolescents with depression and anxiety during the COVID-19 pandemic: Feasibility and acceptability study. *JMIR Formative Research, 6*(11), e40242. https://doi.org/10.2196/40242

Olawade, D. B., Wada, O. Z., Odetayo, A., David-Olawade, A. C., Asaolu, F., & Eberhardt, J. (2024). Enhancing mental health with artificial intelligence: Current trends and future prospects. *Journal of Medicine, Surgery, and Public Health*, 100099. https://doi.org/10.1016/j.glmedi.2024.100099

Park, S. H., & Han, K. (2018). Methodologic guide for evaluating clinical performance and effect of artificial intelligence technology for medical diagnosis and prediction. *Radiology, 286*(3), 800–809. https://doi.org/10.1148/radiol.2017171920

Patel, J., Hung, C., & Katapally, T. R. (2024). Evaluating predictive artificial intelligence approaches used in mobile health platforms to forecast mental health symptoms among youth: A systematic review. *Psychiatry Research*, 116277. https://doi.org/10.1016/j.psychres.2024.116277

Peng, W., Lee, H. R., & Lim, S. (2024). Leveraging chatbots to combat health misinformation for older adults: Participatory design study. *JMIR Formative Research, 8*(1), e60712. https://doi.org/10.2196/60712

Peter, S., Riemer, K., & West, J. D. (2025). The benefits and dangers of anthropomorphic conversational agents. *Proceedings of the National Academy of Sciences, 122*(22), e2415898122. https://doi.org/10.1073/pnas.2415898122

Rashid, M., & Sharma, M. (2025). AI-assisted diagnosis and treatment planning—A discussion of how AI can assist healthcare professionals in making more accurate diagnoses and treatment plans for diseases. *AI in Disease Detection: Advancements and Applications*, 313–336. https://doi.org/10.1002/9781394278695.ch14

Ray, A., Bhardwaj, A., Malik, Y. K., Singh, S., & Gupta, R. (2022). Artificial intelligence and psychiatry: An overview. *Asian Journal of Psychiatry, 70*, 103021. https://doi.org/10.1016/j.ajp.2022.103021

Rogan, J., Bucci, S., & Firth, J. (2024). Health care professionals' views on the use of passive sensing, AI, and machine learning in mental health care: Systematic review with meta-synthesis. *JMIR Mental Health, 11*, e49577. https://doi.org/10.2196/49577

Rollwage, M., Habicht, J., Juechems, K., Carrington, B., Viswanathan, S., Stylianou, M., et al. (2023). Using conversational AI to facilitate mental health assessments and improve clinical efficiency within psychotherapy services: Real-world observational study. *JMIR AI, 2*(1), e44358. https://doi.org/10.2196/44358

Scheinker, D., & Brandeau, M. L. (2020). Implementing analytics projects in a hospital: Successes, failures, and opportunities. *INFORMS Journal on Applied Analytics, 50*(3), 176–189. https://doi.org/10.1287/inte.2020.1036

Schnack, H. G., & Kahn, R. S. (2016). Detecting neuroimaging biomarkers for psychiatric disorders: Sample size matters. *Frontiers in Psychiatry, 7*, 50. https://doi.org/10.3389/fpsyt.2016.00050

Shakespeare, T. (2013). *Disability rights and wrongs revisited.* Routledge. https://doi.org/10.4324/9781315887456

Suharwardy, S., Ramachandran, M., Leonard, S. A., Gunaseelan, A., Lyell, D. J., Darcy, A., et al. (2023). Feasibility and impact of a mental health chatbot on postpartum mental health: A randomized controlled trial. *AJOG Global Reports, 3*(3), 100165. https://doi.org/10.1016/j.xagr.2023.100165

Swaminathan, A., López, I., Mar, R. A. G., Heist, T., McClintock, T., Caoili, K., et al. (2023). Natural language processing system for rapid detection and intervention of mental health crisis chat messages. *npj Digital Medicine, 6*(1), 213. https://doi.org/10.1038/s41746-023-00951-3

Tavory, T. (2024). Regulating AI in mental health: Ethics of care perspective. *JMIR Mental Health, 11*(1), e58493. https://doi.org/10.2196/58493

Thapa, S., & Adhikari, S. (2024). GPT-4o and multimodal large language models as companions for mental wellbeing. *Asian Journal of Psychiatry, 99*, 104157. https://doi.org/10.1016/j.ajp.2024.104157

Thieme, A., Hanratty, M., Lyons, M., Palacios, J., Marques, R. F., Morrison, C., & Doherty, G. (2023). Designing human-centered AI for mental health: Developing clinically relevant applications for online CBT treatment. *ACM Transactions on Computer-Human Interaction, 30*(2), 1–50. https://doi.org/10.1145/3564752

Tsvetanova, A., Sperrin, M., Peek, N., Buchan, I., Hyland, S., & Martin, G. P. (2021). Missing data was handled inconsistently in UK prediction models: A review of method used. *Journal of Clinical Epidemiology, 140*, 149–158. https://doi.org/10.1016/j.jclinepi.2021.09.008

Vertsberger, D., Naor, N., & Winsberg, M. (2022). Adolescents' Well-being while using a mobile artificial intelligence–powered acceptance commitment therapy tool: Evidence from a longitudinal study. *JMIR AI, 1*(1), e38171. https://doi.org/10.2196/38171

Walsh, C. G., Johnson, K. B., Ripperger, M., Sperry, S., Harris, J., Clark, N., et al. (2021). Prospective validation of an electronic health record–based, real-time suicide risk model. *JAMA Network Open, 4*(3), e211428–e211428. https://doi.org/10.1001/jamanetworkopen.2021.1428

Warrier, U., Warrier, A., & Khandelwal, K. (2023). Ethical considerations in the use of artificial intelligence in mental health. *The Egyptian Journal of Neurology, Psychiatry and Neurosurgery, 59*(1), 139. https://doi.org/10.1186/s41983-023-00735-2

Wiens, J., Saria, S., Sendak, M., Ghassemi, M., Liu, V. X., Doshi-Velez, F., et al. (2019). Do no harm: A roadmap for responsible machine learning for health care. *Nature Medicine, 25*(9), 1337–1340. https://doi.org/10.1038/s41591-019-0548-6

World Health Organization. (2021). *Ethics and governance of artificial intelligence for health.* https://www.who.int/publications/i/item/9789240029200

Wysa. (2025). *Wysa: AI for mental health support.* https://www.wysa.com/

Yang, Y., Wang, C., Xiang, X., & An, R. (2025, February). AI applications to reduce loneliness among older adults: A systematic review of effectiveness and technologies. *Healthcare, 13*(5), 446. https://doi.org/10.3390/healthcare13050446

Yang, Z., Reddy, V. J., Kesidi, R., & Jin, F. (2019, August). Addict free-a smart and connected relapse intervention mobile app. In *Proceedings of the 16th international symposium on spatial and temporal databases* (pp. 202–205). doi:10.1145/3340964.3340986.

Yuan, Y., Liu, Z., Miao, W., & Tian, X. (2024). Automatic screening for posttraumatic stress disorder in early adolescents following the ya'an earthquake using text mining techniques. *Frontiers in Psychiatry, 15*, 1439720. https://doi.org/10.3389/fpsyt.2024.1439720

Zhao, G., Li, X., Li, Y., & Pietikäinen, M. (2023). Facial micro-expressions: An overview. *Proceedings of the IEEE, 111*(10), 1215–1235. https://doi.org/10.1109/JPROC.2023.3275192

Zheng, L., Wang, O., Hao, S., Ye, C., Liu, M., Xia, M., et al. (2020). Development of an early-warning system for high-risk patients for suicide attempt using deep learning and electronic health records. *Translational Psychiatry, 10*(1), 72. https://doi.org/10.1038/s41398-020-0684-2

Zidaru, T., Morrow, E. M., & Stockley, R. (2021). Ensuring patient and public involvement in the transition to AI-assisted mental health care: A systematic scoping review and agenda for design justice. *Health Expectations, 24*(4), 1072–1124. https://doi.org/10.1111/hex.13299

Chapter 10
AI in School Social Work

Jingyi Huang and Susan Stone

1 Introduction to AI in School Social Work

Rapid developments in artificial intelligence (AI) present both opportunities and challenges for social work decision-making and service delivery (Dalziel et al., 2024; Reamer, 2023). In the school context, AI is being integrated into school social work—a practice that applies social work theories and methods to help students, families, and school communities address social and psychological issues that can impede student learning and development (Ding et al., 2023; NASW, n.d.). In addition to serving as a bridge between schools, families, and communities, well-trained school social workers can also promote developmental competencies and learning opportunities at both the student and school organizational levels. In addition, because schools are a key youth-serving system, they are also a key node within local resource ecologies related to health, mental health, and youth development programs (School Social Work Association of America, n.d.-a, n.d.-b). Social work practices such as these play a crucial role in creating an educational environment that is supportive and safe for students. As a relatively new area, AI applications in this field have received little attention in the existing literature. Holmes and Tuomi (2022) provide a broad overview of current and emerging applications in education, including opportunities to: (a) individualize learning and support for students, (b) assist teachers and other school staff, and (c) enhance school administrative functions. This scope closely aligns with the entire school social work process. To structure our discussion, we will illustrate AI applications in school social work practices according to their potential functions for students, social workers, and the school system before delving into specific sections.

J. Huang (✉)
Silver School of Social Work, New York University, New York, NY, USA
e-mail: jh9925@nyu.edu

S. Stone
School of Social Welfare, University of California–Berkeley, Berkeley, CA, USA
e-mail: swdean@berkeley.edu

R. An, M. A. Lindsey (eds.), *Artificial Intelligence in Social Work*,
https://doi.org/10.1007/978-3-032-18443-6_10

For students, AI has been proposed as a new approach to customize their learning opportunities and provide targeted mental health support. Compared to traditional methods, these AI-driven solutions can enhance the delivery of social work services to individual students while reducing social workers' workload (Hinostroza Fuentes et al., 2025). Even in settings with poor Internet connectivity or limited technological infrastructure, AI can still provide basic service (Singh & Gill, 2023). As a result, by improving the scalability and accessibility of services, AI holds the potential to promote equity and help close resource gaps among students from different areas.

For a specific school social work system, the integration of AI is being explored to enhance early identification of students at risk in practice. By leveraging technologies such as natural language processing (NLP) and computer vision (CV), AI tools can analyze student activity data and chatbot conversations to provide predictive insights (Labadze et al., 2023). These predictive analytics are crucial for moving from a reactive to a proactive model of care, thereby supporting more data-driven decision-making and enabling the deployment of early, targeted interventions, ultimately helping prevent situations from escalating.

Expanding on this, informed data analytics from AI can help social workers improve comprehensive assessments and optimize interventions. AI models can integrate heterogeneous data—such as behavioral logs, academic records, and socio-emotional indicators—into multidimensional student profiles, allowing social workers to evaluate needs with greater accuracy and contextual sensitivity (Vistorte et al., 2024). This holistic assessment framework not only captures overt risk factors but also reveals latent patterns that may escape conventional evaluation methods (Golden & Aboujaoude, 2024). On the intervention side, AI tools can assist social workers in matching individual needs with evidence-based strategies, dynamically adjusting recommendations as new data emerge, thereby maximizing relevance and effectiveness (Vistorte et al., 2024).

While AI promises to be valuable in school social work, its effective and ethical integration critically depends on addressing underlying technical and deployment limitations. This includes ensuring high-quality data and adequate model design to prevent flawed outcomes, as well as maintaining transparency in operations to build trust and accountability (Aldoseri et al., 2023). Due to these limitations, significant concerns remain regarding ethical issues in AI applications, including the risk of algorithmic bias, which could perpetuate social inequities (Schaeffer et al., 2024), the data security (Pierrès et al., 2024), and the potential for AI to exacerbate educational inequality by widening the gap between well-resourced and under-resourced schools (Wang, 2024). Ultimately, realizing the benefits of AI in this context requires a thoughtful approach that prioritizes both technological advancement and ethical oversight.

This chapter aims to explore opportunities and challenges of AI application in school social work in detail. Aligning with the structure outlined earlier, we will begin with a review of existing practices and research before delving into a critical discussion of key challenges, including robust assessment, equitable access, and data privacy.

2 AI in School Social Work Practice

In this section, evidence from academic research was integrated across various aspects—student services, risk identification, and decision-making support—to illustrate how AI can be applied in school social work practices. Besides addressing traditional limitations, AI also presents drawbacks and risks in practice, which were discussed in this section.

2.1 AI for Customized Learning Opportunities and Mental Health Support

To improve students' opportunities and well-being, schools often face the dual challenge of limited human and material resources, particularly in under-resourced, marginalized areas (Local Burden of Disease Educational Attainment Collaborators [LBDEAC], 2020; Xu et al., 2023). In this context, AI technologies—particularly those accessible via mobile devices—offer a promising supplement to traditional support, including support for mental health and academic performance. (Thakkar et al., 2024; Alowais et al., 2023) By assisting social workers in delivering basic interventions and counselling services, the AI application can partially address the resource shortage of school social work and benefit students' well-being.

2.1.1 AI for Mental Health Interventions and Social-Emotional Learning

Mental health interventions and social-emotional learning (SEL) play an essential role in students' development (Shankland et al., 2024). Traditional service delivery methods for mental health support have limitations, including high costs and limited coverage. Moreover, the effectiveness of conventional approaches can be hindered by stigma and feelings of shame, which may discourage students from seeking help. By providing anonymous, on-demand support, AI-based service delivery is emerging as a promising avenue to reduce these barriers, expand access to care, and deliver timely, scalable mental health interventions (Carter et al., 2021).

Recent reviews and studies underscore AI chatbots' potential to provide mental health support for anxiety, depression, and stress (Gallegos et al., 2024). This AI-driven approach has the potential to complement traditional human interventions, helping underserved populations and reducing barriers related to cost and stigma (Daley et al., 2020; Sethi & Jain, 2024). Emerging evidence, such as a randomized trial with university students by Liu et al. (2022), found that a CBT-based chatbot intervention was associated with a notable reduction in depressive symptoms over 16 weeks and in anxiety in the first 4 weeks, outperforming traditional bibliotherapy. This research also found that patients using chatbots formed stronger therapeutic alliances (Liu et al., 2022). Further highlighting their utility, a mixed-methods study exploring chatbots' emotional support across cultures found that they facilitate users' expression of emotions, particularly sadness and depression. Analyzing extensive data from SimSimi, a global social chatbot, the study indicated users were more willing to share emotional vulnerability with chatbots about depressive or sad moods than on social media. This suggests AI chatbots create a safe space for users to openly express their emotional states (Chin et al., 2023).

In addition, specific AI-based life skills coaching programs helped adolescents improve their social skills and emotional learning. For instance, a study designed an AI-enabled social-emotional game for children with autism spectrum disorder (ASD) to generate personalized stories, which were shown to be an effective way to improve their emotional understanding and social interaction skills (Lyu et al., 2024). A critical review of the intersection of generative AI and social-emotional learning highlighted AI's potential to enhance users' competencies, such as self-awareness, empathy, and social skills, through tools like real-time emotional feedback and personalized learning. However, the review also cautioned against risks such as depersonalization, algorithmic bias, and privacy concerns (Henriksen et al., 2025). Therefore, while the AI's potential for mental health interventions is significant, these tools must undergo ongoing rigorous testing and be implemented ethically, under careful supervision from school social workers, parents, and educators, to ensure student safety and well-being.

2.1.2 AI for Academic Performance Improvement and Skill Training

In the school context, academic performance, student well-being, and the practice of school social work are heavily influenced by the availability of knowledge resources and skills training (Ding et al., 2023). However, disparities in access to quality knowledge and skill training for both students and social workers exacerbate educational inequality and hinder overall development and effective interventions (Golden et al., 2023; Wang et al., 2024).

The rapid advancement of core technologies, like large language models, has positioned AI-powered products as potentially valuable tools for promoting educational equity globally (OECD, 2024). An emerging trend is the use of customized chatbots for skill training across fields such as healthcare, nursing, psychological counseling, and social work education (Labadze et al., 2023; Srinivasan et al., 2024). These chatbots, which track personal data, are designed to offer tailored, interactive learning experiences that help students and professionals improve specific skills. Proponents suggest that such customizable AI approaches could enhance the relevance and effectiveness of training (Tanaka & Nakamura, 2022; Tam et al., 2023). For instance, a review by Labadze et al. (2023) suggests that AI can impact student learning in at least three key areas: homework support, personalized learning, and skill training. Under the supervision of school social workers and educators, AI applications such as chatbots are proposed as tools to support student development and well-being. Beyond student-facing applications, AI tools also serve as a training assistant for professionals. Research by Røed et al. (2023) found that a chatbot could be an efficient medium for training skills in child psychological counseling. Similarly, AI has been explored as a means to enhance parenting skills, thereby strengthening the family-school connection, which is vital for student support (Entenberg et al., 2023). Collectively, these examples illustrate AI's potential to support academic performance, skill development, and the broader educational ecosystem surrounding students.

However, recent evidence highlights AI's limitations in this area. Contrary to the goal of enhancing academic outcomes, some research finds no significant relationship between AI use and performance improvement, suggesting these tools are not a magic key for success without proper pedagogical integration (Bancoro, 2024). This could be partly because AI tools encourage shallow learning and less knowledge retention. For instance, a study found that only 20% of students demonstrated significant retention after an AI-supported semester (AlShibli et al., 2025a, 2025b). Moreover, over-reliance on AI without guidance can erode student skills such as critical thinking and self-regulation (Zhai et al., 2024). Beyond these student-centric limitations, the AI tools themselves present challenges. The quality and neutrality of AI outputs are fundamentally limited by their training data, which can introduce biases or lack deep contextual understanding. This feeds into broader ethical and accessibility concerns, where unequal access and unresolved problems of data privacy and fairness can create new forms of inequity rather than resolve existing ones.

2.2 *AI for Surveillance and Early Identification of Students at Risk*

The foundational first step in school social work interventions is identifying students at risk, a process challenged by the need for accurate, rapid, and widespread screening that adheres to ethical guidelines. Traditionally, the school system relies on student self-reports, teacher referrals, and MTSS-based screenings to identify students' social and emotional problems (Substance Abuse and Mental Health Services Administration [SAMHSA], 2019; Branching Minds, n.d.). However, these traditional approaches encounter significant limitations. Factors such as complex risk indicators, a shortage of trained professionals, and limited access for marginalized groups impede effective screening. Furthermore, reliance on subjective and static self-report data has been shown to limit the accuracy of early mental health identification (Dang et al., 2020; Lira et al., 2022).

Integrating AI into a school's surveillance system can help address specific limitations in current practice. As an automated tool, AI can process complex risk indicators, particularly unstructured data from activity monitoring and chatbots, which would otherwise be difficult and time-consuming to analyze for potential risks. Existing research has shown that AI can accurately identify mental health risks across diverse age groups (Cruz-Gonzalez et al., 2025) and can detect problematic behaviors using multimodal data (Milosevic et al., 2022;

Holmes et al., 2025). Despite certain limitations, such applications have the potential to benefit the school social work system in early identification and surveillance.

2.2.1 AI-Based Early Identification Through Activity Monitoring

By leveraging a combination of cameras, microphones, and mobile Internet, AI models can analyze multimodal data to recognize students' emotions and body movements, thereby assisting in predicting mental health risks and dangerous behaviors. For example, Lorge et al. (2024) evaluated the ability of the GPT-4 model to identify mental health factors in adolescent online forums, finding its performance was comparable to that of human experts on real-world data, while on synthetic data it even outperformed them (Lorge et al., 2024). Similarly, other research has demonstrated that machine learning models, such as logistic regression and support vector machines, can effectively predict an adolescent's mental health condition using social media data (Patel et al., 2025). Akhil et al. (2023) also proposed an AI-driven approach to predict mental disorders and social media addiction among students aged 12–18 based on their social media usage patterns (Akhil et al., 2023).

Beyond mental health, AI has also shown potential for predicting student behavior and attitude. Zhou et al. (2022) developed a novel end-to-end dangerous behavior detection method, named DangerDet, which automatically identifies dangerous behaviors such as fighting and falling from school surveillance videos. Yoon (2024) developed an online tool for detecting gaslighting and verbal abuse in adolescent online activities using a BERT-based classification model, which provides an accuracy rate of 85% when it comes to detecting gaslighting and 87% when it comes to detecting verbal abuse. Using deep learning modeling techniques and supervised learning algorithms, Thao et al. (2023) and Ye et al. (2020) integrated their expertise in object detection into campus cameras to predict the timing and actions of campus violence. The model achieved 97.6% accuracy in identifying violent behavior on campus. K-12 schools, as observed in a systematic review by Ayer et al. (2024), have begun naturally utilizing artificial intelligence tools to identify students at risk of suicide and self-harm because of the COVID-19 pandemic and the global transition to remote education.

While the studies above demonstrate promising capabilities, detection through activity monitoring presents inherent limitations. Monitoring data is often passive, fragmented, and highly context-dependent, making it challenging to accurately assess students' emotional states or psychological distress, hindering the generalizability of findings and the development of more robust detection models. To overcome these challenges, more interactive monitoring approaches—such as AI-driven chatbots—have been introduced, offering a more direct and dynamic way to detect students' mental health.

2.2.2 AI-Based Early Identification Through Chatbots

With the advancement of large language models (LLMs), researchers have demonstrated that AI can identify risks from user interactions with chatbots based on text, speech, and video data (Aggarwal et al., 2023; Haque & Rubya, 2023; Leung et al., 2024), demonstrating particularly strong performance in areas such as anxiety, depression, and suicidal tendencies. According to Weisenburger et al., 90% of chatbot predictions were either in line with self-reports or matched clinical expert opinions (when AI results were inconsistent with self-reports) (Weisenburger et al., 2024). Deshpande et al. developed a chatbot capable of accurately identifying self-harm tendencies in over 92% of cases using their large language models (Deshpande & Warren, 2021).

In the school context, the AI chatbot is being explored in applications for early identification. Chatbots are often introduced to students voluntarily, accessible through school-integrated applications or dedicated platforms, which has the potential to reduce the stigma associated with seeking help and offers students a non-judgmental space for self-expression (Labadze et al., 2023). A chatbot user flow involves the chatbot engaging in a routine conversational assessment. If potential risk indicators are detected in the conversation, the system flags the content and generates an alert. This process requires human professionals to be the primary monitors of interactions, responsible for reviewing flagged conversations, assessing the context and severity of the risk, and providing a human follow-up for students. By developing a collaborative workflow between human professionals and state-of-the-art chatbots, it will be ensured that while AI can assist with initial predictive analysis and early detection, the ultimate decision-making and empathetic support remain within the purview of trained social workers.

While an AI-driven approach has potential in early risk identification, its effectiveness remains constrained when used in isolation. Biased or incomplete data inputs can perpetuate inequalities and misidentify students at risk, posing a significant challenge. This problem is further highlighted by a study from the Rand Corporation, which found that while AI-based suicide risk monitoring can be effective in K-12 schools, these schools and their broader communities often lack adequate resources to address the adolescent mental health challenges that are identified (Diliberti et al., 2024; Ayer et al., 2024). This underscores the need for a holistic and context-sensitive approach to AI integration in school social work. As a powerful tool of data analysis, AI's role could extend beyond early detection to assist in comprehensive assessment and the optimization of intervention plans.

2.3 AI for Comprehensive Assessment and Optimization of Intervention Strategy

After identifying student needs and risks, school social workers need to conduct a comprehensive assessment of each student to determine the appropriate intervention level, estimate intervention outcomes, and optimize the intervention plan (National Association of Social Workers [NASW], n.d.). However, traditional assessment methods face two major limitations. First, the factors influencing intervention outcomes can be highly complex and often involve unstructured data, such as interview records, audio recordings, and images, which are not effectively integrated into traditional statistical analyses (Batko & Ślęzak, 2022). Second, designing optimal intervention plans requires extensive knowledge and analytical skills, which can hinder the adoption of evidence-based practices, particularly in resource-limited areas.

AI tools offer a promising approach, providing quick, stable data analytics to overcome these challenges. Equipped with advanced technologies (e.g., neural network models and natural language processing), AI tools can process multimodal unstructured data and provide a more comprehensive understanding of students' needs and intervention effectiveness (Alqahtani et al., 2023; Olawade et al., 2024), assisting social workers to make better-informed decisions and optimize strategies. For instance, machine learning models have been applied to identify the most effective treatments for depression, such as cognitive behavioral therapy or medication, by analyzing demographic and clinical data (Gunlicks-Stoessel et al., 2020). Moreover, in the school context, AI tools have the potential to create personalized intervention strategies based on data on demographic, mental health, and socio-cultural background (Wang & Yang, 2023). The concept of "digital twins," which uses chatbots to provide continuous responses, is also being explored to optimize student mental health (Abilkaiyrkyzy et al., 2024). Overall, although the application of AI in this area remains an emerging field that requires substantial human guidance and oversight, its potential to enhance assessment and optimize intervention in school social work has already been demonstrated.

In conclusion, AI shows promise as a value-generating tool for school social work practices. On the other hand, technical constraints, resource limitations, and the complexity of student needs—shaped by socio-cultural contexts and individual circumstances—still lead to challenges and risks about AI application in school social work, especially given the "black box" nature of some systems that can obscure their internal workings and decision-making processes. The following section will explore these issues in greater detail.

3 Challenge and Ethical Risk of AI Application in School Social Work

The application of technology never occurs in a vacuum; it is a social process that unfolds through the dynamic interaction between a technology and its socio-cultural context (Kossowska et al., 2023). While the potential of AI in school social work is significant, its responsible and effective implementation hinges on addressing fundamental challenges rooted in the very fabric of AI systems. These challenges can be framed within three critical areas of concern.

First is the adequacy of the data and data sources. The fairness and effectiveness of any AI system are directly contingent on the volume, quality, and representativeness of the data used for model training. Biased data inevitably leads to skewed outcomes. This occurs because machine learning models learn statistical patterns present in the training data; if these patterns are distorted by sampling bias, measurement error, or omission of key variables, the resulting predictions will replicate and even amplify those distortions (Köchling & Wehner, 2020). For example, research has shown that an AI-driven system assigned lower scores to essays by Black students than to those by White students with comparable content, likely reflecting societal biases embedded in the training data. (Yin et al., 2024).

Second is the adequacy of the model itself. Selecting an appropriate AI model and ensuring its technical support are critical to ensuring AI tools perform their intended functions accurately. Certain architectures have inherent limitations that may compromise reliability in specific tasks. For example, Plaat et al. (2025) found that the Transformer—the backbone of most large language models—struggles with tasks that require combining multiple reasoning steps, especially as the problem size grows. This weakness helps explain why such models can sometimes "hallucinate" or give wrong answers in complex reasoning tasks.

Third is the necessity of a sound assessment of AI applications. The AI model's performance needs to be rigorously and continuously evaluated in specific school settings by professionals from both AI and social work to ensure its accuracy, reliability, and generalizability across diverse student populations. However, evaluation itself is not straightforward. AI assessment methods often originate in different research traditions, use inconsistent terms, and rarely share insights, leading to confusion and unrealistic expectations for deployed systems (Burden et al., 2025). In addition, many AI models—especially those used in decision-making—are "black boxes" that are difficult to interpret, making it challenging to identify errors and collaborate (Hassija et al., 2024).

These significant methodological challenges give rise to the specific limitations and ethical risks discussed in this section. The subsequent analysis will explore how these general issues of AI manifest as challenges in navigating complex sociocultural factors, the inexplicability of "black box" algorithms, the propagation of bias and inequity, and risks to data security.

3.1 *From Pattern Matching to Black Boxes: The Challenge of Interpretability in Expert Decision-Making*

A primary challenge in applying AI to school social work lies in reconciling the technology's capability—correlational pattern matching—with the causal reasoning that defines social worker decision-making. Until now, AI systems excel at processing vast datasets to identify statistical patterns and predict based on them, such as the correlation between declining grades and potential mental health risks (Tulğan & Pak Güre, 2024). These patterns and predictions, however, are merely correlational and cannot explain causation. In the real-world context, a student's well-being is shaped by a complex, intersecting web of psychological, familial, and socio-cultural factors that an algorithm cannot fully comprehend (Nuwasiima et al., 2024). For example, an AI tool might flag a student whose attendance has dropped by 20%. It is the social worker who ultimately needs to conduct causal analysis and determine if the cause is a family condition or a personal health issue, each requiring a completely different intervention, and must be person-centered to ensure the student's well-being. Expanding on this, the critical risk is mistaking AI's predictive patterns for a holistic, causal understanding of a student's situation.

Moreover, this challenge is significantly exacerbated by the "black box" phenomenon, in which AI systems operate in ways obscured by technical complexity or commercial confidentiality (Hassija et al., 2024). When the mechanism behind an AI's predication is inexplicable, it becomes difficult for social workers to evaluate it critically. Such abdication of clinical decision-making not only endangers student well-being but also hinders the development of contextual interventions and risks accelerating data colonialism in global health (Sekalala & Chatikobo, 2024).

Therefore, addressing the dual challenge of causal analysis limitations and operational opacity requires a multifaceted approach. It is crucial to develop and demand AI tools that are transparent, interpretable, and accountable. This necessitates emphasizing collaboration between governments, schools, and AI technology companies. Concurrently, social workers should improve their AI literacy to engage with AI tools critically, ensuring they enhance rather than replace social workers' professional decision-making, which is essential for protecting students' well-being.

3.2 *Bias, Neutrality, and the Risk of Education Inequity*

A third challenge is the potential bias in AI applications to create or exacerbate educational inequities. The perceived objectivity of AI often obscures its inherent value-laden nature, and the issue is conceptualized as the "paradox of technological neutrality" (Comeig et al., 2022). This paradox challenges the traditional view that technology is merely a tool (Vogels et al., 2020), prompting a deeper examination of how bias manifests in the development of technical products. Expanding on this, AI-driven bias in school social work can be analyzed at three distinct levels: bias inherent in the AI application's design, bias arising from its application context, and bias that becomes entrenched and amplified over time.

First, bias is often embedded in the initial design of an AI system. Developers' cultural, economic, and political assumptions, along with training data from human history, can introduce inherent biases (Ferrara, 2023). For instance, a mental health screening tool trained on biased data might disproportionately flag students from minority groups, such as LGBTQ+ youth as "at risk," thereby creating discriminatory outcomes and reinforcing educational inequities (Timmons et al., 2023).

Second, bias can arise from the specific context in which an AI tool is deployed. The technology that appears beneficial in one setting can become harmful in another, depending on a society's socio-cultural context or power structure. For instance, AI-based facial recognition is a neutral tool to enhance school security. However, when deployed within an authoritarian context, its function shifts from protection to surveillance and control, exploiting students rather than serving them. In such scenarios, AI applications can reinforce existing power imbalances and compromise students' autonomy (Hanna et al., 2025).

Third, an AI application can solidify biases over the long term. When an AI system with inherent biases is integrated into school social work, its responses may perpetuate those biases over time. Consequently, these algorithmically reinforced patterns are possible to become entrenched in institutional practices, making them beyond merely AI model inherent biases, cementing systemic inequities for future generations (Vicente & Matute, 2023; Qian et al., 2024).

To avoid AI bias and address the risk of educational inequity, a critical approach is essential. School social workers and educators need to remain vigilant to prevent AI from perpetuating societal biases, ensuring AI systems are regularly assessed and updated. This vigilance is crucial to ensure that AI serves to promote fairness rather than reinforce patterns of discrimination or oppression.

3.3 *Privacy and Data Safety*

A further critical challenge lies in protecting student privacy and data safety, an issue that becomes particularly acute in the high-stakes context of school social work. In general, AI systems require vast amounts of student data to function effectively. Compared to commercial applications, student data often includes psychological assessments, behavioral patterns, family situations, and social interactions, which can be more private and sensitive. The mishandling of that data through security breaches can risk exposing a student to long-term stigmatization and emotional distress, impacting their future educational and life opportunities (Time, 2024).

The sensitivity of user data profoundly complicates the concept of "informed consent." Within the imbalanced power dynamic of a school system, it can be challenging to ensure that consent given by students or their families is truly voluntary. There is a tangible risk that they may feel pressured to agree to data collection to access essential AI support services. Furthermore, the operational logic of many AI models—enlarge the volume of data as much as possible—directly conflicts with the privacy principle of data minimization (Herres et al., 2024). This disconnect can lead to excessive collection of student personal information, collecting data far beyond the scope of the intended intervention, thereby increasing the risk surface for both breaches and misinterpretation (Elliott & Soifer, 2022).

In addition, the long-term risk can be "function creep" (Koops, 2021), where data collected for a beneficial purpose, such as identifying mental health needs, is later repurposed for entirely different functions, such as student discipline or sharing with external law enforcement agencies. This potential for misuse without specific, renewed consent fundamentally erodes the foundation of trust between students and the school social work services that are meant to protect them. It transforms a tool of support into a potential instrument of surveillance and control.

To address these multifaceted risks, establishing clear guidelines and robust data protection regulations is a necessary first step. However, a more fundamental mitigation strategy lies in adopting the principles of user-centered design (UCD). Rather than relying solely on post-hoc regulations, a UCD approach embeds ethical protections directly into the technology's architecture. It proactively confronts these challenges by enforcing strict data minimization, designing transparent interfaces that facilitate meaningful, non-coercive consent, and providing clear controls for all users—students, families, and social workers alike (Bonet-Olivencia et al., 2024).

Overall, by enhancing decision-making and service delivery, AI has shown promising potential to improve school social work practices. However, methodological limitations continue to pose significant challenges, particularly in interpretability, equity, and data privacy. In the future, advancing technical robustness, strengthening ethical safeguards, and ensuring meaningful human oversight will be essential to realizing AI's benefits while mitigating its risks.

Competing Interests The authors have no conflicts of interest to declare that are relevant to the content of this chapter.

References

Abilkaiyrkyzy, A., Laamarti, F., Hamdi, M., & Saddik, A. E. (2024). Dialogue system for early mental illness detection: Toward a digital twin solution. *IEEE Access, 12*, 2007–2024. https://doi.org/10.1109/ACCESS.2023.3348783

Aggarwal, A., Tam, C. C., Wu, D., Li, X., & Qiao, S. (2023). Artificial intelligence-based chatbots for promoting health behavioral changes: Systematic review. *Journal of Medical Internet Research, 25*, e40789. https://doi.org/10.2196/40789

Akhil, K., Sireesha, J., Sai, G. V., Reddy, K. S. S., & Haripriya, J. (2023). Harnessing artificial intelligence for preventing and detecting addiction in digital healthcare and social media among students of age group 12 to 18. In *Proceedings of the 5th International Conference on Advances in Computing, Communication Control and Networking (ICAC3N), Greater Noida, India* (pp. 936–942). https://doi.org/10.1109/ICAC3N60023.2023.10541714

Aldoseri, A., Al-Khalifa, K. N., & Hamouda, A. M. (2023). Re-thinking data strategy and integration for artificial intelligence: Concepts, opportunities, and challenges. *Applied Sciences, 13*(12), 7082. https://doi.org/10.3390/app13127082

Alowais, S. A., Alghamdi, S. S., Alsuhebany, N., Alqahtani, T., Alshaya, A. I., Almohareb, S. N., Aldairem, A., Alrashed, M., Bin Saleh, K., Badreldin, H. A., Al Yami, M. S., Al Harbi, S., & Albekairy, A. M. (2023). Revolutionizing healthcare: The role of artificial intelligence in clinical practice. *BMC Medical Education, 23*, Article 689. https://doi.org/10.1186/s12909-023-04698-z

Alqahtani, T., Badreldin, H. A., Alrashed, M., Alshaya, A. I., Alghamdi, S. S., Bin Saleh, K., Alowais, S. A., Alshaya, O. A., Rahman, I., Al Yami, M. S., & Albekairy, A. M. (2023). The emergent role of artificial intelligence, natural language processing, and large language models in higher education and research. *Research in Social and Administrative Pharmacy, 19*(8), 1236–1242. https://doi.org/10.1016/j.sapharm.2023.05.016

AlShibli, A. S., Al Shibli, M., & Al Harthi, A. (2025a). Exploring the impact of artificial intelligence on student academic performance. *Artificial Intelligence & Robotics Development Journal, 5*(3), 383–395. https://doi.org/10.52098/airdj.20233343

AlShibli, A. S., Al Shibli, M., & Al Harthi, A. (2025b). Exploring the impact of artificial intelligence on student academic performance. *Artificial Intelligence & Robotics Development Journal, 15*(3), 343. https://doi.org/10.52098/airdj.20233343

Ayer, L., Boudreaux, B., Welburn Paige, J., Holmes, P., Blagg, T. L., & Mendon-Plasek, S. J. (2024). Artificial intelligence-based student activity monitoring for suicide risk: Considerations for K-12 schools, caregivers, government, and technology developers. *RAND Health Quarterly, 11*(2), Article 2. Retrieved from https://pubmed.ncbi.nlm.nih.gov/38601718/

Bancoro, J. C. M. (2024). The relationship between artificial intelligence (AI) usage and academic performance of Business Administration students. *International Journal of Asian Business and Management, 3*(1), 27–48. https://doi.org/10.55927/ijabm.v3i1.7876

Batko, K., & Ślęzak, A. (2022). The use of big data analytics in healthcare. *Journal of Big Data, 9*(1), 3. https://doi.org/10.1186/s40537-021-00553-4

Bonet-Olivencia, S., Carrillo-Leal, J., Rao, A., & Sasangohar, F. (2024). User-centered design of a diabetes self-management tool for underserved populations. *Journal of Diabetes Science and Technology, 18*(1), 22–29. https://doi.org/10.1177/19322968231212220

Branching Minds. (n.d.). *Guide to social, emotional, and behavioral universal screening*. Retrieved March 31, 2025, from https://www.branchingminds.com/social-emotional-behavioral-universal-screening-guide

Burden, J., Tešić, M., & Pacchiardi, L. (2025). Paradigms of AI evaluation: Mapping goals, methodologies and culture. *ArXiv*. Retrieved from https://arxiv.org/abs/2502.15620

Carter, H., Araya, R., Anjur, K., Deng, D., & Naslund, J. A. (2021). The emergence of digital mental health in low-income and middle-income countries: A review of recent advances and implications for the treatment and prevention of mental disorders. *Journal of Psychiatric Research, 133*, 223–246. https://doi.org/10.1016/j.jpsychires.2020.12.016

Chin, H., Song, H., Baek, G., Shin, M., Jung, C., Cha, M., Choi, J., & Cha, C. (2023). The potential of chatbots for emotional support and promoting mental well-being in different cultures: Mixed methods study. *Journal of Medical Internet Research, 25*, e51712. https://doi.org/10.2196/51712

Comeig, I., Klaser, K., & Pinar, L. D. (2022). The paradox of (Inter)net neutrality: An experiment on ex-ante antitrust regulation. *Technological Forecasting and Social Change, 175*, 121405. https://doi.org/10.1016/j.techfore.2021.121405

Cruz-Gonzalez, P., He, A. W.-J., Lam, E. P., Ng, I. M. C., Li, M. W., Hou, R., Chan, J. N.-M., Sahni, Y., Vinas Guasch, N., Miller, T., Lau, B. W.-M., & Sánchez Vidaña, D. I. (2025). Artificial intelligence in mental health care: A systematic review of diagnosis, monitoring, and intervention applications. *Psychological Medicine, 55*, e18. https://doi.org/10.1017/S0033291724003295

Daley, K., Hungerbuehler, I., Cavanagh, K., Claro, H. G., Swinton, P. A., & Kapps, M. (2020). Preliminary Evaluation of the Engagement and Effectiveness of a Mental Health Chatbot. *Frontiers in Digital Health, 2*, 576361. https://doi.org/10.3389/fdgth.2020.576361

Dalziel, M. V., Schaffer, K., & Martin, N. (2024). Navigating AI in social work and beyond: A multidisciplinary review. *ArXiv*. Retrieved from https://arxiv.org/abs/2411.07245

Dang, J., King, K. M., & Inzlicht, M. (2020). Why are self-report and behavioral measures weakly correlated? *Trends in Cognitive Sciences, 24*(4), 267–269. https://doi.org/10.1016/j.tics.2020.01.007

Deshpande, S., & Warren, J. (2021). Self-harm detection for mental health chatbots. In *Public health and informatics* (Vol. 281, pp. 48–52). IOS Press. https://doi.org/10.3233/SHTI210118

Diliberti, M. K., Schwartz, H. L., Doan, S., Shapiro, A., Rainey, L. R., & Lake, R. J. (2024). *Using artificial intelligence tools in K–12 classrooms (RR-A956-21)*. RAND Corporation. Retrieved from https://www.rand.org/pubs/research_reports/RRA956-21.html

Ding, X., Lightfoot, E., Berkowitz, R., Guz, S., Franklin, C., & DiNitto, D. M. (2023). Characteristics and outcomes of school social work services: A scoping review of published evidence 2000–June 2022. *School Mental Health, 15*, 787–811. https://doi.org/10.1007/s12310-023-09584-z

Elliott, D., & Soifer, E. (2022). AI Technologies, Privacy, and Security. *Frontiers in Artificial Intelligence, 5*, 826737. https://doi.org/10.3389/frai.2022.826737

Entenberg, G. A., Mizrahi, S., Walker, H., Aghakhani, S., Mostovoy, K., Carre, N., Marshall, Z., Dosovitsky, G., Benfica, D., Rousseau, A., Lin, G., & Bunge, E. L. (2023). AI-based chatbot micro-intervention for parents: Meaningful engagement, learning, and efficacy. *Frontiers in Psychiatry, 14*, 1080770. https://doi.org/10.3389/fpsyt.2023.1080770

Ferrara, E. (2023). Should ChatGPT be biased? Challenges and risks of bias in large language models. *ArXiv*. https://doi.org/10.5210/fm.v28i11.13346

Gallegos, C., Kausler, R., Alderden, J., Davis, M., & Wang, L. (2024). Can artificial intelligence chatbots improve mental health? A scoping review. *CIN: Computers, Informatics, Nursing, 42*(10), 731–736. https://doi.org/10.1097/CIN.0000000000001155

Golden, A., & Aboujaoude, E. (2024). Describing the framework for AI tool assessment in mental health and applying it to a generative AI obsessive-compulsive disorder platform: Tutorial. *JMIR Formative Research, 8*, e62963. https://doi.org/10.2196/62963

Golden, A. R., Srisarajivakul, E. N., Hasselle, A. J., Pfund, R. A., & Knox, J. (2023). What was a gap is now a chasm: Remote schooling, the digital divide, and educational inequities resulting from the COVID-19 pandemic. *Current Opinion in Psychology, 52*, 101632. https://doi.org/10.1016/j.copsyc.2023.101632

Gunlicks-Stoessel, M., Klimes-Dougan, B., VanZomeren, A., & Ma, S. (2020). Developing a data-driven algorithm for guiding selection between cognitive behavioral therapy, fluoxetine, and combination treatment for adolescent depression. *Translational Psychiatry, 10*, Article 321. https://doi.org/10.1038/s41398-020-01005-y

Hanna, M. G., Pantanowitz, L., Jackson, B., Pantanowitz, J., Deebajah, M., & Rashidi, H. H. (2025). Ethical and bias considerations in artificial intelligence/machine learning. *Modern Pathology, 38*(3), 100686. https://doi.org/10.1016/j.modpat.2024.100686

Haque, M. D. R., & Rubya, S. (2023). An overview of chatbot-based mobile mental health apps: Insights from app description and user reviews. *JMIR mHealth and uHealth, 11*(1), e44838. https://doi.org/10.2196/44838

Hassija, V., Chamola, V., Mahapatra, A., Singal, A., Goel, D., Huang, K., Scardapane, S., Spinelli, I., Mahmud, M., & Hussain, A. (2024). Interpreting black-box models: A review on explainable artificial intelligence. *Cognitive Computation, 16*, 45–74. https://doi.org/10.1007/s12559-023-10179-8

Henriksen, D., Creely, E., Gruber, N., & Leahy, S. (2025). Social-emotional learning and generative AI: A critical literature review and framework for teacher education. *Journal of Teacher Education, 76*(3), 312–328. https://doi.org/10.1177/00224871251325058

Herres, B., Poschen, C., & Knorr, K. (2024). Privacy-preserving search on medical data. In *Digital health and informatics innovations for sustainable health care systems* (Vol. 316, pp. 252–256). IOS Press. https://doi.org/10.3233/SHTI240392

Hinostroza Fuentes, V. G., Karim, H. A., Tan, M. J. T., & AlDahoul, N. (2025). AI with agency: A vision for adaptive, efficient, and ethical healthcare. *Frontiers in Digital Health, 7*, 1600216. https://doi.org/10.3389/fdgth.2025.1600216

Holmes, W., & Tuomi, I. (2022). State of the art and practice in AI in education. *European Journal of Education, 57*(4), 542–570. https://doi.org/10.1111/ejed.12533

Holmes, G., Tang, B., Gupta, S., Venkatesh, S., Christensen, H., & Whitton, A. (2025). Applications of large language models in the field of suicide prevention: Scoping review. *Journal of Medical Internet Research, 27*(1), e63126. https://doi.org/10.2196/63126

Köchling, A., & Wehner, M. C. (2020). Discriminated by an algorithm: A systematic review of discrimination and fairness by algorithmic decision-making in the context of HR recruitment and HR development. *Business Research, 13*, 795–848. https://doi.org/10.1007/s40685-020-00134-w

Koops, B.-J. (2021). The concept of function creep. *International Review of Law, Computers & Technology, 35*(1), 29–56. https://doi.org/10.1080/17579961.2021.1898299

Kossowska, M., Kłodkowski, P., Siewierska-Chmaj, A., Guinote, A., Kessels, U., Moyano, M., & Strömbäck, J. (2023). Internet-based micro-identities as a driver of societal disintegration. *Humanities and Social Sciences Communications, 10*, Article 955. https://doi.org/10.1057/s41599-023-02573-3

Labadze, L., Grigolia, M., & Machaidze, L. (2023). Role of AI chatbots in education: Systematic literature review. *International Journal of Educational Technology in Higher Education, 20*(1), 1–17. https://doi.org/10.1186/s41239-023-00426-1

Leung, W., Lam, S. C., Ng, F., Yip, C. C. K., & Chan, C.-K. (2024). Effectiveness of chatbot-based interventions on mental well-being of the general population in Asia: Protocol for a systematic review and meta-analysis of randomised controlled trials. *BMJ Health & Care Informatics, 31*(1), e101148. https://doi.org/10.1136/bmjhci-2024-101148

Lira, B., O'Brien, J. M., Peña, P. A., Galla, B. M., D'Mello, S., Yeager, D. S., Defnet, A., Kautz, T., Munkacsy, K., & Duckworth, A. L. (2022). Large studies reveal how reference bias limits policy applications of self-report measures. *Scientific Reports, 12*, Article 19189. https://doi.org/10.1038/s41598-022-23929-4

Liu, H., Peng, H., Song, X., Xu, C., & Zhang, M. (2022). Using AI chatbots to provide self-help depression interventions for university students: A randomized trial of effectiveness. *Internet Interventions, 27*, 100495. https://doi.org/10.1016/j.invent.2022.100495

Local Burden of Disease Educational Attainment Collaborators. (2020). Mapping disparities in education across low- and middle-income countries. *Nature, 577*, 235–238. https://doi.org/10.1038/s41586-019-1872-1

Lorge, I., Joyce, D. W., & Kormilitzin, A. (2024, April 26). Large language models perform on par with experts identifying mental health factors in adolescent online forums. *arXiv*. Retrieved from https://arxiv.org/abs/2404.16461

Lyu, Y., An, P., Zhang, H., Katsuragawa, K., & Zhao, J. (2024, April 24). Designing AI-enabled games to support social-emotional learning for children with autism spectrum disorders. *arXiv*. Retrieved from https://arxiv.org/abs/2404.15576

Milosevic, T., Van Royen, K., & Davis, B. (2022). Artificial intelligence to address cyberbullying, harassment and abuse: New directions in the midst of complexity. *International Journal of Bullying Prevention, 4*, 1–5. https://doi.org/10.1007/s42380-022-00117-x

National Association of Social Workers. (n.d.). *NASW standards for school social work services*. Retrieved March 31, 2025, from https://www.socialworkers.org/Practice/NASW-Practice-Standards-Guidelines/NASW-Standards-for-School-Social-Work-Service

Nuwasiima, M., Ahonon, M. P., & Kadiri, C. (2024). The role of artificial intelligence (AI) and machine learning in social work practice. *World Journal of Advanced Research and Reviews, 24*(1), 80–97. https://doi.org/10.30574/wjarr.2024.24.1.2998

OECD. (2024). *The potential impact of artificial intelligence on equity and inclusion in education* (OECD Artificial Intelligence Papers, No. 23). Organisation for Economic Co-operation and Development. Retrieved from https://www.oecd.org/content/dam/oecd/en/publications/reports/2024/08/the-potential-impact-of-artificial-intelligence-on-equity-and-inclusion-in-education_0d7e9e00/15df715b-en.pdf

Olawade, D. B., Wada, O. Z., Odetayo, A., David-Olawade, A. C., Asaolu, F., & Eberhardt, J. (2024). Enhancing mental health with artificial intelligence: Current trends and future prospects. *Journal of Medicine, Surgery, and Public Health, 3*, 100099. https://doi.org/10.1016/j.jmsph.2024.100099

Patel, J., Hung, C., & Katapally, T. R. (2025). Evaluating predictive artificial intelligence approaches used in mobile health platforms to forecast mental health symptoms among youth: A systematic review. *Psychiatry Research, 343*, 116277. https://doi.org/10.1016/j.psychres.2024.116277

Pierrès, O., Christen, M., Schmitt-Koopmann, F. M., & Darvishy, A. (2024). Could the use of AI in higher education hinder students with disabilities? A scoping review. *IEEE Access, 12*, 24221–24233. https://doi.org/10.1109/ACCESS.2024.10433192

Plaat, A., Wong, A., & Verberne, S. (2025). Multi-step reasoning with large language models: A survey. arXiv preprint *arXiv*:2407.11511. Retrieved from https://arxiv.org/abs/2407.11511

Qian, Y., Siau, K. L., & Nah, F. F. (2024). Societal impacts of artificial intelligence: Ethical, legal, and governance issues. *Societal Impacts, 3*, 100040. https://doi.org/10.1016/j.socimp.2024.100040

Reamer, F. G. (2023). Artificial intelligence in social work: Emerging ethical issues. *Journal of Social Work Values and Ethics, 20*(2), Article 5. https://doi.org/10.55521/10-020-205

Røed, R. K., Baugerud, G. A., Hassan, S. Z., Sabet, S. S., Salehi, P., Powell, M. B., Riegler, M. A., Halvorsen, P., & Johnson, M. S. (2023). Enhancing questioning skills through child avatar chatbot training with feedback. *Frontiers in Psychology, 14*, 1198235. https://doi.org/10.3389/fpsyg.2023.1198235

Schaeffer, D., Coombs, L., Luckett, J., Marin, M., & Olson, P. (2024). Risks of AI applications used in higher education. *Electronic Journal of e-Learning, 22*(6), 491–502. https://doi.org/10.34190/ejel.22.6.3457

School Social Work Association of America. (n.d.-a). *National SSW model*. Retrieved March 31, 2025, from https://www.sswaa.org/ssw-model

School Social Work Association of America. (n.d.-b). *School social work*. Retrieved March 31, 2025, from https://www.sswaa.org/school-social-work

Sekalala, S., & Chatikobo, T. (2024). Colonialism in the new digital health agenda. *BMJ Global Health, 9*(2), e014131. https://doi.org/10.1136/bmjgh-2023-014131

Sethi, S. S., & Jain, K. (2024). AI technologies for social emotional learning: Recent research and future directions. *Journal of Research in Innovative Teaching & Learning, 17*(2), 213–225. https://doi.org/10.1108/JRIT-03-2024-0073

Shankland, R., Haag, P., Tessier, D., Buchs, C., El-Jor, C., & Mazza, S. (2024). Review of the effects of social and emotional learning on mental health and academic outcomes: The role of teacher training and supportive interactions. *Journal of Epidemiology and Population Health, 72*(3), 202750. https://doi.org/10.1016/j.jeph.2024.202750

Singh, R., & Gill, S. S. (2023). Edge AI: A survey. *Internet of Things and Cyber-Physical Systems, 3*, 71–92. https://doi.org/10.1016/j.iotcps.2023.02.004

Srinivasan, M., Venugopal, A., Venkatesan, L., & Kumar, R. (2024). Navigating the pedagogical landscape: Exploring the implications of AI and chatbots in nursing education. *JMIR Nursing, 7*(1), e52105. https://doi.org/10.2196/52105

Substance Abuse and Mental Health Services Administration. (2019). *Ready, set, go, review: Screening for behavioral health risk in schools*. Office of the Chief Medical Officer, Substance Abuse and Mental Health Services Administration. Retrieved from https://www.samhsa.gov/sites/default/files/ready-set-go-review-mh-screening-schools.pdf

Tam, W., Huynh, T., Tang, A., Luong, S., Khatri, Y., & Zhou, W. (2023). Nursing education in the age of artificial intelligence powered chatbots (AI-chatbots): Are we ready yet? *Nurse Education Today, 129*, 105917. https://doi.org/10.1016/j.nedt.2023.105917

Tanaka, H., & Nakamura, S. (2022). The acceptability of virtual characters as social skills trainers: Usability study. *JMIR Human Factors, 9*(1), e35358. https://doi.org/10.2196/35358

Thakkar, A., Gupta, A., & De Sousa, A. (2024). Artificial intelligence in positive mental health: A narrative review. *Frontiers in Digital Health, 6*, 1280235. https://doi.org/10.3389/fdgth.2024.1280235

Thao, L. Q., Diep, N. T. B., Bach, N. C., Linh, L. K., & Giang, N. D. H. (2023). FightNet deep learning strategy: An innovative solution to prevent school fighting violence. *Journal of Intelligent & Fuzzy Systems, 45*(4), 1. https://doi.org/10.3233/JIFS-232480

Time. (2024, March 29). Schools let AI spy on kids who may be considering suicide. But at what cost? *Time*. Retrieved from https://time.com/6694425/ai-monitoring-school-suicide-cost-essay/

Timmons, A. C., Duong, J. B., Simo Fiallo, N., Lee, T., Vo, H. P. Q., Ahle, M. W., Comer, J. S., Brewer, L. P. C., Frazier, S. L., & Chaspari, T. (2023). A call to action on assessing and mitigating bias in artificial intelligence applications for mental health. *Perspectives on Psychological Science, 18*(5), 1062–1096. https://doi.org/10.1177/17456916221134490

Tulğan, B., & Pak Güre, M. D. (2024). In the echoes of tomorrow: The intersection of social work and artificial intelligence through the eyes of Turkish students. *Journal of Social Service Research, 50*(4), 620–636. https://doi.org/10.1080/01488376.2024.2354930

Vicente, L., & Matute, H. (2023). Humans inherit artificial intelligence biases. *Scientific Reports, 13*, Article 15737. https://doi.org/10.1038/s41598-023-42384-8

Vistorte, A. O. R., Deroncele-Acosta, A., Ayala, J. L. M., Barrasa, A., López-Granero, C., & Martí-González, M. (2024). Integrating artificial intelligence to assess emotions in learning environments: A systematic literature review. *Frontiers in Psychology, 15*, 1387089. https://doi.org/10.3389/fpsyg.2024.1387089

Vogels, E. A., Rainie, L., & Anderson, J. (2020, June 30). *Tech is (just) a tool.* Pew Research Center. Retrieved from https://www.pewresearch.org/internet/2020/06/30/tech-is-just-a-tool/

Wang, Y. (2024). The impact of AI application in education on students. In *Proceedings of the 2nd International Conference on Innovation Management.* Psychology, Education and Sociology (IMPES 2024). https://doi.org/10.54097/gg1d3q19

Wang, C., & Yang, T. (2023). Research on mental health situations of college students based on machine learning algorithm. In *2023 International Conference on Ambient Intelligence, Knowledge Informatics and Industrial Electronics (AIKIIE)* (pp. 1–6). IEEE. https://doi.org/10.1109/AIKIIE60097.2023.10389910

Wang, F., Ni, X., Zhang, M., & Zhang, J. (2024). Educational digital inequality: A meta-analysis of the relationship between digital device use and academic performance in adolescents. *Computers & Education, 213*, 105003. https://doi.org/10.1016/j.compedu.2024.105003

Weisenburger, R. L., Mullarkey, M. C., Labrada, J., Labrousse, D., Yang, M. Y., Huff MacPherson, A., Hsu, K. J., Ugail, H., Shumake, J., & Beevers, C. G. (2024). Conversational assessment using artificial intelligence is as clinically useful as depression scales and preferred by users. *Journal of Affective Disorders, 351*, 489–498. https://doi.org/10.1016/j.jad.2024.01.212

Xu, M., Chen, S., Chen, J., & Zhang, T. (2023). Non-linear links between human capital, educational inequality and income inequality: Evidence from China. *PLoS One, 18*(8), e0288966. https://doi.org/10.1371/journal.pone.0288966

Ye, L., Wang, L., Ferdinando, H., Seppänen, T., & Alasaarela, E. (2020). A video-based DT–SVM school violence detecting algorithm. *Sensors, 20*(7), 2018. https://doi.org/10.3390/s20072018

Yin, Z., Chinta, S. V., Wang, Z., Gonzalez, M., & Zhang, W. (2024). FairAIED: Navigating fairness, bias, and ethics in educational AI applications. *ArXiv*. Retrieved from https://arxiv.org/abs/2407.18745

Yoon, S. (2024). AI-based digital therapeutics for adolescent mental health management and disaster response. *Information, 15*(10), 620. https://doi.org/10.3390/info15100620

Zhai, C., Wibowo, S., & Li, L. D. (2024). The effects of over-reliance on AI dialogue systems on students' cognitive abilities: A systematic review. *Smart Learning Environments, 11*, Article 28. https://doi.org/10.1186/s40561-024-00316-7

Zhou, H., Jiang, F., & Lu, H. (2022). Student dangerous behavior detection in school. arXiv preprint *arXiv*:2202.09550. https://doi.org/10.48550/arXiv.2202.09550

Chapter 11
AI in Substance Use and Addiction Prevention

Shaddy Saba and George Leibowitz

1 Introduction

Substance use disorder (SUD) represents a critical and entrenched social welfare challenge, with nearly 50 million individuals meeting criteria in the United States (US) (Substance Abuse and Mental Health Services Administration [SAMHSA], 2024). Driven by complex biological, psychological, and social factors, SUD can be especially difficult to assess, prevent, and treat among marginalized communities (Leibowitz et al., 2023; Schoenfeld et al., 2019; Skewes & Gonzalez, 2013). Artificial intelligence (AI), with its rapidly advancing role in healthcare, has the potential to transform how social workers, allied professionals, and community members understand and address SUD (Poalelungi et al., 2023; Goldkind, 2021).

AI is a broad umbrella term that refers to computer and software systems built to mimic human behavior or solve complex problems that would otherwise require human intelligence (Russell & Norvig, 2021). Many contemporary AI applications for SUD rely on machine learning, a method that combines statistical techniques with computer algorithms. Machine learning can detect patterns in data and make predictions, such as whether a client is at risk of a SUD, or assist with decision-making, such as selecting an optimal evidence-based treatment (Suva & Bhatia, 2024). There has also been growth in the use of deep learning, an advanced form of machine learning that uses layers of connected "neurons" (similar to how the human brain works) to automatically uncover patterns in increasingly complex data like brain scans or audio recordings from client encounters (LeCun et al., 2015).

S. Saba (✉)
Silver School of Social Work, New York University, New York, NY, USA
e-mail: sks9496@nyu.edu

G. Leibowitz
School of Social Work, Rutgers University–New Brunswick, New Brunswick, NJ, USA
e-mail: george.leibowitz@rutgers.edu

R. An, M. A. Lindsey (eds.), *Artificial Intelligence in Social Work*,
https://doi.org/10.1007/978-3-032-18443-6_11

In this chapter, we aim to explore both AI's promise and looming challenges for addressing the problematic or harmful use of psychoactive substances, including alcohol, opioids, cannabis, stimulants, and other drugs, and we consider the implications of AI for vulnerable substance using populations. For context, we first provide background information on SUD and traditional treatment and prevention strategies. Then, we review advances in AI and their applications to SUD, explore ethical considerations of AI and the importance of engaging stakeholders and clients in AI development, and consider the future of this field.

Below, we examine how AI is being used for risk assessment, treatment, and relapse prevention, and focus especially on prevention, early intervention, and harm reduction to align with contemporary best practices in social work and public health that emphasize making available a continuum of strategies to meet individuals where they are (Paquette et al., 2022; Stallvik et al., 2015; Vakharia & Little, 2017). As we demonstrate, while most work on AI for SUD has been limited to research settings, AI is beginning to impact real-world practice and shows compelling potential. At this juncture, it is imperative that ethics not take a back seat to technological advancement. In line with social work's core values of promoting human dignity, social justice, and community well-being (National Association of Social Workers [NASW], 2021), we highlight how AI, when ethically implemented, can help make SUD treatment and prevention practices more equitable, accessible, and relevant for vulnerable populations.

2 Contextualizing Substance Use Disorders

2.1 *SUD Definitions, Epidemiology, and Social Welfare Burden*

SUD is a diagnostic classification with criteria set by the American Psychiatric Association's Diagnostic and Statistical Manual of Mental Disorders (the DSM-5; American Psychiatric Association [APA], 2013), which is used by US mental health practitioners, including licensed clinical social workers, to identify clinical disorders. To meet criteria for SUD, a client must demonstrate symptoms related to the use of substances (e.g., taking more of a substance than initially intended, challenges controlling use, cravings, tolerance, and withdrawal symptoms), along with health and social consequences of use, and continued use despite these consequences (APA, 2013). Within the DSM-5, there are separate SUD diagnoses for each specific substance (e.g., *alcohol* use disorder for SUD involving alcohol, *opioid* use disorder for SUD involving opioids, etc.).

There are several other terms used in clinical and research settings to refer to the problematic use of substances, some of which are at times used interchangeably with "SUD," including "dependence," "addiction," "misuse," "abuse," "heavy use," "risky use," and "problematic use" (Rehm et al., 2013). Though a full discussion of these terms is beyond the scope of this chapter, unless otherwise specified, we will refer to "SUD" when discussing problematic substance use that meets criteria for a clinical disorder and "problematic substance use" as a catch-all umbrella phrase that includes SUD as well as less severe symptom presentations.

SUD is a widespread, deeply entrenched, and challenging social welfare problem. Over 2.2% of the world's population meets criteria for SUD, with global prevalence steadily rising over the past several decades (Castaldelli-Maia & Bhugra, 2022; Pan et al., 2020). In the United States, over 48 million individuals had SUD in 2023, and rates have more than doubled over the past 10 years (SAMHSA, 2024). Alcohol has consistently been the primary driver of SUD, with over half of cases involving alcohol, followed by cannabis and opioids (SAMHSA, 2024). An increasing prevalence of cannabis use disorder in the United States (SAMHSA, 2024), including among young people (Han et al., 2017), may be due in part to the changing legal status of cannabis in recent years. The opioid epidemic, involving high rates of opioid use disorder and deaths due to overdose, represents one of the most difficult public health challenges the United States has faced in recent years (Skolnick, 2018). Emerging adults (18–25 years old) have had the highest rates of nonmedical use of prescription opioids (NUPO) and, compared with older age groups, may experience barriers to effective care (Tapscott & Schepis, 2013; Schuman-Olivier et al., 2014). Encouragingly, recent data indicate a downward trend in NUPO, and improvements in treatment and prevention (such as through technology and AI) could further ameliorate the problem (McCabe et al., 2025; Saxon et al., 2025).

SUDs impose a significant societal burden, resulting in billions of dollars in annual costs due to lost productivity and increased utilization of the healthcare and criminal justice systems (Manthey et al., 2021). The adverse effects of SUD on individuals, families, and communities include hindering physical and mental health, contributing to early mortality, and disrupting interpersonal and social functioning (Newcomb & Locke, 2005). Critically for social workers, many vulnerable and marginalized populations are at heightened risk of SUD, including individuals experiencing poverty (Baptiste-Roberts & Hossain, 2018), sexual and gender minorities (Connolly & Gilchrist, 2020; Hughto et al., 2021), American Indian/Alaska Native people (Soto et al., 2022), trauma survivors (Levin et al., 2021), and those with a history of incarceration (Fazel et al., 2017) or homelessness (Gutwinski et al., 2021). These individuals are, in turn, vulnerable to experiencing stigma, criminalization, and barriers to necessary healthcare because of their substance use (Newcomb & Locke, 2005).

2.2 *Biopsychosocial Determinants of SUD*

To understand the persistence of SUD as a social welfare problem and to inform effective intervention and prevention, it is critical to have an accurate grasp of its etiology and the factors that contribute to SUD. Problematic substance use is often progressive in terms of severity, with individuals transitioning from substance use initiation to greater levels of consumption, then developing mild and then more severe SUD (Lee et al., 2019). In terms of *why* some individuals develop SUD, traditional biomedical models emphasize physiological causes, including a genetic predisposition and substance-related changes to the brain (Skewes & Gonzalez, 2013). In contrast, a contemporary, biopsychosocial understanding of SUD espouses that psychological, sociocultural, *and* biological factors interact in complex ways to confer risk for the development, maintenance, and recurrence of SUD (Skewes & Gonzalez, 2013). Notably and in line with biopsychosocial models of health, 80% of health outcomes are explained by social determinants rather than clinical or biological factors (Greer et al., 2023). Social workers have a substantial role to play in integrated SUD care where multiple disciplines collaborate to address these risk factors holistically (Kaur & Maleckas, 2025), given the profession's focus on social functioning and training in biopsychosocial models of health.

There is a robust empirical literature substantiating the biopsychosocial view of SUD. Recent research confirms there are genetic risk factors for SUD (Hancock et al., 2018) and chronic substance use reshapes reward and stress circuits in the brain (Volkow et al., 2016; Koob & Volkow, 2016), but these changes only partially explain SUD risk. A breadth of psychological and sociocultural risk factors for SUD have been identified, ranging from trauma exposure and mental health conditions to peer and family influences and neighborhood disadvantage (Belfiore et al., 2024). Researchers have also demonstrated how biological and social factors *interact*, for instance, via large-scale adoption studies showing that familial challenges can lead to worse outcomes among those who are genetically predisposed to SUD (Kendler et al., 2012). Substance use and exposure to risk factors can also have differential influences on the risk of developing SUD, depending on an individual's age and developmental stage (Lee et al., 2019). It is also important to note that macro-level policy influences SUD risk to a large extent, such as via drug availability, criminality, and access to treatment (Strang et al., 2012).

Many biopsychosocial determinants of SUD may especially heighten risk among marginalized populations. These populations often have higher rates of trauma exposure, mental health conditions, and neighborhood disadvantages, which are all associated with SUD (George et al., 2023; Mikhail et al., 2018). Individuals experiencing poverty may lack access to healthcare, including SUD treatment (Olfson et al., 2022), and discrimination in healthcare settings contributes to disparities in treatment quality among racial/ethnic minority individuals (Mays et al., 2017). Minority stress models, developed to characterize the unique psychological and social stressors that sexual minority individuals face, may in part explain substance use in this population (Goldbach et al., 2014). It is also vital to consider how identifying with multiple marginalized identities likely confers unique SUD-related risks, in line with an intersectional perspective (Otiniano Verissimo et al., 2023; Schilt-Solberg et al., 2025).

2.3 Contemporary Treatment and Prevention Approaches

Contemporary SUD treatment exists on a continuum, ranging from low-intensity, brief interventions or outpatient treatment to more intensive inpatient or residential programs (Mee-Lee et al., 2013; McLellan et al., 2000). Care recommendations are ideally made based on an individual's symptom severity and biopsychosocial risk factors such as co-occurring mental health conditions and social challenges (Mee-Lee et al., 2013; McLellan et al., 2000). Psychological interventions—such as cognitive-behavioral therapy (CBT), motivational interviewing, and contingency management—are commonly used to enhance motivation for change, build coping and recovery skills, and help individuals in remission avoid relapse (Carroll & Onken, 2005; Magill et al., 2019). For individuals with moderate to severe SUD (particularly opioid use disorder), evidence supports medication-assisted treatment (MAT), in which clients receive medications such as buprenorphine or naltrexone to block cravings and prevent misuse (SAMHSA, 2021; Maisel et al., 2013).

Integrated care approaches that combine MAT, psychological interventions, and social support have been associated with improved retention in care, reduced substance use, and fewer relapse events, likely because they more fully address the biological, psychological, and social dimensions of SUD (Leibowitz et al., 2023; National Institute on Drug Abuse [NIDA], 2018; Sharma et al., 2020). Hub and spoke models, implemented in Vermont and nationally, represent an effective systems-based approach to treating opioid use disorder, integrating medical, behavioral, and wellness care (Brooklyn & Sigmon, 2017). Regional hubs include specialty opioid treatment programs providing intensive services, including induction and dosing of medication, and spokes include community-based healthcare settings that support patient self-efficacy and recovery capital (Best & Nisic, 2022). While traditional SUD treatment has focused on immediate cessation of use and abstinence, MAT and hub and spoke programs prioritize a low-barrier approach and easy access to effective treatment. Such programs are consistent with harm reduction principles when they minimize stigma and the negative consequences of substance use, even for those not motivated to pursue abstinence (Hawk et al., 2015).

Strategies to prevent SUD from developing in the first place also exist on a continuum (Volkow & Blanco, 2023). Universal prevention programs aim to decrease risk among an entire population, such as school-based curricula to enhance psychosocial skills or mass media campaigns to reduce early experimentation. Selective prevention programs target specific groups with known biopsychosocial risk factors, such as programs targeting youth in disadvantaged neighborhoods or children of caregivers with SUD. Even more targeted, indicated prevention programs focus on individuals who exhibit early signs of problematic substance use but do not yet meet criteria for SUD, such as through screening and brief intervention for problematic use in a healthcare setting. The most common prevention programs are universal, school-based education programs targeting all children and adolescents, rather than those with specific risks (Faggiano et al., 2014). Relatively successful programs often target multiple risk and protective factors at once, in line with biopsychosocial models of SUD (Faggiano et al., 2014; Volkow & Blanco, 2023).

Unfortunately, SUD treatment and prevention programs show only modest success, as evidenced by the high and increasing prevalence of SUD (SAMHSA, 2024), challenges engaging individuals in interventions, and often low levels of intervention effectiveness (Farhoudian et al., 2022). Because SUD is a multifactorial biopsychosocial problem (with many potential intersecting risk factors) and it often develops gradually over time, it is difficult to predict who will develop SUD, who will respond well to treatment, and for whom SUD will recur after treatment (Stallvik et al., 2015; McCabe et al., 2018). Once SUD develops and becomes severe, it can be challenging to treat and to maintain recovery (Restrepo-Guzman et al., 2020). A lack of access to care, stigma around substance use, and competing psychosocial demands can serve as barriers to initiating and staying engaged in treatment, particularly for marginalized populations (Farhoudian et al., 2022; Husain et al., 2023). Screening for problematic use is also time and resource-intensive for health and social service systems.

Prevention brings additional challenges. While clinically validated tools are available to identify current problematic use, providers are less equipped to identify those at risk of developing it later. And while preventative interventions primarily target young people, many are at risk for SUD throughout the life course, and there is a need to disseminate prevention strategies for other age groups and settings (Volkow & Blanco, 2023). In both prevention and treatment, progress has been made in considering the range of biopsychosocial risk factors and targeting them across prevention and integrated treatment strategies. However, the field could benefit from a more personalized approach that assesses and addresses individuals' specific needs and preferences in an increasingly holistic and time-sensitive manner (Marchand et al., 2019). AI has the potential to transform SUD treatment and prevention, specifically in this way.

3 Emergence of AI in SUD Treatment and Prevention

3.1 Historical Overview of AI in Medicine and Behavioral Health

AI has been applied in medicine and behavioral healthcare throughout its history and evolution. In the mid-1960s, the first chatbot, ELIZA, was designed to mimic psychotherapy by recognizing simple word patterns and generating predefined responses (Weizenbaum, 1966). During this era, medical research databases and health records became increasingly digitized, laying the foundation for future developments in healthcare data science and AI (Kulikowski, 2019). In the 1970s, AI research in medicine continued to emerge with the development of expert systems like MYCIN, which used rule-based reasoning to diagnose and recommend treatment for bacterial infections (Kaul et al., 2020). Methodological advances in the 1990s and 2000s enabled AI to analyze complex datasets, leading to breakthroughs in medical applications, including in medical imaging and diagnostics, genomics, and personalized and precision medicine (Kaul et al., 2020).

The 2010s saw rapid growth in the use of AI for behavioral health, including substance use research. At that time, researchers began to demonstrate how AI algorithms can be applied to accurately predict risk for mental health conditions, including depression, schizophrenia, and suicide (Abd Rahman et al., 2020). Concurrently, there was renewed interest in developing AI-powered treatment applications, such as improved chatbots, for mental health disorders (Moore & Caudill, 2019); the earliest efforts related to SUD involved using AI algorithms to improve screening for problematic substance use. One early study demonstrated how an AI model could identify heavy drinkers and delineate risk and protective factors for drinking among college students (Zuba et al., 2012); another used AI to categorize individuals based on the characteristics of their opioid use disorder to better determine the influence of genetics (Sun et al., 2012). A 2016 study reported one of the first AI treatment applications for SUD, a chatbot to assess problematic alcohol use among young adults and provide them with education on responsible drinking (Elmasri & Maeder, 2016).

Increasingly, AI has garnered interdisciplinary interest, including among social workers. The Grand Challenges for Social Work include a call to "harness technology for social good," acknowledging that technologies such as AI, when deployed ethically, can help address challenging social problems in new ways (American Academy of Social Work and Social Welfare, n.d.). In cutting-edge university research laboratories, social work scientists lead teams involving engineers, computer scientists, and informaticists to advance such "social good" applications of AI, including SUD (Tambe & Rice, 2018; Davis et al., 2022). Critically, social work scholars are also centering the voices of vulnerable populations who may be affected by AI and advocating that AI applications are ethical, trustworthy, and unbiased (Goldkind et al., 2025). While some may view AI as primarily within the purview of technical disciplines, social workers have much to contribute through dynamic research methodologies, an orientation towards team science and practice, and critical perspectives on social justice.

3.2 *AI Tools and Techniques*

Before reviewing contemporary applications of AI to substance use and SUD, it is necessary to describe and delineate the relevant core methodologies of AI. Early AI systems, including the psychotherapy chatbot ELIZA, relied on "knowledge base" approaches, where experts manually encoded rules for the application to follow (e.g., IF the user's statement includes the word "sad" THEN ask "What makes you feel sad?"). However, this method was limited because humans often draw on unspoken or hard-to-describe knowledge when solving problems. For example, a clinician treating SUD may make different care recommendations based on nuanced differences in complex biopsychosocial factors and their combinations.

Machine learning, with its ability to learn directly from data and better capture the complexities of real-world decision-making, represents an advance from "knowledge-based" approaches (Suva & Bhatia, 2024). Today, the most common AI applications for SUD involve machine learning (Ng et al., 2025; Garbin et al., 2023; Ebrahimi et al., 2021). As an advanced type of machine learning, deep learning is a powerful paradigm for making accurate predictions with complex data (LeCun et al., 2015). We note, however, that as methodologies become increasingly complex, it can become harder to understand how predictions are made (known as the "black box" problem) (Sendak et al., 2020). This is problematic in care settings, where clinicians and clients need meaningful, actionable knowledge to trust AI predictions.

The rapid proliferation of data and technology is broadly enabling these advances in AI and its applications to SUD. Increased digitization and the rise of big data ecosystems across a variety of domains (e.g., research, healthcare settings, social datasets, and consumer devices) provide ever-expanding sources of data for the development of machine learning models that rely on them to make predictions. Data sources that have been used to develop these models in the field of SUD are as wide-ranging as electronic medical records, including records of diagnoses, prescriptions, and provider notes (Ellis et al., 2019); data on social networks from social media platforms (Hassanpour et al., 2019); survey studies, epidemiological, and large publicly available datasets (Davis et al., 2022; Oliva et al., 2022); and physiological data, including from brain scans (Yang et al., 2023), wearable sensors (Davis-Martin et al., 2021), and genomic records (Hatoum et al., 2021). The ubiquity of smartphones and Internet access also allows for advances in intervention delivery, including AI-enabled treatments delivered via mobile devices (Brezing & Brixner, 2022).

Some algorithmic and hardware tools are especially well-equipped for specific types of data: natural language processing is a machine learning approach that extracts meaning from text data—such as from provider notes, transcripts of audio recordings, or social media posts—and this approach can be used to uncover risk for SUD in both micro and macro contexts (Singleton et al., 2023). Deep learning models are particularly well-suited for complex multimodal data such as neuroimaging, genomic, or sensor data, from which they can uncover patterns of risk that might be undetectable with traditional analytical methods (Miotto et al., 2018). Consumer wearable devices, such as Apple Watch and FitBit, represent mainstream adoption of wearable sensors and provide an increasingly accessible source of physiological data for continuously monitoring changes in SUD risk and relapse (Oesterle et al., 2022).

3.3 *Promise and Potential*

Enabled by the availability of novel data, the development and adoption of AI has the potential to significantly enhance the understanding, prevention, and treatment of SUD among vulnerable populations. Machine learning models have been developed to screen for current problematic use, detect early signs of SUD, predict who is at future risk of SUD, and assess who might respond well to SUD treatment (Ng et al., 2025; Garbin et al., 2023; Ebrahimi et al., 2021). These models, and AI more broadly, could increasingly be leveraged within health systems, treatments, and prevention efforts to help make interventions more personalized, targeted, and better timed. Among those who have already received treatment for SUD, AI tools, including predictive models that leverage wearable device data, may help monitor for relapse risk (Davis-Martin et al., 2021).

Crucially, the proliferation of data and AI enables the development of tools for prevention and treatment that increasingly adhere to the complex biopsychosocial model of SUD. That is, by leveraging and combining multimodal data sources ranging from psychophysiological data to data on local social environments, AI can model risk based on a range of biological, psychological, and social determinants—and their interactions. This is important for working with marginalized populations, for whom it is critical to address the structural and intersecting roots of SUD risk. Digitally delivered, AI-based interventions can also enhance the ability to reach hard-to-reach populations with better-targeted, more accessible treatments and prevention strategies. In a nutshell, AI has the potential to democratize information and intervention and ground SUD strategies in the realities of risk for vulnerable populations.

4 Identifying High-Risk Individuals

4.1 *Identifying Current Substance Use Problems*

One promising application of AI in the substance use field is in its ability to identify individuals who are currently exhibiting problematic use. Researchers have demonstrated that machine learning models can be trained on a range of data sources to identify individuals with existing SUD or early signs of SUD using characteristics captured in those data. For example, several studies have leveraged electronic medical record data to train machine learning models, including natural language processing to analyze providers' notes and to screen patients for current SUD with a high degree of accuracy (Ridgway et al., 2021; Blackley et al., 2021). One study demonstrated how machine learning can identify individuals with SUD from their social media profiles (Hassanpour et al., 2019). Using advanced deep learning methods with images and text from users' Instagram profiles, researchers were able to identify individuals with likely alcohol use disorder.

As discussed further below, machine learning and deep learning models hold promise for improving collaborative clinician-client decision-making, which is critical for effectively identifying and addressing SUD. Model performance and trust in machine learning are significantly increased when there is a process for incorporating interdisciplinary stakeholder feedback and perspectives throughout model development. These models have potential real-world applications, for example, assisting health or social service providers in identifying individuals or groups with a high likelihood of an SUD and aiding in diagnosis. In addition, with its ability to mine large and complex sets of data to uncover new associations and interactions, machine learning is being used to identify potential biopsychosocial markers of current SUD, including changes in the brain (Yang et al., 2023), demographic and psychological characteristics (Ahn & Vassileva, 2016), and neurocognitive functioning (Ahn et al., 2016). These findings warrant further validation in clinical research and could lead to the development of novel screening and diagnostic instruments for SUD.

4.2 Predicting Future Substance Use Problems

Beyond identifying current problematic use, AI is also being used to predict future outcomes related to SUD. A growing body of research shows how machine learning can predict who may go on to develop an SUD, who might suffer specific consequences of use, and who might or might not respond well to treatment. In one exemplary study, a machine learning model was able to predict from someone's electronic health record data whether they would go on to develop alcohol use disorder with 96% accuracy (Ebrahimi et al., 2022). In another study, machine learning models trained on demographic and psychometric data of clients in psychological treatment for alcohol use disorder could predict treatment outcomes as well as trained clinicians (Symons et al., 2019). Researchers have also applied machine learning to predict whether individuals who have been prescribed opioids would go on to develop opioid use disorder (Dong et al., 2021a) or overdose from opioids (Dong et al., 2021b), with promising results. Machine learning models that combine various multimodal data sources might have especially high predictive power. In a recent study of patients with posttraumatic stress disorder, a deep learning model that integrated electronic health record data with data on one's neighborhood socioeconomic conditions demonstrated very good performance for predicting whether the patient would go on to develop SUD over the subsequent 3-month period (Miranda et al., 2024). As these studies exemplify, machine and deep learning can reveal previously unknown relationships and create high-performance, clinically valid predictive algorithms. These, in turn, can inform targeted prevention and treatment efforts.

Predictive models have wide potential applications in clinical and community settings, where they could help identify at-risk individuals before traditional assessments would flag concerns—or among individuals who are not otherwise engaged in clinical care—and inform early interventions for those most at risk. Just as research on AI-driven screening could help refine markers of current SUD, predictive modeling may also expand knowledge of risk factors for future risk. For example, researchers applied machine learning to data from a longitudinal survey of youth, uncovering 30 lifestyle variables that predicted future SUD (Jing et al., 2020). The nature of these predictors varied with age—shifting from psychological vulnerabilities in late childhood and early adolescence to challenges of socializing in late adolescence and early adulthood—demonstrating how machine learning can enhance nuance in ecological knowledge.

Other innovations include temporal and graphical deep learning-based modeling using large-scale EHR data for predicting opioid use disorder and other medical conditions (Dong et al., 2021a). For example, graph neural networks (GNNs) are a class of deep learning models that analyze data represented as graphs. In these graphs, *nodes* (e.g., individual patients, a treatment provider, and drugs) interact through *edges* (e.g., behavioral patterns and clinical encounters between a patient and a physician or social worker; Wu et al., 2021). Temporal GNNs extend this to capture how graphs evolve, which is critical for predicting future outcomes such as opioid use disorder. While GNNs can predict risk with increasing accuracy, a significant challenge is the need for advanced computing and technical methodologies to analyze the complex relationships embedded in EHR data, including associations between SUD risk and multifaceted predictors such as co-occurring medical conditions, healthcare access, and adverse childhood experiences.

4.3 Effectiveness and Limitations of Risk Identification

A growing body of research demonstrates the utility of machine learning for identifying and predicting SUD risk. The largest number of machine learning studies exists for SUDs involving alcohol, cannabis, and opioids (see Ebrahimi et al., 2021; Ng et al., 2025; Garbin et al., 2023, for literature reviews of machine learning research involving these substances, respectively). Though results vary, machine learning has demonstrated the ability to identify SUD risk with accuracy exceeding 90%. There is reason to be optimistic that machine learning could significantly improve SUD practice and policy by providing powerful tools for identification and prediction used in healthcare applications.

As machine learning for SUD has primarily been deployed in research contexts to date, its applicability in real-world settings is less clear, and several challenges arise for real-world deployment. Machine learning models are only as useful as the data that is available to train them. As diagnoses and terminology used for clinical substance use problems change over time, models trained on historic EHR data may miss contemporary indicators of SUD. One study that explored a limited set of possible predictors for opioid use disorder in an EHR dataset revealed that the top risk factors were other SUDs, opioid overdose, and heavy opioid use, information that would essentially be "too late" to share with a clinician whose goal was prevention

(Liu et al., 2023). Even when results are promising, the vast majority of machine learning research for SUD has involved training and testing models on a single dataset, and therefore models that have been developed with one sample have mostly not been externally validated with other samples (Ebrahimi et al., 2021; Ng et al., 2025; Garbin et al., 2023). Machine learning is susceptible to overfitting, where it can perform very well on training data but do poorly with new, unseen data because it is fit too specifically to the noise and idiosyncrasies of the training data (Ying, 2019). Thus, it is essential to ensure models trained in one context would perform well in real-world settings before they are broadly deployed.

There is also a large variety in types of machine learning models and in the data that they are trained on (Ebrahimi et al., 2021; Ng et al., 2025; Garbin et al., 2023), making it challenging to compare results across studies and to implement a model that was validated in one setting in another setting. To illustrate, if health system A uses a machine learning model trained on their patients' wearable device data, but health system B does not collect this type of data, a model trained in health system A would be infeasible to deploy in health system B. Many machine learning models also have low interpretability, making it difficult to understand why they make certain predictions or how they would behave under different conditions (Carvalho et al., 2019). This may make it harder for practitioners and stakeholders to trust and apply the model in real-world decision-making, especially when the population, substances, underlying data, or assumptions differ across settings.

5 AI-Supported Treatment and Recovery

5.1 *AI-Enabled Treatments*

Beyond identifying risk, AI has the potential to improve the delivery of SUD treatment—both by enabling providers to make better care decisions and by developing novel, technology-delivered treatments. Given the complex, biopsychosocial nature of SUD, clients' unique symptom and risk profiles, and providers' time constraints, it can be challenging to make effective clinical decisions and allot resources. Newly developed clinical decision support tools apply predictive models on client data and up-to-date research on best practices to help tailor treatment recommendations to each patient's unique clinical needs (Tai et al., 2024). Early research on these tools demonstrates they could improve SUD outcomes and satisfaction in care (Tai et al., 2024). One can imagine a social worker with a busy caseload benefiting from such a tool by being better informed about high-risk clients and making more timely, informed care decisions for them.

AI is also helping to drive advances in client-facing digital therapeutics, which are treatment or prevention strategies delivered via technology directly to at-risk populations (Hao et al., 2024). Technology is helping expand how care is offered, including via the Internet, mobile devices, and virtual reality, potentially lowering treatment barriers through telehealth and enabling creative, flexible treatment adaptations for vulnerable populations. Increasingly, AI is being integrated into these systems, allowing for more targeted and engaging digital interventions. A recently developed mobile app intervention uses a chatbot to deliver evidence-based SUD interventions (including cognitive-behavioral therapy and motivational interviewing) in a tailored, responsive manner (Prochaska et al., 2021), which aligns with social work's emphasis on person-centered care. As technologies like this proliferate, they may help make intervention and prevention more accessible for vulnerable populations who otherwise could not access care, and they could also give social workers a rich toolkit of adjunctive treatments to enhance usual care and recovery.

5.2 *Real-Time Monitoring and Relapse Prevention*

Much of the promise of digital therapeutics lies in the potential to integrate rich, frequently collected data to provide timely responsive care. One source of data that could enhance these tools' usefulness is real-time data from users' smartphones and wearable devices such as smartwatches. Smartphones automatically collect data such as individuals' location and social interactions (e.g., calls and text messages), and wearable devices use biosensors to collect physiological and health data on an ongoing basis, including individuals' physical activity, cardiovascular function, and stress reactivity. Research has begun to examine how AI can use this data to identify behavioral and physiological changes that indicate a risk for relapse among individuals in recovery from SUD. One recent study demonstrated that increases in stress reactivity, measured by wearable biosensors, are associated with relapse over the following week (Mahoney et al., 2023). Another study predicted substance craving 90 min into the future with 93% accuracy solely from GPS data (Epstein et al., 2020).

Because smartphones and wearable devices continuously and automatically collect data like this, they can enable real-time monitoring of risk across multiple biopsychosocial domains without requiring user input. AI leveraging this data could power personalized interventions delivered via mobile devices that target specific risk factors in a time-sensitive manner. Such interventions, known as just-in-time adaptive interventions (Carpenter et al., 2020), could leverage smartphone and wearable device data to identify when individuals are most at risk of relapse and intervene effectively. A pilot study explored the use of this strategy with chronic pain patients at risk of problematic substance use, where participants were prompted by a mobile app to practice mindfulness when their wearable biosensors identified heightened stress reactivity (Garland et al., 2023). Practicing mindfulness in those moments was associated with reductions in pain, stress, and craving for substances.

6 Real-World Applications: Opioid Risk Stratification in the Veterans Affairs

Most work using AI to target health outcomes, including problematic substance use, has remained at the research stage, thus far limiting its real-world benefits. However, one early adopter has been the US Department of Veterans Affairs (VA). In the early 2010s, opioid prescriptions increased at the VA, due in part to exceedingly high rates of chronic pain among veterans (Gellad et al., 2017). Many veterans who were prescribed opioids suffered from adverse outcomes, including suicide and overdose, reflecting the broader opioid epidemic in the United States. Seeking new strategies to mitigate the risk of adverse outcomes among veterans who are prescribed opioids, the VA's extensive electronic health records and centralized data infrastructure allowed it to go beyond traditional monitoring approaches.

The VA developed and deployed the Stratification Tool for Opioid Risk Mitigation (STORM) to identify patients with an opioid prescription who are at risk of overdose or suicide (Oliva et al., 2017). STORM leverages a predictive model to calculate an up-to-date risk score for each patient, based on their demographics, prior adverse events, and physical and behavioral health history. The provider-facing STORM dashboard is a clinical decision support tool that displays the risk factors for each patient (e.g., diagnoses, specific medications) and documents whether specific risk-mitigation strategies (e.g., psychosocial treatments) have been employed with the patient. In a randomized evaluation of STORM involving over 44,000 at-risk patients at all 140 VA medical centers, use of the risk stratification tool was associated with a significant decrease in mortality over the next 4 months (Strombotne et al., 2023).

At this early stage of adoption, it is crucial to study the implementation of strategies like STORM and to glean lessons that can be applied as predictive models are deployed more broadly across health and service settings. Supportive implementation, leadership, and sufficient training are crucial. In a study of STORM's implementation in 39 VA facilities, some staff were not fully aware of its clinical importance or evidence base; there were variations in training, guidance, and leadership buy-in for STORM; and there were challenges integrating the tool into existing clinical workflows and priorities (McCarthy et al., 2022). Questions also remain about how such a tool might be applied in settings beyond the VA, especially in lower-resourced settings with a less robust data infrastructure. Still, STORM represents a pioneering example of implementing predictive analytics in substance use-related care, demonstrating how AI-powered risk stratification tools could be integrated into clinical workflows and potentially improve patient outcomes at scale.

7 Ethical Considerations

7.1 *Bias and Equity*

The rising use of AI for SUD prevention and treatment brings with it several ethical concerns, particularly for marginalized and vulnerable populations. These technologies must reduce, rather than reinforce, existing disparities in SUD and other outcomes. Machine learning models are not neutral; they inherit the biases and limitations of their training data. Many machine learning models have been developed using data from predominantly white, higher socioeconomic status populations (Turner Lee, 2018; Juhn et al., 2022). As a result, these models may perform poorly for individuals from underrepresented groups, leading to misclassification and inappropriate interventions. Machine learning can also reinforce disparities in SUD diagnoses, reflecting biases in how society defines and assigns risk. For example, models trained on criminal justice data could disproportionately flag Black and Latino individuals as high-risk due to historical patterns of racialized policing rather than actual substance use behaviors (Huq, 2019).

Beyond biased risk predictions, disparities in access to AI-driven interventions could create additional barriers to equitable care. Many of the same populations most vulnerable to SUD—low-income individuals, rural communities, and people with disabilities—also face structural barriers in accessing both treatment and digital technologies (Lutz, 2019). If AI-powered tools rely on expensive smartphones, stable Internet connections, or wearable devices, they may inadvertently exclude these groups, further widening disparities in care. Many AI-driven treatment tools are developed in well-resourced healthcare settings. They may be challenging to disseminate in lower-resourced settings or in community-based programs serving the most vulnerable. Additionally, policy constraints and funding limitations may determine whether these technologies are integrated into public healthcare systems, potentially perpetuating a two-tiered system in which socioeconomically disadvantaged individuals receive less benefit from advances in AI treatment.

7.2 *Social Construction of Risk*

Moving beyond bias in how AI learns from past data, we must also consider how it can actively construct social narratives of risk, shaping who society views as high-risk, what outcomes are considered problematic, and which treatment approaches are prioritized in SUD care. One issue concerns how "risk" is defined and measured in machine learning models and how this can reinforce society's existing biases against marginalized populations (Rajkomar et al., 2018). To illustrate, a machine learning model that includes race as a possible predictor of adverse SUD outcomes and is deployed in a hospital may "learn" that racial minority patients of that hospital are more likely to develop SUD and may perpetuate an incorrect belief among providers that minorities are doomed to have substance use problems. However, it may, in fact, be the case that living in an economically disadvantaged area is what puts patients at risk, and racial minorities are overrepresented in these areas. Suppose information on area-level economic disadvantage is not included in a predictive model. In that case, the model may learn the wrong lesson and perpetuate stereotypes about race rather than getting to the societal roots of disparities.

Similarly, we must consider how AI systems designed to detect the risk of adverse substance use outcomes automatically may reinforce unhelpful ideas about what constitutes a poor outcome. Importantly, the SUD field has seen advances in harm reduction approaches and an understanding that one size does not fit all when it comes to treatment goals. There is a risk that deploying AI models trained on a singular outcome (such as complete abstinence) will lead to less person-centered care if that outcome differs from the patient's goals. Treatment and prevention decisions driven by AI may be made to meet goals that diverge from a patient's own priorities, such as moderating their use, learning to use more safely, or pursuing specific life goals as a person in recovery.

7.3 Privacy and Surveillance

The implementation of AI systems for SUD also raises substantial privacy concerns, especially for marginalized communities who have historical reasons to distrust health and social service systems (Dovidio et al., 2008). AI applications often rely on collecting sensitive personal data, such as from electronic health records, social media, and consumer electronic devices. Communities can be wary of sharing data this broadly, and leaks or unintended disclosures involving information on substance use could lead to employment discrimination, loss of child custody, or criminal justice involvement (Looi et al., 2024). Further, when an AI system flags an individual as high-risk, this label could follow them through service systems, potentially leading to differential treatment or discrimination. This is particularly concerning for marginalized populations who are already disproportionately surveilled by social systems. For example, research shows that drug testing during pregnancy and at birth disproportionately targets low-income women and women of color, despite similar rates of substance use across demographic groups (Kunins et al., 2007; Chasnoff et al., 1990). AI could perpetuate these unfair practices.

It is critical to consider the broader potential for increased surveillance. Even when care providers have the best of intentions, relapse monitoring systems that track location or wearable device data can be perceived as intrusive (Moore et al., 2021). There is also the possibility that data and monitoring systems may be accessed by law enforcement or used in criminal proceedings. For the sake of communities that have experienced over-policing and disproportionate criminal justice involvement due to substance use, particularly Black and Latino communities, AI monitoring tools must be developed and disseminated with extreme caution (Boehme et al., 2022).

7.4 *Client and Provider Autonomy and Empowerment*

Though AI has the potential to empower individuals with or at risk of SUD, it could also diminish their autonomy. This is of critical concern to social workers, as respect for client autonomy and self-determination is central to social work's ethical code (NASW, 2021). On the one hand, AI systems that leverage clients' own data about their health and functioning may help them and their clinicians make more informed decisions to mitigate the risk of SUD. Wearable devices could enhance individuals' ability to self-monitor their own risk for relapse by deepening their awareness of their moment-to-moment health status. Digital therapeutics could empower individuals by providing greater access to information, support, and treatment options beyond traditional service settings.

On the other hand, AI could undermine autonomy among those with SUD risk if it is deployed unwisely or in support of over-surveillance or coercive treatments. As described above, data and monitoring tools could contribute to punitive surveillance and be used to mandate abstinence in criminal justice or employment settings. There is also a danger that over-relying on AI could diminish clinicians' ability to apply their own clinical wisdom and to have person-centered conversations with patients about their care and lead to inappropriate care decisions (Tiribelli, 2023). While AI-based treatment recommendation systems seek to empower clinicians, some models are based on difficult-to-interpret "black boxes," which might make it hard for patients and providers to understand why specific recommendations are made, to question intervention strategies critically, and to tailor decisions if necessary (Sendak et al., 2020). Suppose patients come to rely on AI to drive health decisions. In that case, they may become increasingly passive recipients of care, leaving them vulnerable to AI interventions that influence their choices without their full awareness or informed consent (Tiribelli, 2023).

8 Future Directions and Recommendations

8.1 *Emerging Trends in AI Technology*

Next, we discuss emerging trends in AI and offer concrete recommendations for social workers as AI proliferates in SUD care. As AI rapidly advances, many next-generation technologies have significant potential to improve SUD prevention and treatment. One prominent area of research, with exciting applications for SUD, is reinforcement learning. While most machine learning models are trained on past data to make predictions, reinforcement learning continues to incorporate feedback after each decision. It adjusts its decision-making approach over time—effectively learning by doing (Shakya et al., 2023). This makes reinforcement learning especially promising for interventions that learn from ongoing user behavior and environmental changes. In SUD treatment, reinforcement learning could power just-in-time adaptive interventions that are especially precise and effective. For example, a just-in-time intervention that uses reinforcement learning might learn, through trial and error, that a person ignores relaxation exercises but responds well to peer support. Because reinforcement learning can try an intervention and observe the results, it can dynamically learn the optimal timing of interventions and how to motivate people to engage in SUD recovery behaviors.

We are also in the midst of an explosion in the use of generative AI. In contrast to traditional AI models that classify information or make predictions, generative AI models are pretrained on vast amounts of diverse data, enabling them to flexibly understand user input and generate new content (Jo, 2023). This technology could drive increasingly interactive and responsive digital therapeutics for SUD. One key area where this could be used is in advanced chatbots, built on text-based generative AI systems known as large language models (LLMs). While earlier chatbots relied on rule-based systems with pre-scripted responses, LLM-based chatbots can engage in more natural, nuanced conversations that adapt more closely to users' specific needs and concerns. An LLM-based chatbot could deliver evidence-based counseling interventions for SUD (such as motivational interviewing or cognitive behavioral therapy) and do so in an increasingly engaging and sophisticated manner. Beyond direct client support, LLMs can assist social workers by synthesizing large volumes of clinical documentation and research. For providers managing large caseloads, LLMs could quickly summarize vast amounts of clinical data, flagging patterns that suggest risk for poor outcomes, and recommend evidence-based interventions tailored to an individual's unique needs.

8.2 *Promoting Harm Reduction with AI*

Much of the focus of work applying AI to problematic substance use has focused on assessing and preventing SUD, preventing relapse, and promoting abstinence. However, AI also has promise for mitigating individual and social consequences of use, in line with team-based harm reduction approaches, which are effective in addressing complex health care needs through integrated care (Leibowitz et al., 2023). AI-powered tools could support harm reduction efforts among social workers, other interdisciplinary practitioners, and policymakers. Preliminary research suggests the uses of AI to support harm reduction are broad and could include not only preventing poor outcomes like overdose in clinical settings (as in the example of the VA's STORM tool, above; Oliva et al., 2017) but also identifying larger geographic areas where risk is rising and informing optimal community resource allocation.

Research is demonstrating how AI models can help identify "hotspots" of increased drug use or overdose, potentially to optimize the distribution of preventive services. Machine learning models are being used to analyze community-level data, such as historical overdose rates, emergency medical services records, and patterns of disease transmission, to predict trends in injection drug use and overdose

(Bartholomew et al., 2022; Prieto et al., 2020). Such models help policymakers determine the most effective allocation of resources, such as safe injection sites and overdose prevention kits, and they enable community service providers to refine staffing and outreach strategies. For preventing overdose at the individual level, wearable biosensors could monitor physiological indicators of overdose, such as breathing rate and oxygen levels, and AI systems could trigger an emergency response (Ezell et al., 2024).

8.3 *Considering Implementation Challenges and Developing Best Practices*

As AI tools for SUD treatment and prevention transition from research to real-world practice settings, their success will depend on careful attention to equity, ethical implementation, and effective integration into existing systems. Deploying and scaling AI will require significant financial and technical investment, which could pose a barrier, especially in low-resource settings where need is often greatest. Without proactive policies to promote equity, AI could reinforce disparities in SUD care rather than helping to close them. Relatedly, discrepancies in data infrastructure across settings may pose a challenge: a tool developed in one setting may not be feasible in another if it relies on resources unavailable there. AI systems that depend on comprehensive, multimodal data may not perform as well in settings where such data are unavailable, incomplete, or inconsistently collected. It will also be critical to ensure that staff with adequate AI expertise are available across systems to facilitate patients' understanding of AI-driven interventions. As many AI models function as complex "black boxes," non-expert social workers and clients may struggle to trust, critically appraise, or implement AI-generated recommendations. Finally, there is a risk of deploying AI that is out of step with social work ethics and values, such as predictive tools that promote bias and impinge on privacy, or treatment applications that diminish personal autonomy and clinical judgment.

It is therefore essential to develop best practices for developing and properly implementing AI tools in the SUD field. Given the early stage of development and rapid growth of AI in this field, the following principles are not meant to be exhaustive but to serve as a starting point for a broader conversation:

- *Multimodal, Biopsychosocial Data Integration*: AI models should incorporate a breadth of data sources to provide a more holistic view of SUD risk and treatment needs. In addition to traditional clinical data, integrating data on area-level social determinants of health, wearable device data, and other factors can help AI systems identify structural and social risks rather than reinforcing individual blame, stigma, and biases.
- *Client and Provider Autonomy and Informed Consent*: AI tools for SUD must be built to promote individual agency and informed decision-making. As these tools are deployed, informed consent procedures should be clear and ensure clients

understand how their data will be stored and used and how they can opt out of AI. The use of punitive, surveillance-based, or mandatory-participation tools should be critically questioned. Clinicians also should not offload their expertise to technology and rely on AI to make decisions for them. Instead, they should learn to critically engage with technology to augment their practice and help enhance their decision-making.

- *Explainable AI, Trustworthiness, and Transparency*: To the extent possible, AI tools should be designed for interpretability, ensuring that both practitioners and individuals receiving care can understand why and how decisions are made and that clients retain shared decision-making power. Developers should prioritize models that generate clear, human-readable explanations of risk and treatment recommendations, enabling clinicians and clients to engage with AI rather than relying on it (Xu et al., 2019). Stakeholder-driven approaches should incorporate patients' perspectives, lived experience, and domain knowledge in SUD into all phases of machine learning model development. This ensures that data (e.g., EHRs) are representative of the population and that models validly predict clinical outcomes and stratify SUD risk. This approach can also enhance interpretability, facilitate engagement, and build trust that models are appropriate for clinical use and align with clinicians' assessments.
- *Addressing Bias and Equity*: AI models should be rigorously tested across diverse populations to identify biases in risk classification and treatment recommendations. Developers must ensure that AI does not disproportionately flag marginalized groups because of systemic biases in training data and instead incorporates structural determinants of risk. Efforts must be made to ensure digital resources, including AI and data systems, are equitably distributed.
- *Personalized and Flexible, Integrated, Team-based Treatment*: As AI systems can consider many biopsychosocial risk and protective factors, research evidence, and clients' preferences concurrently in real time, they could support a revolution in personalized and responsive care for SUD. To this end, AI-driven interventions should adapt to individual goals, needs, and treatment preferences, rather than adopting a one-size-fits-all approach. In line with integrated hub-and-spoke approaches and recognizing that abstinence-only models may exclude many individuals with different goals, AI tools should support harm reduction and recovery capital (Best & Hennessy, 2022). Social workers in both hubs and spokes serve on MAT teams alongside medical providers, promoting integrated behavioral health and interdisciplinary collaboration and linking clients to social services. Similarly, they can facilitate telehealth and digital integration.
- *Inclusive Design and Co-creation*: AI for SUD should be developed in partnership with people with lived experience and those in recovery—especially individuals with intersecting, marginalized identities—as well as SUD service providers and community organizations. AI tools should align with these individuals' real-world needs, preferences, and ethical concerns. Digital therapeutics and clinical decision support tools should be user-friendly, engaging, culturally relevant, interpretable, and intuitive to use to increase engagement, minimize adoption barriers, and reinforce equitable access to care.

8.4 *Implications for Social Work Education and Practice*

AI has the potential to improve SUD prevention and treatment by improving risk assessment, expanding access to services, and supporting targeted biopsychosocial interventions. Given potential ethical challenges and implementation barriers, social workers should have a seat at the table as these technologies are being developed and deployed, and they can help give voice to the needs and concerns of vulnerable populations with SUD. In doing so, social workers can help ensure AI is implemented in a way that supports rather than impinges on health and social justice.

One of the most pressing concerns is the need for enhanced data and technology literacy in social work education (Rodriguez et al., 2024; Creswell Báez et al., 2025). AI tools may increasingly shape clinical decision-making and policy decisions for people at risk of SUD. Yet, social work professional education typically includes little to no formal training on how these systems operate. To effectively inform clients and advocate for ethical AI use, social workers must be equipped with foundational knowledge of AI, predictive modeling, and digital equity. Schools of social work should update their curricula to ensure that graduates are prepared to navigate and critique advances in AI as they relate to practice and policy in SUD and related fields. Practicing social workers should pursue continuing education in this area to stay up to date on these rapidly advancing technologies.

Beyond education, social workers can play an active role in ensuring that AI serves marginalized communities with SUD, rather than reinforcing disadvantages. When working with clients, we must be prepared to help them understand how AI tools collect and use sensitive data, as well as the potential benefits, risks, and shortcomings of these systems. We should also educate our clients on how their data are used, privacy shortcomings and safeguards, and their rights to opt out of specific services or features. As program managers and advocates, we should promote equitable and ethical AI and push for policies that support transparency, mitigate bias, and lower barriers to technology among underserved communities.

Social workers should work closely with stakeholders and technical experts, including data scientists, software developers, and program managers, to ensure that these tools are designed with an accurate grasp of SUD and its etiology. That is, we should advocate for AI tools that align with a biopsychosocial view of SUD and address clients' real-world needs, rather than taking a one-size-fits-all approach. Finally, we should interrogate how AI in legal, medical, and social service settings can reinforce stigma and criminalization among marginalized populations, and we should prioritize empowering and harm reduction-based approaches.

9 Conclusion

In summary, this chapter provides a comprehensive exploration of the current state of AI in SUD treatment and prevention. Advances in AI and related data infrastructures have enormous transformative potential. AI-based tools can match the multifaceted and complex nature of SUD, democratize information and care, more accurately model risk, and make treatment and prevention more personalized, timely, and effective. Yet, these advances must be grounded in social work values to ensure that AI implementation is ethical, equitable, and does not reinforce existing biases and disparities. This chapter begins a conversation on best practices for AI in SUD and considers implications for social work education and practice.

As AI moves beyond controlled research studies into SUD practice settings, we call on social workers to engage with data scientists, technologists, and policymakers and collaborate closely on the development and implementation of these tools. Our expertise can help ensure that AI-based predictive models and digital therapeutics are attuned to the full complexity of SUD as a biopsychosocial problem and are grounded in the real-world challenges and concerns of vulnerable populations. As professionals who routinely interface with and advocate for marginalized communities at risk of SUD, we should view our role primarily as giving voice to these communities and work to ensure that technological advances are not only effective but also balanced with humanity and social justice.

Conflicts of Interest The authors have no conflicts of interest to declare that are relevant to the content of this chapter.

References

Abd Rahman, R., Omar, K., Noah, S. A. M., Danuri, M. S. N. M., & Al-Garadi, M. A. (2020). Application of machine learning methods in mental health detection: A systematic review. *IEEE Access, 8*, 183952–183964. https://doi.org/10.1109/ACCESS.2020.3029154

Ahn, W. Y., & Vassileva, J. (2016). Machine-learning identifies substance-specific behavioral markers for opiate and stimulant dependence. *Drug and Alcohol Dependence, 161*, 247–257. https://doi.org/10.1016/j.drugalcdep.2016.02.008

Ahn, W. Y., Ramesh, D., Moeller, F. G., & Vassileva, J. (2016). Utility of machine-learning approaches to identify behavioral markers for substance use disorders: Impulsivity dimensions as predictors of current cocaine dependence. *Frontiers in Psychiatry, 7*, 34. https://doi.org/10.3389/fpsyt.2016.00034

American Academy of Social Work and Social Welfare. (n.d.). *Grand challenges for social work*. Retrieved from https://grandchallengesforsocialwork.org

American Psychiatric Association. (2013). *Diagnostic and statistical manual of mental disorders* (5th ed.). American Psychiatric Association. https://doi.org/10.1176/appi.books.9780890425596

Baptiste-Roberts, K., & Hossain, M. (2018). Socioeconomic disparities and self-reported substance abuse-related problems. *Addiction & Health, 10*(2), 112–122. https://doi.org/10.22122/ahj.v10i2.561

Bartholomew, T. S., Tookes, H. E., Spencer, E. C., & Feaster, D. J. (2022). Application of machine learning algorithms for localized syringe services program policy implementation—Florida, 2017. *Annals of Medicine, 54*(1), 2137–2150.

Belfiore, C. I., Galofaro, V., Cotroneo, D., Lopis, A., Tringali, I., Denaro, V., & Casu, M. (2024). A multi-level analysis of biological, social, and psychological determinants of substance use disorder and co-occurring mental health outcomes. *Psychoactives, 3*(2), 194–214. https://doi.org/10.3390/psychoactives3020013

Best, D., & Hennessy, E. A. (2022). The science of recovery capital: Where do we go from here? *Addiction, 117*(4), 1139–1145. https://doi.org/10.1111/add.15732

Best, D., & Nisic, M. (2022). Individual paths to recovery from Substance Use Disorder (SUD): What are the implications of the emerging recovery evidence base for addiction psychiatry and practice? *Psychiatric Clinics of North America, 45*(3), 547–556. https://doi.org/10.1016/j.psc.2022.04.006

Blackley, S. V., MacPhaul, E., Martin, B., Song, W., Suzuki, J., & Zhou, L. (2021). Using natural language processing and machine learning to identify hospitalized patients with opioid use disorder. *AMIA Annual Symposium Proceedings, 2020*, 233–242.

Boehme, H. M., Cann, D., & Isom, D. A. (2022). Citizens' perceptions of over-and under-policing: A look at race, ethnicity, and community characteristics. *Crime & Delinquency, 68*(1), 123–154. https://doi.org/10.1177/0011128720974309

Brezing, C. A., & Brixner, D. I. (2022). The rise of prescription digital therapeutics in behavioral health. *Advances in Therapy, 39*(12), 5301–5306. https://doi.org/10.1007/s12325-022-02320-0

Brooklyn, J. R., & Sigmon, S. C. (2017). Vermont hub-and-spoke model of care for opioid use disorder: Development, implementation, and impact. *Journal of Addiction Medicine, 11*(4), 286–292. https://doi.org/10.1097/adm.0000000000000310

Carpenter, S. M., Menictas, M., Nahum-Shani, I., Wetter, D. W., & Murphy, S. A. (2020). Developments in mobile health just-in-time adaptive interventions for addiction science. *Current Addiction Reports, 7*, 280–290. https://doi.org/10.1007/s40429-020-00322-y

Carroll, K. M., & Onken, L. S. (2005). Behavioral therapies for drug abuse. *American Journal of Psychiatry, 162*(8), 1452–1460. https://doi.org/10.1176/appi.ajp.162.8.1452

Carvalho, D. V., Pereira, E. M., & Cardoso, J. S. (2019). Machine learning interpretability: A survey on methods and metrics. *Electronics, 8*(8), 832. https://doi.org/10.3390/electronics8080832

Castaldelli-Maia, J. M., & Bhugra, D. (2022). Analysis of global prevalence of mental and substance use disorders within countries: Focus on sociodemographic characteristics and income levels. *International Review of Psychiatry, 34*(1), 6–15. https://doi.org/10.1080/09540261.2022.2040450

Chasnoff, I. J., Landress, H. J., & Barrett, M. E. (1990). The prevalence of illicit-drug or alcohol use during pregnancy and discrepancies in mandatory reporting in Pinellas County, Florida. *New England Journal of Medicine, 322*(17), 1202–1206. https://doi.org/10.1056/NEJM199004263221706

Connolly, D., & Gilchrist, G. (2020). Prevalence and correlates of substance use among transgender adults: A systematic review. *Addictive Behaviors, 111*, 106544. https://doi.org/10.1016/j.addbeh.2020.106544

Creswell Báez, J., Victor, B. G., Dysart, C., & Goldkind, L. (2025). "I don't understand it, but okay": An empirical study of mental health practitioners' readiness to use large language models. *Journal of Technology in Human Services, 43*(2), 142–160. https://doi.org/10.1080/15228835.2025.2479475

Davis, J. P., Rao, P., Dilkina, B., Prindle, J., Eddie, D., Christie, N. C., DiGuiseppi, G., Saba, S., Ring, C., & Dennis, M. (2022). Identifying individual and environmental predictors of opioid and psychostimulant use among adolescents and young adults following outpatient treatment. *Drug and Alcohol Dependence, 233*, 109359. https://doi.org/10.1016/j.drugalcdep.2022.109359

Davis-Martin, R. E., Alessi, S. M., & Boudreaux, E. D. (2021). Alcohol use disorder in the age of technology: A review of wearable biosensors in alcohol use disorder treatment. *Frontiers in Psychiatry, 12*, 642813. https://doi.org/10.3389/fpsyt.2021.642813

Dong, X., Deng, J., Hou, W., Rashidian, S., Rosenthal, R. N., Saltz, M., et al. (2021a). Predicting opioid overdose risk of patients with opioid prescriptions using electronic health records based on temporal deep learning. *Journal of Biomedical Informatics, 116*, 103725. https://doi.org/10.1016/j.jbi.2021.103725

Dong, X., Deng, J., Rashidian, S., Abell-Hart, K., Hou, W., Rosenthal, R. N., et al. (2021b). Identifying risk of opioid use disorder for patients taking opioid medications with deep learning. *Journal of the American Medical Informatics Association, 28*(8), 1683–1693. https://doi.org/10.1093/jamia/ocab043

Dovidio, J. F., Penner, L. A., Albrecht, T. L., Norton, W. E., Gaertner, S. L., & Shelton, J. N. (2008). Disparities and distrust: The implications of psychological processes for understanding racial disparities in health and health care. *Social Science & Medicine, 67*(3), 478–486.

Ebrahimi, A., Wiil, U. K., Schmidt, T., Naemi, A., Nielsen, A. S., Shaikh, G. M., & Mansourvar, M. (2021). Predicting the risk of alcohol use disorder using machine learning: A systematic literature review. *IEEE Access, 9*, 151697–151712. https://doi.org/10.1109/ACCESS.2021.3126777

Ebrahimi, A., Wiil, U. K., Naemi, A., Mansourvar, M., Andersen, K., & Nielsen, A. S. (2022). Identification of clinical factors related to prediction of alcohol use disorder from electronic health records using feature selection methods. *BMC Medical Informatics and Decision Making, 22*(1), 304. https://doi.org/10.1186/s12911-022-02051-w

Ellis, R. J., Wang, Z., Genes, N., & Ma'ayan, A. (2019). Predicting opioid dependence from electronic health records with machine learning. *BioData Mining, 12*(1), 3. https://doi.org/10.1186/s13040-019-0193-0

Elmasri, D., & Maeder, A. (2016). A conversational agent for an online mental health intervention. In G. A. Ascoli, M. Hawrylycz, H. Ali, D. Khazanchi, & Y. Shi (Eds.), *Brain informatics and health* (pp. 243–251). Springer International Publishing. https://doi.org/10.1007/978-3-319-47103-7_24

Epstein, D. H., Tyburski, M., Kowalczyk, W. J., Burgess-Hull, A. J., Phillips, K. A., Curtis, B. L., & Preston, K. L. (2020). Prediction of stress and drug craving ninety minutes in the future with passively collected GPS data. *NPJ Digital Medicine, 3*(1), 26. https://doi.org/10.1038/s41746-020-0234-6

Ezell, J. M., Ajayi, B. P., Parikh, T., Miller, K., Rains, A., & Scales, D. (2024). Drug use and artificial intelligence: Weighing concerns and possibilities for prevention. *American Journal of Preventive Medicine, 66*(3), 568–572. https://doi.org/10.1016/j.amepre.2023.11.024

Faggiano, F., Minozzi, S., Versino, E., & Buscemi, D. (2014). Universal school-based prevention for illicit drug use. *Cochrane Database of Systematic Reviews, 2014*(12), CD003020. https://doi.org/10.1002/14651858.CD003020.pub3

Farhoudian, A., Razaghi, E., Hooshyari, Z., Noroozi, A., Pilevari, A., Mokri, A., et al. (2022). Barriers and facilitators to substance use disorder treatment: An overview of systematic reviews. *Substance Abuse: Research and Treatment, 16*, 11782218221118462. https://doi.org/10.1177/11782218221118462

Fazel, S., Yoon, I. A., & Hayes, A. J. (2017). Substance use disorders in prisoners: An updated systematic review and meta-regression analysis in recently incarcerated men and women. *Addiction, 112*(10), 1725–1739. https://doi.org/10.1111/add.13877

Garbin, C., Marques, N., & Marques, O. (2023). Machine learning for predicting opioid use disorder from healthcare data: A systematic review. *Computer Methods and Programs in Biomedicine, 236*, 107573. https://doi.org/10.1016/j.cmpb.2023.107573

Garland, E. L., Gullapalli, B. T., Prince, K. C., Hanley, A. W., Sanyer, M., Tuomenoksa, M., & Rahman, T. (2023). Zoom-based mindfulness-oriented recovery enhancement plus just-in-time mindfulness practice triggered by wearable sensors for opioid craving and chronic pain. *Mindfulness, 14*(6), 1329–1345. https://doi.org/10.1007/s12671-023-02137-0

Gellad, W. F., Good, C. B., & Shulkin, D. J. (2017). Addressing the opioid epidemic in the United States: Lessons from the Department of Veterans Affairs. *JAMA Internal Medicine, 177*(5), 611–612. https://doi.org/10.1001/jamainternmed.2017.0147

George, G., Webb, E. K., & Harnett, N. (2023). Neighborhood-level factors in the development and treatment of trauma and stress-related disorders. *Current Treatment Options in Psychiatry, 10*(3), 181–198. https://doi.org/10.1007/s40501-023-00300-x

Goldbach, J. T., Tanner-Smith, E. E., Bagwell, M., & Dunlap, S. (2014). Minority stress and substance use in sexual minority adolescents: A meta-analysis. *Prevention Science, 15*, 350–363. https://doi.org/10.1007/s11121-013-0393-7

Goldkind, L. (2021). Social work and artificial intelligence: Into the matrix. *Social Work, 66*(4), 372–374. https://doi.org/10.1093/sw/swab028

Goldkind, L., Ming, J., & Fink, A. (2025). AI in the nonprofit human services: Distinguishing between hype, harm, and hope. *Human Service Organizations: Management, Leadership & Governance, 49*(3), 225–236. https://doi.org/10.1080/23303131.2024.2427459

Greer, M. L., Garza, M. Y., Sample, S., & Bhattacharyya, S. (2023). Social determinants of health data quality at different levels of geographic detail. *Studies in Health Technology and Informatics, 302*, 217–221. https://doi.org/10.3233/SHTI230106

Gutwinski, S., Schreiter, S., Deutscher, K., & Fazel, S. (2021). The prevalence of mental disorders among homeless people in high-income countries: An updated systematic review and meta-regression analysis. *PLoS Medicine, 18*(8), e1003750. https://doi.org/10.1371/journal.pmed.1003750

Han, B., Compton, W. M., Blanco, C., & DuPont, R. L. (2017). National trends in substance use and use disorders among youth. *Journal of the American Academy of Child & Adolescent Psychiatry, 56*(9), 747–754. https://doi.org/10.1016/j.jaac.2017.06.011

Hancock, D. B., Markunas, C. A., Bierut, L. J., & Johnson, E. O. (2018). Human genetics of addiction: New insights and future directions. *Current Psychiatry Reports, 20*(2), 8. https://doi.org/10.1007/s11920-018-0873-3

Hao, W., Wang, X., Li, D., & Wang, G. (2024). Overview of the expert consensus on the digital therapeutics in addictive-related disorders. *General Psychiatry, 37*(3), e101392. https://doi.org/10.1136/gpsych-2023-101392

Hassanpour, S., Tomita, N., DeLise, T., Crosier, B., & Marsch, L. A. (2019). Identifying substance use risk based on deep neural networks and Instagram social media data. *Neuropsychopharmacology, 44*(3), 487–494. https://doi.org/10.1038/s41386-018-0247-x

Hatoum, A. S., Wendt, F. R., Galimberti, M., Polimanti, R., Neale, B., Kranzler, H. R., Gelernter, J., Edenberg, H. J., & Agrawal, A. (2021). Ancestry may confound genetic machine learning: Candidate-gene prediction of opioid use disorder as an example. *Drug and Alcohol Dependence, 229*, 109115. https://doi.org/10.1016/j.drugalcdep.2021.109115

Hawk, K. F., Vaca, F. E., & D'Onofrio, G. (2015). Focus: Addiction: Reducing fatal opioid overdose: Prevention, treatment and harm reduction strategies. *The Yale Journal of Biology and Medicine, 88*(3), 235–245.

Hughto, J. M., Quinn, E. K., Dunbar, M. S., Rose, A. J., Shireman, T. I., & Jasuja, G. K. (2021). Prevalence and co-occurrence of alcohol, nicotine, and other substance use disorder diagnoses among US transgender and cisgender adults. *JAMA Network Open, 4*(2), e2036512–e2036512. https://doi.org/10.1001/jamanetworkopen.2020.36512

Huq, A. Z. (2019). Racial equity in algorithmic criminal justice. *Duke Law Journal, 68*(6), 1043–1134.

Husain, J. M., Cromartie, D., Fitzelle-Jones, E., Brochier, A., Borba, C. P., & Montalvo, C. (2023). A qualitative analysis of barriers to opioid agonist treatment for racial/ethnic minoritized populations. *Journal of Substance Abuse Treatment, 144*, 108918. https://doi.org/10.1016/j.jsat.2022.108918

Jing, Y., Hu, Z., Fan, P., Xue, Y., Wang, L., Tarter, R. E., Kirisci, L., Wang, J., Vanyukov, M., & Xie, X. Q. (2020). Analysis of substance use and its outcomes by machine learning I. Childhood evaluation of liability to substance use disorder. *Drug and Alcohol Dependence, 206*, 107605. https://doi.org/10.1016/j.drugalcdep.2019.107605

Jo, A. (2023). The promise and peril of generative AI. *Nature, 614*(1), 214–216. https://doi.org/10.1038/d41586-023-00340-6

Juhn, Y. J., Ryu, E., Wi, C. I., King, K. S., Malik, M., Romero-Brufau, S., Weng, C., Sohn, S., Sharp, R. R., & Halamka, J. D. (2022). Assessing socioeconomic bias in machine learning algorithms in health care: A case study of the HOUSES index. *Journal of the American Medical Informatics Association, 29*(7), 1142–1151. https://doi.org/10.1093/jamia/ocac052

Kaul, V., Enslin, S., & Gross, S. A. (2020). History of artificial intelligence in medicine. *Gastrointestinal Endoscopy, 92*(4), 807–812. https://doi.org/10.1016/j.gie.2020.06.040

Kaur, V., & Maleckas, O. (2025). Integrated healthcare and interdisciplinary collaboration for substance use disorder treatment. *Alcoholism Treatment Quarterly, 43*(3), 447–459. https://doi.org/10.1080/07347324.2025.2460820

Kendler, K. S., Sundquist, K., Ohlsson, H., Palmér, K., Maes, H., Winkleby, M. A., & Sundquist, J. (2012). Genetic and familial environmental influences on the risk for drug abuse: A national Swedish adoption study. *Archives of General Psychiatry, 69*(7), 690–697. https://doi.org/10.1001/archgenpsychiatry.2011.2112

Koob, G. F., & Volkow, N. D. (2016). Neurobiology of addiction: A neurocircuitry analysis. *The Lancet Psychiatry, 3*(8), 760–773. https://doi.org/10.1016/S2215-0366(16)00104-8

Kulikowski, C. A. (2019). Beginnings of artificial intelligence in medicine (AIM): Computational artifice assisting scientific inquiry and clinical art—with reflections on present AIM challenges. *Yearbook of Medical Informatics, 28*(01), 249–256. https://doi.org/10.1055/s-0039-1677895

Kunins, H. V., Bellin, E., Chazotte, C., Du, E., & Arnsten, J. H. (2007). The effect of race on provider decisions to test for illicit drug use in the peripartum setting. *Journal of Women's Health, 16*(2), 245–255. https://doi.org/10.1089/jwh.2006.0070

LeCun, Y., Bengio, Y., & Hinton, G. (2015). Deep learning. *Nature, 521*(7553), 436–444. https://doi.org/10.1038/nature14539

Lee, M. R., McDowell, Y. E., & Sher, K. J. (2019). Progression of substance use to substance use disorder. In Z. Sloboda, H. Petras, E. Robertson, & R. Hingson (Eds.), *Prevention of substance use* (pp. 75–97). Springer International Publishing. https://doi.org/10.1007/978-3-030-00627-3_5

Leibowitz, G. S., Turner, W., Bruckenthal, P., Mezzatesta, M., Ramsey, K. S., & Dyer, M. E. (2023). Lessening the impact of opioid misuse at a federally qualified health center in New York: Outcomes of an integrated workforce training program. *Public Health Reports, 138*(1_suppl), 42S–47S. https://doi.org/10.1177/00333549231170216

Levin, Y., Bar-Or, R. L., Forer, R., Vaserman, M., Kor, A., & Lev-Ran, S. (2021). The association between type of trauma, level of exposure and addiction. *Addictive Behaviors, 118*, 106889. https://doi.org/10.1016/j.addbeh.2021.106889

Liu, Y. S., Kiyang, L., Hayward, J., Zhang, Y., Metes, D., Wang, M., et al. (2023). Individualized prospective prediction of opioid use disorder. *The Canadian Journal of Psychiatry, 68*(1), 54–63. https://doi.org/10.1177/07067437221114094

Looi, J. C., Looi, R. C., Maguire, P. A., Kisely, S., Bastiampillai, T., & Allison, S. (2024). Psychiatric electronic health records in the era of data breaches—What are the ramifications for patients, psychiatrists and healthcare systems? *Australasian Psychiatry, 32*(2), 121–124. https://doi.org/10.1177/10398562241230816

Lutz, C. (2019). Digital inequalities in the age of artificial intelligence and big data. *Human Behavior and Emerging Technologies, 1*(2), 141–148. https://doi.org/10.1002/hbe2.140

Magill, M., Ray, L. A., Kiluk, B., Hoadley, A., Bernstein, M., Tonigan, J. S., & Carroll, K. M. (2019). A meta-analysis of cognitive-behavioral therapy for alcohol or other drug use disorders: Treatment efficacy by contrast condition. *Journal of Consulting and Clinical Psychology, 87*(12), 1093–1105. https://doi.org/10.1037/ccp0000447

Mahoney, J. J., 3rd, Finomore, V. S., Marton, J. L., Ramadan, J., Hodder, S. L., Thompson-Lake, D. G. Y., Marsh, C. B., Koch-Gallup, N., Ranjan, M., & Rezai, A. R. (2023). Identifying biomarkers of drug use recurrence using wearable device technologies and phone applications. *Drug and Alcohol Dependence, 249*, 110817. https://doi.org/10.1016/j.drugalcdep.2023.110817

Maisel, N. C., Blodgett, J. C., Wilbourne, P. L., Humphreys, K., & Finney, J. W. (2013). Meta-analysis of naltrexone and acamprosate for treating alcohol use disorders: When are these medications most helpful? *Addiction, 108*(2), 275–293. https://doi.org/10.1111/j.1360-0443.2012.04054.x

Manthey, J., Hassan, S. A., Carr, S., Kilian, C., Kuitunen-Paul, S., & Rehm, J. (2021). Estimating the economic consequences of substance use and substance use disorders. *Expert Review of Pharmacoeconomics & Outcomes Research, 21*(5), 869–876. https://doi.org/10.1080/14737167.2021.1916470

Marchand, K., Beaumont, S., Westfall, J., MacDonald, S., Harrison, S., Marsh, D. C., Schechter, M. T., & Oviedo-Joekes, E. (2019). Conceptualizing patient-centered care for substance use disorder treatment: Findings from a systematic scoping review. *Substance Abuse Treatment, Prevention, and Policy, 14*, 1–15. https://doi.org/10.1186/s13011-019-0227-0

Mays, V. M., Jones, A. L., Delany-Brumsey, A., Coles, C., & Cochran, S. D. (2017). Perceived discrimination in health care and mental health/substance abuse treatment among Blacks, Latinos, and Whites. *Medical Care, 55*(2), 173–181. https://doi.org/10.1097/MLR.0000000000000638

McCabe, S. E., West, B. T., Strobbe, S., & Boyd, C. J. (2018). Persistence/recurrence of and remission from DSM-5 substance use disorders in the United States: Substance-specific and substance-aggregated correlates. *Journal of Substance Abuse Treatment, 93*, 38–48. https://doi.org/10.1016/j.jsat.2018.07.012

McCabe, S. E., Pasman, E., Wilens, T. E., Schepis, T. S., McCabe, V. V., Ford, J. A., Jardine, J., & Veliz, P. T. (2025). Trends in prescription stimulant, opioid, and benzodiazepine use and diversion in US adolescents. *American Journal of Psychiatry, 182*(7), 683–687. https://doi.org/10.1176/appi.ajp.20240674

McCarthy, S. A., Chinman, M., Rogal, S. S., Klima, G., Hausmann, L. R. M., Mor, M. K., Shah, M., Hale, J. A., Zhang, H., Gordon, A. J., & Gellad, W. F. (2022). Tracking the randomized rollout of a Veterans Affairs opioid risk management tool: A multi-method implementation evaluation using the Consolidated Framework for Implementation Research (CFIR). *Implementation Research and Practice, 3*, 26334895221114665. https://doi.org/10.1177/26334895221114665

McLellan, A. T., Lewis, D. C., O'Brien, C. P., & Kleber, H. D. (2000). Drug dependence, a chronic medical illness: Implications for treatment, insurance, and outcomes evaluation. *JAMA, 284*(13), 1689–1695. https://doi.org/10.1001/jama.284.13.1689

Mee-Lee, D., Shulman, G. D., Fishman, M. J., Gastfriend, D. R., & Miller, M. M. (2013). *The ASAM criteria: Treatment criteria for addictive, substance-related, and co-occurring conditions* (3rd ed.). The Change Companies.

Mikhail, J. N., Nemeth, L. S., Mueller, M., Pope, C., & NeSmith, E. G. (2018). The social determinants of trauma: A trauma disparities scoping review and framework. *Journal of Trauma Nursing, 25*(5), 266–281. https://doi.org/10.1097/JTN.0000000000000388

Miotto, R., Wang, F., Wang, S., Jiang, X., & Dudley, J. T. (2018). Deep learning for healthcare: Review, opportunities and challenges. *Briefings in Bioinformatics, 19*(6), 1236–1246. https://doi.org/10.1093/bib/bbx044

Miranda, O., Fan, P., Qi, X., Wang, H., Brannock, M. D., Kosten, T. R., Ryan, N. D., Kirisci, L., & Wang, L. (2024). DeepBiomarker2: Prediction of alcohol and substance use disorder risk in post-traumatic stress disorder patients using electronic medical records and multiple social determinants of health. *Journal of Personalized Medicine, 14*(1), 94. https://doi.org/10.3390/jpm14010094

Moore, J. R., & Caudill, R. (2019). The bot will see you now: A history and review of interactive computerized mental health programs. *Psychiatric Clinics of North America, 42*(4), 627–634. https://doi.org/10.1016/j.psc.2019.08.007

Moore, K., O'Shea, E., Kenny, L., Barton, J., Tedesco, S., Sica, M., Crowe, C., Alamäki, A., Condell, J., Nordström, A., & Timmons, S. (2021). Older adults' experiences with using wearable devices: Qualitative systematic review and meta-synthesis. *JMIR mHealth and uHealth, 9*(6), e23832. https://doi.org/10.2196/23832

National Association of Social Workers. (2021). *NASW code of ethics*. Retrieved from https://www.socialworkers.org/About/Ethics/Code-of-Ethics/Code-of-Ethics-English

National Institute on Drug Abuse (NIDA). (2018). *Principles of drug addiction treatment: A research-based guide* (3rd ed.). National Institutes of Health.

Newcomb, M. D., & Locke, T. (2005). Health, social, and psychological consequences of drug use and abuse. In Z. Sloboda (Ed.), *Epidemiology of drug abuse* (pp. 45–59). Springer. https://doi.org/10.1007/0-387-24416-6_4

Ng, J. Y., Lad, M. M., Patel, D., & Wang, A. (2025). Applications of machine learning in cannabis research: A scoping review. *European Journal of Integrative Medicine, 74*, 102434. https://doi.org/10.1016/j.eujim.2025.102434

Oesterle, T. S., Karpyak, V. M., Coombes, B. J., Athreya, A. P., Breitinger, S. A., Correa da Costa, S., & Gerberi, D. J. (2022). Systematic review: Wearable remote monitoring to detect non-alcohol/nonnicotine-related substance use disorder symptoms. *The American Journal on Addictions, 31*(6), 535–545. https://doi.org/10.1111/ajad.13341

Olfson, M., Mauro, C., Wall, M. M., Choi, C. J., Barry, C. L., & Mojtabai, R. (2022). Healthcare coverage and service access for low-income adults with substance use disorders. *Journal of Substance Abuse Treatment, 137*, 108710. https://doi.org/10.1016/j.jsat.2021.108710

Oliva, E. M., Bowe, T., Tavakoli, S., Martins, S., Lewis, E. T., Paik, M., Wiechers, I., Henderson, P., Harvey, M., Avoundjian, T., Medhanie, A., & Trafton, J. A. (2017). Development and applications of the Veterans Health Administration's Stratification Tool for Opioid Risk Mitigation (STORM) to improve opioid safety and prevent overdose and suicide. *Psychological Services, 14*(1), 34–49. https://doi.org/10.1037/ser0000099

Oliva, V., De Prisco, M., Pons-Cabrera, M. T., Guzmán, P., Anmella, G., Hidalgo-Mazzei, D., Grande, I., Fanelli, G., Fabbri, C., Serretti, A., Fornaro, M., Iasevoli, F., de Bartolomeis, A., Murru, A., Vieta, E., & Fico, G. (2022). Machine learning prediction of comorbid substance use disorders among people with bipolar disorder. *Journal of Clinical Medicine, 11*(14), 3935. https://doi.org/10.3390/jcm11143935

Otiniano Verissimo, A. D., Gee, G. C., & Grella, C. (2023). Examining the relationship between intersectional discrimination and substance use disorders by race/ethnicity and gender. *Cultural Diversity and Ethnic Minority Psychology, 31*(1), 58–68. https://doi.org/10.1037/cdp0000599

Pan, Z., Zhang, J., Cheng, H., Bu, Q., Li, N., Deng, Y., Zhou, L., Dai, Z., & Lyu, J. (2020). Trends of the incidence of drug use disorders from 1990 to 2017: An analysis based on the Global Burden of Disease 2017 data. *Epidemiology and Psychiatric Sciences, 29*, e148. https://doi.org/10.1017/S2045796020000657

Paquette, C. E., Daughters, S. B., & Witkiewitz, K. (2022). Expanding the continuum of substance use disorder treatment: Nonabstinence approaches. *Clinical Psychology Review, 91*, 102110. https://doi.org/10.1016/j.cpr.2021.102110

Poalelungi, D. G., Musat, C. L., Fulga, A., Neagu, M., Neagu, A. I., Piraianu, A. I., & Fulga, I. (2023). Advancing patient care: How artificial intelligence is transforming healthcare. *Journal of Personalized Medicine, 13*(8), 1214. https://doi.org/10.3390/jpm13081214

Prieto, J. T., Scott, K., McEwen, D., Podewils, L. J., Al-Tayyib, A., Robinson, J., Edwards, D., Foldy, S., Shlay, J. C., & Davidson, A. J. (2020). The detection of opioid misuse and heroin use from paramedic response documentation: Machine learning for improved surveillance. *Journal of Medical Internet Research, 22*(1), e15645. https://doi.org/10.2196/15645

Prochaska, J. J., Vogel, E. A., Chieng, A., Kendra, M., Baiocchi, M., Pajarito, S., & Robinson, A. (2021). A therapeutic relational agent for reducing problematic substance use (Woebot): Development and usability study. *Journal of Medical Internet Research, 23*(3), e24850. https://doi.org/10.2196/24850

Rajkomar, A., Hardt, M., Howell, M. D., Corrado, G., & Chin, M. H. (2018). Ensuring fairness in machine learning to advance health equity. *Annals of Internal Medicine, 169*(12), 866–872. https://doi.org/10.7326/M18-1990

Rehm, J., Marmet, S., Anderson, P., Gual, A., Kraus, L., Nutt, D. J., Room, R., Samokhvalov, A. V., Scafato, E., Trapencieris, M., Wiers, R. W., & Gmel, G. (2013). Defining substance use disorders: Do we really need more than heavy use? *Alcohol and Alcoholism, 48*(6), 633–640. https://doi.org/10.1093/alcalc/agt127

Restrepo-Guzman, R., Li, D., & Lynn, G. (2020). Recovery from addiction: Maintenance and preventing relapse. In C. Marienfeld (Ed.), *Absolute addiction psychiatry review: An essential board exam study guide* (pp. 87–101). Springer. https://doi.org/10.1007/978-3-030-33404-8_6

Ridgway, J. P., Uvin, A., Schmitt, J., Oliwa, T., Almirol, E., Devlin, S., & Schneider, J. (2021). Natural language processing of clinical notes to identify mental illness and substance use among people living with HIV: Retrospective cohort study. *JMIR Medical Informatics, 9*(3), e23456. https://doi.org/10.2196/23456

Rodriguez, M. Y., Goldkind, L., Victor, B. G., Hiltz, B., & Perron, B. E. (2024). Introducing generative artificial intelligence into the MSW curriculum: A proposal for the 2029 educational policy and accreditation standards. *Journal of Social Work Education, 60*(2), 174–182. https://doi.org/10.1080/10437797.2024.2340931

Russell, S. J., & Norvig, P. (2021). *Artificial intelligence: A modern approach* (4th ed.). Pearson.

Saxon, A. J., Olfson, M., Hsiao, R., & Hasin, D. S. (2025). Promising opportunities to intervene on adolescent substance use. *American Journal of Psychiatry, 182*(7), 596–598. https://doi.org/10.1176/appi.ajp.20250354

Schilt-Solberg, M. A., Blair, L. M., & Kurzer, J. A. (2025). Intersectionality in substance use disorders: Examining gender, race/ethnicity, and sexual orientation in the 2021–2022 National Survey on Drug Use and Health. *Addictive Behaviors Reports, 21*, 100587. https://doi.org/10.1016/j.abrep.2025.100587

Schoenfeld, E. R., Leibowitz, G. S., Wang, Y., Chen, X., Hou, W., Rashidian, S., Saltz, M. M., Saltz, J. H., & Wang, F. (2019). Geographic, temporal, and sociodemographic differences in opioid poisoning. *American Journal of Preventive Medicine, 57*(2), 153–164. https://doi.org/10.1016/j.amepre.2019.03.020

Schuman-Olivier, Z., Weiss, R. D., Hoeppner, B. B., Borodovsky, J., & Albanese, M. J. (2014). Emerging adult age status predicts poor buprenorphine treatment retention. *Journal of Substance Abuse Treatment, 47*(3), 202–212. https://doi.org/10.1016/j.jsat.2014.04.006

Sendak, M., Elish, M. C., Gao, M., Futoma, J., Ratliff, W., Nichols, M., Bedoya, A., Balu, S., & O'Brien, C. (2020, January). "The human body is a black box" supporting clinical decision-making with deep learning. In *Proceedings of the 2020 Conference on Fairness, Accountability, and Transparency (FAT '20)* (pp. 99–109). Association for Computing Machinery. https://doi.org/10.1145/3351095.3372827

Shakya, A. K., Pillai, G., & Chakrabarty, S. (2023). Reinforcement learning algorithms: A brief survey. *Expert Systems with Applications, 231*, 120495. https://doi.org/10.1016/j.eswa.2023.120495

Sharma, A., Bhowmick, B., & Patnaik, J. (2020). Innovation through hub and spoke model: E-commercializing regional India's handicraft industry. In A. De Nisco (Ed.), *Proceedings of the 15th European Conference on Innovation and Entrepreneurship (ECIE 2020)* (pp. 614–622). Academic Conferences International Limited. https://doi.org/10.34190/EIE.20.174

Singleton, J., Li, C., Akpunonu, P. D., Abner, E. L., & Kucharska-Newton, A. M. (2023). Using natural language processing to identify opioid use disorder in electronic health record data. *International Journal of Medical Informatics, 170*, 104963. https://doi.org/10.1016/j.ijmedinf.2022.104963

Skewes, M. C., & Gonzalez, V. M. (2013). The biopsychosocial model of addiction. In P. M. Miller (Ed.), *Principles of addiction: Comprehensive addictive behaviors and disorders* (Vol. 1, pp. 61–70). Academic Press. https://doi.org/10.1016/B978-0-12-398336-7.00006-1

Skolnick, P. (2018). The opioid epidemic: Crisis and solutions. *Annual Review of Pharmacology and Toxicology, 58*, 143–159. https://doi.org/10.1146/annurev-pharmtox-010617-052534

Soto, C., West, A. E., Ramos, G. G., & Unger, J. B. (2022). Substance and behavioral addictions among American Indian and Alaska Native populations. *International Journal of Environmental Research and Public Health, 19*(5), 2974. https://doi.org/10.3390/ijerph19052974

Stallvik, M., Gastfriend, D. R., & Nordahl, H. M. (2015). Matching patients with substance use disorder to optimal level of care with the ASAM Criteria software. *Journal of Substance Use, 20*(6), 389–398. https://doi.org/10.3109/14659891.2014.934305

Strang, J., Babor, T., Caulkins, J., Fischer, B., Foxcroft, D., & Humphreys, K. (2012). Drug policy and the public good: Evidence for effective interventions. *The Lancet, 379*(9810), 71–83. https://doi.org/10.1016/S0140-6736(11)61674-7

Strombotne, K. L., Legler, A., Minegishi, T., Trafton, J. A., Oliva, E. M., Lewis, E. T., Sohoni, P., Garrido, M. M., Pizer, S. D., & Frakt, A. B. (2023). Effect of a predictive analytics-targeted program in patients on opioids: A stepped-wedge cluster randomized controlled trial. *Journal of General Internal Medicine, 38*(2), 375–381. https://doi.org/10.1007/s11606-022-07617-y

Substance Abuse and Mental Health Services Administration. (2021). *Medications for opioid use disorder* (Treatment Improvement Protocol (TIP) Series 63; Publication No. PEP21-02-01-002). U.S. Department of Health and Human Services. Retrieved from https://library.samhsa.gov/sites/default/files/pep21-02-01-002.pdf

Substance Abuse and Mental Health Services Administration. (2024). *Key substance use and mental health indicators in the United States: Results from the 2023 National Survey on Drug Use and Health* (HHS Publication No. PEP24-07-021, NSDUH Series H-59). Center for Behavioral Health Statistics and Quality, Substance Abuse and Mental Health Services Administration. Retrieved from https://www.samhsa.gov/data/report/2023-nsduh-annual-national-report

Sun, J., Bi, J., Chan, G., Oslin, D., Farrer, L., Gelernter, J., & Kranzler, H. R. (2012). Improved methods to identify stable, highly heritable subtypes of opioid use and related behaviors. *Addictive Behaviors, 37*(10), 1138–1144. https://doi.org/10.1016/j.addbeh.2012.05.010

Suva, M., & Bhatia, G. (2024). Artificial intelligence in addiction: Challenges and opportunities. *Indian Journal of Psychological Medicine*, 02537176241274148. Advance online publication. https://doi.org/10.1177/02537176241274148

Symons, M., Feeney, G. F., Gallagher, M. R., Young, R. M., & Connor, J. P. (2019). Machine learning vs addiction therapists: A pilot study predicting alcohol dependence treatment outcome from patient data in behavior therapy with adjunctive medication. *Journal of Substance Abuse Treatment, 99*, 156–162. https://doi.org/10.1016/j.jsat.2019.01.020

Tai, A. M. Y., Kim, J. J., Schmeckenbecher, J., Kitchin, V., Wang, J., Kazemi, A., Masoudi, R., Fadakar, H., Iorfino, F., & Krausz, R. M. (2024). Clinical decision support systems in addiction and concurrent disorders: A systematic review and meta-analysis. *Journal of Evaluation in Clinical Practice, 30*(8), 1664–1683. https://doi.org/10.1111/jep.14069

Tambe, M., & Rice, E. (Eds.). (2018). *Artificial intelligence and social work.* Cambridge University Press. https://doi.org/10.1017/9781108669016

Tapscott, B. E., & Schepis, T. S. (2013). Nonmedical use of prescription medications in young adults. *Adolescent Medicine: State of the Art Reviews, 24*(3), 597–610.

Tiribelli, S. (2023). The AI ethics principle of autonomy in health recommender systems. *Argumenta (Sassari), 16*, 1–18. https://doi.org/10.14275/2465-2334/20230.TIR

Turner Lee, N. (2018). Detecting racial bias in algorithms and machine learning. *Journal of Information, Communication and Ethics in Society, 16*(3), 252–260. https://doi.org/10.1108/JICES-06-2018-0056

Vakharia, S. P., & Little, J. (2017). Starting where the client is: Harm reduction guidelines for clinical social work practice. *Clinical Social Work Journal, 45*, 65–76. https://doi.org/10.1007/s10615-016-0584-3

Volkow, N. D., & Blanco, C. (2023). Substance use disorders: A comprehensive update of classification, epidemiology, neurobiology, clinical aspects, treatment and prevention. *World Psychiatry, 22*(2), 203–229. https://doi.org/10.1002/wps.21073

Volkow, N. D., Koob, G. F., & McLellan, A. T. (2016). Neurobiologic advances from the brain disease model of addiction. *New England Journal of Medicine, 374*(4), 363–371. https://doi.org/10.1056/NEJMra1511480

Weizenbaum, J. (1966). ELIZA—A computer program for the study of natural language communication between man and machine. *Communications of the ACM, 9*(1), 36–45. https://doi.org/10.1145/365153.365168

Wu, Z., Pan, S., Chen, F., Long, G., Zhang, C., & Yu, P. S. (2021). A comprehensive survey on graph neural networks. *IEEE Transactions on Neural Networks and Learning Systems, 32*(1), 4–24. https://doi.org/10.1109/TNNLS.2020.2978386

Xu, F., Uszkoreit, H., Du, Y., Fan, W., Zhao, D., & Zhu, J. (2019). Explainable AI: A brief survey on history, research areas, approaches and challenges. In J. Tang, M.-Y. Kan, D. Zhao, S. Li, & H. Zan (Eds.), *Natural language processing and chinese computing* (Lecture notes in computer science) (Vol. 11839, pp. 563–574). Springer. https://doi.org/10.1007/978-3-030-32236-6_51

Yang, L., Du, Y., Yang, W., & Liu, J. (2023). Machine learning with neuroimaging biomarkers: Application in the diagnosis and prediction of drug addiction. *Addiction Biology, 28*(2), e13267. https://doi.org/10.1111/adb.13267

Ying, X. (2019). An overview of overfitting and its solutions. *Journal of Physics: Conference Series, 1168*, 022022. https://doi.org/10.1088/1742-6596/1168/2/022022

Zuba, M., Gilbert, J., Wu, Y., Bi, J., Tennen, H., & Armeli, S. (2012). 1-norm support vector machine for college drinking risk factor identification. In G. Luo, J. Liu, & C. C. Yang (Eds.), *Proceedings of the 2nd ACM SIGHIT International Health Informatics Symposium (IHI '12)* (pp. 651–660). Association for Computing Machinery. https://doi.org/10.1145/2110363.2110435

Chapter 12
AI in Serving Older Adults

Jing Shen and Sheara Jennings

1 Introduction

With the continued decline in birth rates and significant increases in life expectancy, the world is rapidly entering an era of population aging. According to the United Nations' World Population Prospects 2022 report, the global population aged 60 and above is projected to reach 2.1 billion by 2050, nearly double the 1 billion recorded in 2020 (Kalache, 2019). While challenges such as chronic diseases, physical decline, cognitive deterioration, and social isolation are inherent to the aging process, the demographic shift will significantly expand the number of older adults affected by these issues. As a result, the strain on healthcare systems, social support networks, and family caregiving structures will intensify. This growing need underscores the increasing demand for effective health management, emotional support, and cognitive maintenance services tailored to the elderly (Li, 2023).

On the other hand, aging populations are placing unprecedented pressure on elder care services due to the reduction in the younger workforce, changes in traditional family structures, and a shortage of professional caregivers (Feng, 2019; Feng & Wu, 2023). Moreover, rising costs of elder care are straining national healthcare systems, social service resources, and public policies. For instance, China's National Healthcare Security Administration recently issued new guidelines for nursing projects and policy adjustments to simplify the nursing service pricing system and improve transparency (China National Healthcare Security Administration, 2024). Additionally, Canada launched its National Housing Strategy in 2017, with one of its priorities being to improve housing outcomes for older adults (Government of

J. Shen (✉)
School of Physical Education, China University of Geosciences Beijing, Beijing, China
e-mail: shenjing@cugb.edu.cn

S. Jennings
School of Social Work, Howard University, Washington, DC, USA
e-mail: sheara.jennings@howard.edu

R. An, M. A. Lindsey (eds.), *Artificial Intelligence in Social Work*,
https://doi.org/10.1007/978-3-032-18443-6_12

Canada, 2024), while Japan's nursing insurance system offers various levels of care services for the elderly (Yamada & Arai, 2020). Singapore, meanwhile, has introduced measures to raise the retirement age and provide skill development opportunities to help older individuals re-enter the workforce (Sun & Usui, 2023). In the U.S., a comprehensive national framework is also underway. The Administration for Community Living, through the Interagency Coordinating Committee (ICC) on Healthy Aging and Age-Friendly Communities, released a Strategic Framework for a National Plan on Aging in 2024 (Administration for Community Living, 2024). This vision promotes coordinated public–private partnership and cross-sector collaboration—including federal agencies, industry, philanthropy, academia, and older adults—and calls for initiatives in age-friendly communities, aligned health and supportive services, coordinated housing, and increased access to long-term care. It emphasizes person-centeredness and respect for older adults' dignity and autonomy, and aims to dismantle ageism and ableism—offering a vital example of how policy frameworks can integrate both humanistic and technological considerations in preparing for population aging in a developed country context.

In recent years, the rapid advancement of artificial intelligence (AI) technology, especially in the healthcare sector, has significantly improved the accuracy of disease diagnosis and the personalization of treatment plans. For example, AI-assisted diagnostic systems analyze medical images and patient data to quickly identify abnormalities, aiding doctors in formulating more effective treatment plans, thereby providing more precise medical services. Furthermore, AI-driven intelligent dialogue systems offer personalized, user-friendly consultation services for patients (Quazi et al., 2024). In terms of cognitive interventions, AI-powered cognitive training platforms can provide customized brain exercises for the elderly, helping slow the progression of cognitive decline (Faria et al., 2024). Compared to traditional methods, AI offers significant efficiency gains. It can tailor care plans to each elderly individual's unique health status and personalized needs, while also providing continuous, dynamic support throughout the care process.

Although existing research has explored the application of AI in elderly care, comprehensive discussions on systematic evaluation, cultural adaptability, and ethical design remain scarce (Asan & Choudhury, 2021; Lukkien et al., 2023). Therefore, this chapter will delve into the practical effects and potential of AI in elderly care, focusing on its innovative applications in health monitoring, social engagement, cognitive support, and aging in place. Additionally, the chapter will include an exploration of challenges related to technical adaptability, ethical concerns, and cultural differences—not only as barriers to AI implementation, but as key areas where social work can play a transformative role. By addressing these challenges, social workers can help ensure that AI technologies support human dignity, equity, and culturally responsive care for older adults.

2 Application of AI in Elderly Care

2.1 *AI in Health Monitoring for Older Adults*

In the field of elderly care, AI technology has become a central application in health monitoring. As the elderly population grows and health needs become more diversified, AI technologies, such as smart wearable devices and mobile applications, enable real-time monitoring and data collection of vital signs in older adults (Awotunde et al., 2022; Sabry et al., 2022). These data are processed and analyzed through cloud-based platforms, using AI algorithms for disease prediction and risk assessment, thereby providing real-time, convenient, personalized, and efficient health monitoring services. AI plays a crucial role in early disease detection, chronic disease management, accident prevention, and personalized health interventions.

2.1.1 Early Disease Detection

AI has significant potential for early disease detection, particularly in predicting and monitoring atrial fibrillation, where its applications are transforming medical diagnostics and management (Salvi et al., 2024; Yao et al., 2023). By analyzing physiological data from wearable devices, such as heart rate, blood pressure, and oxygen saturation, AI can detect potential disease risks. For example, using wavelets and AI on EEG data, atrial fibrillation can be diagnosed early, helping to identify high risk patients and provide timely prevention measures (Serhal et al., 2022). Deep learning techniques have demonstrated excellent performance in the early detection of cardiovascular diseases, identifying high-risk individuals and providing decision support through data analysis (Baikuvekov et al., 2024).

In terms of cognitive function, wearable device activity log data can effectively support early diagnosis of dementia in high-risk older adults, improving healthcare system accessibility and efficiency (Lee & Lee, 2024). Advanced machine learning techniques, using computerized cognitive tests, motion analysis, speech processing, and brain scans, have enabled AI models to detect the risks of Alzheimer's and Parkinson's diseases with high accuracy (Grueso & Viejo-Sobera, 2021; Reddy et al., 2024). Furthermore, AI systems can closely monitor daily activities, social interactions, and emotional fluctuations in older adults to identify early signs of depression and propose appropriate interventions (Su et al., 2020).

2.1.2 Chronic Disease Management

AI plays a key role in managing chronic diseases, particularly in medication management. Older adults often need to take multiple medications for extended periods, and AI systems, through intelligent medication management systems, can provide accurate medication reminders based on treatment plans and make real-time adjustments according to the elderly individual's medication responses (Ciampi et al., 2022; García-Vázquez et al., 2011). For example, AI can precisely adjust medication dosages based on blood glucose monitoring data, significantly reducing the risks of missed or excessive medication (Spanakis et al., 2022). Additionally, by integrating diverse health data, AI can offer personalized management plans for patients with multiple chronic diseases, such as diabetes, heart disease, and hypertension, thereby improving the overall health of older adults (Wu et al., 2021; Majnarić et al., 2021).

2.1.3 Prevention of Accidental Events

AI technology plays a critical role in mitigating accidental events among older adults, such as fall prevention. For example, fall detection systems that integrate AI analysis can monitor the gait and posture of older individuals in real time, predict fall risk, and issue alerts when necessary to reduce fall incidents and related injuries (Cedeno-Moreno et al., 2024; Kiprijanovska et al., 2020). Furthermore, by monitoring physiological data such as heart rate, blood pressure, and EEG, AI technology can provide early warnings of acute health events, such as heart attacks or strokes, and promptly notify the elderly individual, their family, or medical staff for timely intervention (Xavier et al., 2022; Islam et al., 2022). AI, combined with location-tracking devices, can monitor older adults' locations, preventing them from becoming lost or leaving a safe area, which is particularly useful for those with cognitive impairments (Moreno et al., 2015; García-Requejo et al., 2023).

2.1.4 Personalized Health Interventions

Personalized health interventions are one of AI's significant advantages. AI can develop tailored health plans for older adults based on their health data, covering diet, exercise, and medication management (Espín et al., 2016; Zhu et al., 2023). AI health assistants, leveraging real-time monitoring data and long-term accumulated data resources, can provide precise personalized health recommendations and adjust interventions accordingly to ensure efficient health management. For example, by analyzing gait characteristics, physical abilities, and subtle health trends, AI can identify early signs of health deterioration in older adults and design customized rehabilitation training plans based on these data (Ferraris et al., 2022; Kim et al., 2024). AI-IoT-based elderly healthcare programs have significantly improved the management of hypertension, diabetes, physical activity, and nutrition habits in over 97% of participants while effectively reducing frailty (Woo et al., 2024). These personalized interventions not only improve older adults' health management habits but also effectively prevent the further deterioration of health issues, enhance quality of life, and help delay the aging process.

2.2 *AI in Social Engagement for Older Adults*

Mental health concerns, particularly depression and anxiety, represent significant issues among older adults experiencing social isolation and loneliness. Symptoms such as persistent sadness, loss of interest in daily activities, and reduced emotional engagement severely impact their quality of life and increase demands on social work services. Social workers play a critical role in early identification, intervention, and supportive care, and AI technologies can serve as valuable tools to aid these efforts. By reducing feelings of loneliness, fostering social interaction, and providing emotional support, AI systems offer innovative strategies to address the psychosocial needs of older adults and enhance their mental well-being as populations continue to age.

2.2.1 Reducing Feelings of Loneliness

Loneliness is particularly prevalent among older adults, especially when family members are unable to visit frequently due to work, geographical distance, or other commitments, making their sense of isolation even more pronounced. Such loneliness can have serious consequences, including depression, reduced cognitive function, and poorer overall health outcomes. Social robots have emerged as a promising intervention to address social isolation and loneliness among older adults in both pandemic emergencies and aging societies (Jecker, 2020). AI technologies, particularly virtual assistants and social robots, can offer emotional support and companionship, helping alleviate loneliness among older adults (Gasteiger et al., 2021; You & Choi, 2025). Information and communication technology solutions, such as smart homes and robotic pets, can help detect and mitigate loneliness without requiring direct interaction with others (Latikka et al., 2021). These AI systems use voice recognition and natural language processing technologies to interact with older adults, offering care and companionship. For example, social robots can engage in simple conversations with older individuals, helping them cope with loneliness and providing emotional comfort (Pirhonen et al., 2020). Furthermore, AI can use emotional analysis techniques to sensitively detect fluctuations in an older adult's mood and tailor interaction strategies to their emotional needs. Through this emotional support, AI provides greater companionship and emotional connection, thereby alleviating loneliness (Qiu & Carter, 2023).

2.2.2 Promoting Social Interaction

Older adults often face difficulties in actively participating in social activities due to health problems or mobility limitations, leading to social isolation (Mehrabi & Béland, 2020). AI technology can integrate data from wearable devices and home health monitoring tools to provide comprehensive monitoring of an older adult's health status. Moreover, AI can help create social platforms that allow older individuals to maintain connections with distant family members and friends through video calls and online gatherings, enriching their social lives. For instance, systems combining intelligent personal assistants (IPAs) and interactive televisions (iTVs) can facilitate video calls between older adults and their friends or family members, thus promoting social interactions and maintaining their social circles (Camargo et al., 2023). Additionally, AI systems can recommend suitable social activities or community groups based on an older adult's lifestyle, interests, and health status, helping them find appropriate social circles and engage in more interactions (Czaja & Ceruso, 2022; You & Choi, 2025). These carefully recommended social activities help older adults integrate into social groups, enhancing their sense of social participation, while also ensuring that these activities meet their needs and safety standards (Blusi et al., 2018).

2.2.3 Providing Emotional Support

Depressive symptoms are prevalent among socially isolated older adults and may include feelings of sadness, hopelessness, and loss of interest. These symptoms significantly affect emotional well-being and overall quality of life. In social work practice, early recognition and sustained emotional support are critical. AI technologies—particularly chatbots and social robots—are emerging as valuable tools in this regard. By continuously monitoring behavioral cues, speech patterns, and daily routines, these systems can detect early signs of depression and anxiety, enabling timely interventions by social workers and caregivers (Andrews et al., 2017; Gomes et al., 2023). For instance, AI-driven conversational agents can analyze data on sleep quality, activity levels, and social withdrawal to trigger alerts for supportive care.

Older adults often face challenges such as health issues, lifestyle changes, and social isolation, making emotional support particularly important. AI-driven social robots and chatbots are emerging as promising tools for providing emotional support and companionship to older adults, particularly those living alone (Hsu & Hsieh, 2022). These technologies include embodied conversational agents and AI robots that engage in dialogue, recommend personalized care, and assist with daily activities (Milne-Ives et al., 2020). Some systems even incorporate anthropomorphic features or mimic pets to strengthen emotional bonds (Chen & Park, 2021). In addition, AI chatbots can provide lighthearted interactions—such as singing or telling jokes—that may help manage some symptoms of dementia (Liu et al., 2018).

AI systems can also analyze real-time changes in an older adult's emotional state. For example, if sadness or apathy is detected, the AI can proactively offer comforting dialogue or suggest coping activities (Wu et al., 2023). This capability is especially important for mental health monitoring, as AI can process behavioral signals like sleep quality, physical activity, and social withdrawal to detect possible signs of depression or anxiety. When necessary, it can alert caregivers or family members for timely human support (Andrews et al., 2017; Gomes et al., 2023).

Importantly, these technologies should be viewed as assistive tools rather than replacements for human care. Social workers play an essential role in interpreting AI-generated insights, assessing emotional and contextual factors, and designing individualized support plans grounded in empathy and ethical practice. AI-assisted interventions must align with the principles of person-centered care, ensuring that technological support reinforces rather than overrides professional judgment and human relationships.

Ultimately, AI-enabled emotional care, when guided by social work values, can enhance older adults' sense of dignity, connection, and psychological security. By blending continuous, adaptive monitoring with compassionate professional oversight, these technologies have the potential to improve mental health outcomes and reduce the emotional toll of aging in isolation.

2.3 *AI in Cognitive Support for Older Adults*

As populations age and the proportion of older adults increases, age-related conditions such as cognitive decline—particularly cognitive frailty—have become significant factors affecting the quality of life for older adults (Wilson et al., 2013). Many older adults face cognitive challenges, including memory loss, decreased attention span, and reduced mental flexibility, which not only affect their daily lives but may also lead to mental health issues (Aajami et al., 2020). AI has shown great potential for cognitive support in older adults, particularly in three key areas: cognitive assessment, intervention, and recovery, helping them maintain cognitive function, delay cognitive decline, and ultimately improve their quality of life.

2.3.1 Cognitive Assessment

Cognitive assessment is the foundation of AI applications in cognitive support, as it helps efficiently and accurately identify early signs of cognitive impairment or decline. Traditional cognitive assessments often rely on manual evaluations or standardized tests. At the same time, AI technologies can analyze large datasets to provide more comprehensive and personalized assessments, detecting early signs of cognitive issues (Graham et al., 2019). Additionally, traditional methods often rely on single tests and lack long-term tracking and personalized analysis. In contrast, AI's advantage lies in providing real-time data and dynamic assessments, enabling continuous monitoring of the elderly's cognitive health (Pollack, 2005).

AI's application in cognitive assessment primarily focuses on two aspects: data collection and intelligent analysis, such as the use of machine learning models to interpret behavioral and physiological data to identify patterns, detect anomalies, and predict cognitive decline. Wearable devices, smart home systems, and mobile applications can continuously monitor the physiological and behavioral data of older adults, including gait, sleep, physical activity, and social behaviors. These data accurately reflect daily activities and cognitive changes, enabling healthcare professionals to perform more precise cognitive assessments. Research has developed cognitive health assessment systems that combine wearable physiological sensors with environmental sensors, enabling automated cognitive health assessments within the natural living environments of older adults (Arif Ul Alam et al., 2020). AI systems can also analyze changes in gait, walking speed, and response time to help detect potential cognitive decline or other issues (Obuchi et al., 2024).

2.3.2 Cognitive Intervention

Cognitive intervention is another important application of AI in cognitive support for older adults. AI not only assesses cognitive health, but it also tailors cognitive training and intervention plans based on the assessment results. These plans are designed to help older adults maintain or enhance cognitive function and slow cognitive decline through personalized training.

AI-driven cognitive intervention systems use machine learning algorithms to automatically adjust the content and difficulty of training based on an older adult's cognitive level, health status, and personal needs (Arango et al., 2025; Kitakoshi et al., 2015). These cognitive exercises are often gamified to increase engagement and interest among older adults (Eun et al., 2022). For example, AI systems can design memory training, attention exercises, and problem-solving tasks to help older adults exercise their brains and enhance cognitive abilities (Kitakoshi et al., 2015). Through personalized, dynamically adjusted cognitive training, older adults can maintain challenge while avoiding frustration from tasks that are too difficult.

Furthermore, AI technologies can provide more flexible intervention forms through emotional analysis and natural language processing. Social robots and virtual assistants engage in daily conversations with older adults, providing cognitive training tasks alongside emotional support (Tokunaga et al., 2021). These interactive smart devices not only offer emotional companionship but also perform simple daily assistant tasks, such as medication reminders, playing music, and video calls (Magnenat-Thalmann & Zhang, 2014). Studies have shown that social robot interventions significantly reduce older adults' depression, irritability, and anxiety scores (Yen et al., 2024). This multidimensional approach to cognitive intervention not only improves cognitive functioning but also provides greater emotional support.

2.3.3 Cognitive Recovery

Cognitive recovery is an advanced application of AI in cognitive support for older adults, focusing on restoring or improving cognitive abilities that have declined due to aging or disease (Vogan et al., 2020). Unlike traditional cognitive interventions, cognitive recovery aims to use concentrated and systematic training methods to restore as much cognitive function as possible and help older adults regain their ability to live independently (Hill et al., 2000).

AI applications in cognitive recovery primarily involve integrating virtual reality (VR) and augmented reality (AR) technologies (Catania et al., 2024). Virtual reality provides older adults with an immersive cognitive training experience, allowing them to exercise memory, spatial awareness, and problem-solving abilities through interactive games, simulated tasks, and virtual environments (García-Betances et al., 2015). AI-based cognitive training devices for older adults can flexibly adjust the difficulty of training based on the individual's cognitive condition, ensuring the challenge is appropriate while preventing undue psychological burden (Cai et al., 2023). These virtual training systems significantly enhance older adults' engagement and motivation while improving cognitive functioning (Bapka et al., 2018).

Additionally, AI-driven social robots are also essential tools in cognitive recovery. These robots, through anthropomorphic interaction patterns, assist older adults in effective cognitive recovery training (Pino et al., 2020). Unlike traditional rehabilitation training, social robots enhance older adults' social skills and cognitive flexibility through language and emotional communication (Góngora Alonso et al., 2019). This training not only helps improve cognitive abilities but also reduces feelings of loneliness and anxiety, promoting mental health (Lim, 2023; Hutson et al., 2011).

By combining personalized training plans, virtual reality, and social interaction, AI applications in cognitive recovery not only improve cognitive functioning but also promote greater engagement and accomplishment among older adults, supporting more effective recovery outcomes (Li & Liao, 2025). As technology continues to advance, AI's potential for cognitive recovery will grow, providing more comprehensive and effective cognitive support for older adults.

In summary, AI's applications in cognitive support for older adults primarily focus on assessment, intervention, and recovery. With precise cognitive assessment technologies, AI can facilitate early diagnoses and health management services; through personalized cognitive interventions, AI helps maintain and enhance cognitive function, effectively slowing cognitive decline; and through cognitive recovery systems, AI enables systematic training to maximize the restoration of cognitive abilities. As AI technology continues to progress, its applications in cognitive health management will become more widespread, helping older adults improve their quality of life and achieve healthier aging.

3 Potential Risks of AI in Elderly Care

3.1 Cultural Bias and Diversity Considerations in AI for Elderly Care

Cultural differences are significant factors influencing the quality of care when applying AI in elderly care (Li & Xu, 2021). For example, AI applications in elderly health management, daily care, and emotional support must consider the needs and preferences of older adults from different cultural backgrounds to ensure more personalized and effective care (Huang et al., 2019). Older adults from other cultures have varying care needs, health beliefs, and lifestyles, which necessitate that AI systems be designed with cultural adaptability in mind to ensure their effectiveness and acceptance (Sgorbissa et al., 2018). In addition, health outcomes themselves may be shaped by culture, race, and ethnicity—leading to disparities that must be acknowledged in AI system design. Without intentionally including diverse data, AI algorithms risk producing biased recommendations that fail to meet the needs of underrepresented populations.

However, these cultural factors are not adequately addressed. In that case, AI systems may inadvertently embed cultural bias—such as prioritizing Western medical paradigms, communication norms, or care preferences—at the expense of more diverse or non-dominant cultural practices. These biases can manifest in mismatched care recommendations, reduced trust and usability among minority populations, or even exclusion from AI-enabled services. As such, addressing cultural bias is not only a design issue but a matter of equity and justice in aging services.

First, cultural differences significantly impact the care needs of older adults. In some cultures, older adults are more likely to rely on family members for care, with family members often assuming responsibility for health management rather than seeking professional external care (Liu, 2000). This reliance on family-based caregiving can sometimes conflict with the personalized care recommendations provided by AI systems (Chen & Hou, 2023). To address this, AI technology needs to be designed to align with family care models. Furthermore, some cultures prefer traditional medicine to modern medical practices, so AI care systems must respect these traditional health beliefs and integrate both conventional and contemporary medical knowledge. Equally important, in many cultures, human contact is itself a valued part of care. Emotional connection, physical presence, and interpersonal trust are deeply embedded in caregiving traditions, and AI should be positioned as a supplement rather than a replacement for the human element.

Moreover, the acceptance of AI technology varies across cultures. In some cultures, older adults generally exhibit low acceptance of modern technology, especially when they are not proficient in its use. AI technology is often viewed as difficult to trust and cumbersome to operate (Cotten et al., 2024). Therefore, AI systems need to focus on simplifying user interfaces, reducing complexity, and providing multi-language support to ensure that all older adults can use these technologies more easily.

In conclusion, applying AI in elderly care requires not only sensitivity to cultural diversity but also critical awareness of potential cultural bias embedded in technology. Social workers and technologists must work collaboratively to ensure that AI systems are culturally inclusive, respectful of diverse values, and capable of delivering equitable care to all older adults—regardless of cultural background.

3.2 *Privacy Concerns in AI for Elderly Care*

As AI becomes increasingly integrated into elderly care, privacy protection and data security have emerged as critical ethical challenges. While real-time monitoring and personalized care improve efficiency and responsiveness, they also involve extensive data collection that may compromise the privacy of older adults (Bartoletti, 2019; Htet et al., 2024). Many older adults appreciate the benefits of AI-assisted technologies but remain concerned about potential misuse of their personal information (Hu & Chen, 2024).

To ensure trust and ethical integration, AI systems must balance effective data use with transparency, security, and respect for personal control. This section explores three major dimensions of privacy in AI for elderly care—each carrying significant implications for social work: informed consent and transparency, data security and risk prevention, and autonomy and ethical governance.

3.2.1 Informed Consent and Data Transparency

The application of AI in elderly care requires the collection and use of large amounts of sensitive personal data, including physiological indicators, behavioral patterns, and emotional states. Suppose data collection and use processes are not transparent. In that case, older adults and their families may lack clarity about how their data is handled, for how long it is stored, and whether it might be shared or used for commercial purposes (Huang et al., 2019). This lack of transparency can erode trust and disempower users.

To respect privacy rights, AI developers and care providers must establish clear, accessible, and culturally appropriate informed consent processes (Friedman et al., 2022). These processes should explain in plain language who will have access to health data, how it will be used, and under what circumstances it might be shared or revoked. This is a critical area where social workers play a key role in advocating for and facilitating meaningful informed consent for older adults and their caregivers. In addition to obtaining informed consent, ongoing education and support are essential to help older adults and their caregivers understand how AI technologies function, the potential risks involved, and how they can exercise control over their personal data. This educational component is critical to empowering users and ensuring that consent is documented and meaningfully informed.

3.2.2 Data Security and Risk Prevention

AI systems often rely on cloud platforms and large-scale data processing, which introduces significant cybersecurity risks (Murdoch, 2021). Health data is particularly sensitive and valuable, making it a prime target for breaches and cyberattacks. For example, a significant data leak in 2024 exposed millions of health records, including information on elderly individuals and their caregivers (Wan, 2024; Alder, 2025).

Older adults may be especially vulnerable due to limited digital literacy or awareness of cybersecurity risks. Therefore, it is essential to implement strong encryption protocols, multi-layered authentication, and regular security audits to safeguard data integrity. These measures should be paired with user education and institutional accountability to reduce vulnerabilities and prevent misuse.

3.2.3 Autonomy and Ethical Governance

Beyond transparency and technical safeguards, AI systems must uphold the ethical principle of autonomy. As AI becomes more involved in recommending or executing care decisions, there is a risk that older adults—particularly those with cognitive decline—may lose meaningful control over their personal data and decisions (Mukaetova-Ladinska et al., 2020; O'Connor, 2022).

Ethical governance should ensure that older adults retain decision-making power over how their data is used and shared. When individuals are no longer able to exercise this control, mechanisms such as digital advance directives or designated data proxies can help ensure their wishes are respected (Duque & Otaegui, 2023). Social workers can act as key intermediaries in this process—interpreting AI-generated insights, ensuring alignment with the individual's values, and safeguarding ethical boundaries.

AI-related privacy concerns in elderly care are multifaceted—spanning transparency, technical security, and ethical control. Addressing them requires not only technological safeguards but also inclusive and culturally competent legal-ethical frameworks. Social workers are essential actors in this process, helping older adults navigate complex systems, advocating for informed consent, and ensuring that privacy and autonomy remain central to AI-enabled care.

3.3 Technology Dependence in Elderly Care

As AI becomes more widely used in elderly care, the issue of technology dependence is increasingly becoming a significant concern. While AI has improved the efficiency and convenience of care, excessive reliance on technology has raised concerns about the loss of autonomy for older adults, increased risk of technical failures, and potential social isolation (Salomé & Monfort, 2023). Moreover, as older adults become more reliant on AI systems, the risk of digital exploitation, fraud, or abuse increases—particularly when safeguards and oversight are lacking.

3.3.1 Impact of Technology Dependence on Autonomy

In elderly care, although AI provides conveniences such as health monitoring and medication management, over-reliance on technology may undermine older adults' autonomy (Duque & Otaegui, 2023). While smart devices and virtual assistants offer numerous benefits, they can inadvertently weaken older adults' ability to manage their own health and make independent decisions actively (Dahlke & Ory, 2017). For instance, if older adults overly rely on AI systems for medication reminders, they may become less engaged with their health, leading to a decrease in their sense of autonomy and, ultimately, a reduction in quality of life (Stypińska & Franke, 2023).

3.3.2 Risks of Technical Failures and Dependence

As reliance on AI technology increases, the risks associated with technical failures and operational errors also rise (Arnold & Toner, 2021). Older adults often lack proficiency with technology, and if AI health devices malfunction or data is lost, health warnings may be overlooked, delaying critical treatments (Huang et al., 2019). For example, if monitoring devices fail, older adults may not receive timely health alerts or instructions, increasing the risk of delayed medical response and adverse health outcomes (Illario et al., 2016). The occurrence of technical failures often leaves older adults feeling helpless, deepening their dependence on technology (Claßen, 2013).

3.3.3 Potential for Social Isolation Due to Technology Dependence

Although AI can help older adults maintain certain social connections through virtual companionship and remote healthcare, prolonged reliance on technology may reduce face-to-face interactions with family and friends, leading to social isolation (Khosravi et al., 2016). Virtual interactions lack emotional depth and warmth and cannot replace genuine human social experiences. Prolonged reliance on AI for communication and health management may lead older adults to become more isolated, negatively affecting their mental and emotional health and their sense of social participation (Latikka et al., 2021).

In conclusion, while AI technology in elderly care offers significant conveniences, over-dependence can lead to diminished autonomy, increased risks from technical failures, and heightened social isolation. Therefore, AI care solutions should balance technological support with interpersonal interaction, focus on fostering older adults' independence, reduce the risk of technical failures, and ensure that older adults maintain social and emotional connections.

4 Designing Ethical AI Care Systems that Respect the Autonomy and Dignity of Older Adults

As the global population ages, demand for elderly care continues to rise, while traditional care models struggle to meet increasingly complex needs. In this context, AI has demonstrated significant potential—offering innovative solutions that support daily functioning, health monitoring, and personalized care for older adults.

However, integrating AI into elderly care must go beyond technical efficiency. To truly serve aging populations, AI systems should be guided by humanistic principles—especially the values of autonomy and dignity, which are foundational to social work practice. These principles, embedded in the Social Work Code of Ethics, emphasize respect for older adults' rights, preferences, and lived experiences.

Designing ethical AI care systems that uphold these values not only enhances quality of life but also fosters independence and promotes healthy aging (Hwang et al., 2025). As such, this section explores how ethical, social, and technological considerations can be integrated to ensure that AI innovations align with the human-centered mission of social work.

4.1 *Human-Centered Design and Ethical Considerations*

When applying AI technology in elderly care, it is crucial to comprehensively address ethical issues, particularly those related to privacy, consent, and bias elimination (Iqbal, 2023). AI should be viewed as a semi-autonomous participant capable of influencing older adults' functional and social relationships. Therefore, when designing AI care technologies, it is essential to focus on human-centered attributes, values, and design principles to ensure they meet ethical standards and align with societal needs (Dignum, 2017). The goal of ethical design is to ensure that technology supports rather than undermines the freedom and dignity of older adults, helping them maintain autonomy while respecting their values (Zhou & Salvendy, 2019).

4.2 *AI Supporting Independent Living for Older Adults*

AI technology provides strong support for older adults in maintaining independent living, especially in areas such as health monitoring, accident risk alerting, and personalized care. With real-time monitoring and precise health status detection capabilities, AI can seamlessly integrate into older adults' daily lives and provide appropriate support. For example, AI can play an essential role in elderly health management by monitoring physiological data such as heart rate, blood pressure, and oxygen saturation levels and using wearable devices or sensors to provide early warnings for abnormal health conditions (Yan et al., 2015). Additionally, AI can offer personalized care recommendations, such as predicting potential health risks based on physiological parameters and assisting in developing personalized rehabilitation plans (Puaschunder & Feierabend, 2019). For example, AI has been used in fall detection and Alzheimer's disease prevention, achieving more than 98% accuracy through technologies such as thermal imaging sensors and millimeter-wave radar, enabling timely health interventions (Li, 2024). This AI design approach not only enhances the usability of technology but also increases older adults' sense of participation, reducing their dependence on others, boosting their confidence, and improving their quality of life (Luo et al., 2025).

4.3 Maintaining Autonomy and Dignity

Protecting the autonomy and dignity of older adults is a core element in AI care design (Mhlanga, 2023). In elderly care, healthcare professionals should work with older patients and their significant others to ensure that the wishes and needs of older adults are fully considered in care decision-making processes (Aita, 2013). This not only fosters the development of personalized care decisions but also enhances the autonomy and sense of dignity of older adults, thereby improving their health and quality of life (Nikolidakis et al., 2010). AI systems should allow older adults to participate in care decisions and avoid excessive interference in their daily lives (Zhu et al., 2022). Ensuring that older adults feel fully respected and supported in the caregiving process has a positive impact on their overall well-being (Czaja & Ceruso, 2022). In the design process, particular attention should be given to avoiding over-dominating technology to ensure that older adults still retain control over their health care decisions. By integrating user-centered design, AI technologies can better meet the needs of older adults for independent living while maintaining their dignity and autonomy (Wang et al., 2019).

4.4 Multidisciplinary Collaboration and Participatory Design

The successful application of AI technology in serving older adults also depends on multidisciplinary collaboration, including the involvement of clinical doctors, psychologists, ethicists, and engineers (Wu et al., 2018). Cross-disciplinary partnership helps ensure that the practical application of technology aligns with ethical and professional standards (Yigit et al., 2025). Additionally, older adults' participation in the design, implementation, and evaluation of AI systems is crucial. Incorporating the needs and real-life feedback from older adults is essential to addressing challenges such as the digital divide and inequality, ensuring that AI system designs truly align with their daily experiences and evolving care needs (Demiris, 2024). This participatory approach reflects the principles of participatory action research, which centers the voices of those most affected and promotes more equitable, responsive system design.

As shown, designing AI care technologies that respect the autonomy and dignity of older adults requires a comprehensive, inclusive approach that considers ethics, human-centered and user-centered design, and multidisciplinary collaboration. Through these methods, AI technology can effectively support older adults in maintaining independent living and enhance their quality of life and well-being. As technology continues to develop, AI care systems will play an increasingly important role in promoting healthy aging while respecting the autonomy and dignity of older adults.

5 Conclusion

As the global aging population continues to grow, the demand for elderly care is increasing, and traditional caregiving models face numerous challenges. The application of AI in elderly care offers innovative solutions, particularly in health monitoring, social support, and the maintenance of cognitive function, demonstrating immense potential. AI not only significantly improves the efficiency of caregiving but also enhances personalized services, enabling older adults to make more informed choices. This, in turn, greatly strengthens their ability to live independently and significantly improves their overall quality of life.

However, there remains a gap between the widespread adoption of AI technology and its adaptability among older adults. This may affect their ability to use AI technologies effectively. Furthermore, during the design phase, AI technology needs to balance ease of use and intuitive functionality to reduce technological barriers and improve quality of life. While AI can offer some emotional support, it is inherently limited in replicating the depth and authenticity of human interaction—and from a humanistic perspective, it should not be expected to do so thoroughly.

Additionally, as AI technology becomes more widely applied in the caregiving field, privacy protection and ethical concerns are becoming increasingly important. Data security and algorithmic ethics have become crucial factors in balancing technological innovation with the protection of personal privacy. When AI systems analyze patient data to support diagnosis, it is essential to ensure that data collection and processing adhere to strict privacy principles. Furthermore, the development and application of AI algorithms must respect individual privacy, proactively address algorithmic bias, and ensure interpretability and transparency. If left unaddressed, algorithmic bias can compromise both the accuracy of AI decision-making and the effectiveness of care recommendations, particularly for underserved or underrepresented older adults. Ensuring fairness in AI outcomes is therefore a fundamental part of building trustworthy and inclusive AI systems for aging populations.

To address these issues, future research should further focus on the adaptability of AI systems, cultural differences, ethical design, and privacy protection. Moreover,

AI should be integrated with human caregiving to ensure that technology does not excessively interfere with older adults' autonomy and social interaction. Through multidisciplinary collaboration and technological optimization, AI will become more widespread in elderly care, offering more comprehensive and personalized caregiving services to older adults and ultimately achieving the goal of healthy aging.

Conflicts of Interest The authors have no conflicts of interest to declare that are relevant to the content of this chapter.

References

Aajami, Z., Kazazi, L., Toroski, M., Bahrami, M., & Borhaninejad, V. (2020). Relationship between depression and cognitive impairment among elderly: A cross-sectional study. *Journal of Caring Sciences, 9*(3), 148–153. https://doi.org/10.34172/jcs.2020.022

Administration for Community Living. (2024). *Strategic framework: National plan on aging.* U.S. Department of Health and Human Services. Retrieved from https://acl.gov/sites/default/files/ICC-Aging/StrategicFramework-NationalPlanOnAging-2024.pdf

Aita, K. (2013). How to provide medical and nursing care that respects the wishes of older patients with diminished competence. *Japanese Journal of Geriatrics, 50*(4), 487–490. https://doi.org/10.3143/geriatrics.50.487

Alder, S. (2025, March 19). The Biggest healthcare data breaches of 2024. *HIPAA Journal.* Retrieved from https://www.hipaajournal.com/biggest-healthcare-data-breaches-2024/

Andrews, J., Astell, A., Brown, L., Harrison, R., & Hawley, M. (2017). Technology for early detection of depression and anxiety in older people. *Studies in Health Technology and Informatics, 242*, 374–380. https://doi.org/10.3233/978-1-61499-798-6-374

Arango, J., Marco-Detchart, C., & Inglada, V. (2025). Personalized cognitive support via social robots. *Sensors, 25*(3), 888. https://doi.org/10.3390/s25030888

Arif Ul Alam, M., Roy, N., Holmes, S., Gangopadhyay, A., & Galik, E. (2020). AutoCogniSys: IoT assisted context-aware automatic cognitive health assessment. *arXiv.* Retrieved from https://arxiv.org/abs/2003.07492

Arnold, Z., & Toner, H. (2021). *AI accidents: An emerging threat.* Center for Security and Emerging Technology. https://doi.org/10.51593/20200072

Asan, O., & Choudhury, A. (2021). Research trends in artificial intelligence applications in human factors health care: Mapping review. *JMIR Human Factors, 8*(2), e28236. https://doi.org/10.2196/28236

Awotunde, J. B., Ajagbe, S. A., & Florez, H. (2022). Internet of Things with wearable devices and artificial intelligence for elderly uninterrupted healthcare monitoring systems. In H. Florez & H. Gomez (Eds.), *Applied informatics. ICAI 2022. Communications in computer and information science* (Vol. 1643, pp. 278–291). Springer. https://doi.org/10.1007/978-3-031-19647-8_20

Baikuvekov, M., Tursynova, A., & Yespayev, G. (2024). A deep learning for cardiovascular diseases detection on wearable devices data. In *2024 IEEE 4th international conference on Smart Information Systems and Technologies (SIST)* (pp. 272–277). IEEE. https://doi.org/10.1109/SIST61555.2024.10629525

Bapka, V., Bika, I., Kavouras, C., Savvidis, T., Konstantinidis, E. I., Bamidis, P. D., Papantoniou, G., Masoura, E., & Moraitou, D. (2018). Brain plasticity in older adults: Could it be better enhanced by cognitive training via an adaptation of the virtual reality platform FitForAll or via a commercial video game? In M. Auer & T. Tsiatsos (Eds.), *Interactive mobile communication technologies and learning. IMCL 2017. Advances in intelligent systems and computing* (Vol. 725, pp. 728–742). Springer. https://doi.org/10.1007/978-3-319-75175-7_72

Bartoletti, I. (2019). AI in healthcare: Ethical and privacy challenges. In D. Riaño, S. Wilk, & A. ten Teije (Eds.), *Artificial intelligence in medicine. AIME 2019* (Lecture notes in computer science) (Vol. 11526, pp. 7–10). Springer. https://doi.org/10.1007/978-3-030-21642-9_2

Blusi, M., Nilsson, I., & Lindgren, H. (2018). Older adults co-creating meaningful individualized social activities online for healthy ageing. *Studies in Health Technology and Informatics, 247*, 775–779. https://doi.org/10.3233/978-1-61499-852-5-775

Cai, Y., Cai, X., Zheng, X., Li, X., Wang, Y., & Ji, Y. (2023). Develop cognitive games for older people based on dynamic difficulty adjustment to motivate them to train. In Q. Gao & J. Zhou (Eds.), *Human aspects of IT for the aged population. HCII 2023* (Lecture notes in computer science) (Vol. 14042, pp. 405–419). Springer. https://doi.org/10.1007/978-3-031-34866-2_29

Camargo, J., Silva, T., & Abreu, J. (2023). Interconnecting personal assistants and TVs: A friendly approach to connect generations. In *Proceedings of the 2023 ACM international conference on interactive media experiences*. https://doi.org/10.1145/3573381.3596469

Catania, V., Rundo, F., Panerai, S., & Ferri, R. (2024). Virtual reality for the rehabilitation of acquired cognitive disorders: A narrative review. *Bioengineering, 11*(1), 35. https://doi.org/10.3390/bioengineering11010035

Cedeno-Moreno, R., Malagon-Barillas, D., Morales-Hernández, L., Gonzalez-Hernandez, M., & Cruz-Albarrán, I. (2024). Computer vision system based on the analysis of gait features for fall risk assessment in elderly people. *Applied Sciences, 14*(9), 3867. https://doi.org/10.3390/app14093867

Chen, H.-M., & Hou, S.-I. (2023). A systematic review on aging in the community and culture among Chinese older adults. *Innovation in Aging, 7*(S1), 355–356. https://doi.org/10.1093/geroni/igad104.1182

Chen, Q., & Park, H. (2021). How anthropomorphism affects trust in intelligent personal assistants. *Industrial Management & Data Systems, 121*, 2722–2737. https://doi.org/10.1108/IMDS-12-2020-0761

China National Healthcare Security Bureau. (2024, October 26). *Incremental policy: Nursing prices better reflect technical labor value and support hospitals to provide "care without companion" services*. Retrieved from https://www.gov.cn/zhengce/202410/content_6983136.htm

Ciampi, M., Coronato, A., Naeem, M., & Silvestri, S. (2022). An intelligent environment for preventing medication errors in home treatment. *Expert Systems with Applications, 193*, 116434. https://doi.org/10.1016/j.eswa.2021.116434

Claßen, K. (2013). *Psychological factors and technology acceptance in older age: The role of technology generations* (Doctoral dissertation). Universität Heidelberg. https://doi.org/10.11588/heidok.00014295

Cotten, S., Khan, A., Mobley, C., Jing, X., Obeid, J., Goodrich, G., Baker, H., & Hubig, N. (2024). Ethics and acceptance of AI. *Innovation in Aging, 8*(S1), 280. https://doi.org/10.1093/geroni/igae098.0911

Czaja, S. J., & Ceruso, M. (2022). The promise of artificial intelligence in supporting an aging population. *Journal of Cognitive Engineering and Decision Making, 16*(4), 182–193. https://doi.org/10.1177/15553434221129914

Dahlke, D. V., & Ory, M. G. (2017). Emerging opportunities and challenges in optimal aging with virtual personal assistants. *Public Policy & Aging Report, 27*(2), 68–73. https://doi.org/10.1093/ppar/prx004

Demiris, G. (2024). Stakeholder engagement for the design of generative AI tools: Inclusive design approaches. *Innovation in Aging, 8*(S1), 585–586. https://doi.org/10.1093/geroni/igae098.1918

Dignum, V. (2017). Responsible artificial intelligence: Designing AI for human values. *ITU Journal: ICT Discoveries, 1*, 1–8. http://handle.itu.int/11.1002/pub/8129fdfb-en

Duque, M., & Otaegui, A. (2023). Digital dependency as a burden: Impact of active aging for tech adoption in Brazil and Chile. *Anthropology & Aging, 44*(2), 28–44. https://doi.org/10.5195/aa.2023.422

Espín, V., Hurtado, M., & Noguera, M. (2016). Nutrition for elder care: A nutritional semantic recommender system for the elderly. *Expert Systems, 33*(2), 201–210. https://doi.org/10.1111/exsy.12143

Eun, S. J., Kim, E. J., & Kim, J. Y. (2022). Development and evaluation of an artificial intelligence-based cognitive exercise game: A pilot study. *Journal of Environmental and Public Health, 2022*, 4403976. https://doi.org/10.1155/2022/4403976

Faria, A. L., Almeida, Y., Branco, D., Câmara, J., Cameirão, M., Ferreira, L., Moreira, A., Paulino, T., Rodrigues, P., Spinola, M., Vilar, M., Badia, B. I., & S., Simões, M., & Fermé, E. (2024). NeuroAIreh@b: An artificial intelligence-based methodology for personalized and adaptive neurorehabilitation. *Frontiers in Neurology, 14*, 1258323. https://doi.org/10.3389/fneur.2023.1258323

Feng, Z. (2019). Global convergence: Aging and long-term care policy challenges in the developing world. *Journal of Aging & Social Policy, 31*(4), 291–297. https://doi.org/10.1080/08959420.2019.1626205

Feng, Z., & Wu, B. (2023). Embracing challenges for population aging in China: Building scientific evidence to inform long-term care policymaking and practice. *Journal of Aging & Social Policy, 35*(4), 543–553. https://doi.org/10.1080/08959420.2023.2217979

Ferraris, C., Amprimo, G., Pettiti, G., Masi, G., & Priano, L. (2022). *Automatic detector of gait alterations using RGB-D sensor and supervised classifiers: A preliminary study*. 2022 IEEE Symposium on Computers and Communications (ISCC) (pp. 1–6). https://doi.org/10.1109/ISCC55528.2022.9912923

Friedman, A. B., Pathmanabhan, C., Glicksman, A., Demiris, G., Cappola, A. R., & McCoy, M. S. (2022). Addressing online health privacy risks for older adults: A perspective on ethical considerations and recommendations. *Gerontology and Geriatric Medicine, 8*. https://doi.org/10.1177/23337214221095705

García-Betances, R. I., Jiménez-Mixco, V., Arredondo, M. T., & Cabrera-Umpiérrez, M. F. (2015). Using virtual reality for cognitive training of the elderly. *American Journal of Alzheimer's Disease and Other Dementias, 30*(1), 49–54. https://doi.org/10.1177/1533317514545866

García-Requejo, A., Pérez-Rubio, M., Villadangos, J., & Hernández, Á. (2023). Activity monitoring and location sensory system for people with mild cognitive impairments. *IEEE Sensors Journal, 23*(5), 5448–5458. https://doi.org/10.1109/JSEN.2023.3239980

García-Vázquez, J., Rodríguez, M., Andrade, Á., & Bravo, J. (2011). Supporting the strategies to improve elders' medication compliance by providing ambient aids. *Personal and Ubiquitous Computing, 15*, 389–397. https://doi.org/10.1007/s00779-010-0362-0

Gasteiger, N., Loveys, K., Law, M., & Broadbent, E. (2021). Friends from the future: A scoping review of research into robots and computer agents to combat loneliness in older people. *Clinical Interventions in Aging, 16*, 941–971. https://doi.org/10.2147/CIA.S282709

Gomes, S., Von Schantz, M., & Leocadio-Miguel, M. (2023). Predicting depressive symptoms in middle-aged and elderly adults using sleep data and clinical health markers: A machine learning approach. *Sleep Medicine, 102*, 123–131. https://doi.org/10.1016/j.sleep.2023.01.002

Góngora Alonso, S., Hamrioui, S., de la Torre Díez, I., Motta Cruz, E., López-Coronado, M., & Franco, M. (2019). Social robots for people with aging and dementia: A systematic review of literature. *Telemedicine Journal and E-Health, 25*(7), 533–540. https://doi.org/10.1089/tmj.2018.0051

Government of Canada. (2024, December). *Progress on the National Housing Strategy*. Housing, Infrastructure and Communities Canada. Retrieved from https://housing-infrastructure.canada.ca/housing-logement/ptch-csd/reports-rapports/prog-nhs-dec-2024-dec-snl-eng.html

Graham, S., Lee, E., Jeste, D., Patten, R., Twamley, E., Nebeker, C., Yamada, Y., Kim, H., & Depp, C. (2019). Artificial intelligence approaches to predicting and detecting cognitive decline in older adults: A conceptual review. *Psychiatry Research, 284*, 112732. https://doi.org/10.1016/j.psychres.2019.112732

Grueso, S., & Viejo-Sobera, R. (2021). Machine learning methods for predicting progression from mild cognitive impairment to Alzheimer's disease dementia: A systematic review. *Alzheimer's Research & Therapy, 13*, 162. https://doi.org/10.1186/s13195-021-00900-w

Hill, R. D., Bäckman, L., & Stigsdotter-Neely, A. (Eds.). (2000). *Cognitive rehabilitation in old age*. Oxford University Press.

Hsu, T., & Hsieh, C. (2022). Socially assistive robots assisting older adults in an internet and smart healthcare era: A literature review. In *2022 IEEE 4th Eurasia Conference on IOT, Communication and Engineering (ECICE)* (pp. 591–594). IEEE. https://doi.org/10.1109/ECICE55674.2022.10042947

Htet, Y., Zin, T. T., Tin, P., Tamura, H., Kondo, K., & Watanabe, S. (2024). Smarter aging: Developing a foundational elderly activity monitoring system with AI and GUI interface. *IEEE Access, 12*, 74499–74523. https://doi.org/10.1109/ACCESS.2024.3405954

Hu, Y., & Chen, I. (2024). Older adults' perspectives on using an AI-aided smartphone. *Innovation in Aging, 8*(S1), 1262. https://doi.org/10.1093/geroni/igae098.4035

Huang, G., Luo, Y. Z., & Qian, Z. W. (2019). Critical factors in the application of artificial intelligence to establish health care systems for seniors. *Revista de Cercetare si Interventie Sociala, 65*, 51–59. https://doi.org/10.33788/rcis.65.4

Hutson, S., Lim, S. L., Bentley, P. J., Bianchi-Berthouze, N., & Bowling, A. (2011). Investigating the suitability of social robots for the wellbeing of the elderly. In S. D'Mello, A. Graesser, B. Schuller, & J. C. Martin (Eds.), *Affective computing and intelligent interaction. ACII 2011* (Lecture notes in computer science) (Vol. 6974, pp. 578–587). Springer. https://doi.org/10.1007/978-3-642-24600-5_61

Hwang, A. S., Tannou, T., Nanthakumar, J., Cao, W., Chu, C. H., Zeytinoglu Atici, C., Scane, K., Yu, A., Tsang, W., Chan, J., Lea, P., Harris, Z., & Wang, R. H. (2025). Co-creating humanistic AI AgeTech to support dynamic care ecosystems: A preliminary guiding model. *The Gerontologist, 65*(1), gnae093. https://doi.org/10.1093/geront/gnae093

Illario, M., Vollenbroek-Hutten, M. M. R., Molloy, D. W., Menditto, E., Iaccarino, G., & Eklund, P. (2016). Active and healthy ageing and independent living 2016. *Journal of Aging Research, 2016*, 8062079. https://doi.org/10.1155/2016/8062079

Iqbal, S. (2023). Artificial intelligence tools and applications for elderly healthcare-review. In *Proceedings of the 2023 9th International Conference on Computing and Artificial Intelligence (ICCAI '23)* (pp. 394–397). Association for Computing Machinery. https://doi.org/10.1145/3594315.3594347

Islam, M., Hussain, I., Rahman, M., Park, S., & Hossain, M. (2022). Explainable artificial intelligence model for stroke prediction using EEG signal. *Sensors, 22*(24), 9859. https://doi.org/10.3390/s22249859

Jecker, N. (2020). You've got a friend in me: Sociable robots for older adults in an age of global pandemics. *Ethics and Information Technology, 23*, 35–43. https://doi.org/10.1007/s10676-020-09546-y

Kalache, A. (2019). An education revolution in response to the longevity revolution. *Revista Brasileira de Geriatria e Gerontologia, 22*(4), e190213. https://doi.org/10.1590/1981-22562019022.190213

Khosravi, P., Rezvani, A., & Wiewiora, A. (2016). The impact of technology on older adults' social isolation. *Computers in Human Behavior, 63*, 594–603. https://doi.org/10.1016/j.chb.2016.05.092

Kim, B., Youm, C., Park, H., Choi, H., & Shin, S. (2024). Machine learning approach to classifying declines of physical function and muscle strength associated with cognitive function in older women. *Frontiers in Public Health, 12*, 1376736. https://doi.org/10.3389/fpubh.2024.1376736

Kiprijanovska, I., Gjoreski, H., & Gams, M. (2020). Detection of gait abnormalities for fall risk assessment using wrist-worn inertial sensors and deep learning. *Sensors, 20*(18), 5373. https://doi.org/10.3390/s20185373

Kitakoshi, D., Hanada, R., Iwata, K., & Suzuki, M. (2015). Cognitive training system for dementia prevention using memory game based on the concept of human-agent interaction. *Journal of Advanced Computational Intelligence and Intelligent Informatics, 19*(6), 727–737. https://doi.org/10.20965/jaciii.2015.p0727

Latikka, R., Rubio-Hernández, R., Lohan, E., Rantala, J., Fernández, F., Laitinen, A., & Oksanen, A. (2021). Older adults' loneliness, social isolation, and physical information and communication technology in ambient assisted living: A systematic literature review. *Journal of Medical Internet Research, 23*(12), e28022. https://doi.org/10.2196/28022

Lee, J., & Lee, S. (2024). Development of an AI-based predictive algorithm for early diagnosis of high-risk dementia groups among the elderly: Utilizing health lifelog data. *Healthcare, 12*(18), 1872. https://doi.org/10.3390/healthcare12181872

Li, D. (2023). Research on the current situation of mental health management of the elderly under the background of population aging. *International Journal of Education and Humanities, 6*(3), 120–122. https://doi.org/10.54097/ijeh.v6i3.4760

Li, K. N. (2024). Research on deep learning-based sensor technology for falls in elderly communities. *International Advanced Research Journal in Science, Engineering and Technology, 11*(4). https://doi.org/10.17148/IARJSET.2024.11403

Li, H. H., & Liao, Y. H. (2025). Application and effectiveness of adaptive AI in elderly healthcare. *Psychogeriatrics, 25*(1), e13214. https://doi.org/10.1111/psyg.13214

Li, C., & Xu, S. (2021). How older adults' user experiences of smart healthcare system are affected by their cultural differences. In *Proceedings of the 2021 IEEE 3rd Eurasia Conference on Biomedical Engineering, Healthcare and Sustainability (ECBIOS)* (pp. 100–104). IEEE. https://doi.org/10.1109/ECBIOS51820.2021.9510513

Lim, J. (2023). Effects of a cognitive-based intervention program using social robot PIO on cognitive function, depression, loneliness, and quality of life of older adults living alone. *Frontiers in Public Health, 11*, 1097485. https://doi.org/10.3389/fpubh.2023.1097485

Liu, W. T. (2000). Values and caregiving burden: The significance of filial piety in elder care. In W. T. Liu & H. Kendig (Eds.), *Who should care for the elderly?* (pp. 183–199). World Scientific. https://doi.org/10.1142/9789812793591_0010

Liu, W., Chuang, K., & Chen, K. (2018). The design and implementation of a chatbot's character for elderly care. In *In 2018 International Conference on System Science and Engineering (ICSSE)* (pp. 1–5). IEEE. https://doi.org/10.1109/ICSSE.2018.8520008

Lukkien, D. R. M., Nap, H. H., Buimer, H. P., Peine, A., Boon, W. P. C., Ket, J. C. F., Minkman, M. M. N., & Moors, E. H. M. (2023). Toward responsible artificial intelligence in long-term care: A scoping review on practical approaches. *The Gerontologist, 63*(1), 155–168. https://doi.org/10.1093/geront/gnab180

Luo, J., Zhang, K., Huang, Q., Jiang, S., & Pan, Y. (2025). From acceptance to dependence: Exploring influences of smart healthcare on continuous use intention of mobile health services among older adults with chronic illnesses in China. *Behavioral Sciences, 15*(1), 19. https://doi.org/10.3390/bs15010019

Magnenat-Thalmann, N., & Zhang, Z. (2014). Social robots and virtual humans as assistive tools for improving our quality of life. In *In 2014 5th International Conference on Digital Home (ICDH)* (pp. 1–7). IEEE. https://doi.org/10.1109/ICDH.2014.8

Majnarić, L., Babič, F., O'Sullivan, S., & Holzinger, A. (2021). AI and big data in healthcare: Towards a more comprehensive research framework for multimorbidity. *Journal of Clinical Medicine, 10*(4), 766. https://doi.org/10.3390/jcm10040766

Mehrabi, F., & Béland, F. (2020). Effects of social isolation, loneliness and frailty on health outcomes and their possible mediators and moderators in community-dwelling older adults: A scoping review. *Archives of Gerontology and Geriatrics, 90*, 104119. https://doi.org/10.1016/j.archger.2020.104119

Mhlanga, D. (2023, December 26). *Artificial intelligence in elderly care: Navigating ethical and responsible AI adoption for seniors*. SSRN. https://doi.org/10.2139/ssrn.4675564

Milne-Ives, M., De Cock, C., Lim, E., Shehadeh, M., De Pennington, N., Mole, G., Normando, E., & Meinert, E. (2020). The effectiveness of artificial intelligence conversational agents in health care: Systematic review. *Journal of Medical Internet Research, 22*(10), e20346. https://doi.org/10.2196/20346

Moreno, P., Hernando, M., & Gómez, E. (2015). Design and technical evaluation of an enhanced location-awareness service enabler for spatial disorientation management of elderly with mild cognitive impairment. *IEEE Journal of Biomedical and Health Informatics, 19*(1), 37–43. https://doi.org/10.1109/JBHI.2014.2327638

Mukaetova-Ladinska, E. B., Harwood, T., & Maltby, J. (2020). Artificial Intelligence in the health-care of older people. *Archives of Psychiatric Mental Health, 4*, 7–13. https://doi.org/10.29328/journal.apmh.1001011

Murdoch, B. (2021). Privacy and artificial intelligence: Challenges for protecting health information in a new era. *BMC Medical Ethics, 22*(1), 122. https://doi.org/10.1186/s12910-021-00687-3

Nikolidakis, S., Vergados, D. D., & Anagnostopoulos, I. (2010). Health care web information systems and personalized services for assisting living of elderly people at nursing homes. In M. Wallace, I. E. Anagnostopoulos, P. Mylonas, & M. Bieliková (Eds.), *Semantics in adaptive and personalized services* (Vol. 279, pp. 121–134). Springer. https://doi.org/10.1007/978-3-642-11684-1_9

O'Connor, S. (2022). Artificial intelligence for older adult health: Opportunities for advancing gerontological nursing practice. *Journal of Gerontological Nursing, 48*(12), 3–5. https://doi.org/10.3928/00989134-20221107-01

Obuchi, S., Kojima, M., Suzuki, H., Garbalosa, J., Imamura, K., Ihara, K., Hirano, H., Sasai, H., Fujiwara, Y., & Kawai, H. (2024). Artificial intelligence detection of cognitive impairment in older adults during walking. *Alzheimer's & Dementia: Diagnosis, Assessment & Disease Monitoring, 16*, e070012. https://doi.org/10.1002/dad2.70012

Pino, O., Palestra, G., Carolis, B.D., Carofiglio, V., & Macchiarulo, N. (2020). Social robots in cognitive interventions: Advances, problems and perspectives. In *Proceedings of the Workshop on Artificial Intelligence for an Ageing Society (AIxAS 2020)*. CEUR Workshop Proceedings. Retrieved from http://ceur-ws.org/Vol-2804/paper8.pdf

Pirhonen, J., Tiilikainen, E., Pekkarinen, S., Lemivaara, M., & Melkas, H. (2020). Can robots tackle late-life loneliness? Scanning of future opportunities and challenges in assisted living facilities. *Futures, 124*, 102640. https://doi.org/10.1016/j.futures.2020.102640

Pollack, M. E. (2005). Intelligent technology for an aging population: The use of AI to assist elders with cognitive impairment. *AI Magazine, 26*(2), 9–24. https://doi.org/10.1609/aimag.v26i2.1810

Puaschunder, J. M., & Feierabend, D. (2019). Artificial intelligence in the healthcare sector. In Proceedings of the International RAIS Conference on Social Sciences and Humanities, Johns Hopkins University, Montgomery County Campus, Rockville, MD, November 6–7, 2019. *Scientia Moralitas: International Journal of Multidisciplinary Research, 2*(4), 1–14. https://doi.org/10.2139/ssrn.3469423

Qiu, T., & Carter, D. (2023). An emotion detection mobile application to decrease potential mental disorder among seniors using sentiment analysis from audio data. *Advanced Computer Science and Information Technology Trends, 13*(13), 30. https://doi.org/10.5121/csit.2023.131330

Quazi, F., Mohammed, A. S., & Gorrepati, N. (2024). Transforming treatment and diagnosis in healthcare through AI. *International Journal of Global Innovations and Solutions*. https://doi.org/10.21428/e90189c8.072ffbe8

Reddy, A., Reddy, R., Roghani, A., Garcia, R., Khemka, S., Pattoor, V., Jacob, M., Reddy, P., & Sehar, U. (2024). Artificial intelligence in Parkinson's disease: Early detection and diagnostic advancements. *Ageing Research Reviews, 99*, 102410. https://doi.org/10.1016/j.arr.2024.102410

Sabry, F., Eltaras, T., Labda, W., Alzoubi, K., & Malluhi, Q. (2022). Machine learning for healthcare wearable devices: The big picture. *Journal of Healthcare Engineering, 2022*, 4653923. https://doi.org/10.1155/2022/4653923

Salomé, S., & Monfort, E. (2023). Révolution numérique et âgisme: Les enjeux éthiques de l'intelligence artificielle pour les personnes âgées [The digital revolution and ageism: The ethical challenges of artificial intelligence for older people]. *NPG Neurologie—Psychiatrie—Gériatrie, 23*(138), 383–387. https://doi.org/10.1016/j.npg.2023.09.004

Salvi, M., Acharya, M., Seoni, S., Faust, O., Tan, R., Barua, P., García, S., Molinari, F., & Acharya, U. (2024). Artificial intelligence for atrial fibrillation detection, prediction, and treatment: A systematic review of the last decade (2013–2023). *Wiley Interdisciplinary Reviews: Data Mining and Knowledge Discovery, 14*, e1530. https://doi.org/10.1002/widm.1530

Serhal, H., Abdallah, N., Marion, J., Chauvet, P., Oueidat, M., & Humeau-Heurtier, A. (2022). Overview on prediction, detection, and classification of atrial fibrillation using wavelets and AI on ECG. *Computers in Biology and Medicine, 142*, 105168. https://doi.org/10.1016/j.compbiomed.2021.105168

Sgorbissa, A., Papadopoulos, I., Bruno, B., Koulouglioti, C., & Recchiuto, C. T. (2018). Encoding guidelines for a culturally competent robot for elderly care. In *Proceedings of the 2018 IEEE/RSJ International Conference on Intelligent Robots and Systems (IROS), 1988–1995.* IEEE. https://doi.org/10.1109/IROS.2018.8593856

Stypińska, J., & Franke, A. (2023). AI revolution in healthcare and medicine and the (re-)emergence of inequalities and disadvantages for ageing population. Frontiers in Sociology, 7, 1038854. https://doi.org/10.3389/fsoc.2022.1038854.

Spanakis, E., Urrutia, A., Galindo, R., Vellanki, P., Migdal, A., Davis, G., et al. (2022). Continuous glucose monitoring–guided insulin administration in hospitalized patients with diabetes: A randomized clinical trial. *Diabetes Care, 45*(10), 2369–2375. https://doi.org/10.2337/dc22-0716

Su, D., Zhang, X., He, K., & Chen, Y. (2020). Use of machine learning approach to predict depression in the elderly in China: A longitudinal study. *Journal of Affective Disorders, 282*, 289–298. https://doi.org/10.1016/j.jad.2020.12.160

Sun, Y., & Usui, E. (2023). *The effectiveness of flexible retirement in promoting older workers' employment: Evidence from Singapore*. Working paper. SSRN. https://doi.org/10.2139/ssrn.4389582

Tokunaga, S., Tamura, K., & Otake-Matsuura, M. (2021). A dialogue-based system with photo and storytelling for older adults: Toward daily cognitive training. *Frontiers in Robotics and AI, 8*, 644964. https://doi.org/10.3389/frobt.2021.644964

Vogan, A. A., Alnajjar, F., Gochoo, M., & Khalid, S. (2020). Robots, AI, and cognitive training in an era of mass age-related cognitive decline: A systematic review. *IEEE Access, 8*, 18284–18304. https://doi.org/10.1109/ACCESS.2020.2966819

Wan, H. (2024). Overview of big data information privacy protection technology and challenges. *Science and Technology of Engineering, Chemistry and Environmental Protection, 1*(1). https://doi.org/10.61173/6eyzr869

Wang, S., Bolling, K., Mao, W., Reichstadt, J., Jeste, D., Kim, H. C., & Nebeker, C. (2019). Technology to support aging in place: Older adults' perspectives. *Healthcare, 7*(2), 60. https://doi.org/10.3390/healthcare7020060

Wilson, R., Boyle, P., Segawa, E., Yu, L., Begeny, C., Anagnos, S., & Bennett, D. (2013). The influence of cognitive decline on well-being in old age. *Psychology and Aging, 28*(2), 304–313. https://doi.org/10.1037/a0031196

Woo, Y., Choi, J., & Kim, D. (2024). Effectiveness analysis of AI-IoT based public health care service for elderly in Korea [Conference presentation abstract]. *Archives of Physical Medicine and Rehabilitation, 105*(4, Suppl. 1), e14. https://doi.org/10.1016/j.apmr.2024.02.038

Wu, J. T., Dernoncourt, F., Gehrmann, S., Tyler, P. D., Moseley, E. T., Carlson, E. T., Grant, D. W., Li, Y., Welt, J., & Celi, L. A. (2018). Behind the scenes: A medical natural language processing project. *International Journal of Medical Informatics, 112*, 68–73. https://doi.org/10.1016/j.ijmedinf.2017.12.003

Wu, J., Chang, L., & Yu, G. (2021). Effective Data Decision-Making and Transmission System Based on Mobile Health for Chronic Disease Management in the Elderly. *IEEE Systems Journal, 15*(4), 5537–5548. https://doi.org/10.1109/JSYST.2020.3024816

Wu, W., Hu, J., He, Y., Wang, M., & Huang, Y. (2023). Artificial intelligence-based intelligent elderly care system. In *Proceedings of the third international conference on Artificial Intelligence, Virtual Reality, and Visualization (AIVRV 2023)* (Vol. 12923, Paper 129230J). SPIE. https://doi.org/10.1117/12.3011680

Xavier, J. F., Kamsin, I. F., Zainal Abidin, Z. M., & Vasudavan, H. (2022). AI stroke detection and emergency response system. *International Journal of Data Science and Advanced Analytics, 4*(4), 113–116. https://doi.org/10.69511/ijdsaa.v4i4.101

Yamada, M., & Arai, H. (2020). Long-term care system in Japan. *Annals of Geriatric Medicine and Research, 24*(3), 174–180. https://doi.org/10.4235/agmr.20.0037

Yan, H., Xu, L. D., Bi, Z., Pang, Z., Zhang, J., & Chen, Y. (2015). An emerging technology—Wearable wireless sensor networks with applications in human health condition monitoring. *Journal of Management Analytics, 2*(2), 121–137. https://doi.org/10.1080/23270012.2015.1029550

Yao, X., Attia, Z., Behnken, E., Hart, M., Inselman, S., Weber, K., Li, F., Stricker, N., Stricker, J., Friedman, P., & Noseworthy, P. (2023). Realtime diagnosis from electrocardiogram artificial intelligence-guided screening for atrial fibrillation with long follow-up (REGAL): Rationale and design of a pragmatic, decentralized, randomized controlled trial. *American Heart Journal, 267*, 62–69. https://doi.org/10.1016/j.ahj.2023.10.005

Yen, H. Y., Huang, C. W., Chiu, H. L., & Jin, G. (2024). The effect of social robots on depression and loneliness for older residents in long-term care facilities: A meta-analysis of randomized controlled trials. *Journal of the American Medical Directors Association, 25*(6), 104979. https://doi.org/10.1016/j.jamda.2024.02.017

Yigit, Y., Kaynak, M. F., Alkahlout, B., Ahmed, S., Günay, S., & Ozbek, A. E. (2025). AI-assisted decision-making in mild traumatic brain injury. *BMC Emergency Medicine, 25*(1), 43. https://doi.org/10.1186/s12873-024-01159-8

You, S., & Choi, H. (2025). A sociocultural perspective on AI assistive technology for older adults' social connectedness: A scoping review. *Family Relations, 74*(3), 1080–1097. https://doi.org/10.1111/fare.13128

Zhou, J., & Salvendy, G. (Eds.). (2019). *Human aspects of IT for the aged population: Design for the elderly and technology acceptance* (Vol. 11592). Springer. https://doi.org/10.1007/978-3-030-22012-9

Zhu, J., Shi, K., Yang, C., Niu, Y., Zeng, Y., Zhang, N., Liu, T., & Chu, C. H. (2022). Ethical issues of smart home-based elderly care: A scoping review. *Journal of Nursing Management, 30*(8), 3686–3699. https://doi.org/10.1111/jonm.13521

Zhu, F., Wang, J., Cheng, C., Zhu, C., Yuan, S., Li, H., & Feng, J. (2023). Design of AI in the health and elderly care service platform in the big data environment. In *Proceedings of the 2023 IEEE International Conference on Power Systems and Information Technology Applications in Green Society (ICPSITIAGS)* (pp. 111–116). IEEE. https://doi.org/10.1109/ICPSITIAGS59213.2023.10527766

Chapter 13
AI in Communities at Risk and Housing Stability

Jong Cheol Shin and Kirk A. Foster

1 Introduction

Housing instability, broadly defined to include homelessness, overcrowding, substandard conditions, frequent residential moves, and significant cost burdens (Keene & Blankenship, 2023), remains a critical societal challenge, affecting millions globally and disproportionately impacting specific vulnerable populations. Various factors—such as poverty, insufficient affordable housing supply, gentrification, discriminatory redevelopment policies, and systemic inequities—combine to create precarious living conditions, ranging from struggles to afford rent to prolonged periods of homelessness. Within this multifaceted issue, "communities at risk" encompass diverse groups that are particularly vulnerable. These groups include, but are not limited to, low-income households facing affordability challenges, residents living in substandard or disaster-prone housing, racial and ethnic minorities confronting historical and ongoing discrimination, immigrants navigating unfamiliar or exclusionary housing systems, individuals with disabilities requiring tailored accommodations, veterans experiencing unique re-entry barriers, and populations currently experiencing homelessness. The intersection of economic hardship, environmental risks, and structural inequities disproportionately exacerbates housing precarity among these communities. Therefore, housing stability signifies more than mere shelter; it encompasses secure tenure, affordability, safe and healthy living conditions, and equitable access to essential community resources.

Jong Cheol Shin (✉)
Department of Population Health, Lehigh University, Bethlehem, PA, USA
e-mail: jos322@lehigh.edu

K. A. Foster
School of Social Work, The University of Texas at Arlington, Arlington, TX, USA
e-mail: kirk.foster@uta.edu

R. An, M. A. Lindsey (eds.), *Artificial Intelligence in Social Work*,
https://doi.org/10.1007/978-3-032-18443-6_13

Housing instability is also deeply associated with a variety of public health outcomes. Chronic housing insecurity acts as a significant stressor, progressively impairing individuals' self-rated health the longer instability persists (Bhat et al., 2022). This chronic stress elevates the risk for severe health conditions—including hypertension, obesity, and diabetes—through mechanisms such as increased financial constraints limiting access to health-promoting resources, forced relocation leading to disadvantaged living environments, and heightened psychological stress and mental health challenges directly resulting from housing instability (Gu et al., 2023). Moreover, unstable housing negatively impacts chronic disease management, increasing disease prevalence among housing-insecure populations and complicating symptom control and treatment adherence (Nyamathi & Salem, 2021). Beyond direct health implications, housing instability is associated with increased vulnerability to violence, disrupted educational attainment and employment stability, and perpetuated intergenerational cycles of poverty (Olawade et al., 2023). Furthermore, poor-quality housing—a frequently overlooked aspect of housing insecurity—has direct links to respiratory illnesses, lead poisoning, injuries, and deteriorating mental health (Bashir, 2022). Exposure to hazardous environmental conditions due to substandard housing intensifies long-term health disparities (Anyanwu & Beyer, 2024). Thus, prolonged housing instability is not merely a socioeconomic hardship but also a critical determinant of public health, underscoring the importance of housing security and community well-being.

In recent years, artificial intelligence (AI)—encompassing methodologies such as machine learning, predictive analytics, natural language processing (NLP), and computer vision—has emerged as a promising set of tools to address aspects of the housing stability crisis. Advocates argue that AI can increase efficiency in resource management, yield data-driven insights into complex social patterns, and optimize the allocation of housing support and services. The appeal lies in the potential to leverage computational capacity to identify risks earlier, target interventions more accurately, and reduce the administrative burdens often experienced by service providers and recipients alike. For example, AI might be used to predict individual homelessness risk, expedite tenant screening, optimize the distribution of housing vouchers based on nuanced needs assessments, or monitor neighborhood conditions to guide targeted investments.

Nevertheless, deploying AI in the context of housing stability and vulnerable populations necessitates careful, critical examination. While AI offers potential operational advantages, its application carries profound ethical concerns. These include the risk not only of reflecting but also of amplifying existing societal inequities, creating new forms of exclusion, compromising individual privacy, and undermining critical principles such as fairness, transparency, and accountability. Algorithms, which often appear objective, can inadvertently mask biases and value judgments, making discriminatory or harmful outcomes harder to detect and challenge. Thus, this chapter advocates a critical, cautious, and fundamentally human-centered approach to AI, emphasizing equity and ethical considerations in its design, deployment, and governance within the housing sector.

The following sections provide an overview of primary AI techniques applied or proposed within housing contexts, detailing their functions, potential applications, and inherent limitations. Subsequently, the chapter explores specific applications of these technologies, assessing documented and anticipated impacts on various at-risk populations. Next, cross-cutting ethical, social, and governance challenges—such as algorithmic bias, transparency shortcomings, data privacy risks, surveillance concerns, the need for human oversight, and the importance of meaningful community participation in technology development—are examined in detail. Finally, the chapter concludes by summarizing key findings, acknowledging limitations, and offering recommendations for future research directions, policy development, and responsible AI practices. The overarching aim is to cultivate a nuanced understanding of AI's role in promoting housing stability—moving beyond simplified narratives of technological solutionism toward frameworks rooted in social justice, ethical accountability, and human dignity.

2 Overview of AI Techniques in Housing Stability

This chapter provides a foundational understanding of the key artificial intelligence methodologies relevant to housing stability challenges. The aim is an exhaustive technical exposition of these techniques and their potential applications, while simultaneously introducing the inherent limitations and risks that warrant critical scrutiny, particularly when deployed in contexts affecting vulnerable populations.

2.1 Predictive Analytics and Machine Learning

Predictive analytics involves using statistical algorithms and machine learning techniques to analyze historical and current data to forecast future events or outcomes. Machine learning (ML), a subset of AI, enables computer systems to learn patterns from data without being explicitly programmed for each task. Common techniques include regression analysis (predicting continuous values, such as rent prices or the duration of homelessness) and classification algorithms (assigning data points to predefined categories, such as "high risk" vs. "low risk" of eviction).

In the housing domain, these techniques are envisioned for applications such as early identification of individuals or families deemed at high risk of experiencing homelessness. By analyzing patterns in historical data, potentially including shelter usage history, interactions with social services, hospital visits, or criminal justice involvement, models aim to predict who might need preventive support. For example, a jurisdiction might use an ML model to flag at-risk households so that outreach teams can intervene with rental assistance or social support before an eviction or housing loss occurs (Byrne et al., 2019). Similarly, predictive analytics could forecast neighborhood trends related to housing market changes; for instance, identifying areas potentially facing rapid gentrification or decline, ostensibly to inform urban planning or resource allocation decisions (Robb et al., 2022). One recent study demonstrated an AI model that could recognize early visual indicators of gentrification from Google Street View images, correctly predicting areas that would later undergo gentrification about 74% of the time (Huang et al., 2022). The potential benefit of such predictive approaches lies in moving from reactive crisis management to proactive intervention, thereby optimizing the use of limited preventive resources.

However, the efficacy and ethics of predictive systems are critically dependent on the data they consume. If the historical data reflects systemic biases, the models trained on it will inevitably learn and replicate those biases. For example, data drawn from criminal justice or emergency health services possibly over-represent marginalized communities due to factors like targeted policing or unequal access to primary healthcare, rather than reflecting any inherent predisposition to housing instability (Shaw et al., 2025). Consequently, predictive models might disproportionately flag individuals from these groups not because they are intrinsically more likely to become homeless, but because they are more visible to the systems generating the data. This act of forecasting future instability, based on a past shaped by systemic injustice, risks amplifying those injustices. In short, predictive modeling may improve efficiency, but without careful design and oversight, it can also entrench pre-existing biases under the guise of objectivity.

2.2 *Algorithmic Scoring and Ranking*

Building on predictive analytics, many housing-related systems employ algorithmic scoring and ranking to inform decisions. Tenant screening represents a widespread use of algorithmic scoring in the housing sector. Automated systems assess potential tenants based on factors like credit scores, income verification, eviction history, and criminal background checks, generating a score or recommendation (e.g., "accept," "accept with conditions," or "deny") for each applicant, which landlords or property managers use to make leasing decisions. Similarly, algorithms are employed by housing authorities or social service agencies to prioritize applicants for scarce resources, such as housing vouchers, subsidized units, or supportive services. These systems often calculate a 'vulnerability' or 'need' score based on various indicators, ranking applicants to determine their place on waiting lists or eligibility for specific programs. The purported advantages are increased speed, consistency, and objectivity compared to manual review processes.

Despite the appeal of efficiency and objectivity, algorithmic scoring systems are fraught with potential pitfalls. By design, they reduce complex human circumstances and multifaceted needs to a single (often opaque) numerical value. The choice of which input variables to include and how to weigh them embeds specific value judgments about what factors matter most—judgments that can inadvertently introduce or amplify bias. For instance, credit scores and eviction histories are often strongly correlated with race and income due to historical redlining, discriminatory lending practices, and economic inequality (Linde et al., 2023; Schneider, 2020). Criminal history and race reflect significant disparities in rental experiences, which are evident even among exonerees when they attempt to secure housing after release (Zannella et al., 2020). Using these factors heavily in a tenant screening score effectively encodes societal biases into the algorithm, meaning the resulting 'objective' score can produce discriminatory outcomes in practice.

A similar concern applies to scoring systems used for resource allocation: everything hinges on how concepts like "vulnerability" or "deservingness" are quantified. If an algorithmic formula prioritizes easily quantifiable indicators or those already captured in administrative databases, it may fail to account for more complex, intersectional needs. In one notable study on homelessness services, researchers developed a machine learning allocation system intended to minimize returns to homelessness (Kube et al., 2019); while it improved overall efficiency, they found that a significant fraction of households were algorithmically assigned to interventions that increased their risk of returning to homelessness, highlighting difficult trade-offs between efficiency and equity.

2.3 *Natural Language Processing (NLP)*

NLP is a branch of AI focused on enabling computers to understand, interpret, and generate human language. NLP techniques include methods like sentiment analysis (determining the emotional tone or attitude in text), topic modeling (discovering key themes in a large collection of documents), named entity recognition (extracting specific information such as names, locations, or dates from text), and machine translation (automatically translating text from one language to another), among others.

In the housing context, NLP can be applied to analyze large volumes of text that were previously difficult to review systematically. For example, property management companies or public agencies might use NLP tools to examine tenant communications—including emails, maintenance requests, complaint logs, and online reviews—to identify patterns and actionable insights. Furthermore, NLP methods have been used to develop models that identify overlooked case law regarding housing accessibility and eviction issues from extensive legal databases (Mohammadi et al., 2025). These applications facilitate a more comprehensive analysis of human rights jurisprudence related to housing. An NLP model might automatically flag recurring maintenance issues across multiple units or buildings, detect emerging disputes between tenants and landlords, gauge overall tenant sentiment or satisfaction, or even predict lease violations or the risk of eviction based on the content and tone of communications. Another potential application involves NLP-powered chatbots to handle routine inquiries—answering frequently asked questions about housing applications, eligibility criteria, lease terms, renters' rights, or available services. Such chatbots could provide quick, 24/7 responses and reduce the workload on housing office staff, theoretically improving responsiveness for tenants and applicants.

While NLP offers opportunities to extract insights from unstructured text data, its application in sensitive areas such as tenant communications raises significant concerns. The accuracy of NLP interpretation can be limited, particularly in nuance, sarcasm, language variations across cultures, and context-specific jargon, potentially leading to misinterpretations that could negatively affect tenants. More fundamentally, the systematic analysis of tenant communications constitutes surveillance, raising serious privacy concerns. Tenants may feel inhibited from raising legitimate concerns or complaints if they know their language is being algorithmically monitored and potentially used to assess them as "problematic." This chilling effect undermines open communication, which is vital for healthy landlord-tenant relationships and timely issue resolution. The collection and analysis of such personal communication data require robust safeguards against misuse and breaches, particularly given the sensitive nature of housing-related issues. Therefore, any benefits in efficiency must be weighed against the erosion of privacy and trust between tenants and housing providers.

2.4 Computer Vision

Computer vision involves training AI systems to interpret and understand information from digital images or videos. Techniques include object detection (identifying specific objects within an image), image classification (categorizing images based on content), and scene analysis (interpreting the context and relationships within an image).

In urban studies and housing policy, computer vision has been explored as a tool for analyzing large-scale visual datasets, such as satellite imagery, aerial photos, and publicly available street-level images (e.g., Google Street View). Algorithms can be trained to identify visual indicators associated with neighborhood conditions—such as building upkeep (are roofs and exteriors intact or in disrepair?), the presence of litter or graffiti (often labeled as signs of "blight"), the amount of green space or tree cover, the condition of roads and sidewalks, the presence of abandoned cars, and so on. For instance, a study used pre- and post-disaster satellite images to assess hurricane damage in Florida, a task that might be difficult to achieve solely through manual surveys (Weber & Kané, 2020). Also, a city could use computer vision to scan current satellite imagery and detect properties with specific risk factors (e.g., tarp-covered roofs or structural damage) to prioritize housing code inspections or repairs (Deng et al., 2022). Researchers used a combination of Google Street View imagery and satellite data, along with CNNs, to estimate property values in London. Features such as garden size and building condition explained 68% of the price variance, aiding equitable tax assessments (Law et al., 2019). This kind of urban visual intelligence could provide planners and policymakers with broad, data-driven insights into the physical environment relevant to housing stability and community well-being.

Despite these promising applications, relying on computer vision for neighborhood assessment carries inherent risks and limitations. Visual data alone provides an incomplete picture of community well-being, often overlooking crucial social factors such as community cohesion, informal support networks, and access to services—factors not visible in an image. Moreover, the interpretation of visual cues like "blight" or "disrepair" can be highly subjective and culturally biased. Algorithms trained on datasets labeled according to dominant aesthetic norms might unfairly penalize neighborhoods with different cultural expressions or predominantly lower-income areas, whose properties may look different but still provide stable homes. Such algorithmic assessments risk automating and scaling subjective judgments, potentially reinforcing spatial stigma and justifying disinvestment or gentrification pressures in areas algorithmically labeled as 'declining' based on superficial visual indicators. Without careful validation, ground-truthing, and consideration of context, computer vision analysis of neighborhoods could perpetuate, rather than challenge, spatial inequalities.

2.5 *Reinforcement Learning (RL)*

RL is a machine learning approach in which an AI agent learns optimal decision-making through environmental interaction and feedback, including rewards and penalties. Unlike traditional models using static datasets, RL employs a dynamic trial-and-error methodology: the agent acts, evaluates the outcome (including a reward signal indicating relative success), and progressively refines its strategy to maximize cumulative rewards. This approach has demonstrated efficacy across complex sequential decision-making tasks, including gaming, robotics, and resource allocation.

In the context of housing stability, while RL applications remain nascent, the potential is significant. Housing systems feature dynamic interactions—individuals navigating shelter systems, program applications, and market responses to policy changes—making them theoretically suitable for RL optimization. An RL model could be trained within agent-based simulations of eviction-prevention programs or homelessness systems to identify optimal intervention policies that minimize housing instability or improve resource allocation efficiency (Sarkar et al., 2024). Recent research in the UK incorporated RL algorithms into housing market simulations to analyze how the market adapts to economic disruptions (Olmez et al., 2024). Additionally, RL has demonstrated the capacity to design more equitable resource distribution frameworks, as evidenced by its application to optimize the geographic placement of refugees to enhance employment outcomes (Bansak et al., 2018). RL's ability to balance immediate and long-term rewards aligns well with policy planning requirements.

Nevertheless, RL implementation presents substantial challenges. The reward function, which defines success, requires meticulous design, as imprecise specifications can lead to unintended consequences. Furthermore, effective RL training necessitates simulation environments that accurately reflect real-world conditions, which proves especially difficult for complex social systems like housing. Biased or incomplete simulation data will inevitably lead to flawed RL policies. Finally, the decision-making processes of RL systems, similar to other sophisticated AI models, often lack transparency, potentially complicating accountability when determining why specific allocation strategies are recommended.

3 AI Applications and Differential Impacts by Population

Moving from general AI capabilities to their concrete use in the housing sector, this section examines how these technologies are being applied (or proposed) in real-world scenarios, with a focus on impacts across various at-risk populations and communities.

3.1 Homelessness Prevention and Support

One of the most prominent emerging applications of AI in this domain is the use of predictive models to prevent homelessness. AI-driven predictive analytics systems are being developed and deployed to identify individuals and families at high risk of homelessness, enabling preventive interventions before a crisis hits. These systems typically analyze large administrative datasets, drawing on a combination of data sources, including homeless shelter intakes, subsidized housing waitlists, interactions with social services, healthcare utilization (e.g., emergency room visits, mental health services), and, sometimes, encounters with the criminal justice system.

By detecting patterns (for example, a history of eviction filings or frequent address changes coupled with hospital visits), the model generates a risk score or flag for those it deems most likely to experience homelessness in the near future (Byrne et al., 2019; VanBerlo et al., 2021). Social service providers can then target outreach and support to high-risk individuals, offering case management, short-term financial assistance (such as help with rent or utility arrears), or referrals to programs, such as landlord mediation, before those individuals lose their current housing.

On the back end, such algorithms may also be used to optimize resource allocation for those already experiencing homelessness. For instance, if shelter beds or transitional housing units are limited, an algorithm might prioritize who should receive these resources by predicting which individuals would benefit most or have nowhere else to go (Kube et al., 2023). These efforts can shift the homelessness response from reactive to proactive and use data to deploy scarce resources in the most effective way possible. In Los Angeles County, for example, a pilot AI program called Housing for Health has been used to predict which residents are most likely to lose their housing and then provide financial assistance and services to those individuals. Early reports indicate that since 2021, the program has enrolled over 700 people identified by the algorithm, and about 86% of them have retained their housing, suggesting some success in preventing new homelessness cases (Kendall, 2024). Beyond the resource relocation, the UCLA California Policy Lab used an AI-powered predictive analytics system to identify individuals at the highest risk of homelessness. This system achieved nearly 3.5 times the accuracy of trained social workers.

3.2 *Natural Disaster Victims: AI for Disaster Risk Management and Resilient Housing*

Communities that are prone to natural disasters (such as hurricanes, floods, wildfires, or earthquakes) face unique risks to housing stability. In recent years, AI has been increasingly applied to disaster risk management, with implications for protecting housing and communities in hazard-prone areas (Sun et al., 2020). These applications are especially relevant for residents of disaster-prone regions, who are often among the most vulnerable to sudden homelessness or long-term displacement when disaster strikes.

One major use of AI here is in predictive forecasting and early warning systems. Machine learning models can be trained on vast datasets of weather patterns, geological data, and historical disaster impacts to improve the prediction of events such as floods, storms, and landslides (Zhu et al., 2019). For example, AI models have been developed that analyze meteorological data in real time to predict the likelihood and severity of extreme weather events (such as heavy rainfall leading to floods, drought, etc.) more accurately and earlier than traditional models (Adikari et al., 2021). By providing more timely and precise warnings, these AI systems enable at-risk residents to evacuate or reinforce their homes sooner, potentially saving lives and reducing housing damage. Early warning can be critical for low-income or elderly residents who need more time to move to safety.

Another application is risk mapping: AI can integrate diverse data (topography, soil, drainage, building characteristics, and socioeconomic data) to identify which neighborhoods or buildings are most vulnerable to future disasters. This information helps officials target pre-disaster mitigation efforts, such as strengthening infrastructure or prioritizing buildings for retrofits. Researchers at Texas A&M, for example, have used AI and Google Street View imagery to assess flood risk at a very local level, aiming to pinpoint community vulnerabilities that current broad flood maps might miss (Ho et al., 2024). By identifying that, the map also serves as a valuable supplement and reference to support forecasting extreme disasters, to shore up the community, or at least to ensure its residents have evacuation and recovery plans (Emami & Marzban, 2023).

AI is also being harnessed during and after disasters to aid response and recovery. Computer vision algorithms have been used on satellite and aerial imagery to rapidly assess damage after a disaster, for example, detecting which buildings are destroyed or uninhabitable in the aftermath of a flood or earthquake (Jing et al., 2022; Kim et al., 2022). This can significantly speed up damage assessments, allowing emergency managers to allocate shelter and repair resources to the hardest-hit areas without waiting for manual inspections of every structure. AI analysis of social media and emergency calls can likewise help first responders identify where people are trapped or in urgent need of help during an unfolding disaster (Imran et al., 2020). All these efforts contribute to stabilizing housing for survivors by getting aid where it is needed faster and moving affected individuals into stable housing.

3.3 Housing Service Applicant and Refugees: Resource Allocation for Housing Services

Housing and social service agencies often face the challenging task of allocating insufficient resources; housing vouchers, public housing units, and supportive program placements are consistently inadequate to meet the needs of all qualified applicants. Traditionally, allocation decisions—determining priority access and waitlist positioning—have relied on first-come-first-served approaches, categorical preferences (such as prioritizing families with children or veterans), and individual caseworker judgment. However, the sector is increasingly exploring AI and algorithmic solutions to manage resource distribution more systematically and to prioritize applicants based on assessed need or anticipated benefit (Chui et al., 2018; Yigitcanlar et al., 2020). Consider a public housing authority with 100 rental vouchers available for 1000 eligible applicants. An algorithmic ranking system could assign each applicant a comprehensive vulnerability score to determine assistance priority. This score might incorporate multiple factors, including current housing status (homeless, doubled-up, cost-burdened), income-to-poverty ratio, number of dependents, health conditions, disability status, and application longevity. In theory, this approach promotes consistency through standardized evaluation criteria and enhances efficiency by directing limited resources to the most urgent cases, potentially preventing further hardship.

Real-world implementations include coordinated entry systems for homelessness services that use standardized assessment tools to generate vulnerability scores that guide program placements (Kube et al., 2023). Some jurisdictions are enhancing these systems with machine learning models that predict the specific interventions most likely to prevent individuals from returning to homelessness, allocating resources accordingly. During the COVID-19 pandemic, government entities such as the Colorado Division of Housing, faced with unprecedented demand for emergency rental assistance, employed algorithms to evaluate and prioritize applicants in cohorts, aiming to identify those with the greatest need and highest likelihood of successful outcomes while ensuring equitable distribution across neighborhoods and demographic groups (Chuang, 2021). AI applications also extend to refugee housing allocation, supporting the development of adequate low-income housing solutions to prevent slum formation (Marji & Kohout, 2023) while simultaneously enhancing employment opportunities (Bansak et al., 2018; Ahani et al., 2021).

3.4 Tenant Screening and Housing Access: AI Systems, Eviction Risk, and Demographic Disparities

The adoption of automated tenant screening software represents one of the most pervasive and consequential applications of artificial intelligence within the housing market. Property managers and landlords increasingly use these technological tools to evaluate prospective tenants more efficiently. These screening systems aggregate and analyze comprehensive data from multiple sources—credit reports, eviction histories in public records databases, criminal background checks, income verification services, and occasionally social media platforms or third-party data brokers. Upon processing this information, the software generates an applicant assessment in the form of a numerical score, a rating, or a categorical recommendation (e.g., approve, deny, or approve with additional conditions).

From the property owner's perspective, these automated systems offer significant operational advantages through accelerated processing capabilities and perceived objectivity—applications can be evaluated within minutes, ostensibly reducing the risk of leasing to individuals who might default on rental payments or create management challenges. However, the widespread implementation of algorithmic tenant screening potentially erects substantial barriers to housing accessibility, particularly affecting historically disadvantaged populations (Schneider, 2020).

Beyond individual tenant screening, artificial intelligence applications now extend to property-level eviction risk prediction by integrating diverse datasets, including spatiotemporal public records and municipal data. By synthesizing neighborhood characteristics, property ownership data, and historical eviction patterns, these predictive models enable social service professionals to target at-risk households more strategically, thereby enhancing intervention efficiency and effectiveness (Robb et al., 2022; Mashiat et al., 2024). Nevertheless, these eviction records and predictions can simultaneously function as mechanisms for applicant exclusion or tenant stigmatization. Research employing natural language processing to extract and analyze nationwide eviction filings from court records has uncovered systematic inequities, including unlawful eviction proceedings and disproportionately elevated eviction rates among non-English-speaking tenant populations (Thomas et al., 2024).

4 Cross-Cutting Ethical, Social, and Governance Issues

The specific applications we have examined point toward several recurring, cross-cutting themes that demand deeper reflection. These themes relate to the fundamental nature of algorithmic bias, the challenges of transparency and accountability, data privacy and surveillance implications, the complexities of human-AI interaction in decision-making, and the critical role of power dynamics and community participation in shaping technological outcomes. In this section, we synthesize broader issues that cut across the specific use cases to understand the societal and ethical stakes involved in deploying AI in the sensitive domain of housing stability.

4.1 Algorithmic Bias and Fairness Challenges

A central theme emerging from the previous section is that algorithmic bias is not merely an occasional error but a systemic issue often deeply embedded in AI systems used in the housing context. This bias arises when AI systems learn from data that reflects existing societal inequities. From homelessness prediction to tenant screening, we have seen how algorithms trained on historical data that reflects society's inequities will inevitably reproduce those inequities. The data itself is not neutral, and it captures past and present discrimination in policing, lending, healthcare access, and housing patterns. Consequently, even if AI models do not explicitly use protected characteristics such as race, they can still produce discriminatory outcomes. This occurs through reliance on proxy variables—like zip codes, income levels, criminal records, or even names—that correlate strongly with sensitive traits. For example, a tenant screening algorithm might exclude race as a direct input. Yet, if it heavily weighs credit scores, criminal histories, and prior evictions—factors already influenced by systemic racial disparities—the algorithm will likely yield disproportionately harmful outcomes for minority or low-income applicants, effectively engaging in proxy discrimination.

Addressing such pervasive bias is a complex, twofold challenge: first, to minimize bias within AI systems themselves, and second, to address the societal biases AI observes. For the former, AI practitioners are developing technical "debiasing" methods, conducting bias audits before and during deployment (which involve examining error rates and outcomes across demographic groups), incorporating domain experts and affected communities in defining fairness criteria, and implementing safeguards like removing specific inputs or using post-processing techniques to balance outcomes. Regulatory bodies are also increasingly considering algorithmic accountability laws that would mandate impact assessments for bias in high-stakes AI systems.

The latter challenge—eliminating bias from the world AI observes—is a broader societal endeavor. For communities at risk, it is crucial that any AI deployed in housing actively counteracts historical injustices rather than inadvertently perpetuating them. Achieving this requires robust interdisciplinary collaboration: technologists must work alongside substantive experts, legal experts, and the affected communities to define fair outcomes and continuously adapt systems toward these goals.

4.2 *Transparency, Explainability, and Accountability*

Another cross-cutting concern is the lack of transparency and explainability surrounding many AI systems used in housing decisions. Whether due to the inherent complexity of machine learning models ("black box" algorithms issue) or the protection of proprietary algorithms, the reasoning behind automated decisions is often opaque to those affected by them. This problem, in context, is that there is no explanation for tenant screening rejections or for resource allocation priorities. This opacity poses fundamental challenges to accountability and procedural justice in housing. When individuals cannot understand why a decision impacting their housing stability was made, they are effectively denied the ability to identify potential errors, contest unfair biases, or meaningfully exercise their right to appeal. This lack of transparency is not merely a technical inconvenience; it undermines fundamental principles of due process, particularly when basic needs are at stake.

Meaningful transparency requires not only open-sourcing code but also explanations understandable to non-experts that detail how specific inputs led to a particular outcome. Different levels of explanation may be needed for various audiences, ranging from understanding the system's general logic to obtaining a specific rationale for an individual decision. Achieving this is not trivial, of course, especially for complex machine learning models that even their creators might struggle to interpret precisely.

Furthermore, even if explanations are provided, effective recourse requires accessible and timely mechanisms for appeal and correction. Without robust transparency and avenues for redress, AI systems risk operating as unaccountable arbiters of housing opportunity, disproportionately harming vulnerable individuals who often lack the resources or technical literacy to challenge opaque algorithmic decisions. This is particularly problematic for vulnerable individuals who often lack resources or technical literacy to navigate complicated systems. Suppose the computer's logic is secret or unintelligible. In that case, it may be hard to hold anyone accountable and accept the denial as final, even if it was in error or unfair. The right to shelter is so fundamental that any decision-making process must be seen as legitimate and fair.

4.3 Data Privacy, Surveillance, and Data Governance

The deployment of AI systems in the housing sector relies heavily on the collection and analysis of vast amounts of personal data. Whether this involves individual financial, health, and behavioral data for predictive modeling and tenant screening, or aggregated data on communities and properties for neighborhood analysis, the drive to enhance algorithmic performance often leads to more expansive and potentially invasive data-gathering practices. This trend raises significant concerns regarding privacy, informed consent, and effective data governance, particularly when applied to vulnerable populations who may have limited capacity to refuse data collection due to their need for assistance or housing.

Consider the types of data we discussed: homeless service databases may contain detailed personal histories, including interactions with shelters and outreach services, as well as information on mental health or substance use. Tenant screening processes access credit reports, criminal records, and eviction histories. Resource allocation algorithms might utilize health records or disability status. Furthermore, neighborhood surveillance for monitoring purposes can capture images or sensor data from public spaces that inadvertently record individuals' daily activities.

The aggregation of such extensive personal data into centralized systems creates substantial risks, including data breaches and misuse. There is also the prevalent risk of "function creep," where data collected for a specific, stated purpose is later repurposed for unrelated uses without individuals' explicit consent. Marginalized communities have historically been disproportionately subjected to such practices and heightened surveillance. These privacy risks are particularly acute for at-risk individuals because they often face a coercive dynamic. For example, accessing essential services like rental assistance may be contingent on signing broad data-release forms, effectively trading privacy for basic needs.

To mitigate these dangers, robust data governance frameworks are indispensable. Such frameworks should include clear rules on data minimization (collecting only what is strictly necessary for the defined purpose), purpose limitation (using data solely for its original purpose unless new, informed consent is obtained), and secure data storage and handling procedures to protect against breaches. Strict limitations on data sharing, especially between different agencies and with law enforcement (unless mandated by due legal process), are crucial to prevent function creep. Furthermore, individuals whose data is used in algorithmic decision-making should have the right to access, review, and correct their data, a principle closely tied to transparency and accountability. Without these comprehensive safeguards, the increasing datafication driven by AI adoption could significantly erode privacy, expand surveillance, and further marginalize already vulnerable populations.

4.4 Human Agency, Oversight, and Automation Bias

Given the complexities and potential biases in AI decision-making within the housing sector, a frequently proposed safeguard is the integration of "human-in-the-loop" systems. This approach ensures that human judgment and oversight remain integral to AI-driven processes. Theoretically, human case workers, housing officers, or managers can complement algorithmic recommendations by applying contextual understanding, empathy, and the ability to identify errors or extenuating circumstances that an algorithm might overlook. For instance, if an algorithm deems an applicant ineligible for a housing program, a human reviewer could investigate further, potentially uncovering data errors or specific situations not accounted for by the model.

However, achieving meaningful human oversight in practice is challenging and not automatically guaranteed by simply including a human in the process. A significant hurdle is "automation bias"—the documented human tendency to over-trust or unduly defer to automated systems' suggestions, even when these suggestions may be flawed. In high-pressure environments like busy housing offices, staff might treat algorithmic outputs (e.g., risk scores or eligibility recommendations) as definitive and approve them without thorough scrutiny, particularly if they face time constraints or staffing levels have been reduced under the assumption that AI is efficient. This can lead to an "automation paradox": while a human is theoretically in the loop, their practical reliance on automation can diminish the value and effectiveness of their oversight.

For human-in-the-loop oversight to be genuinely effective, several conditions are essential. First, human reviewers require adequate training to understand the AI system's functionality, strengths, and limitations, and the true implications of its outputs. Access to information is also critical; reviewers should understand the rationale behind an algorithm's conclusion (linking back to transparency and explainability) and be able to consider supplementary details not included in the algorithm's dataset. Furthermore, sufficient time and resources must be allocated for thoughtful review; perfunctory oversight due to excessive workloads will not be meaningful.

Crucially, human reviewers must possess the authority and organizational support to override algorithmic recommendations when appropriate, without fear of negative repercussions. If an organization discourages or penalizes staff for deviating from AI-generated suggestions, the oversight function becomes performative. Conversely, if overriding the algorithm is accepted and even encouraged in suitable situations, human judgment can serve as a vital check. Policies could mandate, for example, that any application denied by an algorithm undergoes automatic human review before final rejection, or that humans randomly audit a certain percentage of all algorithmic decisions (approvals and denials) to detect errors.

In summary, while maintaining a human presence in AI-driven housing decisions is necessary, it is not, by itself, sufficient to ensure fairness and accuracy. The implementation must thoughtfully empower human judgment rather than marginalizing it. This requires careful design of the human-AI interface, comprehensive training programs, and clear protocols for decision-making and appeals to ensure that human agency is preserved and enhanced, not undermined by automation.

4.5 Power Asymmetries and Community Participation

A fundamental cross-cutting issue in the deployment of AI systems within the housing sector is the inherent power imbalance among stakeholders. Those typically driving AI adoption—technology companies, government agencies seeking efficiencies, or large property management firms—often possess significantly more power, resources, and technical expertise than the tenants, applicants, and community members whose lives are directly impacted by these systems. This asymmetry can shape which priorities are encoded into AI systems, whose values are reflected in their design, and which concerns are addressed and which are overlooked. Consequently, AI systems may be developed in a top-down manner, prioritizing institutional goals such as efficiency, cost savings, and risk management, potentially without adequate regard for residents' needs and rights, including secure housing, dignity, and autonomy.

Inclusive design principles and meaningful community participation are increasingly recognized as essential correctives to these power imbalances. The core idea is that individuals most affected by an AI system—for example, public housing residents subject to new monitoring technologies, or homeless individuals whose data informs risk prediction models—should have a significant, empowered voice throughout the technology's lifecycle. This includes problem identification, system design and testing, deployment, and ongoing governance and oversight. Such participation must extend beyond tokenistic gestures, such as superficial focus groups; it requires genuine power-sharing in decision-making.

Achieving meaningful community participation involves overcoming several challenges. Firstly, bridging the knowledge gap is crucial; communities may require resources and support to understand complex AI technologies and their potential impacts, enabling them to engage as informed and equal partners. This could involve public education initiatives or funding for community organizations to access independent technical expertise. Secondly, participation must be early and continuous, not merely an afterthought or consultation once a system is already developed; belated input often cannot substantively alter core design choices.

Moreover, community input must have tangible influence, leading to fundamental changes in system design or deployment decisions, rather than being a procedural checkbox. This may require agencies to be willing to halt or significantly modify AI deployments in response to strong community opposition or concerns. It could also involve granting community oversight bodies the authority to audit AI systems or even mandate their discontinuation if they prove harmful.

This participatory approach is not only ethically imperative but can also lead to more effective and equitable outcomes by diversifying the perspectives involved in problem-solving and system design. Building trust is a key benefit; if communities perceive that AI systems are developed with their input and genuinely serve their needs, rather than primarily functioning as tools for surveillance or control, then acceptance and collaboration are more likely.

5 Conclusion

This chapter has critically examined AI's role in housing for at-risk communities, revealing a landscape where promised efficiencies often collide with significant ethical risks. Key findings highlight that AI systems, by ingesting data reflecting societal biases, can amplify inequities related to race, income, and disability. This can create new barriers to housing, unfairly target vulnerable groups, and undermine due process due to opaque algorithms. The extensive data required also raises serious privacy and surveillance concerns, particularly for marginalized populations.

The central argument is that a critical, human-centered, and equity-focused approach is vital. Technological solutions must be rigorously weighed against potential harm to fairness, justice, and human dignity, and inherently balanced with human knowledge and experience. This necessitates independent research on AI's real-world impacts, including bias audits and the development of context-aware fairness frameworks. Stronger regulatory oversight is needed, mandating transparency, accountability, non-discrimination, and robust data protection. Housing agencies and practitioners must prioritize ethical guidelines, ongoing monitoring for bias, staff training on AI limitations, and meaningful community participation in the deployment of technology.

Ultimately, AI is a tool; its value in addressing housing instability hinges on its alignment with principles of equity and justice. Without such commitment, AI risks entrenching disadvantages rather than fostering the right to safe, stable housing for all.

Competing Interests The authors have no conflicts of interest to declare that are relevant to the content of this chapter.

References

Adikari, K. E., Shrestha, S., Ratnayake, D. T., Budhathoki, A., Mohanasundaram, S., & Dailey, M. N. (2021). Evaluation of artificial intelligence models for flood and drought forecasting in arid and tropical regions. *Environmental Modelling & Software, 144*, 105136.

Ahani, N., Andersson, T., Martinello, A., Teytelboym, A., & Trapp, A. C. (2021). Placement optimization in refugee resettlement. *Operations Research, 69*(5), 1468–1486.

Anyanwu, C., & Beyer, K. M. (2024). Intersections among housing, environmental conditions, and health equity: a conceptual model for environmental justice policy. *Social Sciences & Humanities Open, 9*, 100845.

Bansak, K., Ferwerda, J., Hainmueller, J., Dillon, A., Hangartner, D., Lawrence, D., & Weinstein, J. (2018). Improving refugee integration through data-driven algorithmic assignment. *Science, 359*(6373), 325–329.

Bashir, S. A. (2022). Home is where the harm is: Inadequate housing as a public health crisis: American Journal of Public Health, 2002. In *The Affordable Housing Reader (pp. 123-129).* Routledge.

Bhat, A. C., Almeida, D. M., Fenelon, A., & Santos-Lozada, A. R. (2022). A longitudinal analysis of the relationship between housing insecurity and physical health among midlife and aging adults in the United States. *SSM-Population Health, 18*, 101128.

Byrne, T., Montgomery, A. E., & Fargo, J. D. (2019). Predictive modeling of housing instability and homelessness in the Veterans Health Administration. *Health services research, 54*(1), 75–85.

Chui, M., Harryson, M., Valley, S., Manyika, J., & Roberts, R. (2018). *Notes from the AI frontier applying AI for social good.*

Chuang T. (2021, October 25) *Colorado's COVID rent-assistance program may have paid up to $4.4 million in error, audit finds.* The Colorado Sun https://coloradosun.com/2021/10/25/pandemic-rent-assistance-covid-error-auditor-landlord/

Deng, J., Singh, A., Zhou, Y., Lu, Y., & Lee, V. C. S. (2022). Review on computer vision-based crack detection and quantification methodologies for civil structures. *Construction and Building Materials, 356*, 129238.

Emami, P., & Marzban, A. (2023). The synergy of artificial intelligence (AI) and geographic information systems (GIS) for enhanced disaster management: opportunities and challenges. *Disaster Medicine and Public Health Preparedness, 17*, e507.

Ho, Y. H., Lee, C. C., Diaz, N., Brody, S., & Mostafavi, A. (2024). Elev-vision: Automated lowest floor elevation estimation from segmenting street view images. *ACM Journal on Computing and Sustainable Societies, 2*(2), 1–18.

Gu, K. D., Faulkner, K. C., & Thorndike, A. N. (2023). Housing instability and cardiometabolic health in the United States: a narrative review of the literature. *BMC Public Health, 23*(1), 931.

Huang, T., Dai, T., Wang, Z., Yoon, H., Sheng, H., Ng, A. Y., et al. (2022). Detecting neighborhood gentrification at scale via street-level visual data. In *2022 IEEE International Conference on Big Data (Big Data)* (pp. 1632–1640). IEEE.

Imran, M., Ofli, F., Caragea, D., & Torralba, A. (2020). Using AI and social media multimodal content for disaster response and management: Opportunities, challenges, and future directions. *Information Processing & Management, 57*(5), 102261.

Jing, Y., Ren, Y., Liu, Y., Wang, D., & Yu, L. (2022). Automatic extraction of damaged houses by earthquake based on improved YOLOv5: A case study in Yangbi. *Remote Sensing, 14*(2), 382.

Keene, D. E., & Blankenship, K. M. (2023). The affordable rental housing crisis and population health equity: A multidimensional and multilevel framework. *Journal of Urban Health, 100*(6), 1212–1223.

Kendall, M. (2024, March 6) *This California county is testing AI's ability to prevent homelessness* https://calmatters.org/housing/homelessness/2024/03/california-homeless-los-angeles-ai/

Kim, D., Won, J., Lee, E., Park, K. R., Kim, J., Park, S., et al. (2022). Disaster assessment using computer vision and satellite imagery: Applications in detecting water-related building damages. *Frontiers in Environmental Science, 10*, 969758.

Kube, A., Das, S., & Fowler, P. J. (2019). Allocating interventions based on predicted outcomes: A case study on homelessness services. In *Proceedings of the AAAI Conference on Artificial Intelligence* (Vol. 33, No. 01, pp. 622-629).

Kube, A. R., Das, S., & Fowler, P. J. (2023). Community-and data-driven homelessness prevention and service delivery: optimizing for equity. *Journal of the American Medical Informatics Association, 30*(6), 1032–1041.

Law, S., Paige, B., & Russell, C. (2019). Take a look around: using street view and satellite images to estimate house prices. *ACM Transactions on Intelligent Systems and Technology (TIST), 10*(5), 1–19.

Linde, S., Walker, R. J., Campbell, J. A., & Egede, L. E. (2023). Historic residential redlining and present-day social determinants of health, home evictions, and food insecurity within US neighborhoods. *Journal of General Internal Medicine, 38*(15), 3321–3328.

Marji, N., & Kohout, M. (2023). Optimizing the Spatial Organization of Refugee Camps in Jordan Through Artificial Intelligence. In *World Congress of Architects* (pp. 393–404). Springer International Publishing.

Mashiat, T., DiChristofano, A., Fowler, P. J., & Das, S. (2024, June). Beyond eviction prediction: Leveraging local spatiotemporal public records to inform action. In *Proceedings of the 2024 ACM Conference on Fairness, Accountability, and Transparency* (pp. 1383-1394).

Mohammadi, M., Wieling, M., & Vols, M. (2025). An interpretable approach to detect case law on housing and eviction issues within the HUDOC database. *Artificial Intelligence and Law*, 1–22.

Nyamathi, A. M., & Salem, B. E. (2021). The impact of unstable housing on health. *The Lancet Public Health, 6*(5), e265–e266.

Olawade, D. B., Wada, O. J., David-Olawade, A. C., Kunonga, E., Abaire, O., & Ling, J. (2023). Using artificial intelligence to improve public health: a narrative review. *Frontiers in Public Health, 11*, 1196397.

Olmez, S., Heppenstall, A., Ge, J., Elsenbroich, C., & Birks, D. (2024). Mitigating housing market shocks: an agentbased reinforcement learning approach with implications for real-time decision support. *Journal of Simulation*, 18(6), 921–939.

Robb, K., Amigo, N. D., Marcoux, A., McAteer, M., & De Jong, J. (2022). Using integrated city data and machine learning to identify and intervene early on housing-related public health problems. *Journal of Public Health Management and Practice, 28*(2), E497–E505.

Sarkar, A., DiChristofano, A., Das, S., Fowler, P. J., Jacobs, N., & Vorobeychik, Y. (2024, May). Geospatial active search for preventing evictions. In *Proceedings of the 23rd International Conference on Autonomous Agents and Multiagent Systems* (pp. 2456-2458).

Schneider, V. (2020). Locked out by big data: how big data algorithms and machine learning may undermine housing justice. *Columbia Human Rights Law Review, 52*, 251.

Shaw, C., Janeway, H., Preston-Suni, K., & Ryus, C. R. (2025). Exploring the complexity of homelessness in emergency medicine: Dissecting myths, evidence, and solutions. *AEM Education and Training, 9*, S108–S115.

Sun, W., Bocchini, P., & Davison, B. D. (2020). Applications of artificial intelligence for disaster management. *Natural Hazards, 103*(3), 2631–2689.

Thomas, T., Ramiller, A., Ren, C., & Toomet, O. (2024). Toward a national eviction data collection strategy using natural language processing. *Cityscape, 26*(1), 241–260.

VanBerlo, B., Ross, M. A., Rivard, J., & Booker, R. (2021). Interpretable machine learning approaches to prediction of chronic homelessness. *Engineering Applications of Artificial Intelligence, 102*, 104243.

Weber, E., & Kané, H. (2020). Building disaster damage assessment in satellite imagery with multi-temporal fusion. *arXiv.* https://arxiv.org/abs/2004.05525

Yigitcanlar, T., Desouza, K. C., Butler, L., & Roozkhosh, F. (2020). Contributions and risks of artificial intelligence (AI) in building smarter cities: Insights from a systematic review of the literature. *Energies, 13*(6), 1473.

Zannella, L., Clow, K., Rempel, E., Hamovitch, L., & Hall, V. (2020). The effects of race and criminal history on landlords'(un) willingness to rent to exonerees. *Law and Human Behavior, 44*(4), 300.

Zhu, X., Zhang, G., & Sun, B. (2019). A comprehensive literature review of the demand forecasting methods of emergency resources from the perspective of artificial intelligence. *Natural Hazards, 97*, 65–82.

Chapter 14
AI in Criminal Justice and Rehabilitation

Eunhye Ahn and Beth Angell

1 Introduction

The growing integration of artificial intelligence (AI) in U.S. criminal justice demands thoughtful evaluation from social workers, because these systems deeply affect individuals, families, and communities while intersecting with economic inequality, racial disparities, mental health issues, and housing insecurity. Social work plays a pivotal role at these intersections with a holistic, person-in-environment perspective, recognizing that an individual's criminal behavior and system involvement may stem from untreated mental illness, addiction, financial insecurity, trauma, or lack of support (Pettus-Davis & Epperson, 2015). Social workers seek to address these root causes to decrease system engagement and support rehabilitation. They also recognize the systemic injustices that contribute to crime, from structural racism to social service gaps, and advocate change. Whether working with justice-involved individuals, victims, family members of those involved in the system, or communities, social workers bring a focus on rehabilitation, prevention, and social justice that complements the legal system's emphasis on accountability (Butters & Vaughan-Eden, 2011; Sheehan, 2012).

Given the intimate relationship between criminal justice and social work, the rapid integration of AI and data analytics into the justice systems demand close and critical attention from the social work profession. These technological developments have emerged primarily from computer science, statistics, and legal domains, with little involvement of social work despite its central role in criminal justice rehabilitation and support services. Current AI applications range from predictive

E. Ahn (✉)
School of Human Ecology, University of Wisconsin-Madison, Madison, MI, USA
e-mail: eunhye.ahn@wisc.edu

B. Angell
School of Social Work, University of Michigan–Ann Arbor, Ann Arbor, MI, USA
e-mail: bangell@umich.edu

R. An, M. A. Lindsey (eds.), *Artificial Intelligence in Social Work*,
https://doi.org/10.1007/978-3-032-18443-6_14

policing algorithms that inform patrol deployments to risk assessment instruments used in pre-trial release, sentencing, and community supervision decisions (Silverman, 2023; U.S. Department of Justice, 2024). These technological developments have generated significant debate regarding fairness and ethics, particularly because these tools directly affect vulnerable populations (Angwin et al., 2016; Chouldechova, 2017; Corbett-Davies et al., 2017). The central concern extends beyond technical bias in algorithms to whether AI systems trained on historical criminal justice data inevitably reproduce, or potentially amplify, the structural racism and disparities long documented in U.S. criminal justice systems (Neil & Zanger-Tishler, 2025).

2 Social Work, Criminal and Juvenile Justice, and Rehabilitation

To understand how social work interventions are typically used in criminal justice and rehabilitation systems, it is helpful to have a basic overview of the system's process. The U.S. criminal justice system is a complex network of agencies and processes designed to control crime and impose penalties on those who violate laws. Understanding this system is essential for social workers who operate in this domain, because they often serve as bridges between justice-involved individuals and the services they need to rehabilitate and reintegrate into society.

2.1 U.S. Criminal and Juvenile Justice System

As of 2021, the United States held approximately 1.8 million people in prison and jails—a rate of 531 per 100,000—significantly exceeding other Western nations (Fair & Walmsley, 2024). Mass incarceration in the United States is deeply connected to structural racism, which systematically disadvantages racial minorities, particularly Black Americans (Lee, 2024). Despite comprising only 13% of the U.S. population, Black people account for 34% of those held in local jails, an incarceration rate more than three times that of White people and are disproportionately represented throughout all levels of the justice system, perpetuating racial disparities and adversely affecting individual and community well-being (Zeng & Minton, 2021).

Mass incarceration significantly affects families and communities, with more than 2.7 million children impacted by parental incarceration (Ghandnoosh et al., 2021). Many women serving prison sentences were primary caregivers before sentencing (Kendrick, 2024), and their incarceration can profoundly disrupt family dynamics and negatively affect children's emotional and social development (Miller, 2006). Structural inequalities are further intensified by the school-to-prison pipeline, which disproportionately channels marginalized youth into the juvenile justice system, limiting their opportunities and contributing to ongoing cycles of disadvantage (Hinton & Cook, 2021; Mallett, 2016). Mental health and substance use disorders are common among individuals involved with the justice system. Approximately 44% of people in jail have a diagnosed mental illness, and 63% face challenges with substance use disorders (Bronson & Berzofsky, 2017; Substance Abuse and Mental Health Services Administration, 2024). The justice system's fragmented structure often disrupts treatment, adversely affecting continuity of care as people transition through the system, such as from incarceration to community reentry (Reingle Gonzalez & Connell, 2014). Furthermore, marginalized populations, including individuals experiencing homelessness (Herbert et al., 2015), those who identify as LGBTQ+ (Brown & Jenness, 2020), immigrants, veterans (Blonigen et al., 2016), and people with intellectual disabilities (Salekin et al., 2010), face compounded structural challenges. These groups typically encounter inadequate resources and persistent barriers when navigating service systems.

The criminal justice process follows a relatively standard sequence of events, though procedures can vary across jurisdictions. The process begins when a crime is reported or observed by law enforcement. An investigation follows, which may lead to an arrest if sufficient evidence exists. However, many reported crimes remain unsolved or result in no arrest. Once arrested, a suspect faces an initial appearance before a judge. Charges are filed and decisions are made about pretrial release, including whether to grant bail or order detention. Some cases may be diverted at this stage through programs that offer alternatives to traditional prosecution. Adjudication involves formal court proceedings to determine guilt. It includes arraignment, where charges are formally presented, followed by either a trial or plea negotiations. Cases may be dismissed, or defendants may be acquitted or convicted. If convicted, the individual receives a sentence that may include incarceration in jail or prison, probation, fines, or other sanctions depending on the severity of the offense and individual factors. The final phase encompasses the implementation of a sentence, whether in an institutional setting like jail or prison or community supervision such as probation or parole. It also includes reentry services when individuals transition back to the community after incarceration.

The juvenile justice system operates as a parallel structure with similar stages but different terminology and a stronger emphasis on rehabilitation rather than punishment. For example, juvenile proceedings use terms like "adjudication" rather than "conviction" and "disposition" instead of "sentencing," reflecting the system's theoretical focus on the best interests of the child.

2.2 *Social Work Interventions in the Criminal Justice System*

Throughout this process, social work interventions typically occur at multiple points. Social workers serve as partners across the criminal justice continuum, engaging at critical intervention points including diversion programs, probation services, institutional rehabilitation, and re-entry support (Dowden & Andrews, 2004;

Sheehan, 2012). In the justice system, social workers perform comprehensive assessments, deliver mental health services, facilitate substance abuse treatment, and link justice-involved individuals with community resources while implementing evidence-based practices to reduce recidivism and promote rehabilitation (Ward & Maruna, 2007). Their involvement often begins before formal entry into the system through diversion initiatives that redirect individuals, particularly those with mental illness, substance use disorders, or minor offenses, toward treatment rather than incarceration (Lamberti, 2016). As clients navigate the system, social workers in probation settings balance surveillance requirements with case management services whereas those in correctional facilities offer therapeutic programming, crisis intervention, and family support that mitigate the harmful effects of institutional confinement (Patterson, 2019). During the challenging transition from incarceration to community, social workers coordinate comprehensive reentry planning addressing employment, housing, healthcare, and continued treatment needs (Andrews & Bonta, 2010; Jonson & Cullen, 2015).

3 AI in Criminal Justice and Rehabilitation

Advancements in AI, especially in machine learning and data analytics, are transforming the criminal justice system by enhancing efficiency, predictive accuracy, and consistency across various stages—from policing and pretrial processes to sentencing, corrections, and reentry. At the same time, these technologies raise critical ethical and human rights concerns related to bias, transparency, and fairness that require a human-centered approach. This section provides a concise overview of historical and current AI applications in criminal justice and rehabilitation, drawing on real-world case studies. It explores these applications at key stages: policing and investigation, arrest and pretrial processes, sentencing, probation and parole, and rehabilitation and reentry, including some cases in the juvenile justice systems—noting the goals of these tools and evidence of their impacts.

3.1 AI in Policing and Investigation

Predictive policing emerged as one of the earliest and most contested applications of AI in law enforcement. Although there is no comprehensive federal definition of predictive policing, local jurisdictions have defined it as the use of computer algorithms to forecast crime trends (Silverman, 2023). Bratton and Malinowski (2008) popularized this concept, describing how these systems analyze crime data, such as incident times, locations, and offense types, to identify potential "hot spots" or people of interest, with the goal of optimizing resource allocation and crime prevention. For instance, PredPol (rebranded as Geolitica) generated daily risk maps to guide patrol deployments. In Plainfield, New Jersey, the system's real-world performance revealed significant limitations—fewer than 0.5% of predictions corresponded to actual crimes, with more than 99% of forecasts failing to materialize (Sankin & Mattu, 2023). More troublingly, researchers found that the system consistently directed police away from predominantly White neighborhoods while heavily targeting areas with higher Black and Latino populations. These performance and bias concerns led to its termination in Plainfield and similarly contributed to the discontinuation of related initiatives in other cities (Sankin & Mattu, 2023).

In Los Angeles, early experiments with predictive policing included Operation LASER, launched in 2011. Utilizing software from Palantir to create a "chronic offender score" based on criminal history, social media activity, and license plates, LASER was initially heralded as a breakthrough. However, investigations revealed that the technology reinforced policing biases and obscured the actual impact of its data-driven decisions, leading to its shutdown in 2019 (Thomas, 2024). Chicago's experience further underscores these issues. Starting in 2012, the city's "heat list"—an algorithm designed to predict criminal involvement—disproportionately targeted Black men and was ultimately discontinued in 2019 following inspector general concerns (Charles, 2020).

Facial recognition technology has also become a prominent tool in AI-powered policing. Agencies compile extensive databases from mugshots, driver's licenses, and social media images to identify suspects. The technology's limitations became evident in 2020 when Robert Williams, a Black man in Detroit, was wrongfully arrested after an incorrect system match to a surveillance image of a shoplifter (Hill, 2024). Detroit has experienced at least two additional mistaken arrests of Black men, reflecting broader research showing these systems are less accurate for women and people with darker skin tones (Buolamwini & Gebru, 2018). In response, the Detroit Police Department (2024) revised its policies, prohibiting arrests based solely on facial recognition matches. Officers must now secure independent corroborating evidence, such as location data or DNA, before making an arrest.

Among facial recognition surveillance technologies, Clearview AI has emerged as the most controversial and troubling example. Founded in 2016 by Hoan Ton-That with early funding from Palantir co-founder Peter Thiel, Clearview AI's business model represents an unprecedented invasion of privacy (Hill, 2023). The company has amassed a staggering database of more than 30 billion facial images by scraping photos from social media platforms, all without users' consent or knowledge. Clearview AI has continued its aggressive data harvesting practices, operating primarily outside meaningful regulatory oversight.

Automated surveillance tools extend beyond facial recognition. Automated license plate readers scan thousands of plates per minute to identify stolen or wanted vehicles, while simultaneously generating comprehensive databases that track the movement of citizens (Finklea, 2024). Recent legislative efforts in multiple states have aimed to restrict data retention practices for these plate readers, yet the technology remains widely in use (Dattani, 2022). Acoustic gunshot detection systems like ShotSpotter are now active in more than 100 U.S. cities. These systems use sound pattern recognition to pinpoint gunfire; however, reports indicate false positive rates as high as 99% in some areas, with the technology often mistaking other sounds, such as fireworks or backfiring cars, for gunshots (Kang & Hudson, 2024). Moreover, ShotSpotter's deployment is heavily concentrated in predominantly Black and Latino neighborhoods, raising significant concerns about racial bias. In Chicago, for example, false alerts have led to wrongful arrests and strained community–police relations, prompting class action lawsuits against the system (Burke et al., 2022). More recently, Chicago ended its contract with ShotSpotter after research and activism highlighted its unjust outcomes (Thomas, 2024).

One prominent example of surveillance technology is the New York Police Department's Domain Awareness System (New York Police Department, 2021). This tool operates with more than 25,500 closed-circuit surveillance cameras across New York (Amnesty International, 2022) and integrates real-time video, license plate data, and gunshot detection alerts acoustic sensors to help detectives piece together events and track suspects. Although the system quickly highlights potential leads, the final decision to make an arrest remains firmly in the hands of human officers. This approach illustrates how AI can augment investigative work by rapidly processing vast amounts of data, allowing law enforcement to focus on interpretation and action without relinquishing control (New York Police Department, 2021). However, concerns persist regarding mass surveillance, privacy, and potential overpolicing, particularly in heavily monitored communities.

3.2 AI in Arrest and Pre-Trial Processes

The pretrial phase represents one of the most significant areas of AI implementation in criminal justice, particularly through risk assessment tools that inform bail and detention decisions. Traditionally, judges relied on their experience and subjective judgment, sometimes following preset bail schedules (standardized lists that assign fixed bail amounts to specific offenses), to determine whether a defendant should be released before trial. However, concerns about the inequities of cash bail, whereby defendants with financial means can secure their release whereas individuals with fewer resources remain incarcerated, have driven jurisdictions to seek more objective and data-driven approaches.

A widely used example is the Public Safety Assessment, developed by the Arnold Foundation (now Arnold Ventures), which evaluates nine factors drawn from criminal history and demographic data to predict two outcomes: failure to appear in court and engagement in new criminal activity while awaiting trial (Brittain et al., 2021). New Jersey's pretrial reform provides a case study. In 2017, after virtually eliminating cash bail and implementing the assessment statewide, the state experienced a dramatic drop in its pretrial jail population without increasing crime or failure to appear (Anderson et al., 2019). In other words, judges could release many more defendants who prior to reform would have been detained on bail that they could not afford, and yet public safety did not suffer. Defendants returned to court at a similar rate and did not commit new crimes at a higher rate.

Beyond the Public Ssafety Assessment program, other risk assessment tools illustrate AI's expanding role in both arrest and pretrial processes. In Alaska, for instance, state-developed pretrial tools combine static factors (such as past convictions) with dynamic variables (such as employment status and community ties) to assess flight risk and recidivism (Electronic Privacy Information Center, 2020). Similarly, the DC Risk Assessment Instrument, developed collaboratively by local agencies and independent researchers, employs localized validation studies to tailor pretrial decisions to each jurisdiction's specific conditions (Electronic Privacy Information Center, 2020).

However, the use of AI in pretrial assessment has not been without controversy, as such tools may perpetuate racial disparities present in the data. In New Jersey, although the overall jail population declined, the racial makeup of those detained did not change, indicating that the tool helped reduce jail numbers, but it did not reduce the disparity between Black and White detention rates (Hamilton, 2021; ACLU of New Jersey, 2022). The algorithm may be "fair" in a narrow technical sense because it doesn't consider race and ethnicity and it might have similar accuracy for all racial and ethnic groups, but because the underlying data reflect societal inequities, the outcomes still show racial imbalance.

In another critical example, the Chicago Police Department implemented its Strategic Subject List, or "heat list," that algorithmically identified individuals at risk of involvement in gun violence (González, 2024). In Robert McDaniel's case, being placed on the list led to unexpected police visits and community suspicion. Though he had no violent criminal history, McDaniel was later shot in the legs after being falsely perceived as a police informant due to these visits, raising questions about whether the algorithm's identification contributed to rather than prevented harm (Stroud, 2021).

3.3 *AI in Sentencing*

At the sentencing stage, the most well-known example of technology intervention is the use of risk assessment tools to inform sentencing decisions. In some jurisdictions, judges receive a risk score for a defendant (often the same kind of score used in pretrial or probation contexts) before issuing a sentence, with the intention of guiding them toward appropriate sentencing, such as diverting lower-risk offenders to community penalties and reserving prison for higher risk individuals (Fazel et al., 2022). Correctional Offender Management Profiling for Alternative Sanctions (COMPAS) is one such tool that has been used during sentencing in states like Wisconsin. COMPAS generates risk scores for general recidivism, violent recidivism, and other categories based on a lengthy questionnaire and criminal history data (Brennan et al., 2009). Judges may consider these scores when determining whether to impose incarceration or alternative sanctions.

The use of COMPAS in sentencing came under national scrutiny after a 2016 investigative report by ProPublica, which found racial disparities in the risk scores assigned to defendants in Broward County, Florida (Angwin et al., 2016). Specifically, the analysis showed that Black defendants who did not reoffend were far more likely than White defendants to have been classified as "high risk" by COMPAS (false positive), whereas White defendants who reoffended were more likely than Black defendants to have been mistakenly classified as "low risk" (false negative). This finding sparked a debate on algorithmic fairness that has come to serve as a touchstone in discussions about AI in criminal justice. For example, research has shown that a risk assessment tool can be well-calibrated—in other words, the likelihood of recidivism is similar across groups—yet still shows imbalances in error rates when base rates differ between racial and ethnic groups (Chouldechova, 2017).

Transparency further complicates the fairness debate. As argued by Rudin et al. (2020), the proprietary and opaque nature of algorithms like COMPAS limits defendants' ability to understand or contest the basis of their risk scores. This lack of transparency not only hinders external scrutiny but also raises serious due process concerns. For instance, in State v. Loomis (2016), the defendant challenged his sentence on the grounds that it was partly determined by a secret algorithm he could not examine. Although the court upheld the use of COMPAS, it emphasized that such scores must not serve as the sole determinant in sentencing and that their limitations should be clearly communicated.

3.4 AI in Probation and Parole

Probation and parole officers are responsible for determining supervision intensity, identifying early signs of non-compliance, and making informed responses to violations. Traditional actuarial risk assessments, such as the Level of Service Inventory-Revised and the Ohio Risk Assessment System, have long guided classification into risk categories (Desmarais et al., 2018). AI is increasingly being integrated into probation and parole systems, influencing supervision strategies, recidivism risk prediction, and decision-making processes.

One notable use of AI involves the Pennsylvania Board of Probation and Parole, which since 2013 has employed machine learning forecasts to inform parole eligibility decisions. To assess individuals' eligibility for parole and distinguish between those likely to be rearrested for violent versus nonviolent offenses, the board uses algorithms. These algorithms analyze diverse factors, including the individual's potential for violence, sex offender status, behavior while incarcerated, criminal history, age, intelligence, and insights derived from personal interviews (Berk, 2017). An evaluation report on this tool indicated that although the overall number of people granted parole remained stable, AI integration changed the composition of those receiving parole: individuals assessed as having lower violent recidivism risks became more likely to be granted parole, while higher-risk individuals were less likely (Berk, 2017). Follow-up analyses found reductions in rearrests for both nonviolent and violent crimes, reflecting how AI can inform parole decision-making.

However, similar to other stages, concerns exist in probation and parole settings. If historical data used to train AI models reflect systemic biases, such as racial disparities in probation revocations, the AI system may perpetuate or even exacerbate those inequities. Research has shown that predictive models can disproportionately categorize individuals from marginalized groups as higher risk due to biased data inputs (Rudin et al., 2020). Although the Pennsylvania study did not explicitly address racial disparities (Berk, 2017), these general concerns emphasize the importance of scrutinizing AI-driven tools for unintended biases. Moreover, the transparency and accountability of AI systems involve are significant challenges. Silverman (2023) underscored how proprietary or opaque algorithms complicate transparency, making it challenging for parole boards, probation officers, and social workers to understand or question the basis of AI-generated recommendations. This can inadvertently push probation and parole systems toward increased surveillance rather than personalized rehabilitative support. Such surveillance-oriented approaches might negatively affect the essential client–officer relationship by limiting the professional discretion of officers to adapt supervision plans to individual contexts. Overreliance on AI risks overlooking important nuances, such as an individual's personal progress, unique struggles, or rehabilitative milestones (Silverman, 2023). This underscores the necessity of careful integration of AI tools alongside robust human judgment and social work practices.

3.5 AI in Rehabilitation and Re-entry

AI applications in rehabilitation and reentry are still emerging, but they show promise in facilitating personalized interventions and improving program effectiveness. Virtual reality (VR) technology is increasingly being integrated into rehabilitation and reentry programs, offering safe, controlled environments in which individuals can learn and practice essential skills. For instance, VR is used to prevent and manage aggression through programs like Virtual Reality Aggression Prevention Training, during which offenders engage in simulated scenarios designed to help them recognize, regulate, and deescalate aggressive responses with real-time biometric feedback, specifically heart rate and galvanic skin response, which allow patients and therapists to monitor physiological arousal during role-plays and identify early signs of escalation (Klein Tuente et al., 2018). Additionally, immersive VR environments facilitate risk assessment by enabling practitioners to observe behavioral responses in realistic yet ethically safe scenarios, thereby informing tailored intervention strategies and enhancing re-entry readiness (Cornet & Van Gelder, 2020). VR-based exposure therapy is being employed to treat anxiety disorders, posttraumatic stress disorder, and specific phobias among offender populations, offering controlled exposure that supports desensitization and improved emotional regulation (Ticknor, 2019).

VR also shows the potential to transform therapeutic interventions. For example, VR can enhance cognitive behavioral therapy by enabling role-play scenarios that allow offenders to practice new strategies with immediate, tailored feedback (Ticknor, 2019). In substance abuse treatment, VR can enable controlled exposure to substance-related cues to help manage cravings and reduce relapse risk. Additionally, VR can facilitate remote group therapy and skill development, overcoming challenges such as geographic isolation and limited local resources—a critical advantage for reentry programs (Ticknor, 2019). By simulating real-world scenarios like job interviews and community interactions, VR can equip individuals for successful reintegration through practical, hands-on experiences that build confidence and promote long-term success (Cornet & Van Gelder, 2020).

4 Algorithmic Fairness and Ethics in AI-Driven Criminal Justice

The increasing deployment of AI in criminal justice has precipitated debate and challenges, particularly regarding algorithmic fairness and ethics. This section critically discusses major controversies, the importance of transparency and due process, sources and mechanisms of algorithmic bias, and policy implications with a special emphasis on social work.

4.1 Major Debates and Controversies in Algorithmic Fairness

One influential discussion about algorithmic bias in criminal justice systems began with a study by Angwin et al. (2016). Their investigation of the COMPAS risk assessment tool, which is used to predict the likelihood of reoffending, found that the tool was more likely to classify Black defendants as high risk than White defendants, even when both groups had similar rates of reoffending. For example, imagine two individuals, one who is Black and one who is White, with identical criminal histories and behaviors; the tool would tend to assign a higher risk score to the Black individual, raising concerns that the technology might inadvertently reinforce disparities (Angwin et al., 2016). In response, Northpointe, the developer of COMPAS, argued that the tool was "calibrated" across racial and ethnic groups, meaning that for any given risk score, the actual rate of reoffending is similar regardless of racial and ethnic groups.

Although there is no universally accepted definition of fairness, a wide range of algorithmic fairness metrics have been proposed, including calibration, equalized odds, demographic parity, and predictive parity (Mehrabi et al., 2019).

However, this response also highlights a key challenge: Different methods for measuring fairness can conflict. One approach focuses on overall accuracy, whereas another emphasizes ensuring that errors (such as false positives, such that a person is wrongly labeled as high risk) occur at comparable rates across groups. Achieving both simultaneously can be highly challenging. Chouldechova (2017) further explained this dilemma, also referred to as the impossibility theorem, by demonstrating mathematically that when the base rates of reoffending differ between groups, it is impossible to achieve both perfect calibration and equal error rates. In other words, if the data reflect systemic inequities, such as differences in how communities are policed, then any algorithm may face inherent tradeoffs in fairness (Kleinberg et al., 2016). Thus, focusing on one statistical definition of fairness might lead to unintended consequences, such as inadvertently increasing risk estimates for some populations in an effort to balance error rates (Corbett-Davies et al., 2017).

These debates have far-reaching implications that extend beyond criminal justice research; they shape public policy, legal challenges, and the everyday practices of professionals in fields like social work. For social work professionals, understanding these debates is crucial because the outcomes influenced by such technologies can profoundly affect the lives of the people they serve, making it essential to advocate systems that enhance fairness rather than perpetuate inequalities (Bricout & Goldkind, 2024; Coulton et al., 2015).

4.2 Sources and Mechanisms of Algorithmic Bias

Understanding why and how algorithmic bias arises in criminal justice systems is vital for social work practitioners and researchers, particularly given the well-documented racial and ethnic disparities throughout the U.S. criminal justice system. These disparities, from disproportionate policing to inequitable sentencing, have profound implications for community well-being and policy reform (Pierson et al., 2020). In their comprehensive review, Neil and Zanger-Tishler (2025) suggested that these systemic inequities are embedded in the data used to train risk assessment tools. Although most research has focused on biases in the algorithms, these authors highlighted a more fundamental problem by identifying three distinct pathways through which racial bias in arrest records produces algorithmic bias in criminal justice settings.

Label bias, which poses severe concerns, occurs when the outcome variable that a model seeks to predict—typically arrests, charges, or convictions—is not a direct measure of actual criminal behavior but a proxy that is skewed by systemic inequities. Most risk assessment tools are intended to predict future criminal behavior but are actually trained to predict arrests. Neil and Zanger-Tishler (2025) highlighted that this substitution leads to a fundamental measurement problem when arrest data do not equally reflect actual criminal behavior across racial groups. Arrest records capture only a subset of offending: some people are arrested without having committed the crime, while many who do offend are never arrested at all. This creates a particularly challenging problem because, unlike in some fields where obtaining better outcome measures might be possible, true criminal offending remains largely unobservable.

The second mechanism is feature bias, which arises when the predictors used in risk assessment tools, such as prior arrests and charges, inherit systemic racial disparities. This is particularly critical in criminal justice because, in many risk assessment tools, past arrests are the most important predictors. Although feature bias could theoretically be addressed by allowing for a race-specific coefficient that adjust for racial differences in predictive power, the authors cautioned that this approach may be normatively problematic because it requires explicitly incorporating race and ethnicity into the model (Neil & Zanger-Tishler, 2025).

The third pathway, sample bias, occurs when the training data are not representative of the population to which the algorithm will be applied. Neil and Zanger-Tishler (2025) discussed how racial bias in sampling can produce complex, sometimes counter-intuitive effects because racial differences in arrest patterns can influence which individuals are included in training datasets.

Neil & Zanger-Tishler's (2025) key insight is that many studies in algorithmic fairness in criminal justice systems treat arrest data as if they reflect an unbiased ground truth—a notion that clashes with extensive criminological evidence of systemic bias in policing (Lee, 2024). This oversight can lead to the development of risk assessment instruments that not only fail to mitigate disparities but also may perpetuate them. For social workers and researchers, understanding these nuances is essential because it equips them to advocate data practices and policy reforms that address the root causes of bias, rather than merely its symptoms.

5 Future Directions and Opportunities

Advancing AI in criminal justice requires prioritizing human-centered approaches that empower individuals, advance social justice, and enhance client well-being, rather than solely emphasizing administrative efficiency. Social workers and community partners are uniquely positioned to reenvision these technologies to improve outcomes meaningfully for justice-involved individuals and their communities (Pettus-Davis & Epperson, 2015).

5.1 Critically Understanding and Mitigating Algorithmic Bias in AI

Addressing algorithmic bias in AI systems is essential to achieving fairness and equity in criminal justice outcomes. Neil and Zanger-Tishler (2025) outlined several practical suggestions for identifying and mitigating algorithmic bias resulting from biased data. First, risk assessment tools should regularly update their training data to ensure they accurately reflect the populations with which they are used, thereby minimizing sample bias. Although conceptually straightforward, this practice remains uncommon. Second, practitioners must examine whether predictors, such as arrest records, hold the same predictive validity across racial groups, thereby identifying and potentially mitigating feature bias. This process involves checking for discrepancies in predictive outcomes across racial groups and making necessary adjustments, although it is important to recognize that outcomes may suffer from inherent biases. Third, practitioners should limit AI prediction to more serious crimes, avoiding less serious offenses such as drug-related arrests, which are subject to greater policy discretion and less directly relevant to public safety outcomes. Fourth, sensitivity analyses should be employed to understand how hypothetical variations in label bias, whereby arrests imperfectly represent actual criminal behavior, might affect algorithmic fairness. Last, conducting surveys that link official arrest records with self-reported criminal activity is crucial for validating and calibrating AI systems.

5.2 Innovative Applications of Human-Centered AI

Shifting AI applications toward human-centered technologies presents numerous opportunities aligned with social work values such as empowerment, social justice, and enhancing client well-being. Promising examples include AI-driven early warning systems that identify police officers at risk of misconduct by analyzing patterns in use-of-force incidents and complaints, facilitating early interventions to promote accountability and improve officer–community relationships. Similarly, natural language processing can analyze police reports and emergency calls, effectively distinguishing cases that require social services or mental health interventions programs, allowing individuals to practice emotional regulation, job interviews, and essential life skills in controlled, supportive environments (Cornet & Van Gelder, 2020; Ticknor, 2019).

Chohlas-Wood et al. (2024) provided a compelling example of equitable AI applications through their consequentialist framework. Instead of rigidly adhering to formal constraints such as spending parity (equal resource allocation across groups) or equal error rates (equal mistake rates across groups), they advocated an approach that prioritizes stakeholder preferences regarding outcomes. For instance, in a hypothetical program that offers transportation assistance to attend court appearances, their consequentialist framework emphasizes evaluating the real-world impacts of decisions and explicitly considering stakeholder preferences on trade-offs, such as whether to prioritize increasing overall court appearances or to ensure each group receives equal funding. Stakeholders in this context, including defendants, their families, and court administrators, may weigh these tradeoffs differently. This approach would allow for the optimization of policies through a data-driven, transparent, and stakeholder-informed process, for example, by surveying affected communities on their priorities and tuning the allocation model accordingly.

6 Conclusion and Implications for Social Work

For social workers, evaluating and understanding algorithmic bias and fairness in criminal justice systems carries profound implications for ethical practice, advocacy, and human rights. As algorithmic decision-making tools become increasingly prevalent across domains such as criminal justice, child welfare, and social services, social workers are compelled to cultivate competencies to critically analyze these technologies and their impact on client outcomes (Ahn et al., 2025; Bricout & Goldkind, 2024). Algorithmic systems that leverage vast datasets and machine learning techniques to assess risks, such as recidivism, can inform criminal justice decision-making by enhancing consistency and efficiency (Berk, 2017; Bratton & Malinowski, 2008). However, if not carefully monitored, these tools risk embedding and perpetuating historical biases and discriminatory practices, often disproportionately affecting marginalized groups, including racial minorities and economically disadvantaged communities (Eubanks, 2019; Farayola et al., 2023; O'Neil, 2016; Rudin et al., 2020).

For example, as previously discussed, widely utilized risk assessment tools such as COMPAS have come under scrutiny due to evidence that they may produce a higher false positive rate for Black defendants, inadvertently amplifying racial inequalities despite the appearance of objectivity (Angwin et al., 2016). Similarly, the broader adoption of predictive policing methods, including acoustic gunshot detection and facial recognition software, highlights how ostensibly neutral technologies can exacerbate disparities in surveillance and law enforcement attention, particularly targeting minority communities (González, 2024; Hill, 2024; Thomas, 2024). Such tools often reinforce a feedback loop whereby neighborhoods with historically high arrest rates, reflective of past policing patterns rather than objective crime incidence, continue to be disproportionately monitored, creating cycles of overpolicing and marginalization (Neil & Zanger-Tishler, 2025).

Given their professional commitment to social justice and human dignity, social workers are uniquely positioned to assess these tools critically through a comprehensive, person-in-environment perspective (Mathiyazhagan & Patton, 2024). By highlighting how algorithmic assessments often overlook structural inequalities and environmental factors, social workers can effectively advocate more equitable and transparent deployment of technology. Furthermore, social work education must evolve to integrate algorithmic literacy, equipping future practitioners with competencies necessary to identify and challenge technological practices that compromise fairness and transparency in criminal justice contexts (Ahn et al., 2025; Rodriguez et al., 2024). Educators and scholars have underscored how fostering algorithmic literacy is crucial, as it enables social workers to recognize the limitations of these predictive tools, challenge assumptions of their neutrality, and proactively demand accountability from developers and policymakers (Bricout & Goldkind, 2024).

By understanding the complexities and technological mechanisms underlying algorithmic bias, social workers can advocate essential reforms, such as transparent reporting practices, regular independent audits, inclusive community involvement, and ethical oversight in the development and deployment of AI systems. Thus, the integration of nuanced algorithmic literacy into social work training programs is not merely an educational priority but an ethical imperative. It equips practitioners to safeguard marginalized populations from discriminatory effects embedded in algorithmic decision-making, ensuring these systems align with principles of justice, fairness, and human-centered practice.

Competing Interests The authors have no conflicts of interest to declare that are relevant to the content of this chapter.

References

ACLU of New Jersey. (2022, August 30). *How New Jersey used an algorithm to drastically reduce its jail population–and why it might not be the right tool for the job*. ACLU of New Jersey. https://www.aclu-nj.org/news/how-new-jersey-used-algorithm-drastically-reduce-its-jail-population-and-why-it-might-not-be/

Amnesty International. (2022). *Inside the NYPD's surveillance machine*. https://banthescan.amnesty.org/decode/

Ahn, E., Choi, M., Fowler, P., & Song, I. (2025). Artificial intelligence (AI) literacy for social work: Implications for core competencies. *Journal of the Society for Social Work and Research, 16*(1), 735187. https://doi.org/10.1086/735187

Anderson, C., Redcross, C., Valentine, E., & Miratrix, L. (2019). *Evaluation of pretrial justice system reforms that use the public safety assessment*. MDRC Center for Criminal Justice Research. https://nocache.mdrc.org/sites/default/files/PSA_New_Jersey_Report_%231.pdf

Andrews, D. A., & Bonta, J. (2010). Rehabilitating criminal justice policy and practice. *Psychology, Public Policy, and Law, 16*(1), 39–55. https://doi.org/10.1037/a0018362

Angwin, J., Larson, J., Mattu, S., & Kirchner, L. (2016, May). Machine bias: There's software used across the country to predict future criminals. And it's biased against Blacks. *ProPublica*. https://www.propublica.org/article/machine-bias-risk-assessments-in-criminal-sentencing

Berk, R. (2017). An impact assessment of machine learning risk forecasts on parole board decisions and recidivism. *Journal of Experimental Criminology, 13*(2), 193–216. https://doi.org/10.1007/s11292-017-9286-2

Blonigen, D. M., Bui, L., Elbogen, E. B., Blodgett, J. C., Maisel, N. C., Midboe, A. M., Asch, S. M., McGuire, J. F., & Timko, C. (2016). Risk of recidivism among justice-involved veterans: A systematic review of the literature. *Criminal Justice Policy Review, 27*(8), 812–837. https://doi.org/10.1177/0887403414562602

Bratton, W. J., & Malinowski, S. W. (2008). Police performance management in practice: Taking COMPSTAT to the next level. *Policing, 2*(3), 259–265. https://doi.org/10.1093/police/pan036

Brennan, T., Dieterich, W., & Ehret, B. (2009). Evaluating the predictive validity of the COMPAS risk and needs assessment system. *Criminal Justice and Behavior, 36*(1), 21–40. https://doi.org/10.1177/0093854808326545

Bricout, J., & Goldkind, L. (2024). *Meeting the grand challenge to harness technology for social good: Social workers support vulnerable community members' rights to access safe, beneficent and effective AI*. American Academy of Social Work & Social Welfare. http://grandchallengesforsocialwork.org/wp-content/uploads/2024/07/240730_Harness-Tech_FINAL.pdf

Brittain, B. J., Georges, L., & Martin, J. (2021). Examining the predictive validity of the public safety assessment. *Criminal Justice and Behavior, 48*(10), 1431–1449. https://doi.org/10.1177/00938548211005836

Bronson, J., & Berzofsky, M. (2017). *Indicators of mental health problems reported by prisoners and jail inmates, 2011–12*. Bureau of Justice Statistics, Office of Justice Programs, U.S. Department of Justice. https://bjs.ojp.gov/content/pub/pdf/imhprpji1112.pdf

Brown, J. A., & Jenness, V. (2020). LGBT people in prison: Management strategies, human rights violations, and political mobilization. In H. N. Pontell (Ed.), *Oxford research encyclopedia of criminology and criminal justice*. Oxford University Press. https://doi.org/10.1093/acrefore/9780190264079.013.647

Buolamwini, J., & Gebru, T. (2018). Gender shades: Intersectional accuracy disparities in commercial gender classification. In S. A. Friedler & C. Wilson (Eds.), *Proceedings of the 1st Conference on Fairness, Accountability and Transparency (Vol. 81, pp. 77–91)*. PMLR. https://proceedings.mlr.press/v81/buolamwini18a.html

Burke, G., Mendoza, M., Linderman, J., & Tarm, M. (2022, March 5). How AI-powered tech landed man in jail with scant evidence. *AP News*. https://apnews.com/article/artificial-intelligence-algorithm-technology-police-crime-7e3345485aa668c97606d4b54f9b6220

Butters, R., & Vaughan-Eden, V. (2011). Ethics of practicing forensic social work. *Journal of Forensic Social Work, 1*(1), 61–72. https://doi.org/10.1080/1936928X.2011.541202

Charles, S. (2020, January 27). CPD decommissions 'Strategic Subject List.' *Chicago Sun-Times*. https://chicago.suntimes.com/city-hall/2020/1/27/21084030/chicago-police-strategic-subject-list-party-to-violence-inspector-general-joe-ferguson

Chohlas-Wood, A., Coots, M., Zhu, H., Brunskill, E., & Goel, S. (2024). Learning to be fair: A consequentialist approach to equitable decision making. *Management Science, 7*(2), 456–473. https://doi.org/10.1287/mnsc.2022.00345.

Chouldechova, A. (2017). Fair prediction with disparate impact: A study of bias in recidivism prediction instruments. *Big Data, 5*(2), 153–163. https://doi.org/10.1089/big.2016.0047

Corbett-Davies, S., Pierson, E., Feller, A., Goel, S., & Huq, A. (2017). Algorithmic decision making and the cost of fairness. In S. Matwin, S. Yu, & F. Farooq (Eds.), *Proceedings of the 23rd ACM SIGKDD International Conference on Knowledge Discovery and Data Mining* (pp. 797–806). ACM. https://doi.org/10.1145/3097983.3098095

Cornet, L. J. M., & Van Gelder, J.-L. (2020). Virtual reality: A use case for criminal justice practice. *Psychology, Crime & Law, 26*(7), 631–647. https://doi.org/10.1080/1068316X.2019.1708357

Coulton, C., Goerge, R., Putnam-Hornstein, E., & de Hann, B. (2015). *Harnessing big data for social good: A grand challenge for social work*. American Academy of Social Welfare & Social Work. https://grandchallengesforsocialwork.org/wp-content/uploads/2015/12/WP11-with-cover.pdf

Dattani, Y. (2022). Big brother is scanning: The widespread implementation of ALPR technology in America's police forces. *The Vanderbilt Journal of Entertainment and Technology Law, 24*(4), 3. https://scholarship.law.vanderbilt.edu/cgi/viewcontent.cgi?article=1581&context=jetlaw

Desmarais, S. L., Johnson, K. L., & Singh, J. P. (2018). Performance of recidivism risk assessment instruments in U.S. correctional settings. In J. P. Singh, D. G. Kroner, J. S. Wormith,

S. L. Desmarais, & Z. Hamilton (Eds.), *Handbook of recidivism risk/needs assessment tools* (pp. 1–29). Wiley. https://doi.org/10.1002/9781119184256.ch1

Detroit Police Department. (2024). *Facial recognition policy 307.5*. https://detroitmi.gov/sites/detroitmi.localhost/files/2024-05/DPD%20REVISION%20307.5%20FACIAL%20RECOGNITION.pdf

Dowden, C., & Andrews, D. A. (2004). The importance of staff practice in delivering effective correctional treatment: A meta-analytic review of core correctional practice. *International Journal of Offender Therapy and Comparative Criminology, 48*(2), 203–214. https://doi.org/10.1177/0306624X03257765

Electronic Privacy Information Center. (2020). *Liberty at risk: Pretrial risk assessment tools in the U.S.* https://epic.org/documents/liberty-at-risk/

Eubanks, V. (2019). *Automating inequality: How high-tech tools profile, police, and punish the poor*. St. Martin's Press.

Fair, H., & Walmsley, R. (2024). *World prison population list* (14th ed). Institute for Crime & Justice Policy Research. https://eprints.bbk.ac.uk/id/eprint/53464/

Farayola, M. M., Tal, I., Malika, B., Saber, T., & Connolly, R. (2023). Fairness of AI in predicting the risk of recidivism: Review and phase mapping of AI fairness techniques. In M. Laurent & R. Scandariato (Eds.), *Proceedings of the 18th International Conference on Availability, Reliability and Security* (Article 76). ACM. https://doi.org/10.1145/3600160.3605033

Fazel, S., Burghart, M., Fanshawe, T., Gil, S. D., Monahan, J., & Yu, R. (2022). The predictive performance of criminal risk assessment tools used at sentencing: Systematic review of validation studies. *Journal of Criminal Justice, 81*, 101902. https://doi.org/10.1016/j.jcrimjus.2022.101902

Finklea, K. (2024). *Law enforcement and technology: Use of automated license plate readers*. Congressional Research Service. https://crsreports.congress.gov/product/pdf/R/R48160

Ghandnoosh, N., Stammen, E., & Muhitch, K. (2021). *Parents in prison*. The sentencing project. https://www.sentencingproject.org/app/uploads/2022/09/Parents-in-Prison.pdf

González, R. J. (2024). Algorithmic policing: Part 1. Tech startups, venture capital and law enforcement in America. *Anthropology Today, 40*(5), 23–27. https://doi.org/10.1111/1467-8322.12916

Hamilton, M. (2021). Evaluating algorithmic risk assessment. *New Criminal Law Review, 24*(2), 156–211. https://doi.org/10.1525/nclr.2021.24.2.156

Herbert, C. W., Morenoff, J. D., & Harding, D. J. (2015). Homelessness and housing insecurity among former prisoners. *RSF: The Russell Sage Foundation Journal of the Social Sciences, 1*(2), 44–79. https://doi.org/10.7758/RSF.2015.1.2.04

Hill, K. (2023, September 11). *The technology Facebook and Google didn't dare release*. *The New York Times*. https://www.nytimes.com/2023/09/09/technology/google-facebook-facial-recognition.html

Hill, K. (2024, June 29). Facial recognition led to wrongful arrests. So Detroit is making changes. *The New York Times*. https://www.nytimes.com/2024/06/29/technology/detroit-facial-recognition-false-arrests.html

Hinton, E., & Cook, D. (2021). The mass criminalization of Black Americans: A historical overview. *Annual Review of Criminology, 4*(1), 261–286. https://doi.org/10.1146/annurev-criminol-060520-033306

Jonson, C. L., & Cullen, F. T. (2015). Prisoner reentry programs. *Crime and Justice, 44*(1), 517–575. https://doi.org/10.1086/681554

Kang, E. B., & Hudson, S. (2024). Audible crime scenes: ShotSpotter as diagnostic, policing, and space-making infrastructure. *Science, Technology, & Human Values, 49*(3), 646–672. https://doi.org/10.1177/01622439221143217

Kendrick, C. (2024, May 10). The painful reality of being an incarcerated mother. *ACLU*. https://www.aclu.org/news/prisoners-rights/the-painful-reality-of-being-an-incarcerated-mother

Klein Tuente, S., Bogaerts, S., Van IJzendoorn, S., & Veling, W. (2018). Effect of virtual reality aggression prevention training for forensic psychiatric patients (VRAPT): Study protocol of a multi-center RCT. *BMC Psychiatry, 18*, 251. https://doi.org/10.1186/s12888-018-1830-8

Kleinberg, J., Mullainathan, S., & Raghavan, M. (2016). Inherent trade-offs in the fair determination of risk scores. *arXiv*. http://arxiv.org/abs/1609.05807

Lamberti, J. S. (2016). Preventing criminal recidivism through mental health and criminal justice collaboration. *Psychiatric Services, 67*(11), 1206–1212. https://doi.org/10.1176/appi.ps.201500384

Lee, H. (2024). How does structural racism operate (in) the contemporary US criminal justice system? *Annual Review of Criminology, 7*(1), 233–255. https://doi.org/10.1146/annurev-criminol-022422-015019

Mallett, C. A. (2016). The school-to-prison pipeline: A critical review of the punitive paradigm shift. *Child and Adolescent Social Work Journal, 33*(1), 15–24. https://doi.org/10.1007/s10560-015-0397-1

Mathiyazhagan, S., & Patton, D. U. (2024). Towards just and equitable Web3: Social work recommendations for inclusive practice of AI policies. *AI & Society, 40*, 1549–1551. https://doi.org/10.1007/s00146-024-01994-0.

Mehrabi, N., Morstatter, F., Saxena, N., Lerman, K., & Galstyan, A. (2019). A survey on bias and fairness in machine learning. *arXiv.* https://arxiv.org/abs/1908.09635

Miller, K. M. (2006). The impact of parental incarceration on children: An emerging need for effective interventions. *Child and Adolescent Social Work Journal, 23*(4), 472–486. https://doi.org/10.1007/s10560-006-0065-6

New York Police Department. (2021). *Domain Awareness System: Impact and use policy.* https://www.nyc.gov/assets/nypd/downloads/pdf/public_information/post-final/domain-awareness-system-das-nypd-impact-and-use-policy_4.9.21_final.pdf

Neil, R., & Zanger-Tishler, M. (2025). Algorithmic bias in criminal risk assessment: The consequences of racial differences in arrest as a measure of crime. *Annual Review of Criminology, 8*(1), 97–119. https://doi.org/10.1146/annurev-criminol-022422-125019

O'Neil, C. (2016). *Weapons of math destruction: How big data increases inequality and threatens democracy*. Crown.

Patterson, G. T. (2019). *Social work practice in the criminal justice system* (2nd ed.). Routledge. https://doi.org/10.4324/9780429278099

Pettus-Davis, C., & Epperson, M. W. (2015). *From mass incarceration to smart decarceration (Grand Challenges for Social Work Initiative Working Paper No. 4)*. American Academy of Social Work and Social Welfare.

Pierson, E., Simoiu, C., Overgoor, J., Corbett-Davies, S., Jenson, D., Shoemaker, A., Ramachandran, V., Barghouty, P., Phillips, C., Shroff, R., & Goel, S. (2020). A large-scale analysis of racial disparities in police stops across the United States. *Nature Human Behaviour, 4*(7), 736–745. https://doi.org/10.1038/s41562-020-0858-1

Reingle Gonzalez, J. M., & Connell, N. M. (2014). Mental health of prisoners: Identifying barriers to mental health treatment and medication continuity. *American Journal of Public Health, 104*(12), 2328–2333. https://doi.org/10.2105/AJPH.2014.302043

Rodriguez, M. Y., Goldkind, L., Victor, B. G., Hiltz, B., & Perron, B. E. (2024). Introducing generative artificial intelligence into the MSW curriculum: A proposal for the 2029 educational policy and accreditation standards. *Journal of Social Work Education, 60*(2), 174–182. https://doi.org/10.1080/10437797.2024.2340931

Rudin, C., Wang, C., & Coker, B. (2020). The age of secrecy and unfairness in recidivism prediction. *Harvard Data Science Review, 2*(1). https://doi.org/10.1162/99608f92.6ed64b30

Salekin, K. L., Olley, J. G., & Hedge, K. A. (2010). Offenders with intellectual disability: Characteristics, prevalence, and issues in forensic assessment. *Journal of Mental Health Research in Intellectual Disabilities, 3*(2), 97–116. https://doi.org/10.1080/19315861003695769

Sankin, A., & Mattu, S. (2023, October 2). *Predictive policing software terrible at predicting crimes.–The Markup.* https://themarkup.org/prediction-bias/2023/10/02/predictive-policing-software-terrible-at-predicting-crimes

Sheehan, R. (2012). Forensic social work: A distinctive framework for intervention. *Social Work in Mental Health, 10*(5), 409–425. https://doi.org/10.1080/15332985.2012.678571

Silverman, E. (2023). Predictive justice in the United States of America. In J. Lelieur (Ed.), *Artificial intelligence and administration of criminal justice* (pp. 211–254). Maklu. https://pure.eur.nl/ws/portalfiles/portal/125457157/E-version_RIDP_2023.2_AI_and_administration_of_criminal_justice.pdf

State v. Loomis, 881 N.W.2d 749 (Wis. 2016).

Stroud, M. (2021, May 24). Heat listed. *The Verge.* https://www.theverge.com/c/22444020/chicago-pd-predictive-policing-heat-list

Substance Abuse and Mental Health Services Administration. (2024). *About criminal and juvenile justice.* https://www.samhsa.gov/communities/criminal-juvenile-justice/about

Thomas, G. (2024, October 15). Politicians move to limit predictive policing after years of controversial failures. *Tech Policy.* https://www.techpolicy.press/politicians-move-to-limit-predictive-policing-after-years-of-controversial-failures/

Ticknor, B. (2019). Virtual reality and correctional rehabilitation: A game changer. *Criminal Justice and Behavior, 46*(9), 1319–1336. https://doi.org/10.1177/0093854819842588

U.S. Department of Justice. (2024). *Artificial intelligence and criminal justice: Final report.* https://www.justice.gov/olp/media/1381796/dl

Ward, T., & Maruna, S. (2007). *Rehabilitation: Beyond the risk paradigm.* Routledge. https://doi.org/10.4324/9780203962176

Zeng, Z., & Minton, T. (2021). *Census of jails, 2005–2019—statistical tables.* Bureau of Justice Statistics, Office of Justice Programs, U.S. Department of Justice. https://bjs.ojp.gov/media/65261/download

Chapter 15
AI in Human Trafficking Prevention and Safety

Xi Wang and Noelle E. Fearn

1 Introduction

Human trafficking (HT) remains one of the most pervasive and complex human rights violations in the modern world, affecting millions globally through sexual exploitation, forced labor, child trafficking, and other forms of coercion (United Nations, 2023). Traditional methods of detection and prevention—reliant on manual investigation, victim testimony, and fragmented reporting—have proven insufficient against the evolving tactics of traffickers, who increasingly leverage digital platforms, encrypted communications, and international mobility (United Nations, n.d.). In response, artificial intelligence (AI) has emerged as a robust set of tools that can augment human capabilities to identify trafficking networks, support victims, and disrupt the systems that enable exploitation (Akinsuli, 2022). This chapter is based on a review of 46 peer-reviewed articles published between 2020 and 2025, identified through systematic searches across five major academic databases: EBSCO, PubMed, ProQuest, Scopus, and Web of Science. These sources provided a multidisciplinary foundation for analyzing current trends, technologies, and ethical challenges in the use of AI for anti-trafficking purposes. Table 15.1 summarizes the geographic focus, AI techniques, application domains, and key outcomes of the peer-reviewed studies included in this review.

This chapter explores how AI is being used to address human trafficking across multiple domains. It examines AI-powered techniques for identifying trafficking networks, enhancing law enforcement capacity, and supporting victim recovery. It further interrogates the ethical risks associated with these technologies, including

X. Wang (✉)
School of Social Work, Boston College, Chestnut Hill, MA, USA
e-mail: wx@bc.edu

N. E. Fearn
School of Social Work, St. Louis University, St. Louis, MO, USA
e-mail: noelle.fearn@slu.edu

R. An, M. A. Lindsey (eds.), *Artificial Intelligence in Social Work*,
https://doi.org/10.1007/978-3-032-18443-6_15

Table 15.1 Summary of included studies on AI in human trafficking prevention and safety

Study/ authors	Region	AI method(s) used	Application/ goal	Key outcome(s)
Aarthee and Ezhilmaran (2020)	India	Agglomerative hierarchical clustering for location, multivariate linear regression for age, OneR algorithm for health symptoms	Analyze risk regions for women crimes	Identified key locations and age groups and map health symptoms affecting sex trafficking victims
Akinsuli (2022)	Global (case studies from USA, UK, international)	Machine learning (ML), natural language processing (NLP), data mining, predictive analytics, facial recognition, data anonymization (data masking, pseudonymization, differential privacy, and federated learning)	Identify and track human trafficking networks; secure victim identities; disrupt illicit activities in real-time	Increased detection rates (Polaris +20%, International Organization for Migration +30%, National Crime Agency +40%), up to 97% anonymization accuracy, disrupted up to 200 networks, reduced response time to 3 h, user satisfaction up to 4.8/5
Anda et al. (2020)	Ireland	ResNet50 (DeepUAge); DCA (deep cropping with artistic proportion) technique	Assist law enforcement in investigating child sexual exploitation material (CSEM), a domain that is often intertwined with child trafficking and exploitation	The model achieves state-of-the-art accuracy (MAE = 2.73 years) for subjects aged 1 to 18
Bermeo et al. (2023)	Ecuador	Review: Supervised, unsupervised, Semisupervised ML	Detect trafficking on social media platforms	Highlights strengths and weaknesses across ML techniques for detection
Bhavanasi and Stylianou (2023)	USA	Object-centric ensemble deep learning	Hotel recognition in trafficking investigations	Outperforms image-only methods on occluded data from hotel-ID dataset

(continued)

Table 15.1 (continued)

Study/ authors	Region	AI method(s) used	Application/ goal	Key outcome(s)
Borrelli and Caltagirone (2020)	USA	ML classifier (Artemis) + kill chain methodology	Disrupt trafficking networks using defense strategies	Artemis classifier offers predictive disruption applicable to other threats
Bouma et al. (2021)	Europe	AI-based anomaly detection + travel pattern recognition	Detect anomalies in travel documents for fraud/ trafficking risk	Can extract useful travel behavior patterns; supports faster risk assessment
Deb et al. (2020)	USA	Feature aging module+ feature-to-image aging guidance + face matcher: CosFace	Match children's faces over time: Cross-age face recognition	Improved identification in long-time gaps
Dhinakaran et al. (2021)	India	CNN + crowdsource Mobile app	Real-time child trafficking detection via crowdsourced images	CNN classifies gender, age, impairments; public acts as real-time reporters
Diaz and Panangadan (2020)	USA	NLP + bag-of-words + random Forest (RF)	Identify illegal business ads related to trafficking (yelp reviews)	Random Forest preform best among four models, F1-score 0.77; feature reduction possible; effective for detecting suspicious businesses
Gagneja (2024)	India	ML + big data analytics	Detect patterns in child trafficking/ abduction	Identified patterns involving time, location, transportation
Graham (2023) (dissertation)	USA	Comparative analysis of AI platforms (e.g., spotlight, DIG)	Assess law enforcement tools for HT ad detection	AI platforms enhanced efficiency, accuracy, and iterative system design
Granizo et al. (2020)	Ecuador	Text: SVM/naïve Bayes; image: SVM + CNN + Haar features	Detect twitter content promoting child exploitation	Lower quality image and text: Torso-based SVM model outperformed CNN; CNN excelling on clearer images

(continued)

Table 15.1 (continued)

Study/ authors	Region	AI method(s) used	Application/ goal	Key outcome(s)
Hartawan et al. (2023)	Indonesia	Naïve Bayes, random Forest, decision tree	Detect HTSE-related ads via linguistic patterns	RF achieved highest F1 (0.962); detailed algorithm performance comparison
Helderop et al. (2023)	USA (Chicago)	ML classifiers + criminogenic features; logistic regression model vs. artificial neural network (ANN) model	Predict areas of prostitution to identify sex trafficking risks	Spatially lagged logit regression model (ML) had an 81% efficiency; best ANN model (shallow ANN) predicted with 94% accuracy; identifies key correlates of prostitution
Hemadri et al. (2022)	India	CENSER system: MTCNN, MSRHN (ScatterNet + ResNet), cosine similarity, dropout-based uncertainty, false positive filtering	Match trafficked children via images/ sketches	93.17% accuracy on kinship recognition; 12–18fps real-time speed; aided rescue of 13 trafficked children
Hernández-Álvarez et al. (2021)	Not specified	NLP, image processing, Haar filters, SVM	Detect trafficking messages on twitter, identify age/gender	Multiphase system identifies content and demographics using facial geometry
Ing et al. (2023)	France	Decision tree, RF, gradient boosting, SVM, KNN	Detect human Trafficking networks (HTNs) in legal data	Reformulated legal data for better classification; interpretable models provided
Kjellgren (2025)	UK	Web scraping, social network analysis, PCA (Principal component analysis)	Analyze complexity and geographical patterning of online sex networks	Digital traces reveal structure and heterogeneity of online sex networks
Li et al. (2022)	Canada	Rule-based + dictionary + contextual language model	Extract person names from escort ads (NEAT)	NEAT improved F1 scores by 19% over prior methods in name extraction

(continued)

Table 15.1 (continued)

Study/ authors	Region	AI method(s) used	Application/ goal	Key outcome(s)
Li et al. (2023)	USA	Ensemble models: Lexicon models + BERT (embedding model) + Doc2Vec (embedding model)	Detect human trafficking in yelp reviews	Ensemble models(E2/E3) achieved best performance among seven models on accuracy precision and F1 score. Embedding model (M3: BERT) is good at recall
Liu et al. (2023)	Canada	Weak supervision + LLMs + rule-based matching	Extract names from escort ads (SWEET)	Outperformed prior SOTA by 9% F1; released HTGEN dataset
Makka et al. (2025)	India	AI Surveillance system + computer vision	Real-time detection of trafficking and emergencies	Accelerates response times via AI-assisted alerts to police/ hospitals
McDonald et al. (2021)	USA (global fishing industry)	Machine Learning + remote sensing: PU learning, random Forest, bagging, feature engineering	Identify forced labor on fishing vessels	Detected 14–26% of vessels as high-risk; mapped fishing routes and port visits
Moore (2024)	USA	Thematic analysis + data analysis and ML	Analyze traffickers' use of social media algorithms	Suggests algorithms can be exploited; supports proactive intervention strategies
Mukherjee et al. (2021)	USA	ML pipeline (image classifiers): VGG16 + FC for uniform detection; custom CNN for multilabel clothing attribute classification; mask-RCNN for person segmentation	Detect school uniforms for child ID	Supports victim location inference: 96% accuracy for uniform detection; attribute model outperforms random and baseline models on all clothing types

(continued)

Table 15.1 (continued)

Study/ authors	Region	AI method(s) used	Application/ goal	Key outcome(s)
O'Keefe et al. (2022)	USA	AI-based risk Assessment systems	Detect money laundering linked to HT	Case study shows AI'S power and ethical risks in finance–trafficking link
Ouyang (2023)	USA	NLP (bag-of-words, Word2Vec), ML + agent-based modeling	Track spatiotemporal trends in illicit massage industry (IMI)	Released synthetic datasets; explored language/labor pressures
Perez et al. (2023)	USA	Longformer, XLNet, RoBERTa, ALBERT, BERT, BigBird, GPT-2, CANINE; tokenization: Byte-level BPE, WordPiece, SentencePiece, character-based	Detect HT signals in online sex ads (CSAs): To extract key entities from obfuscated sex ads using transformer--based NER models for trafficking detection.	Longformer best (F1: 0.815); effective NER in obfuscated CSAs for trafficking detection
Ray et al. (2024)	India–Nepal border, global seafood industry	ML models for cross-context detection	Evaluate HT model applicability in tech-facilitated and human--facilitated detection	Models adapt across sectors; detection errors remain concern
Razi et al. (2021)	USA	Literature review + data annotation	Classify types of sexual risk (e.g., grooming, trafficking)	93% focus on predator detection; gap in victim prevention approaches
Román and Cuenca (2023)	Ecuador	ML and DL (especially transformer-based)	Detect illicit twitter messages related to trafficking	Found DL methods more adaptive and effective than traditional ML
Saxena et al. (2023)	USA	DeCLUTR-small + style representation	Identify HT vendors in escort ads (IDTraffickers dataset)	Achieved macro-F1 0.8656 (closed-set); r-precision 0.8852 (open-set)

(continued)

Table 15.1 (continued)

Study/ authors	Region	AI method(s) used	Application/ goal	Key outcome(s)
Sharma et al. (2024)	India	Gesture detection + ML	Detect trafficking via behavior analysis in an app	Promotes ML-based gesture analysis as a prevention tool
Summers et al. (2023)	USA	Multi-input deep learning (DL) binary classification models: Recurrent neural networks (RNN) + CNN (EfficientNetB6) + NN; RNN for text classification, convolutional neural networks (CNN, specifically EfficientNetB6 or ENET) for image/emoji classification, and neural networks (NN) for feature classification.	Classify escort ads for sex trafficking (ST) association	Multi-input DL model 5 (ENET + RNN) performs the best among seven models: Was able to correctly identify all 14 of the observations associated with the estimated probability of 0.845 or greater (1.00 precision)
Sunde and Sunde (2021)	Norway	PrevBOT (authorship analysis + ML): Authorship analysis (author profiling and attribution), Stylometry, ML classification on chat features	Detect child sexual exploitation and abuse (CSEA) offenders online	Predictive support for police: ML can identify sexualized speech, false age/ gender, and recidivist CSEA offenders in chatrooms. PrevBOT shows potential as a crime-preventive tool for online CSEA
Tambe and Tambay (2020)	India	AI + Blockchain + digital identity: CNNs (VGG-16, VGG-19, AlexNet, inception), RNN-based activity recognition, object and motion detection in video (video analytics)	Monitor hidden modern slavery: Meet the requirements for supply chain compliance and supervision in Indian enterprises	Enables low-cost continuous monitoring
Thinyane and Sassetti (2020)	Thailand	Expert system (apprise)	Screen for forced labor victims via multilingual AI system	Highlights ethical concerns; stresses need to address pre-existing inequalities

(continued)

Table 15.1 (continued)

Study/ authors	Region	AI method(s) used	Application/ goal	Key outcome(s)
Tobey (2023)	USA	Lexicon-based NLP, logistic regression, random Forest, active learning with deep reinforcement learning	Identify human trafficking risk in yelp reviews of massage businesses; assess business-level risk of IMBs	Developed interpretable models to detect illicit reviews and risky businesses; reinforced learning improved data labeling efficiency; models support scalable, automated law enforcement interventions
Van der Watt (2023)	USA	AI, NLP, Chatbots, ML, data aggregation	To examine how augmented intelligence—Combining human insight with AI, NLP, and chatbots—Can be used to reduce demand for sex trafficking by proactively deterring potential buyers	Chatbots and NLP-based systems deterred sex buyers in 78 U.S. cities; 6000+ predators intercepted; demonstrates scalable, collaborative AI-human counter--trafficking tools
Volodko et al. (2020)	Lithuania	Statistical analysis (initial)	Analyze trafficking indicators in online job ads	Identifies weak but significant correlations; suggests potential for automation
Weinberg et al. (2020)	UK	NLP + AI: Weak supervision for generate labeled training data + supervised learning to classify modern slavery reports + text feature extraction (TF-IDF) to convert report text for machine learning models + N-gram modeling	Analyze modern slavery reports: To automate the assessment of corporate modern slavery statements for legal compliance and supply chain accountability using AI techniques	Improves monitoring compliance

(continued)

Table 15.1 (continued)

Study/ authors	Region	AI method(s) used	Application/ goal	Key outcome(s)
Wiriyakun and Kurutach (2021)	Thailand	LIME-based feature selection, naive Bayes (NB), decision tree (DT), neural network (NN; 3-layer, 128 nodes each) on trafficking-10 k (dataset)	Identifying human trafficking--related advertisements on the internet (especially those for sex trade)	All models' accuracy improved: Accuracy improved to 73% (NB), 72% (DT), and 77% (NN) using LIME
Woolf (2025)	Not specified	General AI tools	Use AI in criminal investigations, risk assessments, victim support	Stresses holistic potential of AI for law enforcement and services
Yagci Sokat et al. (2024)	USA	Predictive Analytics + multitarget metric	Evaluate transit-based anti-trafficking interventions	Early example of predictive evaluation incorporating cost, goals, and org factors
Yao et al. (2021)	China	Random Forest (RF) models using spatiotemporal data	Predict transfer routes and cities for missing persons related to trafficking	High accuracy in predicting destination cities; integrated RF model proves effective
Zhou (2022)	China	Improved SVM with Laplacian regularization, SVM, RBF (Radial Basis Function), KNN (K-Nearest Neighbors); NLP-based feature extraction including keyword patterns and complexity theory	Classify online advertisements for trafficking detection	Effective for law enforcement surveillance: The improved SVM achieved 92% accuracy and AUC (Area Under the Curve), outperforming standard SVM, RBF, and KNN models in identifying trafficking-related online ads

misidentification, data misuse, and the erosion of privacy and dignity. While AI offers unprecedented opportunities for scalability and efficiency, its deployment must be grounded in survivor-centered values, legal accountability, and cross-sector cooperation. By synthesizing findings from recent studies, this chapter aims to provide a critical yet constructive overview of how AI can both illuminate and complicate the global fight against human trafficking.

2 Major AI-Powered Methods for Detecting and Disrupting Human Trafficking

Section 2 outlines the principal categories of artificial intelligence methods used to detect and disrupt human trafficking networks. It is organized into three main parts: Section 2.1 examines machine learning techniques for detecting trafficking patterns across modalities and platforms; Section 2.2 focuses on deep learning and neural network architectures, emphasizing their role in automating visual, textual, and real-time surveillance tasks; Section 2.3 highlights hybrid and ensemble models that integrate multiple approaches to enhance robustness and interpretability; and Section 2.4 synthesizes the geographic and sector-specific applications of these technologies, as well as their observed real-world outcomes.

2.1 Machine Learning and Trafficking Pattern Detection

This section focuses specifically on machine learning applications, including multimodal victim identification, spatial prediction of trafficking patterns, and online surveillance of illicit content. These approaches highlight AI's growing role in supporting law enforcement, public health, and corporate accountability efforts worldwide.

2.1.1 Multimodal Detection and Age Estimation Technologies

Recent innovations leverage multimodal machine learning to identify victims of human trafficking in real-world digital environments. Granizo et al. (2020) proposed a combined Support Vector Machine (SVM) and Convolutional Neural Network (CNN) framework to classify tweets and detect minors in images. Specifically, the system classifies tweets based on whether they contain content potentially related to child trafficking—such as suspicious language, hashtags, or user behavior patterns—while concurrently analyzing accompanying images for age estimation. Even when faces are obscured, the model uses upper-body Haar features—a set of mathematically defined visual patterns used to detect structured elements like shoulders and torso contours—to substitute for facial cues in estimating age and gender. Similarly, Deb et al. (2020) introduced a feature aging module that enhances deep face embeddings to improve cross-age identification, crucial for recognizing children years after abduction. Anda et al. (2020) extended age estimation using DeepUAge, a deep learning model based on ResNet50, a 50-layer residual neural network architecture commonly used in image classification tasks. DeepUAge was trained on the VisAGe dataset, a publicly available facial image dataset containing labeled age information, and achieved state-of-the-art results in underage facial analysis. Together, these studies highlight the potential of Artificial Intelligence (AI) to support law enforcement through robust identification systems that operate effectively across age gaps, varying image quality, and privacy constraints.

2.1.2 Spatial Prediction and Public Health Surveillance

Machine learning has also enabled spatially aware, demographically informed predictions of trafficking patterns. Yao et al. (2021) developed a multimodel random forest system for forecasting likely destination cities of trafficked children in China, combining spatial grids and vector directions to enhance predictive accuracy. In the Indian context, Aarthee and Ezhilmaran (2020) applied hierarchical clustering and regression analysis to identify high-incidence regions and the most vulnerable age groups (women aged 18–30), linking trafficking exposure to health outcomes like PTSD and HIV. In the USA, Helderop et al. (2023) used artificial neural networks with fine-grained urban geocoding to map prostitution activity in Chicago with 94% accuracy, surpassing the accuracy of traditional regression models. These studies demonstrate the utility of machine learning for policy-relevant spatial surveillance and proactive deployment of anti-trafficking resources.

2.1.3 Online Trafficking Detection and Corporate Accountability

Machine learning is increasingly applied to online textual and visual data to detect illicit trafficking-related content and to enhance corporate accountability, that is, ensuring that companies meet their legal and ethical obligations to prevent modern slavery and exploitation within their platforms or supply chains. Summers et al. (2023) built multi-input deep learning models combining EfficientNet—a convolutional neural network optimized for performance and computational efficiency—with bidirectional Recurrent Neural Networks (RNNs) to analyze escort advertisements. The model correctly identified all 14 observations with an estimated probability of 0.845 or higher (precision of 1.00), which is essential for law enforcement, as a lack of precision can lead to wasted effort. This enables prioritizing high--risk ads in resource-constrained enforcement settings. Li et al. (2023) developed a hybrid lexicon-based and embedding-based classification system to detect illicit massage business (IMB) reviews on public platforms, using ensemble methods to balance precision and recall. Diaz and Panangadan (2020) proposed a scalable Random Forest (RF) classifier trained on publicly available reviews from Yelp and Rubmaps—a review platform focused on adult-oriented massage businesses. This model achieved an F1-score of 0.77, indicating a balanced trade-off between precision and recall and reflecting robust classification performance in a domain with highly imbalanced, noisy data. Beyond direct detection, Weinberg et al. (2020) and Tambe (2020) introduced AI frameworks for monitoring modern slavery compliance in corporate reports and supply chains, respectively, integrating blockchain and human-in-the-loop validation to scale ethical due diligence. These approaches reflect the growing potential of AI for systemic intervention across both public platforms and private sectors.

2.2 *Deep Learning and Neural Networks in Trafficking Detection*

This section delves into the application of deep learning architectures—including CNNs, RNNs, and transformer models—to detect and disrupt human trafficking. Subsections cover visual recognition using CNNs, textual analysis through recurrent and transformer-based models, real-time surveillance systems, and ongoing challenges regarding interpretability and ethics. Together, these approaches demonstrate the power and limitations of deep neural networks in high-stakes and complex trafficking contexts.

2.2.1 Convolutional Neural Networks (CNNs) for Image-Based Identification

Convolutional Neural Networks (CNNs) have emerged as powerful tools in visual--based detection of trafficking victims. These models are especially effective in processing and classifying images, which is crucial for identifying trafficked children or missing persons whose photographs may be outdated or obscured. Anda et al. (2020) introduced DeepUAge, a ResNet50-based model trained on the VisAGe dataset, specifically designed for underage facial images. Compared to existing commercial and academic age estimators—such as Microsoft Azure Face API (mean absolute error [MAE]: 3.60), Amazon Rekognition (MAE: 3.74), and IMDB--WIKI WideResNet (MAE: 20.43)—DeepUAge achieved a significantly lower mean absolute error (MAE) of 2.73, representing a 24.2% improvement over Microsoft Azure and 27% over Amazon Rekognition. This accuracy enables law enforcement to more reliably estimate a subject's age and thus better determine whether an image qualifies as child sexual exploitation material (CSEM), which in turn improves the classification and triage of digital evidence compared to earlier, less specialized models. Similarly, Deb et al. (2020) utilized CNN-based models to implement feature aging techniques, improving cross-age face recognition. Hemadri et al. (2022) introduced a hybrid network that incorporated CNNs to compare present-day photos with sketches and images from earlier years, supporting re-identification over time.

CNNs have also been deployed in mobile-based crowdsourcing applications, such as the system developed by Dhinakaran et al. (2021), which classifies geotagged images uploaded by citizens to support the detection of trafficked or exploited minors. Their model, DesecrateNet, is a 54-layer convolutional neural network designed to identify children under 18 and assess facial impairments or physical disabilities. In performance evaluations, the system achieved an accurate improvement from 92.4% to 96.5%, outperforming popular models such as Inception V3 and MobileNet, while requiring fewer training samples due to efficient use of max pooling and data augmentation techniques. This improvement enables law enforcement to more accurately triage digital evidence, identify minors involved in child sexual exploitation material (CSEM), and prioritize high-risk cases more effectively than with traditional manual screening or generic CNN models. These efforts significantly reduce manual labor for law enforcement and increase the scope of victim identification, particularly in densely populated or resource-constrained regions. Despite their accuracy, CNN-based systems must navigate ethical issues surrounding image storage, consent, and potential misuse. Nonetheless, CNNs remain a cornerstone technology in the domain of trafficking detection, combining automation with high-precision visual analysis.

2.2.2 Recurrent and Transformer Models for Textual Pattern Recognition

While CNNs are optimized for extracting spatial features from images, RNNs are designed to model temporal or sequential dependencies in text or time-series data—making them complementary tools in AI-powered human trafficking detection systems. In the realm of textual analysis, recurrent models such as Recurrent Neural Networks (RNNs)—which process sequential data by retaining information from previous time steps—have enabled significant advances in detecting trafficking--related language online. More recently, transformer-based models (e.g., BERT or Longformer), which rely on self-attention mechanisms rather than recurrence to model contextual relationships, have further improved performance on long and obfuscated text commonly found in illicit online content.

Summers et al. (2023) applied a hybrid deep learning model combining RNNs and CNNs to escort advertisements, capturing temporal and contextual patterns in both textual and visual content. Transformer architectures like BERT and Longformer, as used by Perez et al. (2023), have been particularly effective at handling long, obfuscated sequences common in commercial sex advertisements. These models are trained on large corpora—collections of textual data compiled for natural language processing (NLP) tasks—and fine-tuned for domain-specific tasks such as name extraction, location recognition, and traffic probability classification. Liu et al. (2023) introduced Supervise Weakly for Entity Extraction to fight Trafficking (SWEET), a weak supervision pipeline—an approach that leverages limited labeled data, heuristic rules, and indirect signals rather than fully annotated datasets—for effectively extracting person names from noisy escort advertisements. Similarly, Li et al. (2022) developed Name Extraction Against Trafficking (NEAT), a hybrid Named Entity Recognition (NER) system that merges rule-based and contextual language models to identify ambiguous or obfuscated names in escort ads, achieving a 19% improvement over previous benchmarks. Their attention mechanisms allow them to focus on semantically rich portions of the text, improving detection accuracy. However, such deep learning applications depend heavily on annotated datasets, often derived from ethically complex sources. Studies conducted in Ecuador (Granizo et al., 2020; Hernández-Álvarez et al., 2021) further demonstrated the utility of transformer models and natural language processing (NLP) pipelines for analyzing Twitter content related to human trafficking, particularly involving minors. These systems employed real-time tweet mining, acronym normalization, and age-group detection using both textual and visual inputs. Bermeo et al. (2023) and Román and Cuenca (2023) contributed insights into Spanish-language trafficking detection systems, analyzing how regional linguistic variation across Latin America affects the accuracy and fairness of transformer-based NLP models. Their work highlights the need for culturally adaptive AI systems in multilingual contexts. Concerns remain about algorithmic bias and transparency, particularly when these models are deployed in law enforcement settings. For example, predictive models may underperform on linguistic or demographic subgroups or produce black-box decisions that are difficult to audit in legal proceedings. These concerns raise essential ethical questions, which are addressed in more detail later in the chapter. Nevertheless, their strong performance on text classification tasks makes them vital in decoding the complex linguistic markers of human trafficking.

2.2.3 Deep Learning in Real-Time Surveillance and Detection Systems

Deep learning models are increasingly integrated into real-time surveillance and emergency response systems to detect trafficking and related crimes. Makka et al. (2025) developed a CNN-based surveillance system capable of identifying incidents such as human trafficking, accidents, and medical emergencies, and automatically sending alerts to nearby authorities. These systems integrate multiple inputs, including video feeds and sensor data, to continuously monitor high-risk areas. Sharma et al. (2024) suggested a data science–based approach that analyzes images — including potential gesture detection — to identify possible human trafficking cases. This approach emphasizes portable, user-facing AI tools that can be deployed in field investigations or emergency reporting apps. In public transit contexts, similar AI models are used to intercept trafficking attempts, as shown in Yagci Sokat et al. (2024). Moreover, projects such as the school uniform recognition pipeline (Mukherjee et al., 2021) use CNNs to help identify trafficking victims by matching clothing patterns in images. Similarly, Hartawan et al. (2023) applied a deep learning ensemble to analyze online sex trade advertisements in Indonesia, demonstrating how linguistic and structural patterns can be leveraged for real-time risk classification and disruption of trafficking-related postings. In another example, Granizo et al. (2020) developed a two-phase real-time detection system that intercepts trafficking-related content on Twitter, identifies suspicious posts, and estimates user characteristics such as age and gender through image processing and Support Vector Machine (SVM) classification. While highly effective, these models raise significant ethical questions regarding surveillance, data retention, and individual privacy. For example, scraping user images without consent and profiling minors based on their appearance may infringe on individual privacy and data protection norms. As real-time systems gain prominence, developing transparent oversight mechanisms becomes crucial. These concerns are discussed in greater depth later in this chapter. Nonetheless, such applications underscore the transformative potential of deep learning in both proactive and reactive anti-trafficking interventions.

2.2.4 Challenges of Interpretability and Ethical Considerations in Deep Learning

Despite their impressive performance, deep learning models often face criticism for being "black boxes," making their internal logic difficult to interpret and audit (Hassija et al., 2024). This limitation poses challenges for law enforcement and judicial processes that demand transparency and accountability. Razi et al. (2021), in a systematic review of online sexual risk detection systems, found that many models prioritized algorithmic performance over user-centered evaluation, raising concerns about the societal impacts of such deployments. To address this issue, researchers such as Wiriyakun and Kurutach (2021) advocate integrating explainable artificial intelligence (XAI)—a set of techniques and methodologies that make the outputs and internal logic of AI models interpretable to humans. XAI methods attempt to clarify the decision-making process of deep learning models by visualizing feature importance, simplifying model structures, or generating human-readable explanations.

Additionally, ethical concerns abound in the use of deep learning for trafficking detection, including data privacy, informed consent, surveillance overreach, and the potential criminalization of vulnerable populations. Thinyane and Sassetti (2020) highlighted that AI systems, if not carefully designed, may amplify existing structural inequalities and marginalize vulnerable groups, advocating for a human rights-based approach to system design and deployment. For instance, when models are trained on escort advertisement data or social media content, the ethical sourcing and annotation of such data must be scrutinized. Sunde and Sunde (2021), in developing the PrevBOT tool for early detection of online child sexual exploitation, emphasized the legal tensions between proactive surveillance and ensuring suspects' fair trial rights, calling for new governance frameworks around predictive AI tools. As these technologies continue to evolve, incorporating interdisciplinary oversight, community input, and robust ethical frameworks is essential to ensure their responsible use in combating human trafficking.

2.3 *Hybrid and Ensemble Approaches in Human Trafficking Detection*

This section explores the growing use of hybrid and ensemble strategies to enhance the effectiveness, adaptability, and transparency of AI systems for trafficking detection. It highlights multi-input models that combine visual, textual, and metadata signals; ensemble learning techniques to improve robustness; rule-based and machine-learning integration; and real-world case studies that demonstrate operational deployment. These approaches aim to bridge the gap between precision and generalizability in applied AI.

2.3.1 Multi-Input Models Combining Text, Image, and Metadata

Multi-input models have proven effective in synthesizing diverse data types—textual, visual, and contextual—for trafficking detection. Summers et al. (2023) developed a hybrid architecture integrating CNNs for visual content, RNNs for sequential text data, and structured metadata inputs, enhancing the detection of trafficking signals in escort advertisements. Such architectures enable the simultaneous processing of emojis, keywords, and geographic information, thereby improving contextual understanding and minimizing false positives. Tobey (2023) developed multi-input models that integrate Natural Language Processing (NLP)-based keyword detection, business-level metrics, and spatial data to assess trafficking risks in illicit massage businesses. These models provide interpretable and actionable insights for resource allocation—such as flagging businesses that use trafficking-related euphemisms in online advertisements, identifying clusters of high-risk locations near transportation hubs, or detecting businesses with unusually long operating hours that suggest exploitative practices. Such insights enable law enforcement agencies and social service organizations to strategically prioritize site visits, allocate investigative resources, and design targeted outreach efforts. Complementing this, Ouyang (2023) combined textual analysis, financial records, and image data to detect structural indicators of labor exploitation within the illicit massage industry, showcasing the practical power of multimodal AI pipelines.

Another example is the school uniform identification system (Mukherjee et al., 2021), which extracts clothing texture, color, and logo patterns from images to match schools. These models reflect the real-world complexity of data and offer a more holistic approach to trafficking detection. However, multi-input models are often resource intensive and require well-curated, annotated datasets for effective training. Their implementation in practice calls for interdisciplinary collaboration among technologists, law enforcement, and civil society to ensure usability and fairness.

2.3.2 Ensemble Learning for Robustness in Trafficking Detection

Ensemble learning, which combines the strengths of multiple models, has shown promise in improving the robustness of trafficking detection systems. Techniques such as bagging, boosting, and voting ensembles aggregate predictions from multiple classifiers, reducing overfitting and enhancing generalizability. For example, Bhavanasi and Stylianou (2023) implemented an ensemble model combining predictions from object-centric classifiers to improve hotel recognition accuracy in trafficking investigations. Rather than analyzing entire images, their approach detects and isolates specific objects commonly found in hotel rooms—such as beds, lamps, artwork, floors, curtains, shelves, and seating—using an open-set object detection model (Grounding DINO). For each object type, a separate deep learning model is trained to recognize hotel-specific patterns based solely on that object (e.g., the design of a headboard or the color and shape of a lamp). At inference time, predictions from each visible object in the query image are aggregated to identify the most likely hotel. This ensemble method significantly improves robustness in real-world scenarios where victim images are heavily occluded, and traditional full-image models fail, enabling investigators to geolocate scenes using partial yet distinctive visual cues. Similarly, Zhou (2022) employed ensemble methods—an approach that combines multiple classifiers to improve predictive performance and robustness—to analyze classified web advertisements and online behavioral data (e.g., advertisement language patterns, frequently used words and phrases, victim descriptions, referenced websites, and geographic indicators) to detect patterns indicative of human trafficking. Hartawan et al. (2023) evaluated several ensemble classifiers, including Random Forest and Decision Trees, to detect trafficking-related linguistic cues in Indonesian online advertisements. The Random Forest model achieved a high F1 score of up to 0.962, indicating a strong balance between precision and recall in identifying trafficking-related language. These results were maintained even in adversarial text environments—contexts where traffickers deliberately obscure meaning through misspellings, slang, emojis, and coded language to evade detection. These models perform exceptionally well in noisy environments characterized by informal, inconsistent, and unstructured advertisement texts. Data heterogeneity posed a challenge due to variations in ad formats, writing styles, and linguistic patterns across platforms, unlike standardized corpora, where language is more uniform. Despite their benefits, ensemble models can be computationally demanding and difficult to interpret, which may limit their transparency and scalability in field settings. Nonetheless, their superior performance makes them valuable assets in law enforcement toolkits, especially for cross-platform and high-stakes detection tasks.

2.3.3 Integration of Rule-Based Systems with Machine Learning

Combining rule-based systems with machine learning is another common hybrid strategy that balances precision with adaptability. Rule-based systems, rooted in domain knowledge and expert heuristics, are effective at capturing explicit trafficking indicators—such as specific keywords, phone numbers, or linguistic patterns. Liu et al. (2023) utilized rule-based tagging in combination with large language models in their SWEET pipeline to extract names from escort ads. Similarly, Li et al. (2022) developed NEAT (Name Extraction Against Trafficking), a hybrid NER system that merges dictionary-based approaches with contextual NLP models to detect person names with improved accuracy. Kjellgren (2025) employed a hybrid analytical approach that combined rule-based classification with social network and component analysis to uncover structural relationships within online off--street sex markets, providing new insights into hidden trafficking dynamics—such as the presence of centrally positioned brokers, overlapping advertisement networks, and geographic clustering of illicit services across urban hubs. These hybrid models are particularly useful when labeled data is sparse or adversarial obfuscation is prevalent, as is the case when traffickers use vague language, coded emojis, or alias switching to evade detection. However, such systems require continuous updating as trafficking language and tactics evolve. They also necessitate close collaboration with domain experts to ensure rule relevance—that is, the continued applicability and accuracy of manually crafted classification rules for detecting evolving trafficking cues—and to prevent bias.

2.3.4 Case Studies: From Escort Ad Analysis to School Uniform Recognition

Several case studies exemplify the practical deployment of hybrid and ensemble methods in real-world settings. The Global Emancipation Network's collaboration with UK police (Mukherjee et al., 2021) automated school identification from photos of trafficked children, using two complementary AI models—one to detect school uniforms and another to classify their attributes. In the context of commercial sex advertisements, hybrid models developed by Summers et al. (2023) and Liu et al. (2023) effectively linked disparate data sources to flag high-risk postings and detect coordinated trafficking activity. These examples demonstrate the value of hybrid systems not only in improving model performance but also in translating technical capabilities into operational insights. Volodko et al. (2020) conducted a case study in Lithuania analyzing over 6000 job ads, in which automated methods flagged 98% of posts as containing at least one labor trafficking indicator, demonstrating the importance of hybrid tools in labor-focused detection. Clearly, these applications underscore the need for human-in-the-loop systems to validate AI outputs and ensure victim-centered approaches.

2.4 *Geographic Focus and Observed Outcomes*

This final section synthesizes the implementation of AI-powered anti-trafficking technologies across geographic regions and economic sectors. It examines regional applications in South/Southeast Asia and Western countries, specialized use cases in high-risk industries such as fisheries and illicit massage businesses, and assessments of real-world impact. By contextualizing these systems, the section highlights how local needs, infrastructure, and policy landscapes shape both the success and limitations of AI interventions in trafficking contexts.

2.4.1 Regional Applications: South and Southeast Asia

South and Southeast Asia represent prominent focus areas in AI-assisted trafficking detection due to high trafficking prevalence and diverse cross-border dynamics. Aarthee and Ezhilmaran (2020) applied hierarchical clustering and regression analysis to investigate patterns of female trafficking in India, identifying high-risk states and correlating victim demographics with post-trafficking health outcomes. Hemadri et al. (2022) and Gagneja (2024) worked on systems in India incorporating facial recognition and GPS tracking to identify trafficked children and enable rapid intervention. At the India–Nepal border, Ray et al. (2024) developed machine learning models for optimal resource allocation in detecting trafficking in transit zones. In Thailand, the Apprise system (Thinyane & Sassetti, 2020) applied multilingual AI tools to screen potential victims of forced labor. Complementing this, Wiriyakun and Kurutach (2021) used explainable AI techniques—models that provide human-interpretable reasoning for their predictions—to enhance the detection of trafficking-related features in Thai online sex advertisements, thereby improving the interpretability of predictive models. In Indonesia, Hartawan et al. (2023) employed an ensemble of machine learning models to classify sex trade advertisements, demonstrating the region's growing use of AI to detect online forms of trafficking. These regional initiatives emphasize early intervention and cross-border coordination, while also raising essential questions about infrastructure and data accessibility in low-resource settings—challenges that are further explored in the ethical considerations and limitations section.

2.4.2 Western Contexts: USA, Canada, and Europe

In Western contexts, AI systems are often applied to digital surveillance, criminal investigations, and corporate accountability. In the USA, platforms such as TraffickCam and IDTraffickers (Graham, 2023; Saxena et al., 2023) support law enforcement by linking escort ads and hotel images to known trafficking cases. Perez et al. (2023) used Longformer-based NLP models to improve the detection of obfuscated language in commercial sex advertisements, while Razi et al. (2021) reviewed online sexual exploitation detection models, criticizing the lack of victim-centered evaluations. In Canada, Liu et al. (2023) and Li et al. (2022) developed SWEET and NEAT to extract person names from escort ads using hybrid NER models. In Ireland, Anda et al. (2020) proposed DeepUAge for more accurate age estimation in CSEM investigations. In Lithuania, Volodko et al. (2020) identified labor trafficking patterns in job ads, showing that AI can reveal exploitation indicators in the formal labor market, such as subminimum wages, excessive hours, and high worker dependence through accommodation and wage deductions. Across the UK and continental Europe, technologies such as blockchain-based monitoring systems that trace labor supply chains for ethical sourcing compliance (Tambe & Tambay, 2020) and document authentication tools using semantic text analysis to verify migrant work permits (Bouma et al., 2021) have been proposed to identify trafficking within corporate and cross-border infrastructures. While these efforts reflect a maturing technical landscape, they also raise emerging concerns about civil liberties and ethical AI use—issues that are further discussed later in this chapter, in the section on challenges and limitations.

2.4.3 Sector-Specific Hotspots: Fisheries, Construction, and IMBs

Certain industries have been identified as hotspots for trafficking, prompting the development of specialized AI detection tools. McDonald et al. (2021) used satellite vessel monitoring data and machine learning to identify high-risk fishing vessels engaged in forced labor. In the illicit massage business (IMB) sector, Tobey (2023) and Ouyang (2023) developed hybrid models integrating business metadata, customer reviews, geospatial features, and financial patterns to assess trafficking risks. Financial surveillance offers another lens: O'Keefe et al. (2022) proposed integrating AI into regulatory systems to detect patterns linked to trafficking operations in banking and compliance data. Tambe and Tambay (2020) developed a blockchain-based due diligence tool to identify signs of modern slavery in UK supply chains. These industry-specific applications demonstrate how AI can adapt to the unique features, risks, and data structures of different sectors. However, their real-world effectiveness depends on interorganizational coordination—such as data sharing between regulators, law enforcement, and private entities—and robust policy alignment to ensure that AI-generated alerts translate into legal action or protective measures. Without such integration, AI tools risk becoming siloed or underutilized, limiting their impact on actual trafficking prevention and prosecution.

2.4.4 Impact Assessment: Rescue Rates, Legal Outcomes, and Policy Uptake

While technical progress in AI models is well documented, their real-world effectiveness remains poorly evaluated in terms of rescue outcomes, legal accountability, and policy integration. Hemadri et al. (2022) noted that AI-assisted facial recognition tools helped law enforcement act swiftly on trafficking suspicions, highlighting their potential operational impact. In Thailand, Thinyane and Sassetti (2020) reported improved multilingual screening of likely trafficking victims using Apprise. Weinberg et al. (2020) analyzed corporate compliance with modern slavery legislation and demonstrated that AI-supported monitoring improved reporting quality. Graham (2023) assessed tools like TraffickCam and Domain Insight Graph (DIG), calling for more rigorous performance validation in law enforcement settings. Finally, Borrelli and Caltagirone (2020) introduced the human trafficking "kill chain" model and advocated for centralizing data collection, promoting cross-sector collaboration, and embedding cybersecurity principles into AI deployment. These examples illustrate both the promise and the current limitations of AI technologies in influencing systemic change and improving outcomes for trafficking survivors.

3 AI in Law Enforcement and Victim Support

3.1 Enhancing Investigative Intelligence and Surveillance Capacity

AI technologies are transforming how law enforcement agencies gather, process, and act on intelligence related to human trafficking. By automating surveillance, synthesizing fragmented digital evidence, and revealing hidden network structures, AI enables more proactive, targeted, and timely interventions. This section discusses key domains where AI augments investigative capabilities.

3.1.1 Network Analysis and Intelligence Augmentation

Several studies apply AI to unravel hidden trafficking networks embedded in online platforms and physical operations, such as off-street sex markets, digital escort services, and loosely connected transit hubs. Kjellgren (2025) used principal component analysis and web scraping to analyze over 15,000 UK-based off-street sex networks, identifying patterns of co-occurrence among actors and services. While not focused on real-time detection, Ing et al. (2023) demonstrate how AI can be used to extract and visualize relational patterns from legal case data, offering retrospective insights into trafficking networks based on confirmed judicial evidence. Ing et al. (2023) employed natural language processing and vector-based classification models to analyze legal cases in France, constructing interpretable knowledge graphs that reveal relational links among suspects, locations, and victim profiles. These approaches help identify organized criminal structures that may otherwise remain obscured through manual casework. Furthermore, Graham (2023) evaluated platforms such as the Domain Insight Graph (DIG), which uses AI to connect disparate digital indicators across escort ads, hotel data, and user behavior, offering law enforcement a visual interface for real-time intelligence tracking. These tools enable officers to spot evolving trafficking networks, even when their digital footprints are intentionally fragmented across jurisdictions or platforms.

3.1.2 Surveillance, Early Warning, and Predictive Monitoring

AI-enhanced surveillance systems provide continuous monitoring and early warning capabilities that support trafficking intervention. Makka et al. (2025) developed a real-time CNN-based surveillance system that detects human trafficking and emergency incidents through public camera feeds, generating alerts for nearby responders. In the maritime domain, McDonald et al. (2021) leveraged satellite data and machine learning to identify fishing vessels likely engaged in forced labor based on movement patterns and labor ratios. Thinyane and Sassetti (2020) introduced the Apprise tool, a multilingual expert system used at checkpoints in Thailand to screen potential victims using smartphones, enabling frontline responders to access AI-enhanced risk assessments. Sharma et al. (2024) conceptually proposed incorporating gesture detection into an image analysis framework to help identify potential indicators of human trafficking, although this functionality was not yet implemented in their prototype. These systems exemplify how AI can support proactive and reactive interventions by monitoring risky environments and supporting frontline decision-making.

3.1.3 Document Authentication and Systemic Coordination

AI also supports investigative infrastructure by enhancing document verification and enabling multiagency collaboration. Bouma et al. (2021) proposed using multimodal machine learning to verify travel and identity documents, thereby improving the detection of fraudulent or forged records at border crossings. Meanwhile, Borrelli and Caltagirone (2020) proposed a "human trafficking kill chain" model, adapted from military cyber defense, to guide inter-agency collaboration and centralized intelligence sharing. The model emphasizes a prevention-oriented approach that integrates AI-enabled signals across the trafficking timeline—from recruitment to transport to exploitation. Collectively, these technologies expand law enforcement's operational capacity from reactive casework to predictive, intelligence-led intervention. However, concerns remain around due process, data privacy, surveillance overreach, and the potential for algorithmic bias—especially when AI tools are used in real-time decision-making or inter-agency data sharing. These risks raise critical questions about transparency and accountability in AI-driven policing.

3.2 *Supporting Victim Identification and Recovery*

AI systems currently play a vital role in assisting law enforcement and service providers in identifying, locating, and supporting victims of trafficking. From facial recognition technologies to multilingual screening tools, AI facilitates more efficient interventions while raising critical ethical questions regarding privacy, consent, and justice. Key concerns include the risk of misidentifying victims through biased algorithms, the use of surveillance tools without informed consent, and the potential retraumatization or criminalization of victims during automated data processing. These challenges underscore the importance of ensuring that AI deployment aligns with victim-centered principles and legal safeguards. This section outlines key technological approaches and their practical contributions to victim-centered strategies.

3.2.1 Facial Recognition and Image Matching Technologies

Facial recognition technologies are increasingly used to match current images of missing or trafficked individuals with past photos, sketches, or kinship-based reconstructions. Hemadri et al. (2022) developed the ChildrEN SafEty and Rescue (CENSER) system using the Augmented ScatterNet ResNet Hybrid (MSRHN) framework, enabling comparisons between current-day images and older or partial images, including sketches provided by families.

Deb et al. (2020) advanced cross-age face recognition by introducing a feature aging module that learns to project facial features into deep space, thereby enhancing recognition of children whose appearance has changed over time. Their system incorporates both feature-level transformation and image-level synthesis to simulate facial aging while preserving identity. Tested on child-specific datasets such as Child Face Aging (CFA) and In-the-Wild Child Celebrity (ITWCC), their model boosted CosFace's open-set identification accuracy from 22.91% to 25.04% when the time gap exceeded 10 years. Moreover, their approach outperformed commercial matchers on benchmark datasets such as FG-NET and CACD-VS, achieving rank-1 accuracies of 95.91% on FG-NET and 99.58% on CACD-VS. These results demonstrate significant advancement in long-term re-identification of missing children—an area where conventional models often fail due to aging variability.

Anda et al. (2020) contributed DeepUAge, a ResNet50-based deep learning model trained on a large-scale underage facial dataset (VisAGe) for precise age estimation in child sexual exploitation material (CSEM) investigations. Their system achieved a mean absolute error (MAE) of 2.73 years, outperforming Microsoft Azure and Amazon Rekognition services. Unlike generic cloud-based age predictors, DeepUAge was specifically tailored for underage faces and optimized for forensic use. The authors also developed a novel offline facial preprocessing technique (DCA) suitable for privacy-sensitive law enforcement contexts, enabling better alignment and accuracy on images collected from diverse, unconstrained sources.

These technologies improve investigative efficiency, especially in large-scale datasets where manual identification would be infeasible. Mukherjee et al. (2021), in collaboration with UK police, implemented an automated school uniform recognition system that uses CNNs to identify educational institutions from images of children, further aiding in victim tracing and contextual identification. Together, these visual-based approaches offer scalable tools for locating victims—especially minors—when other forms of identification are unavailable or less than optimal.

3.2.2 Natural Language Processing and Name Recognition

Text-based detection tools also support victim identification, particularly within the digital sex trade. Liu et al. (2023) introduced SWEET, a weak supervision pipeline—an approach that leverages limited labeled data, heuristic rules, and indirect signals rather than fully annotated datasets—that combines rule-based and language model-based tagging to extract names from escort advertisements. Li et al. (2022) proposed NEAT, a hybrid NER system that merges dictionary methods and contextual embedding models to improve person name extraction, even when identifiers are obfuscated. These tools not only aid law enforcement in linking cases across platforms but also help reunite victims with families by identifying aliases and coded references. Thinyane and Sassetti's (2020) case study of the Apprise platform offers a multilingual, mobile-based expert system for screening potential victims of human trafficking and forced labor in field settings—such as seafood factories, industrial zones, and informal labor sites—where privacy, trust, and communication barriers often hinder victim identification. By integrating AI-driven question flow and language translation, Apprise helps non-specialist frontline workers—such as labor inspectors, nongovernmental organization (NGO) staff, and intergovernmental organization (IGO) personnel—identify victims of forced labor or sexual exploitation, even when they lack formal training in trafficking detection.

Wiriyakun and Kurutach (2021) extended this work by applying explainable AI Local Interpretable Model-Agnostic Explanations (LIME) to the classification of online escort advertisements in Thailand—specifically from the trafficking-10 k dataset. Their explainable artificial Intelligence (XAI)-based feature selection method improved interpretability by identifying and ranking important keywords influencing classification outcomes, while also enhancing model accuracy across Naive Bayes (from 68% to 73%), Decision Tree (71% to 72%), and Neural Network models (72% to 77%) compared to a prior baseline.

3.2.3 Ethical Considerations in Victim-Centered AI Design

Despite their potential, these technologies raise critical ethical concerns. Facial recognition models can misidentify individuals, especially across and within racial or age groups, and their use without consent can retraumatize survivors. Projects like PrevBOT (Sunde & Sunde, 2021), although aimed at identifying online offenders, underscore the legal dilemmas surrounding data use and suspects' rights to a fair trial. These include concerns about privacy violations through the automated processing of personal and biometric data, the risk of police provocation if AI avatars pose as children, and the admissibility of chat logs as evidence without violating the suspect's right against self-incrimination. While PrevBOT operates under human oversight, its deployment must comply with strict safeguards under the EU Law Enforcement Directive and the ECHR to ensure legality and fairness. Razi et al. (2021) emphasized that many existing tools prioritize detection efficiency over user-centered outcomes, suggesting a need for frameworks that evaluate tools from victims' perspectives. To ensure that AI-driven systems genuinely support both recovery and dignity for survivors, and also contribute to the identification and apprehension of perpetrators to prevent further harm, interdisciplinary governance is essential. This includes oversight from legal, social work, and survivor-led organizations, as well as technologists. As AI becomes embedded in frontline work, systems must balance predictive accuracy with fairness, transparency, justice, and the protection of survivors' rights.

3.3 Demand-Side Disruption and Preventive Engagement

While most anti-trafficking interventions focus on identifying victims and prosecuting traffickers, AI is also being employed to address demand-side dynamics—such as identifying exploiters, disrupting illicit markets, and preventing future offenses. These tools offer new opportunities for proactive engagement, deterrence, and systemic reform, but also require careful consideration of civil liberties, transparency, and unintended consequences.

3.3.1 Offender Profiling and Online Predator Detection

AI technologies are increasingly used to monitor online environments for exploitative behavior and to identify individuals at risk of committing trafficking-related offenses. Sunde and Sunde (2021) developed PrevBOT, a proactive AI tool designed to detect potential child sexual exploitation offenders in Norway by analyzing digital behavior patterns, such as linguistic cues, age deception, and attempts to move conversations to private channels. The system incorporates ethical and legal safeguards, including data minimization and fair trial protections—such as avoiding entrapment, ensuring human oversight in decision-making, and restricting the use of chat logs unless suspects initiate contact—to ensure human rights compliance in predictive law enforcement. Similarly, Razi et al. (2021) reviewed a broad range of online predator detection systems in the USA, critiquing the lack of victim-centered evaluations and calling for more socially responsible model development.

These efforts reflect a shift from reactive investigation to preventative policing, offering tools to intervene before harm occurs. However, they also raise significant concerns regarding false positives, due process, and the stigmatization of individuals based on probabilistic modeling. Ethical considerations include the risk of reinforcing bias in training data, lack of transparency in algorithmic decision-making, and insufficient mechanisms for accountability or redress when errors occur.

3.3.2 Disrupting Illicit Markets and Commercial Platforms

Several AI systems target the platforms and commercial ecosystems that facilitate trafficking. Liu et al. (2023), Li et al. (2022), and Perez et al. (2023) developed tools to monitor and extract information from escort advertisements, helping identify trafficking-related patterns and language. Tobey (2023) and Ouyang (2023) focused on the illicit massage business (IMB) sector, leveraging a combination of geospatial, financial, and lexical indicators to flag suspicious establishments and inform regulatory action. Geospatial features included proximity to truck stops, military bases, and highway exits; financial indicators involved anomalous business patterns such as high cash flow or frequent late operating hours; and lexical features drew on terms in online reviews—such as euphemistic phrases or references to ethnicity—that are statistically associated with commercial sex activity.

Graham (2023) evaluated the Domain Insight Graph (DIG), a user-friendly platform that enables law enforcement agencies to analyze patterns in online sex advertisements—including obscure data such as special characters and phone numbers—using cluster queries to help uncover trafficking operations. Sharma et al. (2024) developed a machine learning–based web application that analyzes hotel room images to detect potential trafficking indicators. Although the authors mention gesture detection as a possible analytical component, their system remains a technical prototype rather than a community-facing or real-time reporting tool.

These models broaden the focus beyond individual actors to include structural and infrastructural components of the trafficking economy, facilitating systemic disruption alongside case-by-case prosecution.

3.3.3 Transparency, Accountability, and Public Participation

Demand-side interventions must be governed by principles of transparency and community accountability. Dhinakaran et al. (2021) proposed a citizen-focused mobile app that allows users to report suspicious activities by submitting geotagged images, which are processed by AI models for signs of exploitation—for example, indicators such as visible physical impairments, facial scars, or signs of forced child begging. This participatory approach democratizes trafficking detection and enhances early community-based intervention.

Weinberg et al. (2020) developed Project Artificial Intelligence against Modern Slavery (AIMS) to help businesses monitor their supply chains of goods and services—such as seafood from Thailand, electronics from Malaysia and China, textiles from India, and wood from Brazil—for human rights violations, offering dashboards for transparency, risk mapping, and compliance tracking. Tambe and Tambay (2020) proposed integrating AI and blockchain in corporate due diligence processes to address forced labor in supply chains. These initiatives highlight how AI can serve as a tool not just for detection but also for accountability and prevention through structural transformation. For example, their proposed framework combines a self-sovereign digital identity system to verify worker age and consent at hiring, an AI-based monitoring system that analyzes workplace CCTV and payroll data to flag excessive hours, unsafe conditions, or wage violations, and a permissioned blockchain to store verified incidents and evidence in an immutable, transparent ledger accessible to regulators and supply chain partners.

As AI tools become embedded in commercial, legal, and civic infrastructures, it is critical to ensure public transparency, institutional oversight, and survivor-informed design to prevent misuse—such as invasive surveillance of vulnerable populations or biased decision-making that reinforces discrimination—and to enhance long-term impact.

4 Ethical and Privacy Challenges

4.1 Risks of Misidentification and Bias

AI systems used in trafficking detection are vulnerable to algorithmic bias, misidentification, and unfair profiling—risks that disproportionately affect marginalized populations (Anda et al., 2020; Deb et al., 2020; Razi et al., 2021; Thinyane & Sassetti, 2020). These risks are particularly acute in face recognition systems and natural language processing tools when datasets are limited, imbalanced, or nonrepresentative.

4.1.1 Facial Recognition Bias and Cross-Age Inaccuracy

Facial recognition tools used to identify victims across age and time are susceptible to errors. Deb et al. (2020) acknowledged that cross-age face recognition can degrade when dealing with older photos, especially in nonwhite populations. Anda et al. (2020) addressed this issue with DeepUAge, a system trained on underage facial data for CSEM investigations. Still, even this model faces challenges in distinguishing minors across ethnicities and varying image quality. Misidentification not only delays victim recovery but may also lead to wrongful targeting, retraumatization, or privacy violations.

4.1.2 Discriminatory Patterns in Text-Based AI Models

Textual models can also embed bias, particularly when trained on skewed or adversarial datasets —for example, corpora dominated by language from a single demographic or region, which underrepresents other groups (skewed), or datasets intentionally seeded with misleading, discriminatory, or inflammatory content to influence model behavior (adversarial). Razi et al. (2021) observed that many online predator-detection systems emphasize offender profiling while failing to assess the impact on misclassified individuals and innocent users. NLP models used to classify escort ads (e.g., Li et al., 2022; Liu et al., 2023; Perez et al., 2023) may reinforce linguistic and cultural stereotypes—especially when relying on obfuscated or coded language common in marginalized communities.

4.1.3 Need for Explainability and Human Oversight

The use of "black-box" models in high-stakes environments, such as law enforcement, has prompted calls for greater transparency. Wiriyakun and Kurutach (2021) demonstrated that explainable AI (XAI) can improve the interpretability of classification models used in the Thai sex trade context by using Local Interpretable Model-Agnostic Explanations (LIME) to identify and rank the specific words in online escort advertisements that most influence the model's decision. By showing the contribution of each word to a "trafficking" or "not trafficking" classification, investigators and law enforcement can understand why the model reached a given outcome, making the decision process more transparent, fostering trust in automated detection, and enabling accountability in model deployment. Sunde and Sunde (2021) echoed this concern in the PrevBOT system, advocating for legal safeguards to protect fair trial rights. Across systems, explainability and human-in-the-loop review processes are essential to counteract error propagation and ensure ethical AI implementation.

In sum, the risk of algorithmic bias and misidentification remains a fundamental ethical challenge in applying AI to trafficking detection. Addressing it requires not only diversified training data, explainable models, and robust mechanisms for redress when harms occur, but also well-defined training protocols, independent oversight, and procedural guardrails to ensure consistent, accountable, and fair system performance over time.

4.2 Data Misuse and Security Concerns

The deployment of AI systems in anti-trafficking contexts involves handling highly sensitive data, including personal images, behavioral patterns, financial records, and location traces. While such data are vital for detection and intervention, its misuse—either through inadequate security, lack of consent, or overreach—can endanger victims, violate privacy, and erode trust in interventions (Diaz & Panangadan, 2020; Gagneja, 2024; Hemadri et al., 2022; Woolf, 2025; Zhou, 2022).

4.2.1 Sensitive and Ethically Sourced Data

Many AI systems rely on data scraped from escort advertisements, job platforms, social media, or public reviews—often without explicit consent from the individuals involved. Li et al. (2022), Liu et al. (2023), and Perez et al. (2023) use obfuscated language and indirect identifiers from commercial sex ads to train detection models, such as deliberate misspellings ("mizz" for "miss"), symbolic substitutions (e.g., a rose emoji to denote payment), or using names that double as common nouns ("Amber," "Hazel," etc.) to disguise individuals' identities. Although these datasets are rich in signals, they risk misclassifying consensual sex workers or exposing vulnerable individuals to law enforcement surveillance. Razi et al. (2021) and Thinyane and Sassetti (2020) cautioned that using such data without strong ethical frameworks may reproduce structural inequalities and undermine survivor dignity.

4.2.2 Surveillance Overreach and Community Risk

AI-based tools such as Dhinakaran et al.'s (2021) citizen reporting app and Sharma et al.'s (2024) mobile gesture detection model raise concerns about surveillance overreach and misuse. While enabling public participation in trafficking detection, these tools can be misused to report false positives or racially profile individuals in public spaces. Furthermore, McDonald et al.'s (2021) satellite monitoring of fishing vessels, while effective, raises legal questions about the right to commercial privacy in unregulated zones, among others. These concerns underscore the need for robust governance, especially when technologies are deployed outside formal regulatory structures.

4.2.3 Data Security, Retention, and Anonymization

Storing and managing sensitive data—such as facial images of minors (Anda et al., 2020; Hemadri et al., 2022), or financial transactions (O'Keefe et al., 2022)—requires strict security protocols and anonymization standards. Many current systems lack clear guidelines on data retention periods, audit trails, or mechanisms for data subject redress. Weinberg et al. (2020) and Tambe and Tambay (2020) proposed transparency-enhancing tools in corporate and supply chain contexts, but similar measures are needed across all AI applications handling personal and biometric data.

As AI tools grow more pervasive in the anti-trafficking ecosystem, ensuring responsible data stewardship becomes an ethical imperative. This includes building privacy-by-design architectures—systems that integrate privacy safeguards from the outset, such as anonymizing personal identifiers before storage or processing, and limiting access through role-based permissions—enforcing secure data-handling standards, and empowering individuals and communities with rights over how their data is used.

4.3 Cross-Sector Collaboration and Accountability

Effective and ethical use of AI in combating trafficking requires coordination across sectors—law enforcement, civil society, technology developers, policy makers, and affected communities. Cross-sector collaboration can enhance system design, improve oversight, and ensure that AI tools align with both operational goals and human rights principles. However, such a partnership must also clarify lines of accountability, especially when AI systems produce (or have the potential to create) harmful outcomes or operate across jurisdictions. Van der Watt (2023) examined how augmented intelligence can be integrated into anti-trafficking strategies through cross-sector collaboration involving law enforcement, civil society, technology developers, policymakers, and affected communities. For example, in the Street Grace "Transaction Intercept" initiative, technology developers built an AI chatbot that mimics underage personas to engage suspected buyers online, while law enforcement monitors conversations in real time and can intervene to make arrests; civil society organizations coordinate the outreach component and, informed by survivor input, craft deterrence messages that are both realistic and respectful; and policymakers draw on the operational data to design privacy regulations and accountability frameworks. He underscores that such collaboration must include clear lines of accountability, ethical safeguards, and survivor-informed practices, ensuring that technological innovation advances justice and human rights rather than producing harmful outcomes.

4.3.1 Interagency Intelligence Sharing and Standardization

AI systems function best when supported by a coherent data infrastructure and interagency cooperation. Borrelli and Caltagirone (2020) proposed a "human trafficking kill chain" model that applies cybersecurity principles to map and disrupt trafficking stages, requiring intelligence sharing between local law enforcement, federal agencies, and nongovernmental organizations (NGOs). Graham's (2023) evaluation of platforms such as TraffickCam and DIG highlighted the benefits of integrated data systems for improving investigative coordination across state lines. However, differing standards for data access, evidence admissibility, and privacy can hamper collaboration.

Bouma et al. (2021) presented a suite of AI-enabled, multisource techniques for authenticating travel and breeder documents—including visual security feature analysis, breeder document verification, travel pattern extraction, blockchain-based inspection records, and ePassport chip security checks—designed for integration into standardized border control systems. By aligning with internationally recognized specifications, such as the International Civil Aviation Organization (ICAO) ePassport standards, these approaches promote the development of interoperable protocols—that is, common technical rules and data exchange guidelines (e.g., standardized chip data structures, unified scanner output formats, and consistent metadata fields) that enable different agencies and national systems to interpret and use each other's verification results. Such technical alignment facilitates cross-border information sharing and operational consistency, supporting interagency collaboration in transnational security contexts.

4.3.2 Corporate Responsibility and Supply Chain Monitoring

As noted in Sect. 2.1.3, AI tools have also been applied in the private sector to strengthen corporate accountability and identify trafficking risks within global supply chains. For example, Weinberg et al. (2020) developed Project AIMS to provide dashboards and risk maps that enable companies to monitor for modern slavery violations, while Tambe and Tambay (2020) proposed integrating AI with blockchain and self-sovereign identity tools to automate corporate due diligence and increase transparency. Moore (2024) examined the institutional and legal constraints of algorithmic audits in corporate anti-trafficking compliance, arguing that current frameworks lack enforceable transparency and accountability provisions, leaving affected workers without adequate protections. Collectively, these tools encourage firms to move beyond compliance checklists toward proactive detection and remediation.

However, voluntary adoption remains uneven—global benchmarks show that over 80% of companies fail to meet even fundamental human rights due diligence indicators, and only 6% have fully implemented all core steps (World Benchmarking Alliance [WBA], n.d.-a). Public accountability mechanisms are also scarce: in 2023, just 27% of companies engaged directly with rights-holders during due diligence processes (WBA, n.d.-b). These low adoption rates, despite years of nonbinding guidelines, illustrate the limits of voluntary action; without regulatory mandates or public oversight, corporate-led AI systems are likely to prioritize reputational risk management over substantive worker protection.

4.3.3 Survivor-Led Oversight and Participatory Design

Centering survivors in AI system design is essential for building ethically grounded tools. Thinyane and Sassetti (2020) emphasized a rights-based approach that foregrounds survivor agency and context-sensitive screening methods. Sunde and Sunde (2022) incorporated legal safeguards and fair trial protections into the PrevBOT system (e.g., ensuring meaningful human oversight in decision-making, strict limits on biometric data processing under the Law Enforcement Directive, safeguards against police provocation, protection against self-incrimination, and clear data retention/deletion rules), demonstrating that accountability mechanisms can be embedded into technical design. Dhinakaran et al.'s (2021) participatory mobile app model further illustrates how community members can contribute meaningfully to anti-trafficking efforts when provided with safe, structured tools, clear usage guidelines, and appropriate training to ensure effective and responsible participation. Woolf (2025) advocated for trauma-informed AI design grounded in survivor-led participation. Her research emphasizes that codesign with trafficking survivors can help mitigate retraumatization risks and improve trust in AI systems designed to support vulnerable communities.

Ensuring accountability in AI deployment requires robust governance frameworks, community engagement, and multistakeholder audits. As AI becomes more embedded in anti-trafficking strategies, aligning technological innovation with justice-oriented values remains an urgent priority.

5 Conclusion

Artificial intelligence is rapidly transforming the global response to human trafficking. From enhancing surveillance and investigative capabilities to identifying victims and monitoring supply chains, AI technologies offer innovative ways to detect, disrupt, and ultimately prevent exploitation. This chapter has shown how AI can illuminate hidden trafficking networks, empower law enforcement, and extend support to victims across diverse sectors and regions. It has also highlighted the critical importance of ensuring that these tools are used responsibly.

Despite the promise of AI, the ethical risks are considerable. Misidentification, algorithmic bias, data misuse, and insufficient accountability can undermine the very protections these technologies seek to provide. As trafficking becomes increasingly digital, so too must our ethical and legal frameworks evolve. Achieving effective, just, and humane anti-trafficking outcomes will require not only technical innovation but also survivor-informed governance, multisector collaboration, and a commitment to transparency, equity, and human rights.

Looking ahead, AI's role in anti-trafficking efforts should be guided by a dual imperative: to enhance the precision and reach of intervention systems and to safeguard the dignity, autonomy, and safety of those most affected. With careful design and responsible implementation, AI can become a vital ally in the ongoing struggle to dismantle trafficking networks and support those they harm.

Competing Interests The authors have no conflicts of interest to declare that are relevant to the content of this chapter.

References

Aarthee, R., & Ezhilmaran, D. (2020). Analysis of sex trafficking in India: A view on the health care context. *International Journal on Emerging Technologies, 11*(1), 54–61.

Akinsuli, O. (2022). AI and the fight against human trafficking: Securing victim identities and disrupting illicit networks. *Iconic Research and Engineering Journals, 5*(10), 287–303.

Anda, F., Le-Khac, N.-A., & Scanlon, M. (2020). DeepUAge: Improving underage age estimation accuracy to aid CSEM investigation. *Forensic Science International: Digital Investigation, 32*. https://doi.org/10.1016/j.fsidi.2020.300921

Bermeo, M., Escobar, S., & Cuenca, E. (2023). Human trafficking in social networks: A review of machine learning techniques. In J. Maldonado-Mahauad, J. Herrera-Tapia, J. L. Zambrano-Martínez, & S. Berrezueta (Eds.), *Information and Communication Technologies. TICEC 2023. Communications in Computer and Information Science* (Vol. 1885). Springer. https://doi.org/10.1007/978-3-031-45438-7_2

Bhavanasi, S. S., & Stylianou, A. (2023). Hotel recognition using object ensembles. *Proc. Appl. Imagery Pattern. Recogn. Workshop*. Proceedings–Applied Imagery Pattern Recognition Workshop. https://doi.org/10.1109/AIPR60534.2023.10440661.

Borrelli, D., & Caltagirone, S. (2020). Non traditional cyber adversaries: Combatting human trafficking through data science. *Cyber Security: A Peer-Reviewed Journal, 4*(1), 77–90.

Bouma, H., Reuter, A., Brouwer, P., George, M., Ferryman, J., Boyle, J., Juršėnas, A., Karinsalo, A., Pruim, R., van Rooijen, A., ten Hove, J.-M., van Mil, J., Gicic, D., Goller, G., Ledinauskas, E., Ruseckas, J., Kromhout, B., de Moel, H., & Dolstra, N. (2021). Authentication of travel and breeder documents. *Proc SPIE Int Soc Opt Eng, 11869, Counterterrorism, Crime Fighting, Forensics, and Surveillance Technologies V, 118690G* (12 September 2021). https://doi.org/10.1117/12.2598143.

Deb, D., Aggarwal, D., & Jain, A. K. (2020). Identifying missing children: Face age-progression via deep feature aging. In *25th International Conference on Pattern Recognition (ICPR)* (pp. 10540–10547). https://doi.org/10.1109/ICPR48806.2021.9411913

Dhinakaran, K., Udhayakumar, S., Nedunchelian, R., Varshini, V. J., & Swathi, D. (2021). Crowdsourced mobile service for preventing child trafficking using image analytics. In *Communications in Computer and Information Science* (Vol. 1393). Springer. https://doi.org/10.1007/978-981-16-3660-8_43

Diaz, M., & Panangadan, A. (2020). Natural language-based integration of online review datasets for identification of sex trafficking businesses. In *2020 IEEE 21st International Conference on Information Reuse and Integration for Data Science (IRI)* (pp. 259–264). https://doi.org/10.1109/IRI49571.2020.00044

Gagneja, K. (2024). Artificial intelligence and big data based algorithm to track child abduction and child trafficking patterns using sensors. In *2024 Second International Conference on Emerging Trends in Information Technology and Engineering (ICETITE)* (pp. 1–6). https://doi.org/10.1109/ic-ETITE58242.2024.10493744

Graham, J. K. (2023). *Graham, Jamie Kay,* The Dark Web and Human Trafficking. *Doctoral Dissertations and Projects. 4215*. https://digitalcommons.liberty.edu/doctoral/4215

Granizo, S. L., Caraguay, A. L. V., Lopez, L. I. B., & Hernandez-Alvarez, M. (2020). Detection of possible illicit messages using natural language processing and computer vision on twitter and linked websites. *in IEEE Access, vol. 8, pp. 44534–44546, 2020,* https://doi.org/10.1109/ACCESS.2020.2976530.

Hartawan, D. A., Santoso, B. J., & Pratomo, B. A. (2023). Comparative study of machine learning algorithm on linguistic distinctions over text related to human trafficking and sexual exploitation. In *2023 International Conference on Advanced Mechatronics, Intelligent Manufacture and Industrial Automation (ICAMIMIA)* (pp. 442–447). https://doi.org/10.1109/ICAMIMIA60881.2023.10427655

Hassija, V., Chamola, V., Mahapatra, A., Singal, A., Goel, D., Huang, K., Scardapane, S., Spinelli, I., Mahmud, M., & Hussain, A. (2024). Interpreting black-box models: a review on explainable artificial intelligence. *Cognitive Computation, 16*(1), 45–74. https://doi.org/10.1007/s12559-023-10179-8

Helderop, E., Grubesic, T. H., Roe-Sepowitz, D., & Sefair, J. A. (2023). Prostitution arrest spatial forecasting in an era of increasing decriminalization. *Urban Science, 7*(1), 2. https://doi.org/10.3390/urbansci7010002

Hemadri, R. V., Singh, A., & Singh, A. (2022). ChildrEN SafEty and Rescue (CENSER) system for trafficked children from brothels in India. *Proceedings of the AAAI Conference on Artificial Intelligence, 36*(11), 11917–11925. https://doi.org/10.1609/aaai.v36i11.21449

Hernández-Álvarez, M., Granizo, S. L., & Ahram, T. (2021). *Advances in Artificial Intelligence Software and Systems Engineering Proceedings of the AHFE 2020 Virtual Conferences on Software and Systems Engineering and Artificial Intelligence and Social Computing July 16-20 2020* .USA Detection of Human Trafficking Ads in Twitter Using Natural Language Processing and Image Processing. Springer International Publishing Cham 77–83

Ing, D., Delorme, F., Jabbour, S., Robin, N., & Sais, L. (2023). Classification with explanation for human trafficking networks. In *2023 IEEE 10th International Conference on Data Science and Advanced Analytics (DSAA)* (pp. 1–10). https://doi.org/10.1109/DSAA60987.2023.10302606

Kjellgren, R. (2025). The geographies and complexities of online networks in the off-street sex market. *Criminology & Criminal Justice: CCJ, 25*(1), 81–103. https://doi.org/10.1177/17488958241245287

Li, R., Tobey, M., Mayorga, M. E., Caltagirone, S., & Özaltın, O. Y. (2023). Detecting human trafficking: Automated classification of online customer reviews of massage businesses. *Manufacturing & Service Operations Management, 25*(3), 1051–1065. https://doi.org/10.1287/msom.2023.1196

Li, Y., Nair, P., Pelrine, K., & Rabbany, R. (2022). Extracting person names from user generated text: Named-entity recognition for combating human trafficking. In *Findings of the association for computational linguistics: ACL 2022* (pp. 2854–2868). https://doi.org/10.18653/v1/2022.findings-acl.225

Liu, J., Yu, H., Sujaya, V., Nair, P., Pelrine, K., & Rabbany, R. (2023). SWEET: Weakly supervised person name extraction for fighting human trafficking. *In Findings of the Association for Computational Linguistics: EMNLP 2023*, 3355–3367. Association for Computational Linguistics. https://doi.org/10.18653/v1/2023.findings-emnlp.219

Makka, S., Sowmya, A., Vishwanath, S., Snigdha, K., & Charan, V. (2025). Advanced AI surveillance for human trafficking and accident prevention. In *BROADNETS 2024. Lecture Notes of the Institute for Computer Sciences, Social Informatics and Telecommunications Engineering, vol 602*. Springer. https://doi.org/10.1007/978-3-031-81171-5_13

McDonald, G. G., Costello, C., Bone, J., Cabral, R. B., Farabee, V., Hochberg, T., Kroodsma, D., Mangin, T., Meng, K. C., & Zahn, O. (2021). Satellites can reveal global extent of forced labor in the world's fishing fleet. *Proceedings of the National Academy of Sciences of the United States of America, 118*(3). https://doi.org/10.1073/pnas.2016238117

Moore, D. M. (2024). Algorithmic exploitation in social media human trafficking and strategies for regulation. *Laws, 13*(3), 31. https://doi.org/10.3390/laws13030031

Mukherjee, S., Sederholm, T., Roman, A. C., Sankar, R., Caltagirone, S., & Ferres, J. L. (2021). A machine learning pipeline for aiding school identification from child trafficking images. *GoodIT–Proceedings of the Conference on Information Technology for Social Good Pages 297–300*. https://doi.org/10.1145/3462203.3475924.

O'Keefe, E., Carter, J., Byrne, S., Meeks, B., Stoker, J., & Shields, R. (2022). Can we keep up with the machines? Stronger and faster artificial intelligence systems require robust risk management practices. *Journal of Financial Compliance, 5*(4), 294–306. https://doi.org/10.69554/stgq8141

Ouyang, R. (2023). *Machine learning for tangible effects: Natural language processing for uncovering the illicit massage industry & computer vision for tactile sensing* (No. https://arxiv.org/abs/2309.03470). arXiv. https://doi.org/10.48550/arXiv.2309.03470 https://arxiv.org/abs/2309.03470 [cs]

Perez, A. R., Rivas, P., Turek, J., Sooksatra, K., Quevedo, E., Bichler, G., Cerny, T., Giddens, L., & Petter, S. (2023). Decoding the obfuscated: Advanced NER techniques on commercial sex advertisement data. In *2023 International Conference on Computational Science and Computational Intelligence (CSCI)* (pp. 144–151). https://doi.org/10.1109/CSCI62032.2023.00029

Ray, A., Arora, V., Maass, K., & Ventresca, M. (2024). Optimal resource allocation to minimize errors when detecting human trafficking. *IISE Transactions, 56*(3), 325–339. https://doi.org/10.1080/24725854.2023.2177364

Razi, A., Kim, S., Alsoubai, A., Stringhini, G., Solorio, T., De Choudhury, M., & Wisniewski, P. J. (2021). A Human-centered systematic literature review of the computational approaches for online sexual risk detection. *Proceedings of the ACM on Human-Computer Interaction, 5*(CSCW2). https://doi.org/10.1145/3479609.

Román, S., & Cuenca, E. (2023). A review of techniques for detecting illicit messages on Twitter. *ECTM–IEEE Ecuador Tech. Chapters Meet.* ECTM 2023–2023 IEEE 7th Ecuador Technical Chapters Meeting. https://doi.org/10.1109/ETCM58927.2023.10309025.

Saxena, V., Bashpole, B., Van Dijck, G., & Spanakis, G. (2023). IDTraffickers: An authorship attribution dataset to link and connect potential human-trafficking operations on text escort advertisements. In *Proceedings of the 2023 Conference on Empirical Methods in Natural Language Processing*, pages 8444–8464. Association for Computational Linguistics. https://doi.org/10.18653/v1/2023.emnlp-main.524

Sharma, S., Ritik, S. S., Kumar Rai, B., Pathak, R., & Kumar, G. (2024). Image analysis for human trafficking prediction. In A. Kumar & S. Mozar (Eds.), *Proceedings of the 6th International Conference on Communications and Cyber Physical Engineering. ICCCE 2024. Lecture Notes in Electrical Engineering, vol 1096*. Springer. https://doi.org/10.1007/978-981-99-7137-4_84

Summers, L., Shallenberger, A. N., Cruz, J., & Fulton, L. V. (2023). A multi-input machine learning approach to classifying sex trafficking from online escort advertisements. *Machine Learning and Knowledge Extraction, 5*(2), 460. https://doi.org/10.3390/make5020028

Sunde, I. M., & Sunde, N. (2022). Conceptualizing an AI-based police robot for preventing online child sexual exploitation and abuse. *Nordic Journal of Studies in Policing, 9*(1), 1–15. https://doi.org/10.18261/njsp.9.1.11

Sunde, N., & Sunde, I. M. (2021). Conceptualizing an AI-based police robot for preventing online child sexual exploitation and abuse: Part I–The theoretical and technical foundations for prevBOT. *Nordic Journal of Studies in Policing, 8*(2). https://doi.org/10.18261/ISSN.2703-7045-2021-02-01

Tambe, P., & Tambay, P. (2020). Reducing modern slavery using AI and blockchain. In *2020 IEEE / ITU International Conference on Artificial Intelligence for Good (AI4G)* (pp. 22–27). https://doi.org/10.1109/AI4G50087.2020.9311031

Thinyane, H., & Sassetti, F. (2020). Towards a human rights-based approach to AI: Case study of apprise. *Communications in Computer and Information Science, 1236, 33–47*. https://doi.org/10.1007/978-3-030-52014-4_3

Tobey, M. (2023). *Data science and machine learning methodologies for detecting human trafficking risk in the illicit massage industry.* North Carolina State University. https://www.lib.ncsu.edu/resolver/1840.20/41052

United Nations. (n.d.). *Understanding human trafficking*. Retrieved August 10, 2025, from https://www.un.org/en/peace-and-security/understanding-human-trafficking

United Nations Office on Drugs and Crime. (2023). An introduction to human trafficking: vulnerability, impact and action. *Security Research Hub Reports.*. https://digitalcommons.fiu.edu/srhreports/human-rights/human-rights/85

Van der Watt, M. (2023). Discouraging the demand that fosters sex trafficking: Collaboration through augmented intelligence. *Societies, 13*(4), 94. https://doi.org/10.3390/soc13040094

Volodko, A., Cockbain, E., & Kleinberg, B. (2020). "Spotting the signs" of trafficking recruitment online: Exploring the characteristics of advertisements targeted at migrant job-seekers. *Trends in Organized Crime, 23*(1), 7–35. https://doi.org/10.1007/s12117-019-09376-5

Weinberg, N., Bora, A., Sassetti, F., Bryant, K., Rootalu, E., Bikziantieieva, K., van Breen, L., Carrier, P., Lannquist, Y., & Miailhe, N. (2020). AI against modern slavery: Digital insights into modern slavery reporting–challenges and opportunities. *CEUR Workshop Proc., 2884*.

Wiriyakun, C., & Kurutach, W. (2021). Feature selection for human trafficking detection models. *2021 IEEE/ACIS 20th International Fall Conference on Computer and Information Science* (ICIS Fall), Xi'an, China, 2021, pp. 131–135, https://doi.org/10.1109/ICISFall51598.2021.9627435.

World Benchmarking Alliance. (n.d.-a). 80% of companies fail on human rights due diligence—regulations, guidance and pressure are needed to accelerate change. *World Benchmarking Alliance*. Retrieved August 10, 2025, from https://www.worldbenchmarkingalliance.org/publication/social/findings/80-of-companies-fail-on-human-rights-due-diligence-regulations-guidance-and-pressure-are-needed-to-accelerate-change/

World Benchmarking Alliance. (n.d.-b). Most companies fail to include rightsholders in their human rights due diligence processes. *World Benchmarking Alliance*. Retrieved August 10, 2025, from https://www.worldbenchmarkingalliance.org/publication/chrb/findings/most-companies-fail-to-include-rightsholders-in-their-human-rights-due-diligence-processes/

Woolf, A. (2025). The dual impact of artificial intelligence on violence against women and girls: Risks and opportunities. *Assessment & Development Matters, 17*(1), 23–28. https://doi.org/10.53841/bpsadm.2025.17.1.23

Yagci Sokat, K., Chi, M., & Hudlow, J. (2024). Transit monitoring capacity expansion: Analytics for combating human trafficking. *Transportation Research Interdisciplinary Perspectives, 24*, 101032. https://doi.org/10.1016/j.trip.2024.101032

Yao, Y., Liu, Y., Guan, Q., Hong, Y., Wang, R., Wang, R., & Liang, X. (2021). Spatiotemporal distribution of human trafficking in China and predicting the locations of missing persons. *Computers, Environment and Urban Systems, 85*. https://doi.org/10.1016/j.compenvurbsys.2020.101567

Zhou, Q. (2022). A study on human transiting based on big data and web semantics: Distinguishment and detection. *International Journal on. Semantic Web and Information Systems, 18*(1). https://doi.org/10.4018/IJSWIS.310055

Part III
AI and Social Justice in Changing Contexts

Chapter 16
AI in Advocacy and Social Justice

Charles Alba and Henrika McCoy

1 Introduction

Advocacy and social justice are critical to fostering equity, protecting human rights, and empowering marginalized communities (Selvam, 2024). Through advocacy and social justice, communities can challenge systemic inequalities and drive meaningful policy change to alleviate poverty (Desai & Solas, 2012; Jimenez et al., 2014), upholding justice for all and strengthening democratic participation (Miller, 1978). Advocacy and social justice are core to social work and guide social workers in addressing structural inequalities and empowering vulnerable populations (Dalrymple & Boylan, 2013; Watts & Hodgson, 2019). As advocates for individual and community rights, champions of public policies that promote economic and social equity, and community organizers dedicated to systemic change and human dignity, advocacy and social justice directly underpin these vital roles (Dalrymple & Boylan, 2013; Watts & Hodgson, 2019).

Artificial intelligence (AI), defined as the use of computational systems to perform tasks often associated with human intelligence, such as learning, problem-solving, and decision-making (Russell & Norvig, 2016), holds promise in facilitating change in advocacy and social justice. The depth and advances of AI enable it to robustly handle complex data types and constraints via sophisticated reasoning and analytical capabilities. This can range from text-based data using natural language processing techniques to satellite data and imagery employing remote sensing and computer vision to algorithmic economics addressing problems of equitable

C. Alba (✉)
Division of Computational and Data Sciences, Washington University in St. Louis, St. Louis, MO, USA
e-mail: alba@wustl.edu

H. McCoy
Graduate School of Social Work, University of Denver, Denver, CO, USA
e-mail: GSSWDean@du.edu

R. An, M. A. Lindsey (eds.), *Artificial Intelligence in Social Work*,
https://doi.org/10.1007/978-3-032-18443-6_16

resource allocation, fairness, and systemic inequality. Thus, AI has significant potential to inform and enhance advocacy and social justice efforts by providing robust predictions, data-driven insights, and supporting evidence-based decision-making across diverse settings. These settings range from online social movements and legal contexts in judicial processes to forced migration and humanitarian assistance and the prevention of human rights violations and homelessness. AI technologies can automate and scale routine tasks, which could help relieve the excessive workload and burnout faced in social work (Lloyd et al., 2002), humanitarian assistance (Jachens et al., 2019), and legal services (Tsai et al., 2009). AI also possesses the potential to uncover valuable insights from complex data, make robust predictions to guide strategic interventions, and facilitate equitable outcomes through optimized resource allocation. Hence, this study aims to review efforts employing AI in the context of advocacy and social justice. First, we seek to summarize and categorize AI methodologies applied across a broad spectrum of applications, spanning advocacy and social justice. We define advocacy and social justice as the fight for and promotion of fairness, equity, and rights for marginalized or vulnerable groups, ensuring that individuals' civil and economic rights are recognized and protected. To remain aligned with the focus on advocacy and social justice, we primarily emphasize contexts related broadly to social equity and justice.

Second, we aim to comprehensively discuss the limitations and gaps in the application of AI in advocacy and social justice, with an emphasis on ethical considerations, including fairness, inclusivity, and strategies to ensure culturally sensitive advocacy efforts. The goal of this review is to gain a comprehensive understanding of the AI methods applied across specific domains of advocacy and social justice. These AI methods have been deployed, or have the potential to be deployed, across professions in these fields, including, but not limited to, social work. While not every social work professional will directly utilize all these AI methods, our review aims to help them understand the tools available to promote advocacy and social justice in their specialty area; empower them to leverage AI's potential in advancing these causes; and ensure they are aware of the advantages and limitations of such tools to evaluate and effectively integrate AI-driven solutions into their practice critically.

2 Background and Context

While AI has gained significant traction in recent years with the emergence of technologies such as OpenAI's ChatGPT and Google's Gemini, artificial intelligence, defined as the use of computational systems to mimic human intelligence, has been progressing steadily since its conceptualization at the "Dartmouth Workshop" in 1956 (McCarthy et al., 1956). Research applying AI to advocacy and social justice, as defined above, has been documented since the 1990s, with much of the early work relying on "rule-based" approaches, in which a set of rigorously defined rules was stored in a computer and applied to data to achieve outcomes, for example, in housing (Barta & Kheng, 1997). This approach was dominant across many fields of applied AI research, as computers at the time lacked the processing power to support more complex methods. As such, works that apply AI tools and techniques to advocacy and social justice issues were limited, posing challenges for their application across diverse subjects in this field. At the turn of the twenty-first century, research began to advance as the rise of social media and the emergence of more powerful computing systems enabled the adoption of statistical methods to analyze different modalities of data (e.g., tabular data, text, and images), giving interdisciplinary researchers the ability and resources to analyze large volumes of diverse data—such as text, images, social networks, and tabular records—and uncover patterns or insights toward targeted issues of advocacy and social justice (Chen et al., 2008; Mochales-Palau & Moens, 2007; Fu & Chen, 2008). Such abilities to uncover insights from vast amounts of data complement the application of AI methods to social justice and advocacy issues, as context and nuance can be more effectively incorporated into analyses of systemic inequalities, public discourse, and institutional practices, thereby enabling researchers and practitioners to understand emerging challenges better, design evidence-based interventions, and strengthen advocacy strategies across diverse domains. Slightly over a decade later, the combination of far more powerful computers and advances in deep learning research (LeCun et al., 2015). The growing movement toward open-source data (Anokwa et al., 2009) enabled researchers to use AI systems to not only extract insights from complex data sources [e.g., satellite imagery (Braun et al., 2019; Redmond, 2021; McDonald et al., 2021; Mueller et al., 2021)], but also to deliver strong predictive capabilities—where models anticipate outcomes [e.g., predicting court decisions from case files (Yang et al., 2024a, 2024b)], identify trends [e.g., online networks of social movements (Suk et al., 2021; Sanghi et al., 2021; Venkatesan et al., 2021; Wahyuningroem et al., 2024)], and generate new content [e.g., chatbots used to assist advocacy groups (Pillis et al., 2024)]. We will elaborate on these in the "Results" section. These advancements, coupled with the democratization of data and tools, have made AI more accessible for social work and interdisciplinary researchers, positioning it as a powerful new "tool" to advance their work. Despite these growing promises, several dangers warrant attention. First, many open-source AI models increasingly adopted for advocacy purposes are trained on large-scale Internet data. Such data often reproduces historical and structural biases, including racist, sexist, or exclusionary content (Hofmann et al., 2024). When these models are applied directly in advocacy or social justice contexts, they risk perpetuating or even amplifying the very inequalities they are meant to address (Hofmann et al., 2024; Chanda & Banerjee, 2024). Second, just like statistical models, AI models are typically developed within specific contexts or assumptions. Transferring these systems to a different setting can lead to serious misinterpretations or inappropriate outcomes, as the assumptions baked into these methods may no longer hold (Wang et al., 2022; Chanda & Banerjee, 2024). What appears to be a reliable pattern in one environment can become a distortion in another, introducing risks for both practitioners and the communities they serve.

These risks highlight the imperative for social workers, advocates, and interdisciplinary researchers to critically evaluate how AI tools and methods are used. It is essential to ask under what scenarios these systems are appropriate and to avoid treating them as one-size-fits-all solutions. Rather than blindly applying such technologies, practitioners must remain attentive to their limitations, contexts of use, and the ethical consequences of their deployment. These risks make it essential for social workers, advocates, and interdisciplinary researchers to know when and how to use AI tools. Hence, this chapter aims to highlight both the opportunities and limitations of AI in advocacy and social justice by reviewing existing methods, applications, and future directions to inform practitioners, policymakers, and researchers on how these tools can be responsibly leveraged to advance equity, protect human rights, and support vulnerable populations.

3 Methods

3.1 Study Selection Criteria

3.1.1 Inclusion Criteria

Studies that met all of the following criteria were included in the review: (1) Analytical approach: AI; (2) Outcomes: social advocacy and social justice; (3) Time window of search: peer-reviewed articles published from the inception of a bibliographic database until February 2025; (4) Language: English; and (5) Article type: peer-reviewed journal publications, book chapters, or peer-reviewed conference proceedings. Regarding article type (5), note that, although it is common practice to exclude conference proceedings in social science-oriented reviews, we opted to include them because computer science research is frequently published in conference proceedings rather than journal articles. Furthermore, given that "AI for Social Good" has emerged as a prevalent theme across numerous computer science conferences, incorporating conference proceedings ensures comprehensive coverage of relevant, state-of-the-art contributions from the interdisciplinary literature.

3.1.2 Exclusion Criteria

Studies that met any of the following criteria were excluded from the review: (1) letters to the editor, dissertations, or case reports; (2) preprint articles; and (3) studies focusing on advocacy and justice within adjacent domains not directly related to social advocacy and justice. (Refer to the later chapter for climate advocacy and justice and prior chapters for works concerning healthcare/clinical advocacy and justice.)

3.2 *Search Strategy*

3.2.1 Databases

A keyword search was performed across seven electronic bibliographic databases: PubMed, Web of Science (WoS), EBSCO, Scopus, Cochrane Library, Association for Computing Machinery (ACM) Digital Library (DL), and Institute of Electrical and Electronics Engineers (IEEE) Xplore, reflecting a balanced selection of both computer science conference-based publications and non-computer science journal-based sources to comprehensively capture the diverse publication avenues across this interdisciplinary research area.

3.2.2 Keyword Search

The search strategy included comprehensive keyword combinations from two primary conceptual groups: (1) Artificial Intelligence (AI) and related methodological terms and (2) advocacy and social justice. For the AI domain, we included broad terms such as "Artificial Intelligence" and "Machine Learning"; specific subdisciplines, including "Natural Language Processing," "Computer Vision," and "Deep Learning"; related methodological concepts such as "Data Mining," including "Text Mining" and "Social Media Mining"; and "Big Data." For the Advocacy and Social Justice domain, we first considered terms explicitly related to advocacy, including "Advocacy," "Social Movement," and "Marginalized," and terms directly related to social justice, including "Social Justice," "Racial Justice," "Racial Movement," "Human Rights," and "Civil Rights." All keywords in PubMed were searched with the "[Title/Abstract]" tag, which is processed using Automatic Term Mapping. The search function TS = Topic was used in Web of Science, EBSCO, Scopus, Cochrane Library, ACM DL, and IEEE Xplore, which searches for topic terms across the title, abstract, and keywords fields. The search algorithm for spanning these five electronic bibliographic databases is reported in the Supplemental Materials.

4 Results

4.1 *Literature Search*

Figure 16.1 presents the PRISMA flow diagram. We identified 7715 articles through keyword searches, including 2505 from Scopus, 1963 from EBSCO, 1426 from Web of Science, 960 from IEEE Xplore, 443 from PubMed, 399 from the ACM Digital Library, and 19 from the Cochrane Library. After removing 2516 duplicate articles and 2 retracted articles, 5197 articles were retained for screening.

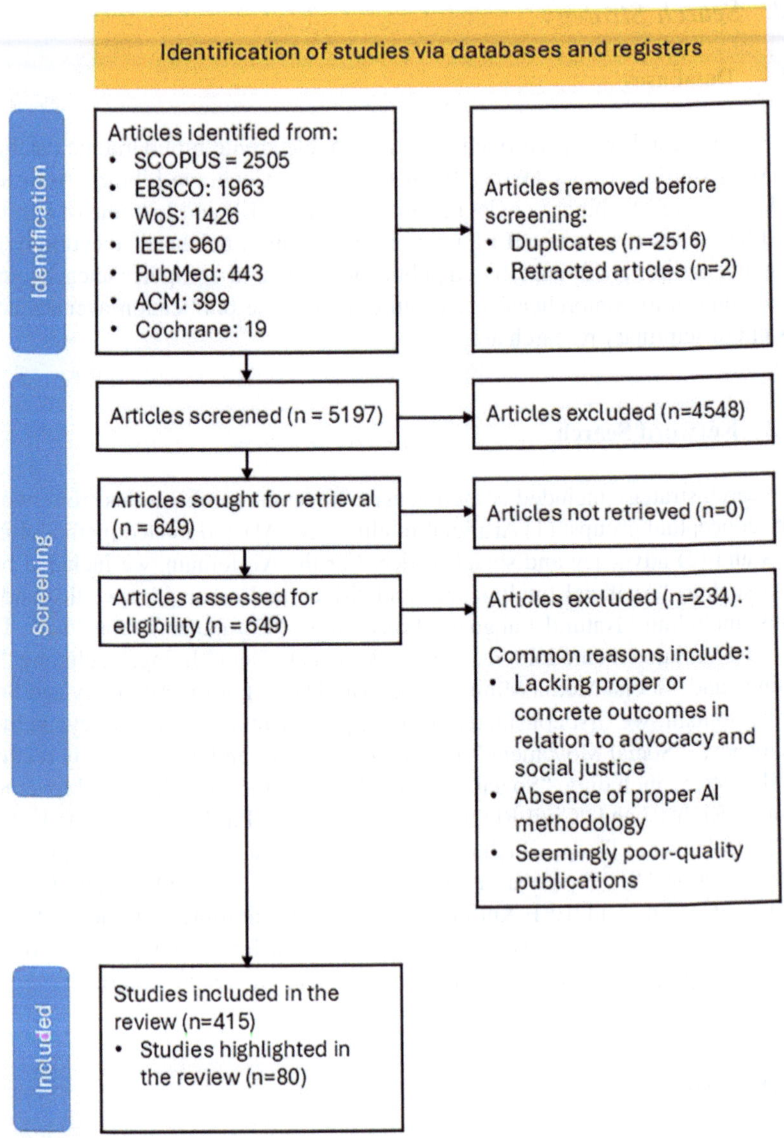

Fig. 16.1 PRISMA diagram

These articles underwent title and abstract screening, thereby eliminating 4548 articles. Common reasons for the exclusion of these articles included (1) no relation to social justice or advocacy (e.g., articles where these terms were used passively), (2) papers that were purely computational in nature, (3) articles concerning the implications of AI in social justice and advocacy as opposed to its application, (4) articles concerning other aspects of advocacy and justice (refer to prior chapters for works concerning healthcare advocacy and the later chapter for climate advocacy), and (5) articles for which the main text was unavailable in English. Subsequently, 649 articles were selected for full-text reviews, of which 234 were excluded for common reasons including, but not limited to, (1) lacking proper or concrete outcomes in relation to advocacy and social justice, (2) the absence or lack of proper AI methodology (e.g., using basic regression techniques as part of the methodology while using the terms "AI" and "statistical analysis" interchangeably), and (3) seemingly poor quality publications. As a result, 415 articles were included in this review.

Due to the sheer number of papers on this topic, we opt to highlight representative and prominent examples within each methodology cluster with respect to their relevant applications, as outlined in the subsequent subsections below. In total, we highlighted 80 studies.

4.2 Study Characteristics

Figure 16.2 shows the trends of the number of papers surrounding AI for advocacy and social justice published over the past 15 years, reflecting a steady exponential increase. Specifically, over the past 10 years: 12 were published in 2016, 18 were

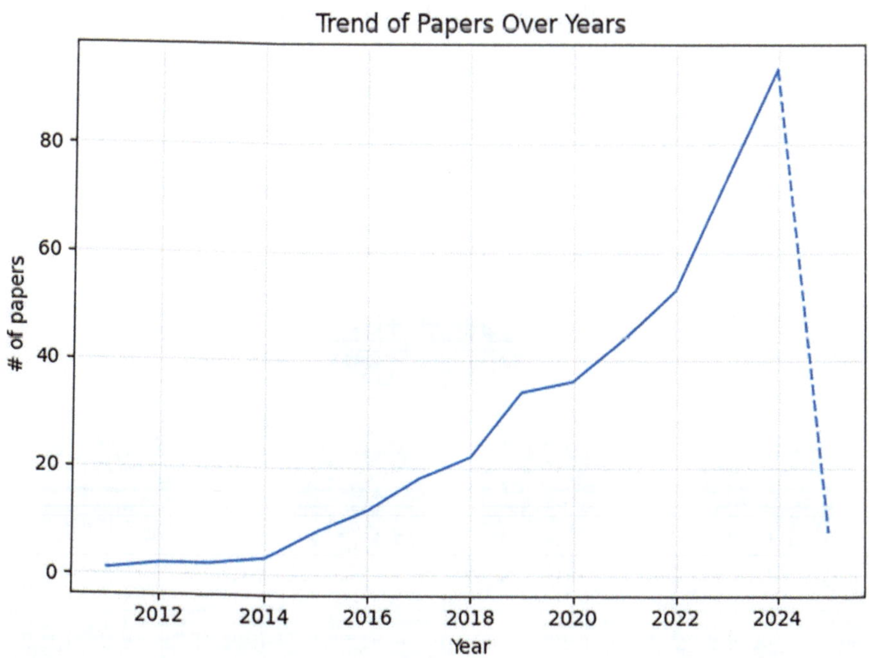

Fig. 16.2 15-year trend of the number of papers surrounding AI for Advocacy and Social Justice published

published in 2017, 22 were published in 2018, 34 were published in 2019, 36 were published in 2020, 44 were published in 2021, 53 were published in 2022, 71 were published in 2023, 94 were published in 2024, and 8 papers have been published thus far in 2025.

Of the papers filtered through our inclusion and exclusion criteria, 217 were conference proceedings, 197 were journal articles, and 1 was a book chapter, reflecting a balance between computer science-focused publication avenues, which typically emphasize computational innovations and methodological advancements, and journal articles that are the preferred publication avenues among social scientists and social work academics.

4.3 *Overview of Distinct AI Methods Used to Advance Advocacy and Social Justice*

Among the papers selected for review, we grouped them into distinct categories based on AI methodologies and their respective applications toward advancing advocacy and social justice: (1) Web and social media mining applications for advocacy (n = 204), (2) NLP applications assisting legal efforts in pursuing social justice (n = 79), (3) Computer vision and remote sensing applications solving humanitarian challenges (n = 33), (4) Virtual reality and chatbots supporting advocates and stakeholders (n = 11), and (5) others (n = 88). We illustrate this categorization as a conceptual framework in Fig. 16.3.

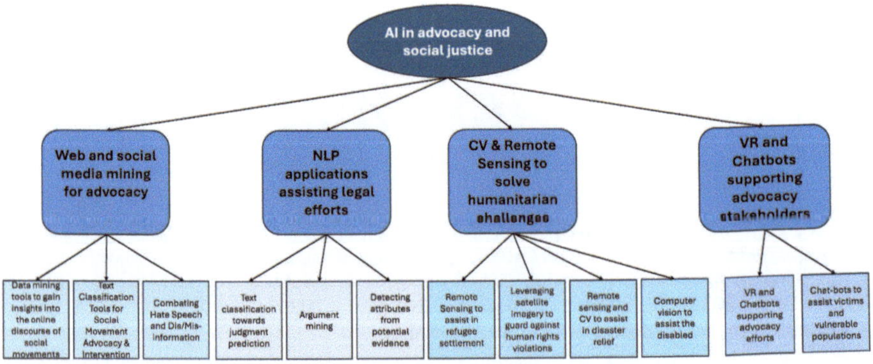

Fig. 16.3 Distinct buckets of AI methodologies and their respective applications

4.3.1 Web and Social Media Mining Applications for Advocacy

Social media has emerged as a prominent platform for organizing, amplifying, or complementing modern social movements. It raises awareness, highlights lived experiences, and expresses diverse opinions on various movements. Platforms like X and Reddit provide avenues for individuals to voice their opinions or experiences on a massive scale, uncovering diverse perspectives that traditional surveys, often constrained by limited sample sizes, might overlook (Alba & An, 2023). Additionally, social media's global connectivity allows researchers to better understand complex social phenomena through methods such as community detection, network analysis, and social network visualization, thereby enhancing the depth and breadth of advocacy-related insights.

Advancements in data mining methods have created opportunities for researchers to apply sophisticated analytical techniques to harness insights from "big data" to inform actionable interventions in social media. This is otherwise known as "social media mining," which is the process of collecting and analyzing user-generated content from online platforms, including social networking sites (e.g., Facebook, X), online forums (e.g., Reddit), video-sharing platforms (e.g., YouTube), and search engines (e.g., Google Trends), to identify and interpret patterns, trends, and actionable insights. Unlike some of the later-mentioned techniques, social media mining does not rely on a single method; rather, it is an interdisciplinary approach that integrates various analytical tools, including natural language processing and social network analysis, to leverage social media data effectively.

Data Mining Tools to Gain Insights into the Online Discourse of Social Movements

Data mining tools offer opportunities to amplify voices within social movements by leveraging insights from vast volumes of user-generated content, providing a scalable approach to understanding collective opinions and identifying key messages from marginalized groups.

Network analysis is a popular data-mining tool used to analyze connections across online interactions and the dynamics among individuals, groups, and key actors within social movements. By drawing on critical insights into online community structures and sources of influence, advocates can identify and target influential leaders to support online collaborative efforts and strengthen community resilience. For example, Jeon (2020) utilized network analysis to examine the interplay between narratives and entities in personal accounts of sexual violence in sports, following revelations related to Olympic gold medalist speed skater Suk-Hee Shim. Similarly, Suk et al. (2021) leveraged network analysis to understand how shared personal experiences of sexual violence and harassment on Twitter during the #MeToo movement transcended into calls for action across a range of institutions and communities. This allowed advocates to identify key discourses, actors, and themes associated with shared experiences surrounding the #MeToo movement.

Network analysis was also employed across a variety of political and democratic movements (Sanghi et al., 2021; Venkatesan et al., 2021; Wahyuningroem et al., 2024). For instance, Wahyuningroem et al. (2024) used network analysis to examine the influential role of youth participants in Indonesia's #ReformasiDikorupsi movement.

Topic modeling is another popular tool for uncovering the major themes and narratives in social movements. In summary, topic modeling helps identify prevalent themes or "topics" within vast collections of user-generated online texts, enabling advocates to distill complex volumes of online discussions into targeted, actionable insights that directly inform strategy, communication, and outreach efforts. For instance, Lee and Jang (2023) and Tong et al. (2022) applied topic modeling to identify central topics in personal narratives and broader social media discourse related to the #StopAsianHate and #BlackLivesMatter movements. Similarly, Umel (2024) used topic modeling to understand the struggles of Filipino migrants in Germany. These examples illustrate how themes derived from topic modeling provide systematic, yet insightful summaries of the dominant concerns, experiences, and perceptions expressed on social media, enabling nonprofits and advocacy groups to make informed decisions and implement strategic interventions.

Leveraging Text Classification Tools for Social Movement Advocacy and Intervention

Text classification involves leveraging machine learning tools to classify text into predefined categories. This capability helps researchers and practitioners systematically detect critical events, sensitive content, and specific behaviors across large volumes of online communication, facilitating timely interventions and targeted responses to emerging issues. For instance, Khatua et al. (2018) and Sawhney et al. (2021) employed text classification techniques to identify places (e.g., workplace, home, public spaces) and emotions linked to personal narratives of sexual violence arising from the #MeToo movement. Similarly, Subramani et al. (2019) developed text classifiers to identify the communicative strategies in online posts from victims or supporters of domestic violence, ranging from awareness to empathy to personal stories. These efforts could enable the early identification of emotional triggers and communication patterns associated with sexual and domestic violence, thus informing proactive strategies such as targeted awareness campaigns, educational programs, and community interventions designed to mitigate risk factors and foster environments that deter such violence. In another application, Stuart et al. (2020) employed text classification techniques to detect social media texts associated with traumatic grief from Chicago gang territories. The authors utilized insights gathered from in-depth interviews with neighborhood youths and observations from stakeholders (gangs, participants of violence-reduction programs, and workers of violence prevention organizations) to inform the development of their algorithms, capturing how traumatic grief is expressed on social media among residents in gang territories. These machine learning algorithms were deployed at scale to systematically analyze online data and gather critical insights, which were subsequently used to assist community organizations and violence prevention initiatives in developing more effective tools—including trauma-informed intervention applications—for victims of gang violence. *Sentiment analysis* is another popular text classification tool used to analyze evolving public sentiments toward social movements. In another instance, Haimson (2019) used sentiment analysis on Tumblr blogs to identify sentiment patterns associated with transgender identity disclosures and social support among transgender individuals, while Swanson et al. (2023) and Sabatovych (2019) used sentiment analysis to capture the prevailing emotional attitudes toward abortion rights movements following the Dobbs v. Jackson Women's Health Organization ruling. These examples illustrate how sentiment analysis could help women's and LGBTQ advocates capture emotional trends and shifts in public opinion, enabling targeted interventions, outreach, and inclusive policymaking.

Combating Hate Speech and Dis/Misinformation

Detecting hate and offensive speech, particularly targeting marginalized or minority communities and individuals, remains a core component of social media mining efforts in advocacy and social justice. While the rapid rise of social media has enhanced societal connectivity, the anonymous and non-face-to-face nature of interactions in the digital realm has facilitated an increase in hateful and offensive speech. AI could therefore be used to detect and filter such hateful and offensive online texts, including women-targeted online abuse (Rathod et al., 2023) and misogynistic aggression (Li, 2022), hate speech toward LGBTQIA+ individuals (Bozhidarova et al., 2023), and racially motivated offensive speech or slurs (Gupta et al., 2023).

Similarly, social media's rapid ability to disseminate information, often with minimal accountability, has facilitated the rise of misinformation and disinformation, which can undermine trust, distort public perception, and hinder efforts to achieve equitable and just outcomes in communities. Although no unified method exists to combat hate speech and misinformation, advancements in artificial intelligence, including some of the previously discussed techniques, offer promising avenues to address these challenges. While detecting hate speech remains challenging due to evolving slang and contexts, recent advances in language models have significantly enhanced identification and response capabilities. For instance, Anandhi et al. (2024), Chit et al. (2022), and Hüsünbeyi et al. (2022) leveraged advanced text classification methods to detect hate speech online, revealing nuanced patterns of discriminatory language and enabling quicker intervention. Similarly, tools such as social network analysis (Sivasankari & Vadivu, 2022) have been deployed to combat mis/disinformation by tracing the propagation paths of false information, identifying influential sources responsible for its widespread dissemination, and thereby enabling targeted interventions to disrupt online misinformation networks effectively. More recently, Generative AI, a type of AI technology capable of producing original content, such as ChatGPT, has also been employed to combat misinformation and disinformation (Jaidka et al., 2025) by generating fact-checking and explanatory content to debunk false claims proactively, address misconceptions, and promote digital literacy initiatives.

4.3.2 NLP Applications Assisting Legal Efforts

A variety of NLP tools are employed to predict, gain insights, and interpret legal documents and judicial processes. These methods range from forecasting judicial outcomes based on the presented arguments to leveraging historical data to recommend arguments to prosecutors and defenders. Collectively, these approaches could aid the pursuit of social justice by facilitating, assisting, and expediting legal processes, thereby striving toward accountability for human rights violations and protecting the innocent, while promoting fair and equitable trials.

Text Classification Toward Judgment Prediction

Building models capable of predicting court decisions remains a prominent text classification application in the legal domain. Typically, these models incorporate case law documents as input, including facts, legal arguments, judicial reasoning, interpretations, and verdicts, and can subsequently assist defenders and prosecutors by forecasting case outcomes based on proposed arguments and existing case files. This predictive capability enables legal professionals to prepare their cases better, develop stronger arguments, and strategize more effectively, ultimately promoting fairer and more informed judicial processes. This predictive capability may further enable proponents of social justice to achieve favorable judicial outcomes, such as Supreme Court rulings supporting civil rights, equal protection, and antidiscrimination efforts. Advancements in language models, specifically designed to process textual inputs and generate predictions with accuracy rates up to 91.8% (Yang et al., 2024a, 2024b), have enabled more reliable deployment of judgment prediction tools, significantly aiding legal professionals, including forensic and legal social workers, in effectively preparing for court cases. Such models have been built to predict judgments across a variety of countries and levels of government, ranging from the European Court of Human Rights (ECHR) to Supreme Court rulings in the United States (Yang et al., 2024a, 2024b), China (Wang et al., 2024), and India (Yang et al., 2024a, 2024b), to rulings made in local courts in Indonesia (Sari et al., 2022).

While accurate predictions offer considerable value, understanding the underlying reasons behind a model's predictions remains essential. Explainable AI (xAI) addresses this by clarifying how specific arguments or legal factors influence the model's judgment prediction outcomes. Such insights empower legal and forensic social workers to strategically assess case strengths, refine advocacy strategies, and promote greater transparency and fairness in judicial processes. Consequently, XAI is becoming increasingly valuable in legal decision-making, transitioning from traditional black-box predictions to transparent, interpretable explanations that are critical for trustworthy forecasting in legal contexts. Several methods and frameworks, such as Abstract Dialectical Frameworks (ADFs) (Collenette et al., 2023; Mumford et al., 2023) and the ANGELIC methodology (Dupré, 2023; Mumford et al., 2023), have been developed to elucidate the complex legal reasoning underlying AI prediction models. For instance, the latter's ANGELIC methodology organizes legal reasoning hierarchically—from verdicts to issues, abstract factors, and factual base-level factors—and produces natural language, step-by-step explanations as part of its prediction process, clearly showing how the model arrives at its decisions (Dupré, 2023; Mumford et al., 2023). Beyond predicting judgments from case law documents, these advancements in language models have also enabled the identification of specific violations detailed within court documents. Such capabilities allow forensic and legal social workers to swiftly identify relevant human rights violations, expediting the pursuit of justice, facilitating timely interventions, and potentially integrating directly into judicial workflows to enhance court efficiency and accuracy. This approach has been demonstrated effectively in identifying specific articles of violation in judgments issued by the European Court of Human Rights (ECHR) (Imran et al., 2023; Kaur & Bozic, 2019; Mumford et al., 2024; Quemy & Wrembel, 2020; Santosh et al., 2024; Xu et al., 2024; Yıldırım et al., 2023), made possible due to openly available court documents and transparency in the ECHR judicial processes.

Collectively, these AI-driven methodologies for legal prediction can support social justice advocates by enabling more accurate forecasting of judicial outcomes and by strengthening the preparation of evidence-based arguments, ultimately helping advocates secure favorable court decisions that advance social justice.

Argument Mining

Argument mining is another valuable methodology that can help legal professionals identify key aspects of arguments, evidence, and reasoning in court cases. Unlike the aforementioned text classification approaches, which primarily focus on predicting court outcomes, argument mining mainly focuses on extracting, clustering, and distinguishing the characteristics of arguments that influence a verdict. These features provide valuable insights to help advocates and legal social workers enhance their strategic argumentation and decision-making in their pursuit of fair and equitable judicial outcomes. There are various methodological approaches to argument mining. One method is to train a text classifier to identify predefined argumentative characteristics in a given piece of text. This is exemplified by Habernal et al. (2024), who developed a multitask text classification model capable of identifying a variety of precise argument types, such as interpretive methods, principles of proportionality, and institutional arguments, that are associated with distinct judicial actors and outcomes. These classifications could assist justice advocates and legal social workers in strategically identifying and strengthening their arguments in their pursuit of legal justice.

Another approach is to employ unsupervised clustering methods that naturally group sentences into argumentative categories based on their similarity. Unlike the above-mentioned approach, which classifies a piece of text into a predefined category, unsupervised methods cluster text with similar argumentative patterns "naturally" into groups, allowing legal social workers and advocates to flexibly explore emerging or previously unidentified argumentative themes without being constrained by the predefined classifications used in previous methods. For instance, Poudyal et al. (2019) developed unsupervised clustering algorithms to distinguish legal arguments related to human rights violations in legal documents. Specifically, they exploited the "Fuzzy" algorithms to account for the fact that a single sentence could encompass multiple arguments, thereby effectively addressing overlapping argumentative content often seen in legal contexts, enabling social workers and legal advocates to better recognize and navigate complex legal reasoning patterns in court cases.

Developing comprehensive yet accessible argument-mining tools is crucial for enabling legal social workers and advocates to easily deploy them across diverse legal scenarios. This is exemplified by Poudyal (2015), who developed a comprehensive argument-mining tool that consists of an (1) Argument Element Identifier (AEI), which uses machine learning algorithms to distinguish argumentative from non-argumentative sentences; (2) Argument Builder (AB), which employs the aforementioned unsupervised algorithms to group similar argumentative sentences into related clusters; and (3) Argument Structurer (AS), which uses word detection and contextual analysis to differentiate between premises and conclusions within argumentative clusters. Such comprehensive argument-mining tools create an integrated pipeline to streamline legal analysis and strategically identify key argumentative characteristics, thereby assisting legal social workers in building stronger cases in a time-efficient manner in their pursuit of social justice.

Detecting Attributes from Potential Evidence

Leveraging AI models to detect critical indicators, such as specific elements of torture, trauma, and abuse within extensive text-based evidence documents, can assist prosecutors, legal professionals, or forensic social workers in gathering relevant evidence. Such techniques not only streamline the evidence review process but also enhance accountability in the pursuit of justice. For instance, Gokhale and Fasli (2017), Kihlman and Fasli (2019), and Gokhale and Fasli (2018) developed text classification models that can detect and identify torture mechanisms such as hooding, blackened goggles, plastic blindfold, and sight deprivation by other means, which are types of sensory deprivation, from testimonies and survivor stories. Similarly, Schirmer et al. (2024) developed GENTRAC, a language model that detects trauma from genocide and mass atrocity court transcripts. Such models could henceforth amplify the voices of marginalized victims, empower survivors by validating their experiences, and enable advocates and legal social workers to pursue accountability and systemic change through robust, evidence-based advocacy.

Additionally, models can also be deployed to assist judges, legal professionals, and forensic social workers in evaluating the reliability and credibility of witness testimony. For instance, Gustafsson et al. (2025) developed machine learning models capable of predicting the accuracy of eyewitness statements based on 94 distinct acoustic features extracted from audio recordings. This demonstrates the potential of using AI to support the legal system in evaluating witness credibility, thereby contributing to fairer judicial outcomes and processes in the pursuit of social justice.

4.3.3 Computer Vision and Remote Sensing to Solve Humanitarian Challenges

Every second, millions of images are captured worldwide, ranging from satellite imagery to ground-based photographs. Each image inherently "contains a thousand words," offering rich information that can address some of the most pressing humanitarian challenges of our time, including refugee settlement planning, detection of human rights violations, disaster relief coordination, and accessibility for individuals with disabilities. However, manually extracting actionable information from such vast amounts of dense imagery can be laborious and time-consuming. For instance, analyzing satellite images manually after natural disasters to identify damaged infrastructure or optimal relief routes can significantly delay response efforts, potentially endangering lives. In critical contexts where human rights and lives hang in the balance, timely intervention is paramount, as delays can lead to increased suffering, prolonged displacement, and preventable loss of life. Therefore, computer vision, a field within AI focused on enabling machines to interpret and predict visual information from images or videos, and remote sensing, the discipline involving the acquisition of information remotely through satellite or aerial imagery, can provide invaluable assistance by enabling the rapid extraction of crucial insights to enhance the effectiveness and timeliness of humanitarian responses and interventions by authorities, NGOs, and advocacy groups dedicated to achieving social justice.

Remote Sensing to Assist in Refugee Settlement

Satellite imagery provides critical information to monitor refugee movements, detect and map settlement expansion, assess environmental impacts, and identify specific infrastructure within refugee or internally displaced people (IDP) settlements. Remote sensing techniques, which analyze and interpret satellite imagery to extract meaningful insights, play a crucial role in translating raw satellite data into actionable information. Such information can greatly benefit humanitarian workers by enhancing their situational awareness, informing efficient resource allocation, and ultimately improving response times and effectiveness during refugee crises.

For instance, Braun et al. (2019) used remote sensing to assess refugee camp expansion and associated environmental changes with the refugee crisis in

Kutupalong, Bangladesh, in lieu of the Rohingya genocide from neighboring Myanmar. The results showed a significant expansion of the refugee camp area, increasing from approximately 36 hectares in early 2016 to over 1850 hectares by early 2019, and a corresponding vegetation loss of about 1500 hectares, highlighting severe environmental impacts associated with rapid refugee influx. These insights can help humanitarian and social justice advocates build stronger cases for international support and peace advocacy, as well as enable more informed planning and resource allocation to manage settlement expansions and associated humanitarian needs effectively. Similarly, Quinn et al. (2018) employed computer vision techniques on high-resolution imagery from 13 refugee/IDP settlements in South Sudan, Iraq, and Nigeria to quantify the distinct structural types within these settlements. Automating this otherwise labor-intensive manual task can assist humanitarian social workers in settlement monitoring, resource and infrastructure planning, and vulnerability and needs assessment.

Additionally, Moser et al. (2022) demonstrated the effectiveness, robustness, and accuracy of advanced computer vision models for identifying small vessels in satellite imagery, with the ultimate aim of leveraging these techniques to enable NGOs and the public to detect refugee boats more effectively. These advancements strengthen humanitarian responses, support timely rescue interventions, and safeguard refugees in vulnerable situations at sea, equipping social workers with critical insights to advocate effectively for humane migration policies and greater international accountability.

Leveraging Satellite Imagery to Guard Against Human Rights Violations

Satellite imagery provides essential data for detecting, classifying, and documenting human rights violations, such as forced displacement, violent conflict, and forced labor. Leveraging remote sensing and computer vision techniques, AI can rapidly deliver predictive insights to humanitarian workers, facilitating urgent, evidence-based interventions and accountability. Such timely intelligence supports social justice by ensuring transparent monitoring, equitable protection, and swift responses to human rights abuses.

Redmond (2021) used remote sensing on satellite imagery to monitor violent conflict targeting civilians during the Rohingya genocide by assessing the destruction of settlements in Rakhine State. Specifically, through semantic segmentation, where each pixel in a captured satellite image was classified as either damaged or undamaged, Redmond was able to quantify and geo-reference the precise amount of damage in Rakhine State at the time the image was captured. By scaling this across satellite imagery captured at different times spanning the genocide, humanitarian workers could assess the scale of civilian displacement and identify affected areas, enabling social and humanitarian workers to direct timely assistance and targeted interventions to those most in need.

Similarly, McDonald et al. (2021) used satellite-based vessel-tracking data, combined with machine learning, to identify globally high-risk fishing vessels.

Specifically, they analyzed data from over 16,000 industrial fishing vessels to detect behavioral patterns indicative of forced labor, including extended time at sea, infrequent port visits, and transmission gaps. Their approach provides targeted insights that can assist humanitarian and social workers in identifying vulnerable populations, guiding resource allocation, planning effective interventions, and advocating effectively for the protection and rights of at-risk maritime workers.

On the other hand, Kalliatakis et al. (2017, 2019) demonstrated the effectiveness of leveraging advanced computer vision techniques to identify human rights violations, including but not limited to child labor, police violence, refugees, child soldiers, forced child marriages, and displacements from images. Such advancements could enhance advocacy efforts by strengthening documentation of abuses, mobilizing timely humanitarian responses, and supporting evidence-based campaigns to protect vulnerable populations and promote accountability for human rights violations in pursuit of social justice.

Remote Sensing and Computer Vision to Assist in Disaster Relief

Satellite imagery provides critical information to monitor disaster events, detect and map affected infrastructure, assess the extent of damage, and identify safe evacuation routes and areas requiring urgent assistance. Therefore, remote sensing and computer vision techniques, including classification, segmentation, and object detection algorithms, could play a crucial role in converting raw satellite imagery into actionable humanitarian intelligence. Such information empowers humanitarian social workers by providing accurate and timely assessments of disaster impacts, enabling targeted interventions, informed evacuation planning, and the efficient allocation of relief resources. For affected populations, this translates into improved safety, timely support, and more effective recovery and reconstruction efforts.

Remote sensing is widely used to support humanitarian relief efforts by providing timely, accurate data for monitoring, assessing, and responding to natural disasters, including floods. For instance, Alizadeh et al. (2022) used advanced computer vision algorithms to estimate floodwater depth by analyzing paired images of submerged stop signs and augmenting flood gauge data. They complemented these data with classical computational algorithms to identify optimized, flood-free evacuation routes. The research incorporated participatory feedback from local residents and rescuers to enhance the practical applicability and effectiveness of evacuation planning. Similarly, Schneibel et al. (2022) demonstrated the use of remote sensing to automate flood monitoring for rapid situational awareness and to provide quick damage assessment of buildings and infrastructure, using satellite data from the Cyclone Idai disaster in Mozambique. By demonstrating high accuracy in flood monitoring (IoU of 80%) and damage assessment for road (IoU of 65.64%) and building detection (F1 score of 71.34%), such algorithms could be confidently deployed to enhance the rapid provision of reliable and accessible crisis information. This could directly support humanitarian relief operations conducted by

NGO's through rapid situation assessments, optimizing the allocation of relief resources and enhancing overall decision-making capabilities.

Similarly, remote sensing can assist in humanitarian relief and human rights monitoring in the aftermath of human-made disasters, such as wars, as exemplified by Mueller et al. (2021), who used advanced computer vision algorithms to identify destroyed buildings from patch-level satellite imagery collected during the Syrian War in Aleppo. By validating the generalizability and robustness of their model against external bombing event data, Mueller et al. (2021) demonstrated that their approach could be reliably deployed in real-world scenarios, thereby offering the potential to support humanitarian efforts through prioritized aid delivery, streamlined resource allocation, and accelerated post-conflict reconstruction planning.

Computer Vision to Assist People with Disability

Computer vision techniques can facilitate solutions to assist individuals with disabilities by enhancing accessibility and inclusion, bridging communication gaps, identifying barriers, and promoting equitable social participation and mobility. The utilization of computer vision to assist deaf and mute individuals through sign language detection—where sign language gestures are automatically recognized and translated into text (Swaroop et al., 2024) or speech (Rajanishree et al., 2022), understandable by individuals unfamiliar with sign language—highlights AI's potential to bridge communication barriers and promote equitable social inclusion. Open-access and deployable tools, such as OpenCV, have enabled seamless integration between gesture recognition algorithms and real-time video processing (Vasanth Kumar & Fawziya, 2024; Swaroop et al., 2024).

In addition, computer vision can assist individuals with disabilities, as demonstrated by Wu et al. (2019), who employed image classification techniques to identify buildings across Milwaukee, Chicago, Los Angeles, and other urban areas based on the presence of handicap-accessible ramps. Such technology could be integrated into future applications to provide real-time, location-based accessibility information, enabling individuals with disabilities to navigate urban environments better.

4.3.4 Virtual Reality and Chatbots to Assist Advocacy Stakeholders

The advanced reasoning capabilities of LLMs and CV have paved the way for generative tools—such as OpenAI's ChatGPT—to develop reliable chatbots and VR experiences. These innovative tools significantly enhance the capacity of advocacy groups and NGOs, effectively supporting advocates and staff through interactive training and educational resources, while simultaneously providing meaningful assistance and timely guidance to victims and the vulnerable populations they serve.

Virtual Reality and Chatbots Supporting Advocacy Efforts

Virtual Reality and chatbots can assist NGOs in training and recruiting advocates by enabling them to practice advocacy in simulated environments. For instance, Pillis et al. developed the "LGBTQIA+ Advocacy Simulator," which utilizes AI-generated virtual characters powered by generative conversational AI. Advocates engaged with realistic simulations of workplace interactions centered around scenarios such as conversations about "coming out." This was accomplished through interactive, web-based technologies that allowed users to either directly control a virtual character's dialogue ("First Person" mode) or guide character interactions indirectly by instructing AI-generated responses ("Third Person" mode). Results indicated significant improvements in advocates' empathy and sympathy, with a mean increase of up to 0.73 (on a scale of 7), demonstrating safe and educational practice of advocacy skills in sensitive social contexts.

Similarly, Baugerud et al. developed an AI-based child avatar system designed to help forensic interviewers practice interviewing techniques with simulated child victims of abuse. The system does so through a "virtual child avatar" trained on 741 mock forensic interviews. Interviewers interacted with the child avatar in immersive VR scenarios simulating sexual and physical abuse disclosures, allowing realistic question-and-response exchanges. Results showed that interviewers asked predominantly open-ended questions and rated their interactions positively, finding the avatar's responses realistic (mean realism rating = 3.44 out of 5) and comfortable engaging with the virtual child (mean comfort rating = 3.59 out of 5). This approach highlights the potential for VR and generative AI to significantly improve training effectiveness and enhance advocates' practical skills in sensitive interviewing contexts.

Chatbots to Assist Victims and Vulnerable Populations

Robust chatbots have also been developed to assist advocates in supporting victims and vulnerable populations. For example, Bauer et al. (2020) developed a chatbot to help survivors of sexual harassment by directing them to appropriate institutions and increasing documentation of underreported harassment cases. They achieved this by creating a three-component system consisting of (1) harassment type classification, (2) extracting spatiotemporal information (such as locations, organizations, or individuals involved), and (3) managing dialogues with users. The system achieved approximately 80% accuracy in harassment type classification and over 90% in extracting locations and dates, demonstrating its ability to facilitate precise documentation and timely guidance. Such a system could provide meaningful assistance to survivors, empowering those who may be hesitant to disclose harassment directly to individuals, stepping in to offer immediate support when social workers are not readily available, and swiftly identifying key entities involved to facilitate timely reporting. Consequently, it could significantly enhance social justice and advocacy efforts by increasing awareness, improving documentation accuracy, and accelerating interventions to pursue accountability and protection for victims.

Similarly, Mutinda and Muchiri (2024) developed a multilingual chatbot to support victims of gender-based violence (GBV) in Kenya, designed to provide emotional counseling and immediate referrals to relevant local services. They achieved this by building a chatbot trained on bilingual datasets (English and Kiswahili). The chatbot attained an accuracy of 63%–92%, demonstrating its ability to provide accessible emotional support and tailored referrals in locally prevalent languages, thereby significantly contributing to advocacy efforts and improved outcomes for GBV victims. Specifically, this chatbot could provide crucial support to social workers by extending immediate assistance in rural communities lacking prompt access to services, reducing stigma through anonymity, and systematically documenting cases to strengthen advocacy and social justice initiatives.

Chatbots toward Mental Health Advocacy

The use of chatbots and other AI tools to assist in mental health care is a widely explored topic, as demonstrated by Alathamneh et al. (2024), who developed a chatbot to provide empathetic, contextually relevant conversational support for mental health patients. They accomplished this by training the chatbot on a diverse set of mental health datasets, including mental health counseling conversations, frequently asked questions (FAQs), and anonymized conversational data from various healthcare resources (e.g., WebMD, Mayo Clinic, HealthLine). In doing so, the authors hope to equip the chatbot with professional-level mental health guidance and expert-informed advice, thereby significantly improving access to real-time mental health support, notably in cases where professional counseling services (including Licensed Clinical Social Workers) may not be immediately available or individuals who face stigma and prefer seeking initial support anonymously before gaining the confidence to approach a counselor directly.

Similarly, Broadbent et al. (2024) demonstrated the effectiveness of ElliQ, an AI-driven social robot designed to alleviate loneliness among elderly individuals through personalized companionship, proactive engagement, daily conversation prompts, wellness check-ins, and cognitive stimulation activities. The study showed that 80% of participants reported reduced feelings of loneliness and improved emotional well-being, highlighting the potential of AI-driven assistive robots to address mental health concerns among the elderly. Such proactive, automated interactions could substantially relieve social workers in elderly care facilities of routine responsibilities, enabling them to devote their time and professional expertise to situations requiring specialized intervention.

5 Discussion

This study conducted an extensive review of AI applications toward advocacy and social justice, aiming to assist social workers and professionals from related disciplines in understanding and leveraging AI tools to advance their advocacy objectives and promote social justice. We identified five prevalent areas of AI use in advocacy and social justice: (1) social media mining, (2) computer vision and remote sensing for humanitarian challenges, (3) virtual reality and chatbots for assisting advocacy stakeholders, (4) predictive modeling to address homelessness, and (5) NLP for legal predictions. Through this review, we uncovered key insights into how AI methods are actively employed to promote fairness, enhance advocacy efforts, and support equitable outcomes across various social justice contexts.

The "AI Boom," which has unfolded since the late 2010s, has invited extensive criticism regarding job displacement, ethical concerns, model explainability and transparency, privacy risks arising from the extensive use of training data, and the potential for misuse. These criticisms have intensified significantly following the emergence of generative AI models such as ChatGPT, further raising concerns about the substantial environmental impacts of the resources required to train these large-scale models, alongside other contentious issues, including copyright infringement related to training data. However, despite these valid concerns, our study illustrates that AI, when thoughtfully designed, responsibly implemented, and deployed with intentions for social good, can significantly benefit humanity by advancing social justice initiatives.

While the use of AI in advocacy and social justice remains relatively modest compared to other prominent AI application fields such as healthcare, e-commerce, and social media, continued innovation and mindful application—coupled with reliable and representative data—offer promising opportunities to enhance equity, protect human rights, and empower communities. To effectively execute this vision, it is critical to promote the open availability of AI models and datasets, encourage active collaboration between AI experts and advocacy stakeholders, and develop safe, scalable, and meaningful solutions explicitly aimed at achieving social good.

5.1 *Areas of Success*

Many of the aforementioned AI tools have been extensively adopted across distinct facilities serving vulnerable populations (e.g., elder care facilities), integrated into nonprofit or nongovernmental organizations that advocate social justice (e.g., Amnesty International), or made accessible to the public for use by both social workers and vulnerable populations. These success stories highlight the importance and impact of developing these AI tools beyond academic publications, thereby turning them into actionable goods that can benefit society through advocacy and social justice.

5.1.1 Adoption of AI Tools into Facilities Serving Vulnerable Populations

ElliQ, an AI-driven social robot designed to alleviate loneliness among elderly individuals through personalized companionship, proactive engagement, daily conversation prompts, wellness check-ins, and cognitive stimulation activities (as detailed in the Results section above), has been extensively integrated into multiple elderly care facilities, spanning 15 programs across numerous healthcare organizations in the United States and Canada (Broadbent et al., 2024). Extensive follow-up trials demonstrated its effectiveness in reducing loneliness, improving users' emotional well-being, and reducing social workers' workload in these facilities. This prominent and widespread adoption, supported by evidence beyond algorithmic development, highlights AI's potential to enhance the quality of life for vulnerable populations and support relevant stakeholders when proactively implemented in care environments.

5.1.2 Adoption by Nonprofit Advocacy Organizations Toward the Pursuit of Social Justice

As noted earlier, AI techniques such as social media mining and remote sensing could be effectively leveraged to support humanitarian and advocacy efforts in their pursuit of social justice. When embraced and integrated by nonprofit advocacy organizations, these tools could significantly assist social and humanitarian workers in delivering timely relief while enabling advocates to utilize data-driven insights to raise public awareness of injustices. This is perhaps best exemplified by Amnesty International's digital investigations team, Evidence Lab (https://citizenevidence.org), which actively advances digital methods to support human rights among populations subjected to injustice by employing several of the aforementioned tools, including social media mining and remote sensing.

Amnesty International's effectiveness is exemplified by its successful development and utilization of the "Strike Tracker" in Syria, which leveraged remote sensing techniques (as detailed in the earlier Results section) to systematically detect and document civilian building destruction resulting from air strikes during the recently concluded Syrian Civil War. By training computer vision models to automatically identify damaged structures in satellite imagery in real time, these tools were effectively deployed to support humanitarian workers in aid and rescue efforts. Additionally, the project provided compelling AI-driven evidence of the destruction caused by the Assad regime's unjustifiable attacks on civilian populations, strengthening Amnesty's advocacy against human rights violations. This initiative, alongside other AI-driven projects by Amnesty International and similar organizations, highlights AI's considerable potential to advance advocacy and social justice efforts when proactively embraced by nonprofit organizations.

5.1.3 Making Tools Publicly Accessible for Vulnerable Populations

Beyond demonstrating efficacy through academic publication, translating AI-driven advancements into accessible, open-source, and practically usable tools for vulnerable populations is crucial. Such accessibility ensures that the potential of AI extends beyond theoretical results, effectively addressing real-world humanitarian needs by empowering individuals who are directly affected.

A variety of publicly accessible AI tools already exist, spanning multiple domains of social and humanitarian support. Examples include mental health platforms such as Wysa (https://www.wysa.com/), Woebot (https://woebothealth.com/), and Earkick (https://earkick.com/), as well as initiatives designed specifically to assist victims of abuse, such as Chatbot Sophia (https://springact.org/sophia-chatbot/) and Hope Chat AI (https://www.domesticshelters.org/hope-chat-ai). These tools can be particularly beneficial by offering immediate, anonymous support to vulnerable individuals and providing a safe initial step toward seeking professional help, especially for those who might otherwise be hesitant or fearful to approach traditional services directly (Moore et al., 2025). Other examples include AutoThemeGenerator (Yang et al., 2024a, 2024b), a generative AI-powered tool that assists qualitative researchers in performing thematic analysis more efficiently. Such a tool can help advocacy groups and social researchers rapidly process and interpret large volumes of qualitative data—turning raw testimonies, interview transcripts, or focus group notes into actionable insights—thereby accelerating evidence-based advocacy and enabling faster, better-informed interventions.

The successful deployment and public accessibility of these AI-driven tools have been enabled in significant part by collaborative partnerships between nonprofit organizations and AI researchers. Such collaborations reflect a shared commitment to translating technological advances into practical solutions that directly benefit those in need. Importantly, these tools serve as supplementary resources, providing immediate, accessible support while encouraging users to seek professional intervention when ready (Dakanalis et al., 2024; Moore et al., 2025). As such, they complement rather than replace professional assistance, highlighting AI's potential to enhance existing services rather than substitute critical human expertise (Dakanalis et al., 2024; Moore et al., 2025).

5.2 *Areas for Growth*

5.2.1 Ensuring AI-Led Advocacy Efforts Are Culturally Sensitive

To effectively utilize AI in advocacy and social justice, it is essential to account for cultural factors in human–computer interaction (HCI) (Shafik, 2025). HCI is an interdisciplinary field concerned with designing, evaluating, and implementing interactive computing systems that are accessible, intuitive, and user-friendly. Successful integration of AI-driven solutions into real-world advocacy contexts relies on understanding users' cultural preferences, behaviors, and expectations to ensure that solutions are well received, widely adopted, and effective in practice (Madon, 1992).

Cultural values and norms vary significantly across countries and communities, reflecting distinct cultures and shaping perceptions, attitudes, and responses toward AI technologies and associated policies (Alba & Mittal, 2021). Due to this cultural variability, individuals and groups may interpret, accept, or resist AI-led advocacy efforts differently, depending on their cultural backgrounds. To ensure equitable and effective dissemination, it is crucial to incorporate culturally informed approaches within HCI frameworks during AI development and implementation. Integrating cultural considerations can enhance user trust, improve engagement, and ultimately maximize the social impact of AI in advancing advocacy and social justice initiatives across diverse global contexts.

5.2.2 Trickling Efforts to Low-Resource Communities

A persistent challenge in scaling AI-led advocacy efforts to vulnerable populations is the disproportionate concentration of tools, datasets, and research in high-resource languages (e.g., English). In contrast, low-resource languages remain underrepresented in AI development and deployment (Alam et al., 2024). This disparity can be attributed to several factors: first, low-resource languages often suffer from limited availability of high-quality, annotated datasets, making it challenging to train robust and accurate models; second, organizations and communities that speak these languages may lack the financial resources, technical expertise, or institutional support necessary to develop and maintain such systems (Mothe, 2024).

The resulting imbalance risks exacerbating the existing Global North-Global South divide and deepening the broader digital divide, where populations in low-resource settings, who often face heightened vulnerabilities, are the least likely to benefit from cutting-edge AI solutions (Yu et al., 2023). This is especially concerning in contexts where social service capacity is already strained, and human resources for social workers or humanitarian responders are scarce. Addressing this gap requires deliberate strategies to localize AI tools, expand multilingual datasets, and invest in capacity-building initiatives within underserved regions.

5.3 *Limitations*

5.3.1 Misinformation

Despite the considerable promise of AI for advocacy and social justice, its application poses significant risks when used to leverage large-scale user-generated content from online platforms. Advocacy and social justice groups increasingly rely on AI-driven social media mining and text analysis to rapidly disseminate information, mobilize support, and shape public discourse. However, this reliance can inadvertently amplify misinformation, particularly when out-of-context or misleading narratives are propagated quickly, causing unintended harm to public credibility and diminishing the legitimacy of advocacy efforts. Such misinformation can ultimately undermine trust and credibility in advocacy messages, hindering effective engagement and meaningful social change.

Moreover, modern-day social media algorithms, designed explicitly to personalize content and enhance user engagement, may inadvertently exacerbate the creation of echo chambers—spaces in which users are predominantly exposed to content aligning closely with their existing beliefs. As highlighted by recent research, such personalized algorithmic filtering can significantly heighten polarization and extremity of viewpoints within social networks (Springsteen et al., 2024). This effect is further intensified when negative stereotypes about out-group members or opposing viewpoints permeate the advocacy-driven content, potentially fostering divisiveness rather than understanding and unity. Consequently, misinformation is further perpetuated as users become increasingly insulated from diverse, fact-based perspectives.

To mitigate these risks, AI advocacy stakeholders must critically and continuously assess information validity, context, and sources using advanced AI-driven approaches, including retrieval-augmented generation (RAG) and context-sensitive language models (Deng et al., 2025). These methodologies offer promising avenues for rapidly verifying the accuracy and contextual relevance of information, detecting inconsistencies, and providing balanced perspectives from reliable sources. Such proactive measures can help advocacy groups maintain trust, reduce misinformation, and effectively promote exposure to diverse, credible, and constructive viewpoints.

5.3.2 Fairness and Bias

Another critical limitation concerns the fairness and bias inherent in AI models, arising primarily from historical biases, racism, and systemic inequalities deeply embedded in human-generated data. When AI systems are trained on such historical data, they risk amplifying existing prejudices and discriminatory practices, creating "algorithms of oppression" (Noble, 2018) that systematically disadvantage marginalized or minority communities. A prominent example is the controversy surrounding the Correctional Offender Management Profiling for Alternative Sanctions (COMPAS) software (Brennan & Dieterich, 2018), an AI tool used to assess potential recidivism risk. In a widely publicized case, 41-year-old African American Prater, convicted of shoplifting $86.35 worth of tools, was predicted to have a high risk of future offenses. In contrast, Borden, a white defendant convicted of armed robbery and attempted armed robbery, was predicted as low risk (Angwin et al., 2016).

Contrary to these predictions, Prater committed no subsequent offenses, while Borden is serving an eight-year prison term for later crimes. A follow-up ProPublica study (Angwin et al., 2016) further highlighted that Black defendants were nearly twice as likely as white defendants to be labeled high risk but not actually re-offend. This exemplifies how biases embedded within historical data can perpetuate unjust outcomes when integrated into predictive modeling.

Henceforth, to counteract such biases, AI practitioners must incorporate participatory approaches and critical frameworks into model development, actively engage diverse communities in the design process, and rigorously examine underlying assumptions to create equitable and socially just AI solutions. Additionally, practitioners can leverage Fair ML solutions such as Fairlearn (Bird et al., 2020) and IBM's AI Fairness 360 (Bellamy et al., 2019). These tools enable users to systematically detect, quantify, and mitigate biases through methods such as fairness-aware optimization, bias metrics evaluation, and explainability analyses, thereby promoting equitable outcomes and transparency in AI-driven decision-making.

5.3.3 AI for Social Harm: Using AI to Target Marginalized Individuals

While AI technologies have significant potential for positive social impact, they can also be employed in ways that harm vulnerable or marginalized individuals. Surveillance tools, such as facial recognition and predictive policing algorithms, can be used to disproportionately monitor, track, and discriminate against minority communities, facilitating oppressive practices or serving personal and political agendas. For example, recent reports suggest that the Trump administration has employed AI-driven surveillance to monitor social media activity of foreign nationals, identifying individuals perceived as supporting terror groups such as Hamas, thereby posing significant threats to civil liberties and freedom of expression (Monahan, 2025).

These applications illustrate the critical importance of teaching ethics and social responsibility to AI practitioners and data scientists. Professionals developing AI tools, as well as advocacy and social justice stakeholders who could potentially use these tools, must remain vigilant, foster critical thinking about the contexts in which their innovations are deployed, and ensure transparency in their applications. To prevent misuse and protect human rights, cross-disciplinary collaboration and community-based approaches among AI experts, policymakers, social advocates, and affected communities are essential. Only through rigorous ethical education, active engagement, and mutual accountability can we ensure that AI systems are developed and used in ways that promote social justice rather than undermine it.

6 Future Directions and Challenges

6.1 Open Sourcing Data

As demonstrated by our results, high-quality, representative, and globally diverse data are essential to achieving tangible outcomes in advocacy and social justice applications of AI. Promoting open science principles, particularly the widespread sharing and open sourcing of data, will be instrumental in facilitating collaborative research, innovation, and equitable AI model development across international contexts. However, recent trends toward monetizing previously free data, such as API access from popular social media platforms like X (formerly Twitter) (Center of an Informed Public, 2023), present significant barriers. Such monetization disproportionately impacts researchers from under-resourced countries and institutions, exacerbating global disparities by limiting their access to essential data for advocacy and social justice research. Advocating for policies that encourage open data sharing, providing grants to enable equitable data access, and developing international collaborative frameworks will therefore be critical to ensuring inclusive participation and advancing socially beneficial AI research.

6.2 Implementing Models to Enact Social Good

Successfully translating predictive AI models and analytical insights from academic settings into tangible improvements in people's lives requires active collaboration with authorities, advocacy organizations, community representatives, and other relevant stakeholders. Such multi-stakeholder engagement ensures that AI interventions are aligned with real-world needs, can be feasibly implemented, and are accepted by the communities they aim to benefit. In addition, effective deployment of these AI-driven advocacy solutions demands rigorous attention to human–computer interaction (HCI) research. Integrating user-centered design principles (Gulliksen et al., 2003), behavioral and decision-making concepts (Alba et al., 2024), and cultural dimensions of technology (Shafik, 2025) when implementing these AI models through HCI studies is essential to ensure that solutions are accessible, intuitive, culturally sensitive, and genuinely helpful to the diverse populations they seek to empower.

Additionally, to robustly assess the effectiveness and social impact of AI-driven advocacy tools, empirical validation through randomized controlled trials (RCTs) or rigorous observational studies must become standard practice. Such studies will help systematically assess whether AI interventions produce meaningful, real-world improvements in advocacy and social justice outcomes, while simultaneously identifying areas that need further refinement. Ultimately, rigorous testing and iterative evaluation will be critical to turning theoretical AI advances into scalable and impactful social justice interventions.

6.3 Sustainable and Cost-Effective Solutions

A critical challenge facing AI-driven advocacy and social justice initiatives is ensuring sustainability and affordability. Many contemporary generative AI models, particularly large-scale models, have significant environmental footprints due to the vast computational resources required for training and deployment (Berthelot et al., 2024), including high GPU costs and substantial energy consumption. This presents a paradox: leveraging AI for social good may inadvertently exacerbate environmental harm and widen existing digital divides, especially disadvantaging resource-scarce countries or communities lacking necessary infrastructure. Addressing this paradox requires a shift toward more sustainable AI practices, such as developing smaller yet robust models (Schick & Schütze, 2021) or employing resource-efficient techniques that enable these large AI models to be trained in an environmentally and cost-efficient manner (Han et al., 2024). These strategies not only reduce computational demands and environmental impact but also promote greater accessibility and practical implementation across diverse global settings, aligning AI-driven advocacy more closely with principles of equity and environmental responsibility.

References

Alam, F., Chowdhury, S. A., Boughorbel, S., & Hasanain, M. (2024, March). LLMs for low resource languages in multilingual, multimodal and dialectal settings. In *Proceedings of the 18th conference of the European chapter of the association for computational linguistics: tutorial abstracts*, pp. 27–33. https://doi.org/10.18653/v1/2024.eacl-tutorials.5

Alathamneh, R., Al Ameri, S., & Al Obeidat, F. (2024). Artificial intelligence in mental health care: The t5 chatbot project. In *2024 11th International Conference on Social Networks Analysis, Management and Security (SNAMS)*, pp. 212–218. https://doi.org/10.1109/SNAMS64316.2024.10883804

Alba, C., & An, R. (2023). Using mobile phone data to assess socio-economic disparities in unhealthy food reliance during the COVID-19 pandemic. *Health Data Science, 3*, 0101. https://doi.org/10.34133/hds.0101

Alba, C., & Mittal, M. M. (2021). Sociocultural behavioral traits in modelling the prediction of COVID-19 infection rates. *Journal of Humanities and Applied Social Sciences, 3*(5), 339–355. https://doi.org/10.1108/JHASS-07-2021-0128

Alba, C., Walasek, L., & Spektor, M. S. (2024). Attention-driven imitation in consumer reviews. *Decision*. https://doi.org/10.1037/dec0000238

Alizadeh, B., Li, D., Hillin, J., Meyer, M. A., Thompson, C. M., Zhang, Z., & Behzadan, A. H. (2022). Human-centered flood mapping and intelligent routing through augmenting flood gauge data with crowdsourced street photos. *Advanced Engineering Informatics, 54*, 101730. https://doi.org/10.1016/j.aei.2022.101730

Anandhi, R., Devi, V. A., Devi, B. K., Kavin, B. P., & Seng, G. H. (2024). Croa-based feature selection with bert model for detecting the offensive speech in twitter data. *Journal of Autonomous Intelligence, 7*(3), 1122. https://doi.org/10.32629/jai.v7i3.1122

Angwin, J., Larson, J., Mattu, S., & Kirchner, L. (2016). *Machine bias*. Propublica. Retrieved April 19, 2019, from https://www.propublica.org/article/machine-bias-risk-assessments-in-criminal-sentencing

Anokwa, Y., Hartung, C., Brunette, W., Borriello, G., & Lerer, A. (2009). Open source data collection in the developing world. *Computer, 42*(10), 97–99. https://doi.org/10.1109/MC.2009.328

Barta, T., & Kheng, J. H. (1997). A knowledge-based housing discrimination advisory system. *New Review of Applied Expert Systems, 3*, 97–108.

Bauer, T., Devrim, E., Glazunov, M., Jaramillo, W. L., Mohan, B., & Spanakis, G. (2020). #metoomaastricht: Building a chatbot to assist survivors of sexual harassment. In *Machine learning and knowledge discovery in databases: International workshops of ECML PKDD*

2019, Würzburg, Germany, September 16–20, 2019, proceedings, Part I, pp. 503–521. https://doi.org/10.1007/978-3-030-43823-4_41

Bellamy, R. K., Dey, K., Hind, M., Hoffman, S. C., Houde, S., Kannan, K., Lohia, P., Martino, J., Mehta, S., Mojsilović, A., et al. (2019). Ai fairness 360: An extensible toolkit for detecting and mitigating algorithmic bias. *IBM Journal of Research and Development, 63*(4/5), 4–1. https://doi.org/10.1147/JRD.2019.2942287

Berthelot, A., Caron, E., Jay, M., & Lefèvre, L. (2024). Estimating the environmental impact of generative-AI services using an lca-based methodology. *Procedia CIRP, 122*, 707–712. https://doi.org/10.1016/j.procir.2024.01.098

Bird, S., Dudík, M., Edgar, R., Horn, B., Lutz, R., Milan, V., Sameki, M., Wallach, H., & Walker, K. (2020). *Fairlearn: A toolkit for assessing and improving fairness in AI.* Microsoft, Technical Report MSR-TR-2020-32. https://www.jmlr.org/papers/volume24/23-0389/23-0389.pdf

Bozhidarova, M., Chang, J., Ale-Rasool, A., Liu, Y., Ma, C., Bertozzi, A. L., Brantingham, P. J., Lin, J., & Krishnagopal, S. (2023). Hate speech and hate crimes: A data-driven study of evolving discourse around marginalized groups. In *2023 IEEE International Conference on Big Data (BigData)*, pp. 3107–3116. https://doi.org/10.1109/BigData59044.2023.10386312

Braun, A., Fakhri, F., & Hochschild, V. (2019). Refugee camp monitoring and environmental change assessment of Kutupalong, Bangladesh, based on radar imagery of sentinel-1 and alos-2. *Remote Sensing, 11*(17), 2047. https://doi.org/10.3390/rs11172047

Brennan, T., & Dieterich, W. (2018). Correctional offender management profiles for alternative sanctions (compas). In *Handbook of recidivism risk/needs assessment tools* (pp. 49–75). Wiley. https://doi.org/10.1002/9781119184256.ch3

Broadbent, E., Loveys, K., Ilan, G., Chen, G., Chilukuri, M., Boardman, S., Doraiswamy, P., & Skuler, D. (2024). Elliq, an AI-driven social robot to alleviate loneliness: Progress and lessons learned. *The Journal of Aging Research & Lifestyle, 13*, 22–28. https://doi.org/10.14283/jarlife.2024.2

Center of an Informed Public. (2023). *Twitter's API access changes could mark 'end of an era' in academic research on the platform.* https://www.cip.uw.edu/2023/02/02/twitters-api-access-changes-academic-research/

Chanda, S. S., & Banerjee, D. N. (2024). Omission and commission errors underlying AI failures. *AI & Society, 39*(3), 937–960. https://doi.org/10.1007/s00146-022-01585-x

Chen, Y. D., Abbasi, A., & Chen, H. (2008). Developing ideological networks using social network analysis and writeprints: A case study of the international Falun Gong movement. In *2008 IEEE International Conference on Intelligence and Security Informatics* (pp. 7–12). IEEE. https://doi.org/10.1109/ISI.2008.4565021

Chit, K. M. M., Shein, Y. Y. C. M. W., Yan, W., & Khine, A. H. (2022). Siren! detecting Burmese hate speech comments on social media. In *2022 14th International Conference on Knowledge and Smart Technology (KST)*, pp. 119–124. https://doi.org/10.1109/KST53302.2022.9729075

Collenette, J., Atkinson, K., & Bench-Capon, T. (2023). Explainable AI tools for legal reasoning about cases: A study on the European court of human rights. *Artificial Intelligence, 317*, 103861. https://doi.org/10.1016/j.artint.2023.103861

Dakanalis, A., Wiederhold, B. K., & Riva, G. (2024). Artificial intelligence: A game-changer for mental health care. *Cyberpsychology, Behavior, and Social Networking, 27*(2), 100–104. https://doi.org/10.1089/cyber.2023.0723

Dalrymple, J., & Boylan, J. (2013). *Effective advocacy in social work.* Sage https://uk.sagepub.com/en-gb/eur/effective-advocacy-in-social-work/book236728

Deng, B., Wang, W., Zhu, F., Wang, Q., & Feng, F. (2025). Cram: Credibility-aware attention modification in LLMs for combating misinformation in rag. *Proceedings of the AAAI Conference on Artificial Intelligence, 39*(22), 23760–23768. https://doi.org/10.1609/aaai.v39i22.34547

Desai, M., & Solas, J. (2012). Poverty, development and social justice. In *The SAGE handbook of international social work* (pp. 85–99). Sage. https://doi.org/10.4135/9781446247594.n5

Dupré, D. T. (2023). Explainable answer set programming for legal decision support. *CILC.* https://doi.org/10.3233/FAIA230994

Fu, T., & Chen, H. (2008, June). Analysis of cyberactivism: A case study of online free Tibet activities. In *2008 IEEE International Conference on Intelligence and Security Informatics* (pp. 1–6). IEEE. https://doi.org/10.1109/ISI.2008.4565020

Gokhale, R., & Fasli, M. (2017). Deploying a co-training algorithm to classify human-rights abuses. In *2017 International conference on the frontiers and advances in data science (FADS)*, pp. 108–113. https://doi.org/10.1109/FADS.2017.8253206

Gokhale, R., & Fasli, M. (2018). Matrix factorization for co-training algorithm to classify human rights abuses. In *2018 IEEE international conference on big data (big data)*, pp. 2170–2179. https://doi.org/10.1109/BigData.2018.8622397

Gulliksen, J., Göransson, B., Boivie, I., Blomkvist, S., Persson, J., & Cajander, Å. (2003). Key principles for user-centred systems design. *Behaviour and Information Technology, 22*(6), 397–409. https://doi.org/10.1080/01449290310001624329

Gupta, V., Ponsam, J. G., & Vangavarapu, C. (2023). Racial slur detection using natural language processes. In *2023 International Conference on Artificial Intelligence and Knowledge Discovery in Concurrent Engineering (ICECONF)*, pp. 1–9. https://doi.org/10.1109/ICECONF57129.2023.10084027

Gustafsson, P. U., Lachmann, T., & Laukka, P. (2025). Machine learning predicts accuracy in eyewitnesses' voices. *Journal of Nonverbal Behavior, 49*(1), 155–169. https://doi.org/10.1007/s10919-024-00474-9

Habernal, I., Faber, D., Recchia, N., Bretthauer, S., Gurevych, I., Spiecker genannt Döhmann, I., & Burchard, C. (2024). Mining legal arguments in court decisions. *Artificial Intelligence and Law, 32*(3), 1–38. https://doi.org/10.1007/s10506-023-09361-y

Haimson, O. L. (2019). Mapping gender transition sentiment patterns via social media data: Toward decreasing transgender mental health disparities. *Journal of the American Medical Informatics Association, 26*(8–9), 749–758. https://doi.org/10.1093/jamia/ocz056

Han, Z., Gao, C., Liu, J., Zhang, J., & Zhang, S. Q. (2024). Parameter-efficient fine-tuning for large models: A comprehensive survey. *Transactions on Machine Learning Research*. https://openreview.net/pdf?id=lIsCS8b6zj

Hofmann, V., Kalluri, P. R., Jurafsky, D., & King, S. (2024). AI generates covertly racist decisions about people based on their dialect. *Nature, 633*(8028), 147–154. https://doi.org/10.1038/s41586-024-07856-5

Hüsünbeyi, Z. M., Akar, D., & Özgür, A. (2022). Identifying hate speech using neural networks and discourse analysis techniques. In *Proceedings of the first workshop on language technology and resources for a fair, inclusive, and safe society within the 13th language resources and evaluation conference*, pp. 32–41. https://aclanthology.org/2022.lateraisse-1.5/

Imran, A. S., Hodnefjeld, H., Kastrati, Z., Fatima, N., Daudpota, S. M., & Wani, M. A. (2023). Classifying European court of human rights cases using transformer-based techniques. *IEEE Access, 11*, 55664–55676. https://doi.org/10.1109/ACCESS.2023.3279034

Jachens, L., Houdmont, J., & Thomas, R. (2019). Effort–reward imbalance and burnout among humanitarian aid workers. *Disasters, 43*(1), 67–87. https://doi.org/10.1111/disa.12288

Jaidka, K., Chen, T., Chesterman, S., Hsu, W., Kan, M.-Y., Kankanhalli, M., Lee, M. L., Seres, G., Sim, T., Taeihagh, A., et al. (2025). Misinformation, disinformation, and generative AI: Implications for perception and policy. *Digital Government: Research and Practice, 6*(1), 1–15. https://doi.org/10.1145/3689372

Jeon, S.-W. (2020). A study on the social phenomenon and perception of sports sexual violence through big data analysis of social media. *Ethiopian Journal of Health Development, 34*(3) https://www.ajol.info/index.php/ejhd/article/view/198772

Jimenez, J., Pasztor, E. M., Chambers, R. M., & Fujii, C. P. (2014). *Social policy and social change: Toward the creation of social and economic justice*. Sage. https://study.sagepub.com/jimenez2e

Kalliatakis, G., Ehsan, S., Fasli, M., Leonardis, A., Gall, J., & McDonald-Maier, K. D. (2017). Detection of human rights violations in images: Can convolutional neural networks help?

International Conference on Computer Vision Theory and Applications, 6, 289–296. https://doi.org/10.5220/0006133902890296
Kalliatakis, G., Ehsan, S., Leonardis, A., Fasli, M., & McDonald-Maier, K. D. (2019). Exploring object-centric and scene-centric cnn features and their complementarity for human rights violations recognition in images. *IEEE Access, 7*, 10045–10056. https://doi.org/10.1109/ACCESS.2019.2891745
Kaur, A., & Bozic, B. (2019). Convolutional neural network-based automatic prediction of judgments of the European court of human rights. *AICS*, 458–469. https://ceur-ws.org/Vol-2563/aics_42.pdf
Khatua, A., Cambria, E., & Khatua, A. (2018). Sounds of silence breakers: Exploring sexual violence on twitter. In *2018 IEEE/ACM international conference on advances in social networks analysis and mining (ASONAM)*, pp. 397–400. https://doi.org/10.1109/ASONAM.2018.8508576
Kihlman, R., & Fasli, M. (2019). Augmenting co-training with recommendations to classify human rights violations. In *2019 IEEE International Conference on Big Data (Big Data)*, pp. 2299–2308. https://doi.org/10.1109/BigData47090.2019.9005478
LeCun, Y., Bengio, Y., & Hinton, G. (2015). Deep learning. *Nature, 521*(7553), 436–444. https://doi.org/10.1038/nature14539
Lee, C. S., & Jang, A. (2023). Questing for justice on twitter: Topic modeling of# stopasianhate discourses in the wake of Atlanta shooting. *Crime & Delinquency, 69*(13–14), 2874–2900. https://doi.org/10.1177/00111287211057855
Li, K. (2022). An evaluation of automation on misogyny identification (AMI) and deep-learning approaches for hate speech-highlight on graph convolutional networks and neural networks. In *2022 International Conference on Computers, Information Processing and Advanced Education (CIPAE)*, pp. 239–244. https://doi.org/10.1109/CIPAE55637.2022.00058
Lloyd, C., King, R., & Chenoweth, L. (2002). Social work, stress and burnout: A review. *Journal of Mental Health, 11*(3), 255–265. https://doi.org/10.1080/09638230020023642
Madon, S. (1992). Computer-based information systems for development planning: The significance of cultural factors. *The Journal of Strategic Information Systems, 1*(5), 250–257. https://doi.org/10.1016/0963-8687(92)90014-N
McCarthy, J., Rochester, N., & Shannon, C. (1956). *Dartmouth workshop*. http://aigraph.cslt.org/courses/06/Dartmouth_workshop.pdf
McDonald, G. G., Costello, C., Bone, J., Cabral, R. B., Farabee, V., Hochberg, T., Kroodsma, D., Mangin, T., Meng, K. C., & Zahn, O. (2021). Satellites can reveal global extent of forced labor in the world's fishing fleet. *Proceedings of the National Academy of Sciences, 118*(3), e2016238117. https://doi.org/10.1073/pnas.2016238117
Miller, D. (1978). Democracy and social justice. *British Journal of Political Science, 8*(1), 1–19. https://doi.org/10.1017/S0007123400001198
Mochales-Palau, R., & Moens, M. F. (2007). Study on sentence relations in the automatic detection of argumentation in legal cases. In *Proceedings of the 2007 conference on Legal Knowledge and Information Systems: JURIX 2007: The Twentieth Annual Conference*, pp. 89–98. https://dl.acm.org/doi/10.5555/1565610.1565624
Monahan, T. (2025). *Surveillance in Trump's America*. https://doi.org/10.24908/ss.v23i1.19220
Moore, B., Herington, J., & Tekin, Ş. (2025). The integration of artificial intelligence-powered psychotherapy Chatbots in pediatric care: Scaffold or substitute? *The Journal of Pediatrics, 280*. https://doi.org/10.1016/j.jpeds.2025.114509
Moser, E., Meyer, S., Schmidhuber, M., Ketterer, D., & Eberhardt, M. (2022). Argo: Towards small vessel detection for humanitarian purposes. *IJCAI, 2022*, 5245–5248. https://doi.org/10.24963/ijcai.2022/728
Mothe, J. (2024). Shaping the future of endangered and low-resource languages---Our role in the age of LLMs: A keynote at ECIR 2024. In *ACM SIGIR Forum* (Vol. 58, pp. 1–13). ACM. https://doi.org/10.1145/3687273.3687280

Mueller, H., Groeger, A., Hersh, J., Matranga, A., & Serrat, J. (2021). Monitoring war destruction from space using machine learning. *Proceedings of the National Academy of Sciences, 118*(23), e2025400118. https://doi.org/10.1073/pnas.2025400118

Mumford, J., Atkinson, K., & Bench-Capon, T. (2023). Combining a legal knowledge model with machine learning for reasoning with legal cases. In *Proceedings of the Nineteenth International Conference on Artificial Intelligence and Law*, pp. 167–176. https://doi.org/10.1145/3594536.3595158

Mumford, J., Atkinson, K., & Bench-Capon, T. (2024). Annotated insights into legal reasoning: A dataset of article 6 echr cases. *Argument & Computation, 15*(2), 113–119. https://doi.org/10.3233/AAC-240002

Mutinda, S., & Muchiri, H. (2024). A bi-lingual counselling chatbot application for support of gender based violence victims in Kenya. In *2024 5th International Conference on Smart Sensors and Application (ICSSA)*, pp. 1–6. https://doi.org/10.1109/ICSSA62312.2024.10788649

Noble, S. U. (2018). Algorithms of oppression: How search engines reinforce racism. In *Algorithms of oppression*. New York University Press. https://doi.org/10.2307/j.ctt1pwt9w5

Pillis, D., Pataranutaporn, P., Maes, P., & Sra, M. (2024, March). AI comes out of the closet: Using AI-generated virtual characters to help individuals practice LGBTQIA+ advocacy. In *Proceedings of the 29th International Conference on Intelligent User Interfaces*, pp. 686–698. https://doi.org/10.1145/3640543.3645213

Poudyal, P., Gonçalves, T., & Quaresma, P. (2019). Using clustering techniques to identify arguments in legal documents. *ASAIL@ ICAIL, 2385*. https://ceur-ws.org/Vol-2385/paper2.pdf

Purao, S., Garfield, M., Gu, X., & Bhetwal, P. (2019). Predicting the slide to long-term homelessness: Model and validation. In *2019 IEEE 21st Conference on Business Informatics (CBI)*, Vol. 1, pp. 31–40. https://doi.org/10.1109/CBI.2019.00011

Quemy, A., & Wrembel, R. (2020). On integrating and classifying legal text documents. In *International Conference on Database and Expert Systems Applications*, pp. 385–399. https://doi.org/10.1007/978-3-030-59003-1_25

Quinn, J. A., Nyhan, M. M., Navarro, C., Coluccia, D., Bromley, L., & Luengo-Oroz, M. (2018). Humanitarian applications of machine learning with remote-sensing data: Review and case study in refugee settlement mapping. *Philosophical Transactions of the Royal Society A: Mathematical, Physical and Engineering Sciences, 376*(2128), 20170363. https://doi.org/10.1098/rsta.2017.0363

Rajanishree, M., Ahmed, N. N., Panchani, Y., Aravindan, S., & Jadhav, V. (2022). Sign language conversion to speech with the application of knn algorithm. In *2022 Sixth International Conference on I-SMAC (IoT in Social, Mobile, Analytics and Cloud)(I-SMAC)*, pp. 886–890. https://doi.org/10.1109/I-SMAC55078.2022.9987421

Rathod, R. G., Barve, Y., Saini, J. R., & Rathod, S. (2023). From data pre-processing to hate speech detection: An interdisciplinary study on women-targeted online abuse. In *2023 3rd International conference on intelligent technologies (CONIT)*, pp. 1–8. https://doi.org/10.1109/CONIT59222.2023.10205571

Redmond, J. (2021). Moderate resolution remote sensing and machine learning for human rights monitoring: The case of Rakhine State, Myanmar. In *2021 IEEE International Geoscience and Remote Sensing Symposium IGARSS*, pp. 2317–2320. https://doi.org/10.1109/IGARSS47720.2021.9553953

Russell, S. J., & Norvig, P. (2016). *Artificial intelligence: A modern approach*. Pearson.

Sabatovych, I. (2019). Do social media create revolutions? using twitter sentiment analysis for predicting the maidan revolution in Ukraine. *Global Media and Communication, 15*(3), 275–283. https://doi.org/10.1177/1742766519872780

Sanghi, A., Sinha, A., Venkatesh, A., & Das, B. (2021). A framework to capture the shift in dynamics of a multi-phase protest—a case study of Hong Kong protests. *Emerging Technologies in Data Mining and Information Security: Proceedings of IEMIS 2020, 3*, 95–110. https://doi.org/10.1007/978-981-15-9774-9_10

Santosh, T., Chowdhury, I., Xu, S., & Grabmair, M. (2024). The craft of selective prediction: Towards reliable case outcome classification - An empirical study on European court of human rights cases. In *Findings of the Association for Computational Linguistics: EMNLP 2024*, pp. 3656–3674. https://doi.org/10.18653/v1/2024.findings-emnlp.208

Sari, I., Kosasih, R., & Fahrurozi, A. (2022). Implementation of Machine Learning in Predicting Length of Punishment at Bandung Court. In *2022 International Conference of Science and Information Technology in Smart Administration (ICSINTESA)* (pp. 12–17). IEEE. https://doi.org/10.1109/ICSINTESA56431.2022.10041693

Sawhney, R., Mathur, P., Jain, T., Gautam, A. K., & Shah, R. (2021). Multitask learning for emotionally analyzing sexual abuse disclosures. In *Proceedings of the 2021 Conference of the North American Chapter of the Association for Computational Linguistics: Human Language Technologies*, pp. 4881–4892. https://doi.org/10.18653/v1/2021.naacl-main.387

Schick, T., & Schütze, H. (2021). It's not just size that matters: Small language models are also few-shot learners. In *Proceedings of the 2021 Conference of the North American Chapter of the Association for Computational Linguistics: Human Language Technologies*, 2339–2352. https://doi.org/10.18653/v1/2021.naacl-main.185

Schirmer, M., Brechenmacher, C., Jashari, E., & Pfeffer, J. (2024, May). GENTRAC: A tool for tracing trauma in genocide and mass atrocity court transcripts.

Schneibel, A., Merkle, N., Wieland, M., Lechner, K., Azimi, S., Henkel, F., Henry, C., Kiefl, R., Yuan, X., & Gaehler, M. (2022). User-driven flood response & monitoring information–key findings of the data 4human project. In *2022 IEEE Global Humanitarian Technology Conference (GHTC)*, pp. 46–53. https://doi.org/10.1109/GHTC55712.2022.9911021

Selvam, V. N. (2024). "Empowering communities": Harnessing energy for human rights and social justice. *International Journal of Law Management & Humanities, 7*(1), 353. https://doi.org/10.10000/IJLMH.116705

Shafik, W. (2025). Human-computer interaction (HCI) technologies in socially-enabled artificial intelligence. In *Future of digital technology and AI in social sectors* (pp. 121–150). IGI Global. https://doi.org/10.4018/979-8-3693-5533-6.ch005

Sivasankari, S., & Vadivu, G. (2022). Tracing the fake news propagation path using social network analysis. *Soft Computing, 26*(23), 12883–12891. https://doi.org/10.1007/s00500-021-06043-2

Springsteen, J., Yeoh, W., & Christenson, D. (2024). Algorithmic filtering, out-group stereotype, and polarization on social media. In *Proceedings of the 23rd International Conference on Autonomous Agents and Multiagent Systems*, pp. 1782–1790. https://doi.org/10.5555/3635637.3663040

Stuart, F., Riley, A., & Pourreza, H. (2020). A human-machine partnered approach for identifying social media signals of elevated traumatic grief in Chicago gang territories. *PLoS One, 15*(7), e0236625. https://doi.org/10.1371/journal.pone.0236625

Subramani, S., Michalska, S., Wang, H., Du, J., Zhang, Y., & Shakeel, H. (2019). Deep learning for multi-class identification from domestic violence online posts. *IEEE Access, 7*, 46210–46224. https://doi.org/10.1109/ACCESS.2019.2908827

Suk, J., Abhishek, A., Zhang, Y., Ahn, S. Y., Correa, T., Garlough, C., & Shah, D. V. (2021). #metoo, networked acknowledgment, and connective action: How "empowerment through empathy" launched a social movement. *Social Science Computer Review, 39*(2), 276–294. https://doi.org/10.1177/0894439319864882

Swanson, K., Ravi, A., Saleh, S., Weia, B., Pleasants, E., & Arvisais-Anhalt, S. (2023). Effect of recent abortion legislation on twitter user engagement, sentiment, and expressions of trust in clinicians and privacy of health information: Content analysis. *Journal of Medical Internet Research, 25*, e46655. https://doi.org/10.2196/46655

Swaroop, S., Prasad, K. Y., Reddy, G. S. S., Rachavelpula, M., & Jogalekar, U. A. (2024). Real time sign language detection. In *2024 International Conference on Artificial Intelligence, Computer, Data Sciences and Applications (ACDSA)*, pp. 1–7. https://doi.org/10.1109/ACDSA59508.2024.10467736

Tong, X., Li, Y., Li, J., Bei, R., & Zhang, L. (2022). What are people talking about in #backlivesmatter and #stopasianhate? Exploring and categorizing twitter topics emerged in online social movements through the latent Dirichlet allocation model. In *Proceedings of the 2022 AAAI/ACM Conference on AI, Ethics, and Society*, pp. 723–738. https://doi.org/10.1145/3514094.3534202

Tsai, F.-J., Huang, W.-L., & Chan, C.-C. (2009). Occupational stress and burnout of lawyers. *Journal of Occupational Health, 51*(5), 443–450. https://doi.org/10.1539/joh.l8179

Umel, A. (2024). Facebook and social representations of Filipino migrant life in Germany: A reflexive computational approach. *Frontiers in Human Dynamics, 5*, 1284711. https://doi.org/10.3389/fhumd.2023.1284711

Vasanth Kumar C., & Fawziya, A. (2024). Ai-enhanced sign language interpreter. In *International Conference on Computer, Communication, and Signal Processing*, pp. 186–198. https://doi.org/10.1007/978-3-031-73617-9_15

Venkatesan, S., Valecha, R., Yaraghi, N., Oh, O., & Rao, H. R. (2021). Influence in social media: An investigation of tweets spanning the 2011 Egyptian revolution. *MIS Quarterly, 45*(4). https://doi.org/10.25300/MISQ/2021/15297

Wahyuningroem, S. L., Sirait, R., Uljanatunnisa, U., & Heryadi, D. (2024). Youth political participation and digital movement in Indonesia: The case of #reformasidikorupsi and #tolakomnibuslaw. *F1000Research, 12*, 543. https://doi.org/10.12688/f1000research.122669.3

Wang, J., Lan, C., Liu, C., Ouyang, Y., Qin, T., Lu, W., Chen, Y., Zeng, W., & Yu, P. S. (2022). Generalizing to unseen domains: A survey on domain generalization. *IEEE Transactions on Knowledge and Data Engineering, 35*(8), 8052–8072. https://doi.org/10.1109/TKDE.2022.3178128

Wang, X., Zhang, X., Hoo, V., Shao, Z., & Zhang, X. (2024). Legalreasoner: A multi-stage framework for legal judgment prediction via large language models and knowledge integration. *IEEE Access*. https://doi.org/10.1109/ACCESS.2024.3496666

Watts, L., & Hodgson, D. (2019). *Social justice theory and practice for social work*. Springer. https://doi.org/10.1007/978-981-13-3621-8

Wu, J., Hu, W., Coelho, J., Nitu, P., Paul, H. R., Madiraju, P., Smith, R. O., & Ahamed, S. I. (2019). Identifying buildings with ramp entrances using convolutional neural networks. In *2019 IEEE 43rd Annual Computer Software and Applications Conference (COMPSAC)*, Vol. 2, pp. 74–79. https://doi.org/10.1109/COMPSAC.2019.10186

Xu, S., Tyss, S., Ichim, O., Plank, B., & Grabmair, M. (2024). Through the lens of split vote: Exploring disagreement, difficulty and calibration in legal case outcome classification. In *Proceedings of the 62nd Annual Meeting of the Association for Computational Linguistics (Volume 1: Long Papers)*, pp. 199–216. https://doi.org/10.18653/v1/2024.acl-long.13

Yang, B., Chen, G., & Luo, X. (2024a). A legal judgment prediction model based on bert, attention, and graph convolutional network. In *2024 IEEE 36th International Conference on Tools with Artificial Intelligence (ICTAI)*, pp. 303–310. https://doi.org/10.1109/ICTAI62512.2024.00052

Yang, Y., Alba, C., Wang, C., Wang, X., Anderson, J., & An, R. (2024b). GPT models can perform thematic analysis in public health studies, akin to qualitative researchers. *Journal of Social Computing, 5*(4), 293–312. https://doi.org/10.23919/JSC.2024.0024

Yıldırım, E., Sert, M. F., Kartal, B., & Çalış, Ş. (2023). Non-compliance of the European court of human rights decisions: A machine learning analysis. *International Review of Law and Economics, 76*, 106167. https://doi.org/10.1016/j.irle.2023.106167

Yu, D., Rosenfeld, H., & Gupta, A. (2023). The 'AI divide' between the global north and global south. In *World Economic Forum* (Vol. 16). https://www.weforum.org/stories/2023/01/davos23-ai-divide-global-north-global-south/

Chapter 17
AI in Environmental Social Work and Climate Change

Siva Mathiyazhagan, Vaiju Raja, and Gautam N. Yadama

1 Introduction

The world is currently confronting an unprecedented convergence of social and environmental crises, including climate change, pandemics, rising global inequality, and geopolitical instability (International Federation of Social Workers [IFSW], 2022). These interconnected challenges are not only transforming human and ecological systems but are also worsening vulnerabilities among already marginalized populations. The climate crisis is intensifying existing social and economic inequalities and causing increased emotional, ecological, and financial distress across communities worldwide (IFSW, 2022; UN Security Council, 2021). The root causes of many of these crises are deeply rooted in historical and systemic structures, such as colonial exploitation and neoliberal economic policies (Billiot et al., 2019; Rao et al., 2022; Martinez & Irfan, 2021). Climate change poses a serious threat to both ecosystems and human well-being. It acts as a "crisis multiplier," heightening conflicts over limited resources, increasing displacement, and driving humanitarian emergencies (UN Security Council, 2021).

Social workers are increasingly working with vulnerable populations and new technology tools, including artificial intelligence (AI), for their professional practice. However, social work interventions in the environment and in technology are limited, often focusing on disaster relief, rehabilitation, and advocacy during emergencies. Traditional social work has been criticized for focusing primarily on the

S. Mathiyazhagan (✉)
School of Social Policy and Practice, University of Pennsylvania, Philadelphia, PA, USA
e-mail: sivam@upenn.edu

V. Raja
Mailman School of Public Health, Columbia University, New York, NY, USA

G. N. Yadama
School of Social Work, Boston College, Chestnut Hill, MA, USA
e-mail: gautam.yadama@bc.edu

R. An, M. A. Lindsey (eds.), *Artificial Intelligence in Social Work*,
https://doi.org/10.1007/978-3-032-18443-6_17

social dimensions of a person's environment while neglecting the natural environment, which is essential to holistic well-being. The social work critique argues that the neoliberal economic model equates well-being with economic growth, but it has contributed to deepening injustice and neglecting holistic well-being (Boetto, 2017; Peeters, 2012; Powers et al., 2021). On the other hand, social work is far behind in adopting emerging technologies and in contributing to ethical innovations in AI for social justice. When it comes to AI and environmental social work, we are still in the ideation phase. Considering the limited literature and evidence-based practice, in this chapter, we try to provide a comprehensive knowledge and understanding of eco-social work, potential avenues for AI in environmental social work in response to climate change, highlighting some of the AI innovations for climate adaptation, the role of social work at the micro- and macro-levels, ethical considerations, and the way forward for environmental justice.

1.1 Eco-Social Work

Eco-Social Work, a form of environmental social work, is an emerging theoretical and practical framework that combines environmental sustainability with social justice, highlighting the interconnectedness of ecological and social systems (Boetto, 2017; Fato, 2024). This framework challenges traditional social work boundaries by recognizing that environmental issues directly impact human well-being, especially among marginalized populations (Gartshore, 2022; Matties et al., 2001; Närhi & Matthies 2016a, 2016b). The roots of Eco-Social Work stem from the Ecological Systems Theory (Bronfenbrenner, 1977), which views individuals as part of dynamic systems influenced by their environment. This perspective helps social workers understand the broader ecological contexts affecting communities and supports the creation of sustainable interventions (Coates & Gray, 2012; Peeters, 2012). Boetto (2017) outlines three levels: personal being, professional thinking, and practical doing. The individual level involves recognizing one's identity as connected to nature, influencing lifestyle choices. The thinking level calls for a transformation in professional values and ethics, including appreciation for traditional Indigenous knowledge and a commitment to global environmental justice (Billiot et al., 2019). The doing level involves implementing practice strategies that incorporate ecological considerations into daily social work interventions (Gartstore, 2022). Thysell and Cuadra (2023) further describe five types of eco-social work, ranging from a holistic approach, where human and ecological interests are inseparable, to various views that favor one dimension over the other.

Eco-Social Work takes a holistic view, recognizing that individual well-being is deeply influenced by environmental, social, cultural, and economic factors (Matties et al., 2001; Närhi & Matthies 2016a, 2016b; Powers et al., 2021). The Environmental Justice Framework (Lee, 1992; Van Horne et al., 2023) enhances Eco-Social Work by tackling the unequal distribution of environmental harms. It emphasizes how vulnerable groups often suffer the most from pollution and ecological damage.

Practitioners use this framework to promote equity and amplify the voices of those most affected (Schmitz et al., 2012). These interconnected factors influence access to vital resources, educational and job opportunities, social support networks, and the state of one's physical environment. Instead of focusing solely on individual challenges, this approach allows social workers to address both immediate issues and their systemic roots (Ungar, 2002). It also enables practitioners to challenge and change broader systems of inequality and environmental harm that disproportionately impact marginalized communities (Belchior Rocha, 2018). Additionally, this approach encourages society to use natural resources wisely, cut carbon footprints, and pursue overall well-being for everyone (Wang & Altanbulag, 2022).

This comprehensive lens supports more effective and sustainable interventions that are sensitive to the complex realities of people's lives. Intersectionality is fundamental to Eco-Social Work, as it recognizes the overlapping systems of oppression, such as race, caste, gender, sexuality, abilities, legal status, and class, that influence environmental vulnerabilities. By applying an intersectional perspective, Eco-Social Work seeks to create more inclusive and equitable pathways toward sustainable development (Norton, 2012; Shackelford et al., 2024). Although Eco-Social Work is still in its early stages, now is the right time to introduce AI and emerging technologies into the intervention process, as they can multiply their impact on ecosystems, communities, and vulnerable populations worldwide. The following sections will explore real-world AI innovation examples, potential opportunities, challenges, and ethical considerations for the effective integration of AI in Eco-Social Work.

2 Integrating AI in Eco-Social Work

Environmental social work, grounded in its enduring "person-in-environment" perspective, has traditionally focused on sociopolitical and economic systems. Yet in the past decade and a half, scholars have increasingly recognized the equally urgent importance of the natural environment in shaping human well-being (Mason et al., 2017; Rao et al., 2022; Shackelford et al., 2024). For frontline communities—especially those living in flood-prone coastal areas, wildfire corridors, or drought-affected agricultural regions—environmental degradation is not a distant abstraction. Environmental degradation, a daily, material concern, is interwoven with housing insecurity, food access, public health, and displacement (Billiot et al., 2019; Camps-Valls et al., 2025; Kumar et al., 2019; Yadama, 2013). In recent years, AI has increasingly been integrated into environmental efforts, creating new opportunities for disaster preparedness, resource management, and climate adaptation. AI-driven systems can analyze large volumes of environmental data, predict extreme weather events, optimize resource allocation, and support decision-making. AI's role in climate action is especially relevant to social work, as practitioners work to ensure equitable access to technology-driven solutions while protecting the rights of vulnerable populations (Ren & Wierman, 2024). Incorporating AI into Eco-Social

Work offers significant potential to improve both micro- and macro-level interventions focused on environmental sustainability and social justice. At the micro-level, AI can help social workers deliver personalized, data-driven interventions that account for ecological and social factors that affect well-being. For example, AI tools can analyze patterns in environmental and social data—such as housing quality, heat islands, pollution exposure, or access to green spaces—to identify at-risk individuals and guide early intervention efforts (Naslund et al., 2020). These tools can also enable remote counseling, digital case management, and predictive modeling to better understand how ecological issues, such as climate change, disproportionately impact marginalized groups (Coates & Gray, 2012). At the macro-level, AI can support policymakers and organizations in identifying and tackling systemic environmental injustices. AI applications in environmental monitoring, resource allocation, and climate risk assessment can inform data-driven policies that prioritize equity and sustainability (Närhi & Matthies 2016a, 2016b). For instance, AI-powered geographic information systems can map areas experiencing high ecological degradation and socioeconomic disadvantage, facilitating targeted interventions and fair resource distribution (Peeters, 2012). Macro-level social workers can partner with technologists to ensure AI systems' design and development reflect diverse perspectives and needs, especially those of historically marginalized communities (Mathiyazhagan, 2021).

Additionally, AI can bolster advocacy efforts by creating compelling data visualizations and predictive scenarios that highlight the urgency of eco-social issues to stakeholders and the public (Schmitz et al., 2012). However, practitioners must remain vigilant in ensuring responsible AI use, including safeguarding privacy and avoiding algorithmic bias that could deepen marginalization of vulnerable groups (Jatobá et al., 2021). Incorporating AI into Eco-Social Work requires a deliberate commitment to ethical practices, inclusivity, and sustainability. AI tools must be designed, developed, and implemented with input from affected communities to ensure cultural relevance and reduce technological exclusion.

3 AI and Climate Change

AI-powered climate models analyze vast datasets from satellites, sensors, and meteorological sources to identify patterns and predict long-term climate trends (Olawade et al., 2024). One notable example is the International Methane Emissions Observatory, which leverages AI to monitor methane emissions, a potent greenhouse gas contributing to global warming (Rolnick et al., 2022); United Nations Environment Programme [UNEP], 2025). Machine learning algorithms also enhance forecasting accuracy for hurricanes, wildfires, and floods, allowing for more timely interventions (Wang et al., 2023). The European Centre for Medium-Range Weather Forecasts (ECMWF) (n.d.) has developed AI-driven climate models that improve predictions of extreme weather events, helping policymakers and emergency responders prepare more effectively (Zewe, 2025).

AI tools are also increasingly embedded in disaster management. For example, Marine Sand Watch (UNEP, n.d.; UNEP, 2024) uses AI to track sand extraction from marine environments, helping to prevent ecosystem destruction. AI-powered satellite imaging can detect rising water levels and predict flooding patterns, improving response time and mitigating damage (Wang et al., 2023). Similarly, AI models analyze temperature, wind patterns, and vegetation dryness to anticipate wildfires, improving wildfire prediction efforts (Ren & Wierman, 2024). In hurricane-prone regions, AI-driven simulations enhance hurricane path prediction and emergency planning, aiding disaster response teams (ECMWF, 2024). For eco-social workers engaged in crisis intervention, AI can provide real-time data on affected populations, identify the most vulnerable areas, and help streamline aid distribution (Dominelli, 2018).

3.1 *Resource Management*

AI's contributions to resource management and climate adaptation are extensive, offering innovative solutions to address environmental challenges. AI optimizes natural resource allocation by managing water distribution and detecting leaks to conserve resources (Kamyab et al., 2023). Traditional methods of water management often rely on manual inspections and historical data, which can be inefficient and prone to errors. AI-driven systems, however, can analyze real-time data from sensors and satellite imagery to identify leaks, predict water demand, and optimize distribution networks. Smart water grids, for instance, use machine learning algorithms to detect anomalies in water pressure and flow, allowing for rapid intervention and minimizing water loss.

These systems can also forecast water demand based on weather patterns, population density, and seasonal variations, ensuring efficient allocation and preventing shortages. Similarly, AI enhances energy efficiency in smart grids by balancing supply and demand, reducing waste, and improving sustainability (Zewe, 2025). Traditional energy grids often struggle to adapt to dynamic supply and demand patterns, especially when integrating renewable energy sources. AI-powered smart grids can analyze real-time data from sensors and smart meters to predict energy needs, optimize energy distribution, and detect grid disturbances. These systems contribute to reliable energy access, which is crucial for community resilience.

3.2 *Land Use Planning*

AI supports land-use planning for sustainable urban development by analyzing geographic and demographic data to inform infrastructure projects (Ren & Wierman, 2024). Urban planning often involves complex decisions with long-term environmental and social consequences. AI can aid urban planners by analyzing large datasets on population density, traffic patterns, environmental conditions, and economic activity (Son et al., 2023). For example, AI can identify optimal locations for new infrastructure projects, such as public transportation, parks, and affordable housing, minimizing environmental impact and maximizing social benefits (Cina et al., 2025).

Moreover, AI can assess the vulnerability of different areas to climate change impacts, such as flooding, heatwaves, and sea-level rise, and recommend appropriate adaptation measures (Camps-Valls et al., 2025; Yadama, 2013). For environmental social workers, these tools can support efforts to advocate for climate-resilient infrastructure in underserved neighborhoods, ensure inclusive community engagement in planning processes, and safeguard vulnerable populations from displacement (Billiot et al., 2019).

3.3 *Localized Climate Adaptation Strategies and Predictive Analytics*

For marginalized communities disproportionately affected by environmental degradation, AI can provide tailored solutions, such as localized climate adaptation strategies (Rolnick et al., 2022). Climate change impacts are often felt most acutely by marginalized communities, who may lack the resources and infrastructure to adapt to changing conditions (Mason et al., 2017; Rao et al., 2022). AI can help these communities by providing localized climate adaptation strategies tailored to their specific needs and circumstances.

Predictive analytics powered by AI are enabling a new scale and scope of environmental modeling for climate adaptation. In water-scarce regions, for example, AI applications in climate-resilient water management have demonstrated significant potential to improve adaptation outcomes. Abdulameer et al. (2025) found that long short-term memory (LSTM) and hybrid physics-informed neural networks achieved higher accuracy in hydrological forecasting (Nash–Sutcliffe efficiency >0.90), enabling early warnings for droughts and floods. In agricultural settings, Internet-of-Things-integrated AI systems reduced water waste by 20%–40% and optimization models improved the distribution efficiency by up to 30%. Yet the study also highlighted significant challenges: 70% of AI tools remain concentrated in data-rich, temperate zones, leaving arid and low-income communities largely underserved. These disparities underscore the need for decentralized data ecosystems and policy alignment to ensure marginalized communities benefit from AI interventions.

While traditional farming practices often rely on generic approaches that can be inefficient and environmentally damaging, precision agriculture systems use AI to analyze data on soil conditions, weather patterns, and crop health to optimize irrigation, fertilization, and pest control (Wang et al., 2023). For example, Hultgren et al. (2025) projected climate change impacts on agricultural yields across 24,378 global regions using 33 climate models and nearly 2000 Monte Carlo simulations per crop. These projections account for adaptation, income growth, and CO_2 fertilization, while providing granular insights invaluable to environmental social workers addressing food insecurity in climate-stressed communities. These systems can also provide farmers with real-time recommendations on when to plant, harvest, and rotate crops, maximizing yields and minimizing environmental impact (Pandian, 2025). For environmental social workers, such insights are crucial for advocating equitable resource governance while co-designing interventions that build trust in technological systems.

4 AI Intervention for Climate Adoption

The AI-driven eco-social work models enhance marginalized community capacity to support disaster preparedness, advocate for policy changes, and promote sustainable solutions. AI-driven disaster response systems can assist social workers in tracking displaced individuals, coordinating emergency housing, and ensuring equitable resource distribution (Albahri et al., 2024; Haykal et al., 2025; Zewe, 2025). AI-driven wildfire detection systems help social workers support displaced communities by coordinating shelter, medical aid, and mental health services for affected individuals in California. AI-enhanced water management systems help social workers address drought crises by ensuring an equitable distribution of water resources and reducing the burden on impoverished communities. AI-driven deforestation monitoring enables social workers and Indigenous rights advocates to track environmental destruction, protect vulnerable communities, and push for policy interventions. AI-powered flood prediction models assist NGOs and social workers in implementing preemptive measures, reducing harm to vulnerable populations by facilitating early evacuations and resource allocation. The following real-world examples highlight AI-powered disaster preparedness and climate adaptation worldwide, exploring the possible role of eco-social workers.

4.1 Wildfire Detection Systems in California, USA

Many wildfire-prone regions like California face an escalating wildfire crisis due to prolonged droughts, rising temperatures, and land-use changes driven by climate change. In the last decade, the state experienced 15 of the 20 most destructive wildfires in its history, with over 11 million acres burned between 2017 and 2021 alone (California Department of Forestry and Fire Protection [CAL FIRE], 2025). These fires have displaced more than 150,000 people, destroyed thousands of homes, and disproportionately impacted rural, low-income, and Indigenous communities just in 2025 (Batko & McTarnaghan, 2025). Nonetheless, AI-driven wildfire detection systems are transforming how early warnings and resource deployments are handled.

Traditional wildfire monitoring, which relied heavily on human surveillance, satellite imagery, and static sensor networks, often faced delays in detection and had limited accuracy, especially in remote areas (Alkhatib, 2014; Di Giuseppe et al., 2025; Jen, 2024). However, AI-enabled wildfire detection systems analyze real-time data from ground sensors, drones, and satellite imagery to identify ignition points and smoke plumes within minutes—far faster than human responders. Programs like ALERTCalifornia, Google's FireSat, IBM's Geospatial Analytics, and University of Southern California's conditional Wasserstein Generative Adversarial Network (cWGAN) model use machine learning to detect anomalies and predict fire spread based on variables such as wind speed, humidity, and vegetation density (ALERTCalifornia, 2025; Brodsky, 2025; Di Giuseppe et al., 2025; Google Research, n.d.-a, n.d.-b; IBM Environmental Intelligence Suite, 2025; Jen, 2024; Raffio, 2024).

One of the most impactful implementations has been the ALERTCalifornia platform at the University of California, San Diego, recognized as one of TIME Magazine's best inventions of 2023 (Dixit, 2023). This system uses over 1100 high-definition cameras paired with AI algorithms to detect smoke plumes and analyze environmental risk factors across the state. Combined with satellite data and community-based response apps, ALERTCalifornia has helped reduce emergency response times and improve coordination among emergency services, social workers, and local governments. The system works by flagging potential fire outbreaks, which are then rapidly reviewed by trained personnel, reducing false positives and cutting detection time to under 60 s in many cases (ALERTCalifornia, 2025).

AI-driven wildfire detection systems also help social workers support displaced communities by coordinating shelter, medical aid, and mental health services for affected individuals (Ren & Wierman, 2024). By forecasting fire spread and high-risk zones, these systems enable preemptive evacuations and resource distribution, minimizing chaos during crises. They allow social workers and local responders to use predictive mapping to direct at-risk residents, such as the older and undocumented individuals, to safety before evacuation routes close (Bell, 2021). AI-enabled alerts also help agencies anticipate housing, food, and counseling needs in advance, rather than responding reactively once a fire has already displaced people. Recent advancements in deep learning have significantly improved the accuracy and speed of wildfire detection using satellite imagery (Matias, 2023).

Another notable development was the creation of the California Wildfire GeoImaging Dataset (CWGID), a large-scale, annotated dataset comprising more than 100,000 pairs of high-resolution, temporally matched satellite images (Martin et al., 2024a). This system captures the same geographic area at different times for each image pair, enabling AI models to learn how wildfires visually manifest and evolve across landscapes. The dataset also includes pre-fire, active fire, and post-fire imagery, providing a robust foundation for supervised learning (Martin et al., 2024b). Using this dataset, researchers implemented EfficientNet-B0, a convolutional neural network architecture known for its optimal trade-off between accuracy and computational efficiency (Klingler, 2024). The model achieved over 92% accuracy in wildfire detection tasks, outperforming traditional image classifiers and demonstrating robust generalization across diverse terrain and environmental conditions (Martin et al., 2024a). The success of such models lies in their ability to detect subtle changes in thermal signatures, smoke trails, and vegetation reflectance that may not be visible to human observers or older detection systems (Giannakidou et al., 2024).

Beyond emergency response, AI technologies are also supporting longer-term social work efforts. By identifying fire-prone zones and socioeconomically vulnerable populations, AI can inform resilience-building programs—such as fire-resistant infrastructure upgrades, insurance subsidies, and trauma-informed mental health services tailored to disaster survivors (Ren & Wierman, 2024). Research shows that anticipatory action, when supported by innovations such as AI-driven forecasting, can significantly reduce disaster-related losses and strengthen community preparedness by improving the effectiveness of early warning systems (de Pérez et al., 2022; United Nations Framework Convention on Climate Change [UNFCCC], 2024). Thereby, California's integration of AI into wildfire detection offers a compelling model for combining environmental science and eco-social work service delivery.

4.2 *Flood Prediction Models in Bangladesh*

Traditional flood warning systems often rely on historical data and manual monitoring, which can be slow and inaccurate (Nearing et al., 2024). AI-powered flood prediction models can analyze real-time data from weather stations, river gauges, and satellite imagery to predict flood events with greater accuracy and speed (Liu et al., 2024). These models, such as FloodSENS, MIT's Earth Intelligence Engine, and Google's Flood Hub, can also identify the most vulnerable areas to flooding, allowing social workers to target interventions and prioritize evacuations (The European Space Agency [ESA], 2020; Chu, 2024; Matias, 2021).

In 2018, Google launched the Flood Forecasting Initiative, an AI-driven system designed to combine hydrologic models (predicting water flow) with inundation models (predicting flood spread), blending conventional physics-based approaches with machine learning trained on satellite and river data to improve the accuracy and reach of flood early warning systems (Matias, 2021; Nevo et al., 2022). Nevo et al. (2022) explain how Google's operational flood warning system uses LSTM networks and manifold models to predict both river stage and inundation depth with high precision. During the 2021 monsoon season, this system covered 470,000 km^2 in India and Bangladesh, issuing over 100 million alerts to over 350 million people. Crucially, these alerts were delivered not only to government authorities but also directly to residents via mobile platforms, including community-based WhatsApp groups and SMS systems accessible in low-bandwidth settings. These timely alerts, often provided up to five days in advance, helped residents evacuate safely, protect livestock, and secure property (Chowdhury, 2021; Liu et al., 2024; Nevo et al., 2022).

Moreover, Google expanded this initiative by launching Flood Hub, a platform designed to provide real-time flood forecasts and early warnings to over 100 countries, and reaching more than 700 million people worldwide (Google Research, 2025; Matias, 2024; Nearing et al., 2024). Studies and field reports have shown that the system has increased trust in flood warnings, improved response coordination among local agencies, and reduced flood-related fatalities by 43% (Chowdhury, 2021; Nearing et al., 2024). Notably, in the Jamuna River basin of Bangladesh, organizations like GiveDirectly have used Flood Hub's forecasts to make anticipatory cash transfers to vulnerable communities before the July flood season, allowing families to safeguard their homes and livelihoods (ESG News, 2025). Flood Hub exemplifies how AI can bolster climate resilience, especially in regions lacking extensive hydrological infrastructure. By providing precise and timely flood forecasts via open access, Flood Hub illustrates how predictive analytics can strengthen disaster response at scale, empowering communities to mitigate climate-related disasters and supporting researchers and policymakers in developing more effective disaster preparedness and response strategies (Google Research, 2025).

4.3 Rainforest and Deforestation Monitoring in the Amazon

Deforestation in the Amazon rainforest is a major environmental and social problem, threatening biodiversity, climate stability, and the livelihoods and autonomy of Indigenous communities. Forests cover 31% of global land area, with 497 million hectares or 12.2% of this forest area found in Brazil (Abdenur, 2020; Food and Agriculture Organization of the United Nations [FAO], 2020). However, deforestation accounts for 12%–20% of global greenhouse gas emissions (FAO, 2020; Gerber & Foley, 2025). Driven primarily by illegal activities including induced forest fires, illegal mining and logging, and land invasions, the commodification and degradation of forests are further expedited by legal agriculture and livestock production industries (FAO, 2020, 2022; Gerber & Foley, 2025).

As local communities and Indigenous Peoples either own or manage nearly half, 4.35 billion hectares, of the world's forest and farm landscapes, yet contribute nothing to deforestation, working with Indigenous rights advocates and social workers to track environmental destruction, protect vulnerable communities, and push for policy interventions is crucial for deforestation monitoring (FAO, 2022; Rolnick et al., 2022). Traditional forest monitoring methods often relied on ground surveys, delayed satellite data, or manual reporting, which were insufficient given the scale and speed of forest loss (Global Conservation, 2024; Global Forest Watch, n.d.; Ennes & Chaves, 2021). However, these ground-based methods also provide critical insights: communities that depend on forests for food, fiber, and income often detect ecological changes long before satellite imagery does. For example, in dry tropical forests of the Eastern Ghats, researchers partnered with local communities to assess the impact of harvesting on endemic tree species. Their findings revealed species-specific vulnerabilities and the demographic consequences of non-timber harvesting—information essential to conservation and predictive modeling (Neeraja et al., 2022). Community-led forest health monitoring provides granular, context-specific data, including threats such as fire, soil erosion, and grazing, which may not be visible through remote sensing alone. These insights are also relevant to IUCN red-list assessments and sustainable harvesting guidelines.

In contrast, AI systems analyze satellite imagery, audio inputs, and predictive models to detect illegal logging early, alert indigenous groups, and guide policy response (Rolnick et al., 2022). Collaborative platforms like PrevisIA, developed by the Brazilian NGO Imazon and Microsoft, analyze high-resolution satellite imagery and land-use patterns to identify unauthorized roads and other indicators of deforestation risk in real time (Imazon, 2022; PrevisIA, n.d.; Smith, 2023). Similarly, Rainforest Connection (RFCx) uses real-time bioacoustic monitoring to combat illegal deforestation in the Amazon and other biodiverse regions. The non-profit utilizes recycled, solar-powered recording devices known as "Guardians," which are installed high in the forest canopy of protected territories to continuously capture environmental sounds, including chainsaws, gunshots, and vehicle engines (Rainforest Connection, 2025). RFCx's technology transmits immediate alerts to local first responders, NGOs, and Indigenous forest rangers via mobile networks (Goldapple, 2021; Rainforest Connection, 2025). These sensors also generate a forensic record of illegal activity that can be used in court (Goldapple, 2021). In Brazil, indigenous groups such as the Tembé have adopted the system to strengthen their surveillance and document invasions for use in legal and advocacy efforts (Abdenur, 2020).

Moreover, the platform promotes a participatory and rights-based model by keeping data control within the community and supporting self-determined environmental governance (Abdenur, 2020; Prestes et al., 2024). The integration of AI with community-based knowledge and field action has not only enhanced the precision of forest monitoring but also empowered indigenous populations to protect their land more effectively (Abdenur, 2020). Open-access tools like Global Forest Watch further amplify these efforts by providing transparent, actionable data to researchers, policymakers, and activists worldwide (Abdenur, 2020; Global Forest Watch, n.d.). These examples exemplify how AI, when ethically and inclusively deployed, can empower marginalized groups and support environmental justice.

4.4 *Drought Monitoring in Sub-Saharan Africa*

Sub-Saharan Africa faces increasingly frequent and severe droughts due to anthropogenic climate change, affecting the livelihoods of over 61 million people (International Centre of Expertise in Montreal on Artificial Intelligence, 2024; United Nations Office for the Coordination of Humanitarian Affairs [UN OCHA] & Regional Interagency Standing Committee [RIASCO], 2024). An estimated $71 billion has been lost over the last 50 years, disproportionately affecting smallholder farmers, pastoralists, and other communities that rely on subsistence farming, with about 23% of sub-Saharan Africa's GDP coming from agriculture (Goedde et al.,

2019; Okoth, 2024). Traditional drought monitoring methods—such as rain gauge data, farmer surveys, or manual soil assessments—are often reactive, fragmented, and lack regional coordination (Le Coz & van de Giesen, 2020). These limitations hinder timely interventions, leaving vulnerable populations without adequate early warning, crop planning tools, or water resource management.

The human toll of these droughts is profound. In 2024, Southern Africa experienced its worst drought in decades, exacerbated by El Niño, leaving over 27 million people facing acute food insecurity and 21 million children suffering from severe malnutrition (Imray, 2024; Sinyangwe & Savage, 2024). Countries such as Zambia, Malawi, and Zimbabwe declared national disasters as crops failed and water sources dwindled (Khorsandi, 2024). Social workers play a critical role in ensuring these populations receive timely, culturally sensitive support, yet fragmented data and delayed crisis recognition often hinder their efforts. However, AI-informed early warning systems allow practitioners to shift from reactive to anticipatory responses, enabling the mobilization of cash transfers, psychosocial support, nutritional aid, and water provision before conditions deteriorate (Kühnle, 2024).

AI-driven models also integrate satellite imagery, weather forecasts, and soil moisture data to provide early warnings and inform resource allocation (International Centre of Expertise in Montreal on Artificial Intelligence, 2024; Sheffield et al., 2014). For instance, the African Flood & Drought Monitor utilizes machine learning algorithms to deliver real-time drought assessments and up to 6 months of forecasts, aiding farmers, social workers, and policymakers in timely decision-making processes (Sheffield et al., 2014; United Nations Convention to Combat Desertification [UNCCD], n.d.). Additionally, the Food and Agriculture Organization's Water Productivity Open-access Portal (WaPOR) uses remote sensing and AI analytics to provide near real-time data on evapotranspiration, biomass production, and water use efficiency across Africa and the Near East (FAO, 2024). These insights help governments and humanitarian agencies manage irrigation systems, prioritize high-risk areas, and optimize land productivity during droughts.

A notable case study is the implementation of AI-based drought prediction models in Kenya. Researchers developed an LSTM neural network to forecast vegetation health using satellite-derived indices. This model achieved an accuracy of 78.3% in predicting drought conditions, enabling timely interventions for pastoral communities dependent on livestock and agriculture (Barrett et al., 2019). The benefits of anticipatory action using AI models are substantial. Improved early warning systems have contributed to a threefold decrease in deaths from weather, climate, and water-related hazards over the past 50 years, despite an increase in the frequency of such events (World Meteorological Organization [WMO], 2024). Taken together, these AI-powered tools help bridge the gap between early warning and early action, offering data-driven support for drought resilience efforts in one of the world's most climate-vulnerable regions. These examples demonstrate AI's potential to enhance social work efforts in climate-related interventions. However, AI solutions must be designed inclusively to prevent exacerbating inequalities and ensure equitable access to resources.

4.5 Ethical Considerations for Environmental Justice

AI has the potential to advance environmental justice by tracking pollution in low-income areas and holding corporations accountable for environmental harm (Ren & Wierman, 2024). The rapid development of AI raises serious ethical concerns regarding data ownership, privacy, and the risk of surveillance disproportionately targeting marginalized communities (Zewe, 2025). AI-driven environmental monitoring tools must be designed with transparency and accountability to prevent the reinforcement of existing environmental injustices (Li et al., 2025). Data ownership and privacy are major concerns, as AI systems often collect and analyze large amounts of personal data. AI-driven environmental monitoring tools could be used to monitor the activities of activists and community organizers, chilling free speech and undermining environmental justice efforts. To prevent these problems, AI-driven environmental monitoring tools must be co-designed with impacted communities with complete transparency and collective accountability. This includes ensuring that data are collected and used responsibly, and that communities have meaningful opportunities to participate in how AI systems are developed and deployed.

4.5.1 Technology Access Gap

Ensuring equitable access to AI-driven resources remains a challenge that must be addressed through inclusive policymaking and equitable AI governance (Dominelli, 2018). Marginalized communities often lack the resources and infrastructure to access and benefit from AI-driven solutions. Addressing this challenge requires capacity building, infrastructure development, access to advanced devices, and inclusive policymaking that prioritizes the needs of marginalized communities and ensures equitable resource allocations to enable access to AI technologies. Equitable AI governance is also essential to prevent AI from exacerbating existing inequalities. This includes ensuring that AI systems are designed, developed, and deployed in a transparent and accountable manner, and that the voices of marginalized communities are heard in decision-making processes.

4.5.2 Bias in AI Models

AI-driven environmental monitoring may reflect biases in training data, leading to inaccurate or unjust outcomes (Ren & Wierman, 2024). AI models rely on extensive datasets, but biases in data collection can lead to erroneous predictions that disproportionately impact marginalized communities (Li et al., 2025). For example, suppose an AI-driven environmental monitoring system is trained on data that underrepresents pollution levels in low-income areas. In that case, it may underestimate the environmental risks these communities face.

4.5.3 The Digital Divide

Access to AI-driven climate solutions is uneven, often favoring wealthier nations and communities while leaving others vulnerable (Zewe, 2025). The digital divide refers to the gap between those who have access to digital technologies, such as computers and the Internet, and those who do not. This divide can exacerbate existing inequalities, as marginalized communities may lack the resources and infrastructure to access and benefit from AI-driven climate solutions.

4.5.4 Environmental Impact of AI

The environmental impact of AI itself cannot be overlooked. AI systems rely on critical minerals, contributing to mining-related environmental degradation (Corrigan & Ikonnikova, 2024). The computational demands of AI contribute to environmental degradation, as training large-scale models requires substantial energy and resources (Olawade et al., 2024). The production and disposal of AI hardware generate electronic waste containing toxic substances like lead and mercury (Corrigan & Ikonnikova, 2024; Iqbal, 2024). AI consumes significant electricity, with data centers requiring extensive energy resources. Moreover, CO_2 emissions and water usage in AI operations are another primary concern. For instance, Google's U.S. data centers alone consumed an estimated 12.7 billion liters of fresh water in 2021 to cool servers (Kirkpatrick, 2023; Li et al., 2025). It is essential to consider energy-efficient AI models to reduce the environmental impact of AI technologies.

5 Role of Social Work

Social workers play a critical role in climate change preparedness and in supporting vulnerable communities in adopting climate change measures. Social workers, deeply committed to principles of justice, equity, and human rights, play a vital role in addressing the complex challenges of climate change through eco-social work practice (The Social Work Graduate, 2023; Timariu, 2022; Ungar, 2002). As climate-related disasters grow in frequency and intensity, integrating AI offers transformative potential to enhance social work's impact on disaster preparedness, adaptation, and policy development. Through ethical application, community engagement, and rights-based advocacy, social workers can ensure that AI is harnessed not merely as a technological tool but as a catalyst for equity-driven, sustainable transformation. In this section, we envision the role of social work in three levels: (1) the role of social work in AI system development, (2) the use of AI in eco-social work practice, and (3) addressing the digital divide for digital inclusion.

5.1 Role of Social Workers in AI Development

As a practice-centric profession grounded in transdisciplinary theories, the adoption of indigenous knowledge, and ongoing community engagement, social workers play a critical role in the AI development cycle for climate change preparedness tools by incorporating human rights and social justice values to ensure AI models and tools are inclusive, equitable, and socio-culturally responsive. Social workers also act as advocates for vulnerable populations and actively incorporate indigenous knowledge and community perspectives to align AI systems with community needs and ethical standards throughout the development process (Harms, 2007). Table 17.1

Table 17.1 Role of social workers in the AI development process

AI development cycle	Role of social workers
Planning	Help identifying high risk and vulnerable population and meaningfully engage them in the planning process to make sure that AI tools meet the community needs and reduce disproportionate impact to the vulnerable populations. Support in required capacity building of communities. Equitable compensation model for community engagement.
Design	Adapt design justice principles for meaningful engagement of communities and support co-design process with communities, designers, and technologies to ensure design frameworks meets the community needs.
Data collection	Support to ensure that data are gathered ethically and reflects the lived realities of diverse communities impacted by climate related disasters. Ensure under/over-representations of certain social groups.
Data analysis	Support developers to look for people behind the data and help them understand local socioeconomic cultural contexts, sensitivities, and barriers in accessing resources and technologies.
Model development	Collaborate with AI developers to identify possible bias, harms, and unintended consequences of AI predictive models.
Validation	Support to validate the AI models and tools with communities to ensure diversity, inclusion, accessibility requirements and ensure that intended people can use it with context.
Implementation	Act as bridge between communities and AI developers. Support with education, capacity building and outreach to promote the responsible use of tools.
Evaluation	Assessing social and environmental impact, gathering community feedback, and recommending adjustments to ensure fairness, usability, and effectiveness.
Use of data	Ensure user data is not used beyond indented purpose and equitable compensation for the community data. Support to reduce carbon footprint, e-waste, energy conservation.

explains the role of social workers in each AI development cycle to ensure that climate change preparedness tools become more just, responsive, and impactful in building community resilience.

5.2 Use of AI in Eco-Social Work Practice

Social workers can leverage AI in multiple dimensions of climate change mitigation and adaptation. At the micro-level, AI-powered tools such as predictive analytics can help identify individuals and households most vulnerable to climate-related risks, enabling targeted interventions. For example, machine learning algorithms can assess socio-environmental data—such as health records, housing stability, and geographical exposure—to anticipate impacts of heatwaves, floods, or wildfires (Vinuesa et al., 2020). Social workers can then mobilize resources and develop personalized action plans to enhance individual and community resilience. On the mezzo level, social workers collaborate with community organizations to implement AI-driven early warning systems and decision-support tools. These systems can provide real-time risk assessments and guide evacuation strategies, resource allocation, and community education. Social workers play a critical role in translating complex data into accessible information and ensuring that marginalized populations—often excluded from technological benefits—receive timely and culturally appropriate support (Bulkeley et al., 2013). At the macro-level, social workers advocate for inclusive and ethical AI policy frameworks in disaster risk reduction and climate adaptation. They engage with governments and global organizations to ensure that AI technologies do not perpetuate existing social inequities. AI tools used in environmental planning and disaster management must be co-designed with communities, centering local knowledge and participatory governance (Eubanks, 2018). Social work's commitment to human rights and social justice ensures that technological innovation aligns with the broader goal of building a new eco-social world where no one is left behind. Moreover, integrating AI into eco-social work practice supports capacity-building and long-term sustainability. Training programs and interdisciplinary collaborations can equip social workers with digital literacy and technological fluency, enabling them to meaningfully contribute to AI development and deployment (IFSW, 2022). This integration reinforces the role of social workers as facilitators of social and environmental protection, advancing policy innovation to address the intersecting crises of climate change, inequality, and systemic disempowerment.

5.3 Addressing Digital Divide for AI-Supported Climate Adoption

Digital divide is a human rights issue (Sanders & Scanlon, 2021). Social workers' intervention is essential for AI solutions to reach and benefit all segments of society, particularly vulnerable and marginalized communities. Social workers actively work with vulnerable populations and marginalized communities. There has been a social voice calling for action to address the digital divide. To make AI in eco-social work practice a reality, it is vital to educate communities, and social workers are better positioned to help individuals understand and use AI tools designed for climate risk alerts, resource management, or early warning systems, ensuring that no group is left behind due to a lack of digital skills. When AI tools are introduced, social workers assist individuals and communities in navigating transitions, reducing resistance, and encouraging adoption to reduce climate-related risk and damage. Social workers advocate for equitable access to digital infrastructure and for fair resource allocation. Social workers collaborate with policymakers to prioritize Internet connectivity, device access, and inclusive digital services in underserved areas—prerequisites for communities to engage with AI-driven climate tools.

6 Conclusion

Environmental social work is increasingly grappling with the intensifying complexities of climate change, not only as an ecological crisis but also as a profoundly social one. As rising temperatures, violent storms, wildfires, and chronic water scarcity disproportionately impact vulnerable populations, practitioners are being called to address these cascading threats through both immediate and anticipatory frameworks. The integration of AI into eco-social work holds significant, transformative promise—not as a detached technological fix, but as a part of a hybrid approach that complements Indigenous and community-based knowledge systems. When combined, these knowledge forms can generate more comprehensive strategies for climate adaptation and resilience. For instance, AI-driven flood forecasting models or deforestation monitoring platforms are most effective when interpreted and operationalized alongside local observations, cultural practices, and social work's relational expertise. The focus, then, is not solely on demonstrating that AI can be beneficial but on identifying emerging examples where AI-enabled insights can be translated into concrete interventions at multiple levels: warning systems that help households evacuate or safeguard assets, adaptation strategies that amplify community resilience, and landscape-scale monitoring that supports policy and ecosystem-level interventions. Yet challenges remain. Gaps in the literature highlight the need for participatory AI approaches that actively involve community stakeholders in design and governance (Rolnick et al., 2022). Strengthening interdisciplinary collaborations between social workers, AI developers, and environmental scientists is essential to align technological solutions with social and ecological goals (Dominelli, 2018; Mason et al., 2017). Moreover, policies must ensure that AI-driven environmental interventions are ethical, inclusive, and sustainable (Zewe, 2025). As AI continues to evolve, the credibility of this field will depend on moving beyond broad claims and instead demonstrating where and how AI, environmental work, and social work intersect in practice, particularly at the community and household level, where climate impacts are most acutely felt. By integrating Indigenous knowledge with predictive analytics and community-based social work, environmental interventions can become more accurate, just, and durable, offering pathways to resilience that ensure equitable climate solutions.

References

Abdenur, A. E. (2020, November 23). *How can artificial intelligence help curb deforestation in the Amazon?* International Peace Institute: The Global Observatory. https://theglobalobservatory.org/2020/11/how-can-artificial-intelligence-help-curb-deforestation-amazon/

Abdulameer, L., Al-Khafaji, M. S., Al-Awadi, A. T., Al Maimuri, N. M. L., Al-Shammari, M., Al-Dujaili, A. N., & Al-Jumeily, D. (2025). Artificial intelligence in climate-resilient water management: A systematic review of applications, challenges, and future directions. *Water Conservation Science and Engineering, 10*, 44. https://doi.org/10.1007/s41101-025-00371-2

Albahri, A. S., Khaleel, Y. L., Habeeb, M. A., Ismael, R. D., Hameed, Q. A., Deveci, M., Homod, R. Z., Albahri, O. S., Alamoodi, A. H., & Alzubaidi, L. (2024). A systematic review of trustworthy artificial intelligence applications in natural disasters. *Computers and Electrical Engineering, 118*(Part B), 109409. https://doi.org/10.1016/j.compeleceng.2024.109409

ALERTCalifornia. (2025). *ALERTCalifornia*. https://alertcalifornia.org/

Alkhatib, A. A. A. (2014). A review on forest fire detection techniques. *International Journal of Distributed Sensor Networks, 10*(3). https://doi.org/10.1155/2014/597368

Barrett, A. B., Duivenvoorden, S., Salakpi, E. E., Muthoka, J. M., Mwangi, J., Oliver, S., & Rowhani, P. (2019). Forecasting vegetation condition for drought early warning systems in pastoral communities in Kenya. *arXiv*. https://doi.org/10.48550/arXiv.1911.10339

Batko, S., & McTarnaghan, S. (2025, January 15). *How the Los Angeles fires are compounding the risk of homelessness*. Urban Institute. https://www.urban.org/urban-wire/how-los-angeles-fires-are-compounding-risk-homelessness

Belchior Rocha, D. M. (2018). Environmental social work and the challenges of socio-environmental conflicts in Brazil. *Critical and Radical Social Work, 6*(2), 211–226.

Bell, B. (2021, May 30). California wildfires disproportionately affect elderly and poor residents, UCI study finds. *UC Irvine News*. https://news.uci.edu/2021/05/30/california-wildfires-disproportionately-affect-elderly-and-poor-residents-uci-study-finds/

Billiot, S., Beltrán, R., Brown, D., Mitchell, F. M., & Fernandez, A. (2019). Indigenous perspectives for strengthening social responses to global environmental changes: A response to the social work grand challenge on environmental change. *Journal of Community Practice, 27*(3–4), 296–316. https://doi.org/10.1080/10705422.2019.1658677

Boetto, H. (2017). A transformative eco-social model: Challenging modernist assumptions in social work. *British Journal of Social Work, 47*, 48–67. https://doi.org/10.1093/bjsw/bcw149

Brodsky, S. (2025, January 20). *California fires drive race for AI detection tools*. IBM. https://www.ibm.com/think/news/ai-fire-prediction

Bronfenbrenner, U. (1977). Toward an experimental ecology of human development. *American Psychologist, 32*(7), 513–531. https://doi.org/10.1037/0003-066X.32.7.513

Bulkeley, H., Edwards, G. A., & Fuller, S. (2013). Climate justice and global cities: Mapping the emerging discourses. *Global Environmental Change, 23*(5), 914–925.

California Department of Forestry and Fire Protection. (2025, April 14). *Statistics*. https://www.fire.ca.gov/our-impact/statistics

Camps-Valls, G., Fernández-Torres, M. Á., Cohrs, K. H., Höhl, A., Castelletti, A., Pacal, A., Robin, C., Martinuzzi, F., Papoutsis, I., Prapas, I., Pérez-Aracil, J., Weigel, K., Gonzalez-Calabuig, M., Reichstein, M., Rabel, M., Giuliani, M., Mahecha, M. D., Popescu, O., Pellicer-Valero, O. J., Ouala, S., Salcedo-Sanz, S., Sippel, S., Kondylatos, S., Happé, T., & Williams, T. (2025). Artificial intelligence for modeling and understanding extreme weather and climate events. *Nature Communications, 16*, 1919. https://doi.org/10.1038/s41467-025-56573-8

Chowdhury, A. (2021, October 22). *Climate change, Google and Bangladesh Floods*. United Nations Development Programme. https://www.undp.org/bangladesh/blog/climate-change-google-and-bangladesh-floods

Chu, J. (2024, November 25). New AI tool generates realistic satellite images of future flooding. *MIT News*. https://news.mit.edu/2024/new-ai-tool-generates-realistic-satellite-images-future-flooding-1125

Cina, E., Elbasi, E., Elmazi, G., & Al Arnaout, Z. (2025). The role of AI in predictive modelling for sustainable urban development: Challenges and opportunities. *Sustainability, 17*(11), 5148. https://doi.org/10.3390/su17115148

Coates, J., & Gray, M. (2012). The environment and social work: An overview and introduction. *International Journal of Social Welfare, 21*(3), 230–238. https://doi.org/10.1111/j.1468-2397.2011.00851.x

Corrigan, C. C., & Ikonnikova, S. A. (2024). A review of the use of AI in the mining industry: Insights and ethical considerations for multi-objective optimization. *The Extractive Industries and Society, 17*, 101440. https://doi.org/10.1016/j.exis.2024.101440

de Pérez, E. C., Harrison, L., Berse, K., Easton-Calabria, E., Marunye, J., Marake, M., Murshed, S. B., Shampa, & Zauisomue, E. H. (2022). Adapting to climate change through anticipatory action: The potential use of weather based early warnings. *Weather and Climate Extremes, 38*, 100508. https://doi.org/10.1016/j.wace.2022.100508

Di Giuseppe, F., McNorton, J., Lombardi, A., & Wetterhall, F. (2025). Global data-driven prediction of fire activity. *Nature Communications, 16*, 2918. https://doi.org/10.1038/s41467-025-58097-7

Dixit, P. (2023, October 24). Stopping wildfires: AlertCalifornia and Cal Fire AI wildfire detector. *TIME*. https://time.com/collection/best-inventions-2023/6327137/alertcalifornia-ai-wildfire-detector/

Dominelli, L. (2018). *Green social work: From environmental crises to environmental justice*. Polity Press.

ESG News. (2025, February 19). *Google expands flood hub to strengthen flood preparedness for vulnerable communities*. https://esgnews.com/google-expands-flood-hub-to-strengthen-flood-preparedness-for-vulnerable-communities/

Ennes, J., & Chaves, L. (2021, November 10). Indigenous agents fight deforestation with drones and AI in Brazilian Amazon. *Mongabay*. https://news.mongabay.com/2021/11/indigenous-agents-fight-deforestation-with-drones-and-ai-in-brazilian-amazon/

European Centre for Medium-Range Weather Forecasts [ECMWF]. (n.d.). *About us*. https://www.ecmwf.int/en/about

Eubanks, V. (2018). *Automating inequality: How high-tech tools profile, police, and punish the poor*. Picador.

Fato, E. (2024). Eco-social work: Theoretical foundations and implications for sustainable inclusion. In F. Calabrò, L. Madureira, F. C. Morabito, & M. J. Piñeira Mantiñán (Eds.), *Networks, markets & people. NMP 2024* (Lecture Notes in Networks and Systems) (Vol. 1186, pp. 429–440). Springer. https://doi.org/10.1007/978-3-031-74679-6_42

Food and Agriculture Organization of the United Nations (2024, May 6). *WaPOR (Water Productivity through Open access of remotely sensed derived data)*. GEO Knowledge Hub. https://gkhub.earthobservations.org/packages/4dkpz-75t98

Food and Agriculture Organization of the United Nations & United Nations Environment Programme. (2020). *The state of the world's forests 2020. Forests, biodiversity and people*. FAO. https://doi.org/10.4060/ca8642en

Food and Agriculture Organization of the United Nations & United Nations Environment Programme. (2022). *The state of the world's forests 2022. Forest pathways for green recovery and building inclusive, resilient and sustainable economies*. FAO. https://doi.org/10.4060/cb9360en

Gartshore, S. (2022). *Eco-social work: Environmental and sustainable social work in everyday practice*. Research Gate Technical Report. https://doi.org/10.13140/RG.2.2.26847.33445

Gerber, J., & Foley, J. (2025, March 4). *How stopping deforestation is a powerful "emergency brake" climate solution*. Project Drawdown. https://drawdown.org/insights/how-stopping-deforestation-is-a-powerful-%E2%80%9Cemergency-brake%E2%80%9D-climate-solution

Giannakidou, S., Radoglou-Grammatikis, P., Lagkas, T., Argyriou, V., Goudos, S., Markakis, E. K., & Sarigiannidis, P. (2024). Leveraging the power of internet of things and artificial intelligence in forest fire prevention, detection, and restoration: A comprehensive survey. *Internet of Things, 26*, 101171. https://doi.org/10.1016/j.iot.2024.101171

Global Conservation. (2024). *Tech for parks: Global forest watch*. https://globalconservation.org/global-forest-watch

Global Forest Watch. (n.d.). *About*. https://www.globalforestwatch.org/about

Goedde, L., Ooko-Ombaka, A., & Pais, G. (2019, February 15). *Winning in Africa's agricultural market*. McKinsey & Company. https://www.mckinsey.com/industries/agriculture/our-insights/winning-in-africas-agricultural-market#/

Goldapple, L. (2021, February 1). *Saving the rainforests with AI: Rainforest connection*. Atlas of the Future. https://atlasofthefuture.org/project/rainforest-connection

Google Research. (2025). *Flood hub*. https://sites.research.google/floods/l/0/0/3

Google Research. (n.d.-a). *FireSat*. https://sites.research.google/gr/wildfires/firesat/

Google Research. (n.d.-b). *Flood forecasting*. https://sites.research.google/gr/floodforecasting/

Harms, L. (2007). *Working with people: Communication skills for reflective practice*. Oxford University Press.

Haykal, D., Goldust, M., Cartier, H., & Treacy, P. (2025). AI in humanitarian healthcare: A game changer for crisis response. *Frontiers in Artificial Intelligence, 8*, 1627773. https://doi.org/10.3389/frai.2025.1627773

Hultgren, A., Carleton, T., Delgado, M., Gergel, D. R., Greenstone, M., Houser, T., Hsiang, S., Jina, A., Kopp, R. E., Malevich, S. B., McCusker, K. E., Mayer, T., Nath, I., Rising, J., Rode, A., & Yuan, J. (2025). Impacts of climate change on global agriculture accounting for adaptation. *Nature, 642*(8068), 644–652. https://doi.org/10.1038/s41586-025-09085-w

IBM Environmental Intelligence Suite. (2025, January 9). *Geospatial analytics*. https://www.ibm.com/docs/en/environmental-intel-suite?topic=components-geospatial-analytics

Imazon. (2022, February 17). *Artificial intelligence platform estimates deforestation risk of 15 thousand km^2 in the Brazilian Amazon in 2022*. https://imazon.fly.dev/imprensa/artificial-intelligence-platform-estimates-deforestation-risk-of-15-thousand-km%C2%B2-in-the-brazilian-amazon-in-2022

Imray, G. (2024, October 15). *Southern Africa is enduring its worst hunger crisis in decades due to El Niño, the UN says*. The Associated Press. https://apnews.com/article/drought-southern-africa-food-el-nino-hunger-6a2c8eb3db2e909f098db3a5ce71f6e4

International Centre of Expertise in Montreal on Artificial Intelligence. (2024). *State of AI in agriculture in Sub-Saharan Africa*. https://doi.org/10.5281/zenodo.13144813

International Federation of Social Workers. (2022, May 24). *The role of social workers in advancing a new eco-social world*. www.ifsw.org/the-role-of-social-workers-in-advancing-a-new-eco-social-world/

Iqbal, S. S. (2024, November 14). Generative AI Could Generate Millions More Tons of E-Waste by 2030. *Scientific American Special Editions, 34*(1). 98. https://doi.org/10.1038/scientificamerican032025-4qVfc0k2DymNMNjxFzj3Vy

Jatobá, A., Souza, R., & Mendes, R. (2021). Ethical challenges in AI: Reflections for social work. *Revista Katálysis, 24*(1), 45–53.

Jen, D. (2024, November 14). *Artificial intelligence detects fires early, protecting people and infrastructure.* American Society of Civil Engineers. https://www.asce.org/publications-and-news/civil-engineering-source/article/2024/11/14/artificial-intelligence-detects-fires-early-protecting-people-infrastructure

Kamyab, H., Khademi, T., Chelliapan, S., SaberiKamarposhti, M., Rezania, S., Yusuf, M., Farajnezhad, M., Abbas, M., Hun Jeon, B., & Ahn, Y. (2023). The latest innovative avenues for the utilization of artificial Intelligence and big data analytics in water resource management. *Results in Engineering, 20*, 101566. https://doi.org/10.1016/j.rineng.2023.101566

Khorsandi, P. (2024, May 15). *In Southern Africa, El Niño drought leaves a trail of scorched harvests and hunger.* World Food Programme. https://www.wfp.org/stories/southern-africa-el-nino-drought-leaves-trail-scorched-harvests-and-hunger

Kirkpatrick, K. (2023, August 1). The carbon footprint of artificial intelligence. *Communications of the ACM.* https://cacm.acm.org/news/the-carbon-footprint-of-artificial-intelligence/

Klingler, N. (2024, March 18). *EfficientNet: Optimizing deep learning efficiency.* viso.ai. https://viso.ai/deep-learning/efficientnet/

Kühnle, J. (2024, February). *Ahead of the curve: What can anticipatory humanitarian action achieve?* Welthungerhilfe. https://www.welthungerhilfe.org/global-food-journal/rubrics/crises-humanitarian-aid/what-can-anticipatory-humanitarian-action-achieve

Kumar, P., Rao, S., & Yadama, G. (2019, September 30). Energy poverty in India. In *Encyclopedia of social work.* https://oxfordre.com/socialwork/view/10.1093/acrefore/9780199975839.001.0001/acrefore-9780199975839-e-1298

Le Coz, C., & van de Giesen, N. (2020). Comparison of Rainfall Products over Sub-Saharan Africa. *Journal of Hydrometeorology, 21*(4), 553–596. https://doi.org/10.1175/JHM-D-18-0256.1

Lee, C. (Ed.). (1992). *Proceedings of the first national people of color environmental leadership summit.* United Church of Christ Commission for Racial Justice.

Li, P., Yang, J., Islam, M.A., & Ren, S. (2025). Making AI less "thirsty": Uncovering and addressing the secret water footprint of AI models. *arXiv.* https://doi.org/10.48550/arXiv.2304.03271

Liu, Z., Coleman, N., Patrascu, F. I., Yin, K., Li, X., & Mostafavi, A. (2024). Artificial intelligence for flood risk management: A comprehensive state-of-the-art review and future directions. *International Journal of Disaster Risk Reduction, 117*, 105110. https://doi.org/10.1016/j.ijdrr.2024.105110

Martin, V., Venable, K.B., & Morgan, D. (2024a). Development and application of a Sentinel-2 satellite imagery dataset for deep-learning driven forest wildfire detection. *arXiv.* https://doi.org/10.48550/arXiv.2409.16380

Martin, V., Morgan, D., & Venable, K.B. (2024b). Python-based GeoImagery dataset development for deep learning-driven forest wildfire detection. *SciPy Proceedings.* https://proceedings.scipy.org/articles/YADT7194

Martinez, D., & Irfan, A. (2021, November 4). *Colonialism, the climate crisis, and the need to center indigenous voices.* Environmental Health News. https://www.ehn.org/indigenous-people-and-climate-change-2655479728/american-settler-colonialism

Mason, L. R., Shires, M. K., Arwood, C., & Borst, A. (2017). Social work research and global environmental change. *Journal of the Society for Social Work & Research, 8*(4), 645–672. https://doi.org/10.1086/694789

Mathiyazhagan, S. (2021). Field practice, emerging technologies, and human rights: The emergence of tech social workers. *Journal of Human Rights and Social Work.* https://doi.org/10.1007/s41134-021-00190-0

Matias, Y. (2021, November 9). *Expanding our ML-based flood forecasting.* Google Research. https://blog.google/technology/ai/expanding-our-ml-based-flood-forecasting/

Matias, Y. (2023, October 10). *How we're using AI to combat floods, wildfires and extreme heat.* Google Research. https://blog.google/outreach-initiatives/sustainability/google-ai-climate-change-solutions/

Matias, Y. (2024, November 11). *How we're helping partners with improved and expanded AI-based flood forecasting.* Google Research. https://blog.google/technology/ai/expanding-flood-forecasting-coverage-helping-partners/

Matthies, A.-L., Närhi, K., & Ward, D. (2001). *The eco-social approach in social work.* SoPhi.

Närhi, K., & Matthies, A.-L. (2016a). Conceptual and historical analysis of ecological social work. In J. McKinnon & M. Alston (Eds.), *Ecological social work: Towards sustainability* (pp. 21–38). Palgrave Macmillan. https://doi.org/10.1007/978-1-137-40136-6_2

Närhi, K., & Matthies, A. L. (2016b). *The ecosocial transition of societies: The contribution of social work and social policy*. Routledge.

Naslund, J. A., Aschbrenner, K. A., Marsch, L. A., & Bartels, S. J. (2020). The future of mental health care: Peer-to-peer support and social media. *Epidemiology and Psychiatric Sciences, 25*(2), 113–122. https://doi.org/10.1017/S2045796015001067

Nearing, G., Cohen, D., Dube, V., Gauch, M., Gilon, O., Harrigan, S., Hassidim, A., Klotz, D., Kratzert, F., Metzger, A., Nevo, S., Pappenberger, F., Prudhomme, C., Shalev, G., Shenzis, S., Tekalign, T. Y., Weitzner, D., & Matias, Y. (2024). Global prediction of extreme floods in ungauged watersheds. *Nature, 627*, 559–563. https://doi.org/10.1038/s41586-024-07145-1

Neeraja, U. V., Saneesh, C. S., Dyda, V., Reddy, H., Yadama, G. N., & Knight, T. M. (2022). Harvesting has variable effects on demographic rates and population growth across three dry forest tree species. *Biotropica, 54*(6), 1376–1389. https://doi.org/10.1111/btp.13135

Nevo, S., Morin, E., Gerzi Rosenthal, A., Metzger, A., Barshai, C., Weitzner, D., Voloshin, D., Kratzert, F., Elidan, G., Dror, G., Begelman, G., Nearing, G., Shalev, G., Noga, H., Shavitt, I., Yuklea, L., Royz, M., Giladi, N., Peled Levi, N., et al. (2022). Flood forecasting with machine learning models in an operational framework. *Hydrology and Earth System Sciences, 26*(15), 4013–4032. https://doi.org/10.5194/hess-26-4013-2022

Norton, C. L. (2012). Social work and the environment: An ecosocial approach. *International Journal of Social Welfare, 21*(3), 299–308. https://doi.org/10.1111/j.1468-2397.2011.00853.x

Okoth, D. (2024, March 4). The cost of African drought. *Nature*. https://www.nature.com/articles/d44148-024-00075-0

Olawade, D. B., Wada, O. Z., Ige, A. O., Egbewole, B. I., Olojo, A., & Oladapo, B. I. (2024). Artificial intelligence in environmental monitoring: Advancements, challenges, and future directions. *Hygiene and Environmental Health Advances, 12*, 100114. https://doi.org/10.1016/j.heha.2024.100114

Pandian, S. (2025, February 12). *Precision agriculture powered by AI for climate-resilient crops.* Data Science Central. https://www.datasciencecentral.com/precision-agriculture-powered-by-ai-for-climate-resilient-crops/

Peeters, J. (2012). The place of social work in sustainable development: Towards ecosocial practice. *International Journal of Social Welfare, 21*, 287–298. https://doi.org/10.1111/j.1468-2397.2011.00856.x

Powers, M., Rinkel, M., & Kumar, P. (2021). Co-creating a "sustainable new normal" for social work and beyond: Embracing an ecosocial worldview. *Sustainability, 13*(19), 10941. https://doi.org/10.3390/su131910941

Prestes, E., Barbosa, L.V.F., Del Grossi, V.C.D., de Azevedo, C.P.G., Macedo, G., & Maffei, R. (2024, July 31). *AI and Brazil's indigenous populations: A call for participation*. United Nations Educational, Scientific and Cultural Organization. https://www.unesco.org/en/articles/ai-and-brazils-indigenous-populations-call-participation

PrevisIA. (n.d.). *PrevisIA*. https://previsia.org.br/

Raffio, N. (2024, July 22). USC scientists use AI to predict a wildfire's next move. *USC Today*. https://today.usc.edu/using-ai-to-predict-wildfires/

Rainforest Connection. (2025). *What we do.* https://rfcx.org

Rao, S., Billiot, S., & Teixeira, S. (2022). *Social work and environmental justice: Expanding critical social work.* Taylor & Francis. https://doi.org/10.4324/9781003211969-53

Ren, S., & Wierman, A. (2024, July 15). The uneven distribution of AI's environmental impacts. *Harvard Business Review.* https://hbr.org/2024/07/the-uneven-distribution-of-ais-environmental-impacts

Rolnick, D., Donti, P. L., Kaack, L. H., Kochanski, K., Lacoste, A., Sankaran, K., Slavin Ross, A., Milojevic-Dupont, N., Jaques, N., Waldman-Brown, A., Luccioni, A. S., Maharaj, T., Sherwin, E. D., Mukkavilli, S. K., Kording, K. P., Gomes, C. P., Ng, A. Y., Hassabis, D., Platt, J. C., et al. (2022). Tackling climate change with machine learning. *ACM Computing Surveys, 55*(2), 1–96. https://doi.org/10.1145/3485128

Sanders, C. K., & Scanlon, E. (2021). The digital divide is a human rights issue: Advancing social inclusion through social work advocacy. *Journal of Human Rights and Social Work, 6*(2), 130–143. https://doi.org/10.1007/s41134-020-00147-9

Schmitz, C. L., Matyók, T., Sloan, L., & James, C. D. (2012). The relationship between social work and environmental sustainability: Implications for interdisciplinary practice. *International Journal of Social Welfare, 21*(3), 278–286. https://doi.org/10.1111/j.1468-2397.2011.00855.x

Shackelford, A., Rao, S., Krings, A., & Frances, K. (2024). Abolitionism and ecosocial work: Towards equity, liberation and environmental justice. *The British Journal of Social Work, 54*(4), 1402–1419. https://doi.org/10.1093/bjsw/bcad247

Sheffield, J., Wood, E. F., Chaney, N., Guan, K., Sadri, S., Yuan, X., Olang, L., Amani, A., Ali, A., Demuth, S., & Ogallo, L. (2014). A drought monitoring and forecasting system for Sub-Sahara African water resources and food security. *Bulletin of the American Meteorological Society, 95*(6), 861–882. https://doi.org/10.1175/BAMS-D-12-00124.1

Sinyangwe, C. & Savage, R. (2024, November 14). 'I have lost everything': Southern Africa battles hunger amid historic drought. *The Guardian*. https://www.theguardian.com/global-development/2024/nov/14/lost-everything-southern-africa-battles-hunger-amid-historic-drought

Smith, E. (2023, September 6). *AI may hold a key to the preservation of the Amazon rainforest*. Microsoft. https://news.microsoft.com/source/latam/features/ai/amazon-ai-rainforest-deforestation/

Son, T. H., Weedon, Z., Yigitcanlar, T., Sanchez, T., Corchado, J. M., & Mehmood, R. (2023). Algorithmic urban planning for smart and sustainable development: Systematic review of the literature. *Sustainable Cities and Society, 94*, 104562. https://doi.org/10.1016/j.scs.2023.104562

The European Space Agency. (2020). *FloodSENS: Smart sensing of floods*. https://incubed.esa.int/portfolio/floodsens/

The Social Work Graduate. (2023, October 27). *Eco social work*. www.thesocialworkgraduate.com/post/eco-social-work

Thysell, M., & Cuadra, C. B. (2023). Imagining the ecosocial within social work. *International Journal of Social Welfare, 32*, 455–472. https://doi.org/10.1111/ijsw.12571

Timariu, D. (2022). *Reflective supervision: Learning hub*. Research in Practice. https://www.practice-supervisors.rip.org.uk

Ungar, M. (2002). A deeper, more social ecological social work practice. *Social Service Review, 76*(3), 480–497. https://www.jstor.org/stable/10.1086/341185

United Nations Convention to Combat Desertification. (n.d.). *African flood and drought monitor*. https://www.unccd.int/land-and-life/drought/toolbox/african-flood-and-drought-monitor

United Nations Environment Programme. (2024, September 21). *AI has an environmental problem. Here's what the world can do about that*. https://www.unep.org/news-and-stories/story/ai-has-environmental-problem-heres-what-world-can-do-about

United Nations Environment Programme. (2025, March 12). *International methane emissions observatory*. https://www.unep.org/topics/energy/methane/international-methane-emissions-observatory

United Nations Environment Programme. (n.d.). *Marine sand watch*. https://unepgrid.ch/en/marinesandwatch

United Nations Framework Convention on Climate Change [UNFCC]. (2024). *Artificial intelligence for climate action in developing countries: opportunities, challenges and risks*. https://unfccc.int/ttclear/misc_/StaticFiles/gnwoerk_static/AI4climateaction/28da5d97d7824d16b7f68a225c0e3493/a4553e8f70f74be3bc37c929b73d9974.pdf

United Nations Office for the Coordination of Humanitarian Affairs & Regional Interagency Standing Committee. (2024, May 20). *Southern Africa is in the grip of a severe drought.* https://www.unocha.org/publications/report/madagascar/southern-africa-grip-severe-drought

United Nations Security Council. (2021, February 23). *Climate change 'biggest threat modern humans have ever faced', world-renowned naturalist tells security council, calls for greater global cooperation* [Press Release]. https://www.un.org/press/en/2021/sc14445.doc.htm

Van Horne, Y. O., Alcala, C. S., Peltier, R. E., Quintana, P. J. E., Seto, E., Gonzales, M., Johnston, J. E., Montoya, L. D., Quirós-Alcalá, L., & Beamer, P. I. (2023). An applied environmental justice framework for exposure science. *Journal of exposure science & environmental epidemiology, 33*(1), 1–11. https://doi.org/10.1038/s41370-022-00422-z

Vinuesa, R., Azizpour, H., Leite, I., Balaam, M., Dignum, V., Domisch, S., et al. (2020). The role of artificial intelligence in achieving the sustainable development goals. *Nature Communications, 11*(1), 233.

Wang, P., & Altanbulag, A. (2022). A concern for eco-social sustainability: Background, concepts, values, and perspectives of eco-social work. *Cogent Social Sciences, 8*(2093035), 1–13. https://doi.org/10.1080/23311886.2022.2093035

World Meteorological Organization. (2024). *Early warnings for all.* https://wmo.int/site/frontline-of-climate-action/priorities/early-warnings-all

Yadama, G. N. (2013). *Fires, fuel, and the fate of 3 billion: The state of the energy impoverished.* Oxford University Press.

Zewe, A. (2025, January 17). Explained: Generative AI's environmental impact. *MIT News*. https://news.mit.edu/2025/explained-generative-ai-environmental-impact-0117

Chapter 18
AI in the Evolving Workplace

Peiqi Guo and Philip Young P. Hong

1 Labor Market Disruption in the Age of AI

In this section, we examine the potential effects of artificial intelligence (AI) on labor market disruption. We begin by identifying the underlying causes of labor market disruption and reviewing historical cases to better understand its motivations. We then explore how AI contributes to, or even triggers, such disruption. This section will also highlight current trends and future projections to outline AI's broader impact on the labor market. In addition, we introduce the concepts of job polarization and labor market segmentation. Finally, a set of case studies will be presented to further illustrate and contextualize the key issues discussed above.

1.1 Trends in AI-Driven Automation

1.1.1 Historical Context of Technological Disruption

Disruption in the labor market is neither rare nor unusual. It has consistently accompanied human history, often driven by technological development and evolving social and economic structures. The Industrial Revolution provides a powerful example to illustrate how technological advances have repeatedly caused significant shifts in labor systems. The term "industrial revolution" has been defined as a "step

P. Guo (✉)
School of Public Health, The University of Texas Health Science Center at Houston, Houston, TX, USA
e-mail: peiqi.guo@uth.tmc.edu

P. Y. P. Hong
School of Social Work, University of Georgia, Athens, GA, USA
e-mail: pyphong@uga.edu

R. An, M. A. Lindsey (eds.), *Artificial Intelligence in Social Work*,
https://doi.org/10.1007/978-3-032-18443-6_18

into production technology which was completely different from the past" (Groumpos, 2021).

To date, three industrial revolutions have occurred. The First Industrial Revolution began in the early 1800s, the Second in the late 1800s through the early 1900s, and the Third happened in the late 1900s to early 2000s. As most scholars agree, the First Industrial Revolution originated in Great Britain and was marked by the transition from hand production to machinery. Labor-intensive sectors such as the textile industry were transformed by mechanized power sources, including steam and water power. Large-scale production systems began to emerge, exemplified by mechanized factories. This revolution catalyzed the transition from an agrarian to an industrial economy. Rural populations migrated to urban centers in response to factory labor demands and economic incentives. These migrations and subsequent demographic changes began reshaping the labor market.

The Second Industrial Revolution was characterized by the rise of electricity and the invention and implementation of the assembly line. Some scholars refer to this era as the "Technological Revolution." Electricity became increasingly integrated into daily life, and inventions such as the telephone, electric light bulb, and radio radically reshaped society and accelerated urbanization. As industrialization progressed, labor demand continued to grow, further transforming the labor market.

The Third Industrial Revolution—also known as the Automation Revolution—emerged in the 1950s. It was defined by the use of programmable automation and the introduction of computers, which enabled fully automated production processes. This period also gave rise to foundational digital technologies, including semiconductors, personal computers, smartphones, and the Internet. As the world transitioned into the digital era, labor markets were disrupted and restructured once again. New occupations, such as software engineering, were created. Existing occupations were redefined or diminished, depending on their compatibility with digital workflows.

The Fourth Industrial Revolution is currently unfolding—or may already be well underway. This phase is rooted in digital technologies and is reshaping nearly every aspect of human society. Key innovations include the Internet of Things (IoT), advanced robotics, and perhaps most significantly, artificial intelligence (AI). A growing body of evidence suggests that the development of artificial general intelligence (AGI)—systems possessing human-comparable intelligence—may be on the horizon (McLean et al., 2023). The potential adoption and integration of AGI into daily life remains a subject of considerable debate. Proponents argue that AGI can significantly improve productivity and accelerate scientific progress. However, critics express concern over the social risks it may introduce, including mass unemployment and safety threats to societal stability (Nguyen & Vo, 2022).

As the historical overview above suggests, labor market disruptions are frequently associated with industrial revolutions. At the heart of such disruptions are the emergence and adoption of disruptive technologies. These technologies typically share several defining characteristics: (1) they are innovative and fundamentally transformative; (2) they can be implemented on a large scale; and (3) they possess the capacity to restructure existing workflows. Technologies such as steam power, mechanization, electricity, and automation have all exemplified these traits.

Artificial intelligence also aligns with these characteristics. First, AI is an emerging disruptive technology with the potential to radically alter existing industries—for example, by replacing certain categories of human labor. Second, supporting technologies such as cloud computing and edge deployment have made large-scale AI implementation technically feasible. The widespread adoption of applications like ChatGPT further illustrates its scalability. Third, AI can reshape workflows. Just as human labor was reduced through mechanization and assembly-line production, AI can further displace human involvement in many processes. One key difference between AI and past industrial revolution technologies is the pace of transformation: AI has the potential to bring about widespread change in a significantly shorter timeframe.

1.1.2 Definition and Scope of AI in the Labor Market

We have previously discussed artificial intelligence in earlier sections, but what kinds of AI technologies are we referring to in this context? Here, we refer specifically to those technologies either derived from or powered by artificial intelligence. These include, for example, advanced AI customer service representatives that rely on natural language processing (NLP), AI-assisted medical imaging diagnostics that utilize machine learning, and autonomous robots that integrate robotics with AI's complex problem-solving capabilities. As these examples illustrate, AI technologies are being leveraged to enhance and augment existing occupations. This adaptability is one of AI's defining features: it can be embedded across a wide range of job functions. In this section, we will briefly examine several industries and occupational domains where AI-driven automation is already being adopted. Detailed examples of such applications are provided below.

Services

The service sector is one of the most labor-intensive industries. Typical roles in this sector include retail associates, food service workers, customer representatives, bartenders, baristas, and other public-facing occupations. AI-powered robotics are increasingly capable of replacing portions of these roles. More advanced robotic systems with agile mobility and intelligent processing capabilities are beginning to perform a broader range of service-related tasks—for instance, robotic bartenders, chefs, or even massage robots. Notably, a specialized subfield called embodied artificial intelligence seeks to develop AI systems with physical embodiments that can interact with the material world. Embodied AI holds significant promise for transforming labor demands in the service sector.

Manufacturing

The manufacturing industry is another sector heavily reliant on human labor. It encompasses a broad range of production activities, including electronics, textiles, automobiles, pharmaceuticals, biomedical devices, and chemical goods. As discussed in the historical review of industrial revolutions, manufacturing has long been a labor-dense sector. However, the shift from manual labor to automated machinery accelerated with the development and implementation of advanced semiconductors in industrial automation. AI's role in this transition is already visible, particularly in the context of "advanced manufacturing" or the emergence of the "smart factory." These shifts build on the foundation of traditional automation and deepen its capabilities through machine learning, predictive maintenance, and real-time adaptive control systems (Edlich et al., 2019).

Transportation and Logistics

Transportation and logistics now serve as foundational components of modern life. This includes air travel, rail systems, road-based transit, and the logistics sector, which underpins global supply chains and domestic delivery networks. According to a report by the McKinsey Global Institute, transportation and logistics represent the second-largest potential market for AI applications (Edlich et al., 2019). One prominent example of AI integration in this sector is AI-driven logistics optimization, which can significantly affect labor roles such as route planning, dispatch coordination, and supply chain management. These systems not only enhance operational efficiency but also reshape the responsibilities and demand for certain workforce roles.

The examples above illustrate how AI has impacted specific industries and their associated occupations. However, the influence of AI is not limited to disruption or a sharp reduction in available job positions. Recent research suggests that AI may instead signal a reform of existing industries. Given the nature of this reform and the reallocation of roles, the outcome involves not only layoffs but also the creation of new opportunities. These complex dynamics will be explored further in the following sections. Table 18.1 summarizes historical technological revolutions and their relationship to labor market fluctuations.

1.2 Job Polarization and Labor Segmentation

In the previous section, we explored the historical trajectory of labor market disruptions and the emerging influence of AI technologies on today's employment landscape. In this section, we turn to two increasingly visible phenomena that stem from the growing prevalence of automation and artificial intelligence in workplaces: job

Table 18.1 Historical technological revolutions and labor market disruption (Szeszák et al., 2025)[a]

Revolution	Time period	Key technologies	Labor market disruption
First industrial revolution	Early 1800s	Steam power, mechanized textile production, water power	Marked by the transition from hand production to machinery. Labor-intensive industries like textiles were transformed by steam-powered mechanization. The shift drove population migration from countryside to cities, initiating the transformation from agrarian to industrial economies.
Second industrial revolution	Late 1800s—Early 1900s	Electricity, assembly line, telephone, electric lighting, radio	Characterized by the generalization of electricity and communication technologies. Invention of the assembly line boosted factory efficiency. Urbanization accelerated, and labor demands continued to rise due to mass production and technological advances in daily life.
Third industrial revolution	1950s—Early 2000s	Programmable automation, computers, semiconductors, internet	Initiated the shift to the digital era. Fully automated production processes emerged. New job categories like software engineers were created, while existing roles were restructured or disappeared. Labor markets adapted to growing reliance on digital tools and personal computing.
Fourth industrial revolution	2000s—Present	AI, robotics, IoT, AGI, cloud computing, edge computing	Rooted in digital technologies, this phase is reshaping all aspects of work. AI is seen as disruptive, large scale, and workflow-transforming. Its ability to replace human labor across sectors may lead to rapid, large-scale unemployment and demands for urgent reform.

[a]Adapted from Szeszák et al. (2025, Fig. 1). Some modifications were made. https://doi.org/10.3390/soc15040088, licensed under the terms of the Creative Commons Attribution 4.0 International License (http://creativecommons.org/licenses/by/4.0/)

polarization and labor market segmentation. These structural changes are not only reshaping occupational distributions but are also prompting serious concerns around employment stability, inequality, and long-term social cohesion.

Job polarization refers to the simultaneous expansion of high-skill and low-skill occupations, accompanied by a marked decline in middle-skill jobs. In other words, while demand for top-tier professionals and basic service workers continues to rise, traditionally stable mid-level jobs are diminishing (Goos et al., 2014). This trend reflects more profound transformations in work structures, in which occupations requiring moderate cognitive or manual skills—once considered the backbone of the modern economy—are increasingly susceptible to automation and displacement.

Closely related is the concept of labor segmentation, which describes the growing separation of the labor force into distinct clusters or sub-markets. These sub-markets often differ significantly in terms of job security, wage levels, benefits, and advancement opportunities. Notably, movement between these segments is usually restricted, with structural barriers preventing many workers from accessing better opportunities. In academic discourse, this phenomenon is often referred to as the "dual labor market" model, which differentiates between the primary labor market—characterized by full-time, well-paid, and secure jobs—and the secondary labor market, which comprises part-time, temporary, or unstable jobs with lower compensation and limited protections (Piore, 2014).

One of the primary drivers of job polarization today is the automation of routine tasks, where AI has shown particular strength. Research suggests that AI systems excel at performing repetitive, rule-based tasks—such as data entry, administrative processing, and manufacturing assembly-line work. In contrast, non-routine cognitive tasks, which require creativity, adaptability, or interpersonal engagement—such as education, healthcare, or social work—remain much more resistant to full automation in the short term (Acemoglu & Restrepo, 2018). As a result, the workforce is being pushed toward a bifurcated structure: high-skill roles that complement AI flourish. At the same time, low-skill service jobs persist out of necessity, and many middle-skill jobs face increasing obsolescence.

These structural changes also expose and exacerbate regional and demographic disparities. High-skilled workers in urban centers and developed regions often benefit from the productivity gains and income boosts enabled by AI adoption. In contrast, workers in rural or economically underdeveloped areas face disproportionate risks of job loss and exclusion from digital transformation. Age, educational attainment, and gender further influence how different groups experience and navigate the impacts of AI.

To address these inequities, researchers and policymakers increasingly advocate for robust reskilling and upskilling programs (Li, 2024). These initiatives must go beyond technical training to include social and psychological support—areas where social workers can play a transformative role (Table 18.2). By participating in policy advocacy, providing career transition services, and empowering underserved

Table 18.2 Labor tasks by skill level and automation risk

Skill level	Typical tasks	Automation risk	Labor market segment
High-skill	Creative decision-making, unstructured communication, professional services (e.g., education, nursing)	**Low**—Hard to replace due to complexity, creativity, and interpersonal nature	Primary labor market (stable jobs, high salary, benefits)
Middle-skill	Routine office tasks, data entry, assembly-line work, administrative support	**High**—Highly automatable due to rule-based, repetitive characteristics	Shrinking segment, facing systematic reduction
Low-skill	Manual labor, basic services (e.g., cleaning, food service, delivery)	**Moderate**—Some tasks automatable, others still require physical presence and adaptability	Secondary labor market (part-time, temporary, low wage)

populations, social workers can help mitigate the disruptive effects of AI while fostering greater equity and social inclusion in an evolving labor market.

1.3 Case Studies

The impact of AI technologies on the labor market is reflected not only in systematic restructuring of work but also varies significantly across industries. In this section, we examine specific examples from the manufacturing sector, the retail and service industries, and the healthcare field to explore how AI technologies are transforming work processes and redistributing labor.

1.3.1 Case 1: Manufacturing Industry

In the manufacturing sector, AI technologies have primarily been applied to the operation and maintenance of automation systems. For example, industrial robots are widely used to perform highly repetitive, precision-based tasks on assembly lines. AI-driven smart maintenance systems improve operational efficiency by increasing equipment availability and minimizing malfunction-related interruptions (Chiacchio et al., 2018). These intelligent transformations have significantly enhanced manufacturing productivity. However, they have also resulted in layoffs among middle-skilled workers. Traditional roles in factories—such as assembly workers and inspectors—are gradually becoming obsolete. In response to these challenges, initiatives like Germany's "Industry 4.0" not only promote the development of smart manufacturing but also emphasize the importance of vocational education. These policies encourage skill development in digital tools and advocate for new models of "human-machine collaboration."

1.3.2 Case 2: Retail and Service Industries

The retail and service industries are at the forefront of labor displacement driven by automation. Automated technologies such as self-checkout systems and vending machines are becoming increasingly common in retail environments. At the same time, businesses are adopting AI systems to reduce human resource costs and continuously optimize customer service protocols. Although these technologies bring benefits to companies, they have also reduced labor demand for front-line workers. For instance, in chain supermarkets and fast-food restaurants, traditional cashier and server roles are being phased out in favor of automated systems such as self-order kiosks. Simultaneously, the spread of self-service machines has created new occupations, such as systems operations engineers. These emerging roles typically require higher skill levels, posing additional challenges for less experienced or non-traditional workers.

1.3.3 Case 3: Healthcare Industry

The healthcare industry presents a unique case in which AI brings both enhancement and displacement. Technologies such as AI-assisted diagnostic imaging systems are increasingly being used to support medical image analysis and clinical decision-making. These tools have significantly improved physician efficiency and the overall quality of healthcare delivery. However, at the same time, low-skill roles—such as electronic health record (EHR) recorders, medical coders, insurance reimbursement assistants, and clinical administrators—are gradually being replaced by AI-powered automation software. These changes reduce reliance on backend labor and raise concerns about data security, privacy, and ethical AI governance (Topol, 2019).

Table 18.3 summarizes the aforementioned cases.

To address the challenges brought by AI implementation, governments and enterprises have developed a range of integrative strategies. For instance, several European Union member states have introduced worker-centered skill transformation and upskilling programs that promote internal training and workforce reallocation within the same organizations (Arntz et al., 2016). Social workers play a critical role in this process: not only can they provide counseling services to laid-off or affected workers, but they can also actively engage in policy advocacy and contribute to human-centered market development by building a more equitable and inclusive workplace and technological transition.

Table 18.3 Sectoral case summary: AI impact, response, and outcomes

Sector	AI application	Observed labor impact	Response and outcomes
Manufacturing	Industrial robots on assembly lines; smart maintenance systems	Lay-offs of middle-skilled workers; shrinking demand for assembly workers and inspectors	"Industrial 4.0" promotes vocational training and human-machine cooperation mechanisms (Chiacchio et al., 2018)
Retail & service	Self-checkout machines, vending machines, self-order kiosks; AI-enabled customer service	Reduced demand for front-line workers; replacement of cashiers and servers; emergence of new tech maintenance roles	Emergence of new occupations with higher skill requirements; challenges for less experienced and nontraditional workers
Healthcare	AI-assisted diagnostic systems for imaging and clinical support; automated backend documentation	Enhancement of physician efficiency; job loss for recorders, coders, administrators; concerns over data and AI ethics	Controversy over privacy and data protection; push for balanced automation and ethical governance (Topol, 2019)

2 Labor Rights and Algorithmic Workplaces

As AI technologies continue to permeate the workplace, an increasing number of work procedures and requirements are being delegated to data-driven algorithmic systems. Algorithms are no longer merely tools for decision-making; they have become central drivers of task management and work allocation across industries. These changes are significantly impacting the structure of workers' rights, their day-to-day experiences, and long-term career trajectories. In this chapter, we will examine the challenges that algorithmic workplaces pose to workers by focusing on three key aspects: first, the erosion of worker autonomy due to algorithmic management; second, the intensification of workplace surveillance and the related concerns about data privacy; and third, the presence of algorithmic bias in human resources processes such as recruitment and promotion. This chapter aims to explore how labor rights are being restructured in the age of technological transformation and to discuss potential strategies—such as policy reform, social work interventions, and technological oversight—to promote fairness and justice in AI-mediated work environments.

2.1 Worker Autonomy

The emergence of AI technologies has led to a significant expansion in the adoption of algorithmic management systems across a wide range of workplaces. Algorithmic management refers to end-to-end digitalized management processes powered by big data analytics and automated decision-making systems. These systems oversee task allocation, workflow organization, performance evaluation, scheduling, and even income distribution for workers. Such data-driven management approaches offer substantial advantages for enhancing operational efficiency and reducing costs. They have been widely implemented across sectors such as e-commerce, logistics, retail, manufacturing, and more (Jarrahi et al., 2021).

However, alongside these gains in efficiency, algorithmic management systems have substantially eroded front-line workers' autonomy. In traditional settings, human administrators were responsible for most decisions and communication. Today, those functions have largely been replaced by opaque rating mechanisms, performance indices, and algorithmic recommendations. It has become increasingly complex for workers to understand how decisions about their tasks are made or to question the fairness of those decisions (Kellogg et al., 2020). This issue is particularly prominent in platform-based economies such as ridesharing and food delivery services, where workers are technically classified as "independent operators" but are tightly constrained by platforms' algorithmic management systems.

More importantly, the rise of algorithmic management introduces significant ethical concerns. These systems make decisions based solely on data and historical patterns, without incorporating empathy, context, or ethical reasoning. For instance, algorithms may reinforce systemic biases by assigning unfair weights or relying on historically biased datasets, resulting in discriminatory outcomes against specific groups of workers. Additionally, algorithmic decisions may fail to account for personal emergencies or exceptional circumstances, leading to unjust penalties or performance assessments. Since many of these systems are designed to minimize human oversight, they can further marginalize non-standard workers, such as those who are pregnant or living with physical or mental disabilities, exacerbating inequities in the workplace.

2.2 *Surveillance and Data Privacy*

Workplace surveillance has undergone a profound transformation due to advances in AI and sophisticated image processing. In the past, workplace monitoring primarily relied on human oversight. Today, it has gradually evolved into automated systems powered by intelligent algorithms and sensor technologies. Enterprises now employ facial recognition cameras, real-time location-tracking systems, device activity-monitoring tools, voice recognition systems, and other surveillance technologies to monitor employees' movements, productivity, and even their communication content (Ajunwa et al., 2017).

From a management perspective, these technologies facilitate more timely and quantifiable oversight, enabling firms to evaluate employee performance, monitor work status, and support cost control and operational efficiency. However, these benefits come with significant concerns. The legality and ethical implications of pervasive surveillance have sparked widespread controversy. The growing reliance on continuous monitoring raises critical questions about privacy infringement, informed consent, and the potential erosion of workers' dignity and autonomy in the modern workplace (Table 18.4).

Some scholars have pointed out that beyond improving efficiency and enabling micromanagement, workplace surveillance systems based on behavioral data collection are no longer merely management tools—they represent a form of "Surveillance Capitalism," in which individual privacy is sacrificed to concentrate corporate power and maximize profit (Zuboff, 2019). When legal boundaries remain ambiguous, surveillance practices can more easily overstep legitimate oversight and infringe upon essential privacy rights and human dignity.

Even more far-reaching are the psychological and social consequences of such pervasive, 360 degree surveillance. Research has shown that workers subjected to high-pressure, continuous monitoring environments over the long term are more likely to experience anxiety, depression, burnout, and other emotional disorders (Moore et al., 2018). These adverse outcomes can lead to disengagement and detachment from work. Employees may lose motivation, experience a diminished sense of autonomy, and develop passive or defensive attitudes, which in turn contribute to increased tension and deteriorating workplace relationships.

Table 18.4 Types of workplace Surveillance and risk dimensions (Ball, 2021)[a]

Surveillance type	Technical features	Primary purpose	Associated risks
Face-recognition cameras	Image-based identification powered by AI algorithms	Monitor presence and behavior	Potential violation of privacy rights; controversial in legitimacy and ethical boundaries
Position tracking systems	Location sensors detecting real-time employee movements	Monitor mobility and working hours	Possible over-monitoring and lack of transparency
Working device monitoring systems	Record keyboard, mouse, application usage, system activity	Evaluate efficiency and workflow discipline	Data overcollection; psychological burden due to constant behavioral measurement
Voice recognition systems	Analyze audio inputs to track communication and response times	Improve response efficiency and control protocols	Ethical concerns about monitoring communication contents; employee trust erosion
Integrated AI-based surveillance	Combine multiple sensors and algorithms for 24/7 full-range tracking	Real-time performance metrics and cost control	Risk of psychological pressure, emotional fatigue, anxiety, burnout, and workplace disengagement

[a]Adapted from Ball (2021), Chap. 2: New workplace surveillance practices. Some modifications were made. https://publications.jrc.ec.europa.eu/repository/handle/JRC125716, licensed under the terms of the Creative Commons Attribution 4.0 International License (http://creativecommons.org/licenses/by/4.0/)

2.3 *Bias and Fairness*

In the previous section, we explored how algorithmic management can undermine workers' autonomy and how workplace surveillance can violate employee privacy and harm emotional well-being. Although AI technologies are often portrayed as objective and neutral, their decision-making processes are inherently rooted in existing data and social structures. As a result, algorithmic bias is embedded within systems that may appear fair on the surface.

Barocas and Selbst (2016) examined algorithmic models adopted by numerous companies for human resource functions such as recruitment, screening, and performance evaluation. They found that these models are often trained on historical employee data that already contains various forms of bias—such as information bias, selection bias, and demographic inequalities in gender, ethnicity, and education. When such biased data are used to train AI-powered algorithms, the resulting systems can perpetuate and even amplify discrimination. For instance, studies have shown that some automated hiring systems tend to exclude nontraditional job seekers—such as women applying for technical roles or minority candidates—because they are underrepresented in historical datasets (Raghavan et al., 2020).

To mitigate these biases, scholars have emphasized the importance of transparency and ethical auditing in AI systems that affect workers' rights and livelihoods. Transparency measures may include disclosing the sources of training data and the logic behind algorithmic decisions. Furthermore, implementing fairness evaluation procedures involving multidisciplinary reviewers and introducing human oversight at critical decision points can help ensure accountability.

Social workers can play a vital role in addressing these issues by educating workers about algorithmic bias and their workplace rights (Eubanks, 2018). They may also advocate for ethical AI use by collaborating with government agencies and nonprofit organizations to encourage businesses to incorporate social responsibility as a core consideration when adopting new technologies.

3 Ethical and Societal Implications

In the previous sections, we examined the impact of AI on labor market structures, workers' rights, and the workplace environment. Beyond these direct effects, AI also generates broader influences on society and ethics. In this chapter, we will further explore the ethical and societal implications of AI, focusing on three key areas: economic inequality, responsible AI development, and regulatory and policy interventions.

3.1 Economic Inequality

AI technologies have been regarded as powerful tools for promoting efficiency and increasing profits. However, they also risk widening existing disparities in wealth and opportunity. Research has shown that AI technologies are primarily controlled by major enterprises with advantages in capital, data, and technical expertise (Korinek & Stiglitz, 2021). These benefits tend to accrue first to high-skill workers and capital owners, further empowering already advantaged populations as active users and participants. In contrast, low- and middle-skill workers, along with marginalized populations, resort to being the passive target of AI-based information and organizational decisions, thereby facing significantly greater risks of job loss. The unequal distribution of access and capacity to implement AI further exacerbates technological divides, acting as a powerful amplifier of socio-economic inequality.

3.2 Responsible AI Development

To address the structural imbalances created by AI technologies, both academic and policy communities have increasingly emphasized the need for "Responsible AI." Responsible AI calls for embedding essential ethical values and public interest principles into both technological development and business applications. Researchers such as Jobin et al. have identified several core design principles for responsible AI systems: explainability, fairness, accountability, transparency, and safety (Jobin et al., 2019). These principles are recognized as critical safeguards against AI systems that may harm vulnerable populations, infringe on human rights, or undermine public trust. Furthermore, scholars argue that the governance of AI should not be confined to technical regulation alone but must also address how these technologies are socially embedded and interact with broader societal structures. The development of responsible AI should also be expanded to promote humanistic values in the workplace, so that AI for employee engagement can serve as the foundation upon which enterprise productivity can rest (Hong, 2024). The control mechanism of AI for business interests and efficiency can be offset by AI's role in advancing an inclusive workplace and culture development. A fair AI system should not only be technically controllable but also socially accountable (Crawford & Calo, 2016).

3.3 Regulatory and Policy Interventions

To effectively manage the societal risks posed by AI, a variety of governance frameworks and regulatory strategies have been proposed across different regions. The European Union, for example, introduced one of the world's first comprehensive regulatory efforts through the "Artificial Intelligence Act" (Regulamento da União Europeia (UE), 2024). This act employs a tiered, risk-based framework that reinforces approval and accountability requirements for high-risk AI systems. In contrast, the United States has taken a more market-oriented approach, emphasized innovation, and limited regulatory intervention, thus avoiding a unified legislative framework. In response to these divergent strategies, scholars and policymakers have advocated for a global regulatory approach grounded in human-centered values. Such a framework should prioritize: (1) the development of standardized international regulations for data usage and platform accountability; (2) protections against systematic bias and discrimination, especially for vulnerable populations; and (3) the inclusion of governments and civil society in auditing and screening AI systems during the design phase to prevent large-scale systemic risks (Table 18.5).

Table 18.5 Key points on ethical and societal implications of AI

Section	Main points	Key references	Policy directions/ suggestions
Economic inequality	AI increases efficiency but widens wealth and opportunity gaps. Benefits go to high-skill workers and capitalists; low/mid-skill and marginalized groups face job loss	Korinek and Stiglitz (2021)—AI under control of large enterprises with capital, data, and technology advantages; amplifies socioeconomic disparity	Address technology-driven inequality; mitigate impact on vulnerable populations
Responsible AI development	Embed ethics into AI via explainability, fairness, accountability, transparency, and safety. Focus on social impact, not just technology	Jobin et al. (2019)—Design principles to protect vulnerable groups and human rights; Crawford and Calo (2016)—Focus on social embeddedness of AI	Ensure AI is not only technically controllable but socially accountable
Regulatory and policy interventions	EU adopts risk-based AI act; US favors market-led approach. Global push for human-centered regulation	EU AI Act (2024); USA market-oriented approach	(1) Standardized data regulation and platform accountability; (2) Prevent systematic bias/ discrimination; (3) Encourage ethical review during algorithm design

4 Social Work and AI: Mitigation and Advocacy

AI technologies have garnered increasing attention due to their profound impact on societal structures, including labor market disruptions and ethical concerns. In this context, social support systems—particularly social work—become even more essential alongside technical interventions. Social workers, grounded in justice and human-centered values, play a critical role in addressing current challenges posed by AI and in advocating for and offering equitable, future-oriented solutions.

4.1 Policy Advocacy and Practice

In previous sections, we discussed the impacts of AI technologies on economic structures, technical design, and ethical governance. We also highlighted the associated risks and broader societal influences. However, technical optimization and policy development alone are not sufficient to achieve inclusive technological transformation. Social workers can become a vital force in promoting justice and equitable AI implementation by advocating for socially beneficial policies and practices.

Social workers possess long-standing practical experience in engaging with policymaking processes and addressing structural disparities. They can offer professional, human-centered perspectives in debates concerning AI technologies. Reamer (2023) emphasizes that social workers should participate in shaping governance and public policy. Specifically, they should advocate for the inclusion of social justice, data ethics, and the protection of vulnerable populations within AI-related policies. Such advocacy can take the form of conducting research, delivering conference presentations, participating in community engagement efforts, and translating social observations into policy recommendations with systemic influence.

Social workers should also pay special attention to marginalized populations affected by the AI revolution—such as low-skill workers, older adults, immigrant workers, and people with disabilities. As Wronka (2022) argues, the ethical foundation of social work obliges practitioners to advocate for the rights of minority and vulnerable groups. In the context of labor market challenges caused by automation, algorithmic discrimination, and data exploitation, social workers should actively engage with lawmakers, educational institutions, and nonprofit organizations to ensure these populations are not left behind. Social workers can also directly participate in the practice of developing alternative or competing human-centered algorithms that could generate dynamic information (1) offsetting disadvantages experienced by vulnerable populations in the world of AI and (2) feeding into other AI algorithmic functions as essential data for the larger system level to benefit (Hong, 2024). By having more algorithms at the system level rely on quality human-centered data from marginalized populations, the adverse effects in the labor market caused by automation, algorithmic discrimination, and data exploitation can be minimized.

Equally important, social work practitioners can serve as a bridge between the general public and government institutions. They can help ensure that AI governance reflects public interest by participating in policy discussions, submitting policy memos, or serving as expert consultants on policymaking committees. For example, social workers could recommend developing algorithmic transparency standards, implementing labor data privacy regulations, and participating in AI ethics review boards to safeguard the public good.

In summary, AI governance should not be the exclusive domain of technologists and legislators. Social workers must actively contribute to this mission by leveraging their experience in community engagement and direct service provision. Their involvement in policy advocacy and practice is essential in guiding AI development toward fairness, inclusivity, and responsibility—values that reflect the core mission of social work and promote social justice in an increasingly digital society.

4.2 Supporting Displaced Workers

Traditional labor market structures are undergoing systematic restructuring, driven by the rapid development of artificial intelligence technologies. These unforeseen transformations have led to unprecedented displacement, particularly among middle- and low-skilled workers. Many individuals are now facing the threat of job loss, career disruption, and forced repositioning. These challenges impact not only their emotional well-being but also their ability to adapt socially. At this critical juncture, social work practitioners should serve as first responders, offering direct services and support to affected individuals.

Clients laid off due to AI-related disruptions often experience emotional symptoms similar to those observed in the broader unemployed population. These may include anxiety, denial, self-blame, and helplessness. In more severe cases, individuals may develop symptoms of post-traumatic stress or depression (Dziegielewski, 2013). Drawing on their expertise in psychological and psychosocial support, social workers can provide both individual and group counseling to help unemployed individuals process their feelings, recognize external factors driving these changes, rebuild confidence, and gradually adjust to a new life rhythm. At the same time, social workers can establish "unemployment mutual help clubs" to foster mutual sharing and peer support. For example, an evidence-based social work intervention called Transforming Impossible into Possible (TIP) uses the psychological self-sufficiency (PSS) theory to shift perceived employment barriers into employment hope, supporting individuals who are voluntarily or involuntarily disconnected from the labor market (Hong, 2013, 2016). These community-based interactions can help reduce social isolation and self-blame while enhancing social belonging and psychological resilience.

In addition to providing emotional support, social workers should take a proactive role in position transition programs and digital skills retraining initiatives. The National Association of Social Workers (NASW, 2024) emphasizes that social workers can provide critical services in these areas, including resource referrals, capability assessments, action planning, and support for career reconstruction. Using the same example from above, the PSS framework offers a system for evaluating individualized goal achievement pathways based on perceived employment barriers and employment hope over time (Hong, 2014; Hong et al., 2012, 2014). TIP intervention is designed to strengthen the PSS process for overcoming barriers to hope and achieving disconnected workers' employment goals (Hong, 2016). This involves helping clients identify their core strengths, recognize their potential, and develop realistic, goal-oriented learning plans. Through collaboration with vocational schools, higher education institutions, and nonprofit organizations, social workers can refer clients to appropriate vocational education programs. They can also provide ongoing support, including financial aid application assistance, career counseling, and post-placement support. Such partnership-based collaborative interventions facilitate a shift from passive unemployment to proactive re-engagement with the workforce.

In summary, labor market transformation driven by the AI revolution should not be viewed solely as a structural challenge, but also as a critical opportunity for social work innovation (Table 18.6). By providing emotional support, conducting individualized assessments, referring to job resources, supporting skill development, and fostering community-based networks, social workers can help displaced individuals transition from victims of disruption to adaptive, empowered contributors to the evolving economy.

Table 18.6 Reskilling and support program summary

Action	Brief description	Key resources	Key stakeholders
1. Emotional counseling	Provide individual or group counseling to help process anxiety, denial, self-blame, and rebuild stability.	Counseling rooms, trauma-informed care tools, trained staff	Social workers, mental health professionals
2. Peer support facilitation	Organize mutual help clubs to reduce isolation, foster peer interaction, and build social belonging.	Community centers, facilitation guides, peer leaders	Unemployed clients, community organizers
3. Capability assessment	Support identification of strengths, transferable skills, and adaptability for future planning.	Assessment tools, digital skills frameworks	Social workers, career coaches
4. Learning path planning	Design realistic and goal-oriented reskilling or education plans tailored to client potential.	Education catalogs, skill gap analysis tools	Vocational schools, adult education providers
5. Resource Referral & Ongoing Support	Connect to training programs, assist with financial aid, and offer career navigation support.	Training referrals, funding applications, job navigation tools	NGOs, workforce agencies, financial aid officers

4.3 Empowerment and Education

While the previous section focused on practical short-term interventions, empowerment and education offer broader, long-term strategies for addressing the challenges posed by AI-driven labor market disruption. Empowerment can be fostered through education that promotes digital literacy and strengthens awareness of workplace rights (Finn, 2020).

Social workers can play a key role in this process by organizing workshops and community presentations that help individuals understand how algorithmic systems function and how to identify and respond to technological unfairness in employment contexts. These efforts enable communities to become more informed and resilient in the face of rapid digital transformation.

In addition, social workers can support labor unions and worker-based organizations in rebuilding collective communication mechanisms. This is particularly vital for platform-based workers, who often lack traditional representation. By helping these workers establish mutual support networks and communication channels, social workers contribute to a stronger worker voice and shared problem-solving (Scholz, 2017).

In summary, empowerment and education are essential dimensions of social work practice. They equip individuals and communities with the tools to navigate and challenge the structural inequalities arising from AI adoption, while advancing broader labor market transformation.

5 Future Directions and Recommendations

5.1 Characteristic Shifting of Social Work in AI Labor Market

As AI becomes more deeply embedded into workplace structures, the practice model of social work faces unprecedented challenges—alongside valuable opportunities. Traditionally, social work has focused primarily on providing individualized services, including incident-based interventions and resource referrals, with relatively less attention to group-level or systemic advocacy. However, in the current context, where AI is reshaping the labor market and workplace governance, social workers must expand their roles to engage more actively in structural systems and contribute their expertise to building ethically grounded smart workplaces.

As discussed in previous sections, social work practitioners should proactively participate in algorithmic systems review processes, particularly for AI systems used in recruitment, performance evaluation, and platform-based task assignment—all of which are directly tied to workers' income and employment stability. Social workers can advocate for the integration of transparent, explainable algorithms and support the development of fair mechanisms that include specialized indexes, such as a "vulnerable population impact assessment." One such example presented earlier is the overtime PSS measures of perceived employment barriers and employment hope that can be incorporated into the algorithm for employee success on the job (Hong, 2024). Introducing such considerations early in the design phase can help mitigate biases and discriminatory outcomes that may be embedded in the historical data used to train AI models.

Moreover, social workers should broaden their professional boundaries by collaborating within interdisciplinary research teams that include data ethicists, AI engineers, policy analysts, business leaders, human resource specialists, and lawmakers. These interdisciplinary teams can collaborate to develop human-centered governance frameworks for AI-integrated workplaces. For example, social workers can help design and implement community-based support projects tailored to emerging labor arrangements such as part-time gig work, platform-based economies, and remote employment.

These support initiatives should offer not only material resources but also psychological resilience counseling and career navigation services. By strengthening workers' negotiation and bargaining capacity in algorithm-dominated work environments, social workers can help enhance civic participation and social protection in the era of intelligent labor systems.

5.2 Future Research and Interdisciplinary Cooperation

Although current studies have begun to explore the impact of AI technologies on the labor market, many critical questions remain insufficiently addressed. One key research priority is to understand AI's influence on occupational identity, self-perception, and long-term emotional well-being. In particular, within nontraditional employment models—such as platform economies and flexible or precarious work arrangements—there is a lack of systematic assessment of how unstable job conditions and social isolation affect workers over time. These conditions may be captured by interdisciplinary collaborations to study various dimensions of employment barriers in both individual and structural contexts (Hong et al., 2021).

Furthermore, research is needed to explore how social work can be systematically embedded within AI governance systems. This includes going beyond individual counseling to contribute meaningfully to policy development, ethical algorithm review, and inclusive workflow design. Social workers must not only respond to the impacts of technology but also proactively shape the environments in which such technologies are deployed. This would also mean that social workers need to contribute to business decisions by proactively investing in AI algorithms for human-centered career development processes, from employee hiring and retention to career advancement, that will ultimately benefit productivity (Hong, 2024).

Emerging scholarship suggests that future AI governance will require deep and sustained collaboration between technological development and social science inquiry (Serena & Kneesc, 2024). To foster this interdisciplinary integration, it is essential to establish virtual and institutional collaboration models—what might be called a "Social Work–AI–Policy" triad—that promotes the meaningful inclusion of social workers in shaping equitable AI-driven workplace transitions.

Social workers can also collaborate with institutions of higher education to co-develop academic programs such as "AI and Social Justice." Such curricula can prepare a new generation of interdisciplinary scholars and practitioners who possess both ethical sensitivity and technical fluency in evolving technologies.

In short, the AI-driven transformation of the workplace is an irreversible trend (Table 18.7). This moment offers a rare and valuable opportunity for social work

Table 18.7 Summary of future directions and cooperation methods

Future direction	Key actions	Cooperation methods
1. Embed social work into AI governance systems	Expand social work roles to include policymaking, ethics review, and workflow design	Joint taskforces with tech developers, ethics boards, and public agencies
2. Build "social work—AI—Policymaking" collaborative workflows	Develop systematic collaboration models for just and equitable AI-driven workplace transitions	Establish cross-sector virtual labs with social workers, AI engineers, and public policymakers
3. Assess AI's impact on occupational identity and well-being	Study the psychological and emotional effects of flexible/platform work and technological displacement	Interdisciplinary research involving social work, sociology, and occupational psychology

practitioners to solidify their role in the governance of future smart societies. By engaging in research, education, and policy, social workers can help lead the transition toward more just, inclusive, and sustainable digital labor systems.

6 Summary

To address the challenges posed by the AI-driven workplace revolution, social workers should proactively engage in interdisciplinary research, business engagement, and policy and community advocacy. By leveraging their expertise in counseling, organizational, community, and policy practice, they can support individuals in transition and help build a more inclusive, just, and sustainable workplace environment.

Competing Interests The authors have no conflicts of interest to declare that are relevant to the content of this chapter.

References

Acemoglu, D., & Restrepo, P. (2018). Low-skill and high-skill automation. *Journal of Human Capital, 12*(2), 204–232. https://doi.org/10.1086/697242

Ajunwa, I., Crawford, K., & Schultz, J. (2017). Limitless worker surveillance. *California Law Review, 105*, 735. https://doi.org/10.15779/Z38BR8MF94

Arntz, M., Gregory, T., & Zierahn, U. (2016, May 13). *SeloVerde uses geospatial big data and AI/ML to monitor deforestation in supply chains, powered by AWS*. https://www.oecd.org/en/publications/the-risk-of-automation-for-jobs-in-oecd-countries_5jlz9h56dvq7-en.html

Ball, K. (2021). *Electronic monitoring and surveillance in the workplace. Literature review and policy recommendations*. Publications Office of the European Union. https://doi.org/10.2760/5137. ISBN 978-92-76-43340-8.

Barocas, S., & Selbst, A. D. (2016). Big data's disparate impact. *California Law Review, 104*, 671.

Chiacchio, F., Petropoulos, G., & Pichler, D. (2018). *The impact of industrial robots on EU employment and wages: A local labour market approach (working paper 2018/02)*. Bruegel Working Paper. https://www.econstor.eu/handle/10419/207001

Crawford, K., & Calo, R. (2016). There is a blind spot in AI research. *Nature, 538*(7625), 311–313. https://doi.org/10.1038/538311a

Dziegielewski, S. F. (2013). *DSM-IV-TR in action: Includes DSM-5 update chapter*. Wiley.

Edlich, A., Phalin, G., Jogani, R., & Kaniyar, S. (2019). *Driving impact at scale from automation and AI*.

Eubanks, V. (2018). *Automating inequality: How high-tech tools profile, police, and punish the poor*. St. Martin's Press.

Finn, J. L. (2020). *Just practice: A social justice approach to social work*. Oxford University Press.

Goos, M., Manning, A., & Salomons, A. (2014). Explaining job polarization: Routine-biased technological change and offshoring. *American Economic Review, 104*(8), 2509–2526. https://doi.org/10.1257/aer.104.8.2509

Groumpos, P. P. (2021). A critical historical and scientific overview of all industrial revolutions. *IFAC-PapersOnLine, 54*(13), 464–471. https://doi.org/10.1016/j.ifacol.2021.10.492

Hong, P. Y. P. (2013). Toward a client-centered benchmark for self-sufficiency: Evaluating the 'process' of becoming job ready. *Journal of Community Practice, 21*, 356–378.

Hong, P. Y. P. (2014). Employment hope: A path to empowering disconnected workers. In E. J. Clark & E. F. Hoffler (Eds.), *Hope matters: The power of social work* (pp. 143–148). NASW Press.

Hong, P. Y. P. (2016). Transforming impossible into possible (TIP): A bottom-up practice in workforce development for low-income jobseekers. *Environment and Social Psychology, 1*, 93–104.

Hong, P. Y. P. (2024). Transforming opportunities into productivity (TOP): A new social development model for social transformation. *Social Development Issues, 46*, 88–108.

Hong, P. Y. P., Polanin, J. R., & Pigott, T. D. (2012). Validation of the employment hope scale: Measuring psychological self-sufficiency among low-income jobseekers. *Research on Social Work Practice, 22*, 323–332.

Hong, P. Y. P., Polanin, J. R., Key, W., & Choi, S. (2014). Development of the perceived employment barrier scale (PEBS): Measuring psychological self-sufficiency. *Journal of Community Psychology, 42*, 689–706.

Hong, P. Y. P., Gumz, E., Choi, S., Crawley, B., & Cho, J. (2021). Centering on structural and individual employment barriers for social and human development. *Social Development Issues, 43*, 29–53.

Jarrahi, M. H., Newlands, G., Lee, M. K., Wolf, C. T., Kinder, E., & Sutherland, W. (2021). Algorithmic management in a work context. *Big Data & Society, 8*(2), 20539517211020332. https://doi.org/10.1177/20539517211020332

Jobin, A., Ienca, M., & Vayena, E. (2019). The global landscape of AI ethics guidelines. *Nature Machine Intelligence, 1*(9), 389–399. https://doi.org/10.1038/s42256-019-0088-2

Kellogg, K. C., Valentine, M. A., & Christin, A. (2020). Algorithms at work: The new contested terrain of control. *Academy of Management Annals, 14*(1), 366–410. https://doi.org/10.5465/annals.2018.0174

Korinek, A., & Stiglitz, J. E. (2021). *Artificial intelligence, globalization, and strategies for economic development* (working paper 28453). National Bureau of Economic Research. https://doi.org/10.3386/w28453

Li, L. (2024). Reskilling and upskilling the future-ready workforce for industry 4.0 and beyond. *Information Systems Frontiers, 26*(5), 1697–1712. https://doi.org/10.1007/s10796-022-10308-y

McLean, S., Read, G. J., Thompson, J., Baber, C., Stanton, N. A., & Salmon, P. M. (2023). The risks associated with artificial general intelligence: A systematic review. *Journal of Experimental & Theoretical Artificial Intelligence, 35*(5), 649–663. https://doi.org/10.1080/0952813X.2021.1964003

Moore, P. V., Upchurch, M., & Whittaker, X. (2018). Humans and machines at work: Monitoring, surveillance and automation in contemporary capitalism. In P. V. Moore, M. Upchurch, & X. Whittaker (Eds.), *Humans and machines at work: Monitoring, surveillance and automation in contemporary capitalism* (pp. 1–16). Springer. https://doi.org/10.1007/978-3-319-58232-0_1

NASW. (2024). *NASW practice standards & guidelines [guideline]*. NASW. https://www.socialworkers.org/Practice/Practice-Standards-Guidelines

Nguyen, Q. P., & Vo, D. H. (2022). Artificial intelligence and unemployment:An international evidence. *Structural Change and Economic Dynamics, 63*, 40–55. https://doi.org/10.1016/j.strueco.2022.09.003

Piore, M. J. (2014). The dual labor market: Theory and implications. In *Social Stratification* (4th ed.). Routledge.

Raghavan, M., Barocas, S., Kleinberg, J., & Levy, K. (2020). Mitigating bias in algorithmic hiring: Evaluating claims and practices. In *Proceedings of the 2020 Conference on Fairness, Accountability, and Transparency*, pp. 469–481. https://doi.org/10.1145/3351095.3372828

Reamer, F. G. (2023). Artificial intelligence in social work: Emerging ethical issues. *International Journal of Social Work Values and Ethics, 20*(2), 52–71. https://doi.org/10.55521/10-020-205

Regulamento da União Europeia (UE). (2024). *EU Artificial Intelligence Act | Up-to-date developments and analyses of the EU AI Act*. https://artificialintelligenceact.eu/

Scholz, T. (2017). *Uberworked and underpaid: How workers are disrupting the digital economy*. Wiley.

Serena, O., & Kneese, T. (2024, May). *AI governance needs sociotechnical expertise*. Data & Society. https://datasociety.net/library/ai-governance-needs-sociotechnical-expertise/

Szeszák, B. M., Kerékjártó, I. G., Soltész, L., Galambos, P., Szeszák, B. M., Kerékjártó, I. G., Soltész, L., & Galambos, P. (2025). Industrial revolutions and automation: Tracing economic and social transformations of manufacturing. *Societies, 15*(4). https://doi.org/10.3390/soc15040088

Topol, E. J. (2019). High-performance medicine: The convergence of human and artificial intelligence. *Nature Medicine, 25*(1), 44–56. https://doi.org/10.1038/s41591-018-0300-7

Wronka, J. (2022). A human rights framework for integrated practice. In *Human rights and social justice*. Routledge.

Zuboff, S. (2019). Surveillance capitalism and the challenge of collective action. *New Labor Forum, 28*(1), 10–29. https://doi.org/10.1177/1095796018819461

Chapter 19
AI in International Social Work and Global Issues

Fan Yang and Benjamin Lough

1 Introduction

1.1 Overview and Significance

Artificial intelligence (AI) is rapidly transforming various professional fields, including international social work. Defined broadly, AI refers to a suite of algorithmic computing capacities that perform tasks typically requiring human intelligence, such as commercial recommender systems, facial recognition, language processing, and sentiment analysis (Goldkind, 2021).

The relevance of AI to international social work has increased alongside the growing complexity and scale of global social challenges. International social work inherently deals with social issues that transcend national boundaries, such as forced migration, natural disasters, and pandemics. Social workers in international settings coordinate across diverse cultures, language barriers, legal systems, and administrative frameworks. Within this context, AI technologies offer unprecedented capabilities to address transnational social problems on a global scale. However, the application of AI in international contexts demands careful attention to cultural and ethical implications. This critical intersection between technology, ethics, and cultural competence forms a central theme of this chapter.

F. Yang (✉) · B. Lough
School of Social Work, University of Illinois Urbana-Champaign, Urbana, IL, USA
e-mail: fany16@illinois.edu; bjlough@illinois.edu

R. An, M. A. Lindsey (eds.), *Artificial Intelligence in Social Work*,
https://doi.org/10.1007/978-3-032-18443-6_19

1.2 Purpose of the Chapter

The purpose of this chapter is to critically examine the role of AI in addressing global social challenges. It aims to provide a balanced perspective by exploring both the potential of AI to improve responses to issues such as migration, refugee support, and global health and climate crisis and the risks it poses, including bias, data privacy concerns, and the reinforcement of structural inequalities. This chapter emphasizes the importance of culturally responsive usage and introduces ethical collaboration and decolonizing practices as essential pathways toward achieving cultural humility in international social work. Through real-world examples and critical analysis, it seeks to guide readers toward the responsible and inclusive integration of AI into international social work.

2 AI's Role in Addressing Global Challenges

AI has increasingly become a tool for tackling complex social problems that transcend borders. From managing migration flows to coordinating disaster relief and combating pandemics, AI technologies are being deployed to augment human efforts worldwide. This section explores three critical global challenges: migration and refugee crises, humanitarian aid in disasters, and international health emergencies and how AI offers innovative solutions in each. While highlighting the benefits of these AI-driven approaches, we also acknowledge the challenges that must be addressed, including data privacy, bias, and ethical dilemmas, setting the stage for a more detailed discussion of ethics later in the chapter.

2.1 Migration and Refugee Issues

AI is increasingly being utilized globally to enhance migration management and support services for refugees. In this context, AI primarily contributes through three significant applications: (1) predictive analytics, which enable the forecasting of migration flows and humanitarian needs, (2) AI-powered case management systems that effectively match refugees with essential services, and (3) AI-driven communication and assistance tools designed to improve interactions and facilitate access to support services for refugees.

Predictive analytics are employed to forecast migration flows and humanitarian needs, thereby enabling policymakers and aid organizations to prepare proactively. For instance, the Foresight project uses machine learning to analyze over 120 indicators and predict potential changes in migration patterns over time (Nair et al., 2023). These AI-driven models can identify tipping points and combinations of conflict, famine, or economic stress that may precipitate mass migration, thereby facilitating earlier interventions. In East Africa, United Nations agencies have implemented similar approaches to anticipate displacement from regions such as Somalia by integrating climate and violence data, thereby transitioning humanitarian response from reactive to anticipatory.

AI-powered case management systems are being developed to enhance support for refugees by prioritizing vulnerable cases and matching them to appropriate services through data-driven algorithms. One notable example is GeoMatch, an AI-driven matching tool that recommends optimal resettlement locations for refugees (Achugamonu, 2025; Ferweda et al., 2022). Developed by researchers at Stanford's Immigration Policy Lab, GeoMatch analyzes refugees' background characteristics alongside historical integration outcomes, such as employment, to identify host communities where individuals are most likely to thrive. Notably, while the system supports decision-making, final determinations remain the responsibility of human case officers.

Another growing application is AI-driven communication and assistance tools for migrants and asylum seekers. Natural language processing and chatbot systems can help refugees navigate legal processes and access information. For instance, a WhatsApp-based chatbot called Sésamo was developed by the Sesame Workshop and the Norwegian Refugee Council to support Venezuelan migrant families (Ruvin, Hallie, 2021). This AI-powered chatbot provides easy access to educational content and vital information through mobile messaging, helping children and caregivers in displacement to learn and connect in their own language.

2.2 *Humanitarian Aid and Disaster Response*

AI is also transforming how social work professionals prepare for and respond to disasters and humanitarian crises worldwide. In disaster management, timing and information are everything. AI systems excel at rapidly analyzing data to support quick decision-making.

Machine learning models are increasingly being trained to predict events such as famines, floods, or conflict outbreaks before they occur, facilitating a shift from reactive relief to anticipatory action. For instance, humanitarian organizations employ predictive analytics to assess the potential impacts of drought on food security, enabling them to allocate aid—such as food supplies and cash assistance—before hunger sets in. This proactive approach enables aid organizations to mitigate the adverse effects of disasters by acting in advance (Jelonek, 2023).

During acute crises, AI technology significantly enhances situational awareness and damage assessment. Satellite imagery and computer vision are commonly utilized to map disaster impacts in real time. A notable initiative in this domain is the United Nations Global Pulse's PulseSatellite system, which integrates human analysis with AI-driven models to accelerate damage assessment. PulseSatellite can map structures within refugee settlements, detect roof damage, and segment flood extents from satellite imagery (Logar et al., 2020). This approach significantly reduces the time required for manual counting and analysis, allowing humanitarian teams to quickly estimate the number of affected individuals and prioritize rescue operations. For example, during Cyclone Idai's flooding in Mozambique, AI-powered satellite mapping rapidly identified isolated communities, guiding helicopter relief missions (Charrua et al., 2021). Similarly, computer vision techniques have been employed to monitor refugee camps, including mapping tent locations and tracking camp growth, thereby informing camp management and infrastructure planning (Achugamonu, 2025; Ferweda et al., 2022).

These examples underscore the transformative potential of AI in enhancing the efficiency and effectiveness of humanitarian responses. Nonetheless, challenges persist. AI systems are only as good as the data they learn from; thus, in many low-income regions, data scarcity can limit model accuracy. As will be discussed later in this chapter, there are also concerns about the ethical use of AI. For instance, algorithms must be transparent and free of bias to ensure equitable aid so that no vulnerable group is left unseen by a "black-box" decision (Pasipamire & Muroyiwa, 2024). These issues are prompting initiatives to develop responsible AI guidelines for humanitarian use. Overall, AI's role in disaster relief is already proving transformative: enhancing early warning, sharpening situational awareness, and optimizing life-saving operations on a global scale.

2.3 Global Health Crises

Global health emergencies, such as pandemics, pose immense challenges that AI is increasingly helping address. In recent international health crises, from Ebola to COVID-19, AI tools have augmented epidemiological analysis, accelerated diagnostics, and supported healthcare delivery, especially in resource-strapped settings.

One key contribution of AI is in disease outbreak prediction and monitoring. Machine learning models have been employed to analyze extensive datasets, including online behavior and mobility data, to detect early signals of emerging epidemics. For instance, AI-based digital surveillance systems have been developed to detect early signs of outbreaks by processing open-source data, including news reports and social media data (MacIntyre et al., 2023). These systems can trigger early investigation, diagnostics, and responses at the regional level, complementing traditional research methods. Additionally, AI has been integrated into epidemic and pandemic early warning systems, identifying patterns in data that signal the onset of outbreaks. By analyzing travel and mobility data, AI can predict potential disease hotspots, model disease spread, and inform public health interventions (El Morr et al., 2024; Zhao et al., 2024).

Once a health crisis is underway, AI-powered diagnostics and screening become crucial. AI algorithms have demonstrated proficiency in analyzing medical images and other health data at speeds beyond those achievable by human experts alone. In the 2020 pandemic, AI models were used to read chest X-rays and CT scans for COVID-19 pneumonia signs, aiding radiologists in triaging patients when thousands of scans needed review. Some hospitals deployed AI-driven thermal cameras and computer vision to identify people with fevers in crowds (Borkowski, 2020). In low-resource settings where doctors are scarce, these AI chatbots and diagnostic apps have become front-line tools for disseminating public health guidance and combating misinformation. Case studies from the Ebola response in West Africa similarly show AI's impact: a machine learning model used by UNICEF analyzed streams of text messages from the public to identify regions with spikes in certain Ebola symptoms, helping target community health outreach (Pasipamire & Muroyiwa, 2024).

On the healthcare delivery side, telehealth and telemedicine saw a boost from AI during global crises. AI-powered diagnostic tools have been deployed on tablets to assist community health workers in detecting diseases in diverse settings, from refugee camps to rural villages. These innovations have improved access to care, especially when traditional health systems are under strain. For instance, AI algorithms can rapidly assess and prioritize patients based on the severity of their conditions, aiding overwhelmed healthcare providers with effective triage and ensuring timely care for those in critical condition (Zuhair et al., 2024).

In summary, AI's role in global health crises has been multifaceted, strengthening preparedness, detection, and response. These benefits need to be weighed against challenges, including data privacy, algorithmic bias, and the need for validation to avoid false results. However, as later sections will discuss, with proper ethical guardrails, AI can be deployed responsibly in healthcare.

3 Key Risks and Barriers to Equitable AI Use in International Social Work

While AI holds promises for advancing social work globally, it also introduces significant challenges and risks. In international social work, these concerns are magnified. Key areas of caution include algorithmic bias and fairness, data privacy and security, and the digital divide and global inequities. Each of these issues can limit AI's usefulness and pose ethical dilemmas for practitioners. The following sections discuss these challenges, emphasizing their relevance to international social work and humanitarian contexts.

3.1 Bias and Fairness in Algorithms

One critical concern is the potential for AI systems to reinforce bias and discrimination. AI models learn from existing data, and if that data reflects historical prejudices or the underrepresentation of certain groups, the algorithms can reproduce and even amplify those biases (Reamer, 2023). In international social work, this means an AI tool used for risk assessment or resource allocation might unfairly disadvantage marginalized communities. For instance, in international social work contexts involving refugees and immigrants, the use of AI in asylum and border management systems has raised significant ethical concerns. If AI algorithms inaccurately assess asylum seekers, they might be incorrectly returned to their countries of origin or sent to unsafe regions where they could face persecution or severe human rights violations, a harmful outcome known as refoulement (Forster & House, 2022).

Additionally, employing AI in asylum procedures raises critical issues regarding fairness and due process, potentially exacerbating existing structural inequities rather than alleviating them. Affected communities may be unable to interrogate, contest, or correct the algorithms and thus the decisions made "on their behalf," thus further disempowering already marginalized groups. Biased algorithms could therefore unintentionally reinforce the very inequalities that international social work endeavors to eliminate. Moreover, in the context of global climate crises, AI systems designed to predict and manage disaster responses may not adequately account for the vulnerabilities of marginalized communities. Without careful design and oversight, these systems could allocate resources inequitably, exacerbating existing disparities. The International Committee of the Red Cross has emphasized the need to address risks, such as algorithmic bias and data privacy concerns, when deploying AI in humanitarian operations (Beduschi, 2022).

These examples underscore the necessity for rigorous evaluation and mitigation of biases in AI systems within international social work. In a global context, such biases may be exacerbated when AI tools developed in one cultural setting are applied in another. Ensuring that AI tools are equitable and bias-free requires continuous scrutiny and the implementation of measures to prevent the perpetuation of systemic inequalities (Reamer, 2023).

3.2 *Data Privacy and Security*

The integration of AI into international social work, particularly in contexts involving refugees, immigrants, climate change, and health crises, raises significant concerns about privacy, confidentiality, and data security. Social workers frequently handle sensitive personal information related to clients' health, familial, and legal statuses. Integrating AI tools, such as predictive analytics or case management systems, may result in large amounts of client data being collected, stored, or analyzed digitally. Protecting this data is paramount. International social workers have an ethical duty to ensure that any AI software or platform they use has robust security measures: encryption, access controls, and protection against breaches (Reamer, 2023). Unauthorized access or cyberattacks could expose vulnerable populations to risks like identity theft, stigmatization, or persecution (Lubin, 2022). For instance, the leakage of information regarding a refugee's location or a survivor of domestic violence's shelter could result in severe harm. Adherence to social work ethical codes globally underscores the importance of confidentiality; thus, the adoption of AI does not absolve professionals from this responsibility.

Privacy concerns are more complicated in international contexts where legal protections vary significantly. For example, in some countries, comprehensive data protection laws, such as the European Union's General Data Protection Regulation, provide strict guidelines on handling personal data, whereas other regions may have weak or nonexistent privacy regulations (Sartor & Lagioia, 2020). This inconsistency suggests that cross-border humanitarian projects using AI may operate in legal gray areas regarding data handling. Additionally, there exists the threat of surveillance and data misuse. Analyses caution that AI systems can be repurposed by third parties for surveillance without consent. Therefore, the security of data within AI systems transcends technical issues and becomes a matter of human rights (Ahmad, 2020). International social workers must exercise caution to ensure that the technologies they employ do not inadvertently expose clients to danger.

3.3 *Digital Divide and Global Inequity*

AI has the potential to exacerbate the existing digital divide and amplify global inequities. Access to AI technologies and the infrastructure is markedly uneven worldwide (Okolo, 2023). In high-income countries, fixed broadband costs constitute approximately 1% of monthly gross national income per capita. In contrast, in low-income countries, these costs can exceed 30% of the monthly gross national income per capita (Schellekens & Skilling, 2024). This significant disparity implies that AI-driven interventions, which often depend on reliable Internet connectivity and substantial computational resources, remain inaccessible to regions that could benefit most from them (Dychiao et al., 2024). Consequently, while wealthy nations advance in deploying AI across sectors such as healthcare, education, and social services, lower-income countries risk falling further behind, thereby missing out on the potential benefits of these technologies. This emerging AI divide threatens to deepen existing global inequalities (Berg et al., 2024). A United Nations report highlights that, without intentional efforts, high-income countries are poised to disproportionately reap AI's rewards, leaving developing nations at a disadvantage due to uneven investment and adoption (Berg et al., 2024). For instance, a social work agency in a well-resourced urban area might use AI to predict and prevent public health crises, whereas a similar agency in a low-resource setting cannot do so, thereby widening the disparity in community outcomes (Schellekens & Skilling, 2024; Vázquez & García, 2021).

Within individual countries, the digital divide further marginalizes rural and underserved populations by limiting their access to AI-assisted services (Perez et al., 2025). International social workers frequently serve refugees, disaster survivors, and individuals in remote areas where Internet and electricity access are unreliable. In such humanitarian contexts, the limitations of AI become particularly evident. AI tools typically require extensive data and stable connectivity—resources are often scarce in crisis zones. Moreover, existing data in these settings may be incomplete or biased, undermining the effectiveness of AI applications (Maita et al., 2024). A study published in the *International Review of the Red Cross* emphasizes that "poor data quality generates poor outcomes that may directly affect populations in an already vulnerable situation due to conflicts or crises" (Beduschi, 2022). For example, if a disaster relief algorithm is trained predominantly on data from wealthier regions, it may fail to accurately prioritize needs across different cultural or economic contexts. AI is not a panacea for humanitarian challenges; in fact, it may create new forms of inequality if certain groups consistently benefit from AI-driven services while others are excluded.

Critically, this uneven distribution and utilization of AI technology must be understood within a broader context of global power dynamics. AI is built upon infrastructures and dependencies that reflect, and may reproduce, existing global power hierarchies. This critical frame recognizes that the development and deployment of AI is shaped by a transnational political economy dominated by powerful states, Big Tech monopolies, and venture capital interests. Embracing AI without interrogating these foundations risks aligning practice with the logics of technocratic control and risks complicity in the infrastructures that reproduce global inequality, including knowledge structures. This frame calls for social workers to decenter these dependencies. It also calls on us to balance the scale and speed that AI promises with the relational and justice-oriented practices that define the field.

4 Cultural Competence and Ethical Collaboration in AI-Driven International Social Work

As AI-driven interventions become more common in international social work, ensuring cultural competence and ethical practices is paramount. Cultural competence refers to the ability to understand and respect the values, norms, and needs of diverse populations (Cai, 2016). This section discusses how AI tools and programs can be developed and implemented to honor local cultures and empower communities. We highlight that effective AI for social good must be not only technologically sound but also culturally sensitive and ethically grounded. This ensures AI augments social work in an inclusive, fair manner that respects the dignity and agency of all communities served.

4.1 Importance of Cultural Competence in the Era of AI

In international social work, cultural competence is considered an essential pillar of effective and ethical practice. This concept emphasizes that social interventions must resonate with local values and traditions to succeed (Nadan, 2017). It signifies a social worker's ability to appreciate and work within the cultural contexts of the communities they serve (Davis, 2020).

When introducing AI tools into international social work, the same principle applies: these technologies should be designed and adapted with a keen awareness of cultural differences. AI systems are not culturally neutral; everything from the data used to train them to the way their interface is presented carries assumptions that may or may not fit the local context (UNESCO, 2021). For example, a mental health support chatbot developed in one country might assume a direct communication style, but in another culture, people may prefer a more indirect or formal approach when discussing personal issues (Chin et al., 2023; Folk et al., 2025). Culturally competent AI design would take such scenarios into account—perhaps by adjusting language, adopting local idioms or symbols, and aligning with community norms of interaction.

Ensuring cultural relevance goes beyond mere language translation or superficial adjustments to imagery. It requires integrating AI systems with "indigenous" epistemological frameworks that reflect local ways of knowing and interpreting and aligning interventions with community norms, values, and social structures (Akter, 2024). In practice, this could mean engaging cultural advisors or representatives from the target community during the AI development process (Nadan, 2017). For instance, an AI-driven counseling app for refugees should reflect an understanding of the refugees' cultural background and trauma experiences, as well as their conceptions of healing and family, so that the recommendations it provides feel trustworthy. If an AI tool ignores cultural context, it risks imposing external values or misinterpreting users' needs, leading to low adoption or even harm. Thus, cultural competence acts as a quality check: AI solutions must be vetted for cultural sensitivity and appropriateness just as they are for technical accuracy. This means recognizing the diversity within cultural groups and avoiding stereotypes in algorithm design (Williams & Shipley, 2021). Ultimately, prioritizing cultural competence in AI-driven social work interventions helps ensure that technology augments rather than disrupts local practices and that communities feel respected and understood. This lays a foundation of trust, which is critical for any social program's success.

4.2 *Ethical Collaboration with Communities*

Achieving cultural competence and ethical AI deployment requires a sustained commitment to collaboration with local communities throughout every stage of development. Rather than imposing externally developed high-tech solutions, social workers and technologists are increasingly adopting participatory approaches that actively involve the people who will use or be affected by AI systems. This approach aligns with well-established traditions in international social work, such as participatory action research and community engagement, which emphasize shifting decision-making power to those most directly impacted by interventions (Bazzano et al., 2025). In the context of AI, participatory design entails involving community members, front-line social workers, and local organizations in defining the problem, shaping the AI solution, and governing its implementation (Tan et al., 2025). By centering community voices and perspectives, the resulting AI tool is more likely to address genuine needs and gain community acceptance. For instance, when developing an AI system to allocate humanitarian aid in a specific region, a participatory approach would involve inviting local leaders and residents to share their insights on traditional aid distribution methods, local conceptions of fairness, and the outcomes that matter most to them. This inclusive process ensures that the algorithm's objectives and constraints are informed by community priorities, fostering an AI system that is contextually relevant and ethically sound (Okolo, 2023). By embedding participatory methodologies within AI development, implementation, and interpretation, social work practitioners and technologists not only enhance the relevance and acceptance of AI solutions but also uphold the fundamental principles of cultural competence and community self-determination.

Ethical collaboration also encompasses informed consent and transparency. Communities must be clearly informed about how an AI application functions, what data it collects and utilizes, and the intended purpose of its deployment. This information should be conveyed in a language and manner that is easily understood by community members (Nankya et al., 2025). Just as with any social intervention, practitioners must explain the objectives of the AI-driven program and obtain informed consent from the individuals or communities involved. Transparency also entails openly discussing the AI system's limitations and establishing a straightforward process for community feedback or complaints. One effective strategy could be creating community advisory boards specifically for AI projects. These advisory bodies can oversee project progress, address emerging concerns, and ensure that the technology remains accountable to the people it is intended to serve. Furthermore, international guidelines emphasize the necessity of diverse stakeholder participation to foster inclusive AI governance (UNESCO, 2021). This participatory approach ensures that AI systems are not only ethically sound but also practically relevant to the communities they serve.

4.3 Cultural Competence Training and Capacity Building

To ensure AI is used sustainably and equitably in international social work, cultural competence and capacity building are essential. This means training social workers to effectively engage with diverse communities, especially in contexts such as migration, health crises, and climate challenges, and to apply AI in ethical and culturally appropriate ways (Safodien, 2021). Capacity building empowers professionals and community leaders to use and oversee AI tools, reducing reliance on external experts. This begins with foundational AI literacy, which includes understanding fundamental AI concepts, how algorithms make decisions, and recognizing the strengths and limitations of these technologies (Mackline Nuwasiima et al., 2024).

Developing AI literacy allows social workers to critically assess AI outputs and make informed decisions, thereby maintaining professional judgment and ethical standards rather than passively accepting automated recommendations (Åhs et al., 2022).

Global initiatives increasingly recognize the importance of building digital and AI capacity among social workers and related professionals, especially in international social work. For instance, UNESCO has implemented digital capacity-building programs that include AI literacy components tailored for government and NGO staff, teachers, and educators in low-resource settings, often focusing on humanitarian contexts related to migration, disaster response, and public health emergencies (UNESCO Institute for Lifelong Learning, 2022a, 2022b). These programs use real-world scenarios, such as using AI to facilitate language learning for refugees or to prioritize healthcare interventions, to enhance participants' competencies in applying data-driven solutions effectively. In addition to structured training initiatives, practical on-the-job capacity building is critical. An effective approach involves embedding data scientists or IT specialists within social work teams to provide hands-on mentorship and support. A study highlights that embedding data science teams within specific departments fosters agility and cultivates specialized expertise, leading to more responsive and customized analytics outcomes (Stelmaszak & Klinc, 2023). Additionally, fostering local technological talent with a focus on social impact can further enhance capacity.

Social work education institutions play a crucial role in preparing professionals to engage effectively with emerging technologies. Standards such as the Council on Social Work Education's 2022 Educational Policy and Accreditation Standards (EPAS) explicitly emphasize technological competence and ethical use of technology in social work practice (Council on Social Work Education, 2022). Aligning higher education curricula with these standards ensures social workers are better equipped to navigate and critically assess technological advancements. To further bridge theoretical learning and practical application, interdisciplinary university programs can be established to train future engineers and social workers collaboratively in "AI for social good" projects. Such interdisciplinary training cultivates a workforce that is not only technically proficient but also deeply attuned to community needs and ethical considerations. Continuous capacity building and professional development reinforce these skills, enabling social workers to effectively integrate AI technologies into practice while maintaining cultural competence and accountability to the communities they serve.

5 Decolonizing Practices: Toward Cultural Humility

Decolonizing practice is essential to achieving cultural humility in international social work, particularly in contexts involving migrants, refugees, climate crises, and health emergencies, as it moves beyond traditional cultural competence frameworks that imply mastery rather than ongoing learning (Fong, 2001; Tamburro, 2013). Traditional cultural competence models often carry problematic assumptions, positioning practitioners as able to grasp or master another group's culture fully. This viewpoint inadvertently perpetuates hierarchical power dynamics, reinforcing Western-centric approaches and marginalizing local and Indigenous knowledge (Tamburro, 2013). Furthermore, existing social work theories, methodologies, and educational curricula predominantly originate from Western contexts, leading to the exclusion or marginalization of non-Western epistemologies. Such exclusion not only maintains existing global power imbalances but also limits the effectiveness and relevance of interventions in culturally diverse and resource-constrained settings (Bennett et al., 2024).

Additionally, the growing reliance on AI technologies, often developed and controlled by powerful global actors, risks amplifying existing inequalities and further excluding marginalized populations from equitable benefits. Thus, embracing decolonizing practices requires critically examining these embedded power structures, actively challenging knowledge exclusivity, promoting cultural humility, and authentically integrating local and Indigenous perspectives (Tamburro, 2013). By centering marginalized voices and acknowledging the complexities involved, social workers can better achieve equitable, culturally responsive, and justice-oriented practices.

Traditional cultural competence models often carry problematic assumptions, positioning practitioners as able to grasp or master another group's culture fully. This viewpoint inadvertently perpetuates hierarchical power dynamics, reinforcing Western-centric approaches and marginalizing local and Indigenous knowledge. Furthermore, existing social work theories, methodologies, and educational curricula predominantly originate from Western contexts, leading to the exclusion or marginalization of non-Western epistemologies. Such exclusion not only maintains existing global power imbalances but also limits the effectiveness and relevance of interventions in culturally diverse and resource-constrained settings. Additionally, the growing reliance on AI technologies, often developed and controlled by powerful global actors, risks amplifying existing inequalities and further excluding marginalized populations from equitable benefits. Thus, embracing decolonizing practices requires critically examining these embedded power structures, actively challenging knowledge exclusivity, promoting cultural humility, and authentically integrating local and Indigenous perspectives. By centering marginalized voices and acknowledging the complexities involved, social workers can better achieve equitable, culturally responsive, and justice-oriented practices.

This section explores decolonizing practice from two angles: (1) cultural humility and Indigenous knowledge, which involves ongoing learning, power-sharing, and valuing Indigenous worldviews, and (2) decolonizing data and technology, which emphasizes community data ownership and AI solutions driven by local needs. Together, these approaches push social work beyond cultural competence toward more inclusive, equitable practices.

5.1 Cultural Humility and Integrating Indigenous Knowledge

Decolonizing AI also necessitates embracing cultural humility, which involves recognizing the limitations of one's understanding of another culture and committing to continuous learning and power balancing. Unlike cultural competence, which implies mastery of cultural knowledge, cultural humility emphasizes ongoing self-reflection and the recognition of power imbalances. In social work, this means that technologists and practitioners must acknowledge their gaps in understanding the communities they serve (Ray, 2024). A culturally humble approach begins by asking fundamental questions like: "Should we build this AI system? If so, how can we co-design it with those who will use or be affected by it?"

Integrating Indigenous knowledge systems into AI development is a promising pathway. Indigenous epistemologies—ways of knowing developed over centuries—provide valuable perspectives that challenge Western paradigms (Williams & Shipley, 2021). In practice, this integration might involve consulting Indigenous elders during the design phase, incorporating community-defined data points such as traditional indicators into predictive models, or using local languages and concepts in AI interfaces.

Cultural humility within tech teams means deferring to Indigenous experts on what data is meaningful and what outcomes are desirable. Rather than imposing a generic risk score to predict which families need intervention, a culturally humble AI project in a First Nations context would begin by understanding how the community defines "risk" and "family well being." This approach may reveal protective factors such as community cohesion or connection to land, which are often overlooked in Western models (Asakura et al., 2023). By learning from Indigenous frameworks and integrating AI with community practices of monitoring and mutual aid, technology becomes a tool that enhances local wisdom rather than overriding it.

Moreover, adopting cultural humility and valuing Indigenous knowledge inherently challenges technological solutionism, a belief that assumes complex social problems can be fully or adequately resolved through technological interventions, particularly advanced algorithms (Anka, 2024). Critiquing technological solutionism explicitly acknowledges that technology, especially AI, is neither universally applicable nor inherently neutral and emphasizes that many social issues require culturally informed approaches rather than purely technical solutions (Couldry & Mejias, 2019). Recognizing the limitations of technological approaches underscores the critical importance of genuinely empowering Indigenous communities, enabling their active participation and leadership in deliberations on the appropriateness, boundaries, and ethical implications of technology deployment within their unique contexts. Such involvement ensures technological interventions are culturally responsive, ethically grounded, and aligned with the priorities and values of Indigenous people.

Social workers using AI in international settings should act as facilitators or bridges rather than as authoritative technology implementers. Cultural humility of social workers can help resist the lure of technological solutionism. A humble stance could involve co-training: social work professionals sharing AI literacy with community members while learning from them about local contexts (Hood et al., 2022). This reciprocal learning ensures that AI tools are continuously adapted to meet evolving community needs. Additionally, humility encourages openness to non-technological or hybrid solutions that blend traditional practices with modern technology, which may be more effective in some contexts (Anka, 2024).

In conclusion, decolonizing AI is not an abstract ideal; it is a practical pathway to better outcomes. It shifts power to communities, incorporates a broader range of human knowledge, and produces interventions that are ethical by design. As a result, AI tools developed in this way would better support the goals of international social work—promoting social justice, respecting cultural differences, and empowering communities toward sustainable change. Some argue that decolonizing AI also means recognizing that certain social problems should not be technologized at all, thus resisting the impulse to reduce complex moral and communal challenges to solvable technical issues.

5.2 *Decolonizing Data and Technology*

An antidote to digital colonialism is decolonizing AI from the ground up, particularly with respect to data ownership and the development process. Currently, AI development often mirrors historical patterns of resource extraction, where data is collected from marginalized communities without explicit consent or tangible benefits, a practice scholars refer to as data colonialism (Couldry & Mejias, 2019; Mannuru et al., 2023). For instance, social media or mobile data from communities in low-income countries may be used to train AI systems, or individuals from these regions may be hired for data labeling due to low labor costs. Yet, these communities seldom benefit from the resulting technologies, reflecting a pattern of exploitation that underscores the urgent need for ethical data practices and equitable benefit-sharing (Ateeq et al., 2024).

Decolonizing data and technology involves empowering communities to reclaim ownership, value, and contextual understanding of the data they generate. This approach is not merely an alternative to cultural competence; rather, it is fundamental for achieving authentic cultural competence through ongoing cultural humility and power-sharing. To decolonize technology, community-driven and community-owned approaches to AI development are paramount. Participatory algorithm design is a pivotal strategy that involves local community members in problem definition, setting success criteria, and testing algorithm outputs. This collaborative approach transforms AI from a black-box tool imposed on communities to a co-created asset that reflects their priorities and lived experiences (Williams & Shipley, 2021). This could mean a refugee community helping to develop an algorithm for resource allocation in camps, ensuring it reflects their priorities and lived realities, and ensuring that AI technologies align with community values and ethical considerations.

Data sovereignty is a critical principle in decolonizing AI, asserting that communities, especially Indigenous and marginalized populations, have the inherent right to govern the collection, storage, and utilization of their data. This principle emphasizes that data ownership should remain with the community rather than being exploited by external entities. One challenge is that existing AI ethics frameworks are often rooted in Western values, prioritizing individual autonomy and data privacy while neglecting the communalist perspectives predominant in many regions of the Global South. For example, in African contexts, data governance is embedded in relational ethics; community well-being and collective ownership are often valued over individual rights, making it essential to reinterpret AI ethics frameworks in ways that resonate with local values and cultural norms (Grancia, 2024). This cultural mismatch underscores the importance of developing region-specific guidelines that reflect the lived realities and priorities of local populations, particularly when addressing pressing healthcare challenges. Community oversight is essential to ensuring data sovereignty and making sure that AI serves the interests of those who provide the data.

Ultimately, decolonizing technology involves fundamentally disrupting power dynamics—from AI being imposed upon communities to AI being co-created by them. While co-creation is essential, achieving meaningful change requires deeper structural, societal, and systemic engagement. Although this approach may take more time, the additional effort yields tools that are more contextually appropriate and ethically grounded.

6 Responsible AI: Future Directions for International Social Work

AI presents significant potential for addressing complex global social issues, yet its deployment in international contexts introduces unique ethical, cultural, and practical challenges. To maximize AI's positive impact while mitigating risks, future strategies must focus on refining ethical governance, strengthening professional competencies, promoting inclusive participatory design processes, and enhancing data management infrastructures.

6.1 Ethical Guidelines, Governance, and Advocacy

As AI becomes increasingly embedded in international social work, robust ethical guidelines and governance frameworks are essential to ensure these technologies align with core social work values and responsible use. Currently, the landscape is fragmented, with scattered principles like the "AI for Good" pledges or general technology ethics codes in social work. International social work would greatly benefit from tailored standards that address the unique challenges of social services and humanitarian contexts worldwide.

One notable model to build on is the global effort by UNESCO, which released the first international standard on AI ethics in 2021, the *Recommendation on the Ethics of Artificial Intelligence*, which emphasizes human rights, fairness, and human oversight (UNESCO, 2021). In addition to UNESCO's foundational standards, social work professionals can draw on existing ethics-informed guidelines specifically developed within the field. These frameworks address three primary domains: practice standards, regulatory and licensing standards, and codes of ethics standards (Reamer, 2023). In 2013, recognizing the need for structured guidance on emerging technologies, the Association of Social Work Boards (ASWB) appointed an international task force comprising representatives from diverse areas of social work practice, regulation, and education. By 2015, the task force had developed and adopted detailed ethics guidelines specifically for social workers engaging with digital and electronic technologies. These guidelines emphasized seven core ethical areas that are especially relevant to AI integration into international social work practice: practitioner competence; informed consent; privacy and confidentiality; boundaries, dual relationships, and conflicts of interest; records and documentation; collegial relationships; and social work practice across jurisdictional boundaries (López Peláez & Kirwan, 2023). Building on this foundation, further progress in ethical standard-setting occurred in 2017 through unprecedented collaboration among key U.S. social work organizations, ASWB, the National Association of Social Workers (NASW), Council on Social Work Education (CSWE), and the Clinical Social Work Association (CSWA). These entities worked together to develop comprehensive practice standards that included detailed ethical considerations for the use of technology within social work. The resulting standards addressed critical ethical areas, including informed consent, competent practice, conflicts of interest, privacy and confidentiality, boundaries and professional relationships, record-keeping, and supervision (NASW et al., 2017).

While these frameworks provide valuable guidance, it is essential to acknowledge their limitations. First, many operate primarily as aspirational guidelines rather than enforceable regulations. Building on these foundational ethical guidelines, it is crucial to recognize that although existing frameworks offer a solid foundation, they should not be simply imported from the outside. Instead, they must emerge organically from communities and professional organizations within the Global South, reflecting local realities and knowledge systems. Unlike domestic contexts, international social work often involves complex, dynamic situations involving refugees, immigrants, climate crises, and global health emergencies (Payne & Askeland, 2016). Ethical guidelines developed through a bottom-up approach are better positioned to address the unique challenges of international social work contexts. In refugee and immigrant settings, informed consent should be transparent and culturally sensitive, taking into account language barriers and differing norms. In climate crisis zones, AI-driven decisions must account for disrupted infrastructure and data gaps. During global health emergencies, such as pandemics, data sharing raises confidentiality concerns, requiring strong security to prevent misuse. Social workers must critically assess AI outcomes to ensure context-aware, responsible implementation that prioritizes local leadership and community-driven processes.

Without concrete oversight and accountability mechanisms, particularly in transnational contexts, ethical commitments risk becoming symbolic rather than impactful. This situation can lead to "ethical laundering," where superficial compliance masks potentially harmful or inequitable technological practices. Ethical codes are generally unenforceable, especially across transnational contexts with varying governance structures and legal frameworks. Without clear accountability mechanisms, usually established at localized levels, these codes risk serving more as virtue signaling than as genuine safeguards. Second, the majority of these standards originate from institutions and professional bodies based in the Global North. As a result, they often reflect Northern-centric norms and regulatory priorities that may not align with the cultural values, social realities, or infrastructural conditions of communities in the Global South. These limitations highlight the need for more inclusive, enforceable, and locally grounded frameworks that better reflect the diversity of international practice contexts. Given these limitations, it is necessary to move from a one-size-fits-all ethical approach to one that is responsive to specific practice contexts.

Ultimately, addressing critical limitations—such as the lack of enforceability and Northern-centric biases—while ensuring careful cultural localization of ethical guidelines is essential to support responsible AI use in international social work effectively. Comprehensive guidelines that incorporate enforceable accountability mechanisms and context-specific cultural adaptations will more effectively promote social justice, resilience, and global equity, thereby mitigating rather than exacerbating existing inequalities.

6.2 Capacity Building and Training for International Social Workers

To integrate AI responsibly, both social workers and technologists need training that builds mutual understanding. Social workers should gain basic AI literacy to evaluate technologies critically, while technologists must learn about social work values and contexts. Joint training programs and co-design workshops can foster collaboration, critical thinking, and community-aligned solutions. Additionally, in the future, formal education curricula in social work should incorporate modules on AI ethics, digital literacy, and practical skills for evaluating AI systems (Hodgson et al., 2022; Reamer, 2023; Safodien, 2021). Universities and professional training organizations could collaborate with tech companies and international NGOs to offer certification programs specifically focused on ethical AI integration (Council on Social Work Education, 2022; National Association of Social Workers et al., 2017). Continuous professional development should also be encouraged through regular updates and refresher training on emerging technologies and their ethical implications. Creating an international exchange program for social workers and technologists can further enhance knowledge transfer and cultural competency, thereby ensuring AI solutions are globally informed and locally relevant.

6.3 Inclusive and Participatory Design with Strengthened Data Infrastructure

Inclusive and participatory design is a cornerstone of responsible AI in social work. This approach involves co-developing tools with the communities they aim to serve, ensuring that AI solutions are both relevant and culturally appropriate (Sabater et al., 2025). Community stakeholders should be involved from the start to ensure AI tools reflect local needs. Strong, locally controlled data systems are key to ethical AI use, helping prevent misuse and ensuring accuracy. Building local data capacity and using federated learning can enhance data sovereignty. Clear guidelines on data ownership and consent are also essential. Communities should have transparent control over their data, including the ability to access, correct, and withdraw their data from AI systems (Tan et al., 2025). Building robust governance structures, such as community advisory boards, can facilitate ongoing dialogue between stakeholders, enhancing accountability and trust. Regular audits and evaluations of AI systems by independent bodies can further ensure ethical compliance and effectiveness. To be meaningful, however, participatory design must be adequately resourced. Funders and NGOs must also be willing to retool timelines and metrics to value long-term engagement and locally defined outcomes. Ultimately, empowering communities with the skills and resources necessary to participate meaningfully in AI development will foster inclusive, equitable, and sustainable outcomes in international social work contexts.

In conclusion, integrating AI into international social work offers significant potential to address global challenges. However, achieving responsible and ethical AI use requires clear, enforceable guidelines tailored to international contexts. These guidelines must be culturally responsive, inclusive, and uphold accountability to bridge ethical gaps and mitigate biases effectively. Additionally, building professional competence through targeted AI literacy for social workers and social work training for technologists is essential. Joint educational initiatives and continuous learning opportunities will foster interdisciplinary collaboration and ethical practice. Finally, inclusive participatory design, supported by robust local data infrastructures, ensures that AI solutions are relevant and equitable. Meaningful community involvement and transparent data governance empower communities and build trust, resulting in fairer and more effective outcomes. By prioritizing ethical standards, capacity building, and inclusive design, international social work can harness AI responsibly to advance global social justice and equity.

Competing Interests The authors have no conflicts of interest to declare that are relevant to the content of this chapter.

References

Achugamonu, S. (2025). *Place matters: The possibilities and pitfalls of machine learning algorithms for refugee resettlement.*

Ahmad, N. (2020). Refugees and algorithmic humanitarianism: Applying artificial intelligence to RSD procedures and immigration decisions and making global human rights obligations relevant to AI governance. *International Journal on Minority and Group Rights, 1*(aop), 1–69.

Åhs, F., Mozelius, P., Espvall, M., & Se, P. M. (2022). *Preparing psychologists and social workers for the daily use of AI.*

Akter, S. (2024). Global perspectives on the social impacts of artificial intelligence: A comparative review of regional inequalities and cultural contexts. *Journal of Artificial Intelligence General Science, 5*(1).

Anka, A. (2024). Using the concept of epistemic injustice and cultural humility for understanding why and how social work curricular might be decolonized. *Social Work Education*. https://doi.org/10.1080/02615479.2023.2299245

Asakura, K., Miller, J., Nakash, O., & O'Neill, P. (2023). Toward "decolonizing" clinical social work practice and education. In *Smith college studies in social work* (Vol. 93, Issues 2–4, pp. 73–82). Routledge. https://doi.org/10.1080/00377317.2023.2279389

Ateeq, A., Ahmed Ali, S., Milhem, M., Alzoraik, M., Ateeq, R. A., & Al Asta, A. Y. (2024). Exploring the reality of artificial intelligence in the developing countries: Challenges and opportunities – a scientific perspective. *Pakistan Journal of Life and Social Sciences (PJLSS), 22*(1). https://doi.org/10.57239/pjlss 2024 22.1.00144

Bazzano, A. N., Mantsios, A., Mattei, N., Kosorok, M. R., & Culotta, A. (2025). AI can be a powerful social innovation for public health if community engagement is at the core. *Journal of Medical Internet Research, 27*, e68198. https://doi.org/10.2196/68198

Beduschi, A. (2022). Harnessing the potential of artificial intelligence for humanitarian action: Opportunities and risks. *International Review of the Red Cross, 104*(919), 1149–1169.

Berg, J., Snene, M., & Velasco, L. (2024). *Mind the AI divide: Shaping a global perspective on the future of work.* United Nations. https://www.ilo.org/publications/major-publications/mind-ai-divide-shaping-global-perspective-future-work

Bennett, B., Redfern, H., & Zubrzycki, J. (2024). How do we decolonise the social work curriculum? *Australian Social Work, 77*(1), 1–13. https://doi.org/10.1080/0312407X.2024.2329233

Borkowski, A. (2020). Using artificial intelligence for COVID-19 chest X-ray diagnosis. *Federal Practitioner, 37*(9). https://doi.org/10.12788/fp.0045

Cai, D. Y. (2016). A concept analysis of cultural competence. *International Journal of Nursing Sciences, 3*(3), 268–273. https://doi.org/10.1016/j.ijnss.2016.08.002

Charrua, A. B., Padmanaban, R., Cabral, P., Bandeira, S., & Romeiras, M. M. (2021). Impacts of the tropical cyclone Idai in Mozambique: A multi-temporal landsat satellite imagery analysis. *Remote Sensing, 13*(201).

Chin, H., Song, H., Baek, G., Shin, M., Jung, C., Cha, M., Choi, J., & Cha, C. (2023). The potential of chatbots for emotional support and promoting mental well-being in different cultures: Mixed methods study. *Journal of Medical Internet Research, 25*, e51712. https://doi.org/10.2196/51712

Council on Social Work Education. (2022). *2022 Educational Policy and Accreditation Standards (EPAS).* Council on Social Work Education. https://www.cswe.org/getmedia/bb5d8afe-7680-42dc-a332-a6e6103f4998/2022-EPAS.pdf

Couldry, N., & Mejias, U. A. (2019). Data colonialism: Rethinking big data's relation to the contemporary subject. *Television & New Media, 20*(4), 336–349.

Davis, M. (2020). The "culture" in cultural competence. In *Cultural competence and the higher education sector: Australian perspectives, policies and practice* (pp. 15–29). Springer Singapore. https://doi.org/10.1007/978-981-15-5362-2_2

Dychiao, R. G., Nazer, L., Mlombwa, D., & Celi, L. A. (2024). Artificial intelligence and global health equity. *BMJ, 387*.

El Morr, C., Ozdemir, D., Asdaah, Y., Saab, A., El-Lahib, Y., & Sokhn, E. S. (2024). AI-based epidemic and pandemic early warning systems: A systematic scoping review. *Health Informatics Journal, 30*(3). https://doi.org/10.1177/14604582241275844

Ferweda, J., Finseraas, H., & Christensen, D. A. (2022). *The feasibility of using data-driven algorithmic recommendations for refugee placement in Norway*.

Folk, D., Wu, C., & Heine, S. (2025). Culture and chatbots: Cultural variation in attitudes towards social chatbots. *Journal of Cross-Cultural Psychology*.

Fong, R. (2001). Culturally competent practice: What is it and why does it matter? *Journal of Ethnic & Cultural Diversity in Social Work, 10*(1), 1–10. https://doi.org/10.1300/J051v10n01_01

Forster, M., & House, C. (2022). Refugee protection in the artificial intelligence era. *Research Paper*.

Goldkind, L. (2021). Social work and artificial intelligence: Into the matrix. *Social Work (United States), 66*(4), 372–374. https://doi.org/10.1093/sw/swab028

Grancia, M. K. (2024). Decolonizing AI ethics in Africa's healthcare: An ethical perspective. *AI and Ethics*. https://doi.org/10.1007/s43681-024-00650-z

Hodgson, D., Goldingay, S., Boddy, J., Nipperess, S., & Watts, L. (2022). Problematising artificial intelligence in social work education: Challenges, issues and possibilities. *The British Journal of Social Work, 52*(4), 1878–1895.

Hood, S., Campbell, B., & Baker, K. (2022). *Culturally informed community engagement: Implications for inclusive science and health equity*. https://doi.org/10.3768/rtipress.2023.op.0083.2301

Jelonek, A. C. (2023). *Use of predictive analytics in humanitarian operations*. Fordham University.

Logar, T., Bullock, J., Nemni, E., Bromley, L., Quinn, J. A., & Luengo-Oroz, M. (2020). *PulseSatellite: A tool using human-AI feedback loops for satellite image analysis in humanitarian contexts*. https://ojs.aaai.org/index.php/AAAI/article/view/7101

López Peláez, A., & Kirwan, G. (Eds.). (2023). *The Routledge international handbook of digital social work*. Routledge.

Lubin, A. (2022). The rights to privacy and data protection under international humanitarian law and human rights law. In *Research handbook on human rights and humanitarian law* (pp. 462–491). Edward Elgar.

MacIntyre, C. R., Chen, X., Kunasekaran, M., Quigley, A., Lim, S., Stone, H., Paik, H. Y., Yao, L., Heslop, D., Wei, W., Sarmiento, I., & Gurdasani, D. (2023). Artificial intelligence in public health: The potential of epidemic early warning systems. *Journal of International Medical Research, 51*(3). https://doi.org/10.1177/03000605231159335

Maita, K. C., Forte, A. J., Demaerschalk, B. M., Coffey, J. D., Lunde, J. J., Borna, S., Torres-Guzman, R. A., Maniaci, M. J., Haider, C. R., & Avila, F. R. (2024). The impact of digital health solutions on bridging the health care gap in rural areas: A scoping review. *The Permanente Journal, 28*(3), 130–143.

Mannuru, N. R., Shahriar, S., Teel, Z. A., Wang, T., Lund, B. D., Tijani, S., Pohboon, C. O., Agbaji, D., Alhassan, J., Galley, J. K., Kousari, R., Ogbadu-Oladapo, L., Saurav, S. K., Srivastava, A., Tummuru, S. P., Uppala, S., & Vaidya, P. (2023). Artificial intelligence in developing countries: The impact of generative artificial intelligence (AI) technologies for development. *Information Development*. https://doi.org/10.1177/02666669231200628

Nadan, Y. (2017). Rethinking 'cultural competence' in international social work. *International Social Work, 60*(1), 74–83. https://doi.org/10.1177/0020872814539986

Nankya, H., Mathews, D., Ferryman, K., Kane, O., & Ali, J. (2025). Community engagement for artificial intelligence health research in Africa. *Wellcome Open Research, 10*, 158. https://doi.org/10.12688/wellcomeopenres.23684.1

Nair, R., Madsen, B., & Kjærum, A. (2023). An explainable forecasting system for humanitarian needs assessment. In *Proceedings of the AAAI Conference on Artificial Intelligence* (Vol. 37, No. 13, pp. 15569–15575).

National Association of Social Workers, Clinical Social Work Association, Council on Social Work Education, & Association of Social Work Boards. (2017). *NASW, ASWB, CSWE, & CSWA standards for technology in social work practice*. National Association of Social Workers. https://www.socialworkers.org/Practice/NASW-Practice-Standards-Guidelines/Standards-for-Technology-in-Social-Work-Practice

Nuwasiima, M., Ahonon, M. P., & Kadiri, C. (2024). The role of artificial intelligence (AI) and machine learning in social work practice. *World Journal of Advanced Research and Reviews, 24*(1), 80–97. https://doi.org/10.30574/wjarr.2024.24.1.2998

Okolo, C. T. (2023). Addressing global inequity in AI development. In *Handbook of critical studies of artificial intelligence* (pp. 378–389). Edward Elgar.

Pasipamire, N., & Muroyiwa, A. (2024). Navigating algorithm bias in AI: Ensuring fairness and trust in Africa. *Frontiers in Research Metrics and Analytics, 9*. https://doi.org/10.3389/frma.2024.1486600

Payne, M., & Askeland, G. A. (2016). *Globalization and international social work: Postmodern change and challenge*. Routledge.

Perez, K., Wisniewski, D., Ari, A., Lee, K., Lieneck, C., & Ramamonjiarivelo, Z. (2025). Investigation into application of AI and telemedicine in rural communities: A systematic literature review. *Healthcare (Switzerland), 13*(3). https://doi.org/10.3390/healthcare13030324

Ray, S. (2024). *Incorporating indigenous knowledge systems into AI governance: Enhancing ethical frameworks with Maori and Navajo perspectives*. https://doi.org/10.20944/preprints202410.2112.v2

Reamer, F. G. (2023). Artificial intelligence in social work: Emerging ethical issues. *International Journal of Social Work Values and Ethics, 20*(2), 52–71.

Ruvin, H. (2021). *Sesame workshop announces new tools to support children and families impacted by the Venezuelan crisis*. Sesame Workshop.

Sabater, A., López, B., Campdepadrós, R., & Sánchez, C. (2025). Participatory action research for AI in social services: An example of local practices from Catalonia. In P. Ahrweiler (Ed.), *Participatory artificial intelligence in public social services: From bias to fairness in assessing beneficiaries* (pp. 79–96). Springer Nature Switzerland. https://doi.org/10.1007/978-3-031-71678-2_4

Safodien, M. (2021). Social work 4.0? The Fourth Industrial Revolution and social work education: A South African perspective. *Social Work, 57*(3), 257–271.

Sartor, G., & Lagioia, F. (2020). *The impact of the General Data Protection Regulation (GDPR) on artificial intelligence*.

Schellekens, P., & Skilling, D. (2024). *Three reasons why AI may widen global inequality*. Center for Global Development.

Stelmaszak, M., & Kline, K. (2023). Managing embedded data science teams for success: How managers can navigate the advantages and challenges of distributed data science. *Harvard Data Science Review, 5*(2). https://doi.org/10.1162/99608f92.1f068331

Tamburro, A. (2013). Including decolonization in social work education and practice. *Journal of Indigenous Social Development, 2*(1), 1–16.

Tan, Y., Soh, K., Zhang, R., Lee, J., Meng, H., Sen, B., & Lee, Y.-C. (2025). *Empowering social service with AI: Insights from a participatory design study with practitioners*. https://doi.org/10.48550/arXiv.2502.19822

UNESCO. (2021). *Recommendation on the ethics of artificial intelligence*. https://unesdoc.unesco.org/ark:/48223/pf0000381137

UNESCO Institute for Lifelong Learning. (2022a). *From radio to artificial intelligence: Review of innovative technology in literacy and education for refugees, migrants and internally displaced persons*. UNESCO. https://doi.org/10.54675/KZHI8494

UNESCO Institute for Lifelong Learning. (2022b). *Leveraging innovative technology in literacy and education programmes for refugees, migrants and internally displaced persons*. UNESCO. https://doi.org/10.54675/IMHD4511

Vázquez González, S. & García Rendón, O.L. (Eds.) (2021). Desafíos del trabajo social digital en Latinoamérica. Thomson Reuters Aranzadi

Williams, D., & Shipley, G. (2021). Enhancing artificial intelligence with indigenous wisdom. *Open Journal of Philosophy, 11*, 43–58.

Zhao, A. P., Li, S., Cao, Z., Hu, P. J.-H., Wang, J., Xiang, Y., Xie, D., & Lu, X. (2024). AI for science: Predicting infectious diseases. *Journal of Safety Science and Resilience, 5*(2), 130–146. https://doi.org/10.1016/j.jnlssr.2024.02.002

Zuhair, V., Babar, A., Ali, R., Oduoye, M. O., Noor, Z., Chris, K., Okon, I. I., & Rehman, L. U. (2024). Exploring the impact of artificial intelligence on global health and enhancing healthcare in developing nations. *Journal of Primary Care and Community Health, 15*. https://doi.org/10.1177/21501319241245847

Part IV
AI in Social Work Education and Research

Chapter 20
AI in Social Work Education

Yue Fang, Cao Fang, and Ruopeng An

1 Introduction

Artificial intelligence (AI) is rapidly transforming higher education, and social work education is no exception. The integration of AI-driven educational technologies, such as large language models (LLMs), chatbots, and immersive virtual reality (VR) simulations, is transforming how students learn, practice, and prepare for professional roles in their fields. These tools are expanding pedagogical possibilities and offering new avenues for experiential learning that go beyond traditional methods.

Historically, social work education has relied on human-based role-play, in-person simulations, and direct field experiences to build practice skills and professional judgment. However, the proliferation of digital technologies is challenging and complementing these conventional approaches. This shift aligns with evolving expectations for technological competence and ethical digital practice as outlined by the National Association of Social Workers (NASW), Association of Social Work Boards (ASWB), Council on Social Work Education (CSWE), and Clinical Social Work Association (CSWA) in their *Standards for Technology in Social Work Practice* (NASW et al., 2017). These standards emphasize the responsible integration of technology to enhance education while upholding the profession's core values.

The COVID-19 pandemic accelerated this digital transformation. Restrictions on in-person field placements and classroom learning forced educators to innovate rapidly. In response, many turned to AI-powered platforms and VR simulations to

Y. Fang (✉) · R. An
Silver School of Social Work, New York University, New York, NY, USA
e-mail: yf2938@nyu.edu; ra4605@nyu.edu

C. Fang
School of Social Work, The University of Texas at Austin, Austin, TX, USA
e-mail: cao.fang@austin.utexas.edu

R. An, M. A. Lindsey (eds.), *Artificial Intelligence in Social Work*,
https://doi.org/10.1007/978-3-032-18443-6_20

create scalable, interactive, and safe environments for skill development. These tools have demonstrated strong potential to improve learning outcomes, foster reflective practice, and bridge the gap between theoretical knowledge and real-world application (Huttar & BrintzenhofeSzoc, 2020; Kourgiantakis & Lee, 2020; Mitchell et al., 2022).

The integration of AI into social work education brings both promise and complexity. On one hand, AI tools can personalize instruction, provide immediate feedback, and simulate complex social scenarios, supporting the development of essential competencies. On the other hand, scholars raise significant ethical, social, and cultural concerns, including issues of privacy, algorithmic bias, transparency, and the potential erosion of human-centered values in social work (Zawacki-Richter et al., 2019). As these technologies become more embedded in educational practice, educators, researchers, and policymakers must engage critically with their implications.

Evidence supporting the effectiveness of AI-enhanced simulations is growing. Recent systematic reviews and meta-analyses show that simulated learning can significantly improve social work student outcomes, particularly for advanced learners and in mental health contexts (S. Zhang & Stepteau-Watson, 2024). This underscores the importance of continued research and critical engagement to ensure AI technologies are deployed responsibly and effectively.

This chapter focuses on AI-driven educational technologies that leverage AI to deliver learning experiences or facilitate the practice of social work skills. This focus differs from AI literacy (covered in Chap. 23), which involves teaching students to comprehend AI concepts and consider their ethical and societal implications. While AI literacy emphasizes critical understanding, the pedagogical use of AI, such as through generative models, intelligent tutoring systems, and immersive simulations, represents a distinct and rapidly evolving dimension of educational practice (Zawacki-Richter et al., 2019).

This chapter provides a comprehensive overview of AI-driven tools used in social work education. It examines their pedagogical affordances, evaluates the current evidence base, explores ethical considerations, and identifies key research gaps. Ultimately, it proposes strategic directions for integrating these technologies into social work curricula that enhance learning while remaining faithful to the profession's core values.

2 Theoretical Foundations for AI-Enabled Learning

AI-enabled learning environments are transforming the education of social work and healthcare professionals. Rooted in longstanding pedagogical theories and simulation-based practices, these environments leverage AI to expand the scope and depth of experiential learning. The integration of AI technologies into education offers new opportunities for scenario realism, responsive feedback, and individualized learning while remaining grounded in proven educational models.

2.1 Simulation-Based Learning (SBL): Historical Use, Benefits, and AI Enhancement

Simulation-based learning (SBL) has played a central role in both healthcare and social work education for decades. Traditionally, SBL relied on live actors, paper-based scenarios, or video recordings to replicate complex client interactions and clinical environments. These tools foster critical competencies, including interviewing, assessment, ethical reasoning, and interprofessional collaboration (Craig et al., 2017; Dodds et al., 2018; Lee et al., 2020; Kourgiantakis et al., 2020; Kourgiantakis & Lee, 2022). More recently, digital and AI-driven simulations have emerged, allowing learners to practice and refine skills in controlled, repeatable, and scalable ways (Egonsdotter & Israelsson, 2024; Jefferies et al., 2024).

Meta-analyses confirm that SBL produces substantial positive effects on complex skill acquisition across various educational domains (Chernikova et al., 2020; S. Zhang & Stepteau-Watson, 2024). These benefits increase further when simulations incorporate technological scaffolding and feedback mechanisms. Comparative studies confirm that well-designed computer-based simulations can match or even surpass traditional actor-led methods in promoting reflective practice and procedural skills (Egonsdotter & Israelsson, 2024; Zhang & Stepteau-Watson, 2024).

AI enhances SBL in three core ways. First, it supports dynamic scenario generation, tailoring learning experiences to meet the individual needs and progress of each student. Second, AI enables real-time, automated feedback, which is critical for developing judgment and clinical reasoning (Guraya, 2024; Q. Wu et al., 2022). Third, AI tools integrated with VR/AR technologies enhance the immersive quality of simulations, thereby increasing learner engagement and the perceived realism of client interactions (Gordon et al., 2024; Share & Pender, 2024). These developments are particularly impactful in interprofessional education, where AI systems can simulate collaborative care planning and cross-disciplinary communication (Asakura et al., 2021).

2.2 Experiential and Constructivist Pedagogies: Kolb's Cycle and AI

The theoretical foundation for simulation and AI-enabled learning environments is strongly influenced by Kolb (1984)'s experiential learning cycle. This model emphasizes learning through doing, structured around four stages: concrete experience, reflective observation, abstract conceptualization, and active experimentation. SBL aligns with this model, offering structured spaces for learners to engage in lifelike scenarios and reflect on their actions (Asakura et al., 2021; Sollars & Xenakis, 2021).

AI technologies enrich each phase of Kolb's cycle. They enable iterative practice through on-demand simulations, support reflection with data-driven feedback, and guide abstraction through performance analytics and prompts. For example, an AI tutor might surface patterns in a student's responses, such as recurring gaps in empathy statements, and then recommend targeted practice. In this way, AI becomes a co-facilitator of learning, aligned with constructivist principles that prioritize learner agency, contextualized knowledge, and co-creation (Matlala, 2021; Egonsdotter & Bengtsson, 2023; Share & Pender, 2024).

Moreover, AI supports participatory pedagogies that are increasingly valued in social work education. These approaches position learners not only as recipients of knowledge but also as active contributors who shape their own learning paths. AI tools can accommodate this by adapting content in real time and offering diverse routes through simulations, thereby fostering autonomy and engagement (Asakura et al., 2021; Gordon et al., 2024).

2.3 Digital Competence and Human–Computer Interaction (HCI)

For AI-enhanced learning to be effective, both learners and educators must possess a baseline level of digital competence. This includes not only operational skills, such as navigating software or using feedback dashboards, but also critical awareness of how digital tools shape learning experiences (Egonsdotter & Israelsson, 2024). In social work education, which is traditionally not tech-centered, these competencies are emerging as essential for the ethical and effective use of AI.

Human–computer interaction (HCI) principles also play a vital role in AI integration. Systems that are unintuitive or poorly designed can increase cognitive load and reduce learner confidence. Research indicates that intuitive interfaces, clear visual feedback, and participatory design strategies enhance learner comfort and effectiveness (Gordon et al., 2024; Wu et al., 2022). When users are involved in shaping how AI tools work through feedback, co-design, or pilot testing, engagement and learning outcomes improve (Asakura et al., 2021).

AI in education must also respect the human-centered values of social work and healthcare professions. Tools should support, not replace, relational skills and ethical decision-making. Participatory design processes help ensure that AI systems align with these values by embedding equity, transparency, and inclusivity from the outset (Gordon et al., 2024; Zhang et al., 2023a).

2.4 Key Research Trends and Emerging Directions

Since 2017, scholarship on SBL and AI in social work and healthcare education has expanded rapidly. Early foundational work (Craig et al., 2017; Dodds et al., 2018) set the stage for broader inquiries into the impact and design of simulations. By

2020–2021, meta-analyses and reflective studies (Chernikova et al., 2020; Sollars & Xenakis, 2021) offered robust evidence of simulation effectiveness and pedagogical alignment. In recent years, research has focused on AI-driven innovation, such as real-time feedback systems (Q. Wu et al., 2022), big data analytics in simulation (Guraya, 2024), and cross-disciplinary simulations with participatory approaches (Gordon et al., 2024; Share & Pender, 2024).

This growth reflects increasing recognition that AI is not just a technological tool but a pedagogical force. It reshapes how knowledge is delivered, how learning is assessed, and how educators engage with students. The current trajectory suggests continued convergence between AI capability, simulation fidelity, and pedagogical intentionality.

3 General-Purpose AI Tools for Learning and Professional Support

This section reviews the major categories of general-purpose AI tools currently influencing higher education, particularly those that can be adapted for social work instruction and practice training. Rather than focusing on proprietary branding, the discussion highlights underlying functions: large language model (LLM) systems that generate knowledge, tools that organize information into pedagogical resources, conversational tutors that facilitate practice, and documentation or productivity assistants that reduce administrative burden. Together, these applications establish the technological foundation for specialized social work simulation platforms.

3.1 Foundational AI Models for Knowledge Access and Educational Support

The most visible entry point for AI in education has been the family of large language models (LLMs) such as ChatGPT, Gemini, and Claude. These systems generate human-like text, answer questions, and synthesize complex information through natural-language interaction. Their capacity to serve simultaneously as information retrievers, writing partners, and reflective interlocutors has quickly positioned them as multipurpose tools for students and educators.

In higher education, comparative classroom and laboratory studies demonstrate that distinct LLM architectures serve complementary pedagogical purposes. A review of early studies on ChatGPT's educational impact (Lo, 2023) identified two broad categories of pedagogical use: teaching preparation and student learning support. Instructors have used ChatGPT to outline syllabi, draft lectures, and design student assessment items; students use it to summarize information, answer questions, and assist with writing (Lo, 2023). Rane (2024) found that Gemini's continuously updated knowledge and adaptive learning design outperform ChatGPT in generating factual, individualized exercises, while ChatGPT remains stronger in creative text generation and formative feedback. Kellaway (2025) utilized Claude 3.5 to support a 3-month English writing program for 45 learners. Claude supplied level-appropriate models and step-by-step scaffolds for short compositions. By the end, all learners met or exceeded the course's target benchmark (EIKEN Grade 4), and 94% reported higher confidence and a wider range of expression. For students, LLMs serve as virtual tutors, capable of clarifying complex concepts, posing practice questions, and generating feedback on drafts. When used intentionally, they can foster metacognition and iterative learning.

However, research also cautions that LLM-generated assessments may overlook targeted learning objectives or produce plausible but inaccurate information, underscoring the need for critical engagement rather than uncritical reliance (Lo, 2023; Rane, 2024). Nevertheless, recent global survey data suggest that educators increasingly perceive the main benefits of generative AI as personalized instruction, support for problem-solving, and enhanced learning engagement (Mohammadi et al., 2026). As these capabilities mature, LLMs provide the backbone for many emerging educational platforms, which are reviewed in the subsequent sections.

3.2 AI-Assisted Knowledge Organization and Content Synthesis

A second class of tools focuses on organizing existing materials to help teachers and students manage knowledge. Google's NotebookLM exemplifies this development by combining generative AI with retrieval-augmented generation (RAG) to summarize, synthesize, and question-answer from user-provided sources. Rather than drawing on the open web, NotebookLM grounds its responses in uploaded readings, syllabi, or reports, thereby improving factual accuracy and contextual relevance (Reyna, 2025).

Educators can upload course outlines, lesson plans, and reference texts; the system then produces draft study guides, questions, and aligned formative assessments (Tufino, 2025). NotebookLM's structured prompts make it especially useful for curriculum mapping and constructive alignment, allowing instructors to trace how learning outcomes connect to activities and assessments. In curriculum review processes, it can flag redundancies or gaps and visualize where graduate attributes, such as critical thinking and ethics, are addressed.

For students, it operates as a contextual tutor. By interacting with their own course materials, they receive explanations and clarifications that stay within the approved content domain. This is an advantage over open-ended chatbots. Pilot studies at several universities have shown that NotebookLM facilitates more responsive and inclusive classroom experiences by freeing faculty from repetitive explanations and enabling individualized guidance through document-grounded dialogue (FGCU Digital Learning Blog, 2024; Reyna, 2025).

3.3 *Conversational Learning Partners and Cognitive Coaching Tools*

The emergence of conversational AI chatbots has opened new possibilities for interactive, student-centered learning. Chatbots powered by large language models (LLMs), such as ChatGPT, Bing Copilot, and Perplexity, are increasingly used as pedagogical assistants. The Stanford Teaching Commons (2023) categorizes their educational roles into seven functional types: mentor (providing formative feedback), tutor (offering adaptive explanations), coach (enhancing self-regulation), teammate (collaborating in group projects), student (eliciting reciprocal teaching), simulator (role-playing complex social or ethical situations), and tool (supporting design and content creation). This spectrum of pedagogical roles illustrates how chatbots extend the learning environment from a one-way transmission model toward a dynamic space for reflective practice.

Emerging studies have shown that generative AI chatbots can strengthen student engagement and professional skill development when used under guided supervision. For instance, Song et al. (2025) observed that generative AI chatbots (built on GPT-4 architectures) encouraged collaborative problem-solving among university students by breaking down complex problems into manageable parts, fostering experimentation, and supporting collective reasoning. Students reported feeling more confident and creative when interacting with dialogic agents capable of empathy and contextual adaptation.

Although current evidence on AI chatbots primarily stems from clinical settings, these innovations hold clear pedagogical value for social work and behavioral health education. Studies on conversational systems, such as ChatGPT (Blease & Torous, 2023), and therapeutic chatbots, like Youper, Woebot, and Wysa (Farzan et al., 2025), demonstrate their ability to model empathetic, structured, and reflective dialogue. When thoughtfully adapted for instruction, such systems can function as low-risk practice spaces where students rehearse interviewing, self-reflection, and rapport-building before engaging with real clients, bridging the gap between theory and practice in professional training.

3.4 *Intelligent Notetaking and Productivity Enhancers*

AI-powered documentation tools are reshaping how educators and practitioners manage administrative and reflective writing tasks, which have long been recognized as significant sources of burden in social services and allied professions (Ausserhofer et al., 2023; Ferraioli, 2025; Tarshish, 2024). Automated notetakers and meeting assistants exemplify this shift from information retrieval to cognitive offloading. Tools such as Magic Notes, Otter, Fireflies, Zoom AI Companion, and Microsoft Copilot utilize speech recognition, natural-language processing, and summarization algorithms to convert spoken or written notes into structured, professional documentation that aligns with institutional standards.

One of the widely discussed examples is Magic Notes. Launched in 2024 and adopted across roughly one-third of England's social-care teams within a year, it enables practitioners to record client meetings with consent and automatically generate structured summaries that conform to council documentation templates (Will, 2025). During the pilot implementation, administrative workload reportedly decreased by 48%, allowing social workers to focus more on direct client contact. The system's language-translation and formatting features have proven especially valuable for workers whose first language is not English, supporting inclusion and accuracy.

Beyond Magic Notes, a growing ecosystem of AI notetaking and meeting-assistant tools, such as Otter, Fireflies, and Sembly, has entered classrooms and field education. These platforms utilize generative AI and natural-language processing to transcribe lectures or group supervision sessions, highlight key concepts, and generate automated summaries. For instructors, they provide searchable records of class discussions and can scaffold formative feedback by surfacing recurring themes or misconceptions. For students, they reduce cognitive load during complex learning tasks, enabling deeper engagement and critical analysis rather than mechanical transcription.

3.5 AI Documentation and Case-Management Solutions in Human Services

In human services, documentation is essential for accountability and care coordination but often consumes a disproportionate share of practitioners' time. New AI-powered documentation tools aim to streamline this process while maintaining ethical and reflective standards of practice. Social Work Magic, for instance, offers AI-assisted templates for progress notes, safety plans, and intervention tracking. It supports professional documentation drafting efficiently while reinforcing appropriate tone and structure. Beyond automation, its creators emphasize digital literacy and ethical integration, framing AI as a partner that enables social workers to dedicate more time to direct engagement rather than administrative repetition (Social Work AI Magic, 2025a, 2025b).

At the organizational level, Netsmart's Bells AI Suite demonstrates how enterprise systems are embedding generative AI within electronic health records. Its components, including Documentation Assistant, Virtual Scribe, and Quality Coach, combine ambient listening, real-time validation, and automated audits to produce compliant records and feedback loops. User data report up to 60% reductions in documentation time and improved adherence to care plans, highlighting the model of augmented intelligence, the technology designed to support, not supplant, professional judgment (Netsmart, 2024).

These documentation platforms signal a broader transformation of human-service workflows into "documentation intelligence" systems that connect observation, analysis, and ethical decision-making. In social work education, such platforms provide authentic practice opportunities: students can critique AI-generated drafts, discuss confidentiality and consent, and explore how automation reshapes professional accountability.

4 Specialized AI Simulation Platforms for Social Work Education

While large language models and productivity assistants have become everyday learning companions, a parallel frontier is emerging in simulation-based education. These specialized platforms employ AI not only to deliver information but also to create experiences, allowing students to practice complex interpersonal, ethical, and analytical skills in controlled, feedback-rich environments. Across social work programs, educators are adapting AI simulations to extend field preparation, enhance reflective learning, and provide equitable access to realistic practice opportunities.

4.1 Platforms for Developing Core Clinical Interviewing Skills

Several AI-powered platforms focus specifically on building foundational and advanced interviewing competencies through conversational simulation and structured feedback.

4.1.1 Culturally Responsive Practice: Empathy Helper

Empathy Helper is a simulation platform built on large language models and agentic AI technologies. Rather than relying on fixed scripts or branching logic, it uses conversational AI to generate client avatars that respond in real time to what the learner says or types. These avatars can be configured with distinct psychosocial histories, cultural identities, and presenting problems, and their narratives can evolve dynamically across an encounter. The platform supports both one-on-one and one-to-many formats that simulate group counseling or psychoeducational sessions, and it is delivered via a web interface that promotes text-based chat or voice input without the need for specialized hardware or standardized patients.

Functionally, Empathy Helper is designed as a complete practice-and-feedback environment for core social work communication skills. Educators can select from or build multiple competency rubrics—such as those based on the Cultural Formulation Interview and other interviewing frameworks and micro-counselling models—and assign them to different training scenarios. Each interaction with an avatar is automatically logged and analyzed against the chosen rubric, producing structured competency scores and detailed qualitative feedback on specific strengths and areas for improvement. A natural-language parser also tallies key behaviors (for example, open and closed questions, simple and complex reflections, and affirmations) and generates global indicators of empathy and acceptance. Learners can review this feedback after a session through an "Evaluate" mode, or they can activate an "Instruction" mode that provides real-time coaching and suggestions while they are still interacting with the virtual client or group.

A pilot study of Empathy Helper was conducted with graduate social work trainees at the Brown School of Washington University in St. Louis (Lindsay et al., n.d.). Over several weeks, participants completed brief online modules. Then they engaged in multiple simulated interviews with distinct client avatars, receiving automated rubric scores, behavioral tallies, and narrative guidance after each encounter. Findings from this pilot indicated that trainees reported greater confidence in their interviewing skills, demonstrated solid performance on rubric-based competency indicators, and frequently used evidence-informed communication behaviors during simulations. Implementation and usability ratings were likewise positive, with participants viewing the platform as acceptable, appropriate for social work training, feasible to integrate into their workload, and easy to use. Together, these results suggest that Empathy Helper offers a practical, scalable adjunct to traditional skills labs and supervision in social work education, and they motivate larger, controlled studies in more diverse instructional settings.

4.1.2 Figment Learning Labs Virtual Patients

Figment Learning Labs (Interprofessional Education Collaborative, 2025) has developed an AI-powered virtual patient platform that demonstrates cross-disciplinary applicability. Usability testing with 60 interprofessional students showed increased engagement, enhanced learning outcomes, and greater confidence in patient interviewing. The platform's generative AI engine creates responsive, life-like virtual clients capable of engaging in free-flowing conversations, with structured debriefing sessions enhancing reflective learning. This model illustrates how AI simulation can prepare students for the interprofessional collaboration increasingly required in integrated care settings.

4.1.3 GenAI QPR for Suicide Prevention

For specialized training contexts, the GenAI Question, Persuade, and Refer (QPR) Simulator targets suicide prevention gatekeeper training using GPT-4o technology (Levkovich et al., 2025). Eighty-nine mental health gatekeepers engaged in three-stage training: conversation with simulated at-risk individuals, automated rubric-based feedback on rapport and risk assessment, and self-efficacy reassessment. Self-efficacy scores increased from 4.96 to 5.88 (Cohen's $d = 1.67$), with participants rating interactions as realistic and emotionally safe. While some expressed concerns about the loss of human nuance, the findings validate generative AI as an effective medium for experiential crisis-response training when accompanied by ethical oversight and debriefing.

4.2 Integrated Field Practice Simulations

Beyond discrete skill development, several platforms simulate comprehensive practice environments that mirror the complexity of actual field placements.

4.2.1 Comprehensive Training Modules: Virtual Social Work Trainer

At the University of Utah, researchers in the College of Social Work and Department of Population Health Sciences have created a suite of AI-enabled learning modules collectively known as the Virtual Social Work Trainer (VSWT) (University of Utah College of Social Work, n.d.). These modules offer structured simulations for essential competencies, including home environment assessment, safety planning, suicide risk evaluation, and motivational interviewing (Mortensen, 2024). The integrated Virtual Motivational Interviewing (VMI) chatbot employs generative AI to simulate diverse client responses and give real-time, theory-grounded feedback. Rather than relying on pre-programmed decision trees, VMI produces unique conversational exchanges informed by motivational-interviewing principles. Students receive immediate feedback on their reflective listening, open-ended questioning, and accuracy in empathy. The developers emphasize that the goal is to provide repeated, low-stakes opportunities for skill refinement.

4.2.2 Agency-Based Learning

Developed at the University of Newcastle (Australia), Social Work Virtual (SWV) is a web-based simulation program designed to build students' digital practice competencies through immersive, case-based learning. Developed during the COVID-19 pandemic, Social Work Virtual (SWV) was designed to replicate the immersive "Big Day In" experiential exercise, which is traditionally conducted in person (Agllias et al., 2021; Heinsch et al., 2023). This 8-week program assigns students to simulated agencies, including community services, mental health teams, school-based centers, and family support units, where they conduct policy research, attend meetings, and interview actors portraying clients via telehealth (Heinsch et al., 2023). These activities reflect the digital tools and processes increasingly used in practice during the pandemic and were designed to support students' readiness for field education as service systems rapidly shifted to online modalities.

To guide their progress, students complete weekly online learning modules that introduce new information related to the case scenario and support their preparation for team meetings and mentor-facilitated reflection (Heinsch et al., 2023, 2024). Evaluation findings indicate that SWV enhanced students' learning experiences, improving their preparedness for digital practice and social work placement (Heinsch et al., 2023). At the same time, both evaluation data and practice-mentor reflections highlight limitations common to virtual simulations, particularly the absence of real-time pressure, emotional intensity, and "in-the-moment" decision-making that characterize frontline practice (Heinsch et al., 2024). These constraints, noted more broadly in virtual simulation literature (Asakura & Bogo, 2021), point to opportunities for future enhancement. Integrating generative AI may help create more spontaneous, emotionally nuanced interactions, offering a richer approximation of real-world practice. As such, the SWV experience underscores both the promise and the current technical limits of virtual approaches to social work education.

4.2.3 Pre-field Preparation

The University of South Florida School of Social Work launched its Virtual Simulation Pilot Project in 2023 to enhance pre-field preparation and lifelong professional development (School of Social Work, 2024). Using an interactive web-based simulation platform, first-semester MSW students practiced with virtual clients exhibiting anxiety, depression, substance misuse, and family conflict. Focus-group data indicated that students valued the ability to rehearse difficult conversations multiple times in a "safe space." Instructors, meanwhile, highlighted the need for ongoing training and technical support to manage technology integration effectively. The project's next phase expands participation and assessment, reflecting the iterative nature of AI adoption in curricula. As USF's faculty notes, simulations complement real practice by providing structured opportunities to test knowledge, build confidence, and internalize professional competencies before field placement.

4.3 Immersive and Virtual Reality Applications

Virtual and immersive reality (VR/IVR) technologies are reshaping social work education by providing experiential, emotionally engaging learning environments that replicate real-world complexities while maintaining safety and control. Across universities, VR simulations now enable students to practice communication, assessment, and decision-making with lifelike clients, bridging the gap between classroom instruction and field practice. These tools leverage advances in AI to create responsive, interprofessional learning experiences that align with competency-based education standards.

4.3.1 Interprofessional VR for Behavioral Health Training

Virtual reality environments push experiential learning further by embedding students within embodied, sensory-rich practice spaces. At George Mason University, 28 MSW students participated in an interprofessional VR case where they engaged a substance-using adolescent in a hospital clinic (Cunningham, 2024). The simulation, developed in partnership with Certified Healthcare Simulation Educators and aligned with healthcare best-practice standards, was framed by pre- and post-simulation debriefs. Students reported gains in rapport-building, adaptability, and confidence in applying behavioral health interventions. Faculty emphasized VR's potential to strengthen resilience and reflective capacity in an increasingly demanding workforce. Building on that success, Mason's team developed a new VR case involving a substance-engaged family and envisions involving peer-recovery coaches in future training cycles (Matto et al., 2024).

4.3.2 Virtual Scenario Development

Georgia State University is exploring accessible approaches to creating virtual scenarios through 3D engine technology. Dr. Seelman and her colleagues are developing immersive virtual productions for social work education, using platforms such as Unreal Engine to create realistic scenarios that eliminate traditional filming requirements, thereby reducing the need for cameras, actors, sets, and production crews (Deupree, 2025). This approach enables individual faculty to create compelling case scenarios and historical narratives for their courses. Current projects include case scenarios addressing adolescent safety risks and a short film about Anna Julia Cooper, a historical advocate for Black youth education. The integration of AI-assisted character animation makes virtual production accessible to educators without technical coding expertise, offering new possibilities for emotionally engaging online students beyond text-based learning. This work illustrates how emerging 3D technologies can democratize immersive content creation in social work education (Deupree, 2025).

4.3.3 AI-Powered VR Simulation Platform

Emerging innovations are also integrating immersive VR with generative AI to create dynamic, responsive practice environments that move beyond pre-scripted scenarios. At New York University, Lanzieri et al. (2025) are developing an AI-powered VR simulation platform in which students interact with a virtual client avatar through real-time speech-to-text and text-to-speech systems. Built using a Retrieval-Augmented Generation (RAG) approach with OpenAI's GPT-4o-mini model, the platform combines a conversational "client" assistant that produces contextually relevant responses and an "evaluator" assistant that analyzes learner communication and intervention skills. A human-in-the-loop architecture allows faculty to guide model outputs, refine client behaviors, and maintain fidelity to social work values and ethical standards (Lanzieri et al., 2025). Currently in development before student piloting, the platform demonstrates how AI-enhanced VR can increase realism by generating spontaneous, emotionally nuanced dialogues that more closely resemble complex practice encounters. This approach also offers scalable opportunities for individualized feedback and repeated practice, addressing longstanding limitations of VR simulations that rely on fixed branching scripts or static content (Lanzieri et al., 2025).

The NYU project illustrates a next-generation direction for immersive learning—one that pairs embodied VR environments with adaptive AI-driven interactions to create more flexible, authentic, and pedagogically rich simulations for social work education. As these platforms evolve, they may offer educators new tools for teaching engagement, assessment, and decision-making in ways that balance experiential realism with controlled, ethically grounded learning conditions.

4.4 AI Literacy and Critical Engagement

As AI systems increasingly influence social service delivery, cultivating critical AI literacy becomes an educational imperative. Share and Pender's (2024) simulation exercise engaged MSW students in role-playing as stakeholders during the deployment of an AI predictive-risk algorithm that identified at-risk families. The experiential exercise highlighted ethical dilemmas surrounding bias, accountability, and transparency while developing students' capacity to advocate for equitable AI implementation. Participants developed critical AI literacy and stakeholder empathy, demonstrating that simulation-based pedagogy can move beyond technical training toward ethical and policy reflexivity. This approach cultivates graduates who are capable of critiquing and shaping AI integration in practical settings.

5 Integrating AI Tools into Social Work Curricula

Recent literature highlights the transformative potential and accompanying challenges of integrating AI into social work education. Key developments center on curriculum design, competency frameworks, and faculty development. Across these areas, AI tools are increasingly used to enhance learning through simulation, feedback, and data-driven personalization, while raising important pedagogical and ethical questions.

5.1 *Curriculum Design and Competency Frameworks*

5.1.1 Competency-Based Education and AI-Driven Simulations

The shift toward competency-based education (CBE) in social work requires methods that promote practical skill development, ongoing assessment, and reflective learning. AI-enabled simulations are emerging as key tools in this transition. Simulations supported by AI or virtual reality provide environments for repeated practice and instant feedback, which are key pillars of CBE, without requiring real-world risk or client exposure. These tools allow students to engage in complex interpersonal scenarios, rehearse clinical skills, and receive detailed performance analytics (Huttar & BrintzenhofeSzoc, 2020; E. Baker & Jenney, 2023; Heinsch et al., 2023).

Virtual simulations enhance learner engagement and can lead to measurable improvements in confidence and competence. For example, Baker and Jenney (2023) found that social work students trained through virtual simulations demonstrated greater readiness to apply trauma-informed care principles. Similarly, Huttar and Brintzenhofeszoc's (2020) systematic review identified simulation as a scalable, effective method for teaching direct practice skills.

Generative AI tools, such as ChatGPT, can provide additional support in CBE frameworks by serving as conversational partners or reflective coaches. These tools can prompt learners to explore ethical dilemmas, assess case studies, or receive feedback on documentation—all tailored to individual learning progress. Chang et al. (2023) highlight that such AI-driven feedback aligns well with self-regulated learning models, supporting goal setting and personalization. Celik et al. (2024) and Singer et al. (2023) further emphasize the importance of aligning these tools with educational theory to avoid shallow engagement or over-reliance.

Still, rigorous longitudinal studies are needed to confirm the long-term effects of AI-based simulation on actual competency development. Craig et al. (2017) caution that while early data are promising, more work is required to ensure consistency, reliability, and generalizability across diverse learner populations.

5.1.2 Virtual Field Placements

The COVID-19 pandemic accelerated the adoption of remote and virtual field placements in the social work field. Once considered temporary adaptations, these models are now recognized as viable components of the practicum landscape (Mitchell et al., 2022). AI tools play a growing role in this space by augmenting placement experiences with pre-placement simulations, interactive decision-making exercises, and real-time documentation support.

Heinsch et al. (2023) found that students in virtual placements developed critical digital competencies, including telehealth communication, electronic record keeping, and cross-site collaboration. Supervisors reported that these experiences often matched or exceeded traditional placements in terms of preparedness and professional identity formation. Mitchell et al. (2022) argue that virtual placements can promote equity by increasing access for students in rural areas or with caregiving responsibilities.

AI-enhanced virtual placements can also serve as a buffer or primer for more complex in-person engagements. When students engage in simulation before live client work, they are better equipped to handle ethical ambiguity, documentation pressures, and interprofessional communication.

5.1.3 Scaffolded Learning with AI Assistants

While generative AI tools hold promise, their educational value depends heavily on thoughtful integration. Chang et al. (2023) emphasize the importance of structured scaffolding to help students navigate and critique AI-generated responses. This involves teaching students how to craft effective prompts, interpret feedback critically, and cross-validate information.

Faculty must also address ethical limitations and potential biases in AI outputs. Singer et al. (2023) note that ChatGPT and similar tools reflect the data on which they are trained, which may embed systemic bias. Therefore, AI tools should be framed as learning aids rather than authorities. Garkisch and Goldkind (2024) emphasize the need for social work education to critically engage with AI technologies within an ethical and human-rights framework, highlighting the importance of interdisciplinary collaboration and ongoing reflection on digital ethics in practice.

Scaffolded use of AI in the classroom enables students to gain confidence in evaluating information quality, managing data privacy, and applying tools appropriately. Celik et al. (2024) emphasize that such practices promote not only digital literacy but broader twenty-first-century skills such as critical thinking, self-direction, and ethical reasoning.

5.2 *Faculty Development and Training*

5.2.1 Ongoing Training and Support

The successful integration of AI in social work curricula depends heavily on faculty readiness. Instructors require ongoing professional development to select suitable AI tools, design pedagogically sound prompts, interpret AI-driven feedback, and address student concerns. Without institutional support, even well-intentioned efforts risk producing inconsistent or superficial learning outcomes.

Qehaja (2025) emphasizes that AI integration in higher education is not a one-time event but a continuous process of strategic adaptation. Similarly, Hazzan-Bishara et al. (2025) highlight that both external determinants (such as institutional support and exposure to credible AI information) and internal determinants (including self-efficacy and intrinsic motivation) influence educators' willingness to adopt AI. Training must therefore include hands-on opportunities for faculty to experiment with AI tools, enabling them to build confidence and pedagogical competence. Cordero et al. (2024) further advocate for interdisciplinary collaboration, engaging experts in media design and computer science to co-develop educationally meaningful and contextually appropriate AI use cases.

5.2.2 Ethical and Practical Considerations

The integration of AI into social work education raises pressing ethical and practical issues. At the institutional level, clear policies are needed to address data security, academic integrity, and equitable access to technology. At the classroom level, instructors must ensure that AI tools do not reinforce biases or marginalize already vulnerable learners. Zhang and Tang (2025) emphasize the need for robust evaluative frameworks to track how AI tools affect different student groups across disciplines. Similarly, Ruiz-Rojas et al. (2024) advocate for transparency in the use of AI-generated content, particularly when it replaces or supplements faculty input.

Faculty co-design and communities of practice are key mechanisms to ensure ethical oversight. Cordero et al. (2024) and Hodgson et al. (2023) recommend that social work programs create interdisciplinary ethics committees to monitor AI use, share best practices, and develop responsive guidelines as technology evolves.

Ultimately, ethical integration is not just about risk mitigation; it's also about modeling professional values. Faculty who critically engage with AI demonstrate to students what responsible, reflective digital practice looks like in action.

6 Ethical, Legal, and Equity Considerations

The integration of AI into social work education requires careful consideration of its ethical, legal, and equity implications. While AI offers new pathways for learning and assessment, it also raises concerns about bias, privacy, consent, and the erosion of human judgment. Moreover, unequal access to technology and unclear regulatory standards risk deepening existing disparities. Addressing these challenges requires a proactive, value-driven approach that aligns AI adoption with social work's commitments to justice, integrity, and inclusivity. The following sections examine key domains shaping this ethical landscape: bias and fairness, privacy and data security, human–AI collaboration, accessibility, and regulatory oversight.

6.1 Bias and Fairness

AI models are only as unbiased as the data and design choices behind them. Numerous studies highlight that AI systems can encode and perpetuate sociocultural biases, especially when training data reflect existing inequalities or lack representation of marginalized groups. In social work, this is particularly concerning, as AI-driven tools may not account for cultural identity, intersectionality, or the lived experiences of diverse populations, potentially reinforcing systemic discrimination (R. S. Baker & Hawn, 2022; Varona & Suárez, 2022; Klimova et al., 2023; Roshanaei, 2024; Saeidnia et al., 2024; Palmquist et al., 2025). For example, Baker and Hawn (2022) document how algorithmic bias in education disproportionately affects students by race, gender, nationality, and disability, while Roshanaei (2024) emphasizes the need for continuous monitoring and bias mitigation to ensure equitable access to higher education.

Mitigating these risks requires deliberate strategies, including the use of diverse and representative datasets, regular bias audits, and the involvement of stakeholders from affected communities in AI design and evaluation. The literature also calls for frameworks that move beyond technical fairness to address equity and justice, ensuring that AI systems not only avoid discrimination but also actively promote inclusion (McDonald & Pan, 2020; Tilmes, 2022; Roshanaei, 2024). Palmquist et al. (2025) and McDonald and Pan (2020) argue for integrating intersectional and identity-based ethics into curricula, equipping students to recognize and challenge bias in AI systems.

6.2 Privacy, Consent, and Data Security

AI tools in social work education often collect sensitive personal data, raising significant concerns about confidentiality, informed consent, and data security. Existing studies stress that students and clients must be fully informed about what data is collected, how it will be used, and the limitations of AI systems before engaging with simulations or digital platforms (Al-Zahrani, 2024; Fedele et al., 2024; Franco D'Souza et al., 2024; Klimova et al., 2023; Saeidnia et al., 2024). D'Souza et al. (2024) recommend explicit, written consent and transparent communication about AI's role in educational processes.

Compliance with legal frameworks such as the Health Insurance Portability and Accountability Act (HIPAA) and the General Data Protection Regulation (GDPR) is essential, especially when AI tools are used for case simulations or assessments involving real or simulated client data. Fedele et al. (2024) highlight the importance of robust data protection measures, including secure storage, encryption, and clear data ownership policies. The risk of data breaches, hacking, or misuse is particularly acute for vulnerable populations, necessitating ongoing vigilance and ethical review (Al-Zahrani, 2024; Fedele et al., 2024; Saeidnia et al., 2024).

6.3 Human–AI Collaboration and Professional Judgment

While AI simulations offer risk-free practice environments, they cannot replicate the complexity, emotional nuance, or ethical ambiguity of real human interactions. Over-reliance on AI may diminish opportunities for developing empathy, critical thinking, and professional judgment. Reimer (2024) and Hodgson et al. (2023) emphasize that AI should augment, rather than replace, human educators and mentors. Effective curricula integrate AI tools with live supervision, group debriefing, and community-based learning to ensure students develop both technical and relational skills (Bankins & Formosa, 2023; Hodgson et al., 2023; Reimer, 2024; Palmquist et al., 2025; Segal, 2025). Segal (2025) finds that while AI can support ethical decision-making, it cannot independently resolve complex dilemmas. Human oversight remains essential for interpreting AI outputs, contextualizing recommendations, and upholding professional values (Bankins & Formosa, 2023; Palmquist et al., 2025; Segal, 2025).

6.4 Accessibility and the Digital Divide

Equitable access to AI-enhanced education is a persistent challenge. Implementing AI tools requires reliable hardware, Internet connectivity, and technical support, which may be lacking in rural or low-income settings (Abulibdeh et al., 2024; Al-Zahrani, 2024; Palmquist et al., 2025). Al-Zahrani (2024) and Abulibdeh et al. (2024) warn that the digital divide can exacerbate existing educational inequalities, limiting the benefits of AI to privileged groups.

To promote equity, programs should provide necessary devices, offer asynchronous and low-bandwidth options, and design interfaces accessible to students with disabilities. Tilmes (2022) critiques current fairness initiatives for often overlooking the needs of students with disabilities and advocates for a disability justice approach that centers on accessibility and inclusion.

6.5 Regulatory and Accreditation Considerations

Regulatory frameworks and accreditation standards often lag behind technological advances. Fedele et al. (2024) note that many professional standards remain silent on AI, creating uncertainty for educators and institutions. However, accreditation bodies are beginning to recognize AI-assisted training, with some offering continuing education credits for AI-powered simulations. Studies recommend updating standards to address the ethical, legal, and pedagogical implications of AI, ensuring that tools comply with data protection laws and professional guidelines. Ongoing collaboration among educators, regulators, and technology developers is essential to align AI integration with the core values of social work, including integrity, justice, and cultural responsiveness (Klimova et al., 2023; Fedele et al., 2024; Franco D'Souza et al., 2024; Saeidnia et al., 2024).

Overall, integrating AI tools into social work curricula demands a proactive, ethically grounded approach. Addressing bias, ensuring privacy and consent, maintaining a human-centered pedagogy, promoting accessibility, and updating regulatory frameworks are essential for responsible and equitable adoption of AI. Ongoing stakeholder engagement, critical digital literacy, and continuous evaluation will enable social work education to harness the benefits of AI while upholding its foundational values.

7 Future Directions and Research Agenda

As AI becomes increasingly embedded in social work education, future research in AI-enhanced social work education must strike a balance between innovation and ethical and pedagogical depth. Key priorities include advancing emotional intelligence in AI, enhancing interoperability across platforms, evaluating long-term learning outcomes, integrating critical AI literacy into curricula, and promoting ethical co-design with service users. Together, these directions aim to ensure that AI integration strengthens empathy, equity, and professional integrity in social work education.

7.1 Advancing Emotional Intelligence in AI

Current AI tools in education, including those for social work, often lack genuine affective and cultural sensitivity. The literature highlights the need to integrate sentiment analysis, affective computing, and culturally contextualized datasets to create more nuanced and empathetic client avatars and simulations. AI-driven emotional assessment is advancing through machine learning, facial recognition, and multimodal emotion recognition, fostering empathy and social cooperation in learning environments. However, challenges remain regarding accuracy, privacy, and cross-cultural validity. Future research should refine AI models for emotion recognition and ensure ethical, culturally sensitive implementation (Vistorte et al., 2024; Henriksen et al., 2025; Palmquist et al., 2025). Integrating social-emotional competencies (SEC) with AI literacy enhances educational outcomes by promoting personalized learning, collaboration, and ethical awareness. Embedding SEC into AI curricula prepares students and educators to navigate both technological and emotional challenges, supporting the development of holistic skills (Henriksen et al., 2025; Palmquist et al., 2025). Teacher education frameworks now emphasize operationalizing cultural sensitivity within AI systems, recognizing the limitations of current technologies in accounting for diverse social and emotional norms (Henriksen et al., 2025).

7.2 Interoperability and Integration

The literature underscores the potential of combining VR, AI chatbots, and documentation assistants into cohesive learning platforms. Studies demonstrate that AI-driven instructor assistants in VR environments can increase student engagement and reduce cognitive load, though improvements in learning outcomes are sometimes modest (Tracy & Spantidi, 2025; Yousif et al., 2025). Systematic reviews of AI chatbots in education reveal benefits for both students and educators, including personalized support, skill development, and time-saving assistance. However, successful integration requires addressing reliability, accuracy, and ethical concerns (Essel et al., 2022; Labadze et al., 2023; Roca et al., 2024). Research suggests that further exploration is needed to understand how these tools interact and impact learning outcomes, particularly in social work education. The integration of AI, AR, and VR has been demonstrated to enhance educational processes across various disciplines, including social work, and supports the achievement of the Sustainable Development Goals (Yousif et al., 2025). Future studies should investigate the design and efficacy of unified platforms that streamline training and assessment.

7.3 Longitudinal Outcomes and Efficacy

Most current studies report immediate improvements in student confidence, self-efficacy, and academic performance following AI-enabled training. For example, the use of chatbots and AI platforms has led to higher academic achievement and increased student satisfaction. However, there is a notable gap in longitudinal research evaluating whether these gains translate into sustained competency, improved client outcomes, or reduced turnover in professional practice (Essel et al., 2022; Palmquist et al., 2025; Yousif et al., 2025). Meta-analyses in related fields suggest that AI interventions can have lasting positive impacts, especially when personalized and adaptive tools are used (X.-Y. Wu, 2024). Future research should prioritize long-term studies that assess the durability of AI-enabled training effects in social work, including impacts on professional practice and client well-being.

7.4 Critical AI Literacy Within AI-Enabled Courses

Embedding critical AI literacy into social work curricula is essential for fostering reflective practitioners. The literature emphasizes the importance of teaching not only technical AI skills but also the ethical, societal, and career implications. Students and educators must be aware of AI's limitations, biases, and social impacts. Professional development programs should include training on AI technology, ethical considerations, and social-emotional learning to equip educators with the necessary skills (Labadze et al., 2023; Mouta et al., 2024; Palmquist et al., 2025). Studies show that integrating ethics and career futures into AI education is effective and age-appropriate, enabling students to recognize and address bias, consider societal impacts, and apply AI knowledge to help their communities (H. Zhang et al., 2023b). Scenario-based toolkits and participatory learning approaches can further enhance critical AI literacy and agency among students and educators (Mouta et al., 2024).

7.5 *Ethical AI Co-design with Service Users*

Participatory, stakeholder-centered design is increasingly recognized as vital to ensuring that AI simulations align with social work values and promote equity. Involving service users, clients, and communities in the co-design of AI tools, such as avatar personas, feedback rubrics, and scenario narratives, can help surface values, address biases, and ensure cultural relevance (H. Zhang et al., 2023b; Mouta et al., 2024; Lindgren et al., 2025). Participatory design processes have been demonstrated to incorporate empathy, social norms, and ethical considerations into AI systems, thereby supporting value-based and equitable outcomes (H. Zhang et al., 2023b; Lindgren et al., 2025). Ethical toolkits and scenario-based resources are being developed to guide educators and developers in implementing AI responsibly, with an emphasis on transparency, stakeholder involvement, and the mitigation of disparities in access and outcomes (Mouta et al., 2024). Future research should further investigate co-design methodologies and their impact on the effectiveness and equity of AI-enabled social work education.

8 Conclusion

AI-driven educational technologies are revolutionizing the way future social workers learn, practice, and reflect. From generative language models that create case vignettes and streamline documentation to simulation platforms such as Empathy Helper, Virtual Social Work Trainer, and Social Work Virtual, these tools provide scalable, immersive, and evidence-informed learning experiences. Virtual reality and AI-powered virtual patients deepen empathy and relational understanding, while agentic AI platforms enable structured micro-skills practice with personalized feedback. Yet realizing AI's full potential requires ethical integration, inclusive design, and sustained mentorship to ensure technology complements the humanistic essence of social work. Moving forward, continued research, participatory co-design, and responsive policy development will be critical to building an equitable, reflective, and ethically grounded future for AI in social work education.

Competing Interests The authors have no conflicts of interest to declare that are relevant to the content of this chapter.

References

Abulibdeh, A., Zaidan, E., & Abulibdeh, R. (2024). Navigating the confluence of artificial intelligence and education for sustainable development in the era of Industry 4.0: Challenges, opportunities, and ethical dimensions. *Journal of Cleaner Production, 437*, 140527. https://doi.org/10.1016/j.jclepro.2023.140527

Agllias, K., Pallas, P., Blakemore, T., & Johnston, L. (2021). Enhancing child protection practice through experience-based simulation learning: The social work big day in. *Social Work Education, 40*(8), 1024–1037. https://doi.org/10.1080/02615479.2020.1771301

Al-Zahrani, A. M. (2024). Unveiling the shadows: Beyond the hype of AI in education. *Heliyon, 10*(9), e30696. https://doi.org/10.1016/j.heliyon.2024.e30696

Asakura, K., Occhiuto, K., Tarshis, S., & Dubrowski, A. (2021). Designing and conducting healthcare simulations: Contributions from social work. *Cureus*. https://doi.org/10.7759/cureus.16193

Asakura, K., & Bogo, M. (2021). Editorial: The use of simulation in advancing clinical social work education and practice. *Clinical Social Work Journal, 49*(2), 111–116. https://doi.org/10.1007/s10615-021-00810-2

Ausserhofer, D., Tappeiner, W., Wieser, H., Serdaly, C., Simon, M., Zúñiga, F., & Favez, L. (2023). Administrative burden in Swiss nursing homes and its association with care workers' outcomes—A multicenter cross-sectional study. *BMC Geriatrics, 23*(1), 347. https://doi.org/10.1186/s12877-023-04022-w

Baker, E., & Jenney, A. (2023). Virtual simulations to train social workers for competency based learning: A scoping review. *Journal of Social Work Education, 59*(1), 8–31. https://doi.org/10.1080/10437797.2022.2039819

Baker, R. S., & Hawn, A. (2022). Algorithmic bias in education. *International Journal of Artificial Intelligence in Education, 32*(4), 1052–1092. https://doi.org/10.1007/s40593-021-00285-9

Bankins, S., & Formosa, P. (2023). The ethical implications of artificial intelligence (AI) for meaningful work. *Journal of Business Ethics, 185*(4), 725–740. https://doi.org/10.1007/s10551-023-05339-7

Berisha Qehaja, A. (2025). Strategic integration of artificial intelligence solutions to transform teaching practices in higher education. *Foresight, 27*(5), 970–991. https://doi.org/10.1108/FS-04-2024-0079

Blease, C., & Torous, J. (2023). ChatGPT and mental healthcare: Balancing benefits with risks of harms. *BMJ Mental Health, 26*(1), e300884. https://doi.org/10.1136/bmjment-2023-300884

Celik, I., Gedrimiene, E., Siklander, S., & Muukkonen, H. (2024). The affordances of artificial intelligence-based tools for supporting 21st-century skills: A systematic review. *Australasian Journal of Educational Technology*. https://doi.org/10.14742/ajet.9069

Chang, D. H., Lin, M. P.-C., Hajian, S., & Wang, Q. Q. (2023). Educational design principles of using AI chatbot that supports self-regulated learning in education: Goal setting, feedback, and personalization. *Sustainability, 15*(17), 12921. https://doi.org/10.3390/su151712921

Chernikova, O., Heitzmann, N., Stadler, M., Holzberger, D., Seidel, T., & Fischer, F. (2020). Simulation-based learning in higher education: A meta-analysis. *Review of Educational Research, 90*(4), 499–541. https://doi.org/10.3102/0034654320933544

Cordero, J., Torres-Zambrano, J., & Cordero-Castillo, A. (2024). Integration of generative artificial intelligence in higher education: Best practices. *Education Sciences, 15*(1), 32. https://doi.org/10.3390/educsci15010032

Craig, S. L., McInroy, L. B., Bogo, M., & Thompson, M. (2017). Enhancing competence in health social work education through simulation-based learning: Strategies from a case study. *Journal of Social Work Education, 53*(Suppl 1), S47–S58. https://doi.org/10.1080/10437797.2017.1288597

Cunningham, M. (2024). *Innovate for good: Social work case simulation goes virtual.* https://www.gmu.edu/news/2024-01/innovate-good-social-work-case-simulation-goes-virtual

Deupree, L. (2025, May 23). *Social work professor taps into teaching potential of virtual reality tools.* https://news.gsu.edu/2025/05/23/social-work-professor-taps-into-teaching-potential-of-virtual-reality-tools

Dodds, C., Heslop, P., & Meredith, C. (2018). Using simulation-based education to help social work students prepare for practice. *Social Work Education, 37*(5), 597–602. https://doi.org/10.1080/02615479.2018.1433158

Egonsdotter, G., & Bengtsson, S. (2023). Reflections in case-based learning: Experiences of computer-based simulations in social work education. *Journal of Social Work Education, 59*(4), 964–976. https://doi.org/10.1080/10437797.2022.2033655

Egonsdotter, G., & Israelsson, M. (2024). Computer-based simulations in social work education: A scoping review. *Research on Social Work Practice, 34*(1), 41–53. https://doi.org/10.1177/10497315221147016

Essel, H. B., Vlachopoulos, D., Tachie-Menson, A., Johnson, E. E., & Baah, P. K. (2022). The impact of a virtual teaching assistant (chatbot) on students' learning. *International Journal of Educational Technology in Higher Education, 19*(1), 57. https://doi.org/10.1186/s41239-022-00362-6

Farzan, M., Ebrahimi, H., Pourali, M., & Sabeti, F. (2025). Artificial intelligence-powered cognitive behavioral therapy chatbots: A systematic review. *Iranian Journal of Psychiatry, 20*(1), 102.

Fedele, A., Punzi, C., & Tramacere, S. (2024). The ALTAI checklist as a tool to assess ethical and legal implications for a trustworthy AI development. *Computer Law & Security Review, 53*, 105986. https://doi.org/10.1016/j.clsr.2024.105986

Ferraioli, F. (2025). Exploring the relationship of administrative burden with doctors' motivation and patients' experience of care. *International Review of Administrative Sciences, 91*(2), 167–183. https://doi.org/10.1177/00208523241302496

FGCU Digital Learning Blog. (2024). *Enhancing teaching with AI: How faculty can leverage NotebookLM.* https://www.fgcu.edu/digitallearning/digital-learning-blog/02-24-2025-notebooklm

Franco D'Souza, R., Mathew, M., Mishra, V., & Surapaneni, K. M. (2024). Twelve tips for addressing ethical concerns in implementing AI in medical education. *Medical Education Online, 29*(1), 2330250. https://doi.org/10.1080/10872981.2024.2330250

Garkisch, M., & Goldkind, L. (2024). Considering a unified model of AI-enhanced social work: A systematic review. *Journal of Human Rights and Social Work, 10*(1), 23–42. https://doi.org/10.1007/s41134-024-00326-y

Gordon, M., Daniel, M., Ajiboye, A., et al. (2024). A scoping review of artificial intelligence in medical education: BEME Guide No. 84. *Medical Teacher, 46*(4), 446–470. https://doi.org/10.1080/0142159X.2024.2314198

Guraya, S. Y. (2024). Transforming simulation in healthcare leveraging AI. *BMC Medical Education, 24*(1), 941. https://doi.org/10.1186/s12909-024-05916-y

Hazzan-Bishara, A., Kol, O., & Levy, S. (2025). The factors affecting teachers' adoption of AI technologies. *Education and Information Technologies, 30*(11), 15043–15069. https://doi.org/10.1007/s10639-025-13393-z

Heinsch, M., Cliff, K., Tickner, C., & Betts, D. (2023). Social work virtual. *Social Work Education*, 1–7. https://doi.org/10.1080/02615479.2023.2254796

Heinsch, M., Tickner, C., Betts, D., Cliff, K., Vincent, K., & Canty, J. (2024). Enhancing simulation in social work education using AI. *Advances in Social Work and Welfare Education, 25*(2) https://www.journal.anzswwer.org/index.php/advances/article/view/352

Henriksen, D., Creely, E., Gruber, N., & Leahy, S. (2025). Social-emotional learning and generative AI. *Journal of Teacher Education, 76*(3), 312–328. https://doi.org/10.1177/00224871251325058

Hodgson, D., Watts, L., & Gair, S. (2023). Artificial intelligence and implications for the Australian social work journal. *Australian Social Work, 76*(4), 425–427. https://doi.org/10.1080/0312407X.2023.2247833

Huttar, C. M., & BrintzenhofeSzoc, K. (2020). Virtual reality and computer simulation in social work education. *Journal of Social Work Education, 56*(1), 131–141. https://doi.org/10.1080/10437797.2019.1648221

Interprofessional Education Collaborative. (2025). *AI-powered virtual patients to enhance learner engagement.* https://summit2025.nexusipe.org/sessions/ai-powered-virtual-patients-enhance-learner-engagement-and-application-knowledge-among

Jefferies, G., Davis, C., Mason, J., & Yadav, R. (2024). Using simulation to prepare social work students for field education. *Social Work Education, 43*(5), 1369–1383. https://doi.org/10.1080/02615479.2023.2185219

Kellaway, H. (2025). Effective utilization of AI tools in university English education. *第一工科大学研究報告 / Daiichi Institute of Technology Annual Report, 37*, 81–96.

Klimova, B., Pikhart, M., & Kacetl, J. (2023). Ethical issues of AI-driven mobile apps. *Frontiers in Public Health, 10*, 1118116. https://doi.org/10.3389/fpubh.2022.1118116

Kolb, D. A. (1984). *Experiential learning: Experience as the source of learning and development.* Prentice Hall.

Kourgiantakis, T., & Lee, E. (2022). Developing mental health competencies using simulation. *Social Work Education, 41*(6), 1351–1366. https://doi.org/10.1080/02615479.2021.1955850

Kourgiantakis, T., & Lee, E. (2020). Social work practice education during the pandemic. *International Social Work, 63*(6), 761–765. https://doi.org/10.1177/0020872820959706

Kourgiantakis, T., Sewell, K. M., Lee, E., et al. (2020). Teaching note—Enhancing social work education in mental health. *Journal of Social Work Education, 56*(3), 587–594. https://doi.org/10.1080/10437797.2019.1656590

Labadze, L., Grigolia, M., & Machaidze, L. (2023). Role of AI chatbots in education. *International Journal of Educational Technology in Higher Education, 20*(1), 56. https://doi.org/10.1186/s41239-023-00426-1

Lanzieri, N., Dempsey, A., Olsen, A. F., Samelson, H., & Plass, J. L. (2025). Creating an AI powered VR simulation platform for social work skill development. *Journal of Technology in Human Services*, 1–29. https://doi.org/10.1080/15228835.2025.2565820

Lee, E., Kourgiantakis, T., & Bogo, M. (2020). Translating knowledge into practice. *Social Work Education, 39*(3), 329–349. https://doi.org/10.1080/02615479.2019.1620723

Levkovich, I., Haber, Y., Levi-Belz, Y., & Elyoseph, Z. (2025). A step toward the future? *Frontiers in Medicine, 12*, 1599900.

Lindgren, H., Lindvall, K., & Richter-Sundberg, L. (2025). Responsible design of an AI system for health behavior change. *Frontiers in Digital Health, 7*, 1436347. https://doi.org/10.3389/fdgth.2025.1436347

Lindsay, R., Yang, Y., & An, R. (n.d.). A pilot study of Empathy Helper. *Journal of Social Work Education*. Under peer review.

Lo, C. K. (2023). What is the impact of ChatGPT on education? A Rapid Review of the Literature. *Education Sciences, 13*(4), 410. https://doi.org/10.3390/educsci13040410

Matlala, S. (2021). Educators' perceptions of problem-based learning via simulation. *Curationis, 44*(1). https://doi.org/10.4102/curationis.v44i1.2094

Matto, H. C., Ihara, E. S., Cieslowski, B., Hines, D. A., & Booth, J. (2024). Virtual reality case simulation. *Social Work Education, 43*(9), 2774–2786. https://doi.org/10.1080/02615479.2023.2289452

McDonald, N., & Pan, S. (2020). Intersectional AI: A Study of How Information Science Students Think about Ethics and Their Impact. 4 (CSCW2), 1–19. https://doi.org/10.1145/3415218

Mitchell, B., Sarfati, D., & Stewart, M. (2022). COVID-19 and beyond. *Clinical Social Work Journal, 50*(1), 3–10. https://doi.org/10.1007/s10615-021-00788-x

Mohammadi, E., Thelwall, M., Cai, Y., Collier, T., Tahamtan, I., & Eftekhar, A. (2026). Is generative AI reshaping academic practices worldwide? *Information Processing & Management, 63*(1), 104350. https://doi.org/10.1016/j.ipm.2025.104350

Mortensen, M. (2024, November 5). *Using AI to train future social workers.* https://attheu.utah.edu/artificial-intelligence/using-ai-to-train-future-social-workers

Mouta, A., Torrecilla-Sánchez, E. M., & Pinto-Llorente, A. M. (2024). Design of a future scenarios toolkit. *Education and Information Technologies, 29*(9), 10473–10498. https://doi.org/10.1007/s10639-023-12229-y

National Association of Social Workers (NASW), Association of Social Work Boards (ASWB), Council on Social Work Education (CSWE), & Clinical Social Work Association (CSWA). (2017). *NASW, ASWB, CSWE, & CSWA standards for technology in social work practice.* https://www.socialworkers.org/LinkClick.aspx?fileticket=bq9JrB-oVm4%3d&portalid=0

Netsmart. (2024). *AI documentation assistant.* https://www.ntst.com/carefabric/careguidance-solutions/ai-documentation-assistant

Palmquist, A., Dis Isfold Sigurdardottir, H., & Myhre, H. (2025). Exploring interfaces and implications for AI literacy. *Journal of Computers in Education.* https://doi.org/10.1007/s40692-025-00354-1

Rane, N. (2024). Enhancing the quality of teaching and learning through generative AI. *TESOL and Technology Studies, 5*(1), 1–6. https://doi.org/10.48185/tts.v5i1.1000

Reimer, E. C. (2024). Examining the role of generative AI in enhancing social work education. *Social Sciences, 13*(12), 648. https://doi.org/10.3390/socsci13120648

Reyna, J. (2025). *The potential of Google NotebookLM for teaching and learning.* https://www.academia.edu/download/123907198/NotebookLM_paper_FINAL_2.pdf

Roca, M. D. L., Chan, M. M., Garcia-Cabot, A., Garcia-Lopez, E., & Amado-Salvatierra, H. (2024). The impact of a chatbot working as an assistant. *Computer Applications in Engineering Education, 32*(5), e22750. https://doi.org/10.1002/cae.22750

Roshanaei, M. (2024). Towards best practices for mitigating AI implicit bias. *Education and Information Technologies, 29*(14), 18959–18984. https://doi.org/10.1007/s10639-024-12605-2

Ruiz-Rojas, L. I., Salvador-Ullauri, L., & Acosta-Vargas, P. (2024). Collaborative working and critical thinking. *Sustainability, 16*(13), 5367. https://doi.org/10.3390/su16135367

Saeidnia, H. R., Hashemi Fotami, S. G., Lund, B., & Ghiasi, N. (2024). Ethical considerations in AI interventions. *Social Sciences, 13*(7), 381. https://doi.org/10.3390/socsci13070381

School of Social Work. (2024). *School of Social Work completes first phase of innovative virtual simulation pilot project.* https://www.usf.edu/cbcs/news/2024/social-work-virtual-simulation-project.aspx

Segal, M. (2025). Confronting and managing ethical dilemmas in social work using ChatGPT. *European Journal of Social Work, 28*(1), 155–167. https://doi.org/10.1080/13691457.2024.2377786

Share, P., & Pender, J. (2024). Role-playing the future: a simulation-based exploration of AI in social work. *Ubiquity Proceedings, 27.* https://doi.org/10.5334/uproc.149

Singer, J. B., Creswell Báez, J., & Rios, J. A. (2023). AI creates the message: Integrating AI Language Learning Models into Social Work Education and Practice. *Journal of Social Work Education, 59*(2), 294–302. https://doi.org/10.1080/10437797.2023.2189878

Social Work AI Magic. (2025a). *Social work tools for effective practices.* https://www.socialworkmagic.com/post/essential-digital-tools-for-enhancing-social-work-practices

Social Work AI Magic. (2025b). *Social work AI tools for simplified workflows.* https://www.socialworkmagic.com/post/simplifying-social-work-with-advanced-technology

Sollars, E. D., & Xenakis, N. (2021). Simulation-based Continuing Education in Health Care Social Work: A Case Study of Clinical Training Innovation. *Clinical Social Work Journal, 49*(2), 162–171. https://doi.org/10.1007/s10615-021-00806-y

Song, Y., Huang, L., Zheng, L., Fan, M., & Liu, Z. (2025). Interactions with generative AI chatbots: unveiling dialogic dynamics, students' perceptions, and practical competencies in creative problem-solving. *International Journal of Educational Technology in Higher Education, 22*(1), 12. https://doi.org/10.1186/s41239-025-00508-2

Stanford Teaching Commons. (2023). *Exploring the pedagogical uses of AI chatbots.* https://teachingcommons.stanford.edu/teaching-guides/artificial-intelligence-teaching-guide/exploring-pedagogical-uses-ai-chatbots

Tarshish, N. (2024). The administrative burden framework: A new horizon for research and practice in social work?. *Social Work, 69*(1), 86–94. https://doi.org/10.1093/sw/swad037

Tilmes, N. (2022). Disability, fairness, and algorithmic bias in AI recruitment. *Ethics and Information Technology, 24*(2), 21. https://doi.org/10.1007/s10676-022-09633-2

Tracy, K., & Spantidi, O. (2025). Impact of GPT-driven teaching assistants. *IEEE Transactions on Learning Technologies, 18*, 192–205. https://doi.org/10.1109/TLT.2025.3539179

Tufino, E. (2025). *NotebookLM as a Socratic physics tutor* [Preprint]. *arXiv.* https://doi.org/10.48550/arXiv.2504.09720

University of Utah College of Social Work. (n.d.). *Virtual skills & workforce trainer.* https://www.vswt.utah.edu/

Varona, D., & Suárez, J. L. (2022). Discrimination, bias, fairness, and trustworthy AI. *Applied Sciences, 12*(12), 5826. https://doi.org/10.3390/app12125826

Vistorte, A. O. R., Deroncele-Acosta, A., Martín Ayala, J. L., Barrasa, A., López-Granero, C., & Martí-González, M. (2024). Integrating artificial intelligence to assess emotions in learning environments. *Frontiers in Psychology, 15*, 1387089. https://doi.org/10.3389/fpsyg.2024.1387089

Will, J. (2025). Social work has a paperwork problem. *Dropbox Blog.* https://blog.dropbox.com/topics/work-culture/social-worker-burnout-ai-tools-casework-documentation

Wu, Q., Wang, Y., Lu, L., Chen, Y., Long, H., & Wang, J. (2022). Virtual simulation in undergraduate medical education. *Frontiers in Medicine, 9*, 855403. https://doi.org/10.3389/fmed.2022.855403

Wu, X.-Y. (2024). Artificial intelligence in L2 learning: a meta-analysis of contextual, instructional, and social-emotional moderators. *System, 126*, 103498. https://doi.org/10.1016/j.system.2024.103498

Yousif, N., Youssef, E., & Gad, S. (2025). E-Kalaiva AI technology in the education of social work students. *European Journal of Education, 60*(1), e12889. https://doi.org/10.1111/ejed.12889

Zawacki-Richter, O., Marín, V. I., Bond, M., & Gouverneur, F. (2019). Systematic review of research on artificial intelligence applications in higher education. *International Journal of Educational Technology in Higher Education, 16*(1), 39. https://doi.org/10.1186/s41239-019-0171-0

Zhang, A., Walker, O., Nguyen, K., Dai, J., Chen, A., & Lee, M. K. (2023a). Deliberating with AI: Improving Decision-Making for the Future through Participatory AI Design and Stakeholder Deliberation. *Proceedings of the ACM on Human-Computer Interaction, 7*(CSCW1), 1–32. https://doi.org/10.1145/3579601

Zhang, H., Lee, I., Ali, S., DiPaola, D., Cheng, Y., & Breazeal, C. (2023b). Integrating ethics and career futures with technical learning. *International Journal of Artificial Intelligence in Education, 33*(2), 290–324. https://doi.org/10.1007/s40593-022-00293-3

Zhang, S., & Stepteau-Watson, D. (2024). A systematic review and meta-analysis of simulated learning's effects. *Journal of Social Work Education, 60*(1), 115–131. https://doi.org/10.1080/10437797.2023.2236675

Zhang, Y., & Tang, Q. (2025). Integrating AI-generated content tools in higher education: A comparative analysis of interdisciplinary learning outcomes. Scientific Reports, 15, Article 25802. https://doi.org/10.1038/s41598-025-10941-y

Chapter 21
AI in Social Work Research

Yuyi Yang, Jingyi Huang, and Ruopeng An

1 Introduction

Artificial intelligence (AI) has evolved from a peripheral innovation into a central methodological component across the social sciences, including social work research. In recent years, scholars have adopted data mining and natural language processing (NLP) to identify social needs in case notes and community narratives. Predictive analytics have been used to model risk and support decision-making for service allocation in high-stakes contexts (Garkisch & Goldkind, 2025). Computer vision and socially assistive robots now enable the observation of social environments and the design of technology-mediated interventions (Hwang & Naik, 2023). Large language models (LLMs) further expand these possibilities by enabling the integration of qualitative and quantitative inquiry. They can assist in coding, synthesis, and hypothesis generation, yet they also raise new concerns about accuracy, bias, and data provenance (Hua et al., 2025). Collectively, these developments create opportunities to analyze complex, multimodal evidence at scale and to generate testable theories on how policies and programs affect individuals and communities.

However, the use of AI in social work also brings forward challenges that are particularly relevant to the profession's human rights mandate. The opacity of

Y. Yang (✉)
Division of Computational and Data Sciences, Washington University in St. Louis, St. Louis, MO, USA
e-mail: y.yuyi@wustl.edu

J. Huang · R. An
Silver School of Social Work, New York University, New York, NY, USA
e-mail: y.yuyi@wustl.edu; ra4605@nyu.edu

R. An, M. A. Lindsey (eds.), *Artificial Intelligence in Social Work*,
https://doi.org/10.1007/978-3-032-18443-6_21

black-box models complicates interpretability and validity (Reamer, 2023). Training data often reproduces structural inequities (Keddell, 2019), while AI-assisted research raises ethical questions about privacy, consent, and governance when sensitive client information is involved. Evidence from applied systems shows that implementation choices, such as model design, threshold selection, and decision support policies, can shape downstream outcomes and equity. Researchers are thus reminded to evaluate not only statistical performance but also institutional context and patterns of human–AI interaction. These methodological, ethical, and epistemological issues determine whether AI strengthens or undermines social work's commitments to dignity, justice, and transparency.

This chapter examines the current state of AI in social work research with three aims. First, it organizes emerging applications through a research design lens: descriptive and exploratory studies that employ data mining and NLP to map needs and narratives; predictive and analytical studies that develop and interrogate risk models across diverse human service systems; experimental and intervention studies that use socially assistive robots (SARs), computer vision, and conversational agents to test technology-mediated practices; and synthesis and conceptual studies that leverage LLMs, retrieval-augmented generation (RAG), and agentic AI to support theory building and knowledge integration. Second, the chapter identifies cross-cutting methodological, ethical, and epistemological challenges, including integrating AI into mixed-methods designs, pursuing reproducibility and interpretability, and protecting privacy, consent, and fairness. Finally, it reflects on how AI reshapes foundational questions of knowledge production through evolving forms of human-AI collaboration. The goal is to offer a critical, practice-informed roadmap for rigorous, transparent, and equity-centered research in social work.

2 Applications of AI in Social Work Research

The applications of AI in social work research are diverse, spanning multiple methodological traditions and analytic goals. Rather than operating as a one-size-fits-all solution, AI serves as a modular methodological partner that can augment different stages of inquiry, from data collection and pattern discovery to prediction, experimentation, and conceptual synthesis. Its usefulness depends on how well specific techniques are aligned with the epistemic aims and design requirements of a given study. The sections that follow examine how AI methods have been integrated into four major research designs in social work: descriptive and exploratory studies that map needs and narratives; predictive and analytical studies that model risks and complex outcomes; experimental and intervention studies that test technology-mediated practices; and synthesis and conceptual studies that use AI to generate, integrate, and refine theoretical frameworks.

2.1 *Descriptive/Exploratory Research*

Descriptive and exploratory studies in social work aim to observe social patterns, identify salient factors, and generate hypotheses without directly testing causal relationships. Traditional methods, such as surveys, administrative reports, and ethnographic fieldwork, have yielded valuable insights but are often constrained by limited sample sizes, subjective coding, and high labor demands. Artificial intelligence offers scalable tools that can process large, unstructured datasets and uncover latent structures. Among these, three techniques have become especially prominent: text mining, natural language processing (NLP), and causal AI.

2.1.1 Text Mining

Text mining refers to a family of computational techniques that transform unstructured text into analyzable data (Zhang & Li, 2023). Before the recent wave of LLMs, most text mining in social work relied on relatively simple but powerful pipelines that combined basic preprocessing, descriptive statistics, and classical machine learning (Hou & Huang, 2025). These methods remain valuable for descriptive and exploratory research because they are transparent, reproducible, and well aligned with qualitative and mixed-methods traditions.

A typical workflow begins with basic text preprocessing and descriptive counts. Researchers tokenize text into words or sentences, convert all characters to lowercase, remove punctuation, and sometimes remove high-frequency stopwords such as "the" or "and." Stemming or lemmatization is used to collapse word variants so that "helping," "helped," and "helps" are treated as instances of the same concept. From there, analysts compute word and phrase frequencies, often examining the most common unigrams, bigrams, and trigrams to gain an initial sense of what respondents discuss in open-ended survey items, case notes, or online discussions. Keyword-in-context (KWIC) or concordance views extend these counts by showing each occurrence of a target term with a small window of surrounding words, which is crucial for qualitative interpretation (Manning & Schütze, 1999). For instance, it is not only how often "violence" or "stigma" appears that matters, but whether these terms are used to describe personal experience, institutional practices, or public discourse.

To move beyond single words, text mining frequently incorporates co-occurrence analysis, collocations, and simple networks. Co-occurrence tables record which words or codes tend to appear within the same sentence, paragraph, or document (Callon et al., 1991). These tables can reveal, for example, that terms related to "stigma" regularly co-occur with "healthcare," "police," or "child welfare," suggesting relationships among concepts that merit deeper qualitative exploration. Collocation and n-gram analysis (Smadja, 1991) help identify multiword expressions such as "food insecurity," "case manager," or "risk assessment" that function as meaningful units in practice settings. Researchers often visualize these relationships as networks, where nodes represent words or codes and edges reflect the strength of co-occurrence. Clusters of tightly connected terms can surface emergent topics, such as intersecting discussions of housing, mental health, and criminal justice, which are then interpreted using domain knowledge and qualitative reading.

Topic modeling and related unsupervised methods offer another set of tools that became popular in mixed-methods work before generative AI. Latent Dirichlet Allocation (LDA) represents documents as mixtures of a small number of topics, each defined by a probabilistic distribution over words (Kaur & Wallace, 2024). In social work research, LDA has been used to identify candidate themes across large corpora of narrative records, such as thousands of case summaries or social media posts, and to compare topic prevalence across time periods, client groups, or intervention conditions (Benites-Lazaro et al., 2018; Sun et al., 2024; Park, 2024).

Structural topic models extend this approach by allowing document-level covariates, such as gender or service setting, to influence topic prevalence and, in some cases, topic content. Earlier work also employed latent semantic analysis and other matrix factorization techniques to uncover latent dimensions in term-document matrices, which can support clustering, visualization, or exploratory scaling of concepts (Qi et al., 2024b; Yeasin et al., 2009). Dictionary-based sentiment analysis tools, which score texts using predefined lexicons of positive and negative words, have been used to approximate attitudes or emotional tone in narratives about policy changes, service experiences, or public campaigns (Hardeniya & Borikar, 2016).

Once some human coding exists, supervised machine learning methods can be trained to predict codes or categories at scale. These approaches typically represent text segments using bag-of-words or TF-IDF vectors, then fit models such as logistic regression, support vector machines, naive Bayes, or tree-based classifiers (Dawar et al., 2023). In social work contexts, such models have been used to predict whether a sentence or note mentions particular constructs, for example, structural racism (Mohebbi et al., 2023), housing instability (Wilson et al., 2020), or intimate partner violence (Ha et al., 2021), and to prioritize ambiguous or high-risk segments for human review through active learning (Hughes et al., 2021). In systematic reviews (Neubauer et al., 2023; Novitzky et al., 2023) of computational text analysis on domestic and intimate partner violence, these supervised models appear alongside unsupervised methods and rule-based systems, illustrating how relatively simple text mining pipelines can scale qualitative coding to tens or hundreds of thousands of documents while still relying on human judgment for interpretation.

Together, these pre-generative AI text mining techniques provide a bridge between traditional qualitative analysis and more advanced NLP methods. They enable social work researchers to summarize large bodies of narrative data, surface candidate themes and relationships, and generate hypotheses for subsequent in-depth qualitative or quantitative investigation, while maintaining a level of methodological transparency that supports critical reflection and community engagement.

2.1.2 Natural Language Processing

NLP is a branch of AI that enables computers to understand, generate, and analyze human language. It integrates techniques from linguistics, computer science, and machine learning to process unstructured text at scale. Modern NLP systems combine rule-based methods, statistical modeling, and deep learning architectures such as transformers to capture syntax, semantics, and context. The recent surge in NLP—accelerated by advances in neural networks and the availability of large textual corpora—has enabled sophisticated linguistic analysis with unprecedented accuracy. These capabilities are particularly valuable in social work research, where much of the field's evidence is embedded in qualitative narratives, clinical notes, and open-ended case reports. By automating the extraction and organization of these narratives, NLP enables researchers to uncover patterns in language use, identify emerging social issues, and transform qualitative insights into analyzable data, thereby offering a promising paradigm to bridge the gap between qualitative inquiry and large-scale quantitative analysis.

In applied research, NLP has been used to convert unstructured text into structured datasets suitable for empirical analysis. Bako and colleagues, for example, developed an NLP and machine learning pipeline to classify social work interventions recorded in electronic health record (EHR) notes (Bako et al., 2021). Their algorithm successfully categorized thousands of intervention descriptions, demonstrating the feasibility of automated extraction. The authors argued that such tools could improve workforce planning and facilitate research on the effectiveness of interventions. Another notable application involves the detection of intimate partner violence (IPV) within health records. Tabaie and colleagues compared structured coding with NLP-based approaches. They found that a rule-based NLP algorithm identified IPV-related emergency-department encounters with 99.5% precision by scanning clinical notes for situational cues (Tabaie et al., 2022). They suggested that near-real-time detection could enhance surveillance and enable faster social work intervention.

Beyond clinical data, NLP has also been applied to analyze social media and police reports (An et al., 2023; Yang et al., 2023). Neubauer and colleagues conducted a systematic review that identified 22 studies using computational text analysis to explore domestic and intimate partner violence (Neubauer et al., 2023). These studies employed a range of techniques under the broader NLP umbrella, combining rule-based classification with machine learning and deep learning, as well as topic modeling for pattern discovery. Such approaches integrate language understanding with statistical and neural representations, enabling researchers to detect patterns that traditional manual coding cannot capture. Most datasets were drawn from social media platforms (15 studies), while others originated from police reports, health records, and social service agencies. Typical research tasks included analyzing the #WhyIStayed campaign to understand reasons for remaining in or leaving abusive relationships and detecting crisis-related posts on Facebook. Together, these studies illustrate how NLP and related AI methods extend text mining capabilities, enabling the systematic exploration of sensitive social issues while underscoring the need for ethical safeguards regarding privacy, consent, and data representativeness.

2.1.3 Causal AI

Causal AI refers to a family of methods that use explicit causal models to move beyond correlation and explore how changes in one part of a system can affect another (Mannava, 2024). Central tools include directed acyclic graphs (DAGs), structural causal models, and potential outcomes frameworks, which allow researchers to encode assumptions about confounders, mediators, and selection mechanisms (Chernozhukov et al., 2024). For descriptive and exploratory social work research, these models are especially valuable because they provide a transparent way to articulate hypothesized causal structures, identify which variables must be measured and adjusted for, and generate testable hypotheses about how policies and programs shape client outcomes.

In practice, DAGs and related causal diagrams can be used to map complex service systems, such as child welfare, homelessness prevention, or integrated behavioral health care. By visually representing relationships among family characteristics, neighborhood conditions, prior system involvement, and service decisions, social work researchers can distinguish between confounders that should be controlled, colliders that should not be conditioned on, and mediators that may carry the effect of an intervention (Austin et al., 2019; Poppe et al., 2025). These diagrams help clarify whether an observed association, such as between screening scores and placement decisions, is plausibly causal or likely to be confounded by unmeasured structural factors. They also inform data collection and model specification by highlighting which variables are essential to include before conducting predictive or evaluative analyses.

Causal AI also encompasses algorithmic approaches that combine machine learning with causal inference to estimate treatment effects and identify heterogeneous impacts across subgroups. Methods such as causal forests, targeted maximum likelihood estimation, and double machine learning can use high-dimensional administrative and narrative data to estimate how specific interventions, such as in-home services versus foster care placement, supportive housing versus usual shelter use, or chatbot-based psychoeducation versus standard information, differentially affect outcomes for clients with distinct profiles (Lechner & Mareckova, 2024; McConnell & Lindner, 2019). These models remain exploratory when used to generate hypotheses about which families or communities are most likely to benefit from a given program. Still, they can guide subsequent confirmatory studies and more rigorous impact evaluations.

Finally, causal discovery techniques use statistical constraints to search for plausible DAG structures directly from data under explicit assumptions. Although still emerging in social work, these methods may help researchers uncover candidate causal pathways in complex systems where theory is underdeveloped, such as the interplay among online misinformation, help-seeking behavior, and service engagement. For example, Tian and Rizoiu (2025) used a structural causal modeling and counterfactual framework to estimate how public attention signals, such as Google search trends, causally shape engagement of misinformation. Their findings show that temporal shifts in information-seeking behavior produce measurable causal effects on online participation, illustrating how causal AI can reveal influence pathways relevant to help-seeking and service engagement. Because causal AI makes assumptions explicit and invites critical scrutiny, it fits well with participatory and community-engaged research traditions. When combined with qualitative inquiry and practitioner knowledge, causal AI can support more transparent theorizing about mechanisms of change and more thoughtful design of interventions that target leverage points within social systems.

2.2 *Predictive/Analytical Research*

Predictive and analytical research in social work uses AI to anticipate future outcomes, characterize risk and resilience profiles, and identify leverage points for intervention. Early work focused on relatively transparent models such as regularized regression and tree-based ensembles built from structured administrative data (Shortreed et al., 2023; Khan et al., 2024b). Over time, however, the methodological repertoire has expanded to include unsupervised learning, dimensionality reduction, multimodal prediction, and forecasting models, as well as privacy-preserving training schemes such as federated learning (Che et al., 2023; Nikolaidis et al., 2023). These approaches allow researchers to discover natural groupings of clients, uncover latent dimensions of need, combine text, images, and sensor streams, and generate short- and long-term forecasts of service demand or risk trajectories. Together, they broaden the ways predictive analytics can inform social work practice, moving beyond single-outcome risk scores toward richer descriptions of patterns, pathways, and potential intervention touchpoints.

2.2.1 Regularized Regression Models and Structured Predictors

Regularized regression approaches, such as LASSO, ridge regression, and elastic net, remain widely used in social service analytics due to their interpretability and ability to handle large predictor sets. One influential example is the Allegheny Family Screening Tool (AFST), which employs regularized logistic regression to estimate the likelihood of adverse child welfare outcomes using hundreds of administrative and demographic variables (Allegheny County Department of Human Services, Office of Analytics, Technology and Planning, 2024). Trained on historical referral data and periodically recalibrated, AFST has been shown to reduce unnecessary investigations for low-risk referrals, improve decision consistency at higher risk levels, and be associated with reduced racial disparities at some decision points. Similarly, Rosholm et al. (2024) analyzed nearly 200,000 child maltreatment referrals in Denmark using logistic regression and LASSO, reporting AUROC values above 0.87 and demonstrating strong correlations between predicted risk and later adverse outcomes. These structured models illustrate how regularized regression can support prioritization, triage, and early-warning analytics while maintaining statistical transparency.

2.2.2 Tree-Based Ensemble Methods

Tree-based ensemble models, such as random forests and gradient boosting, offer a more flexible alternative for capturing nonlinear relationships and complex interactions among risk factors. They have been particularly impactful in homelessness and housing instability research. Byrne et al. (2019) applied random forests to electronic medical records from more than 5.8 million U.S. veterans, achieving substantially higher sensitivity than logistic regression in predicting positive homelessness screens, at the cost of some reduction in specificity. Building on this, Zamora-Resendiz et al. (2023) integrated document features and structured EMR data to predict homelessness risk months before formal screening, with the top 1% of model-identified individuals being 34 times more likely to screen positive than a random selection. Such results demonstrate that ensemble methods offer superior early-detection capability and can uncover latent high-risk groups missed by traditional screening.

2.2.3 Multi-model Decision Support Systems and Placement Optimization

More recent work has explored multi-model systems that combine machine learning predictions with placement decision algorithms. Trudeau et al. (2023) developed 50 random-forest models to predict successful placement for youths entering psychiatric residential treatment or community care, achieving AUROCs of 0.66–0.79. In validation analyses, 80% of youths matched to model-recommended placements exceeded the predicted outcome, suggesting strong alignment between algorithmic recommendations and real-world trajectories. Beyond youth treatment settings, multi-model placement systems incorporate diverse predictors—clinical histories, behavioral indicators, prior service use, and contextual variables—to generate individualized risk-benefit profiles that augment professional judgment. These systems help reduce reliance on subjective heuristics, promote equity in resource allocation, and support multidisciplinary teams in allocating scarce high-intensity services.

2.2.4 Unsupervised, Multimodal, and Privacy-Preserving Predictive Models

In addition to supervised prediction of specific outcomes, social work researchers increasingly use unsupervised learning to explore heterogeneity in client populations and service trajectories (Annaki et al., 2022). Cluster analysis, for example, Fink (2025) applied k-means, Gaussian mixture models, and hierarchical clustering to identify subgroups of individuals who shared similar behavioral and demographic patterns, demonstrating how unsupervised methods can reveal latent structures across many variables within complex social data. Studies have applied these methods to identify distinct profiles of child welfare involvement, combinations of housing instability, mental health symptoms, and justice contact, or trajectories of substance use and treatment engagement (Putnam-Hornstein et al., 2013). Rather than predicting a single binary outcome, clustering reveals naturally occurring subgroups (Chin & Collins, 2024), such as families with high material hardship but low formal system contact, that may require different outreach strategies or policy responses. Mixture models and trajectory clustering extend this logic to longitudinal data, grouping individuals by their patterns of change over time rather than only by their status at a single point in time.

Dimensionality reduction methods such as principal component analysis (PCA) and related factor models provide another set of tools for analytical research. When administrative datasets contain dozens or hundreds of correlated indicators, PCA can summarize them into a smaller number of composite indices that capture underlying constructs such as neighborhood disadvantage, service complexity, or cumulative adversity (Friesen et al., 2016). These latent dimensions can then be used as predictors in outcome models or as grouping variables to examine how intervention effects vary across contexts. In recent work, autoencoder-based representation learning plays a similar role, compressing high-dimensional records or free-text embeddings into dense feature vectors that preserve substantial variation while reducing noise (Kane et al., 2023).

Multimodal predictive models integrate heterogeneous data sources that increasingly characterize social work practice, including structured records, narrative notes, images, audio, and sensor data. For instance, models may combine case characteristics, NLP-processed worker notes, and neighborhood indicators to forecast referrals to child protective services, or they may integrate wearable sensor streams with self-reported mood to predict crisis episodes in community mental health (Kline et al., 2022; Saha et al., 2021). Sequence models and other time-aware architectures can learn temporal patterns in these multimodal streams, improving forecasts of short-term risk or service utilization. For example, Othman et al. (2024) used a multimodal time-series framework combining social media emotion signals and hospital emergency data to forecast public mental health needs during the COVID-19 pandemic in Singapore, showing how external text-derived indicators can anticipate surges in crisis visits. At the system level, Megouo and Pierre (2024) developed an ensemble forecasting model that accurately predicted emergency medical call volumes by integrating temporal, spatial, and environmental features, demonstrating how forecasting methods can support proactive planning of staff and resources across human service agencies.

Finally, federated learning and related privacy-preserving techniques address the reality that much social work data is fragmented across agencies that cannot easily pool records due to legal, ethical, or logistical constraints. In a federated learning setup, models are trained across multiple organizations or jurisdictions without sharing raw data. Each site computes model updates locally, and only encrypted summaries are aggregated, enabling the development of more generalizable risk models or resource allocation tools while limiting data transfer (Loftus et al., 2022). Although still emerging in social work, these approaches are being explored in allied fields such as healthcare and education, and they hold promise for cross-agency predictive analytics in areas such as homelessness prevention, child welfare, and intimate partner violence services (Abbas et al., 2024). At the same time, they raise new questions about governance, equity, and accountability when decision support tools are built from data that no single stakeholder can easily inspect (Eden et al., 2025).

2.3 *Experimental/Intervention Research*

Experimental and intervention research leverages AI-driven technologies to test innovative methods to enhance client well-being, strengthen practitioner competencies, and improve the delivery of social services, unlike predictive analytics, which primarily model risk and outcomes. Experimental approaches use AI as an active component of the intervention itself. A growing set of technologies, such as socially assistive robots, conversational agents, and computer-vision-enabled tools, is increasingly being deployed to deliver therapeutic interactions, provide skills training, monitor behavioral change, and augment frontline practice. These tools are particularly well-suited to social work because they support consistent, scalable, and context-sensitive engagement with clients while addressing longstanding challenges in the field, including workforce shortages, variability in service quality, and the need for culturally responsive and accessible interventions.

2.3.1 Socially Assistive Robots

Socially assistive robots (SARs) integrate AI-based perception, language processing, and adaptive decision-making to provide support through social interaction rather than physical labor (Yang et al., 2025). Contemporary SARs rely on natural language understanding, speech generation, emotion recognition algorithms, and behavior planning models to sustain conversation, respond to user affect, prompt activities, and deliver tailored feedback. These technical affordances make SARs well-suited for experimental research in social work, where investigators can systematically vary the robot's dialogue style, emotional responsiveness, or prompting strategy to test their causal effects on client engagement, psychological well-being, or skill acquisition. A scoping review of SARs in mental health care identifies two primary forms used in such studies: Companion or animal-like robots, which emulate features of animal-assisted therapy without the risks of allergens or care burden; and humanoid or service-oriented robots, which support more natural verbal and nonverbal interaction and can autonomously deliver structured activities (Guemghar et al., 2022). Early experiments show that SARs can reduce distress among hospitalized children (Trost et al., 2019), model social behaviors for youth with autism (Cabibihan et al., 2013), and support exercise adherence and health monitoring among older adults (Gadde et al., 2011). However, empirical evidence remains limited by small samples and narrow diagnostic coverage.

A recent randomized controlled trial by Murayama and Takase (2025) demonstrates how SARs function as an experimental intervention tool. Community-dwelling older adults in Japan were assigned either to a humanoid robot intervention—featuring AI-driven conversation, reminders, and cognitive games—or to care-as-usual. Relative to controls, the robot group reported significant reductions in loneliness and improvements in psychological well-being. Qualitative responses highlighted the robot's perceived emotional support, companionship, and cognitive stimulation. Notably, the study illustrates how SARs enable researchers to isolate the effects of specific communicative or behavioral modules (e.g., empathic responses, motivational prompts) delivered consistently across participants—capabilities that are difficult to achieve with human facilitators. Thus, SARs represent a promising platform for controlled experimentation in social work research, allowing investigators to test theoretically informed mechanisms of social support, engagement, and behavior change within highly standardized yet socially meaningful interactions.

2.3.2 Conversational Agents

Modern conversational agents (CAs) increasingly rely on advanced AI capabilities—including LLMs, context-aware dialogue management, reinforcement learning-based adaptation, and agentic planning systems—to deliver interactive, human-like communication. Unlike earlier rule-based or decision-tree systems, LLM-enabled CAs can interpret open-ended user input, generate personalized responses, and sustain emotionally attuned dialogue. These technologies are highly valuable in experimental social work research because they enable investigators to manipulate variables such as empathic style, motivational strategies, cultural tailoring, or fidelity to therapeutic protocols in a controlled yet scalable manner. In this sense, CAs function not simply as service tools but as experimental instruments: they can standardize intervention delivery, model specific communication mechanisms, and simulate practitioner–client interactions for training, mechanism testing, and causal inference.

A growing body of evidence demonstrates the potential and limitations of these systems. A 2023 meta-analysis of 32 randomized controlled trials found that CA interventions produced modest but significant short-term improvements in depressive symptoms, generalized and specific anxiety, distress, stress, and quality of life, with personalization and empathic responsiveness identified as key active ingredients (He et al., 2023). Related scoping reviews show that AI chatbots used for professional training, often combining elements of cognitive-behavioral therapy and scenario-based simulation, can reduce anxiety and burnout among health and social care workers. However, the evidence remains sparse (Baek et al., 2025). Although these studies primarily examine CAs as therapeutic or training interventions, they also demonstrate that CAs can reliably deliver communicative components, such as empathic responding, motivational prompts, and structured feedback, consistently across participants. This reliability is a necessary methodological condition for using CAs as experimental instruments. For social work research, these findings are significant: CAs allow researchers to experimentally test the effects of communication style, feedback mechanisms, and relational behaviors on client engagement and practitioner skill development; evaluate the scalability and consistency of intervention protocols; and investigate mechanisms of change within digitally mediated helping relationships. As such, AI-powered conversational systems serve as versatile research platforms for probing, refining, and experimentally validating interventions in social work.

2.3.3 Computer Vision-Enabled Interventions

Computer vision refers to methods that allow computers to interpret information from images and video, such as detecting objects, estimating body pose, or recognizing patterns in the built environment (Mendes-Neves et al., 2023). In social work research, computer vision-enabled interventions typically use cameras or other imaging devices to monitor risk, support safety, and augment practitioner judgment in real time (Bernasco et al., 2021; Prakash et al., 2023). These systems do not replace social workers or caregivers. Instead, they provide additional streams of information that can prompt timely follow-up, inform assessment, and guide resource allocation.

A critical application area involves safety monitoring and risk detection in settings such as long-term care facilities, domestic violence shelters, and supported housing (Mantler et al., 2021; Ullah et al., 2025). For example, vision models can be trained to detect falls, wandering, or prolonged inactivity among older adults who live alone or in assisted living. Chen and Fisher (2023) developed the MISO system, which uses RGB-D cameras to monitor inactivity and automatically alert caregivers when it detects prolonged stillness or a possible fall, allowing staff to check in immediately rather than relying on periodic in-person rounds or self-reports. Similar approaches have been explored for detecting aggressive incidents or escalating conflict in residential group homes, where automatic alerts can trigger de-escalation protocols or call additional staff to the scene (Thomas & Balamurugan,

2024). In these applications, computer vision functions as an always-on observer that can recognize predefined risk signatures and route cases to human decision-makers.

A second line of work uses computer vision to assess physical and neighborhood environments that shape social work concerns. Researchers have analyzed street view images, satellite imagery, and building photographs to quantify features such as housing conditions, sidewalk quality, the presence of green space, and signs of physical disorder (Larkin et al., 2025; Suel et al., 2021). These image-based indicators can be linked to administrative data to examine how environmental characteristics relate to crime, child maltreatment reports, chronic disease, and service utilization (Wu & Wang, 2024; Yue et al., 2022). For instance, image-based measures of housing disrepair or neighborhood blight can help identify blocks where housing inspection, lead abatement, or community outreach programs may be most needed. Ercan and Mathyalakan (2024) developed a computer vision-based system that automatically inspects public housing images to detect safety risks such as clutter, obstruction, or structural damage, enabling authorities to prioritize inspections and respond more quickly to potential hazards. In this way, computer vision supports place-based interventions by turning visual cues into structured data that can be mapped and tracked over time.

Computer vision has also been used to support practice and training by analyzing video-recorded interactions. In child welfare, researchers have explored tools that estimate synchrony between caregivers and children during play sessions by tracking gaze, proximity, and body posture (Isaev et al., 2023; Weng et al., 2025). In mental health and school-based counseling, computer vision models have been piloted to detect basic nonverbal cues, such as eye contact, head nods, and extended silences, during simulated sessions (Inoue et al., 2021; Vail et al., 2021). For example, Choi et al. (2024) developed a virtual counseling system that used computer vision to model nonverbal compassion behaviors—such as gaze alignment, facial mimicry, and head-nodding—and found that these cues improved perceived empathy and communication effectiveness in counseling simulations. These signals can be summarized for supervision, providing students and practitioners with structured feedback on engagement patterns that would be difficult to track manually across many sessions. Although such systems are not used to evaluate performance in a high-stakes way, they illustrate how vision-enabled analytics can serve as mirrors that help practitioners reflect on their own practice.

Finally, several computer vision applications aim to promote accessibility and inclusion for people with disabilities, which is a central concern in many social work settings. Mobile applications that recognize printed text, signage, or everyday objects can help people with visual impairments navigate public spaces and service environments (Chimwaza & Jimu, 2024). Sign language recognition and gesture-based interfaces can facilitate communication between deaf or hard-of-hearing clients and providers who do not share a common signed language (Alsharif et al., 2025). In child and adolescent services, vision-based tools have been used experimentally to support social skills training. For example, in the ALTRIRAS system developed by Almeida et al. (2019), which uses real-time facial expression recognition to give children immediate visual feedback during structured emotion recognition games, helping them practice identifying and responding to basic emotions. These interventions blend human support with automated cues to lower barriers to participation and communication.

Together, these examples show that computer vision-enabled interventions can extend social work practice beyond traditional text and tabular data, bringing visual information about bodies, spaces, and interactions into analytic and decision-making systems. They also set the stage for critical ethical questions about surveillance, consent, and potential misuse, including applications such as targeted policing and facial recognition, which are taken up in more detail in later sections on equity and governance.

2.4 Synthesis/Conceptual Research

Synthesis and conceptual research in social work examines how AI systems can generate new knowledge, integrate complex evidence, and contribute to theory building. Unlike descriptive or exploratory analyses that characterize patterns in existing data, this strand of research uses AI as an intellectual instrument: a tool for organizing large bodies of information, surfacing latent patterns, articulating conceptual frameworks, and interrogating underlying assumptions about human behavior and social systems (Alam, 2025; Mökander & Schroeder, 2021). Recent scholarship argues that LLMs can function as synthetic theorists, capable of scanning disciplinary corpora, mapping conceptual spaces, and proposing candidate mechanisms for subsequent evaluation (Zhang et al., 2025). Experimental work in scientific discovery platforms further shows that LLMs can integrate heterogeneous evidence sources to generate plausible hypotheses and identify unrecognized linkages across literatures, suggesting that such systems may assist researchers in developing new theoretical propositions (Jiang et al., 2025; Qi et al., 2024a).

The advantages of AI-driven synthesis are especially salient in a field like social work, where knowledge is fragmented across disciplines and where theories often integrate psychological, relational, structural, and policy-level determinants. Studies evaluating LLM-supported evidence synthesis have shown that models can reconcile conflicting findings, trace multidimensional mechanisms, and generate structured summaries that approximate expert reasoning, thereby supporting conceptual integration across domains (Dennstädt et al., 2024). In related work, multi-agent LLM systems have been used to orchestrate multi-step conceptual tasks such as generating alternative framings, evaluating competing logic models, and constructing causal diagrams from complex policy or program documents (Alba et al., 2025). Through these capabilities—rapid evidence aggregation, counterfactual reasoning, and iterative conceptual refinement—AI serves not merely as a summarization tool but as a collaborator for conceptual innovation, complementing human judgment and extending the methodological repertoire available for theory-driven social work scholarship.

2.4.1 Large Language Model-Based Conceptual Synthesis and Theory Development

LLMs offer powerful capabilities for synthesis and conceptual development because they can process large, interdisciplinary evidence bases and generate structured insights that traditionally required extensive expert labor. In conceptual and theory-building research, particularly in fields such as social work, where explanations span multiple levels of analysis, LLMs enable researchers to rapidly map conceptual linkages, compare competing frameworks, surface latent constructs, and propose theoretical extensions that can later be empirically tested. Compared to manual qualitative synthesis or expert-driven literature reviews, LLMs provide scale, speed, and the ability to integrate heterogeneous sources, reducing human bias while enabling iterative refinement of conceptual models.

For example, a recent study on literature screening workflows demonstrated that LLMs can be used to evaluate the relevance of scientific publications based on title and abstract, achieving high sensitivity in identifying eligible studies for systematic reviews while substantially reducing the number of records that require manual screening (Dennstädt et al., 2024). In that work, the model was prompted to apply prespecified inclusion criteria, assign a relevance score, and generate short justifications, allowing human reviewers to focus on borderline cases and audit the reasoning behind inclusion or exclusion decisions. This type of application illustrates how LLMs can participate in conceptual synthesis not only by summarizing existing studies, but also by shaping the evidence base from which theories and practice guidelines are derived. Another perspective article argues that LLMs are transforming the scientific method, from hypothesis generation through discovery, by enabling automated reasoning across large disciplinary corpora (Zhang et al., 2025). The authors describe pipelines in which LLMs map existing constructs, identify gaps or contradictions in current theories, suggest novel hypotheses, and even propose candidate study designs or measurement strategies that can then be refined and evaluated by human researchers. Finally, in computational social science, a review of LLM applications shows that these models are already being used to generate structured insights from heterogeneous text datasets, supporting tasks such as stance detection, social network inference, and topic modeling in social system research (Thapa et al., 2025). In that literature, LLMs have been used to code frames in protest speech, infer relational ties from co-mentioned actors in news coverage, and derive high-level themes from extensive collections of policy documents, thereby providing building blocks for new theories of polarization, mobilization, and institutional change.

2.4.2 Retrieval-Augmented Generation

Retrieval-Augmented Generation (RAG) frameworks (Gao et al., 2023) are well-suited to social work synthesis and conceptual research because they combine the generative reasoning of LLMs with the evidentiary grounding of retrieval systems.

This allows researchers to produce concept maps, cross-study comparisons, policy analyses, and theoretical arguments that are explicitly tied to cited empirical sources. Whereas traditional LLM-based synthesis may rely on latent statistical patterns learned during pretraining, RAG can systematically retrieve, summarize, and contrast large volumes of research, reducing hallucination and increasing transparency by grounding outputs in verifiable documents.

In healthcare, RAG has been used to reduce factual errors and produce trustworthy, evidence-linked responses. For example, a recent COVID-19 fact-checking study integrating GPT-4 with multiple RAG variants demonstrated substantial gains in accuracy and significant reductions in hallucinations when verifying claims against a corpus of 130,000 peer-reviewed articles, highlighting the value of retrieval grounding for high-stakes scientific synthesis (Li et al., 2025). Building on this logic, a 2024 ACL paper showed that RAG-generated explanations grounded in local news articles about socioeconomic problems were rated higher than standard LLM outputs on factual accuracy, completeness, and contextual relevance. In that work, the system retrieved local reporting about housing, employment, and social programs, then used those documents to generate explanations of neighborhood-level challenges and policy options, illustrating how retrieval grounding can anchor abstract reasoning in place-based evidence (Dumitru et al., 2024).

Emerging applications in social and human services further illustrate the breadth of issues RAG can address. Pilot systems for homelessness services have used RAG to answer questions about shelter availability, eligibility criteria, and local outreach programs by retrieving information from municipal service directories, agency websites, and community resource guides, while linking users back to the underlying sources (Khan et al., 2024a; Singh et al., 2025). In child welfare and family services, prototype tools retrieve policy manuals, case law summaries, and prior assessment reports when workers ask questions about placement options, visitation rules, or mandated timelines, helping align decisions with current regulations and evidence without requiring staff to search multiple databases manually (Wu et al., 2025). In public health and social policy communication, experimental RAG assistants have been designed to respond to questions about social benefits, vaccine safety, and stigma-sensitive topics by retrieving passages from guidelines, systematic reviews, and advocacy reports, then generating tailored explanations that preserve citations and highlight conflicting or conditional findings (Amugongo et al., 2025). Together, these examples suggest that RAG could support social work researchers and practitioners in creating comprehensive evidence syntheses, exploring contradictory findings across disciplines, and generating contextually grounded policy and practice narratives explicitly tied to verifiable documents.

2.4.3 Agentic AI

Agentic AI extends beyond static text generation by enabling multi-step reasoning, planning, tool use, and autonomous execution of research tasks (Ali & Dornaika, 2025). For synthesis and conceptual research in social work, agentic systems offer unique advantages: they can orchestrate literature searches, evaluate the quality of evidence, compare theoretical models, generate alternative conceptual framings, and iteratively refine hypotheses in response to researcher feedback. This workflow-driven autonomy distinguishes agentic AI not only from traditional qualitative synthesis but also from standard LLM or RAG outputs, enabling more systematic exploration of complex social phenomena and multi-level theories.

Emerging evidence shows that agentic AI can support resource-intensive qualitative synthesis tasks (Lee et al., 2025; Xu et al., 2025a). One study evaluating GPT-based agents for thematic analysis demonstrated that carefully designed, stepwise prompting workflows could autonomously extract, synthesize, and justify study-level themes from qualitative interview transcripts. Using a 5-point evaluation scale across 11 published studies, GPT-generated themes achieved an average score of 3.05. The outputs showed strong alignment with researcher-identified themes, high succinctness with minimal redundancy, substantial explanatory depth, and relevant supporting quotations (Yang et al., 2024a). These findings suggest that agentic AI can substantially reduce the manual labor required for qualitative analysis while still producing evaluable, auditable outputs.

Complementary evidence comes from recent work using multi-agent LLM systems to synthesize institutional-level documents. For example, one study analyzing AI policies across the top 50 U.S. universities employed an iterative prompt chaining and self-refinement framework to identify core themes across dozens of policy documents (Alba et al., 2025). The agentic workflow consisted of multiple LLM agents assigned to document summarization, theme proposal, redundancy reduction, and final theme consolidation. This process uncovered seven cross-cutting themes spanning academic integrity, responsible AI use, data privacy, ethical safeguards, and institutional adaptation. The study demonstrates that agentic AI can coordinate multi-step reasoning across large, heterogeneous corpora, producing policy-relevant insights in contexts where manual synthesis would be prohibitively time-consuming.

Although applications directly targeting social work issues remain nascent, several adjacent studies illustrate how agentic AI can be adapted to social service contexts. Multi-agent LLM pipelines have been used to generate and refine causal diagrams, logic models, and program theories for public health and social policy interventions by assigning different agents the roles of theorist, critic, and synthesizer (Dawid et al., 2025; Le et al., 2024). Other human services pilot projects have leveraged agent workflows to map service eligibility rules across fragmented program documents, reconcile conflicting guidelines, and generate client-specific navigation summaries for housing, nutrition, or benefits programs (Barron et al., 2025). In community health research, agentic systems have been used to iteratively cluster, re-cluster, and validate themes across thousands of open-ended responses concerning stigma, barriers to care, and vaccine misinformation, reducing the cognitive burden on researchers while allowing rapid sensitivity analyses across alternative theoretical framings (Gullahorn et al., 2024; Meng et al., 2025). Together, these emerging directions suggest that agentic AI can support social work scholarship by automating early-stage synthesis tasks, generating competing conceptual explanations, and enabling researchers to focus on higher-order interpretation, critique, and integrative theory building.

3 Methodological, Ethical, and Epistemological Challenges

As AI systems become increasingly integrated into social work research, they introduce not only new analytical and conceptual possibilities but also significant methodological, ethical, and epistemological challenges. Unlike conventional tools, AI models, particularly machine learning, LLMs, and agentic systems, shape the research process itself: they influence what can be observed, how constructs are defined, which forms of evidence are prioritized, and how knowledge claims are generated (Barelli et al., 2024; Keyes & Creel, 2022; Lewis et al., 2024). These technologies bring issues such as data bias, opacity, reproducibility, and validity to the forefront of social work scholarship, raising questions about whether AI-enabled findings can be trusted, generalized, or interpreted in ways that remain aligned with social work's values and commitments to equity. At the same time, the scale and automation offered by AI risk amplify existing structural inequalities or embed unexamined assumptions into research designs and theoretical frameworks.

3.1 Methodological Challenges

3.1.1 Integration into Social Research Design

Social work research often relies on small-scale qualitative inquiry, community-based participatory methods, and mixed-methods designs. While AI can extend these approaches by processing large administrative datasets or synthesizing extensive narrative records, effective integration requires attention to alignment with established social research principles at the design stage. Robust frameworks emphasize that AI tools must be embedded into research workflows through transparent protocols for data governance, de-identification, controlled access, baseline model testing, and expert validation. Simply inserting black-box models into qualitative or community-based studies risks privacy breaches, loss of contextual nuance, and unreliable conclusions. Implementation studies in social services further highlight the importance of documenting who uses the AI system, where it is deployed, and for what purpose, as well as developing detailed operational manuals and iterative trial cycles (Nair et al., 2025). These experiences underscore that integration is not merely a technical task: it requires collaborative planning with practitioners and communities, clear articulation of human-AI roles, and research designs that preserve the epistemic values of social work.

3.1.2 Reproducibility, Interpretability, and Validity

Reproducibility and interpretability remain central concerns in AI-supported studies. Many high-performing machine learning and deep learning models operate as opaque systems, making it difficult for researchers to replicate findings or understand how predictions are generated (Takaoka, 2022). To address these limitations, methodological guidance increasingly recommends incorporating interpretable or explainable techniques, such as linear models, decision trees, Shapley additive explanations, and surrogate models, into the analytic pipeline (Basagaoglu et al., 2022; Nambiar et al., 2023). These approaches help clarify the relationship between inputs and outputs (interpretability) and the reasoning behind specific predictions (explainability). Broader research-integrity discussions reinforce that AI-assisted studies must include transparent methodological descriptions (Chen et al., 2024a), detailed reporting of data preprocessing, and explicit justification of model choices. Taken together, these considerations highlight that validity in AI-supported social work research requires open algorithms where possible, standardized evaluation metrics (e.g., ROC and precision-recall curves), robust documentation, and opportunities for independent replication.

3.1.3 Interpretable and Explainable AI (XAI)

Interpretable and explainable AI, often referred to as XAI, has emerged as a primary subdomain that seeks to address the challenges posed by opaque, black-box systems. Rather than focusing solely on predictive accuracy, XAI methods aim to make model behavior more transparent so that researchers, practitioners, and communities can understand how predictions are generated, identify potential sources of bias, and evaluate whether model reasoning is acceptable for high-stakes decisions (Ortigossa et al., 2024). These goals are especially salient in social work, where AI tools may influence access to services, surveillance, and allocation of scarce resources in ways that directly affect vulnerable populations.

One strand of XAI emphasizes inherently interpretable models whose internal structure can be examined directly. Examples include sparse linear models, decision trees, rule-based learners, and constrained gradient boosting models (Behzadimanesh et al., 2025; Yang et al., 2024b). In child welfare and youth justice research, such models have been used to identify combinations of factors, such as prior reports, caregiver characteristics, school engagement, and neighborhood disadvantage, that precede substantiated maltreatment or system contact (Moon et al., 2024; Moreau et al., 2024). Because decision paths and feature weights can be inspected and discussed, practitioners can evaluate whether the model relies on meaningful mechanisms or on proxies that may encode structural inequities. Similar approaches have been used in homelessness and housing services to clarify which patterns of shelter use, eviction history, and health conditions are associated with repeated episodes of homelessness, allowing agencies to scrutinize and revise model-based prioritization criteria (Rahmattalabi et al., 2022; Vajiac et al., 2024). For example, Kube et al. (2023) developed a machine learning system that used shelter histories, eviction records, and health information to identify who was most likely to reenter homelessness. By examining which features drove predictions, agencies could adjust their prioritization rules to balance efficiency with equity and ensure that models did not reinforce existing disparities.

A second strand focuses on post hoc explanations for more complex models, including deep neural networks and large ensembles. Techniques such as Shapley additive explanations, Integrated Gradients, Local Interpretable Model Agnostic Explanations, and counterfactual explanations help clarify how changes in specific inputs influence model outputs (Jin et al., 2023; Salih et al., 2023). In predictive analytics for mental health crisis services, for example, Shapley value-based analyses have been used to examine which features, such as recent emergency visits, missed appointments, or neighborhood-level indicators, contribute most strongly to predictions of near-term crisis risk (Kharrat et al., 2024; Mustapha et al., 2022). Counterfactual explanations can show how a small set of modifiable variables would need to change for a client to move from a high-risk to a lower-risk category or from ineligible to eligible for a program, highlighting levers that practitioners or policymakers can realistically influence (Ahmed et al., 2025).

Emerging work also extends XAI to the group level and structural explanations that are critical for equity-oriented social work. Rather than only examining individual predictions, researchers analyze whether feature attributions and error rates differ across demographic groups, jurisdictions, or agencies (Papanikou et al., 2025; Wang & Wu, 2024). In child protection risk assessment, for instance, XAI tools can reveal whether models systematically assign higher risk scores to families from particular neighborhoods or racial groups even when case characteristics are similar (Keddell, 2019; Papanikou et al., 2025). These findings can inform governance processes, community oversight, and model redesign, for example, by adjusting feature sets, changing loss functions, or constraining how certain variables are used. In this way, XAI becomes a mechanism for auditing and correcting AI systems rather than merely describing them.

Integrating XAI into AI-supported social work research strengthens both methodological rigor and ethical accountability. Interpretable and explainable methods make it easier to document model logic, engage practitioners and community stakeholders in understanding and contesting predictions, and align analytic pipelines with social work values. When combined with transparent reporting and independent replication (Gyevnar et al., 2023), XAI offers a practical pathway for ensuring that AI-augmented decisions are not only accurate but also understandable, contestable, and fair for the populations that social work aims to serve.

3.1.4 Data Quality and Representativeness

The performance and trustworthiness of AI techniques depend heavily on the quality of the data used to train them. Social work datasets often contain small sample sizes, inconsistent documentation, and unstructured narrative text—all of which introduce bias and limit model generalizability. Narrative records, for instance, may vary widely in writing style or omit critical contextual information, restricting a model's ability to learn nuanced patterns (Lukmanjaya et al., 2025). Exclusive reliance on administrative data can likewise misrepresent specific populations and reproduce structural inequities. Ensuring representativeness, therefore, requires combining multiple data sources and adopting culturally informed data practices. It also depends on engaging communities, particularly Indigenous populations and other historically marginalized groups, in decisions about data use. Another emerging methodological risk is anchoring bias, in which researchers may over-weight an AI system's initial output because it appears precise or objective (Carter & Liu, 2025) and overlook contradictory evidence. To counter this tendency, AI-generated results must be approached critically, triangulated across sources, and interpreted through human expertise. These concerns collectively highlight the need for rigorous data curation, reflexive engagement with AI outputs, and conservative claims about what AI-derived insights can validly support.

3.2 *Ethical Challenges*

3.2.1 Privacy, Consent, and Data Governance

AI-assisted social work research often involves highly sensitive information about individuals and communities, raising significant obligations regarding privacy, consent, and data stewardship. Ethical guidance in the field consistently emphasizes that informed consent must be meaningful in technology-mediated settings: participants should understand how their data will be used, what AI systems will access, and what risks, including secondary use and re-identification, may occur. Computer vision applications that rely on continuous video capture, such as fall detection or environmental monitoring, introduce additional challenges because cameras can record bystanders, staff, or residents who have not explicitly agreed to be monitored and whose images can be repurposed in ways they did not anticipate (Moore et al., 2024). These risks are heightened when footage is retained for long periods, combined with other datasets, or shared with external entities, for example, law enforcement agencies or private vendors, potentially enabling forms of targeted surveillance that go well beyond the original care or safety purpose. Robust data governance practices are essential, including strong encryption, secure storage, restricted access protocols, and clear procedures for responding to data breaches. De-identification of narrative records and administrative files is particularly important in domains such as child protection, where rich textual descriptions may inadvertently reveal identities even when obvious identifiers are removed.

Implementation studies in social services demonstrate how these principles can be operationalized (Trinkley et al., 2024), for example, by using closed networks that prevent external access, allowing workers to enter and review information without exposing it to the public Internet (NASW et al., 2017). These approaches highlight that safeguarding privacy is not only a technical matter but also an ethical responsibility that requires transparent communication with participants, organizational policies for breach notification, and ongoing evaluation of data practices as AI systems evolve. Ethical AI research in social work, therefore, demands a combination of procedural rigor, contextual sensitivity, and continuous human oversight to ensure that data use aligns with social work values and community expectations.

3.2.2 Algorithmic Fairness and Equity

AI systems trained on historical data risk reproducing the very inequities that social work seeks to address. When administrative datasets reflect structural racism, class-based disparities, or biased service patterns, predictive models may encode these patterns and treat them as neutral signals. This can produce disproportionate false positives for marginalized groups, reinforce harmful stereotypes, or create feedback loops in which increased surveillance leads to higher recorded risk (Chapman et al., 2022). Analyses of child welfare risk assessment tools illustrate this concern: algorithms often rely on proxies such as previous system involvement, which correlate with socioeconomic disadvantage and can heighten risk scores for families already subject to disproportionate state attention (Stapleton, 2025). Similar concerns arise with computer vision systems deployed for public safety, benefits administration, or institutional security. Facial recognition technologies have repeatedly been shown to perform less accurately for people of color and other marginalized groups, raising the risk of misidentification, unwarranted investigation, or denial of services when such tools are used around public housing, schools, or welfare offices (Amador-Lankster, 2025; Yucer et al., 2023). Vision systems that purport to detect suspicious behavior or loitering can encode stereotypes about who counts as threatening and intensify surveillance in already overpoliced neighborhoods (Wahyono et al., 2023). When these outputs are treated as neutral indicators of risk, they can legitimize discriminatory practices and normalize continuous monitoring of communities that social work aims to support.

Yet empirical evaluations also show that human oversight can mitigate these effects. In a mixed-methods study of the Allegheny Family Screening Tool, Cheng and colleagues compared actual worker decisions with those that would have been made if the algorithm alone had determined which referrals to investigate. They found that the algorithm, by itself, would have produced an approximately 18 percentage-point gap in screen time between Black and White children. In contrast, worker decisions using the tool resulted in a gap of about seven percentage points, because workers frequently overrode high-risk scores for Black families when those scores conflicted with their holistic assessment of the case (Cheng et al., 2022; Stapleton et al., 2022). Similar analyses of Allegheny County's implementation indicate that the introduction of the screening tool, together with continued human discretion, was associated with reductions in Black-White disparities in screening, case openings, and short-term home removals, even though supervisors retained final authority over decisions (Goldhaber-Fiebert & Prince, 2019; Rittenhouse et al., 2023). These cases underscore the importance of human-in-the-loop decision-making rather than fully automated determinations. More broadly, achieving fairness requires systematic auditing, the use of bias detection and mitigation metrics, transparency about model assumptions, and the involvement of affected communities in the design and governance of AI systems (Funda, 2025). Ethical AI in social work must therefore be grounded in participatory processes, culturally responsive data practices, and explicit commitments to equity, ensuring that computational tools support, rather than undermine, social justice aims.

3.3 *Epistemological Challenges*

3.3.1 Shifts in Knowledge Production and Validation

AI technologies are reshaping how knowledge is generated, interpreted, and validated in social work research (Chen et al., 2024b). Automated literature retrieval, predictive risk scoring, and algorithmic pattern recognition can create the impression that data "speak for themselves," encouraging an overly empiricist orientation in which statistical associations are treated as objective facts. Yet AI outputs inevitably reflect assumptions baked into training data, modeling choices, and system design. Overreliance on algorithmic recommendations risks misinterpretation or misclassification, especially when contextual nuance or experiential knowledge is overlooked (Cross et al., 2024). AI has also altered research workflows across disciplines, expanding analytical capacity while introducing new vulnerabilities related to error propagation, academic misconduct, and uncritical acceptance of machine-generated findings (Chakravorti et al., 2025). These shifts highlight the need for AI-generated insights to be situated within theoretical frameworks, interpreted through professional judgment, and subjected to reflexive critique rather than treated as neutral or authoritative knowledge claims.

3.3.2 The "Black-Box" Problem

The opacity of many AI models raises not only practical concerns but also more profound epistemological questions about the kind of knowledge these systems produce (Greif, 2022). While all statistical models involve abstraction, high-performing machine learning and deep learning architectures are distinct in both scale and structure. They often contain millions or even billions of parameters, arranged across many layers of nonlinear transformations. As a result, there is no straightforward way to trace how a particular input feature flows through the network or how combinations of features yield a given output (Chang & Chen, 2024; Søgaard, 2024). This structural complexity makes it difficult for researchers, practitioners, and affected communities to understand why a prediction was made, even when the model's overall accuracy is high.

By contrast, more traditional models such as linear regression, logistic regression, or shallow decision trees provide explicit and relatively stable mappings between inputs and outputs. Coefficients, splits, and rules can be inspected, debated, and related to substantive theory. In complex neural networks, representations are distributed across many units and layers. Individual parameters lack clear meanings, and small changes in inputs can interact in nonintuitive ways (Lange et al., 2022; Xu et al., 2025b). Training procedures are also probabilistic and path dependent, influenced by random initialization, stochastic optimization, and subtle properties of the training data. Two models trained on the same dataset may yield slightly different internal representations and decision boundaries, even if their aggregate performance appears similar (Benzing et al., 2022; Kwok et al., 2025). These features of modern ML and DL make it harder to provide the mechanistic or theory-linked explanations that social work typically expects when justifying interventions or policies.

In social work contexts, the black-box problem is therefore not only about a lack of technical transparency but about who can legitimately interrogate and contest algorithmic reasoning (Busuioc et al., 2022; Hollanek, 2020). When frontline workers are asked to act on predictions from models they cannot explain, they bear responsibility for decisions they cannot articulate to clients, supervisors, or courts. When communities are subject to surveillance or triage by opaque systems, they lack the information needed to challenge potential errors, embedded biases, or harmful feedback loops. Opacity also increases the risk that vulnerabilities in system design, privacy practices, or third-party data flows remain hidden, since even technically sophisticated users may struggle to understand how information is combined and propagated.

To uphold epistemic integrity and institutional accountability, AI used in social research and practice must be paired with forms of transparency meaningful to non-experts. This includes open documentation of training data and model assumptions, explainability tools that reveal how inputs influence outputs at both individual and group levels, and governance arrangements that guarantee a right to explanation and contestation for people whose lives are shaped by algorithmic findings. Without such measures, black-box models threaten to shift social work away from reasoned, accountable judgment toward forms of decision-making that are difficult to justify, scrutinize, or reform.

3.3.3 Reflexivity and Positionality in Human-AI Collaboration

Reflexivity, the critical examination of one's assumptions, standpoint, and interpretive practices, is central to social work scholarship (Rogers & Brown, 2023). AI complicates this process by introducing new forms of cognitive bias and power asymmetry into the production of knowledge. Researchers may inadvertently anchor their interpretations to an initial AI output, overlook omissions, or ascribe unwarranted authority to machine-generated text (Rastogi et al., 2020). These dynamics require heightened reflexive awareness, including careful interrogation of data sources, questioning of model limitations, and triangulation of AI-generated results with independent evidence. Human-AI collaboration in qualitative and conceptual research must treat algorithmic classifications and summaries as provisional, subject to expert review and contextual judgment. Interpretability frameworks underscore that explanations are co-constructed between the system and the user, shaped by the user's positionality, expertise, and expectations (Yang & Ma, 2025). Maintaining epistemic rigor, therefore, requires attention to how human interpretation, institutional context, and structural biases embedded within AI systems jointly shape decisions and knowledge claims.

4 Future Directions

4.1 Human-AI Collaboration in Research Workflows

Looking ahead, AI is likely to function as a collaborative partner rather than a replacement for social work researchers. Future research workflows will increasingly rely on systems that augment professional judgment by streamlining data processing, generating preliminary analyses, and assisting with literature synthesis, while leaving interpretation, contextualization, and ethical decision-making to trained professionals. Human review remains essential: examples from risk assessment practice illustrate that skilled practitioners can identify and correct algorithmic biases, significantly reducing disparities in automated recommendations. To support effective collaboration, research environments will need to incorporate AI literacy training, develop interfaces that facilitate the critical examination of model outputs, and design mechanisms to ensure that machine-generated insights remain transparent, auditable, and open to contestation. In this vision of human-AI partnership, the role of the researcher expands from data analyst to orchestrator of hybrid workflows that combine computational efficiency with relational expertise and ethical judgment.

4.2 Epistemological Renewal and Theoretical Integration

AI's ability to detect cross-cutting patterns in large, heterogeneous datasets invites a reassessment of how social problems are conceptualized. Predictive models may reinforce existing theoretical accounts, reveal discrepancies between assumptions and empirical patterns, or challenge dominant constructs altogether. Such insights create opportunities for scholars to interrogate which variables are being optimized, what forms of harm or resilience are foregrounded, and how structural inequalities shape the datasets that models learn from. At the same time, AI-derived findings must not be treated as definitive: cognitive biases such as anchoring can lead researchers to overvalue the first model output they encounter, while the absence of contextual nuance may obscure mechanisms that matter for theory. Epistemological renewal will therefore require integrating AI-generated evidence with critical, interpretive, and values-based traditions in social work. This means treating AI as a tool for provoking theoretical reflection rather than replacing it—one that can help refine constructs, test conceptual boundaries, and illuminate overlooked dimensions of social experience.

4.3 Interdisciplinary Synthesis and Policy Modeling

The future of AI-assisted social work research depends on sustained collaboration across disciplines. Social problems cut across psychological, technological, legal, and policy domains, and effective AI systems must therefore be co-designed by diverse teams that include social scientists, engineers, ethicists, and community stakeholders. Interdisciplinary collaboration can support the development of fairness and transparency standards, improve the cultural responsiveness of datasets, and ensure that AI models align with human rights and social justice principles. These partnerships are particularly valuable in policy modeling, where AI can simulate the consequences of interventions, explore counterfactual scenarios, and integrate evidence from multiple sectors, including health, education, housing, and legal systems. Coordinated efforts among researchers, practitioners, administrators, and affected communities will be essential for building AI systems that not only advance analytical rigor but also reinforce social work's commitments to dignity, inclusion, and equitable outcomes. Such synthesis offers a pathway toward robust, ethically grounded evidence that can inform policy, strengthen service systems, and deepen the field's theoretical foundations.

5 Conclusion

AI has become an increasingly versatile methodological partner in social work research, extending the field's capacity for descriptive, predictive, experimental, and conceptual inquiry. Techniques such as data mining, NLP, machine learning, socially assistive robotics, computer vision, and LLMs enable analysis and synthesis at scales and granularities previously unattainable. Yet the value of these tools is contingent rather than inherent. Their contributions depend on a transparent research design, equitable data governance, and an epistemic posture that treats AI outputs as provisional insights to be interpreted, rather than definitive truths.

Methodologically, AI is most powerful when embedded within rigorous mixed-methods frameworks that ensure clear data provenance, reproducibility, interpretability, and appropriate model validation. Ethically, its use requires robust safeguards to protect privacy, provide informed consent, promote fairness, and ensure human oversight to mitigate potential harms and support accountability, particularly in settings involving vulnerable populations or sensitive service systems. Epistemologically, AI should function as a catalyst for reflection rather than a substitute for human judgment, encouraging researchers to interrogate assumptions, examine sources of bias, and engage critically with how knowledge is produced through human-machine collaboration.

Looking forward, three priorities stand out. First, advancing human-AI collaboration that enhances rather than replaces the intellectual and relational foundations of social inquiry. Second, pursuing epistemological renewal that integrates computational evidence with theoretical traditions and values central to social work. Third, fostering interdisciplinary collaboration to build transparent, responsible, and equity-centered research infrastructures. When guided by methodological rigor, ethical integrity, and the profession's enduring commitments to dignity, justice, and human rights, AI has the potential to help social work ask more profound questions, generate more actionable insights, and design more just and responsive interventions.

Competing Interests The authors have no conflicts of interest to declare that are relevant to the content of this chapter.

References

Abbas, S., Abbas, Z., Zahir, A., & Lee, S. (2024). Federated learning in smart healthcare: A comprehensive review on privacy, security, and predictive analytics with IoT integration. *Healthcare, 12*. https://doi.org/10.3390/healthcare12242587

Ahmed, A., Saleem, M., Alzeen, M., Birur, B., Fargason, R. E., Burk, B. G., Alhassan, A., & Al-Garadi, M. (2025). Explainable AI for mental health emergency returns: Integrating LLMs with predictive modeling. *arXiv*. https://arxiv.org/abs/2502.00025

Alam, N. (2025). Social work in the age of artificial intelligence: A rights-based framework for evidence-based practice through social psychology, group dynamics, and institutional analysis. *Journal of Evidence-Based Social Work*, 1–12. https://doi.org/10.1080/26408066.2025.2547219

Alba, C., Xi, W., Wang, C., & An, R. (2025, February). ChatGPT comes to campus: Unveiling core themes in AI policies across US universities with large language models. In *Proceedings of the 56th ACM Technical Symposium on Computer Science Education V. 2* (pp. 1359–1360). https://doi.org/10.1145/3641555.3705141

Ali, M. A., & Dornaika, F. (2025). Agentic AI: A comprehensive survey of architectures, applications, and future directions. *Artificial Intelligence Review*. Advance online publication. https://doi.org/10.1007/s10462-025-11422-4

Allegheny County Department of Human Services, Office of Analytics, Technology and Planning. (2024, May 31). *Evaluation findings on the use of predictive risk models in child welfare* [Report]. https://analytics.alleghenycounty.us/2024/05/31/predictive-risk-models-in-child-welfare/Home

Almeida, L., da Silva, D., Theodório, D., Silva, W., Rodrigues, S., Scardovelli, T., Silva, A., & Bissaco, M. (2019). ALTRIRAS: A computer game for training children with autism spectrum disorder in the recognition of basic emotions. *International Journal of Computer Games Technology, 2019*, 4384896. https://doi.org/10.1155/2019/4384896

Alsharif, B., Alalwany, E., Ibrahim, A., Mahgoub, I., & Ilyas, M. (2025). Real-time American Sign Language interpretation using deep learning and keypoint tracking. *Sensors, 25*, 2138. https://doi.org/10.3390/s25072138

Amador-Lankster, V. (2025). Facial recognition in policing: How algorithmic bias targets people of color. *The Undergraduate Law Review at UC San Diego*. https://doi.org/10.5070/lr3.47403

Amugongo, L., Mascheroni, P., Brooks, S., Doering, S., & Seidel, J. (2025). Retrieval augmented generation for large language models in healthcare: A systematic review. *PLoS Digital Health, 4*, e0000877. https://doi.org/10.1371/journal.pdig.0000877

An, R., Yang, Y., Batcheller, Q., & Zhou, Q. (2023). Sentiment analysis of tweets on soda taxes. *Journal of Public Health Management and Practice, 29*(5), 633–639. https://doi.org/10.1097/PHH.0000000000001721

Annaki, I., Rahmoune, M., Bourhaleb, M., Berrich, J., Zaoui, M., Castilla, A., Berthoz, A., & Cohen, B. (2022). Clustering analysis of human navigation trajectories in a visuospatial memory locomotor task using K-means and hierarchical agglomerative clustering. *E3S Web of Conferences*. https://doi.org/10.1051/e3sconf/202235101042

Austin, A. E., Desrosiers, T. A., & Shanahan, M. E. (2019). Directed acyclic graphs: An underutilized tool for child maltreatment research. *Child Abuse & Neglect, 91*, 78–87. https://doi.org/10.1016/j.chiabu.2019.02.011

Baek, G., Cha, C., & Han, J.-H. (2025). AI chatbots for psychological health for health professionals: Scoping review. *JMIR Mental Health, 12*, e67682. https://doi.org/10.2196/67682

Bako, A. T., Taylor, H. L., Wiley, K., Jr., Zheng, J., Walter-McCabe, H., Kasthurirathne, S. N., & Vest, J. R. (2021). Using natural language processing to classify social work interventions. *The American Journal of Managed Care, 27*(1), e24–e31. https://doi.org/10.37765/ajmc.2021.88580

Barelli, E., Lodi, M., Branchetti, L., & Levrini, O. (2024). Epistemic insights as design principles for a teaching-learning module on artificial intelligence. *Science & Education*. Advance online publication. https://doi.org/10.1007/s11191-024-00504-4

Barron, R., Eren, M., Serafimova, O., Matuszek, C., & Alexandrov, B. (2025). Bridging legal knowledge and AI: Retrieval-augmented generation with vector stores, knowledge graphs, and hierarchical non-negative matrix factorization. *arXiv*. https://doi.org/10.48550/arXiv.2502.20364

Basagaoglu, H., Chakraborty, D., Lago, C., Gutierrez, L., Şahinli, M., Giacomoni, M., Furl, C., Mirchi, A., Moriasi, D., & Şengör, S. (2022). A review on interpretable and explainable artificial intelligence in hydroclimatic applications. *Water, 14*(8), 1230. https://doi.org/10.3390/w14081230

Behzadimanesh, S., Bodic, P., Webb, G., & Boley, M. (2025). Interpretable representation learning for additive rule ensembles. *arXiv*. https://doi.org/10.48550/arXiv.2506.20927

Benites-Lazaro, L. L., Giatti, L., & Giarolla, A. (2018). Topic modeling method for analyzing social actor discourses on climate change, energy and food security. *Energy Research & Social Science, 45*, 28–44. https://doi.org/10.1016/j.erss.2018.07.031

Benzing, F., Schug, S., Meier, R., Oswald, J., Akram, Y., Zucchet, N., Aitchison, L., & Steger, A. (2022). Random initialisations performing above chance and how to find them (https://arxiv.org/abs/2209.07509) [Preprint]. *arXiv*. https://doi.org/10.48550/arxiv.2209.07509

Bernasco, W., Hoeben, E., Koelma, D., Liebst, L., Thomas, J., Appelman, J., Snoek, C., & Lindegaard, M. (2021). Promise into practice: Application of computer vision in empirical research on social distancing. *Sociological Methods & Research, 52*, 1239–1287. https://doi.org/10.1177/00491241221099554

Busuioc, M., Curtin, D., & Almada, M. (2022). Reclaiming transparency: Contesting the logics of secrecy within the AI Act. *European Law Open, 2*, 79–105. https://doi.org/10.1017/elo.2022.47

Byrne, T., Montgomery, A. E., & Fargo, J. D. (2019). Predictive modeling of housing instability and homelessness in the Veterans Health Administration. *Health Services Research, 54*(1), 75–85. https://doi.org/10.1111/1475-6773.13050

Cabibihan, J., Javed, H., Ang, M., & Aljunied, S. (2013). Why robots? A survey on the roles and benefits of social robots in the therapy of children with autism. *International Journal of Social Robotics, 5*, 593–618. https://doi.org/10.1007/s12369-013-0202-2

Callon, M., Courtial, J. P., & Laville, F. (1991). Co-word analysis as a tool for describing the network of interactions between basic and technological research: The case of polymer chemistry. *Scientometrics, 22*, 155–205. https://doi.org/10.1007/BF02019280

Carter, L., & Liu, D. (2025). How was my performance? Exploring the role of anchoring bias in AI-assisted decision making. *International Journal of Information Management, 75*, 102875. https://doi.org/10.1016/j.ijinfomgt.2025.102875

Chapman, A., Grylls, P., Ugwudike, P., Gammack, D., & Ayling, J. (2022). A data-driven analysis of the interplay between criminological theory and predictive policing algorithms. In *Proceedings of the 2022 ACM Conference on Fairness, Accountability, and Transparency*. https://doi.org/10.1145/3531146.3533071

Chang, Y., & Chen, S. (2024). Design of a basis-projected layer for sparse datasets in deep learning training using GC–MS spectra as a case study (https://arxiv.org/abs/2403.09188) [Preprint]. *arXiv*. https://doi.org/10.48550/arxiv.2403.09188

Chakravorti, T., Wang, X., Venkit, P., Koneru, S., Munger, K., & Rajtmajer, S. (2025). Social scientists on the role of AI in research. *arXiv*, abs/2506.11255. https://doi.org/10.48550/arxiv.2506.11255

Che, L., Wang, J., Zhou, Y., & Fan, F. (2023). Multimodal federated learning: A survey. *Sensors, 23*, 6986. https://doi.org/10.3390/s23156986

Chen, L., & Fisher, R. (2023). MISO: Monitoring inactivity of single older adults at home using RGB-D technology. *ACM Transactions on Computing for Healthcare, 5*, 1–19. https://doi.org/10.1145/3674848

Chen, H., Ren, X., He, L., & Huang, J. (2024a). Editorial: AI as intelligent technology and agent to understand and be understood by human minds. *Frontiers in Psychology, 15*. https://doi.org/10.3389/fpsyg.2024.1461881

Chen, Z., Chen, C., Yang, G., He, X., Chi, X., Zeng, Z., & Chen, X. (2024b). Research integrity in the era of artificial intelligence: Challenges and responses. *Medicine, 103*(27), e38811. https://doi.org/10.1097/MD.0000000000038811

Cheng, H.-F., Stapleton, L., Kawakami, A., Sivaraman, V., Cheng, Y., Qing, D., Perer, A., Holstein, K., Wu, Z. S., & Zhu, H. (2022). How child welfare workers reduce racial disparities in algorithmic decisions. In *CHI '22: Proceedings of the 2022 CHI Conference on Human Factors in Computing Systems* (Article 162, pp. 1–22). https://doi.org/10.1145/3491102.3501831

Chernozhukov, V., Hansen, C., Kallus, N., Spindler, M., & Syrgkanis, V. (2024). Applied causal inference powered by ML and AI. *arXiv*. https://arxiv.org/abs/2403.02467

Chimwaza, L., & Jimu, P. (2024). Vision Aid: Developing an assistive mobile application for visually impaired individuals. *International Journal of Advanced Research in Science, Communication and Technology*. https://doi.org/10.48175/ijarsct-22228

Chin, S., & Collins, J. E. (2024). Clustering Methods in Rheumatic and Musculoskeletal Disease Research: An Educational Guide to Best Research Practices. *The Journal of rheumatology, 51*(12), 1160–1168. https://doi.org/10.3899/jrheum.2024-0519

Choi, D. S., Park, J., Loeser, M., & Seo, K. (2024). Improving counseling effectiveness with virtual counselors through nonverbal compassion involving eye contact, facial mimicry, and head-nodding. *Scientific Reports, 14*, 506. https://doi.org/10.1038/s41598-023-51115-y

Cross, J., Choma, M., & Onofrey, J. (2024). Bias in medical AI: Implications for clinical decision-making. *PLoS Digital Health, 3*, e0000651. https://doi.org/10.1371/journal.pdig.0000651

Dawar, I., Kumar, N., Negi, S., Pathan, S., & Layek, S. (2023). Text categorization using supervised machine learning techniques. In *2023 Sixth International Conference of Women in Data Science at Prince Sultan University (WiDS PSU)* (pp. 185–190). IEEE. https://doi.org/10.1109/WiDS-PSU57071.2023.00046

Dawid, H., Harting, P., Wang, H., Wang, Z., & Yi, J. (2025). Agentic workflows for economic research: Design and implementation. *arXiv*. https://arxiv.org/abs/2504.09736

Dennstädt, F., Zink, J., Putora, P. M., Hastings, J., & Cihoric, N. (2024). Title and abstract screening for literature reviews using large language models: An exploratory study in the biomedical domain. *Systematic Reviews, 13*, 158. https://doi.org/10.1186/s13643-024-02575-4

Dumitru, R.-G., Alexeeva, M., Alcock, K., Ludgate, N., Jeong, C., Abdurahaman, Z. F., Puri, P., Kirchhoff, B., Sadhu, S., & Surdeanu, M. (2024). Retrieval augmented generation of subjective explanations for socioeconomic scenarios. In D. Card, A. Field, D. Hovy, & K. Keith (Eds.), *Proceedings of the Sixth Workshop on Natural Language Processing and Computational Social Science (NLP+CSS 2024)* (pp. 68–85). Association for Computational Linguistics. https://doi.org/10.18653/v1/2024.nlpcss-1.6

Eden, R., Chukwudi, I., Bain, C., Barbieri, S., Callaway, L., Jersey, S., George, Y., Gorse, A., Lawley, M., Marendy, P., McPhail, S., Nguyen, A., Samadbeik, M., & Sullivan, C. (2025). A scoping review of the governance of federated learning in healthcare. *NPJ Digital Medicine, 8*. https://doi.org/10.1038/s41746-025-01836-3

Ercan, M., & Mathyalakan, A. (2024). Computer vision based safety inspection in public housing. In *TENCON 2024 – 2024 IEEE Region 10 Conference (TENCON)* (pp. 1398–1401). IEEE. https://doi.org/10.1109/tencon61640.2024.10902946

Fink, N. (2025). Unsupervised clustering approaches for autism screening: Achieving 95.31% accuracy with a Gaussian mixture model (https://arxiv.org/abs/2503.05746) [Preprint]. *arXiv*. https://doi.org/10.48550/arxiv.2503.05746

Friesen, C., Seliske, P., & Papadopoulos, A. (2016). Using principal component analysis to identify priority neighbourhoods for health services delivery by ranking socioeconomic status. *Online Journal of Public Health Informatics, 8*. https://doi.org/10.5210/ojphi.v8i2.6733

Funda, V. (2025). A systematic review of algorithm auditing processes to assess bias and risks in AI systems. *Journal of Infrastructure, Policy and Development*. Advance online publication. https://doi.org/10.24294/jipd11489

Gadde, P., Kharrazi, H., Patel, H., & MacDorman, K. (2011). Toward monitoring and increasing exercise adherence in older adults by robotic intervention: A proof of concept study. *Journal of Robotics, 2011*, Article 438514. https://doi.org/10.1155/2011/438514

Gao, Y., Xiong, Y., Gao, X., Jia, K., Pan, J., Bi, Y., Dai, Y., Sun, J., Wang, M., & Wang, H. (2023). Retrieval-augmented generation for large language models: A survey. *arXiv*. https://arxiv.org/abs/2312.10997

Greif, H. (2022). Analogue models and universal machines: Paradigms of epistemic transparency in artificial intelligence. *Minds and Machines, 32*, 111–133. https://doi.org/10.1007/s11023-022-09596-9

Gullahorn, B., Kuo, I., Robinson, A., Bailey, J., Loken, J., & Taggart, T. (2024). Identifying facilitators and barriers to the uptake of medication for opioid use disorder in Washington,

DC: A community-engaged concept mapping approach. *PLoS ONE, 19*, e0306931. https://doi.org/10.1371/journal.pone.0306931
Garkisch, M., & Goldkind, L. (2025). Considering a unified model of artificial intelligence enhanced social work: A systematic review. *Journal of Human Rights and Social Work, 10*, 23–42. https://doi.org/10.1007/s41134-024-00326-y
Guemghar, I., Pires de Oliveira Padilha, P., Abdel-Baki, A., Jutras-Aswad, D., Paquette, J., & Pomey, M. P. (2022). Social robot interventions in mental health care and their outcomes, barriers, and facilitators: Scoping review. *JMIR Mental Health, 9*(4), e36094. https://doi.org/10.2196/36094
Goldhaber-Fiebert, J. D., & Prince, L. (2019, March 20). *Impact evaluation of a predictive risk modeling tool for Allegheny County's Child Welfare Office*. Stanford University. https://www.alleghenycountyanalytics.us/wp-content/uploads/2019/05/Impact-Evaluation-from-16-ACDHS-26_PredictiveRisk_Package_050119_FINAL-6.pdf
Gyevnar, B., Ferguson, N., & Schafer, B. (2023). Bridging the transparency gap: What can explainable AI learn from the AI Act? In *Frontiers in Artificial Intelligence and Applications* (pp. 964–971). https://doi.org/10.3233/FAIA230367
Ha, P., D'silva, R., Chen, E., Koyutürk, M., & Karakurt, G. (2021). Identification of intimate partner violence from free text descriptions in social media. *Journal of Computational Social Science, 5*, 1207–1233. https://doi.org/10.1007/s42001-022-00166-8
Hardeniya, T., & Borikar, D. A. (2016). Dictionary based approach to sentiment analysis: A review. *International Journal of Advanced Engineering, Management and Science, 2*. https://api.semanticscholar.org/CorpusID:213194437
He, Y., Yang, L., Qian, C., Li, T., Su, Z., Zhang, Q., & Hou, X. (2023). Conversational agent interventions for mental health problems: Systematic review and meta-analysis of randomized controlled trials. *Journal of Medical Internet Research, 25*, e43862. https://doi.org/10.2196/43862
Hollanek, T. (2020). AI transparency: A matter of reconciling design with critique. *AI & Society, 38*, 2071–2079. https://doi.org/10.1007/s00146-020-01110-y
Hou, Y., & Huang, J. (2025). Natural language processing for social science research: A comprehensive review. *Chinese Journal of Sociology, 11*(1), 121–157. https://doi.org/10.1177/2057150X241306780
Hua, Y., Na, H., Li, Z., Liu, F., Fang, X., Clifton, D., & Torous, J. (2025). A scoping review of large language models for generative tasks in mental health care. *NPJ Digital Medicine, 8*, 230. https://doi.org/10.1038/s41746-025-01611-4
Hughes, A., Bull, L., Gardner, P., Barthorpe, R., Dervilis, N., & Worden, K. (2021). On risk-based active learning for structural health monitoring. *ArXiv*, abs/2105.05622. https://doi.org/10.1016/j.ymssp.2021.108569.
Hwang, J., & Naik, N. (2023). Systematic social observation at scale: Using crowdsourcing and computer vision to measure visible neighborhood conditions. *Sociological Methodology, 53*(2), 183–216. https://doi.org/10.1177/00811750231160781
Inoue, M., Irino, T., Furuyama, N., & Hanada, R. (2021). Observational and accelerometer analysis of head movement patterns in psychotherapeutic dialogue. *Sensors, 21*, 3162. https://doi.org/10.3390/s21093162
Isaev, D., Sabatos-DeVito, M., Di Martino, M., Carpenter, K., Aiello, R., Compton, S., Davis, N., Franz, L., Sullivan, C., Dawson, G., & Sapiro, G. (2023). Computer vision analysis of caregiver–child interactions in children with neurodevelopmental disorders: A preliminary report. *Journal of Autism and Developmental Disorders*, 1–12. https://doi.org/10.1007/s10803-023-05973-0
Jiang, H., Shi, S., Yao, Y., Jiang, C., & Li, Q. (2025). HypoChainer: A collaborative system combining LLMs and knowledge graphs for hypothesis-driven scientific discovery. *arXiv*. https://arxiv.org/abs/2507.17209
Jin, W., Li, X., Fatehi, M., & Hamarneh, G. (2023). Generating post-hoc explanation from deep neural networks for multi-modal medical image analysis tasks. *MethodsX, 10*, 102009. https://doi.org/10.1016/j.mex.2023.102009

Kane, M., King, C., Esserman, D., Latham, N., Greene, E., & Ganz, D. (2023). A compressed large language model embedding dataset of ICD-10-CM descriptions. *BMC Bioinformatics, 24*. https://doi.org/10.1186/s12859-023-05597-2

Kaur, A., & Wallace, J. R. (2024). Moving beyond LDA: A comparison of unsupervised topic modelling techniques for qualitative data analysis of online communities. *arXiv*. https://arxiv.org/abs/2412.14486

Keddell, E. (2019). Algorithmic justice in child protection: Statistical fairness, social justice and the implications for practice. *Social Sciences, 8*(10), 281. https://doi.org/10.3390/socsci8100281

Keyes, O., & Creel, K. (2022). Artificial knowing otherwise. *Feminist Philosophy Quarterly*. https://doi.org/10.5206/fpq/2022.3/4.14313

Khan, A., Hasan, M., Kemell, K., Rasku, J., & Abrahamsson, P. (2024a). Developing retrieval augmented generation (RAG) based LLM systems from PDFs: An experience report. *arXiv*. https://doi.org/10.48550/arXiv.2410.15944

Khan, Z., Ali, A., Khan, D., & Aldahmani, S. (2024b). Regularized ensemble learning for prediction and risk factors assessment of students at risk in the post-COVID era. *Scientific Reports, 14*, 1–12. https://doi.org/10.1038/s41598-024-66894-1

Kharrat, F., Gagné, C., Lesage, A., Gariépy, G., Pelletier, J., Brousseau-Paradis, C., Rochette, L., Pelletier, É., Lévesque, P., Mohammed, M., & Wang, J. (2024). Explainable artificial intelligence models for predicting risk of suicide using health administrative data in Quebec. *PLoS ONE, 19*, e0301117. https://doi.org/10.1371/journal.pone.0301117

Kline, A., Wang, H., Li, Y., Dennis, S., Hutch, M., Xu, Z., Wang, F., Cheng, F., & Luo, Y. (2022). Multimodal machine learning in precision health (https://arxiv.org/abs/2204.04777) [Preprint]. *arXiv*. https://doi.org/10.48550/arxiv.2204.04777

Kube, A., Das, S., & Fowler, P. (2023). Community- and data-driven homelessness prevention and service delivery: Optimizing for equity. *Journal of the American Medical Informatics Association, 30*, 1032–1041. https://doi.org/10.1093/jamia/ocad052

Kwok, D., Altintas, G., Raffel, C., & Rolnick, D. (2025). The butterfly effect: Neural network training trajectories are highly sensitive to initial conditions (https://arxiv.org/abs/2506.13234) [Preprint]. *arXiv*. https://doi.org/10.48550/arxiv.2506.13234

Lange, R., Matelsky, J., Wang, X., Kwok, D., Rolnick, D., & Kording, K. (2022). Neural networks as paths through the space of representations (https://arxiv.org/abs/2206.10999) [Preprint]. *arXiv*. https://doi.org/10.48550/arxiv.2206.10999

Larkin, A., Huang, T., Chen, L., Lin, P., Hart, J., Zhang, W., Coull, B., Yi, L., Suel, E., Hankey, S., James, P., & Hystad, P. (2025). Developing nationwide estimates of built environment quality characteristics using street-view imagery and computer vision. *Environmental Science & Technology, 59*, 13638–13646. https://doi.org/10.1021/acs.est.5c00966

Le, H., Xia, X., & Chen, Z. (2024). Multi-agent causal discovery using large language models. *arXiv*. https://doi.org/10.48550/arXiv.2407.15073

Lechner, M., & Mareckova, J. (2024). Comprehensive causal machine learning. *arXiv*. https://arxiv.org/abs/2405.10198

Lee, K., Paek, H., Ofoegbu, N., Rube, S., Higashi, M., Dawoud, D., Xu, H., Shi, L., & Wang, X. (2025). A4SLR: An agentic AI-assisted systematic literature review framework to augment evidence synthesis for HEOR and HTA. *Value in Health*. Advance online publication. https://doi.org/10.1016/j.jval.2025.08.002

Lewis, J., Whaanga, H., & Yolgörmez, C. (2024). Abundant intelligences: Placing AI within Indigenous knowledge frameworks. *AI & Society, 40*, 2141–2157. https://doi.org/10.1007/s00146-024-02099-4

Li, H., Huang, J., Ji, M., Yang, Y., & An, R. (2025). Use of retrieval-augmented large language model for COVID-19 fact-checking: Development and usability study. *Journal of Medical Internet Research, 27*, e66098. https://doi.org/10.2196/66098

Loftus, T., Ruppert, M., Shickel, B., Ozrazgat-Baslanti, T., Balch, J., Efron, P., Upchurch, G., Rashidi, P., Tignanelli, C., Bian, J., & Bihorac, A. (2022). Federated learning for preserving data privacy in collaborative healthcare research. *Digital Health, 8*. https://doi.org/10.1177/20552076221134455

Lukmanjaya, W., Butler, T., Cox, S., Perez-Concha, O., Bromfield, L., & Karystianis, G. (2025). Leveraging AI to investigate child maltreatment text narratives: Promising benefits and addressable risks. *JMIR Pediatrics and Parenting, 8*, e73579. https://doi.org/10.2196/73579

Mannava, M. (2024). Causal inference in AI-based decision support: Beyond correlation to causation. In *2024 4th International Conference on Ubiquitous Computing and Intelligent Information Systems (ICUIS)* (pp. 176–181). IEEE. https://doi.org/10.1109/icuis64676.2024.10866582

Manning, C. D., & Schütze, H. (1999). *Foundations of statistical natural language processing*. MIT Press.

Mantler, T., Veenendaal, J., & Wathen, C. (2021). Exploring the use of hotels as alternative housing by domestic violence shelters during COVID-19. *International Journal on Homelessness*. https://doi.org/10.5206/ijoh.2021.1.13642

McConnell, K. J., & Lindner, S. (2019). Estimating treatment effects with machine learning. *Health Services Research, 54*(6), 1273–1282. https://doi.org/10.1111/1475-6773.13212

Megouo, T., & Pierre, S. (2024). A stacking ensemble machine learning model for emergency call forecasting. *IEEE Access, 12*, 115820–115837. https://doi.org/10.1109/access.2024.3445591

Mendes-Neves, T., Meireles, L., & Mendes-Moreira, J. (2023). A survey of advanced computer vision techniques for sports. *arXiv*. https://doi.org/10.48550/arXiv.2301.07583

Meng, H., Zhang, R., Wang, G., Yang, Y., Qin, P., Lee, J., & Lee, Y. (2025). Deconstructing depression stigma: Integrating AI-driven data collection and analysis with causal knowledge graphs. In *Proceedings of the 2025 CHI Conference on Human Factors in Computing Systems*. https://doi.org/10.1145/3706598.3714255

Mohebbi, F., Forati, A., Torres, L., deRoon-Cassini, T., Harris, J., Tomas, C., Mantsch, J., & Ghose, R. (2023). Exploring the association between structural racism and mental health: Geospatial and machine learning analysis. *JMIR Public Health and Surveillance, 10*, e52691. https://doi.org/10.2196/52691

Mökander, J., & Schroeder, R. (2021). AI and social theory. *AI & Society, 37*, 1337–1351. https://doi.org/10.1007/s00146-021-01222-z

Moreau, T., Sinatra, R., & Sekara, V. (2024). Failing our youngest: On the biases, pitfalls, and risks in a decision support algorithm used for child protection. In *Proceedings of the 2024 ACM Conference on Fairness, Accountability, and Transparency*. https://doi.org/10.1145/3630106.3658906.

Moon, E., Saxena, D., Maharaj, T., & Guha, S. (2024). Beyond predictive algorithms in child welfare. In *Proceedings of the 50th Graphics Interface Conference*. https://doi.org/10.1145/3670947.3670976

Moore, J., McMeekin, P., Parkes, T., Walker, R., Morris, R., Stuart, S., Hetherington, V., & Godfrey, A. (2024). Contextualizing remote fall risk: Video data capture and implementing ethical AI. *NPJ Digital Medicine, 7*, 250. https://doi.org/10.1038/s41746-024-01050-7

Murayama, H., & Takase, M. (2025). Evaluating the effectiveness of digital social robots in reducing loneliness among community-dwelling older adults in Japan: Randomized controlled trial and qualitative analysis. *JMIR Aging, 8*, e74422. https://doi.org/10.2196/74422

Mustapha, A., Ikhalea, N., Chianumba, E., & Forkuo, A. (2022). Developing an AI-powered predictive model for mental health disorder diagnosis using electronic health records. *International Journal of Multidisciplinary Research and Growth Evaluation, 3*(1), 914–931. https://doi.org/10.54660/ijmrge.2022.3.1.914-931

Nair, M., Nygren, J., Nilsen, P., Gama, F., Neher, M., Larsson, I., & Svedberg, P. (2025). Critical activities for successful implementation and adoption of AI in healthcare: Towards a process framework for healthcare organizations. *Frontiers in Digital Health, 7*, 1550459. https://doi.org/10.3389/fdgth.2025.1550459

Nambiar, A., Harikrishnaa, S., & Sharanprasath, S. (2023). Model-agnostic explainable artificial intelligence tools for severity prediction and symptom analysis on Indian COVID-19 data. *Frontiers in Artificial Intelligence, 6*, 1272506. https://doi.org/10.3389/frai.2023.1272506

NASW, ASWB, CSWE, & CSWA. (2017). *Standards for technology in social work practice*. National Association of Social Workers. https://www.socialworkers.org/Practice/NASW-Practice-Standards-Guidelines/Standards-for-Technology-in-Social-Work-Practice

Neubauer, L., Straw, I., Mariconti, E., & Tanczer, L. M. (2023). A systematic literature review of the use of computational text analysis methods in intimate partner violence research. *Journal of Family Violence*, 1–20. Advance online publication. https://doi.org/10.1007/s10896-023-00517-7

Nikolaidis, C., Perifanis, V., Pavlidis, N., & Efraimidis, P. (2023). Federated learning for early dropout prediction on healthy ageing applications. In *2023 Eighth International Conference on Fog and Mobile Edge Computing (FMEC)* (pp. 135–142). IEEE. https://doi.org/10.1109/fmec59375.2023.10306129

Novitzky, P., Janssen, J., & Kokkeler, B. (2023). A systematic review of ethical challenges and opportunities of addressing domestic violence with AI-technologies and online tools. *Heliyon, 9*. https://doi.org/10.1016/j.heliyon.2023.e17140

Ortigossa, E., Gonçalves, T., & Nonato, L. (2024). EXplainable Artificial Intelligence (XAI)—From theory to methods and applications. *IEEE Access, 12*, 80799–80846. https://doi.org/10.1109/access.2024.3409843

Othman, N., Panchapakesan, C., Loh, S., Zhang, M., Gupta, R., Martanto, W., Phang, Y., Morris, R., Loke, W., Tan, K., Subramaniam, M., & Yang, Y. (2024). Predicting public mental health needs in a crisis using social media indicators: A Singapore big data study. *Scientific Reports, 14*. https://doi.org/10.1038/s41598-024-73978-5

Papanikou, V., Karidi, D., Pitoura, E., Panagiotou, E., & Ntoutsi, E. (2025). Explanations as bias detectors: A critical study of local post-hoc XAI methods for fairness exploration. *arXiv*, abs/2505.00802. https://doi.org/10.48550/arxiv.2505.00802

Park, T. (2024). COVID-19 research trends in social work: LDA topic modeling analysis in South Korea. *Journal of Social Service Research, 50*(4), 609–619. https://doi.org/10.1080/01488376.2024.2354528

Poppe, L., Steen, J., Loh, W. W., Crombez, G., De Block, F., Jacobs, N., Tennant, P. W. G., Cauwenberg, J. V., & Paepe, A. L. (2025). How to develop causal directed acyclic graphs for observational health research: A scoping review. *Health Psychology Review, 19*(1), 45–65. https://doi.org/10.1080/17437199.2024.2402809

Prakash, V., Kohli, M., Kohli, S., Prathosh, A., Wadhera, T., Panigrahi, D., Vijay, J., Kommu, S., & Prakash, V. (2023). Computer vision-based assessment of autistic children: Analyzing interactions, emotions, human pose, and life skills. *IEEE Access, 11*, 47907–47929. https://doi.org/10.1109/access.2023.3269027

Putnam-Hornstein, E., Needell, B., & Rhodes, A. E. (2013). Understanding risk and protective factors for child maltreatment: The value of integrated, population-based data. *Child Abuse & Neglect, 37*(2–3), 116–119. https://doi.org/10.1016/j.chiabu.2012.08.006

Qi, B., Zhang, K., Tian, K., Li, H., Chen, Z., Zeng, S., Hua, E., Hu, J., & Zhou, B. (2024a). Large language models as biomedical hypothesis generators: A comprehensive evaluation. *arXiv*. https://doi.org/10.48550/arXiv.2407.08940

Qi, Q., Hessen, D. J., Deoskar, T., & van der Heijden, P. G. M. (2024b). A comparison of latent semantic analysis and correspondence analysis of document-term matrices. *Natural Language Engineering, 30*(4), 722–752. https://doi.org/10.1017/S1351324923000244

Rahmattalabi, A., Vayanos, P., Dullerud, K., & Rice, E. (2022). Learning resource allocation policies from observational data with an application to homeless services delivery. In *Proceedings of the 2022 ACM Conference on Fairness, Accountability, and Transparency*. https://doi.org/10.1145/3531146.3533181

Rastogi, C., Zhang, Y., Wei, D., Varshney, K., Dhurandhar, A., & Tomsett, R. (2020). Deciding fast and slow: The role of cognitive biases in AI-assisted decision-making. *Proceedings of the ACM on Human-Computer Interaction, 6*, 1–22. https://doi.org/10.1145/3512930

Reamer, F. G. (2023). Artificial intelligence in social work: Emerging ethical issues. *International Journal of Social Work Values and Ethics, 20*(2), 52–71. https://doi.org/10.55521/10-020-205

Rittenhouse, K., Putnam-Hornstein, E., & Vaithianathan, R. (2023, June 19). *Algorithms, humans and racial disparities in child protection systems: Evidence from the Allegheny Family Screening Tool* [Working paper]. University of California, San Diego; University of North Carolina Chapel Hill; Auckland University of Technology. https://krittenh.github.io/katherine--rittenhouse.com/Algorithms%20Humans%20Racial%20Disparities.pdf

Rogers, M., & Brown, C. (2023). Critical ethical reflexivity (CER) in feminist narrative inquiry: Reflections from cis researchers doing social work research with trans and non-binary people. *International Journal of Social Research Methodology, 27*, 447–461. https://doi.org/10.1080/13645579.2023.2187007

Rosholm, M., Bodilsen, S. T., Michel, B., & Nielsen, A. S. (2024). Predictive risk modeling for child maltreatment detection and enhanced decision-making: Evidence from Danish administrative data. *PLoS ONE, 19*(7), e0305974. https://doi.org/10.1371/journal.pone.0305974

Saha, K., Grover, T., Mattingly, S., Swain, V., Gupta, P., Martínez, G., Robles-Granda, P., Mark, G., Striegel, A., & De Choudhury, M. (2021). Person-centered predictions of psychological constructs with social media contextualized by multimodal sensing. *Proceedings of the ACM on Interactive, Mobile, Wearable and Ubiquitous Technologies, 5*, 1–32. https://doi.org/10.1145/3448117

Salih, A., Raisi-Estabragh, Z., Galazzo, I., Radeva, P., Petersen, S., Lekadir, K., & Menegaz, G. (2023). A perspective on explainable artificial intelligence methods: SHAP and LIME. *Advanced Intelligent Systems, 7*, 2400304. https://doi.org/10.1002/aisy.202400304

Shortreed, S., Walker, R., Johnson, E., Wellman, R., Cruz, M., Ziebell, R., Coley, R., Yaseen, Z., Dharmarajan, S., Penfold, R., Ahmedani, B., Rossom, R., Beck, A., Boggs, J., & Simon, G. (2023). Complex modeling with detailed temporal predictors does not improve health records-based suicide risk prediction. *NPJ Digital Medicine, 6*, 1–9. https://doi.org/10.1038/s41746-023-00772-4

Singh, A., Ehtesham, A., Kumar, S., & Khoei, T. (2025). Agentic retrieval-augmented generation: A survey on agentic RAG. *arXiv*. https://doi.org/10.48550/arXiv.2501.09136

Stapleton, L., Lee, M. H., Qing, D., Wright, M., Chouldechova, A., Holstein, K., Wu, Z. S., & Zhu, H. (2022). Imagining new futures beyond predictive systems in child welfare: A qualitative study with impacted stakeholders. In *Proceedings of the 2022 ACM Conference on Fairness, Accountability, and Transparency* (pp. 1162–1177). https://doi.org/10.1145/3531146.3533177

Stapleton, L. (2025). *How child welfare workers reduce racial disparities in algorithmic decisions*. CW360°: Spring 2025 Edition. Center for Advanced Studies in Child Welfare, University of Minnesota.

Smadja, F. A. (1991). From N-grams to collocations: An evaluation of Xtract. In *Proceedings of the 29th Annual Meeting of the Association for Computational Linguistics* (pp. 279–284). Association for Computational Linguistics. https://doi.org/10.3115/981344.981380

Søgaard, A. (2024). On the opacity of deep neural networks. *Canadian Journal of Philosophy*. Advance online publication. https://doi.org/10.1017/can.2024.1

Suel, E., Bhatt, S., Brauer, M., Flaxman, S., & Ezzati, M. (2021). Multimodal deep learning from satellite and street-level imagery for measuring income, overcrowding, and environmental deprivation in urban areas. *Remote Sensing of Environment, 257*, 112339. https://doi.org/10.1016/j.rse.2021.112339

Sun, S., Zack, T., Williams, C. Y. K., Sushil, M., & Butte, A. J. (2024). Topic modeling on clinical social work notes for exploring social determinants of health factors. *JAMIA Open, 7*(1), ooad112. https://doi.org/10.1093/jamiaopen/ooad112

Tabaie, A., Zeidan, A. J., Evans, D. P., Smith, R. N., & Kamaleswaran, R. (2022). A novel technique to identify intimate partner violence in a hospital setting. *The Western Journal of Emergency Medicine, 23*(5), 781–788. https://doi.org/10.5811/westjem.2022.7.56726

Takaoka, K. (2022). AI implementation science for social issues: Pitfalls and tips. *Journal of Epidemiology, 32*(4), 155–162. https://doi.org/10.2188/jea.JE20210278

Thomas, M., & Balamurugan, P. (2024). Real-time violence detection and alert system using MobileNetV2 and Cloud Firestore. In *2024 2nd International*

Conference on Networking and Communications (ICNWC) (pp. 1–9). IEEE. https://doi.org/10.1109/icnwc60771.2024.10537319

Tian, L., & Rizoiu, M. (2025). Estimating online influence needs causal modeling! Counterfactual analysis of social media engagement. *arXiv*. https://arxiv.org/abs/2505.19355

Thapa, S., Shiwakoti, S., Shah, S. B., Adhikari, S., Veeramani, H., Nasim, M., & Naseem, U. (2025). Large language models (LLM) in computational social science: Prospects, current state, and challenges. *Social Network Analysis and Mining, 15*, 4. https://doi.org/10.1007/s13278-025-01428-9

Trinkley, K. E., An, R., Maw, A. M., Glasgow, R. E., & Brownson, R. C. (2024). Leveraging artificial intelligence to advance implementation science: potential opportunities and cautions. *Implementation Science, 19*(1), 17. https://doi.org/10.1186/s13012-024-01346-y

Trost, M., Ford, A., Kysh, L., Gold, J., & Matarić, M. (2019). Socially assistive robots for helping pediatric distress and pain: A review of current evidence and recommendations for future research and practice. *The Clinical Journal of Pain, 35*, 451–458. https://doi.org/10.1097/ajp.0000000000000688

Trudeau, K. J., Yang, J., Di, J., Lu, Y., & Kraus, D. R. (2023). Predicting successful placements for youth in child welfare with machine learning. *Children and Youth Services Review, 153*, 107117. https://doi.org/10.1016/j.childyouth.2023.107117

Ullah, R., Asghar, I., Akbar, S., Evans, G., Vermaak, J., Alblwi, A., & Bamaqa, A. (2025). Vision-based activity recognition for unobtrusive monitoring of the elderly in care settings. *Technologies, 13*(5), 184. https://doi.org/10.3390/technologies13050184

Vail, A., Girard, J., Bylsma, L., Cohn, J., Fournier, J., Swartz, H., & Morency, L. (2021). Goals, tasks, and bonds: Toward the computational assessment of therapist versus client perception of working alliance. In *2021 16th IEEE International Conference on Automatic Face and Gesture Recognition (FG 2021)* (pp. 1–8). IEEE. https://doi.org/10.1109/fg52635.2021.9667021

Vajiac, C., Frey, A., Baumann, J., Smith, A., Amarasinghe, K., Lai, A., Rodolfa, K., & Ghani, R. (2024). Preventing eviction-caused homelessness through ML-informed distribution of rental assistance. *Proceedings of the AAAI Conference on Artificial Intelligence, 38*(20), 22393–22400. https://doi.org/10.1609/aaai.v38i20.30246

Wahyono, A., Harjoko, A., Dharmawan, A., Adhinata, F. D., Kosala, G., & Jo, K.-H. (2023). Loitering detection using spatial-temporal information for intelligent surveillance systems on a vision sensor. *Journal of Sensor and Actuator Networks, 12*(1), 9. https://doi.org/10.3390/jsan12010009

Wang, S., & Wu, Y. (2024). Achieving equalized explainability through data reconstruction. In *2024 International Joint Conference on Neural Networks (IJCNN)* (pp. 1–8). https://doi.org/10.1109/ijcnn60899.2024.10651184

Weng, Z., Bravo-Sánchez, L., Wang, Z., Howard, C., Xenochristou, M., Meister, N., Kanazawa, A., Milstein, A., Bergelson, E., Humphreys, K., Sanders, L., & Yeung-Levy, S. (2025). Artificial intelligence–powered 3D analysis of video-based caregiver-child interactions. *Science Advances, 11*, eadp4422. https://doi.org/10.1126/sciadv.adp4422

Wilson, P., Thorpe, R., Sharps, P., & Laughon, K. (2020). The relationship between housing instability and intimate partner violence: A retrospective study. *Public Health Nursing*. https://doi.org/10.1111/phn.12819

Wu, D., & Wang, J. (2024). Analyzing urban crime through street view imagery: Insights from urban micro built environment and perceptions. *Urban Science, 8*(4), 247. https://doi.org/10.3390/urbansci8040247

Wu, H., Zhang, H., Chen, W., & Xia, J. (2025). Retrieval augmented decision-making: A requirements-driven, multi-criteria framework for structured decision support. *arXiv*. https://doi.org/10.48550/arXiv.2505.18483

Xu, H., Yi, S., Lim, T., Xu, J., Well, A., Mery, C., Zhang, A., Zhang, Y., Ji, H., Pingali, K., Leng, Y., & Ding, Y. (2025a). TAMA: A human-AI collaborative thematic analysis framework using multi-agent LLMs for clinical interviews. *arXiv*. https://doi.org/10.48550/arXiv.2503.20666

Xu, S., Negri, M., & Roth, V. (2025b). NIMO: A nonlinear interpretable model (https://arxiv.org/abs/2506.05059) [Preprint]. *arXiv*. https://doi.org/10.48550/arxiv.2506.05059

Yang, S., & Ma, R. (2025). Classifying epistemic relationships in human–AI interaction: An exploratory approach (https://arxiv.org/abs/2508.03673) [Preprint]. *arXiv*. https://arxiv.org/abs/2508.03673

Yang, Y., Lin, N., Batcheller, Q., Zhou, Q., Anderson, J., & An, R. (2023). Sentiment analysis of tweets on menu labeling regulations in the US. *Nutrients, 15*(19), 4269. https://doi.org/10.3390/nu15194269

Yang, Y., Alba, C., Wang, C., Wang, X., Anderson, J., & An, R. (2024a). GPT models can perform thematic analysis in public health studies, akin to qualitative researchers. *Journal of Social Computing, 5*(4), 293–312. https://doi.org/10.23919/JSC.2024.0024

Yang, Y., Wang, C., Xiang, X., & An, R. (2025). AI applications to reduce loneliness among older adults: A systematic review of effectiveness and technologies. *Healthcare, 13*(5), 446. https://doi.org/10.3390/healthcare13050446

Yang, Z., Sudjianto, A., Li, X., & Zhang, A. (2024b). Inherently interpretable tree ensemble learning. *arXiv*. https://doi.org/10.48550/arXiv.2410.19098

Yeasin, M., Malempati, H., Homayouni, R., & Sorower, M. S. (2009). A systematic study on latent semantic analysis model parameters for mining biomedical literature. *BMC Bioinformatics, 10*(Suppl 7), A6. https://doi.org/10.1186/1471-2105-10-S7-A6

Yucer, S., Tektas, F., Moubayed, N., & Breckon, T. (2023). Racial bias within face recognition: A survey. *ACM Computing Surveys, 57*, 1–39. https://doi.org/10.1145/3705295

Yue, X., Antonietti, A., Alirezaei, M., Tasdizen, T., Li, D., Nguyen, L., Mane, H., Sun, A., Hu, M., Whitaker, R., & Nguyen, Q. (2022). Using convolutional neural networks to derive neighborhood built environments from Google Street View images and examine their associations with health outcomes. *International Journal of Environmental Research and Public Health, 19*, 12095. https://doi.org/10.3390/ijerph191912095

Zamora-Resendiz, R., Oslin, D. W., Hooshyar, D., Million Veteran Program Suicide Exemplar Work Group, & Crivelli, S. (2023). Using electronic health record metadata to predict housing instability amongst veterans. *Preventive Medicine Reports, 37*, 102505. https://doi.org/10.1016/j.pmedr.2023.102505

Zhang, J., & Li, J. (2023). Compound knowledge mining. In J. Zhang & J. Li (Eds.), *Spatial cognitive engine technology* (pp. 163–168). Academic Press. https://doi.org/10.1016/B978-0-323-95107-4.00002-0

Zhang, Y., Khan, S. A., Mahmud, A., Yang, H., Lavin, A., Levin, M., Frey, J., Dunnmon, J., Evans, J., Bundy, A., Džeroski, S., Tegnér, J., & Zenil, H. (2025). Exploring the role of large language models in the scientific method: From hypothesis to discovery. *NPJ Artificial Intelligence, 1*(1), 14. https://doi.org/10.1038/s44387-025-00019-5

Part V
Ethical Considerations and Future Directions

Chapter 22
Ethical Challenges and AI Governance in Social Work

Jingyi Huang, Fan Yang, and Joyce Lee

1 Introduction to Ethical Principles in AI and Social Work

Artificial intelligence (AI) is increasingly woven into the social work profession, from predictive risk models in child welfare practice and research (Gillingham, 2020) to AI-powered mental health chatbots in practice (Yang et al., 2025) to simulation teaching tools in education (Heinsch et al., 2024). Empirical and conceptual work now describes how AI is being used to conduct risk assessments (Rosholm et al., 2024), triage cases (Cuccaro-Alamin et al., 2017), detect patterns in administrative data (Rosholm et al., 2024), and support remote or automated service delivery (Yang et al., 2025). At the same time, these applications raise specific ethical concerns within the field of social work, including algorithmic bias and discrimination, lack of transparency and explainability, threats to privacy and confidentiality, and the potential erosion of professional judgment and client trust (Saeidnia et al., 2024; Weiner et al., 2024). Professional bodies such as the National Association of Social Workers (NASW) have updated technology standards, reaffirmed digital-age ethical obligations, and begun issuing guidance on AI (NASW et al., 2017), signaling that AI is no longer a speculative issue but a practical governance priority for social work (Reamer, 2013, 2023).

In parallel, a dense landscape of AI ethics and governance frameworks has emerged across sectors. Comparative reviews of national strategies, corporate

J. Huang (✉)
Silver School of Social Work, New York University, New York, NY, USA
e-mail: jh9925@nyu.edu

F. Yang
School of Social Work, University of Illinois Urbana-Champaign, Urbana, IL, USA
e-mail: fany16@illinois.edu

J. Lee
College of Social Work, The Ohio State University, Columbus, OH, USA
e-mail: lee.10148@osu.edu

R. An, M. A. Lindsey (eds.), *Artificial Intelligence in Social Work*,
https://doi.org/10.1007/978-3-032-18443-6_22

guidelines, and civil-society frameworks identify a strong convergence on a small set of recurring principles for "trustworthy AI": fairness and non-discrimination, transparency and explainability, human rights and human-centeredness, accountability, and safety (Corrêa et al., 2023; Fjeld et al., 2020; Jobin et al., 2019; Lee et al., in press). Building on these converging principles, international and regional instruments such as the Organisation for Economic Co-operation and Development (OECD) Recommendation on Artificial Intelligence (OECD, 2025), United Nations Educational, Scientific and Cultural Organization (UNESCO) Recommendation on the Ethics of Artificial Intelligence (UNESCO, 2024), the European Union's General Data Protection Regulation (GDPR) and Artificial Intelligence Act (European Parliament, 2025), and the U.S. National Institute of Standards and Technology (NIST) AI Risk Management Framework (AI RMF; NIST, 2023) codify expectations that AI systems should respect human rights, support inclusive and sustainable development, and be subject to risk-based governance and meaningful human oversight.

Importantly, AI ethics principles reflected in these frameworks closely mirror, rather than replace, the ethical foundations of social work. Social work's ethical codes and standards, such as the NASW Code of Ethics (NASW, n.d.) and the International Federation of Social Workers (IFSW) Global Social Work Statement of Ethical Principles (IFSW, 2018), affirm core commitments to human dignity and worth, human rights, social justice, the importance of human relationships, integrity, competence, and the ethical use of technology in practice (Reamer, 2013; NASW et al., 2017). Fairness and non-discrimination in AI resonate with social work's opposition to structural injustice, equity, and transparency. Moreover, the human-centeredness of AI aligns with person-in-environment perspectives, self-determination, informed consent, and voluntary client participation. Accountability and safety of AI reflect social workers' duties to prevent harm, do good, and answer for decisions that affect people's lives. These have been reflected in recent AI ethical frameworks developed by social workers to inform the responsible use of AI in social work research, teaching, and practice (Ahn et al., 2025; Lee et al., in press; Ricciardelli et al., 2025). For example, social work scholars in collaboration with leaders of the Society for Social Work and Research (SSWR), which is the premier research organization of the social work profession, have developed the Equity, Transparency, Human-Centeredness, Integrity, Collaboration, and Safety (ETHICS) framework, outlining six key ethical principles to uphold in social work research and providing recommendations for their practical applications (Lee et al., in press).

Yet even with this broad alignment of AI principles and social work ethics, applying these ideals in social work presents significant challenges. Bridging the gap between high-level "trustworthy AI" guidelines and real-world social work practice requires grappling with the profession's unique context and responsibilities. Social workers often serve vulnerable populations in situations where trust, empathy, and human relationships are paramount (Garrett, 2025; Patton et al., 2023). Consequently, any AI system introduced into social work practice must be held to higher ethical standards to avoid eroding these foundations. For example, scholars caution that algorithmic tools can conflict with core social work values, raising concerns about client confidentiality, informed consent, self-determination, and treating clients as whole persons (Gabriels et al., 2025; Reamer, 2023). This means social workers have a proactive ethical obligation not only to vet and adapt AI tools carefully, but also to advocate for their appropriate and ethical use (Flaherty & Krishnan, 2025). In fact, if left unchecked, AI could perpetuate biases or reduce the human element of care, undermining social work's commitment to equity, justice, and authentic human connection. Therefore, social workers must take the lead in ensuring AI integration uplifts rather than undermines professional ethics.

This chapter responds to that challenge by linking AI ethics principles with concrete governance arrangements tailored to social work. Section 2 reviews major global and regional AI governance frameworks, including the OECD Principles on AI, UNESCO's Recommendation on the Ethics of AI, the General Data Protection Regulation (GDPR), the EU AI Act, America's AI Action Plan, and the NIST AI Risk Management Framework (European Union, 2024; NIST, 2023; OECD, 2019; UNESCO, 2021; White House, 2025), and considers how they embed fairness, transparency, human-centeredness, accountability, and safety in their frameworks. Section 3 develops an institutional and risk-based AI governance model for social work, distinguishing unacceptable, high, limited, and minimal-risk applications and the corresponding requirements for ethical review and human oversight. Sections 4, 5, 6 examine cross-cutting issues of data governance, privacy protection, transparency, accountability, fairness, inclusion, and participatory governance. Section 7 focuses on the social worker's role in AI governance, while Sect. 8 identifies key challenges, gaps, and directions for future policy, practice, and research. Together, these sections move from principles to practice, offering a framework for ensuring that AI is governed in ways that strengthen, rather than erode, the ethical foundations of social work.

2 Global and Regional AI Governance Frameworks

Over the past five years, AI governance, which refers to the processes, standards, and guardrails to ensure AI systems and tools are ethical and safe (IBM, n.d.), has emerged as a central global priority (Davtyan, 2024; Zhu, 2024). At the international level, the OECD Principles on AI (2019) established the first intergovernmental standard for responsible and human-centered AI. In 2021, UNESCO's Recommendation (United Nations Educational, Scientific and Cultural Organization [UNESCO], 2021) on the Ethics of AI expanded this foundation by emphasizing human rights, transparency, fairness, and oversight.

In Europe, the European Union has led regulatory efforts. *The General Data Protection Regulation* (European Union, 2016) set global benchmarks for data protection (Corning, 2024). Building on this, the *EU Artificial Intelligence Act,* a comprehensive AI act that applies to all 27 EU member states (European Union, 2024), introduced a risk-based approach, with phased implementation from 2025 to 2027, to regulate high-risk and general-purpose AI systems (Lewis et al., 2025).

In the United States, AI governance primarily relies on executive directives and voluntary standards rather than binding legislation. The America's *AI Action Plan* (The White House, 2025) establishes a national policy roadmap that coordinates federal agencies to foster safe, innovative, and globally competitive AI development. On the other hand, the NIST *AI Risk Management Framework* (National Institute of Standards and Technology [NIST], 2023) provides organizations with a practical, risk-based framework for assessing, mitigating, and monitoring AI risks throughout the system lifecycle. At the same time, it is essential to note that, unlike Europe, there is no one overarching federal AI law in the United States, which has led to individual states creating their own regulations and thus resulting in a patchwork of complex and varied AI legislation across the country (Crenshaw & Richards, 2025).

Overall, these frameworks indicate the reflexive evolution of AI governance, establishing a conceptual foundation for regulatory practices across diverse contexts. The following sub-sections outline how major global and regional frameworks translate ethical principles into institutionalized governance mechanisms and concrete policy measures.

2.1 OECD AI Principles and Recommendations for Policymakers

The *Principles on Artificial Intelligence* (2019), adopted by the Organisation for Economic Co-operation and Development (OECD) and endorsed by more than 40 countries, represent the first intergovernmental standard for trustworthy AI. The OECD principles outline five core principles and five corresponding policy recommendations for member states, emphasizing inclusive growth, human-centered values and fairness, transparency, safety, and accountability of AI actors (OECD, 2019).

Table 22.1 shows how the principles of AI are translated into practical policy recommendations that operationalize ethical goals (OECD, 2019). For example, to realize the principles of transparency and explainability, governments are encouraged to establish regulatory sandboxes—controlled environments that allow developers and regulators to test AI systems and decision-making processes, and to refine transparency requirements before real-world deployment (OECD, 2023). Similarly, to ensure human-centered values and fairness, policymakers are advised to create data trusts and shared infrastructures that protect privacy and ensure equitable access to AI resources. The recommendations also call for investment in AI research for social good, capacity building for safety and risk management, and international coordination to harmonize accountability standards (Del Ser et al., 2023).

Table 22.1 OECD AI principles and recommendations for policymakers

OECD AI Principle	Corresponding Recommendation for Policymakers
1. Inclusive growth, sustainable development, and well-being	Invest in AI research and development that advances social good and sustainable outcomes; ensure public and private R&D addresses societal challenges, environmental sustainability, and inclusive economic opportunities
2. Human-centered values and fairness (respect for human rights, diversity, fairness, privacy, and autonomy)	Foster an inclusive AI-enabling ecosystem that protects individual rights and embeds fairness, accessibility, and equity across sectors; promote shared infrastructures (e.g., data trusts) that safeguard privacy and non-discrimination
3. Transparency and explainability	Shape an enabling and interoperable policy and governance environment that mandates transparency, documentation, and accountability; use agile regulation and regulatory sandboxes to ensure explainable and traceable AI deployment
4. Robustness, security, and safety	Build human capacity and prepare for labor-market transformation by enhancing technical competence, safety culture, and risk-management skills; strengthen institutional capability to monitor, test, and certify AI reliability
5. Accountability of AI actors	Encourage international cooperation for trustworthy AI, promoting global alignment on accountability standards, interoperability, and shared auditing practices; support multilateral frameworks for oversight and redress mechanisms

Note. Adapted from OECD Principles on Artificial Intelligence, Organisation for Economic Co-operation and Development (OECD, 2019), https://www.oecd.org/en/topics/sub-issues/ai-principles.html

2.2 *UNESCO Policy and Governance Recommendations on AI*

The United Nations Educational, Scientific and Cultural Organization (UNESCO) *Recommendation on the Ethics of Artificial Intelligence* (2021) advances a broader human rights and social justice perspective. Adopted by 193 member states, it represents the first global normative instrument dedicated to AI governance. Compared to the OECD's development and innovation framework, UNESCO's recommendation centers on protecting human dignity, equality, diversity, and environmental sustainability (Samarawickrama, 2022).

It calls on states to establish national AI ethics councils, implement ethical impact assessments (EIAs), and integrate AI ethics education into curricula and professional training. The document also promotes data responsibility, green AI development, and international, multi-stakeholder cooperation (UNESCO, 2021). To ensure accountability, UNESCO urges continuous monitoring, evaluation, and implementation through national ethics commissions, reporting mechanisms, and multilateral collaboration. Collectively, these measures establish a comprehensive, human-centered governance architecture that links ethics with actionable regulatory practice (Allahrakha, 2024; UNESCO, 2021).

Table 22.2 Seven principles of lawful data processing

Principle	Description
1. Lawfulness, Fairness, and Transparency	Data must be processed lawfully, fairly, and transparently to individuals.
2. Purpose Limitation	Data must be collected for specified, explicit, and legitimate purposes.
3. Data Minimization	Only data necessary for the intended purpose should be processed.
4. Accuracy	Data must be accurate and kept up to date.
5. Storage Limitation	Data must not be stored longer than necessary.
6. Integrity and Confidentiality	Data must be processed securely to prevent unauthorized access or loss.
7. Accountability	Controllers are responsible for demonstrating compliance with all principles.

Note. Adapted from Regulation (EU) 2016/679 of the European Parliament and of the Council of 27 April 2016 on the protection of natural persons with regard to the processing of personal data and on the free movement of such data (General Data Protection Regulation), European Union (2016), Official Journal of the European Union. https://eur-lex.europa.eu/eli/reg/2016/679/oj

2.3 General Data Protection Regulation (GDPR)

The General Data Protection Regulation (GDPR), adopted by Europe Union (EU) in 2016 and enforced since May 25, 2018 (European Union, 2016), is the world's most comprehensive data protection law, establishes legal standards for how personal data are collected, processed, stored, and transferred, emphasizing individual control, transparency, and accountability (Amoo et al., 2024; Sealey, 2020).

The regulation is central to AI governance because most AI systems rely on large volumes of personal or sensitive data (e.g., health, demographic, and behavioral data). By defining seven foundational principles of lawful data processing (Table 22.2), the regulation provides a normative blueprint for safeguarding individual rights and promoting the responsible and ethical development of AI (Cormack, 2021; European Union, 2016).

2.4 EU Artificial Intelligence Act

The European Union Artificial Intelligence Act (2024) is the world's first comprehensive, legally binding framework for AI governance (Smuha, 2025). Unlike voluntary frameworks (e.g., OECD/UNESCO principles), it imposes legal obligations on providers and deployers of AI systems placed on or used in the EU, with prohibitions, risk-tiered duties (especially for high-risk AI), general-purpose AI (GPAI) rules (including a systemic-risk tier), conformity assessment and market surveillance, and significant fines (Butt, 2024; Gstrein et al., 2024).

Table 22.3 Risk-based regulatory framework of the EU AI Act

Risk level	Regulatory intensity	Examples
Unacceptable Risk	Completely prohibited	Social scoring systems, manipulative AI that distorts human behavior, or indiscriminate scraping of facial images to create recognition databases.
High Risk	Strict regulation (mandatory compliance obligations)	AI used for medical diagnosis, recruitment and hiring, judicial decision-making, social welfare allocation, or public security surveillance.
Limited Risk	Transparency obligations	Chatbots, emotion-recognition systems, and AI-generated content (users must be clearly informed).
Minimal or No Risk	Largely unregulated	Game AI, recommendation engines, or spam filters.

Note. Adapted from Regulation (EU) 2024/1689 of the European Parliament and of the Council of 13 June 2024 laying down harmonized rules on artificial intelligence (Artificial Intelligence Act), European Union (2024), Official Journal of the European Union. https://eur-lex.europa.eu/eli/reg/2024/1689/oj

The *EU AI Act* introduces a risk-based regulatory framework based on differentiated levels of governance. As Table 22.3 shows, all AI systems are categorized into four risk levels, each with a corresponding level of legal oversight intensity (European Union, 2024).

This risk-based governance framework allows proportional regulation. The higher the potential risks to fundamental rights and safety, the stricter the oversight, transparency, and accountability mechanisms required (European Union, 2024).

Under the *EU AI Act*, high-risk AI systems, including those in health, employment, and social welfare services, are subject to the strictest regulatory obligations. Developers and deployers must establish risk management frameworks to ensure system safety, data quality, and fairness (European Union, 2024). They are required to maintain technical documentation, guarantee transparency and human oversight, and demonstrate robustness and reliability under diverse contexts (Nolte et al., 2025). Before deployment, high-risk systems must undergo conformity assessment and obtain Conformité Européenne (CE) certification. Continuous monitoring and incident reporting ensure accountability throughout the system's lifecycle (Gornet & Maxwell, 2024). Collectively, these measures aim to make high-risk AI systems safe, traceable, and human-centered within the EU governance framework.

In addition, *the EU AI* Act introduces foundational governance requirements for general-purpose AI (GPAI) systems (European Union, 2024), focusing on transparency, accountability, and traceability across the AI workflow. For GPAI, providers must maintain detailed technical documentation on model design, training, and limitations; ensure compliance with copyright and data-transparency requirements by publishing summaries of training data; and share essential information with downstream users to enable safe deployment. They are also required to monitor performance, address risks, and cooperate with regulators. Until harmonized standards are finalized, GPAI providers should adhere to the approved GPAI Code of

Practice, which promotes adherence to the EU AI Act's legal obligations on safety, transparency, and copyright of GPAI models and serves as evidence of compliance (European Union, 2024, 2025; Nolte et al., 2025).

2.5 America's AI Action Plan (2025)

Released by the White House in July 2025, *America's AI Action Plan* (2025) serves as the United States' first comprehensive national strategy for AI. It outlines a long-term policy framework that integrates innovation, safety, and competitiveness, aiming to strengthen domestic AI capabilities while shaping global governance norms.

In terms of AI governance, *America's AI Action Plan* (2025) presents a non-regulatory, innovation-driven vision, centered on voluntary standards and multi-agency coordination. Governance is framed as a mechanism to promote transparency, safety, and accountability without hindering innovation. The plan designates the White House Office of Science and Technology Policy, the National Institute of Standards and Technology, and the United States Department of Commerce as core governance bodies responsible for developing risk-management protocols, transparency standards, and model evaluation procedures. It institutionalizes four key pillars: (1) risk and safety governance, (2) transparency and accountability, (3) ethical oversight, and (4) public-private collaboration—supported by reporting requirements and incident-monitoring systems (The White House, 2025).

In contrast to the European Union's regulatory framework, which enforces binding, risk-based legal obligations through *the AI Act* (European Union, 2024), the U.S. approach prioritizes flexibility, innovation, and market self-regulation. Rather than prescribing uniform compliance requirements, it relies on industry-led codes of practice, voluntary risk frameworks (e.g., NIST AI RMF), and cross-sectoral cooperation to operationalize accountability (The White House, 2025).

2.6 NIST AI Risk Management Framework

The AI Risk Management Framework (AI RMF) is a voluntary guidance document developed by the U.S. National Institute of Standards and Technology (NIST) and officially released in January 2023 (NIST, 2023). The U.S. National AI Initiative Act of 2020 mandated that organizations identify, assess, manage, and mitigate risks associated with AI systems throughout their lifecycle (NIST, 2023). As a non-prescriptive, flexible, and consensus-based standard for both public and private sectors, the *AI RMF* emphasizes that AI risk management is governance of uncertainty and harm, not mere compliance. It situates risk in a socio-technical context, acknowledging that AI systems' impacts depend not only on code and data, but also

Table 22.4 Four core functions of AI RMF

Function	Purpose
Govern	Establish a culture of AI risk management and governance.
Map	Identify and contextualize AI risks.
Measure	Assess and evaluate risks quantitatively and qualitatively.
Manage	Treat, monitor, and adapt to AI risks over time.

Note. Adapted from Artificial Intelligence Risk Management Framework (AI RMF 1.0) (NIST AI 100–1), by National Institute of Standards and Technology (2023), U.S. Department of Commerce. https://doi.org/10.6028/NIST.AI.100-1

on how humans design, deploy, and interact with them (Dotan et al., 2024; NIST, 2023; Polemi et al., 2024).

NIST structures the *AI RMF*'s operational section around four interrelated core functions that apply across AI system design, development, deployment, and monitoring.

Table 22.4 (NIST, 2023) outlines the four core functions of the NIST *AI RMF*: Govern, Map, Measure, and Manage. These functions construct a continuous process for the development of trustworthy and responsible AI. Govern establishes accountability and ethical oversight; Map identifies potential risks and affected stakeholders; Measure evaluates accuracy, bias, and robustness through systematic assessment; and Manage mitigates and monitors risks throughout the AI lifecycle (NIST, 2023). Collectively, these functions integrate transparency, adaptability, and responsibility into AI governance practices.

3 Institutional and Risk-Based AI Governance in Social Work

AI governance in social work should be institutionalized rather than aspirational. As AI becomes increasingly integrated into social work, it is reshaping key professional processes, including early risk detection, intervention design, decision-making, service delivery, and evaluation (Sigfrids et al., 2022; Wang, 2025). These AI-augmented practices introduce new forms of uncertainty and ethical complexity, highlighting the urgent need for context-specific frameworks and regulatory mechanisms (Lee et al., in press; Reamer, 2022; Ricciardelli et al., 2025). Institutionalized governance can ensure that AI applications in social work remain grounded in ethical values, such as respect for human rights, individual well-being, and social justice, thereby improving social equity and well-being (Wang, 2025; Murko et al., 2024).

To institutionalize AI governance, establishing formal oversight structures, such as AI ethics committees and clear lines of accountability, together with a risk-based governance framework, is essential. Social work operates in ethically sensitive environments where decisions shape individuals' rights, well-being, and life opportunities (Juujärvi et al., 2020). Compared to commercial domains, AI in social work must respond to complex human contexts, where algorithmic bias can cause disproportionate harm to vulnerable populations (Lee et al., in press; Patton et al., 2023; Reamer, 2023). The strength of a risk-based governance approach lies in its capacity to deliver context-specific oversight that distinguishes among varying levels of harm, vulnerability, and professional responsibility. Such a framework enables agencies to adopt proportionate, context-appropriate governance measures, providing a balanced mechanism that protects clients while supporting responsible and ethical innovation.

Inspired by the *EU AI Act* (European Union, 2024), Table 22.5 drafts a social work–specific risk taxonomy that aligns regulatory intensity with ethical risk and potential social impact.

Table 22.5 Proposed social work-specific risk-based AI governance framework

Risk Level	Regulatory	Applications	Governance Requirements
Unacceptable Risk	Prohibited	Profile clients based on race, gender, disability, or socioeconomic status. Manipulative recommendation tools that distort caseworker judgment. Cause unsustainable environmental impact	Must not be developed or deployed; subject to institutional and legal prohibition
High Risk	Strict Regulation (mandatory ethical review and continuous oversight)	Predictive analytics for child welfare, health risk, eligibility assessment for social benefits, chatbots used in therapy or other types of therapeutic treatments, or automated intake triage	Mandatory EIA, algorithmic transparency, data quality validation, fairness audit, and human-in-the-loop decision control
Limited Risk	Moderate Regulation (transparency and accountability obligations)	Chatbots for client communication (e.g., case management, information), emotion analysis tools, or resource recommendation systems	Documentation of model purpose and limitations, explainability assurance, and periodic bias testing
Minimal Risk	Light Governance (self-regulation and monitoring)	Scheduling systems, administrative automation, or workflow optimization tools	Basic ethical compliance declaration, data protection adherence, and internal monitoring for misuse or drift

Note. This framework is an original conceptual synthesis created by the author. While informed by the risk-based approach articulated in the EU AI Act (European Union, 2024), the structure, categories, and governance requirements are newly formulated for social work practice

3.1 *Unacceptable Risk: Ethical Red Lines and Prohibition*

AI systems that fundamentally violate equity or human rights, or pose unacceptable risks, must be strictly prohibited, such as those that profile clients based on race, gender, disability, or socioeconomic status (European Union, 2024). These AI systems are identified as inherently undermining social justice or human dignity, breaching the moral foundation of social work. Institutional policies should explicitly codify ethical "red lines," including prohibitions on AI models with unmitigated bias, discriminatory data, or unsustainable environmental impact (Roy et al., 2025). Social work agencies should adopt a "diagnose–mitigate–document" procedure for dataset evaluation (Ortega-Bolaños et al., 2024). If bias or harm cannot be adequately corrected, the system should not be deployed.

3.2 *High Risk: Mandatory Ethical Review and Human Oversight*

High-risk AI systems, such as predictive analytics for child welfare/protection, mental health triage, chatbots employed in therapeutic processes, or welfare eligibility assessments, directly influence life-altering decisions. As the *EU AI Act* illustrates, the governance of high-risk AI systems must follow the principles of safety, transparency, and human-centeredness (European Union, 2024). Agencies are required to conduct EIAs, submit systems to independent review boards, and maintain human-in-the-loop oversight throughout design to deployment. Multi-stakeholder involvement, including practitioners, ethicists, and affected communities, should guide oversight, insisting on continuous monitoring and corrective accountability rather than one-time compliance.

3.3 *Limited Risk: Transparency and Accountability Obligations*

Limited-risk systems, such as chatbots for lower risk communications (e.g., information sharing, case management tasks), emotional recognition tools, or recommendation systems, may not directly determine outcomes but can still affect communication, trust, and perceived fairness. In line with the transparency and integrity principles of the social work ethical framework (Reamer, 2022), these systems require clear disclosure of AI involvement and limitations. Social workers and clients should be informed when interacting with AI tools, ensuring informed consent and user comprehension. In parallel, periodic fairness and accuracy audits must be conducted, and all deployments should maintain accessible documentation for accountability.

3.4 *Minimal Risk: Ethical Self-Regulation and Professional Learning*

Minimal-risk systems, such as workflow automation or scheduling tools, pose limited direct ethical risks but still require ongoing professional responsibility (European Union, 2024). Risk-based governance requires an emphasis on ethical self-monitoring, compliance documentation, and an internal audit process. Agencies should foster a culture of accountability through AI literacy and training programs (e.g., provision of continuing education credits to maintain social work licensure), enabling social workers to identify potential ethical risks. Even without external regulation, embedding ethical reflection into daily service delivery ensures that low-risk tools continue to uphold social work's core values of trust, transparency, and public service.

This proposed tiered AI risk-governance framework helps translate the six ethical principles—Equity, Transparency, Human-centeredness, Integrity, Collaboration, and Safety (ETHICS) outlined by Lee et al. (in press)—into actionable safeguards tailored for the social work context. As the authors of the ETHICS framework in social work research suggest, ethical AI governance must be proactive, context-sensitive, and value-driven, ensuring that systems that promote efficiency do not erode the core ethics of social work (Lee et al., in press). By calibrating oversight intensity to risk exposure, this AI risk-governance framework preserves innovation while responding to potential ethical risks.

4 Data Governance, Privacy, and Transparency

Building on the institutional principles and AI risk-based regulatory framework, effective AI governance in social work also depends on robust data management, which serves as a foundation for ensuring individual privacy and transparency in AI applications.

4.1 *Data Governance*

Building on the principles of the GDPR, the UNESCO *Recommendation on the Ethics of Artificial Intelligence* (UNESCO, 2021), and the OECD *AI Principles* (OECD, 2019), data governance must be anchored in quality, representativeness, and purpose limitation. Social work AI systems should collect only the data strictly necessary for defined service purposes and ensure that each data use remains consistent with its original ethical intent. In parallel, datasets must be continually audited for accuracy and bias, especially regarding marginalized or underrepresented groups (Knowles et al., 2023).

A robust data-governance framework requires clearly defined responsibilities, including the designation of data stewards or data-protection officers to oversee data flows, metadata documentation, and ethical compliance (Verhulst, 2025). Institutions and agencies should maintain transparent records of data lineage and establish review protocols for data retention and deletion. Following the *NIST AI RMF* (2023), social work agencies should regularly "map" their data sources and document limitations in representation or collection context. Periodic data-quality assessments and human audits can ensure that training data and client information remain trustworthy, minimizing systematic bias in the AI applications.

4.2 Privacy Protection

Given that social work AI applications routinely handle highly sensitive, context-specific information related to health, disability, family safety, and social benefits, individuals' privacy protection must be treated as a core governance pillar. The GDPR and the *EU AI Act* (2024) both require data controllers to demonstrate lawful processing, consent management, and accountability mechanisms for all AI-driven decisions. Social work agencies and organizations should conduct a Data Protection Impact Assessment (DPIA) or EIA before introducing any AI application that could affect clients' rights or access to services (Chang, 2021).

In practice, conducting a DPIA or EIA involves a structured process that begins at the earliest stages of AI design and continues throughout the system's lifecycle. Organizations should first identify the potential ethical, social, and human rights risks posed by the AI application, with particular attention to how it might affect vulnerable or marginalized clients. Based on the findings, social work agencies are expected to document the purposes of data use, risk mitigation strategies, and the justification for decisions in a transparent and auditable manner (Chang, 2021). Continuous monitoring and periodic re-evaluation are essential to maintain ethical alignment as systems evolve, ensuring that AI tools consistently uphold human dignity, fairness, and social justice—the moral foundation of social work practice.

4.3 Transparency and Accountability

Transparency is another foundation of ethical and trustworthy AI (Knowles et al., 2023). According to the OECD AI Principles (OECD, 2019), transparency requires openness about how AI systems operate, what data they apply, and how decisions are generated. The *EU AI Act* (European Union, 2024) further requires providers of general-purpose and high-risk AI systems to disclose documentation regarding their training data, model capabilities, and limitations.

In the social work field, transparency means that both social workers and clients can clearly acknowledge the scope, purpose, and limitations of AI used in service delivery (Devlieghere & Gillingham, 2020). When AI applications are used for assessments, eligibility decisions, or intervention planning in social work practice, explanations must be accessible and culturally sensitive to non-technical audiences. Agencies should document when and how AI systems are involved, disclose the frameworks that guide their outputs, and clarify the mechanisms for human oversight. By embedding the principle of transparency from data collection to results explanation, social workers enhance public trust, informed consent, and professional accountability, ensuring that AI remains ethical and context-aware.

5 Accountability and Oversight

Accountability and oversight are essential to ensuring that AI applications in social work stay ethical and publicly trustworthy. Accountability defines who is responsible for potential ethical outcomes and how oversight of AI is exercised from design to deployment. Building on global frameworks such as the OECD AI Principles, UNESCO's *Recommendation on the Ethics of Artificial Intelligence* (UNESCO, 2021), and the *EU AI Act* (European Union, 2024), accountability in social work requires both institutional structures and professional practices that enable monitoring and correction. This section outlines three complementary dimensions—institutional accountability, professional oversight, and continuous evaluation—that together form a sustainable AI governance architecture to promote accountability.

5.1 Institutional Accountability

Institutionalized structure provides the backbone of accountability and AI governance in social work. According to the OECD AI Principle on Accountability (OECD, 2019) and the UNESCO *Recommendation on the Ethics of AI* (UNESCO, 2021), institutions that design or deploy AI should be able to demonstrate compliance with ethical, legal, and professional standards. This requires clearly defined responsibilities and a reporting mechanism that specifies who is accountable for each stage of the AI lifecycle—from data collection and model training to deployment and monitoring.

Social work agencies should establish AI ethics and oversight committees to review documentation, approve deployments, and coordinate post-deployment audits. These committees serve as independent governance bodies, ensuring that AI systems align with regulatory frameworks (European Union, 2024) and with the ethical principles of social work. Agencies are also required to develop incident-reporting protocols to enable the timely identification and remediation of algorithmic harm (e.g., discriminatory treatment based on race, gender, and other client identities, biased risk assessments, misdiagnosis, breaches of confidentiality, and privacy). Such mechanisms can provide institutionalized accountability as an ongoing governance function rather than a one-time compliance.

5.2 Professional and Procedural Oversight

In real-world practices, accountability extends to social workers and interdisciplinary teams who apply AI tools in daily service delivery. While AI can enhance efficiency and support decision-making, it should not replace professional judgment or the ethical responsibility to contextualize interventions. The NIST AI Risk Management Framework (NIST, 2023) and UNESCO's governance guidance (UNESCO, 2021) emphasize the importance of human-in-the-loop mechanisms that allow users to monitor, override, or recalibrate AI outputs when necessary.

Thereby, social workers should be trained and equipped with AI literacy and ethical reasoning skills to identify biases and inappropriate generalizations in AI models. On the other hand, agencies can promote accountability through standardized documentation, such as recording when AI tools are used in case assessment or decision-making, and maintaining a clear audit trail of human approvals. Embedding these safeguards can transform oversight into a collaborative process, linking technical governance with social work ethical practice.

5.3 Continuous Evaluation and Ethical Learning

Accountability in AI governance does not end at deployment. It requires continuous evaluation, reflexivity, and institutional learning. For instance, the *EU AI Act* mandates post-market monitoring and incident reporting for high-risk systems (European Union, 2024), a regulation that social work agencies can adapt through ongoing ethical audits and periodic performance reviews. These evaluations should assess not only technical reliability but also social outcomes, such as whether AI applications improve accessibility, reduce discrimination, or inadvertently reinforce structural inequities.

Furthermore, social work agencies should maintain transparent channels for clients and social workers to report concerns or unexpected effects of AI applications, thereby reinforcing the accountability loop. Results from these evaluations should inform policy revisions and updates to technical models. This adaptive cycle aligns with the UNESCO framework's call for dynamic and participatory governance (Liu et al., 2024; UNESCO, 2021), which positions accountability not as punishment but as a process of collective reflection and continuous ethical improvement.

6 Fairness, Inclusion, and Participatory Governance

As the core ethics of social work, fairness, inclusion, and participation should be central pillars of AI governance as well (Lee et al., in press; Reamer, 2023). Beyond technical optimization, social work practice requires AI systems that actively promote equity, non-discrimination, and social justice. In parallel, global frameworks such as UNESCO's Inclusion Agenda emphasize participatory and value-sensitive approaches that align AI development with human rights and cultural diversity (UNESCO, 2021). Fair and inclusive governance thus ensures that AI not only avoids harm but also contributes to the advancement of dignity and justice in social systems.

6.1 *Fairness and Non-Discrimination*

Fairness in AI governance refers to both procedural and distributive equity, ensuring that algorithmic processes do not systematically disadvantage any social group, especially historically marginalized and underserved groups (Leslie et al., 2024). According to the OECD AI Principles and the *EU AI Act* (European Union, 2024), fairness requires proactive assessment of bias in data, models, and outcomes. In social work, where professional decisions may affect clients' access to social welfare, mental health resources, or child protection services, even limited algorithmic biases can amplify existing inequities.

To practice fairness, agencies should develop and adopt quantitative fairness metrics, such as equalized odds, demographic parity, or disparate-impact ratios, to evaluate biases in model outputs (Leslie et al., 2024). These metrics must be complemented by qualitative, context-based evaluation that reflects the complex ecology of human need. In addition, periodic fairness audits and impact assessments should become integral to institutional review processes, ensuring that AI outputs align with ethical principles of non-discrimination and equity.

6.2 *Inclusion and Cultural Responsiveness*

Inclusion in AI governance extends beyond representation in data to demand active participation from diverse stakeholders throughout AI applications. The UNESCO *Recommendation on the Ethics of AI* (UNESCO, 2021) calls for participatory approaches that integrate community perspectives into AI system design, evaluation, and policy formation. For social work practices, inclusion means co-designing tools with social workers, clients, and community advocates who understand contextual and cultural nuances best (Tan et al., 2025).

Agencies should establish stakeholder advisory panels that include service users, marginalized groups, and local organizations. These panels can provide continuous feedback on system functionality, fairness, and accessibility. On the other hand, culturally responsive design of AI applications requires contextual and demographic adaptability, ensuring that AI tools respect the diversity of client contexts (Ozegalska-Lukasik & Lukasik, 2023). This participatory engagement transforms AI governance from a top-down regulatory framework into a co-creative process of social accountability.

6.3 Participatory and Reflexive Governance

Participatory governance refers to the process of embedding fairness and inclusion into institutional routines through deliberation, feedback, and collaborative decision-making (Tan et al., 2025). Agencies should incorporate participatory design methodologies, such as stakeholder workshops, value mapping, and ethical impact dialogues, at the early stages of AI system development. These mechanisms are promising for fostering reflexivity, enabling developers and social workers to question embedded assumptions, review design goals, and dynamically adjust AI governance practices.

To institutionalize reflexive AI governance, social work agencies can adopt community-based evaluation frameworks that combine fairness metrics with qualitative feedback from social workers and clients. Evaluation results should be made public through transparent reports, reinforcing trust and accountability (Laufer et al., 2022). As a result, participatory governance can help transform ethical pursuits into measurable, sustained practice, ensuring that AI applications in social work embody the field's enduring commitments to human dignity, justice, and cultural humility.

7 The Social Worker's Role in AI Governance

As AI becomes increasingly embedded in social service systems, social workers are called to take on vital roles in guiding and governing these technologies. This involves not only using AI tools in practice but also ensuring they align with the profession's ethical standards and social justice commitments. Drawing from core social work competencies, this section discusses the social worker's role in AI governance in three key domains: (1) ethical and professional responsibility, (2) participation and evaluation in practice, and (3) social justice and policy engagement.

7.1 Ethical and Value-Based Leadership in AI Integration

Social workers have a professional duty to uphold ethical standards when integrating AI into practice. This begins with recognizing that the ethical imperative is not to avoid AI, but to engage with it responsibly (Flaherty & Krishnan, 2025). Rather than passively reacting to new technologies, practitioners are urged to actively shape AI development in line with social work values (NASW, n.d.; IFSW, 2018). In practical terms, this means social workers must approach AI with the same care and ethical vigilance used in any practice context and intervention, ensuring respect for client rights, transparency, and accountability.

Adherence to professional ethics is paramount. Existing guidelines already extend ethical obligations to technology use. The NASW *Code of Ethics* (revised 2021) explicitly requires informed consent when using electronic interventions and mandates protecting client privacy and confidentiality in digital communications (Reamer, 2023). These standards also apply to AI tools. Core ethical principles like autonomy, beneficence, and justice remain guiding lights. Thus, social workers are responsible for critically assessing AI outputs and not simply accepting automated recommendations without question (Flaherty & Krishnan, 2025). They must be prepared to override or challenge an AI decision if it conflicts with the client's interests or rights, reinforcing that technology should *support rather than supplant* human judgment.

Critically, being an ethical gatekeeper also involves maintaining professional competency in technology. Social workers cannot fulfill their moral duties if they lack an understanding of how AI systems work. Recognizing this, educational bodies have begun identifying the competencies needed for ethical tech integration. A recent Council on Social Work Education (CSWE) task force emphasized foundational digital skills, including digital literacy and information literacy. It also highlighted "*technology-informed professional identity*," integrating technology into one's practice while upholding core values (Council on Social Work Education, Commission on Educational Policy, & Task Force on Technology and Social Work Education [CSWE], 2025). In other words, social workers must continually learn about AI, stay current with emerging technologies, and critically evaluate their benefits and risks (Ahn et al., 2025). This aligns with CSWE's first competency, "ethical and professional behavior," now interpreted in a digital context.

Not all voices in the field are unreservedly optimistic about AI in practice. Some offer cautionary perspectives on technology's impact on social work ethics. Garrett (2025), for instance, warns that an over-reliance on AI "assistants" could lead to a *"disappearance" of social work ethics*, if practitioners become complacent and trust opaque algorithms over their own judgment (Garrett, 2025). This critique underscores that social workers must remain grounded in the profession's humanistic, empathic, and reflective value base, even as they experiment with tools such as chatbots and decision aids. The "art of social work," empathy, contextual understanding, and relational skill, cannot be coded into an algorithm (Nugent, n.d.). Social workers must therefore approach AI with a balanced perspective: Embracing its potential benefits while fiercely protecting the core ethical principles and person-centered focus that define effective practice. By doing so, they serve as a check against both technological utopianism and the risks of ethical complacency in a data-driven era.

7.2 *Participatory Design and Co-leadership in AI Systems*

Beyond upholding ethical standards, social workers play a pivotal role in the participatory design and evaluation of AI interventions. Frontline practitioners possess on-the-ground insights into client needs, community contexts, and systemic barriers, often missing in tech-centric development. When included as co-designers or consultants, social workers help ensure that AI systems are fit for purpose, culturally sensitive, and aligned with real-world social service contexts. For example, if developers are creating an AI triage tool for mental health cases, social workers can advise on psychosocial factors and local resources the algorithm should consider. In such partnerships, social workers function as bridges between technical teams and the community, translating grassroots needs into technical specifications and, in turn, explaining algorithmic outputs in accessible, human terms to colleagues and clients.

Even when not explicitly co-designers, social workers are often the end users integrating AI into practice and thus key to oversight of implementation. In child welfare, social welfare benefits, health care, and other subfields relevant to social work, agencies are adopting machine learning systems for risk assessments or resource allocation. Social workers ensure these tools augment rather than replace professional judgment. Practically, this means treating an AI's recommendation as a hypothesis, one possibility, or one source of information, not an objective truth. For instance, if a predictive model flags a teenager as high risk for school dropout, a social worker will use that flag to inquire further, perhaps visiting the school, speaking with the teenager, family, and teachers, and reviewing the youth's situation holistically before deciding on any intervention. In doing so, the practitioner validates and tests the algorithm's output against reality, thereby conducting ongoing evaluation and improvement of the AI tool. This participatory oversight prevents blind trust in black-box predictions and maintains accountability, keeping humans at the center and in the loop for critical decisions. It also embodies reflexivity, with practitioners continuously reflecting on whether the AI is accurate, fair, and helpful in each case.

Notably, social workers' own perspectives on using AI highlight a preference for human-centered augmentation. In a qualitative study of clinical social workers experimenting with a large language model (ChatGPT), practitioners saw value in using AI to generate ideas and streamline paperwork, but they also raised serious concerns about confidentiality, loss of nuance, and risks of misinformation (Báez et al., 2025). Participants emphasized a "preference for augmentation rather than full automation" of practice tasks, stressing that no AI should replace the therapeutic relationship or their professional judgment. The researchers called for comprehensive training and clear ethical guidelines to support responsible use of such tools (Báez et al., 2025). This frontline insight reinforces the importance of participatory governance: Social workers are willing to innovate with AI, but only in ways that bolster, not erode, key professional values of care, empathy, and client empowerment. In summary, by co-leading design, critically implementing and evaluating AI tools, and voicing practitioner experiences, social workers help steer AI development in a participatory, evidence-informed, and human-centered direction.

8 Challenges, Gaps, and Future Directions

AI's growing role in social work brings enormous promise but also complex ethical challenges. Across multiple AI frameworks, principles for "trustworthy AI," such as fairness, transparency, human-centeredness, accountability, and safety, align closely with social work's core values. Yet applying these ideals in practice is fraught with difficulties. Social workers have already voiced concerns that algorithmic tools could erode foundational ethics, threatening client confidentiality and privacy, limiting self-determination, and failing to engage individuals as "whole persons" (Garrett, 2025). The profession now faces the task of confronting these challenges head-on to ensure technology advances rather than undermines social work's commitment to dignity, justice, and service.

These challenges are compounded by the fact that current ethical standards and guidelines have not caught up with technological reality. Most social work codes of ethics predate the AI era; one recent review found that none of the nine principal social work codes explicitly addressed the use of predictive algorithms in decision-making (Reamer, 2023). Traditional codes provide a strong foundation of professional values, such as justice, dignity, and informed consent, but offer little guidance on AI-specific dilemmas, such as algorithmic transparency and accountability for automated decisions. However, professional organizations are beginning to respond. For instance, NASW updated its technology standards in 2017. It affirmed that digital practices must uphold social work ethics, and CSWE's Taskforce on Technology and Social Work Education recommended that social workers adopt digital and information literacy skills (CSWE, 2025).

Still, these early efforts have yet to fully articulate how practitioners should navigate issues such as data bias, model validation, and clients' rights to know when AI is involved in their care. There is an ethical capacity gap as well: Many social workers have not been trained in data science or AI oversight, leaving them ill-prepared to question or interpret algorithmic outputs. Bridging this gap will require both updating formal standards and building practitioners' literacy in AI ethics. Social workers must be empowered with new competencies to critically assess AI tools and advocate for their clients' interests in increasingly complex technological landscapes.

Looking ahead, a multifaceted effort is needed to strengthen ethical integrity as AI is integrated into social work. Governance and policy will play a key role. Policymakers are increasingly converging on risk-based regulatory approaches that align with social work values. In the European Union, for example, the *EU AI Act* designates certain human services algorithms as "high-risk." It will require strict transparency, oversight, and auditing measures before they can be deployed. Uses of AI deemed fundamentally incompatible with rights are to be banned outright under this law. This precautionary stance aims to prevent harm and bias by design, rather than reacting after violations occur. By contrast, other jurisdictions, such as the United States, have so far favored softer, voluntary guidelines over binding rules. Such frameworks emphasize innovation and self-regulation, but they may lack the power to enforce accountability. In fields like social work, where lives and rights are at stake, many experts argue that purely voluntary ethics are insufficient. Ensuring AI tools are safe, fair, and transparent calls for enforceable standards and legislation. Social work organizations should engage with regulators to advocate for laws and policies that protect clients' rights in algorithmic systems, mirroring the profession's long-standing advocacy for social justice in the policy arena.

At the same time, ethical AI in social work cannot be achieved solely through top-down rules. Practical governance mechanisms are needed within agencies and communities to translate principles into everyday practice. This includes embedding ethics review and oversight into the lifecycle of any AI used in social services. Agencies might establish dedicated AI ethics committees or expand the mandate of existing review boards to vet new tools for bias, privacy, and alignment with social work's mission. Before an algorithm is adopted to allocate resources or assess risks, it should undergo an algorithmic impact assessment, essentially, an ethical audit with input from social workers and, crucially, the clients affected. Monitoring and evaluation must then be continuous. AI systems should be regularly audited and updated as their real-world performance is observed. This proactive stance helps catch emerging biases or errors before they can cause harm, embodying a "not harm" approach in a dynamic sense. Alongside internal oversight, multi-stakeholder participation is key. Including frontline social workers, clients, and community representatives in governance not only grounds AI use in lived experiences, it also builds trust. When those affected have a voice in how an AI tool is designed, deployed, and evaluated, the tool is far more likely to reflect real community needs, cultural responsiveness, and ethical norms. This participatory ethos aligns with social work's collaborative practice models and with international AI ethics guidelines that emphasize human rights, transparency, inclusivity, and human oversight (UNESCO, 2021).

Finally, strengthening ethical integrity in AI in the future will require that the social work profession fully embraces its role as an advocate and innovator in the tech arena. Rather than viewing AI as a threat, social workers can assert their expertise in human welfare and justice to guide technological development in more caring directions. Interdisciplinary collaboration is one avenue: Working alongside data scientists and software developers, social workers can help ensure that AI systems are informed by social context and human values from the ground up. Co-designing AI tools with input from practitioners and service users can surface biases and cultural blind spots early, creating more fair and usable systems. Notably, some scholars argue that social workers' values and skills make them uniquely suited to mediate between technologists and communities, to champion justice and equity in the creation of AI policies and tools (Goldkind, 2021). This forward-looking stance means social workers should be present in legislative halls, research labs, and software design meetings alike. It also means investing in continuous learning within the profession: from ethics training on AI to new social work research on algorithmic impacts to revisions of curricula that prepare future social workers for a data-driven world. The mission of social work has always been to empower individuals, improve well-being, and challenge injustice, and that mission must extend into the realm of AI. By actively engaging in AI governance and development, the social work profession can help ensure these technologies are used in ways that respect human dignity and advance social good.

Competing Interests The authors have no conflicts of interest to declare that are relevant to the content of this chapter.

References

Ahn, E., Choi, M., Fowler, P., & Song, I. H. (2025). Artificial Intelligence (AI) literacy for social work: Implications for core competencies. *Journal of the Society for Social Work and Research, 16*(1), 9–26. https://doi.org/10.1086/735187

Allahrakha, N. (2024). UNESCO's AI ethics principles: Challenges and opportunities. *International Journal of Law and Policy*. https://doi.org/10.59022/ijlp.225

Amoo, O., Atadoga, A., Osasona, F., Abrahams, T., Ayinla, B., & Farayola, O. (2024). GDPR's impact on cybersecurity: A review focusing on USA and European practices. *International Journal of Science and Research Archive, 11*(1), 0220. https://doi.org/10.30574/ijsra.2024.11.1.0220

Báez, J. C., Ahn, E., Tamietti, A., Victor, B. G., & Goldkind, L. (2025). Clinical social workers' perceptions of large language models in practice: Resistance to automation and prospects for integration. *Journal of Evidence-Based Social Work*. Advance online publication, 1–22. https://doi.org/10.1080/26408066.2025.2542450

Butt, J. (2024). Analytical study of the world's first EU Artificial Intelligence (AI) Act, 2024. *International Journal of Research Publication and Reviews, 5*(3), 0914. https://doi.org/10.55248/gengpi.5.0324.0914

Chang, H. (2021). A response to the use of ethics as a data protection building block for AI. *Journal of AI, Robotics & Workplace Automation*. https://doi.org/10.69554/omos9444

Cormack, A. (2021). An introduction to the GDPR (Version 2). *IDPro Body of Knowledge*. https://doi.org/10.55621/idpro.11

Corning, G. (2024). The diffusion of data privacy laws in Southeast Asia: Learning and the extra-territorial reach of the EU's GDPR. *Contemporary Politics, 30*, 656–677. https://doi.org/10.1080/13569775.2024.2310220

Corrêa, N. K., Galvão, C., Santos, J. W., Del Pino, C., Pinto, E. P., Barbosa, C., Massmann, D., Mambrini, R., Galvão, L., Terem, E., & de Oliveira, N. (2023). Worldwide AI ethics: A review of 200 guidelines and recommendations for AI governance. *Patterns, 4*(10), 100857. https://doi.org/10.1016/j.patter.2023.100857

Council on Social Work Education, Commission on Educational Policy, & Task Force on Technology and Social Work Education. (2025). *Technology and social work education report.* CSWE Press. https://www.cswe.org

Crenshaw, J., & Richards, M. (2025). *The hidden cost of 50 state AI laws: A data-driven breakdown.* U.S. Chamber of Commerce. https://www.uschamber.com/technology/the-hidden-cost-of-50-state-ai-laws-a-data-driven-breakdown#:~:text=Unfortunately%2C%20there%20is%20a%20great,leadership%20in%20the%20technology%20sector

Cuccaro-Alamin, S., Foust, R., Vaithianathan, R., & Putnam-Hornstein, E. (2017). Risk assessment and decision making in child protective services: Predictive risk modeling in context. *Children and Youth Services Review, 79*, 291–298. https://doi.org/10.1016/j.childyouth.2017.06.027

Davtyan, T. (2024). An overview of global efforts towards AI regulation. *Bulletin of Yerevan University C: Jurisprudence, 15*(2), 158–170. https://doi.org/10.46991/bysu.c/2024.15.2.158

Del Ser, J., Coeckelbergh, M., De Prado, M. L., & Herrera, F. (2023). Connecting the dots in trustworthy artificial intelligence: From AI principles, ethics, and key requirements to responsible AI systems and regulation [Preprint]. *arXiv*. https://arxiv.org/abs/2305.02231

Devlieghere, J., & Gillingham, P. (2020). Transparency in social work: A critical exploration and reflection. *The British Journal of Social Work*. Advance online publication. https://doi.org/10.1093/bjsw/bcaa166

Dotan, R., Blili-Hamelin, B., Madhavan, R., Matthews, J., & Scarpino, J. (2024). Evolving AI risk management: A maturity model based on the NIST AI Risk Management Framework [Preprint]. *arXiv*. https://doi.org/10.48550/arxiv.2401.15229

European Parliament. (2025). *EU AI Act: First regulation on artificial intelligence*. https://www.europarl.europa.eu/topics/en/article/20230601STO93804/eu-ai-act-first-regulation-on-artificial-intelligence#:~:text=The%20AI%20Act%20includes%20the%20following%20regulations:,with%20transparency%20requirements%20and%20EU%20copyright%20law

European Union. (2016). Regulation (EU) 2016/679 of the European Parliament and of the Council of 27 April 2016 on the protection of natural persons with regard to the processing of personal data and on the free movement of such data (General Data Protection Regulation). *Official Journal of the European Union*. https://eur-lex.europa.eu/eli/reg/2016/679/oj

European Union. (2024). Regulation (EU) 2024/1689 of the European Parliament and of the Council of 13 June 2024 laying down harmonised rules on artificial intelligence (Artificial Intelligence Act). *Official Journal of the European Union*. https://eur-lex.europa.eu/eli/reg/2024/1689/oj

Fjeld, J., Achten, N., Hilligoss, H., Nagy, A., & Srikumar, M. (2020). *Principled artificial intelligence: Mapping consensus in ethical and rights-based approaches to principles for AI.* Berkman Klein Center for Internet & Society. https://dash.harvard.edu/server/api/core/bitstreams/c8d686a8-49e8-4128-969c-cb4a5f2ee145/content

Flaherty, H. B., & Krishnan, P. (2025). Refusing to fall behind: The ethical obligation to embrace AI in mental health social work. *Journal of Evidence-Based Social Work*. Advance online publication, 1–15. https://doi.org/10.1080/26408066.2025.2553018

Gabriels, A., Kuiper, C. H., & Harder, A. T. (2025). Algorithmic tools to help social workers in child protection service make well-informed decisions: A scoping review. *Child Abuse & Neglect, 169*, 107678. https://doi.org/10.1016/j.chiabu.2025.107678

Garrett, P. M. (2025). 'Magic moments': AI and the 'disappearance' of social work ethics? *The British Journal of Social Work*. Advance online publication. https://doi.org/10.1093/bjsw/bcaf230

Gillingham, P. (2020). The development of algorithmically based decision-making systems in children's protective services: Is administrative data good enough? *The British Journal of Social Work, 50*(2), 565–580. https://doi.org/10.1093/bjsw/bcz157

Goldkind, L. (2021). Social work and artificial intelligence: Into the matrix. *Social Work, 66*(4), 372–374. https://doi.org/10.1093/sw/swab028

Gornet, M., & Maxwell, W. (2024). The European approach to regulating AI through technical standards. *Internet Policy Review, 13*(3), 1784. https://doi.org/10.14763/2024.3.1784

Gstrein, O., Haleem, N., & Zwitter, A. (2024). General-purpose AI regulation and the European Union AI Act. *Internet Policy Review, 13*(3), 1790. https://doi.org/10.14763/2024.3.1790
Heinsch, M., Tickner, C., Betts, D., Cliff, K., Vincent, K., & Canty, J. (2024). Enhancing simulation in social work education using artificial intelligence: "Social Work Virtual". *Advances in Social Work & Welfare Education, 25*(2) https://www.journal.anzswwer.org/index.php/advances/article/view/352
IBM. (n.d.). *What is AI governance?* https://www.ibm.com/think/topics/ai-governance
International Federation of Social Workers. (2018, July 2). *Global social work statement of ethical principles*. https://www.ifsw.org/global-social-work-statement-of-ethical-principles/
Jobin, A., Ienca, M., & Vayena, E. (2019). The global landscape of AI ethics guidelines. *Nature Machine Intelligence, 1*(9), 389–399. https://doi.org/10.1038/s42256-019-0088-2
Juujärvi, S., Kallunki, E., & Luostari, H. (2020). Ethical decision-making of social welfare workers in the transition of services: The ethics of care and justice perspectives. *Ethics and Social Welfare, 14*(1), 65–83. https://doi.org/10.1080/17496535.2019.1710546
Knowles, B., Fledderjohann, J., Richards, J., & Varshney, K. R. (2023). Trustworthy AI and the logics of intersectional resistance. In *Proceedings of the 2023 ACM conference on fairness, accountability, and transparency*. https://doi.org/10.1145/3593013.3593986
Laufer, B., Jain, S., Cooper, A., Kleinberg, J., & Heidari, H. (2022). Four years of FAccT: A reflexive, mixed-methods analysis of research contributions, shortcomings, and future prospects. In *Proceedings of the 2022 ACM conference on fairness, accountability, and transparency*. https://doi.org/10.1145/3531146.3533107
Lee, J. T., Pace, G., Cha, H., Rao, S., An, R., & Denby-Brinson, R. (in press). ETHICS: An ethical framework for artificial intelligence (AI) use in social work research. *Journal of the Society of Social Work and Research*. https://doi.org/10.1086/739116
Leslie, D., Rincón, C., Briggs, M., Perini, A., Jayadeva, S., Borda, A., Bennett, S., Burr, C., Aitken, M., Katell, M., Fischer, C., Wong, J., & Garcia, I. (2024). AI fairness in practice [Preprint]. *SSRN*. https://doi.org/10.2139/ssrn.4731838
Lewis, D., Golpayegani, D., & Pandit, H. J. (2025). Mapping the regulatory learning space for the EU AI Act. *arXiv*. https://arxiv.org/abs/2503.05787
Liu, Y., Zheng, W., & Su, Y. (2024). Enhancing ethical governance of artificial intelligence through dynamic feedback mechanism. In I. Sserwanga et al. (Eds.), *Wisdom, well-being, win-win. iConference 2024. Lecture Notes in Computer Science* (Vol. 14598). Springer. https://doi.org/10.1007/978-3-031-57867-0_8
Murko, E., Babšek, M., & Aristovnik, A. (2024). Artificial intelligence and public governance models in socioeconomic welfare: Some insights from Slovenia. *Administratie Si Management Public, 43*, 41–58. https://doi.org/10.24818/amp/2024.43-03
NASW. (n.d.). *Read the code of ethics*. https://www.socialworkers.org/About/Ethics/Code-of-Ethics/Code-of-Ethics-English
National Association of Social Workers, Association of Social Work Boards, Council on Social Work Education, & Clinical Social Work Association. (2017). *Standards for technology in social work practice*. https://www.socialworkers.org/Practice/NASW-Practice-Standards-Guidelines/Standards-for-Technology-in-Social-Work-Practice
National Institute of Standards and Technology. (2023). Artificial Intelligence Risk Management Framework (AI RMF 1.0) (NIST AI 100–1). *U.S. Department of Commerce*. https://doi.org/10.6028/NIST.AI.100-1
Nolte, H., Rateike, M., & Finck, M. (2025). Robustness and cybersecurity in the EU Artificial Intelligence Act. In *Proceedings of the 2025 ACM Conference on Fairness, Accountability, and Transparency*. https://doi.org/10.1145/3715275.3732020
Nugent, K. (n.d.). *Preserving the art of social work in the age of AI*. National Association of Social Workers–Missouri Chapter. https://naswmo.socialworkers.org/News/Preserving-the-Art-of-Social-Work-in-the-Age-of-AI
Organisation for Economic Co-operation and Development (OECD). (2019). *OECD principles on artificial intelligence*. https://www.oecd.org/en/topics/sub-issues/ai-principles.html

Organisation for Economic Co-operation and Development (OECD). (2023). The state of implementation of the OECD AI principles four years on (OECD Artificial Intelligence Papers No. 3). OECD Publishing. https://doi.org/10.1787/835641c9-en

Organisation for Economic Co-operation and Development (OECD). (2025). *Recommendation of the Council on Artificial Intelligence*. https://legalinstruments.oecd.org/en/instruments/oecd-legal-0449

Ortega-Bolaños, R., Bernal-Salcedo, J., Ortiz, M., Sarmiento, J., Ruz, G., & Tabares-Soto, R. (2024). Applying the ethics of AI: A systematic review of tools for developing and assessing AI-based systems. *Artificial Intelligence Review, 57*(110). https://doi.org/10.1007/s10462-024-10740-3

Ozegalska-Lukasik, N., & Lukasik, S. (2023). Culturally responsive artificial intelligence: Problems, challenges and solutions [Preprint]. *arXiv*. https://doi.org/10.48550/arxiv.2312.08467

Patton, D. U., Landau, A. Y., & Mathiyazhagan, S. (2023). ChatGPT for social work science: Ethical challenges and opportunities. *Journal of the Society for Social Work and Research, 14*(3), 553–562. https://doi.org/10.1086/726042

Polemi, N., Praça, I., Kioskli, K., & Bécue, A. (2024). Challenges and efforts in managing AI trustworthiness risks: A state of knowledge. *Frontiers in Big Data, 7*, 1381163. https://doi.org/10.3389/fdata.2024.1381163

Reamer, F. G. (2013). Social work in a digital age: Ethical and risk management challenges. *Social Work, 58*(2), 163–172. https://doi.org/10.1093/sw/swt003

Reamer, F. G. (2022). Managing ethics challenges in social work organizations. *Advances in Social Work, 22*(2), 374–392. https://doi.org/10.18060/25719

Reamer, F. G. (2023). Artificial intelligence in social work: Emerging ethical issues. *International Journal of Social Work Values and Ethics, 20*(2), 52–71. https://doi.org/10.55521/10-020-205

Ricciardelli, L. A., Loy, A., & Bantry-White, E. (2025). Preserving the integrity of evidence-based social work in the age of AI: A proposed ethical framework. *Journal of Evidence-Based Social Work*, 1–20. https://doi.org/10.1080/26408066.2025.2587092

Rosholm, M., Bodilsen, S. T., Michel, B., & Nielsen, A. S. (2024). Predictive risk modeling for child maltreatment detection and enhanced decision-making: Evidence from Danish administrative data. *PLoS One, 19*(7), e0305974. https://doi.org/10.1371/journal.pone.0305974

Roy, A., Rizou, S., Papadopoulos, S., & Ntoutsi, E. (2025). Achieving socio-economic parity through the lens of the EU Artificial Intelligence Act. In *Proceedings of the 2025 ACM Conference on Fairness, Accountability, and Transparency*. https://doi.org/10.1145/3715275.3732125

Saeidnia, H., Fotami, S., Lund, B., & Ghiasi, N. (2024). Ethical considerations in artificial intelligence interventions for mental health and well-being: Ensuring responsible implementation and impact. *Social Sciences, 13*(7), 381. https://doi.org/10.3390/socsci13070381

Samarawickrama, M. (2022). AI governance and ethics framework for sustainable AI and sustainability [Preprint]. *arXiv*. https://arxiv.org/abs/2210.08984

Sealey, B. (2020). Has the 2016 General Data Protection Regulation really given consumers more control over their personal data? *LJMU Student Law Journal, 1*, 17–41. https://doi.org/10.24377/LJMU.SLJ.vol431rticle431

Sigfrids, A., Nieminen, M., Leikas, J., & Pikkuaho, P. (2022). How should public administrations foster the ethical development and use of artificial intelligence? A review of proposals for developing governance of AI. *Frontiers in Human Dynamics, 4*, 858108. https://doi.org/10.3389/fhumd.2022.858108

Smuha, N. (2025). Regulation 2024/1689 of the European Parliament and Council of June 13, 2024 (EU Artificial Intelligence Act). *International Legal Materials*. https://doi.org/10.1017/ilm.2024.46

Tan, Y., Soh, K., Zhang, R., Lee, J., Meng, H., Sen, B., & Lee, Y. (2025). Empowering social service with AI: Insights from a participatory design study with practitioners. In *Extended abstracts of the CHI conference on human factors in computing systems*. https://doi.org/10.1145/3706599.3719736

The White House. (2025, July 23). *Winning the race: America's AI Action Plan*. https://www.whitehouse.gov/wp-content/uploads/2025/07/Americas-AI-Action-Plan.pdf

United Nations Educational, Scientific and Cultural Organization (UNESCO). (2021). *Recommendation on the ethics of artificial intelligence*. https://www.unesco.org/en/artificial-intelligence/recommendation-ethics

United Nations Educational, Scientific and Cultural Organization (UNESCO). (2024). *Recommendations on the ethics of artificial intelligence*. https://www.unesco.org/en/articles/recommendation-ethics-artificial-intelligence

Verhulst, S. (2025). Data stewardship decoded: Mapping its diverse manifestations and emerging relevance at a time of AI [Preprint]. *arXiv*. doi:https://doi.org/10.48550/arxiv.2502.10399.

Wang, W. (2025). The integration of artificial intelligence and social work: Opportunities, risks, and future directions. *Frontiers in Humanities and Social Sciences, 5*(4), 263–269. https://doi.org/10.54691/hx3e5z06

Weiner, E., Dankwa-Mullan, I., Nelson, W., & Hassanpour, S. (2024). Ethical challenges and evolving strategies in the integration of artificial intelligence into clinical practice. *PLOS Digital Health, 4*, e0000810. https://doi.org/10.1371/journal.pdig.0000810

Yang, F., Wang, C., Lindsey, M. A., & An, R. (2025). Use of artificial intelligence-based chatbots to promote physical activity: A systematic review of interventions. *Kinesiology Review, 14*(1), 80–92. https://doi.org/10.1123/kr.2024-0081

Yang, F., Wei, J., Zhao, X., & An, R. (2025). Artificial intelligence-based mobile phone apps for child mental health: Comprehensive review and content analysis. *JMIR mHealth and uHealth, 13*, e58597. https://doi.org/10.2196/58597

Zhu, Z. (2024). Trends and hotspots in global artificial intelligence public policy research (2014–2024): A bibliometric analysis using CiteSpace and VOSviewer. In *Proceedings of the 2024 4th International Conference on Big Data, Artificial Intelligence and Risk Management*. https://doi.org/10.1145/3718751.3718819

Chapter 23
Building AI Literacy and Competency in Social Work

Fan Yang and Janet M. Liechty

1 Introduction

Social workers worldwide live, work, and play in a digital and algorithmic era. This period is defined by the pervasive influence of digital technologies and algorithm-driven decision systems in nearly every aspect of life. The digital age began with the expansion of computers, mobile devices, and the Internet, transforming how people communicate, learn, and access services. The algorithmic age extends this transformation through the widespread use of data analytics, machine learning, and artificial intelligence (AI) to automate decisions, predict behavior, allocate resources, and deliver services. Together, these forces have reshaped how information is produced and shared, how systems are guided, how power and resources are allocated, and how human needs are understood and addressed. For the social work profession, that shift raises practical, ethical, and pedagogical questions about what we need to know and be able to do.

For social workers, this era brings both promise and peril, and the call to "harness technology for social good" has been highlighted as one of the grand challenges for social work. Data-driven, algorithmic tools and systems can improve access to care and training, identify unmet needs, augment learning, facilitate ease of communication, and enhance service coordination and quality. Yet these tools and systems can also perpetuate bias, obscure the sources of information and lines of accountability, and threaten privacy. To act ethically and effectively, social workers and their clients must gain AI literacy to understand how digital and AI systems function, whose values and assumptions are embedded in their design, and how to advocate for transparent, equitable, and human-centered uses of technology. AI literacy and the application of AI competencies have thus become essential for advancing social justice and protecting human dignity in a data-driven world, as well as for

F. Yang (✉) · J. M. Liechty
School of Social Work, University of Illinois Urbana-Champaign, Urbana, IL, USA
e-mail: fany16@illinois.edu; jliechty@illinois.edu

R. An, M. A. Lindsey (eds.), *Artificial Intelligence in Social Work*,
https://doi.org/10.1007/978-3-032-18443-6_23

ensuring the social work profession's relevance and preparedness for the current era and the decades ahead.

AI literacy and the application of AI competencies are therefore essential for advancing social justice, protecting human dignity in the digital and algorithmic era, and ensuring the social work profession's relevance and preparedness now and into the future. Consequently, this chapter focuses on building capacity for AI literacy and competencies. Building on earlier chapters that document where and how AI is already used in practice, our aim here is to demonstrate how the profession can scale learning and workforce development, enabling social workers at every career stage to acquire the orientation and capabilities required for ethical and competent practice.

2 Defining AI Literacy and AI Competency in Social Work

2.1 Definitions: AI Literacy

2.1.1 Background: The Evolution of "Literacy"

The term "literacy" originally referred to the ability to read and write, express oneself, and communicate in writing (Freire, 2007). Over the past several decades, the notion of literacy has been extended to describe a set of abilities enabling individuals to engage meaningfully in specific domains: for example, digital literacy is defined as the capacity to use digital technology, communication tools, and networks; scientific literacy is defined as the ability to understand and engage in science-based reasoning (Laugksch, 2000); and data literacy refers to the ability to read, work with, analyze, and argue with data as part of inquiry (DiSalvo et al., 2014). Advances in technology, changes in work and society, and the proliferation of new forms of knowledge creation have driven this expansion of literacy concepts. Each of these literacies shares a common orientation: enabling expression, communication, and access to knowledge in a given domain.

2.1.2 AI Literacy: Concept and Framework

Under the broader umbrella of literacy, "AI literacy" has emerged as a distinct and critical domain. In essence, AI literacy builds on and extends prior literacies, such as digital and data literacy, by attending to the rapidly evolving characteristics of generative artificial intelligence (AI) technologies: their ability to learn from and act upon data, their autonomous behaviors, their integration into socio-technical systems, and their potential to reshape human tasks, decisions, and social systems.

In their influential work, Duri Long and Brian Magerko (2020) define AI literacy as "a set of competencies that enables individuals to evaluate AI technologies critically; communicate and collaborate effectively with AI; and use AI as a tool online, at home, and in the workplace" (Long & Magerko, 2020). Their framework proposed five thematic dimensions: (1) understanding AI concepts and types, (2) recognizing AI's capabilities and limitations, (3) comprehending underlying AI processes, (4) addressing ethical and societal implications, and (5) examining public perceptions of AI (Long & Magerko, 2020). This work situates AI literacy beyond mere technical or programming knowledge; it emphasizes the capacity for critical engagement, responsible use, and effective human–AI interaction.

Subsequent scholarship has refined this conceptualization. In search of a sound theoretical foundation to define, teach, and evaluate AI literacy, a recent exploratory review was conducted to conceptualize the newly emerging concept "AI literacy." Grounded in a review of 30 existing peer-reviewed articles, this review identifies four core aspects of AI literacy: knowledge/understanding, use/interaction, evaluation, and ethics/reflective awareness (Tsz et al., 2021). Further empirical work situates AI literacy as a multidimensional construct that encompasses effective human-AI collaboration, creative idea generation, content evaluation, and step-by-step collaboration (Liu et al., 2025; Perchik et al., 2023). Thus, the term "literacy" in this context retains its classical grounding while being extended to the domain of AI technologies.

2.2 *Definition of AI Competencies*

2.2.1 Background: Competency in Professional Education

Across different professions, competence is widely defined as the habitual and judicious integration of knowledge, skills, communication, reasoning, values, and reflection in real settings for the benefit of those served (Epstein & Hundert, 2002). This definition emphasizes that competence is not only what a practitioner knows but how that knowledge is enacted responsibly in context. Assessment frameworks further distinguish levels of performance and competence that reflect knowing, knowing how to do something, the ability to show others how, and doing and accomplishing the critical tasks of the domain; thus, these levels underscore that competence is observable in practice and must go beyond factual understanding (Miller, 1990a). Contemporary competency-based education extends these ideas, portraying competencies as multidimensional, developmental, and context-contingent outcomes that organize curricula and accountability (Frank et al., 2010).

2.2.2 AI Competencies: Scope and State of the Literature

Translating these principles, AI competencies refer to the demonstrable ability to apply AI-related knowledge, skills, and values to concrete tasks, such as selecting, configuring, deploying, supervising, and evaluating AI systems, in alignment with professional standards and societal obligations. In education, researchers discuss concepts similar to AI literacy, but with a slightly narrower focus than the above definitions. They distinguish between knowing how AI works and being able to use it responsibly in real-world situations, emphasizing the importance of ethics, evaluation, and keeping people at the center of AI use (Chiu, 2025; Chiu et al., 2024). International policy and standards entities have begun to codify AI competencies for specific audiences. For example, UNESCO's frameworks for students and teachers specify domains such as a human-centered mindset, ethics of AI, AI foundations and applications, AI pedagogy, and professional learning, each with progression levels ranging from acquisition to creation (UNESCO, 2024, 2025). Beyond education, organizational research conceptualizes AI competence as the capability to integrate AI technologies with complementary resources and skills to achieve optimal performance, thereby highlighting that competencies can be defined at both individual and institutional levels (Mikalef et al., 2023).

2.3 AI Literacy and AI Competencies in the Social Work Context: Specificities and Distinctions

General AI literacy frameworks establish a necessary baseline, but the discipline and profession of social work demand tailored adaptations of general AI literacy and competencies frameworks, given the profession's core mission, values, and varied contexts of practice and research. More general approaches define AI literacy as the capacity to understand AI concepts and types, recognize capabilities and limits, grasp underlying processes, and consider societal implications (Liu et al., 2025; Long & Magerko, 2020; Perchik et al., 2023; Tsz et al., 2021); and those components still apply, yet their weighting and practical expression shift in a profession grounded in person-centered, values-driven, context-sensitive practice.

Social work is fundamentally relationship-centered, and so AI literacy and AI competencies in the context of social work must begin with the effects of digital and algorithmic tools on trust, power, and rapport in the worker–client relationship. Research on digitalization in social work documents both benefits and strains for relational practice, making critical reflection on human–AI mediation a core literacy element for social work, rather than an optional add-on (Nordesjö et al., 2022). An AI-literate social worker should be able to anticipate when technology reconfigures attention, authority, and the meaning of presence and human connection in direct practice with individuals and families.

Social workers routinely steward highly sensitive information; therefore, AI literacy and AI competencies in this field must prioritize data flows, consent, retention, secondary use, and the limitations of de-identification, alongside evolving professional standards. Ethics scholarship in social work highlights boundary management, confidentiality, and documentation as recurring challenges intensified by digital tools, and the profession's technology standards set expectations that now extend to algorithmic systems (Reamer, 2013). Practitioners, therefore, need operational literacy in how these standards apply when AI is embedded in assessment, referral, or service delivery.

Many social work agencies operate under tight budgets and uneven IT support; therefore, AI literacy must incorporate practical knowledge about organizational readiness, governance, and maintenance under constrained conditions. Reviews of information and communication technologies used in social work show that without investment in training, supervision, and evaluation, adoption is fragile and uneven (Chan & Holosko, 2016; Perron et al., 2010); literacy thus includes the ability to appraise feasibility, advocate for safeguards, and plan for responsible implementation. This organizational lens transforms generic AI knowledge into field-ready literacy, attuned to the realities of staffing, infrastructure, and accountability.

Because social workers work with clients who are vulnerable to experiencing digital exclusion, AI literacy in social work must be equity-attuned and accessibility-aware. Decades of scholarship on digital inequalities demonstrate how access, skills, and usage patterns track existing social disadvantages. In social work services, this means asking who benefits, who is burdened, and how to redesign or supplement tools to address language access, connectivity, disability accommodations, and cultural fit. Equity, therefore, becomes a baseline condition for AI literacy and AI competencies rather than a downstream consideration.

2.4 *Working Definitions for This Chapter*

For this chapter, we therefore define AI literacy in social work as the integrated knowledge, interpretive judgment, and ethical orientation that enable social work students, practitioners, educators, and researchers to (1) explain, in accessible terms, how AI systems used in human services are designed, trained, validated, and governed; (2) appraise capabilities, limitations, error modes, and fairness implications in context; (3) communicate transparently with clients and interprofessional teams about whether and how AI is used, preserving rapport, client autonomy, and culturally responsive practice; (4) safeguard confidentiality, informed consent, and prudent data stewardship across data life cycles; and (5) anticipate and mitigate inequities in access and outcomes for digitally marginalized populations. This definition extends general AI literacy scholarship by centering on relational practice, ethical research conduct, professional standards, organizational constraints, and digital inclusion as constitutive conditions of literate AI engagement in social work.

AI competencies in social work refer to the enacted, context-appropriate abilities that professionals operationalize AI literacy in practice, teaching, administration, and research, considering organizational, regulatory, and equity constraints. Competent performance is evidenced by the capacity to: (1) select, configure, and integrate AI tools into micro, mezzo, and macro workflows, curricula, and study designs in alignment with agency policy, law, and institutional review requirements; (2) maintain ongoing oversight of system performance, make necessary adjustments, and document procedures using model and dataset records, while auditing for distribution drift, errors, and unequal impacts across groups; (3) protect privacy and consent across data collection, sharing, retention, linkage, and secondary use in service delivery, classrooms, and research; (4) sustain relational integrity and support the autonomy of clients, students, and research participants when digital systems mediate contact; (5) ensure accessibility and inclusion for digitally marginalized populations in services, learning environments, and studies; and (6) participate in governance and accountability, including algorithmic impact assessment, incident response, documentation for reproducibility, and continuous improvement. This performance-focused formulation aligns with competency theory, which emphasizes the observable integration of knowledge, skills, values, and judgment. It also reflects emerging AI competency frameworks that prioritize a human-centered, ethical application and evaluation within the CSWE's outcomes-based approach to professional practice and research.

2.5 Differences and Connections Between AI Literacy and AI Competency in Social Work

AI literacy and AI competency in social work are analytically distinct yet developmentally linked for students, practitioners, educators, and researchers in the field (Table 23.1). Literacy is broad, conceptual, and values attuned. It equips these groups to explain how AI used in human services is designed and governed, to judge capabilities and limits, to communicate use transparently in practice, teaching, and research, and to anticipate equity and privacy risks (Long & Magerko, 2020). AI competency is role-specific and performance-based. This is evidenced by their ability to select and integrate tools into agency workflows, curricula, and study designs; monitor and document impacts, protect confidentiality and consent; sustain relational practice with clients and participants; ensure accessibility; and participate in governance and continuous improvement. In short, literacy orients judgment, while competence demonstrates that judgment operates within organizational, legal, and equitable constraints.

The relationship between literacy and competency is sequential, reciprocal, and situated within the ethical and practical realities of social work (Table 23.1). Literacy is a prerequisite and compass for competent action, steering client-centered, culturally responsive, and human rights-oriented choices in services, classrooms, and studies. Competent performance, in turn, refines literacy by generating situated insights about model behavior, documentation gaps, workflow fit, and unintended effects on rapport and access, which then inform critical understanding, pedagogy, and policy advocacy. The practical implication is a literacy-to-competency pathway aligned with competency-based social work professional education. Programs and agencies should build shared literacy foundations in concepts, ethical reasoning, data stewardship, and equity analysis, then assess competency through observable performance in authentic tasks that develop from understanding core concepts, to being able to explain and design appropriate actions, and finally to confidently and independently performing those actions in classroom, field, and research settings

Table 23.1 AI literacy versus AI competency concepts in social work

Component	AI literacy	AI competency
Definition	Integrated knowledge, interpretive judgment, and ethical orientation that enable social workers to explain how AI systems used in human services are designed, trained, validated, and governed; to appraise capabilities, limitations, error modes, and fairness implications in context; to communicate transparently with clients and teams while preserving rapport and client autonomy; to safeguard confidentiality and informed consent across the data life cycle; and to anticipate and mitigate inequities in access and outcomes	Enacted, context-appropriate abilities through which professionals operationalize AI literacy under organizational, regulatory, and equity constraints. Evidenced by the capacity to select, configure, and integrate tools within workflows; monitor, calibrate, and document system behavior and impact; protect privacy and consent; sustain relational integrity and client self-determination when technology mediates contact; ensure accessibility for digitally marginalized groups; and participate in governance, audit, and continuous improvement
Scope	Broad, conceptual, and value based. Oriented toward understanding, critique, and responsible use	Role-specific and performance-based. Oriented toward effective implementation, evaluation, and innovation
Purpose	To cultivate informed, ethical, and reflective practitioners who can judge the appropriateness of AI, communicate its use transparently, and lay a foundation for safe and equitable adoption aligned with social work values	To develop competent Social Work practitioners, educators, and researchers who can ethically apply AI tools to enhance practice, learning, and knowledge generation

(Council on Social Work Education, 2022; Miller, 1990b). In this model, the purpose of literacy is to enable informed, ethical, and reflective judgment about if and how AI should be used, while the purpose of competency is to ensure that such judgment is enacted safely and effectively to enhance practice quality, mitigate bias, and promote equity.

3 Aligning AI Use and Training with NASW Code of Ethics and CSWE Competencies

3.1 National Association of Social Workers (NASW) Code of Ethics

The NASW Code of Ethics is a "set of standards that guide the professional conduct of social workers" (NASW, 2021). It outlines six core values that can guide social workers' engagement with AI and algorithmic systems: service, social justice, the dignity and worth of the person, the importance of human relationships, integrity, and competence. These values prompt social workers to examine the ethical implications of AI, including privacy, systemic bias, and transparency, and to advocate for the equitable and responsible use of AI. From a social justice perspective, social workers must consider how AI may impact access to services, resource allocation, and ensure that human rights are upheld. The value of dignity and worth of the person invites practitioners to monitor algorithms for unintended harm and to promote client agency in digital environments. Emphasizing the importance of human relationships reminds social workers to use AI to enhance, not replace, empathy and human connection. Competent and ethical practice in the algorithmic era requires AI literacy to evaluate AI tools and their impact on client well-being, dignity, and self-determination. Guided by these core professional values, social workers are uniquely positioned to collaborate with data scientists and AI developers, ensuring that emerging technologies serve clients, honor human relationships, and promote social justice. The Code of Ethics provides both purpose and direction for advancing AI literacy and competency across social work practice, education, and research. The CSWE competencies further translate these values into the specific knowledge, skills, and behaviors needed to practice effectively in an AI-driven environment.

3.2 CSWE Policy and Accreditation (EPAS) Standards Competencies and AI

The CSWE competency model specifies the knowledge and skills expected of graduating social workers (Council on Social Work Education, 2022). In the algorithmic era, the central task for social work educators and accredited programs is to operationalize those competencies within settings where assessment, service delivery, policy, and evaluation are increasingly mediated by AI (Rodriguez et al., 2024). Research suggests that AI literacy should be integrated across core social work competencies, rather than being treated as an elective or a single stand-alone course, and that curricular integration should align with existing accreditation expectations and professional values (Ahn et al., 2025; Rodriguez et al., 2024). Aligning instruction on AI with accreditation standards and risk-sensitive pedagogies can help ensure that graduates are prepared to manage the ethical, equity, and accountability implications of algorithmic systems (Ahn et al., 2025). Consequently, CSWE's vision of competent, ethical, evidence-informed practice should be enacted in the very contexts where algorithmic systems already shape decisions and opportunities (Council on Social Work Education, 2022).

This subsection proceeds in two parts. We first illustrate how each of the nine CSWE EPAS competencies could be updated or enhanced in response to AI's current transformation of practice. Second, we introduce components of a new AI competency for consideration as revisions to the 2029 EPAS are underway.

What follows are suggested contexts and practice behaviors for each of the nine competencies relevant to AI in social work practice (summarized in Table 23.2). AI Literacy would be incorporated into Generalist practice behaviors,

Table 23.2 Integrative framework: AI literacy and AI competence across CSWE nine competencies and NASW Code of Ethics

CSWE EPAS 2022 Competency	Relevant NASW ethical principle	AI literacy (awareness, critical reflection)	AI competence (applied skills, tool mastery, evaluation)
1. Demonstrate ethical and professional behavior	Integrity, competence, service	Understands ethical implications of AI (privacy, bias, transparency); recognizes limits of algorithmic approaches and need for human oversight	Applies ethical reasoning to select, use, and monitor AI tools; maintains transparency, confidentiality, and professional integrity in digital contexts
2. Advance human rights and social, racial, economic, and environmental justice	Social justice, service, political action	Understands how AI affects distribution of resources, surveillance, and social control	Engages in advocacy and policy reform to ensure AI advances human rights and digital equity
3. Engage anti-racism, diversity, equity, and inclusion in practice	Dignity and worth, social justice	Recognizes digital inequities and algorithmic bias as new forms of systemic oppression	Uses and evaluates AI systems to promote inclusion and equity; advocates for bias mitigation and fair access to technology
4. Engage in practice-informed research and research-Informed practice	Competence, integrity, scientific inquiry	Critically interprets AI-based research, data provenance, and potential bias	Uses AI ethically for data analysis, modeling, or evaluation; ensures transparency and validity in AI-driven research
5. Engage in policy practice	Social justice, service, political action	Understands policy implications of AI (data governance, regulation, digital rights, privacy)	Participates in policy analysis and advocacy for equitable and ethical AI use in human services; monitors and assesses equity when systems use AI to identify human needs and allocate resources
6. Engage with individuals, families, groups, organizations, and communities	Dignity and worth, human relationships, service	Recognizes relational and cultural impacts of AI-mediated engagement; reflects on trust and authenticity in digital interactions	Uses AI-enhanced tools (e.g., case management platforms, chatbots) to augment but not replace human empathy and connection
7. Assess individuals, families, groups, organizations, and communities	Integrity, competence, privacy and confidentiality	Understands data-driven assessment tools and their potential biases	Integrates AI-generated insights with professional judgment; ensures validity and fairness in assessment

(continued)

Table 23.2 (continued)

CSWE EPAS 2022 Competency	Relevant NASW ethical principle	AI literacy (awareness, critical reflection)	AI competence (applied skills, tool mastery, evaluation)
8. Intervene with individuals, families, groups, organizations, and communities	Service, dignity and worth, competence	Understands potential benefits and risks of AI-supported interventions	Applies AI tools (e.g., digital therapeutics, predictive supports) ethically, monitors for unintended harm, and centers client agency
9. Evaluate practice with individuals, families, groups, organizations, and communities	Competence, integrity, accountability	Understands how AI informs evaluation metrics and data ethics	Uses AI-driven analytics responsibly to evaluate practice outcomes; collaborates with data experts to ensure ethical use

Note. CSWE competency language and NASW ethical principles are drawn from CSWE (2022) and NASW (2021), respectively. Descriptions of AI literacy and AI competence are author-developed syntheses informed by these documents and the broader interdisciplinary literature on artificial intelligence and professional practice.

and AI Competence into Advanced areas of specialized practice. These contexts and practice behaviors serve as a starting point that reflects knowledge, skills, values, and/or cognitive and affective processes relevant to AI in social work practice.

3.2.1 Competency 1: Demonstrate Ethical and Professional Behavior

AI literacy begins with understanding the ethical implications of algorithmic systems, including privacy, data security, transparency, and bias. Social workers must recognize the limits of automated decision-making and the critical need for human oversight. AI competence involves applying ethical reasoning to the selection, use, and monitoring of AI tools; maintaining professional integrity, confidentiality, and transparency in digital contexts; and ensuring that technology aligns with the NASW Code of Ethics.

3.2.2 Competency 2: Advance Human Rights and Social, Racial, Economic, and Environmental Justice

Social workers with AI literacy understand how algorithmic systems affect the distribution of resources, surveillance practices, and mechanisms of social control. They critically assess whether these tools advance or undermine human rights and social equity. AI-competent social workers engage in advocacy, policy reform, and public education to ensure that AI technologies are used to promote, rather than restrict, rights and opportunities.

3.2.3 Competency 3: Engage Anti-racism, Diversity, Equity, and Inclusion in Practice

AI literacy includes awareness of digital inequities and algorithmic bias as potentially new forms of systemic oppression. Social workers must learn to identify how data and design choices reproduce historical injustices. Building competence involves using and evaluating AI systems to promote inclusion, transparency, and fairness. Practitioners should advocate for mitigating bias, equitable data practices, and fair access to technology that benefits all communities.

3.2.4 Competency 4: Engage in Practice-Informed Research and Research-Informed Practice

An AI-literate social worker critically interprets AI-generated research, understanding issues of data provenance, sampling bias, and algorithmic validity. Competence involves using AI ethically in data analysis, modeling, and evaluation while ensuring that results are grounded in sound social science methods. Social workers contribute to AI-driven research that reflects human values, community priorities, and social good.

3.2.5 Competency 5: Engage in Policy Practice

AI literacy encompasses an understanding of the policy implications of AI, including data governance, regulation, digital rights, and privacy. Social workers must be able to analyze how policy frameworks shape the use of AI in human services. AI competence involves participating in advocacy and policy design to promote equitable and ethical AI use, monitoring the effects of automated systems on service needs identification, and ensuring that AI supports fairness in resource allocation.

3.2.6 Competency 6: Engage with Individuals, Families, Groups, Organizations, and Communities

AI literacy entails awareness of the relational and cultural dimensions of technology-mediated engagement. Social workers reflect on how digital tools affect trust, authenticity, and power in human relationships. Competence means skillfully using AI-enhanced platforms, such as case management systems, chatbots, or telehealth supports, to augment rather than replace human empathy and connection. Technology should complement rather than replace authentic relational practice.

3.2.7 Competency 7: Assess Individuals, Families, Groups, Organizations, and Communities

An AI-literate practitioner understands the structure, purpose, and potential biases of data-driven assessment tools. They recognize when algorithmic recommendations may reinforce inequities or obscure contextual factors. Competence involves integrating AI-generated insights with professional judgment, maintaining fairness and validity in assessment, and ensuring that data use aligns with ethical standards for privacy and confidentiality.

3.2.8 Competency 8: Intervene with Individuals, Families, Groups, Organizations, and Communities

AI literacy includes understanding both the potential benefits and the risks of AI-supported interventions, such as predictive analytics, digital therapeutics, or automated support tools. Competence means applying these tools ethically and responsibly, continuously monitoring for unintended harm, and centering client agency and informed consent. Social workers must ensure that interventions guided by AI are transparent, accountable, and person-centered.

3.2.9 Competency 9: Evaluate Practice with Individuals, Families, Groups, Organizations, and Communities

AI literacy in evaluation involves understanding how AI informs outcome measurement, program analytics, and data ethics. Competent practitioners utilize AI-driven analytical tools to evaluate practice outcomes responsibly and collaborate with data experts to ensure the ethical use of client information. By integrating AI thoughtfully into evaluation processes, social workers can enhance evidence-based practice while upholding values of accountability and integrity.

3.3 Proposing a New Competency for the 2029 EPAS: "Engage AI and Algorithmic Systems Informed Practice"

While AI literacy should be infused throughout the existing competencies (Boetto, 2025; Goldkind, 2021), the pace and scope of technological transformation suggest the need for an explicit competency focused on AI and digital ethics. This new competency would articulate expectations for social workers to understand, evaluate, and apply AI technologies in ways that advance human well-being, promote social justice, and preserve the profession's relational and ethical core.

The Council on Social Work Education (CSWE) is currently updating the Nine Competencies outlined in the 2022 Education and Policy Accreditation Standards (EPAS) (CSWE, 2022). Given the likelihood that AI and the algorithmic era will transform nearly every aspect of social work practice and the practice context in the coming decade, some scholars in the social work profession have been proposing a tenth competency focused on AI (Rodriguez et al., 2024). The tenth competency could be called "Engage AI and Algorithmic Systems Informed Practice."

Under the CSWE EPAS 2022, each of the nine competencies is followed by a set of Practice Behaviors at the Generalist level for all programs. Then, each program develops its own set of Practice Behaviors at the Advanced level for each area of specialized practice it offers. For the proposed tenth competency, we recommend that AI literacy be incorporated into the Generalist practice behaviors and that more advanced applications of AI be developed within a program's areas of specialization. This would ensure basic knowledge at the Generalist level and encourage deeper engagement in areas of specialization. In the proposed three-tier system of AI literacy and competency outlined below, Generalist practice behaviors align with Tier I, which encompasses foundational AI literacy knowledge. In contrast, advanced practice behaviors would reflect Tier II (intermediate) or Tier III (advanced) level AI knowledge, skills, values, and cognitive/affective processes. The levels of AI competency and corresponding training recommendations are described below.

4 Building Capacity for Social Work AI Readiness: A Three-Tier Approach

Modern social work must build capacity for AI readiness through deliberate professional development spanning all levels of practice, research, education, policy, and ethics. As discussed in earlier sections, emerging ethical standards and accreditation guidelines are beginning to acknowledge technology and AI as integral to competent professional formation (Hodgson et al., 2022; Nuwasiima et al., 2024). The Council on Social Work Education (CSWE) has identified increasing knowledge of AI and its implications as a strategic priority for social work programs (Council on Social Work Education, 2025). Likewise, leading scholars argue that social workers in all roles will need at least basic AI literacy, the ability to understand and critically evaluate AI systems, to uphold social justice and effectively advocate for clients in an AI-driven society (Ahn et al., 2025; BASW, 2025; Liu et al., 2025; Rodriguez et al., 2024). Given this broad and cross-cutting impact, it is imperative to prepare the entire workforce, students, practitioners, faculty, and agency leaders to engage with AI ethically and competently. Professional development (PD) for AI readiness thus encompasses both AI literacy (a foundational understanding for all) and AI competency (applied skills for practice) in social work.

This section proposes a three-tier PD framework to scaffold AI readiness, illustrated in Table 23.3: Tier 1 for foundational AI literacy among all social work

Table 23.3 Three-tier approach to building AI literacy and AI competencies in social work

Tier	Level	Audience	Focus of learning	Key learning goals/Outcomes	Examples of application
I	Foundational: Foundational AI Literacy for All Social Workers	All social work students, faculty, field instructors, agency staff, and supervisors	Awareness and basic understanding of AI concepts, benefits, risks, and ethical issues	• Recognize everyday AI applications in professional and personal contexts. • Understand privacy, consent, and data safeguards. • Identify potential bias and ethical implications. • Cultivate curiosity and critical thinking about AI's role in human services.	Recognizing AI features in tools like documentation software, scheduling apps, or case management platforms; following ethical and privacy guidelines in digital communication
II	Intermediate: Applied AI Competencies for Practitioners, Educators, and Researchers	Social work practitioners, educators, researchers, administrators, and policy professionals seeking to integrate AI into their work	Application of AI tools to enhance professional functions and outcomes	• Develop and apply AI-informed tools ethically in service delivery, teaching, or research. • Analyze data responsibly and identify bias. • Use AI to improve efficiency and outcomes while upholding social work values.	Using AI analytics in program evaluation; employing chatbots for resource navigation; integrating AI-assisted writing or learning tools into teaching; employing predictive analytics for policy or community assessment

(continued)

Table 23.3 (continued)

Tier	Level	Audience	Focus of learning	Key learning goals/Outcomes	Examples of application
III	Advanced: Advanced Leadership and Innovation in AI for Social Good	Social work leaders, scholars, researchers, and interdisciplinary innovators	Leadership, innovation, and governance in AI development, policy, and ethical oversight	• Lead interdisciplinary AI projects- Shape ethical AI policies and regulatory practices. • Advocate for human-centered and socially just AI systems. • Conduct or guide AI-related research and innovation.	Developing ethical AI governance policies, contributing to interdisciplinary AI research, designing AI systems that reflect social work's core values and justice-oriented frameworks

professionals; Tier 2 for intermediate training focused on the applied use of AI in practice and administration; and Tier 3 for advanced leadership and governance capacities. This tiered approach aligns with recommendations by social work education experts who outline the need for foundational digital skills, practice-integration competencies, and technology leadership across the profession. By building capacity at these three levels, the social work profession can proactively meet emerging standards and ensure that AI integration aligns with core values and ethical commitments (Reamer, 2023).

4.1 *Tier 1: Foundational AI Literacy for All Social Workers*

Tier 1 focuses on broad foundational AI literacy for the widest audience (see Table 23.3). The audience at this tier includes social work students, educators, researchers, and practitioners across settings who are new to AI concepts. The focus of PD at this tier is basic awareness and conceptual understanding of AI: participants learn fundamental terminology, how AI is being used in society and social services, and core ethical issues. At this foundational level of AI literacy, the aim is to build comfort and dispel myths, ensuring learners understand what AI is and is not capable of. Key learning goals include recognizing common AI applications in social work, understanding the potential benefits and risks of these tools, and developing an initial critical perspective grounded in social work values and ethics. By the end of Tier 1 training, individuals should be able to engage in informed conversations about AI and identify situations in practice or policy where AI might be relevant. As Table 23.3 indicates, Tier 1 is about establishing a baseline upon which more advanced competencies can be built, ensuring that the learning remains accessible and broadly applicable.

Examples of applications at this tier include introductory and low-stakes ones. For instance, a social work program might incorporate a brief AI literacy module into an orientation course, familiarizing all incoming students with AI terminology and ethical dilemmas. Faculty and staff could attend general workshops or lunch-and-learn sessions on "AI essentials" that introduce tools like ChatGPT and discuss their appropriate use in academic or practice settings. In agency contexts, Tier 1 may involve basic training for practitioners on how AI-driven systems work, accompanied by guided discussions on client consent and bias. The goal is not to produce experts, but to ensure everyone in the social work ecosystem shares a common understanding of AI basics. This broad foundation creates a shared language and awareness, which is crucial for scaling up more specialized AI learning in the following tiers.

4.2 Tier 2: Intermediate AI Competencies in Practice, Education, and Research

Building on this foundation, Tier 2, "Applied AI Competencies for Practitioners, Educators, and Researchers" shifts the focus from general literacy to the practical application of AI in specialized social work roles. At this intermediate level, the focus of learning centers on applying AI tools to enhance professional functions and outcomes (see Table 23.3).

In alignment with the six core components of AI competency outlined earlier, Tier 2 training emphasizes the development of skills and ethical practice in the use of AI in real-world social work contexts. Social workers in this tier learn to develop, adapt, and apply AI-informed tools in their specific practice or educational environments, whether in direct service delivery, program administration, teaching, or research, ensuring they are employed in an ethically sound manner that upholds social work's core values. A key learning outcome is the ability to critically analyze data and AI-generated outputs responsibly, which includes identifying biases in data or algorithms and interpreting automated insights with an understanding of context and limitations. Practitioners are also taught to leverage AI to improve the efficiency and effectiveness of interventions or administrative processes, while maintaining a focus on human well-being and social justice.

Participants who complete Tier 2 can translate foundational knowledge into competent action. They not only grasp AI concepts but can also make informed decisions about when and how to use AI in practice, selecting appropriate tools and approaches to solve problems. For instance, a social work program evaluator at this stage might use AI-driven analytics to assess the outcomes of a service program, thereby enhancing program evaluation with data-driven insights that can inform improvements. Likewise, a practitioner could employ a chatbot or virtual assistant to help clients navigate resources and services, provided that the tool is accessible, culturally sensitive, and maintains client confidentiality. In an educational setting, instructors can integrate AI-assisted writing or learning tools to support student learning. At the same time, administrators can use predictive analytics to identify community needs and proactively allocate resources for preventive programs. Taken together, these examples (see Table 23.3) demonstrate how Tier 2 solidifies an intermediate level of AI competence that builds directly upon the Tier 1 literacy foundation, effectively bridging the gap between knowing about AI and adeptly using AI to enhance social work practice.

4.3 Tier 3: Advanced AI Leadership and Innovation

Tier 3, "Advanced Leadership and Innovation in AI for Social Good," represents the highest level of professional development in this model and targets those in leadership and pioneering roles. This tier is designed for social work leaders, senior administrators, experienced scholars, and interdisciplinary innovators who will guide the strategic integration of AI in social services and advocate for the ethical use of technology at organizational and policy levels. The focus of learning at Tier 3 is on leadership, innovation, and governance in AI development, policy, and ethical oversight (see Table 23.3).

Tier 3 training cultivates the capacity to lead and manage AI-driven initiatives. Learners also strengthen the ability to shape ethical AI policies and regulatory practices, positioning themselves as influential voices for human rights and social justice in broader technology governance conversations. Consistent with the highest-level AI competencies previously outlined, Tier 3 emphasizes competencies related to policy advocacy, organizational leadership, and innovation management in the context of AI. Professionals at this level are prepared to champion human-centered and socially just AI systems, ensuring that any AI adoption within their agencies or communities is aligned with core social work values and actively counteracts biases or inequities. Moreover, Tier 3 participants are equipped to conduct or guide AI-related research and development, allowing them to contribute to the evidence base on AI in social work and to supervise interdisciplinary teams in creating new AI tools or approaches grounded in the profession's ethical principles and commitment to social good.

Examples of application at the Tier 3 level (Table 23.3) illustrate the transformative leadership roles envisioned for this stage. For instance, a social work executive or policy leader might lead the development of comprehensive AI governance guidelines for a human services organization or contribute to government regulations that ensure AI tools are used responsibly and equitably in the social sector. A scholar at this level could collaborate with computer scientists to design an AI system that addresses a community issue, such as an algorithm to better target social services to those most in need, while embedding transparency and fairness into its design from the outset. Others may participate in interdisciplinary research initiatives to assess the societal impacts of AI or to develop new AI-driven interventions for the greater good, rigorously examining outcomes and their ethical implications. Through Tier 3, the model produces social work professionals who are not only capable of navigating and utilizing AI in practice but also lead its ethical integration and drive innovation. In doing so, these leaders ensure that the evolution of AI in social work remains grounded in human rights and social justice principles.

4.4 Cross-Tier Regulatory and Ethical Considerations

Across all three tiers of AI readiness, certain regulatory and ethical considerations must be interwoven to ensure compliance with laws and alignment with social work values. Regardless of skill level, social workers using AI are still bound by fundamental regulations, such as applicable privacy rules under the Health Insurance Portability and Accountability Act (HIPAA), the Family Educational Rights and Privacy Act (FERPA), and Institutional Review Board (IRB) standards. These regulations should be emphasized in professional development. At the foundational Tier 1, learners are taught that privacy laws strictly govern health-related client data; thus, entering a client's protected health information into a third-party AI tool would constitute a breach of confidentiality. Similarly, social work educators and students must remember FERPA protections when using AI in educational settings; student records and academic work should not be shared with AI systems in ways that violate privacy or academic policies. These principles are reinforced at Tier 2 and 3 with more nuance. Intermediate practitioners (Tier 2) learn to apply privacy-by-design principles, such as using only de-identified data with AI tools or opting for platforms that offer encryption and compliance features. Advanced leaders (Tier 3) work to establish organizational protocols that clearly instruct staff on these matters; for example, an agency might approve a HIPAA-compliant AI platform for case documentation while banning unvetted apps from handling any sensitive information (Badillo-Diaz, 2025b).

In addition, all tiers need grounding in the ethics of algorithmic fairness and accountability. This involves recognizing and mitigating biases in AI systems and establishing accountability for the decisions made. Social workers are taught to ask: Who is responsible if an algorithm makes an error that causes harm? At the basic level, it's an awareness that AI decisions can be fallible and biased (Badillo-Diaz, 2025b; Hodgson et al., 2022); at the intermediate level, it's learning techniques to audit an AI's decisions and advocate for clients who may be misclassified; at the advanced level, it's implementing governance mechanisms like an ethics review board for AI or bias mitigation requirements in contracts with AI vendors.

Informed consent is another through-line. The NASW Code of Ethics requires that clients or participants be informed of significant procedures that affect them.

Thus, social workers must strive for transparency with clients regarding the use of AI. At Tier 1, this might mean understanding that if an AI is involved in service delivery, clients should be informed in plain language. At Tier 2, practitioners receive training on how to explain AI tools to clients and obtain consent, or at least assent, for their use. For example, a practitioner might say: "We have a new computer program that helps us identify which services you might need. It will analyze some of your information with your permission and give suggestions, which we will then discuss. You can opt out of this at any time." Tier 3 leaders will formalize these expectations in policy, possibly requiring that an opt-out clause and robust informed consent procedures accompany any client-facing AI. In the research realm, Tier 3 experts may guide IRBs to update protocols addressing AI, ensuring research participants are informed if AI will be used in the procedures of their research, and ensuring that such use has been reviewed for ethical soundness.

Finally, a cross-cutting theme is the selection of approved, secure AI systems. Especially in practice, social workers should favor tools that meet security and privacy standards. Tier 2 training can include learning to vet an AI tool, verifying whether it's HIPAA-compliant, checking whether it's been validated in relevant populations, and determining whether it has a mechanism for human override or review. Tier 3 leaders may develop an official list of sanctioned AI tools for their agency or school, collaborating with IT departments to ensure data protection. They also stay up-to-date with evolving regulations (e.g., new laws on AI or data protection) to update their policies accordingly. The overarching principle is that ethical obligations and legal mandates travel with the use of AI: adopting a new technology does not exempt social workers from their duty to protect client welfare, privacy, and self-determination. By embedding regulatory and ethical training at every tier, the three-tier framework ensures that increased technical skill is always paired with increased ethical responsibility. This prepares social workers not only to use AI effectively but to use it conscientiously, upholding the trust placed in our profession as we navigate the algorithmic age.

5 Exploring the Existing Landscape of AI Training and Framework in Social Work

The conversation about AI in social work is no longer theoretical. In recent years, social work has witnessed a concerted effort to build AI literacy and competencies among professionals through education, training programs, and policy frameworks. Globally, institutions are moving beyond theoretical discussions to implement practical training initiatives that equip social workers with the skills to use AI responsibly. These initiatives span formal higher education curricula, continuing professional education courses, in-agency training programs, and the development of competency frameworks by regulatory and professional bodies.

5.1 *Integration of AI Literacy in Social Work Education*

Universities and professional schools of social work have begun integrating AI-related content into their curricula and certificate offerings. In the United States, for example, some Master of Social Work (MSW) programs now include modules on technology and data science, while post-graduate certificate programs specifically targeting AI in practice have emerged. New York University's Silver School of Social Work launched a post-master's certificate in "Using Artificial Intelligence to Support Mental Health," reflecting a growing recognition that social workers need specialized training to harness AI tools in clinical and community settings. Similarly, social work educators have called for embedding generative AI content into core curricula. The Council on Social Work Education's technology task force recommended creating a new competency focused on digital literacy, AI ethics, and responsible technology use in future accreditation standards, to ensure graduates are prepared for ethical digital practice and know how to use AI tools responsibly (Council on Social Work Education, 2025). This push in higher education signals a shift from viewing technology as peripheral to recognizing it as central to contemporary social work competency.

Notably, academic initiatives often involve interdisciplinary collaboration. Social work programs are partnering with data science and engineering experts to design training experiences that bridge technical and practice skills. For example, an AI-powered simulation platform called Empathy Helper was developed by a multidisciplinary team of social work educators, mental health professionals, and AI experts at Washington University at St. Louis Brown School of Social Work to enhance student training. Co-led by faculty from a school of social work and a data science professor, this project enables large language models and agentic AI technologies to create realistic virtual clients, allowing students to practice engagement and assessment in a safe, controlled environment. Such collaborations illustrate how integrating expertise from computer science can help social workers build AI competencies within the context of social work values and client-centered practice (Lindsay et al., 2025). Around the world, other universities have followed suit. In Singapore, the National University of Singapore's Department of Social Work offers a two-day executive course on "Artificial Intelligence for Social Work," taught by a data science expert, to rapidly bring practitioners up to speed on AI project lifecycles, machine learning basics, and best practices in AI ethics and governance. It aims to "empower social workers to leverage AI tools ethically and effectively" while maintaining human-centered care (Council on Social Work Education, 2025). Participants learn key AI concepts, the stages of AI projects, and how to identify opportunities for their organizations. These examples from academia underscore a global trend: professional social work education is increasingly embedding AI literacy and AI competencies, often through cross-disciplinary initiatives, to prepare new social workers for a tech-augmented practice environment.

5.2 Continuing Education and Professional Training Programs

Beyond degree programs, a range of continuing education and training programs has emerged worldwide to build AI literacy among practicing social workers. Many of these programs are driven by the urgent need to close the knowledge gap among current practitioners, as studies have found that many social workers still rate their knowledge of AI as low (Council on Social Work Education, 2025). The goal is to enhance AI literacy, enabling social workers to confidently adopt new tools while upholding their ethical standards.

One notable effort is the proliferation of online continuing education courses specifically about AI in social work. For instance, Walden University developed a one-hour asynchronous micro-course in 2024 called "AI Essentials for the Social Worker," which grants continuing education credit to licensed professionals. This module introduces foundational concepts of generative AI in an accessible manner, aiming to equip practitioners with more informed and confident knowledge about applying AI technologies in social work. As an accredited continuing education course, it aligns with licensure requirements and indicates that AI competency is now an integral part of ongoing professional development.

Open-access and massive open online courses (MOOCs) are also contributing to AI upskilling in the field. A prominent example is the "AI for Social Professionals: Social Work, Psychology, and More" course developed by Vives University College in Belgium. This five-week online course has attracted thousands of enrollees and focuses on leveraging AI responsibly in social services to enhance client care and improve efficiency. The curriculum strikes a balance between practical skills and ethics, where participants explore real-world AI tools for tasks such as client management, documentation, and risk assessment. Through case studies, they learn how to utilize these tools in an ethical and client-centered manner. The popularity of this MOOC suggests a global demand for such knowledge, transcending national boundaries in the social sector.

National professional bodies are likewise providing training resources. In Canada, the Canadian Association of Social Workers hosted webinars as part of an "AI and Social Work Practice" series. One such webinar in March 2025, "Ethical and Responsible Use of AI for Social Work Practice," was designed to introduce practitioners to the "transformative potential of generative AI" across micro, mezzo, and macro practice, while engaging them in critical discussions on ethics. The session emphasized core social work ethics, including privacy, confidentiality, avoidance of bias, and human-centered care, as nonnegotiables when adopting AI tools. It also included live demonstrations and a hands-on prompt guidebook to help participants develop practical skills in using generative AI in everyday practice settings. This reflects a pedagogical shift toward interactive learning, ensuring that social workers not only learn about AI in theory but also practice using it under guidance, always with an eye to ethical standards. Similarly, in the United States, chapters of the National Association of Social Workers have begun offering continuing education webinars on topics like AI ethics and best practices.

For example, the NASW's Wisconsin Chapter featured a 2024 webinar on "AI and Social Work Ethics" to help practitioners navigate emerging dilemmas, such as informed consent, confidentiality, and documentation, in the age of AI. These professional training efforts indicate that continuing education is rapidly evolving to include AI competency, treating it as essential to modern practice alongside traditional skills.

5.3 *Agency Initiatives and Policy Frameworks for AI Competency*

At the organizational and policy level, there is growing recognition that social service agencies and regulatory bodies must establish frameworks to guide AI integration and ensure workforce readiness. When agencies adopt AI-driven systems, they face the challenge of training their staff to use these tools appropriately and ethically. Real-world deployments of AI in social work settings have underscored this need. For example, in the United Kingdom, several local authorities began piloting an AI system called "Magic Notes," which automatically transcribes and summarizes case conversations for social workers. The British Association of Social Workers (BASW) has stressed that such tools "must never replace relationship-based practice and decision-making." Crucially, BASW's first practice guidance on AI calls on employers to provide clear training and support for staff using AI, and to designate leadership (e.g., a principal social worker) to oversee the ethical use of AI within agencies (BASW, 2025). The guidance explicitly states that organizations introducing generative AI should ensure practitioners receive appropriate training, clear guidance, and support on the responsible use of these technologies. This reflects a policy-driven framework where professional bodies are not only cautioning about risks but also actively encouraging capacity-building at the agency level. By embedding training expectations into practice standards, bodies like BASW are influencing how agencies roll out AI, essentially mandating that competency development accompanies any AI deployment.

On the ground, several agency-driven training initiatives have started to emerge. Large social service organizations and government departments are developing internal workshops and protocols for their staff when new AI tools are introduced. For example, child welfare agencies that use predictive analytics models for risk assessment have organized training sessions to help social workers understand model outputs and interpret them critically rather than blindly trust algorithmic recommendations. In healthcare social work, hospital systems that deploy AI-based decision support have integrated an AI orientation into their staff development programs, ensuring social workers learn how to co-utilize these tools while still exercising professional judgment. Though many of these internal training courses are not public-facing, they are increasingly guided by formal frameworks and partnerships. A case in point is the collaboration between social service agencies and academic institutions to develop training curricula. Some jurisdictions have partnered with universities to deliver certification programs for employees on topics like data-informed practice or AI in case management. These partnerships leverage academic expertise and often refer to governance standards to shape content, covering areas such as data privacy law, algorithmic bias, and client consent, which are crucial for agency policy compliance.

Another key aspect of the current landscape is the role of governance and ethical frameworks in shaping the content of training. Professional bodies worldwide are producing guidelines that effectively serve as learning objectives for training programs. The BASW guidance (2025) and NASW's ethical webinars both underscore themes such as bias awareness, transparent use of AI, accountability for decisions, and the primacy of human relationships. These themes are now woven into workshops and courses as standard modules. For example, a continuing education course might include a module on "Ethical Concerns of AI in Social Work," covering privacy, informed consent, and equity issues, echoing the points raised in official standards. Likewise, interdisciplinary bodies have begun issuing broader AI ethics frameworks that social work educators adapt to context-specific training. Social workers are thus being taught not just how to use AI tools but how to evaluate them critically. This capacity for critical appraisal is a competency increasingly highlighted in policy-driven frameworks as essential for the profession's engagement with AI.

In summary, the global landscape reflects a growing, multisectoral effort to develop AI literacy and AI competencies across social work education, training, and practice. Universities are incorporating foundational AI literacy into their curricula, while continuing education programs and professional associations provide applied training to develop role-specific competencies. Agencies and policymakers are beginning to formalize expectations through ethical frameworks and governance tools. Yet, across these efforts, a clear theoretical foundation and cohesive professional guidance remain limited. As a result, many training initiatives operate in silos, underscoring the need for coordinated, evidence-informed strategies that align with the profession's values and standards.

6 From Literacy and Competency to Leadership: A Social Work Professional Agenda for the Algorithmic Age

As this chapter has explored, AI literacy and AI competency form two distinct yet interdependent pillars of social work's digital future. AI literacy provides the knowledge and critical lens, AI competency provides the action orientation and the capacity to implement that knowledge in real-world practice and policy. Together, these two dimensions form a comprehensive framework for professional empowerment in the digital era. Only by maintaining a clear distinction between understanding AI and skillfully using AI can social workers ensure they do not confuse mere familiarity with true capability. The integration of both ensures that social workers not only comprehend the algorithmic tools shaping society but can also harness and guide them in the service of humanity (Badillo-Diaz, 2025a).

The integration of AI literacy and competency positions social workers to confront and mitigate algorithmic injustice. As algorithmic tools become increasingly embedded in child welfare, mental health, benefits eligibility, and criminal justice systems, social workers' dual capacity for ethical discernment and action becomes vital. With these capacities, social workers can critically examine how AI systems may perpetuate or exacerbate structural inequality and take informed steps to prevent or mitigate harm. In practice, this may involve scrutinizing an algorithm's design before implementation, advocating for equity audits and stakeholder consultation, or halting deployment when tools conflict with ethical or legal standards. Far from being passive recipients of innovation, AI-literate and AI-competent social workers act as ethical stewards and co-creators—insisting that technological adoption be guided by relational care, procedural fairness, and community voice (Council on Social Work Education, 2025). In doing so, the profession advances its long-standing commitment to anti-oppressive practice, now extended into the digital domain.

This synthesis of literacy and competency also lays the foundation for a forward-looking professional agenda. To meet the demands of the algorithmic age, these capacities must be intentionally cultivated in education, sustained in practice, and extended through research. Educational programs should embed AI-related knowledge and skills throughout the curriculum. Field placements and continuing education should reinforce this foundation through authentic engagement with AI systems in real-world contexts. Organizations and agencies must invest in workforce development, infrastructure, and participatory design to ensure that ethical use of technology becomes a shared responsibility, not an individual burden. Across all domains, social workers must actively shape research and policy debates by bringing their ethical frameworks and contextual expertise into interdisciplinary conversations on AI governance.

In summary, AI literacy and AI competency are not merely technical supplements to social work; they are essential prerequisites for ethical and effective practice in a rapidly changing world. Their integration enables the profession to respond to rapid technological change not with fear or resignation, but with clarity, confidence, and a deep sense of purpose. This is not simply a matter of adapting to innovation. It is an opportunity for social work to lead: to assert its values, shape the systems that shape lives, and uphold its mission in new and powerful ways in the era of AI.

Competing Interests The authors have no conflicts of interest to declare that are relevant to the content of this chapter.

References

Ahn, E., Choi, M., Fowler, P., & Song, I. H. (2025). Artificial intelligence (AI) literacy for social work: Implications for core competencies. *Journal of the Society for Social Work and Research, 16*(1), 9–26.

Badillo-Diaz, M. (2025a, February 13). Moving beyond AI literacy: Why social workers need AI fluency. — *The AI Social Worker*. https://www.theaisocialworker.com/blog/building-resilient-communities-the-role-of-ai-in-disaster-response-and-recovery-efforts

Badillo-Diaz, M. (2025b, Spring). The impact of AI technology on the social work profession: Benefits, risks, and ethical considerations. *Center for Advanced Studies in Child Welfare CW360* [Newsletter]. https://cascw.umn.edu/cw360deg-spring-2025/impact-ai-technology-social-work-profession-benefits-risks-and-ethical

Boetto, H. (2025). Artificial intelligence in social work: An EPIC model for practice. *Australian Social Work*, 1–14. https://doi.org/10.1080/0312407X.2025.2488345

British Association of Social Workers [BASW]. (2025, March). *Generative AI and Social Work: Initial Guidance for Practice and Ethics*. BASW. https://basw.co.uk/sites/default/files/2025-03/181372%20Generative%20AI%20and%20Social%20Work%20Practice%20Guidance_0.pdf

Chan, C., & Holosko, M. J. (2016). A review of information and communication technology enhanced social work interventions. *Research on Social Work Practice, 26*(1), 88–100. https://doi.org/10.1177/1049731515578

Chiu, T. K. F. (2025). AI literacy and competency: Definitions, frameworks, development and future research directions. *Interactive Learning Environments, 33*(5), 3225–3229. https://doi.org/10.1080/10494820.2025.2514372

Chiu, T. K. F., Ahmad, Z., Ismailov, M., & Sanusi, I. T. (2024). What are artificial intelligence literacy and competency? A comprehensive framework to support them. *Computers and Education Open, 6*, 100171. https://doi.org/10.1016/J.CAEO.2024.100171

Council on Social Work Education. (2022). Educational policy and accreditation standards. In *Council on social work education: Washington, DC, USA*. https://www.cswe.org/getmedia/bb5d8afe-7680-42dc-a332-a6e6103f4998/2022-Educational-Policy-and-Accreditation-Standards-%28EPAS%29.pdf?utm_source=chatgpt.com

Council on Social Work Education. (2025). *CSWE commission on educational policy task force on technology and social work education report*. https://www.cswe.org/getmedia/3785b60b-5fae-4c39-a0ec-c052eddf9588/COEP-Technology-Report.pdf#:~:text=dimensions%20of%20AI,in%20shaping%20AI%20policies%20that

DiSalvo, B., Guzdial, M., Bruckman, A., & McKlin, T. (2014). Saving face while geeking out: Video game testing as a justification for learning computer science. *Journal of the Learning Sciences, 23*(3), 272–315. https://doi.org/10.1080/10508406.2014.893434

Epstein, R. M., & Hundert, E. M. (2002). Defining and assessing professional competence. *JAMA, 287*(2), 226–235. https://doi.org/10.1001/JAMA.287.2.226

Frank, J. R., Snell, L. S., Ten Cate, O., Holmboe, E. S., Carraccio, C., Swing, S. R., Harris, P., Glasgow, N. J., Campbell, C., Dath, D., Harden, R. M., Iobst, W., Long, D. M., Mungroo, R., Richardson, D. L., Sherbino, J., Silver, I., Taber, S., Talbot, M., & Harris, K. A. (2010). Competency-based medical education: Theory to practice. *Medical Teacher, 32*(8), 638–645. https://doi.org/10.3109/0142159X.2010.501190

Freire, P. (2007). Pedagogy of the oppressed. In P. Kuppers & G. Robertson (Eds.), *The community performance reader* (pp. 24–27). Routledge. https://doi.org/10.4324/9781003060635-5

Goldkind, L. (2021). Social work and artificial intelligence: Into the matrix. *Social Work, 66*(4), 372–374. https://doi.org/10.1093/sw/swab028

Hodgson, D., Goldingay, S., Boddy, J., Nipperess, S., & Watts, L. (2022). Problematising Artificial Intelligence in social work education: Challenges, issues and possibilities. *British Journal of Social Work, 52*(4), 1878–1895. https://doi.org/10.1093/BJSW/BCAB168

Laugksch, R. C. (2000). Scientific literacy: A conceptual overview. *Science Education, 84*(1), 71–94.

Lindsay, R., Yang, Y., & An, R. (2025). *A pilot study of empathy helper, a generative Artificial Intelligence platform for communication practice in graduate social work*. [Manuscript submitted for publication, under peer review].

Liu, X., Zhang, L., & Wei, X. (2025). Generative artificial intelligence literacy: Scale development and its effect on job performance. *Behavioral Sciences, 15*(6), 811. https://doi.org/10.3390/BS15060811

Long, D., & Magerko, B. (2020, April 21). What is AI literacy? Competencies and design considerations. *Conference on human factors in computing systems – Proceedings*. https://doi.org/10.1145/3313831.3376727

Mikalef, P., Islam, N., Parida, V., Singh, H., & Altwaijry, N. (2023). Artificial intelligence (AI) competencies for organizational performance: A B2B marketing capabilities perspective. *Journal of Business Research, 164*, 113998. https://doi.org/10.1016/J.JBUSRES.2023.113998

Miller, G. E. (1990a). The assessment of clinical skills/competence/performance. *Academic Medicine: Journal of the Association of American Medical Colleges, 65*(9 Suppl), S63–S67. https://doi.org/10.1097/00001888-199009000-00045

Miller, G. E. (1990b). The assessment of clinical skills/competence/performance. *Academic Medicine, 65*(9), S63–S67. https://doi.org/10.1097/00001888-199009000-00045

National Association of Social Workers [NASW]. (2021). *NASW code of ethics*. https://www.socialworkers.org/About/Ethics/Code-of-Ethics/Code-of-Ethics-English

Nordesjö, K., Scaramuzzino, G., & Ulmestig, R. (2022). The social worker-client relationship in the digital era: A configurative literature review. *European Journal of Social Work, 25*(2), 303–315. https://doi.org/10.1080/13691457.2021.1964445

Nuwasiima, M., Ahonon, M. P., & Kadiri, C. (2024). The role of Artificial Intelligence (AI) and machine learning in social work practice. *World Journal of Advanced Research and Reviews, 24*(1), 080–097. https://doi.org/10.30574/WJARR.2024.24.1.2998

Perchik, J. D., Smith, A. D., Elkassem, A. A., Park, J. M., Rothenberg, S. A., Tanwar, M., Yi, P. H., Sturdivant, A., Tridandapani, S., & Sotoudeh, H. (2023). Artificial Intelligence literacy: Developing a multi-institutional infrastructure for AI education. *Academic Radiology, 30*(7), 1472–1480. https://doi.org/10.1016/J.ACRA.2022.10.002

Perron, B. E., Taylor, H. O., Glass, J. E., & Margerum-Leys, J. (2010). Information and communication technologies in social work. *Advances in Social Work, 11*(2), 67. https://doi.org/10.18060/241

Reamer, F. G. (2013). Social work in a digital age: Ethical and risk management challenges. *Social Work, 58*(2), 163–172. https://doi.org/10.1093/SW/SWT003

Reamer, F. G. (2023). Artificial Intelligence in social work: Emerging ethical issues. *International Journal of Social Work Values and Ethics, 20*(2), 52–71. https://doi.org/10.55521/10-020-205

Rodriguez, M. Y., Goldkind, L., Victor, B. G., Hiltz, B., & Perron, B. E. (2024). Introducing generative artificial intelligence into the MSW curriculum: A proposal for the 2029 educational policy and accreditation standards. *Journal of Social Work Education, 60*(2), 174–182.

Tsz, D., Ng, K., Ka, J., Leung, L., Kai, S., Chu, W., & Shen Qiao, M. (2021). NC-ND license conceptualizing AI literacy: An exploratory review. *Computers and Education: Artificial Intelligence, 2*, 100041. https://doi.org/10.1016/j.caeai.2021.100041

UNESCO. (2024). AI competency framework for students. In *AI competency framework for students*. UNESCO. https://doi.org/10.54675/JKJB9835

UNESCO. (2025, February 20). *What you need to know about UNESCO's new AI competency frameworks for students and teachers*. UNESCO News. https://www.unesco.org/en/articles/what-you-need-know-about-unescos-new-ai-competency-frameworks-students-and-teachers

Chapter 24
Conclusion: Challenges and Opportunities for AI in Social Work

Yuyi Yang, Ruopeng An, and Michael A. Lindsey

1 Reframing AI and Social Work

Artificial intelligence (AI) has entered social work at a moment when the profession is already grappling with widening inequalities, strained service systems, and shifting political and economic conditions (Dalziel et al., 2024). Algorithmic tools now participate in decisions about who is deemed at risk and which families receive preventive support (Reamer, 2023). They also shape how scarce resources are allocated and which narratives about need and responsibility become visible in institutional data (Coeckelbergh, 2023). These developments challenge longstanding assumptions that social work is solely a human, face-to-face enterprise. At the same time, they open the door to new forms of insight, coordination, and collective action.

As the book reveals, AI in social work is not merely a collection of technological projects. Instead, it appears as an emerging ecosystem that links infrastructures, organizations, professional roles, and community struggles. The book shows that AI is already present in the intimate spaces of counseling and casework, in the operational routines of agencies, and in the policy arenas where laws, funding streams, and rights are negotiated. The question is no longer whether AI belongs in social work. Instead, it is how its presence can be understood, contested, and reshaped so that it supports rather than undermines the profession's commitments to equity, justice, and dignity (Boetto, 2025).

Y. Yang (✉)
Division of Computational and Data Sciences, Washington University in St. Louis, St. Louis, MO, USA
e-mail: y.yuyi@wustl.edu

R. An · M. A. Lindsey
Silver School of Social Work, New York University, New York, NY, USA
e-mail: ra4605@nyu.edu; michael.lindsey@nyu.edu

R. An, M. A. Lindsey (eds.), *Artificial Intelligence in Social Work*,
https://doi.org/10.1007/978-3-032-18443-6_24

1.1 From Scattered Pilots to an Emerging Field

Early debates about AI in human services often focused on isolated pilots and prototype tools: a predictive model in one jurisdiction, a chatbot in a particular clinic, or a classification algorithm embedded in a single intake system (Huang & Rust, 2018). Viewed in isolation, such initiatives can appear as technical curiosities or local experiments. When examined collectively, however, they point toward the consolidation of a distinct field of practice and inquiry in which AI and social work are mutually entangled.

Across the book, similar questions recur. How are data about individuals, families, and communities collected, cleaned, and labeled for algorithmic use? Who defines the target outcomes that models are trained to predict? Which errors are considered tolerable and which are framed as unacceptable? These questions signal a shift from ad hoc innovation to a more systematic engagement with AI as part of the infrastructure of social welfare. The emerging field is not defined only by shared tools. It is also characterized by shared dilemmas about risk, responsibility, fairness, and care (Sun, 2025).

Recognizing this shift is essential for at least two reasons. First, it highlights the need for cumulative knowledge rather than one-off evaluations of individual systems. Second, it underscores that decisions about AI in social work are no longer confined to technical teams or individual agencies. They are distributed across professional bodies, regulators, educators, researchers, and communities. The move from scattered pilots to an emerging field is therefore also a move from individual experimentation to collective governance.

1.2 AI and Social Work Values

Much public discourse about AI in the public sector is framed in terms of efficiency, cost savings, and scalability (Kuziemski & Misuraca, 2020). These concerns matter for social work, but they are not the primary lens through which this book views AI. What is at stake is not simply whether AI can help agencies process cases more quickly or extend limited staff capacity. The central question is how algorithmic systems interact with core social work values.

AI systems participate in defining whose needs are recognized and legitimized, which harms are prioritized, and whose accounts are treated as credible. They shape the categories through which people are seen, the thresholds at which intervention is deemed warranted, and the narratives that are encoded in administrative records. In contexts marked by racism, ableism, sexism, classism, and other forms of structural oppression, AI can easily reproduce and amplify existing injustices if left unchecked (Zajko, 2022). At the same time, carefully designed systems can be used to reveal patterns of exclusion, monitor inequities, and support more responsive and inclusive forms of practice (Heeks, 2022).

For these reasons, AI in social work must be evaluated against criteria such as respect for human dignity, promotion of self-determination, advancement of social and economic justice, and commitment to collective well-being. Questions about transparency, accountability, participation, and redress are not auxiliary ethical considerations. They are central to assessing whether AI is compatible with the profession's normative commitments. The chapters in this book repeatedly show that decisions about model design, data governance, and deployment are also decisions about whose lives are made more livable and whose are rendered more precarious.

1.3 Social Workers in the Algorithmic Age

In many policy debates, social workers appear only at the end of the AI pipeline as end users who must adapt to tools designed elsewhere or as potential resisters who may slow implementation. This book advances a different view. Across domains and regions, social workers are already shaping the trajectory of AI by questioning problem framings, advocating for affected communities, co-designing interventions, generating new forms of evidence, and articulating alternative imaginaries of what technology could do.

The chapters position social workers as actors who inhabit multiple roles in the algorithmic age. They are practitioners who navigate human-AI collaboration in everyday encounters with service users. They are organizational leaders who negotiate procurement, implementation, and internal governance of AI systems. They are educators who help students interpret and critique algorithmic tools and researchers who use AI both as an object of study and as a method for inquiry. They are advocates who contest harmful uses of data and build alliances with other professions, social movements, and communities to demand more just technological arrangements.

Seeing social workers in this way has significant implications. It challenges narratives that cast AI as an external force that arrives in human services and emphasizes the agency of professionals and communities in shaping how technology is imagined, built, and governed. It also suggests that the skills and commitments cultivated within social work, including critical reflexivity, relational practice, and attention to power, are not peripheral to debates about AI but indispensable to them.

2 An Integrative View of the Book

2.1 Part I—Foundations of AI in Social Work (Chaps. 1–2)

Part I lays the groundwork for the book by clarifying what is at stake when AI enters social work. The opening chapters frame AI not as a single tool but as a set of computational practices and infrastructures that increasingly structure how information about people, families, and communities is generated, interpreted, and acted upon. Core concepts such as machine learning, natural language processing, and predictive analytics are introduced in relation to everyday social work environments rather than in abstraction. By tracing continuities with earlier information systems and risk assessment tools, Part I situates AI within an extended history of data-driven governance. At the same time, it underscores the new forms of scale, opacity, and automation that distinguish contemporary systems.

Chapter 1 presents AI as a cross-cutting presence in practice, education, and research. In direct practice, algorithmic systems support tasks such as risk stratification, case prioritization, eligibility screening, and resource matching. In some settings, they also mediate client interaction through chatbots and other digital interfaces. In education, AI appears in adaptive learning platforms, automated feedback tools, and simulation-based training. These systems can expand opportunities for skills development but also complicate assessment and professional formation. In research, data-intensive methods extend what can be done with administrative records, text corpora, images, and other complex datasets. They enable more fine-grained analysis of social problems and service trajectories. Throughout, Chap. 1 emphasizes that these developments unfold within social and institutional contexts marked by longstanding inequities, digital divides, and contested histories of state intervention.

Chapter 2 develops a correspondingly multifaceted ethical lens. Established social work values, such as social justice, the dignity and worth of the person, self-determination, the importance of human relationships, and professional integrity, are reinterpreted in an environment where algorithmic classifications and predictions can shape life chances. Value-oriented frameworks from bioethics, trustworthy AI guidelines, and value-sensitive design are brought into conversation with social work codes and traditions. This synthesis foregrounds questions about whose data are collected and for what purposes, how consent and confidentiality can be meaningfully upheld in large, linked datasets, and how responsibility is allocated when automated systems contribute to harmful decisions.

Several domains of ethical concern are examined in detail. The book revisits privacy and data protection in the context of the granular, linked datasets required for AI, which heighten the risks of reidentification and secondary use. Fairness and nondiscrimination are discussed through the lens of algorithmic bias and subgroup disparities in model performance, with attention to how historical patterns of racism, ableism, sexism, and classism can be encoded in training data. Transparency and explainability are treated as prerequisites for informed consent, contestation, and trust. This prompts questions about the appropriateness of highly opaque models in high stakes social work contexts. Accountability is framed as a shared obligation across developers, vendors, agencies, practitioners, and regulators rather than as a purely individual responsibility.

Finally, Part I underscores that ethical engagement with AI must be situated within a global and cultural context. Differences in legal regimes, infrastructural capacity, and cultural norms around privacy, autonomy, and collective responsibility shape how AI systems are designed, deployed, and experienced. The foundational chapters argue for the cultivation of AI-related competencies within social work education and ongoing professional development. These include critical data literacy, the ability to interrogate model behavior, and skills for participating in interdisciplinary collaborations. In doing so, Part I provides a conceptual and normative vocabulary that recurs throughout the book. AI is understood simultaneously as a technical development, a social practice, and a moral and political project. Its legitimacy in social work is assessed by the extent to which it advances or undermines commitments to equity, justice, and human dignity.

2.2 *Part II—AI Applications Responding to Social Needs (Chaps. 3–15)*

Part II shifts from foundational questions to concrete domains of practice where AI is being deployed to address social needs. Across these chapters, AI systems appear in some of the most resource-constrained and ethically charged spaces of social work, including poverty and economic insecurity, child and family welfare, health and disability, LGBTQ+ affirmation, gender-based and intimate partner violence, mental health, school contexts, substance use, aging, housing instability, criminal justice involvement, and human trafficking. The chapters show that AI is rarely introduced in neutral circumstances. It tends to enter settings where institutional mistrust is already high, where services are rationed, and where the consequences of error can be profound. At the same time, these are precisely the contexts where better coordination, earlier risk identification, and more responsive services are urgently needed.

2.2.1 Material Hardship, Health, and Disability (Chaps. 3–6)

This set of chapters examines how AI is used to address material deprivation, health inequities, and diverse forms of disability. Across these contributions, AI is applied to questions of who falls into poverty and gains access to benefits and financial services, who receives timely and appropriate health care, and how physical, cognitive, and developmental challenges are supported across the life course.

Chapter 3 focuses on poverty and economic inequality. AI-driven tools are used to identify at-risk households, forecast the impact of policy changes, detect fraud and underutilization in benefits systems, and tailor financial inclusion initiatives. The promise lies in moving from reactive responses to more anticipatory, data-informed strategies that can flag emerging hardship before it becomes entrenched. Chapter 4, however, highlights the dangers of algorithmic surveillance in welfare and social protection systems. Models can reinforce punitive logics, encode historical discrimination into eligibility rules, and subject poor communities to intensified monitoring. Social work perspectives are used to argue that AI in this domain must be oriented toward economic justice rather than merely administrative efficiency.

Chapter 5 extends this line of analysis into clinical and public health settings. AI is described as a tool for enhancing diagnosis, risk stratification, care coordination, and population health monitoring. Particular attention is paid to how data-driven methods might exacerbate or reduce disparities along race, gender, and other axes of marginalization. Discussions of electronic health records, imaging, and sensor data illustrate the potential for more precise and timely interventions. They also highlight the compounded risks associated with sensitive health information and unequal access to digital infrastructure.

Chapter 6 on physical, cognitive, and developmental challenges emphasizes assistive and rehabilitative applications. AI-enabled devices and systems are described as supporting communication, mobility, and daily living for people with disabilities. At the same time, they generate new forms of data about bodily function and behavior. The analysis foregrounds tensions between empowerment and control, autonomy and paternalism, accessibility and commercialization. Across this cluster, AI is framed as capable of enabling more responsive and individualized forms of support. This potential can only be realized, however, if design and governance center on the voices and priorities of those whose lives are most affected.

2.2.2 Identity, Relationships, and Psychosocial Well-being (Chaps. 7–10)

These chapters focus on identity, relational life, and psychosocial well-being. Here, AI is entangled with how people understand themselves and each other, how stigma and affirmation are mediated, and how interpersonal violence and distress are recognized and addressed. The chapters consider LGBTQ+ communities, sexual and intimate partner violence, mental health services, and school-based social work.

In the context of LGBTQ+ communities, AI appears both as a resource and a threat. Algorithmic methods are used to analyze online discourse, identify needs and patterns of discrimination, and design affirming digital supports. At the same time, classification systems, content moderation tools, and surveillance infrastructures can mislabel, invisibilize, or expose LGBTQ+ individuals, especially in hostile legal and cultural environments. The analysis in Chap. 7 emphasizes the importance of participatory and queer-informed approaches that resist normative assumptions about gender and sexuality.

Chapters 8 and 9 on sexual and intimate partner violence and on mental health describe AI systems that seek to detect risk, support help-seeking, and supplement scarce human resources. Natural language processing and pattern recognition are used to identify indicators of coercion, abuse, or suicidality in text, speech, and behavioral data. Chatbots and digital therapeutics provide psychoeducation, coping strategies, and crisis support. These tools can extend reach and offer greater anonymity, which may be especially valuable for survivors and people experiencing stigma. Yet they also risk trivializing complex relational dynamics, misclassifying nuanced disclosures, and responding in ways that lack cultural and trauma-informed sensitivity.

Chapter 10 examines school-based applications and shows how AI reshapes the ecology in which children and young people grow and learn. Predictive analytics and early warning systems promise to identify students who may be at risk of academic failure, behavioral difficulties, or psychosocial distress. In principle, this can enable more timely support. However, such systems can also contribute to labeling, tracking, and differential treatment, particularly along racial and socioeconomic lines. The chapter underscores that in these relational domains, AI cannot be understood only as a technical instrument. It participates in the construction of categories such as risk, resilience, deviance, and well-being. It therefore must be evaluated in terms of its effects on dignity, belonging, and relational trust.

2.2.3 High Risk, Institutional, and Life Course Contexts (Chaps. 11–15)

The next cluster of chapters follows AI into high-risk environments shaped by powerful institutions, where social workers often operate at the intersection of care and control. These chapters address substance use and addiction, aging and long-term care, housing instability and homelessness, involvement with criminal legal systems, and human trafficking.

In the substance use field, AI is used to detect patterns of use and overdose risk, personalize treatment planning, and monitor adherence and relapse. Data from health records, criminal justice systems, social media, and digital devices are combined to generate risk scores and tailor interventions. The potential benefits include more targeted outreach, better matching of services to individual needs, and earlier identification of crises. Chapter 11 also identifies significant concerns about coercion, criminalization, and the use of algorithmic tools to justify intrusive surveillance or punitive responses, particularly in communities already overpoliced and underserved.

Chapter 12 on aging and long-term care describes AI-supported monitoring, fall detection, cognitive assessment, and social robots in home and institutional settings. These technologies can enhance safety and independence. They also raise questions about privacy, autonomy, the redistribution of caregiving labor, and the risk that technological substitutes replace human contact. Chapter 13 on housing instability and homelessness highlights predictive tools for identifying individuals at risk of eviction or chronic homelessness and for prioritizing access to limited housing resources. While such systems can improve coordination and transparency, they may also encode exclusionary criteria and reproduce structural racism embedded in housing markets and social policies.

Chapters 14 and 15, dealing with criminal justice and human trafficking, bring these tensions into especially stark relief. Risk assessment instruments, predictive policing, and analytic platforms promise more rational and evidence-based decisions about detention, sentencing, supervision, and victim identification. Empirical analyses and critical perspectives, however, show how these systems often rest on historically biased data, intensify surveillance of marginalized communities, and shift discretionary power into opaque technical processes. In work on trafficking, AI is used to mine online advertisements, communications, and movement patterns to identify potential exploitation. It also carries risks of misidentification, collateral harm to sex workers, and expanded policing of already vulnerable populations.

Across these high-risk and institutional contexts, Part II reveals a recurring pattern: AI is deployed at points where eligibility, risk, and deservingness are defined and enforced. The chapters collectively argue that any assessment of AI in these settings must therefore grapple with the politics of classification and control. They call for approaches in which social workers and affected communities actively contest problem framings, reshape data practices, and design systems that prioritize harm reduction, rights protection, and structural transformation over mere efficiency or predictive accuracy.

2.3 *Part III—AI and Social Justice in Changing Contexts (Chaps. 16–19)*

Part III shifts the focus from specific service domains to the wider sociopolitical environments in which AI is developed and deployed. The chapters examine how AI intersects with advocacy, environmental justice, transformations of work, and global social issues. Together, they show that AI is not only a tool used within existing welfare and service systems. It is also a force that reshapes the structural conditions under which social problems emerge, are interpreted, and are contested. Social workers appear here as actors who engage with AI at the level of movements, institutions, and transnational governance, not only at the point of individual service delivery.

Chapter 16 on advocacy and social justice highlights how AI can reconfigure the terrains on which campaigns and movements operate. Data-driven tools are used to monitor policy debates, map networks of influence, analyze social media discourse, and identify emerging narratives and misinformation. Machine learning can identify communities disproportionately affected by policy choices and help tailor messaging or resource allocation to them. At the same time, the analysis warns that the same techniques can be used to manipulate public opinion, segment constituencies in ways that exacerbate polarization, and obscure the structural roots of injustice behind individualized profiling. From a social work perspective, the chapter argues for advocacy practices that appropriate AI for critical and emancipatory purposes. This includes participatory approaches in which communities help define the problems to be analyzed, the indicators of success, and the boundaries of acceptable data use.

Environmental social work and climate change provide a second arena in which AI is deeply entangled with questions of justice. Here, AI is mobilized to analyze remote sensing data, model climate risks, monitor deforestation and pollution, and support early warning systems for disasters. These capabilities can strengthen governments' and communities' ability to anticipate and respond to environmental hazards. They can also document uneven patterns of exposure and vulnerability across regions and populations. Chapter 17, however, shows that such systems are embedded in political economies of extraction and development. Decisions about where to monitor, which risks to prioritize, and how to respond to model outputs are shaped by power relations between states, corporations, and communities. Environmental social work brings an explicitly justice-oriented lens to these developments. It insists that AI-assisted climate action must be accountable to frontline communities, indigenous knowledge systems, and intergenerational equity rather than solely to technocratic metrics of risk reduction or economic efficiency.

Chapter 18 on the evolving workplace traces the implications of AI for labor markets, working conditions, and the dignity of work. Building on histories of industrial and digital transformation, it examines how algorithmic management, platform-mediated labor, and automation alter employment opportunities, job quality, and workers' bargaining power. AI is used to sort applicants, schedule shifts, monitor performance, and optimize workflows. These practices can reinforce precarious employment, intensify surveillance, and widen the gap between high- and low-skilled workers. At the same time, AI can support new forms of training, career navigation, and workplace accommodations, which may benefit workers who face barriers due to disability, migration status, or caregiving responsibilities. The chapter positions social workers as essential actors in advocating for technological fairness. This advocacy includes supporting workers affected by displacement, participating in policy debates about regulation and social protection, and collaborating with unions and community organizations to contest harmful uses of algorithmic control.

International social work and global issues provide a final vantage point in Part III, highlighting applications in humanitarian assistance, conflict and displacement, global health, and transnational governance. Tools such as crisis mapping, early warning systems, translation and communication technologies, and analytic platforms for targeting aid can enhance coordination and responsiveness in complex emergencies. Chapter 19 also shows how these technologies embed the priorities, biases, and security logics of powerful states, donors, and corporations. Data extracted from crisis-affected populations may be repurposed for surveillance or commercial use, while AI-driven classifications influence who is recognized as a legitimate refugee, a security threat, or a deserving recipient of assistance. A decolonial and culturally responsive lens is proposed to counter the uncritical export of AI systems designed in high-income contexts, emphasizing local ownership, self-determination, and solidarity as guiding principles.

Taken together, the chapters in Part III recast AI as part of the structural fabric within which social problems are produced, perceived, and contested. Advocacy, environmental governance, labor markets, and international aid emerge as sites where algorithmic tools can either entrench existing hierarchies or open new spaces for accountability and redistribution of voice. In contrast to the service-oriented applications highlighted in Part II, Part III underscores that social work engagement with AI must extend to these macro-level dynamics, where decisions about data, models, and infrastructures shape the very conditions under which justice claims can be articulated and heard.

2.4 Part IV—AI in Social Work Education and Research (Chaps. 20–21)

Part IV turns to the spaces where social work knowledge and professional identities are produced, examining how AI is reshaping education and research as mutually reinforcing enterprises. Across these chapters, AI is not treated as a peripheral technical topic. It is presented as part of the conditions under which learning, inquiry, and professional judgment now take place. The analysis foregrounds how AI-mediated tools alter pedagogical relationships, research practices, and how evidence and expertise are defined within the profession.

In social work education, AI is situated within a broader transformation of higher learning. Simulation environments, virtual clients, adaptive learning platforms, and generative tools are used to create more varied opportunities for practice, feedback, and reflection. These technologies can diversify exposure to client scenarios, support skills rehearsal in lower-risk settings, and personalize learning pathways for students with different needs and backgrounds. At the same time, they reconfigure assessment, supervision, and academic integrity. This raises questions about what counts as an authentic demonstration of competence and how to evaluate learning in AI-mediated environments. Chapter 20, therefore, emphasizes the need for critical digital pedagogy that teaches students to interpret and interrogate algorithmic systems rather than accepting them as neutral utilities. Faculty development is central, since instructors must learn to integrate AI into curricula in ways that align with social work values, attend to equity and accessibility, and respect the emotional and relational dimensions of learning. Discussions of inclusive design, trauma-informed use of simulations, and participatory curriculum development underscore that the integration of AI into education should itself be guided by principles of co-creation and shared governance.

In social work research, AI is presented as a methodological catalyst that cuts across descriptive, predictive, experimental, and conceptual work. Techniques such as machine learning, natural language processing, and network analysis extend what can be done with administrative records, practice notes, policy documents, social media, and other complex data sources. Researchers employ AI to uncover patterns in service trajectories, model risk and resilience, evaluate interventions, and synthesize large bodies of qualitative and mixed-methods evidence. Chapter 21 is explicit that methodological innovation does not replace the need for careful theorizing, robust research design, and attention to context. Choices about model specification, outcome variables, training data, and evaluation metrics are both technical and conceptual. They determine which realities are rendered visible, which are flattened or obscured, and whose experiences are treated as central. Transparency, reproducibility, and participation are proposed as key criteria for responsible AI-informed research, alongside attention to how data practices intersect with structural inequalities.

Taken together, the chapters in Part IV treat AI in education and research as profoundly interconnected. The tools used to study social problems and interventions help define what counts as legitimate knowledge, and these epistemic hierarchies in turn shape the competencies that education seeks to cultivate. AI thus becomes a lens through which to reconsider longstanding questions about the purposes of social work education and research. These include whose knowledges are centered, how power circulates through evidence-making, and how professional training can prepare practitioners to navigate and critically reshape an increasingly data-saturated world.

2.5 *Part V—Ethical Considerations and Future Directions (Chaps. 22–23)*

Part V returns the book to explicitly normative and forward-looking terrain by focusing on ethical challenges, governance, and the cultivation of AI literacy and competency within the profession. The chapters treat ethics not as a late-stage add-on to technological innovation but as a structuring concern that must shape how AI is imagined, designed, implemented, and evaluated in social work. Together, they ask what kinds of institutional arrangements, professional capacities, and community engagements are required if AI is to support rather than undermine commitments to equity, justice, and human dignity.

Chapter 22 moves beyond general statements of principle to examine how ethical commitments can be translated into concrete institutional and regulatory arrangements. It outlines typologies of risk and proposes ways of distinguishing low-risk from high-risk AI applications in social work, with particular attention to systems that affect liberty, entitlements, and exposure to state intervention. Questions of transparency, contestability, and due process are addressed in relation to procurement, implementation, and oversight practices. The analysis foregrounds the roles of agencies, professional associations, regulators, and technology vendors in establishing clear lines of accountability, creating mechanisms for impact assessment and auditing. It also highlights the need to ensure that affected individuals and communities have avenues for redress. Governance is not treated as a purely top-down affair. The chapter emphasizes participatory and community-based approaches to setting norms for acceptable AI use, including advisory bodies, co-governance structures, and partnerships with civil society organizations. It alerts readers to the risks of ethics washing, in which aspirational guidelines are adopted without substantial changes to data practices or decision-making structures. The chapter argues that effective governance must be resourced, enforceable, and responsive to evolving technological and social conditions.

Chapter 23 turns to the capacities that social workers, educators, researchers, and organizations need to participate meaningfully in this governance landscape and in the design and critique of AI systems. AI literacy is conceptualized as more than basic technical familiarity. It encompasses critical data literacy, understanding of how models are trained and evaluated, awareness of common failure modes and biases, and the ability to interpret and communicate the limitations of algorithmic outputs in specific practice contexts. Competency frameworks are outlined at multiple levels, including individual practitioners and students, supervisory and managerial roles, and organizational and community stakeholders. These discussions stress that AI literacy is inseparable from ethical and political literacy. Being competent with AI involves recognizing how systems interact with structural racism, ableism, class inequality, and other forms of oppression. It also involves knowing when and how to challenge the use of particular tools and being able to advocate for alternatives or safeguards. The chapter proposes strategies for embedding AI-related competencies into pre-service education, continuing professional development, and leadership training. It also highlights the importance of aligning these efforts with broader initiatives in digital inclusion and community technology education.

Taken together, the chapters in Part V position ethical deliberation, governance, and capacity building as central to the future of AI in social work rather than as afterthoughts. They suggest that the trajectories outlined in earlier parts will be shaped not only by technological advances, but also by the extent to which social workers and the communities they serve can develop the knowledge, skills, and institutional leverage needed to steer AI toward purposes that are compatible with the profession's core values. In this framing, future directions for AI in social work are inseparable from the creation of governance structures and literacy initiatives that enable practitioners and communities to act as informed, critical, and collectively empowered participants in technological change.

3 Cross-Cutting Challenges and Future Directions for AI in Social Work

Across this book, AI appears in diverse guises and settings, yet a common set of tensions recurs. These tensions are not simply technical problems to be solved. They are reflections of deeper questions about what kind of social work is enacted when algorithmic systems become part of its infrastructure.

3.1 Human Relationships, Care, and Algorithmic Systems

Many of the chapters in Parts II and IV show AI entering spaces that have historically been organized around face-to-face interaction and relational judgment. These include child welfare investigations, mental health encounters, school consultations, substance use treatment, and supervision and teaching in educational settings. In these domains, AI is often introduced to make work more manageable, to extend limited capacity, or to reduce delays and inconsistency. Risk scores, early warning flags, and triage tools promise to help practitioners identify patterns that might otherwise go unnoticed. Virtual agents and simulations create new opportunities for practice and reflection.

At the same time, the book documents how algorithmic systems can narrow the terms on which people are seen. When complex life circumstances are condensed into risk categories or eligibility thresholds, the narrative and relational aspects of practice can be overshadowed by what is measurable and modeled. Several contributions describe the moral distress that practitioners experience when automated recommendations conflict with their understanding of a client's situation. They also represent the pressure practitioners feel when organizational cultures encourage deference to model outputs even in the face of doubt. In such settings, AI does not simply support care. It can reconfigure what counts as reasonable or defensible care and who bears responsibility when things go wrong.

A key future direction, therefore, is the development of practice models that treat AI as a complement to, rather than a substitute for, relational work (Harayama et al., 2021). This includes designing tools that make their reasoning more transparent and contestable. It also includes embedding procedures that require practitioners to document reasons for agreeing or disagreeing with algorithmic suggestions and creating supervisory structures that support critical reflection on human-AI collaboration rather than equating compliance with good practice. It further requires organizational acknowledgement that some dimensions of professional responsibility cannot be delegated to models. These include negotiating meaning with clients, weighing values in ethically charged decisions, and cultivating trust in communities where institutional credibility is fragile.

3.2 *Data Justice, Structural Inequality, and Evaluation*

A second cross-cutting theme concerns the relationship between AI, data practices, and structural inequality. Across practice domains, the book illustrates how the data used to train and validate AI systems are shaped by histories of racism, ableism, sexism, class stratification, and other forms of oppression. Administrative records reveal uneven patterns of surveillance and intervention across populations (Parayiwa et al., 2022). Policing and criminal justice data encode decades of discriminatory enforcement (Anastasopoulou, 2025). Health records reproduce differential access to care (Getzen et al., 2022). When these datasets become the basis for predictive models, disparities are not only recorded (Getzen et al., 2022). They can also be reproduced and intensified.

The book engages directly with technical approaches to bias detection and mitigation, as well as with fairness metrics that seek to equalize error rates or predictive performance across groups. While such methods are essential, the book suggests that they are insufficient on their own. A model can satisfy formal fairness criteria and still contribute to unjust outcomes if the underlying problem framing is narrow, if its predictions trigger harmful interventions, or if the communities most affected have little say in what is being predicted and why. Contributions on poverty, child welfare, criminal justice, housing, and migration, among others, show that questions of data justice extend to how data are collected and categorized, who has the power to interpret and challenge them, and how they are used to legitimate institutional responses.

Future directions in this domain involve rethinking evaluation as a multi-layered practice. Technical performance metrics remain necessary, but assessments of distributive impact, procedural fairness, and experiential legitimacy must supplement them. Mixed-methods approaches that combine quantitative analysis with qualitative inquiry and community-based evaluation can help reveal whether AI tools are, in fact, reducing inequities, widening access, and diminishing harmful contact with coercive systems. They can also help determine whether AI is reshaping inequalities in less visible ways (Bircan & Özbilgin, 2025). Data justice further implies involving affected communities in decisions about what data should be collected, how long it should be retained, and under what conditions it can be shared or linked. In this sense, the limits of automation are not only computational. They are defined by the boundaries that communities set around acceptable uses of their data and the kinds of social ordering they are willing to endorse.

3.3 *Participation, Governance, and Collective Agency*

The chapters in Parts III and V make clear that the trajectory of AI in social work is not predetermined solely by technological innovation. It is shaped by laws and regulations, procurement contracts, organizational cultures, professional norms, and communities' capacities to contest or appropriate systems that affect them. Yet current governance arrangements often leave social workers and service users at the margins of decision-making. Tools may be selected and deployed by vendors and executives with limited input from frontline staff or people with lived experience. Oversight may focus narrowly on compliance rather than on the broader social and ethical consequences of deployment.

Across domains, the book points toward the need for more participatory and multi-level forms of AI governance. At the organizational level, this includes building impact assessment processes that anticipate potential harms and benefits before systems are rolled out. It also includes establishing ethics and equity review mechanisms that include community representation and creating channels through which practitioners and clients can raise concerns and trigger review or suspension of tools that prove harmful in practice (Al-kfairy et al., 2024). At the professional and policy levels, it involves social work associations and accrediting bodies developing standards and guidance specific to AI. It also consists of advocating for regulations that enshrine transparency, contestability, and meaningful consent, and collaborating with other professions, unions, and civil society groups to influence national and regional frameworks for trustworthy AI (Li et al., 2023).

Crucially, participation in governance depends on the kinds of literacy and competency discussed in Part IV. Social workers, educators, and community organizations need a sufficient understanding of how AI systems work and of the legal and institutional levers available to them to engage in informed critique and negotiation. Future directions, therefore, include investing in AI education that is explicitly linked to questions of power and social justice, supporting community technology initiatives that enable affected groups to audit or co-design systems, and resourcing advocacy and organizing efforts that bring marginalized voices into debates about digital policy (Selwyn, 2022). In this view, the central question is not whether AI can be made perfectly safe or fair. It is whether social work and the communities it serves can build the collective agency required to steer AI toward purposes that align with their visions of justice and care.

4 Conclusion: Cautious Hope and Shared Responsibility

The analyses gathered in this book unsettle any simple story about AI as either a solution to entrenched social problems or a threat to be categorically refused. They demonstrate AI systems that help identify unmet needs, expand access, and enable more timely interventions. They also show systems that intensify surveillance, reproduce structural inequalities, and narrow the terms on which people and communities are recognized. Against this backdrop, cautious hope is warranted, but only if it is coupled with a clear sense of responsibility and an insistence that social work's core commitments remain nonnegotiable. Dignity, self-determination, social and economic justice, and the importance of human relationships cannot be traded away in the name of predictive accuracy or administrative efficiency (Chohlas-Wood et al., 2023).

The chapters also make visible the forms of work that should not be automated. No model can substitute for the ethical discernment involved in weighing harms and benefits in particular lives, for the relational labor of building trust across difference, or for the political work of naming and challenging oppressive structures. AI may assist in organizing information, surfacing patterns, or simulating scenarios. It cannot decide whose suffering matters, who is worthy of solidarity, or what counts as a just distribution of risk and care. Those judgments remain the responsibility of practitioners, communities, and publics and must be made in ways open to contestation and change.

At the same time, the book resists fatalism. It documents many instances in which social workers, educators, researchers, and community partners are already reshaping AI through critical engagement, creative appropriation, and collective organizing. The invitation that emerges from this concluding chapter is to deepen and extend that work. This includes continuing to develop practice models that center relationships, research programs that foreground data justice, educational initiatives that build critical and technical capacities, and governance arrangements that redistribute voice and power. AI will not determine the future of social work on its own. The more pressing question is how social work, in solidarity with those it serves, will decide which futures are acceptable when AI is part of the landscape and what forms of care, accountability, and collective flourishing it will insist on in the process.

Competing Interests The authors have no conflicts of interest to declare that are relevant to the content of this chapter.

References

Al-kfairy, M., Mustafa, D., Kshetri, N., Insiew, M., & Alfandi, O. (2024). Ethical challenges and solutions of generative AI: An interdisciplinary perspective. *Informatics, 11*(3), 58. https://doi.org/10.3390/informatics11030058

Anastasopoulou, M. (2025). Exploring algorithmic governance: The AI Act and new realities for criminal justice, and fundamental rights. *New Journal of European Criminal Law, 16*(2), 176–196. https://doi.org/10.1177/20322844251338627

Bircan, T., & Özbilgin, M. F. (2025). Unmasking inequalities of the code: Disentangling the nexus of AI and inequality. *Technological Forecasting and Social Change, 211*, 123925. https://doi.org/10.1016/j.techfore.2024.123925

Boetto, H. (2025). Artificial intelligence in social work: An EPIC model for practice. *Australian Social Work*, 1–14. https://doi.org/10.1080/0312407X.2025.2488345

Chohlas-Wood, A., Coots, M., Goel, S., & Nyarko, J. (2023). Designing equitable algorithms. *Nature Computational Science, 3*(7), 601–610. https://doi.org/10.1038/s43588-023-00485-4

Coeckelbergh, M. (2023). Narrative responsibility and artificial intelligence: How AI challenges human responsibility and sense-making. *AI & SOCIETY, 38*(6), 2437–2450. https://doi.org/10.1007/s00146-021-01375-x

Dalziel, M. V., Schaffer, K., & Martin, N. (2024). Navigating AI in social work and beyond: A multidisciplinary review. *arXiv preprint* https://arxiv.org/abs/2411.07245. https://doi.org/10.48550/arXiv.2411.07245

Getzen, E., Ungar, L., Mowery, D., Jiang, X., & Long, Q. (2022). Mining for equitable health: Assessing the impact of missing data in electronic health records. *Journal of Biomedical Informatics, 139*, 104269. https://doi.org/10.1101/2022.05.09.22274680

Harayama, Y., Milano, M., Baldwin, R., Antonin, C., Berg, J., Karvar, A., & Wyckoff, A. (2021). Artificial intelligence and the future of work. In B. Braunschweig & M. Ghallab (Eds.), *Reflections on artificial intelligence for humanity* (Vol. 12600, pp. 53–67). Springer. https://doi.org/10.1007/978-3-030-69128-8_4

Heeks, R. (2022). Digital inequality beyond the digital divide: Conceptualizing adverse digital incorporation in the global South. *Information Technology for Development, 28*(4), 688–704. https://doi.org/10.1080/02681102.2022.2068492

Huang, M. H., & Rust, R. T. (2018). Artificial intelligence in service. *Journal of Service Research, 21*(2), 155–172. https://doi.org/10.1177/1094670517752459

Kuziemski, M., & Misuraca, G. (2020). AI governance in the public sector: Three tales from the frontiers of automated decision-making in democratic settings. *Telecommunications Policy, 44*(6), 101976. https://doi.org/10.1016/j.telpol.2020.101976

Li, B., Qi, P., Liu, B., Di, S., Liu, J., Pei, J., Yi, J., & Zhou, B. (2023). Trustworthy AI: From principles to practices. *ACM Computing Surveys, 55*(9), 1–46. https://doi.org/10.1145/3555803

Parayiwa, C., Behie, A., & Lal, A. (2022). Perinatal health surveillance: A spatiotemporal analysis of administrative health records from Queensland, Australia, 2008–2018. *Proceedings of the Royal Society of Queensland, 131*. https://doi.org/10.53060/prsq.2022-09

Reamer, F. G. (2023). Artificial intelligence in social work: Emerging ethical issues. *International Journal of Social Work Values and Ethics, 20*(2), 52–71. https://doi.org/10.55521/10-020-205

Selwyn, N. (2022). The future of AI and education: Some cautionary notes. *European Journal of Education, 57*(4), 620–631. https://doi.org/10.1111/ejed.12532

Sun, Q. (2025). Intelligent social welfare: How AI optimizes social assistance, Elderly Care, and Healthcare Systems. *Digital Society & Virtual Governance, 1*(1), 17–32. https://doi.org/10.6914/dsvg.010102

Zajko, M. (2022). Artificial intelligence, algorithms, and social inequality: Sociological contributions to contemporary debates. *Sociology Compass, 16*(3), e12962. https://doi.org/10.1111/soc4.12962

Index

R. An, M. A. Lindsey (eds.), *Artificial Intelligence in Social Work*,
https://doi.org/10.1007/978-3-032-18443-6

J

L

M

N

O

P

Q

R

V

W

MIX
Papier aus verantwortungsvollen Quellen
Paper from responsible sources
FSC® C105338

If you have any concerns about our products,
you can contact us on
ProductSafety@springernature.com

In case Publisher is established outside the EU,
the EU authorized representative is:
Springer Nature Customer Service Center GmbH
Europaplatz 3, 69115 Heidelberg, Germany

Printed by Libri Plureos GmbH
in Hamburg, Germany